Strategies for Addressing Behavior Problems in the Classroom

FIFTH EDITION

Mary Margaret Kerr
University of Pittsburgh

C. Michael Nelson
University of Kentucky, Emeritus

Upper Saddle River, New Jersey
Columbus, Ohio

Library of Congress Cataloging-in-Publication Data

Kerr, Mary Margaret.
Strategies for addressing behavior problems in the classroom / Mary Margaret Kerr, C. Michael Nelson.-- 5th ed.
p. cm.
Includes bibliographical references and index.
ISBN 0-13-117986-1
1. Classroom management. 2. Behavior disorders in children. 3. Behavior modification. 4. School discipline. I. Nelson, C. Michael (Charles Michael) II. Title.
LB3013.K47 2006
371.5'3--dc22 2005000192

Vice President and Executive Publisher: Jeffery W. Johnston
Senior Editor: Allyson P. Sharp
Editorial Assistant: Kathleen S. Burk
Production Coordination: Lea Baranowski, Carlisle Publishers Services
Production Editor: Linda Hillis Bayma
Design Coordinator: Diane C. Lorenzo
Photo Coordinator: Sandy Schaefer
Cover Designer: Jason Moore
Cover image: © 2001 Nikki Wolfson, oil pastel on paper (24″ × 18″). Image provided courtesy of *VSA arts* (www.vsarts.org)
Production Manager: Laura Messerly
Director of Marketing: Ann Castel Davis
Marketing Manager: Autumn Purdy
Marketing Coordinator: Brian Mounts

This book was set in Garamond by Carlisle Communications, Ltd. It was printed and bound by Courier Stoughton, Inc. The cover was printed by Courier Stoughton, Inc.

Photo Credits: Tom Watson/Merrill, p. 3; Anthony Magnacca/Merrill, pp. 37, 67, 133, 193, 221, 259, 335; David Young-Wolff/PhotoEdit, p. 97; Richard Hutchings/PhotoEdit, p. 161; C. Michael Nelson, p. 198; Kenneth W. Kerr, p. 287; Trish Gant © Dorling Kindersley, p. 317.

Pearson Education Ltd.
Pearson Education Singapore Pte. Ltd.
Pearson Education Canada, Ltd.
Pearson Education—Japan
Pearson Education Australia Pty. Limited
Pearson Education North Asia Ltd.
Pearson Educación de Mexico, S.A. de C.V.
Pearson Education Malaysia Pte. Ltd.

10 9 8 7 6 5 4 3
ISBN: 0-13-117986-1

"Who dares to teach must never cease to learn."

—John Cotton Dana

For Vaughan Stagg

M.M.K.

For my students and colleagues

C.M.N.

DISCOVER THE COMPANION WEBSITE ACCOMPANYING THIS BOOK

THE PRENTICE HALL COMPANION WEBSITE: A VIRTUAL LEARNING ENVIRONMENT

Technology is a constantly growing and changing aspect of our field that is creating a need for content and resources. To address this emerging need, Prentice Hall has developed an online learning environment for students and professors alike—Companion Websites—to support our textbooks.

In creating a Companion Website, our goal is to build on and enhance what the textbook already offers. For this reason, the content for each user-friendly website is organized by chapter and provides the professor and student with a variety of meaningful resources.

For the Professor—

Every Companion Website integrates **Syllabus Manager**™, an online syllabus creation and management utility.

- **Syllabus Manager**™ provides you, the instructor, with an easy, step-by-step process to create and revise syllabi, with direct links into the Companion Website and other online content without having to learn HTML.
- Students may log on to your syllabus during any study session. All they need to know is the web address for the Companion Website and the password you've assigned to your syllabus.
- After you have created a syllabus using **Syllabus Manager**™, students may enter the syllabus for their course section from any point in the Companion Website.
- Clicking on a date, the student is shown the list of activities for the assignment. The activities for each assignment are linked directly to actual content, saving time for students.
- Adding assignments consists of clicking on the desired due date, then filling in the details of the assignment—name of the assignment, instructions, and whether it is a one-time or repeating assignment.
- In addition, links to other activities can be created easily. If the activity is online, a URL can be entered in the space provided, and it will be linked automatically in the final syllabus.
- Your completed syllabus is hosted on our servers, allowing convenient updates from any computer on the Internet. Changes you make to your syllabus are immediately available to your students at their next logon.

Common Companion Website features for students include:

For the Student—

- **Chapter Objectives**—Outline key concepts from the text.
- **Interactive Tutorials**—Complete with hints and automatic grading that provide immediate feedback for students—Multiple Choice, True/False, Short Answer, and Discussion Forums.

After students submit their answers for the multiple choice and true/false tutorials, the Companion Website **Results Reporter** computes a percentage grade, provides a graphic representation of how many questions were answered correctly and incorrectly, and gives a question-by-question analysis of the quiz. Students are given the option to send their quiz to up to four e-mail addresses (professor, teaching assistant, study partner, etc.).

- **Links to the Web**—Links to websites that relate to chapter content.
- **Come into My Classroom**—Critical thinking questions from the case studies featured in the text.
- **Tools for Learning**—Resources, forms, and relevant material that relate to each chapter's content.
- **Glossary**—Terms and definitions related to the book.
- **Message Board**—Virtual bulletin board to post or respond to questions or comments from a national audience.

To take advantage of the many available resources, please visit the *Strategies for Addressing Behavior Problems in the Classroom,* Fifth Edition, Companion Website at

www.prenhall.com/kerr

EDUCATOR LEARNING CENTER: AN INVALUABLE ONLINE RESOURCE

Merrill Education and the Association for Supervision and Curriculum Development (ASCD) invite you to take advantage of a new online resource, one that provides access to the top research and proven strategies associated with ASCD and Merrill—the Educator Learning Center. At **www.educatorlearningcenter.com**, you will find resources that will enhance your students' understanding of course topics and of current educational issues, in addition to being invaluable for further research.

How the Educator Learning Center Will Help Your Students Become Better Teachers

With the combined resources of Merrill Education and ASCD, you and your students will find a wealth of tools and materials to better prepare them for the classroom.

Research

- More than 600 articles from the ASCD journal *Educational Leadership* discuss everyday issues faced by practicing teachers.
- A direct link on the site to Research Navigator™ gives students access to many of the leading education journals as well as extensive content detailing the research process.
- Excerpts from Merrill Education texts give your students insights on important topics of instructional method diverse populations, assessment, classroom management, technology, and refining classroom practice.

Classroom Practice

- Hundreds of lesson plans and teaching strategies are categorized by content area and age range.
- Case studies and classroom video footage provide virtual field experience for student reflection.
- Computer simulations and other electronic tools keep your students abreast of today's classrooms and current technologies.

Look into the Value of Educator Learning Center Yourself

A 4-month subscription to Educator Learning Center is $25 but is **FREE** when packaged with any Merrill Education text. In order for your students to have access to this site, you must use this special value-pack ISBN number **when** placing your textbook order with the bookstore: 0-13-186373-8. Your students will then receive a copy of the text packaged with a free ASCD PIN code. To preview the value of this Website to you and your students, please go to **www.educatorlearningcenter.com** and click on "Demo."

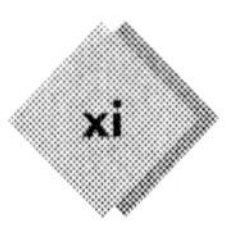

BRIEF CONTENTS

PART 1
FOUNDATIONS OF EFFECTIVE BEHAVIOR MANAGEMENT 1

Chapter 1
IDENTIFYING AND SERVING STUDENTS WITH BEHAVIOR PROBLEMS 2

Chapter 2
SCHOOL- AND CLASSROOM-WIDE POSITIVE BEHAVIOR SUPPORT 36

Chapter 3
PRINCIPLES OF INTERVENTION PLANNING 66

Chapter 4
ASSESSMENT-BASED INTERVENTION PLANNING 96

Chapter 5
MONITORING STUDENT PROGRESS 132

Chapter 6
EVALUATING INTERVENTION EFFECTS 160

PART 2
STRATEGIES FOR SPECIFIC BEHAVIOR PROBLEMS 191

Chapter 7
ADDRESSING DISRUPTIVE BEHAVIORS 192

Chapter 8
IMPROVING SCHOOL SURVIVAL SKILLS AND SOCIAL SKILLS 220

Chapter 9
ADDRESSING AGGRESSIVE BEHAVIORS 258

Chapter 10
DEVELOPING ALTERNATIVES TO SELF-STIMULATORY AND SELF-INJURIOUS BEHAVIOR 286

PART 3
BEYOND THE CLASSROOM 315

Chapter 11
SUPPORTING STUDENTS WITH PSYCHIATRIC PROBLEMS 316

Chapter 12
EXTENDING INTERVENTION EFFECTS 334

EPILOGUE 371

CONTENTS

PART I
FOUNDATIONS OF EFFECTIVE BEHAVIOR MANAGEMENT 1

Chapter 1
IDENTIFYING AND SERVING STUDENTS WITH BEHAVIOR PROBLEMS 2

Outline 2
Objectives 2
Key Terms 3
Come into My Classroom: A Case Study 4
Introduction 5
Positive Behavior Support 6
Implementing Positive Behavior Support 8
Behavior Intervention Planning 9
Legislation Affecting Student Behavior 11
IDEA 2004 Disciplinary Regulations 11
Section 504 and the Americans with Disabilities Act 13
No Child Left Behind Act 13
Behavior Disorders or Problem Behaviors? 14
Identifying Students with Behavioral Disorders 16
Systematic Screening 17
Assessment for Identification 18
Certification 19
Behavior Support in General Education Settings 27
Behavior Problems and Educational Placement 28
Summary 31
Discussion/Application Ideas 31
Notes 32
References 32

Chapter 2
SCHOOL- AND CLASSROOM-WIDE POSITIVE BEHAVIOR SUPPORT 36

Outline 36
Objectives 36
Key Terms 37
Come into My Classroom: A Case Study 38
Introduction 41
Why Emphasize Prevention? 41
Universal Interventions 42
Who Owns the Problem? 42
Prevention and Early Intervention 43
Implementing School-Wide Positive Behavior Support 44
Using Behavior Incident Data 45
Designing School-Wide Systems 47
Implementing Positive Behavior Support in the Classroom 50
Extending School-Wide Strategies 50
Promoting Success in the Classroom 51
Effective Instruction and Student Behavior 52
Group Management Systems in the Classroom 58
Summary 61
Discussion/Application Ideas 61
References 62

Chapter 3
PRINCIPLES OF INTERVENTION PLANNING 66

Outline 66
Objectives 66
Key Terms 67
Come into My Classroom: A Case Study 68
Introduction 69
Principles of Applied Behavior Analysis 69

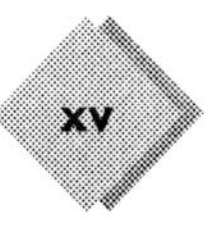

Principle I *69*
Principle II *71*
Principle III *71*
Principle IV *72*
Principle V *73*
Principle VI *73*
Systematic Procedures for Influencing Behavior 73
Behavioral Enhancement Procedures *75*
Behavior Reduction Procedures *79*
Legal and Ethical Guidelines 85
Effective Practices 88
Summary 90
Discussion/Application Ideas 91
References 91

Chapter 4
ASSESSMENT-BASED INTERVENTION PLANNING 96

Outline 96
Objectives 96
Key Terms 97
Come into My Classroom: A Case Study 98
Introduction 101
The Assessment Process 102
Identifying Problem Behavior 103
Standards for Social Behavior *103*
Ruling Out Medical Explanations for Problem Behavior *104*
Social Validation of Problem Behaviors *104*
Screening *106*
Assessment-Based Intervention Planning 110
Step 1: Assess the Student's Behavior *111*
Step 2: Propose a Hypothesis *116*
Step 3: Assess the Validity of the Hypothesis *118*
Step 4: Design an Intervention *120*
Step 5: Collect Data on Intervention Effectiveness and Adjust the Plan as Needed *124*
Step 6: Write Long- and Short-Term Intervention Objectives *125*
Summary 128
Discussion/Application Ideas 128
Notes 128
References 129

Chapter 5
MONITORING STUDENT PROGRESS 132

Outline 132
Objectives 132
Key Terms 133
Come into My Classroom: A Case Study 134
Introduction 136
Overview of Classroom Measurement 137
Teacher Objections to Systematic Measurement of Student Progress *138*
Frequently Asked Questions About Monitoring Student Behavior *139*
Measuring Student Progress 142
Selecting a Monitoring Format and Procedures *142*
Recording Strategies *146*
Observing and Recording Multiple Behaviors of Students *153*
Student Portfolios *153*
Using Technology to Observe and Record Behaviors *156*
Assessing Observer Agreement *156*
Summary 157
Discussion/Application Ideas 157
References 158

Chapter 6
EVALUATING INTERVENTION EFFECTS 160

Outline 160
Objectives 160
Key Terms 161
Come into My Classroom: A Case Study 162
Introduction 164
Graphing and Charting Student Performance 164
Autographing Formats *166*
Graph or Chart? *167*

Types of Graphs and Charts *168*
Guidelines for Graph or Chart Construction *170*
The Role of Program Monitoring and Evaluation in IEPs *172*
Data-Based Decision Making 175
Analyzing Level *179*
Analyzing Data Trends *179*
Single-Subject Research Designs 184
Withdrawal and Reversal Designs *185*
Changing Criterion Design *186*
Alternating Treatments Design *188*
Summary 189
Discussion/Application Ideas 189
References 189

PART 2
STRATEGIES FOR SPECIFIC BEHAVIOR PROBLEMS 191

Chapter 7
ADDRESSING DISRUPTIVE BEHAVIORS 192

Outline 192
Objectives 192
Key Terms 193
Introduction 194
Come into My Classroom: A Case Study 194
Environmentally Mediated Interventions 195
Rules *195*
Teacher Movement Patterns *197*
Teacher-Mediated Interventions 198
Monitoring Teacher Verbal and Nonverbal Behavior *198*
Reprimands *199*
Physical Interactions with Students *199*
High-Probability Request Sequences *200*
The Praise-and-Ignore Approach *200*
Differential Reinforcement of Other Behaviors *200*
Differential Reinforcement of Low Rates of Behavior *201*
Public Posting *201*
Contingency Contracting *202*
Token Economy Programs *202*
Peer-Mediated Interventions 206
Group Goal Setting and Feedback *206*
Peer Monitoring *207*
Peer Management *208*
Group Contingencies *208*
Good Behavior Game *210*
Self-Mediated Interventions 211
Self-Monitoring *211*
Self-Evaluation *212*
Self-Graphing *213*
Self-Instruction *213*
Summary 213
Come into My Classroom: A Case Study 213
Discussion/Application Ideas 218
References 218

Chapter 8
IMPROVING SCHOOL SURVIVAL SKILLS AND SOCIAL SKILLS 220

Outline 220
Objectives 220
Key Terms 221
How This Chapter Is Organized 222
Improving School Survival Skills 222
Assessing School Survival Skills 222
Come into My Classroom: A Case Study 222
Promoting Self-Determination *223*
Teacher-Mediated Strategies 225
General Guidelines *225*
Managing Routines *227*
Homework Strategies *227*
Instructional Modifications *228*
Direct Teaching of School Survival Skills *228*
Combining Contingency Management with Other Strategies *228*
Peer-Mediated Strategies 232
Peer Tutoring *232*
Cooperative Learning *233*
Self-Mediated Strategies 234

Strategies to Improve Social Competence 234
Assessment Considerations 234
Social Withdrawal 238
Teacher-Mediated Strategies 239
Social Skills Instruction *239*
Peer-Mediated Strategies 242
Peers as Instructional Agents *242*
Self-Mediated Strategies 242
Come into My Classroom: A Case Study 248
Summary 254
Discussion/Application Ideas 254
References 254

Chapter 9
ADDRESSING AGGRESSIVE BEHAVIORS 258

Outline 258
Objectives 258
Key Terms 259
Come into My Classroom: A Case Study 260
An Introduction to Antisocial Behavior 260
Documenting and Understanding Aggressive Behavior 261
Teacher-Mediated Strategies 262
Academic Intervention *263*
Verbal De-escalation *263*
Anger Management Training *266*
Social Competence Training *266*
Contingency Management Strategies *266*
Token Reinforcement and Response Cost *269*
Time-Out from Reinforcement *270*
Crisis Interventions *270*
Peer-Mediated Strategies 272
Peer Confrontation *273*
Conflict Resolution Strategies *273*
Peers as Teachers of Anger Management *275*
Self-Mediated Strategies 275
Summary 275
Come into My Classroom: A Case Study 276
Discussion/Application Ideas 285
References 285

Chapter 10
DEVELOPING ALTERNATIVES TO SELF-STIMULATORY AND SELF-INJURIOUS BEHAVIOR 286

Outline 286
Objectives 286
Key Terms 287
Come into My Classroom: A Case Study 288
Introduction 289
Self-Stimulatory Behavior *289*
Self-Injurious Behaviors 292
A Note About SIB and SSB Assessment and Interventions *292*
SSB, SIB, and Functional Relations 294
Motivative Operations 295
Assessment of SSB 296
Intervention Strategies for SSB 297
Enriching the Environment *298*
Social Reinforcement Approaches *298*
Reinforcing Alternative Behaviors *298*
Noncontingent Reinforcement *298*
Perceptual Reinforcement *298*
Stimulus Variation *299*
Sensory Preferences *299*
Response-Reinforcer Procedure *299*
Sensory Reinforcement *299*
Automatic Reinforcement *299*
Sensory Extinction Procedure *300*
Environmental Safety Considerations *300*
Assessment of SIB 300
Intervention Strategies for SIB 301
Environmental Changes *301*
Environmental Safety Considerations *303*
DRO *303*
NCR *304*
Interruption and Redirection *304*
Weakening SIB *304*
Restraint Devices *305*
Movement Suppression Procedure *305*
Summary 306
Come into My Classroom: A Case Study 306
Discussion/Application Ideas 311
Notes 311
References 312

PART 3
BEYOND THE CLASSROOM 315

Chapter 11
SUPPORTING STUDENTS WITH PSYCHIATRIC PROBLEMS 316

Outline 316
Objectives 316
Key Terms 317
Introduction 318
Come into My Classroom: A Case Study 318
Mental Health Prevention Services 319
Identifying Psychological Problems 319
Interview Strategy 319
Depression 321
Bipolar Disorder 323
Suicide 323
Drug and Alcohol Abuse 324
Alcohol and Other Depressants 325
Marijuana 327
Heroin 327
Hallucinogens 327
Inhalants 327
Narcotics 328
Club Drugs 328
Stimulants 328
Steroids 328
Eating Disorders 329
Anxiety Disorders 330
Specific Phobias 331
Summary 331
Come into My Classroom: A Case Study 332
Discussion/Application Ideas 332
References 332

Chapter 12
EXTENDING INTERVENTION EFFECTS 334

Outline 334
Objectives 334
Key Terms 335
Come into My Classroom: A Case Study 336
Introduction 340
Principles of Maintenance and Generalization 341
Take Advantage of Natural Communities of Reinforcement 342
Train Diversely 343
Incorporate Functional Mediators 345
Transition Planning 347
Transitions to Less Restrictive Educational Settings 348
Transitions to Other Settings 353
Effective Collaboration 359
Working with School Personnel 359
Working with Families 361
Working with Community Professionals and Agencies 364
Summary 366
Discussion/Application Ideas 366
Notes 367
References 367

EPILOGUE 371

INDEX 373

Note: Every effort has been made to provide accurate and current Internet information in this book. However, the Internet and information posted on it are constantly changing, so it is inevitable that some of the Internet addresses listed in this textbook will change.

PART 1 FOUNDATIONS OF EFFECTIVE BEHAVIOR MANAGEMENT

Chapter 1 Identifying and Serving Students with Behavior Problems

Chapter 2 School- and Classroom-Wide Positive Behavior Support

Chapter 3 Principles of Intervention Planning

Chapter 4 Assessment-Based Intervention Planning

Chapter 5 Monitoring Student Progress

Chapter 6 Evaluating Intervention Effects

CHAPTER 1

IDENTIFYING AND SERVING STUDENTS WITH BEHAVIOR PROBLEMS

OUTLINE

Introduction
Positive Behavior Support
Legislation Affecting Student Behavior
Behavior Disorders or Problem Behaviors?
Identifying Students with Behavioral Disorders
Behavior Problems and Educational Placement

OBJECTIVES

After completing this chapter, you should be able to

- Describe the process of determining students' needs for behavioral support and educational services, including the assessment data that should be collected and the decisions that should be made.
- Describe the continuum of positive behavior support for students and indicate how decisions should be made regarding which students require what levels of intervention.
- Describe litigation affecting the education of students with emotional or behavioral disorders, including the provisions of the Individuals with Disabilities Education Improvement Act of 2004 (IDEA 2004) that affect school disciplinary practices for students with disabilities.
- Indicate what a definition of behavioral disorders should accomplish and indicate weaknesses of the current federal definition.
- Discuss the role of school-based teams with regard to addressing the needs of students for positive behavior support and for reducing the need to identify, label, and serve students in special education programs.
- Give a rationale for creating systemic changes in schools as a basis for preventing and responding more effectively to challenging student behaviors.

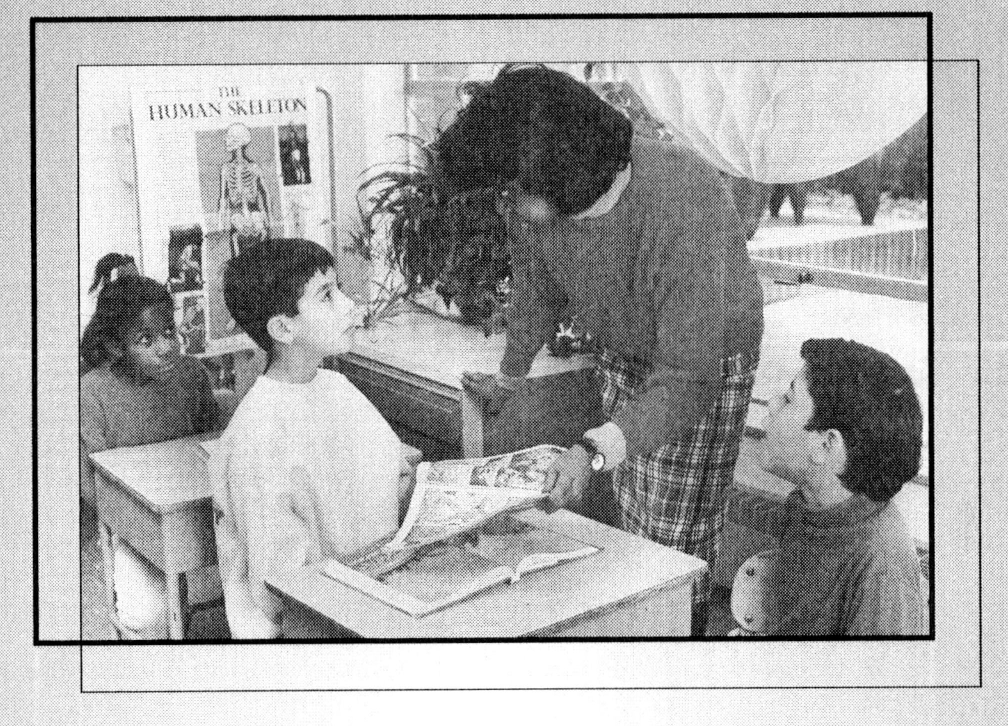

KEY TERMS (refer to the Glossary on the Companion Website for definitions)

accommodation plan
Americans with Disabilities Act
attention-deficit hyperactivity disorder
behavior intervention plans
behavior specialist
Behavior Support Team
communicative function
comorbidity
consulting teacher
Council for Children with Behavioral Disorders
Council for Exceptional Children
Diagnostic and Statistical Manual of Mental Disorders, 4th Edition
effective behavioral support
externalizing
full inclusion
functional behavioral assessment
individualized education plan
Individualized Education Program Team
Individuals with Disabilities Education Act
intensive intervention
interim alternative educational setting
internalizing
least restrictive environment
local educational agency
manifestation determination
No Child Left Behind Act
positive behavior support
pragmatic language skills
prereferral intervention
primary prevention
projective technique
research-validated practices
screening
secondary prevention
Section 504
social competence
supported inclusion
syndrome
systems of care
targeted intervention
tertiary prevention
universal intervention
wraparound plan

If you are reading this book, you have an interest in helping students with problem behaviors. Perhaps you know that a recent U.S. Surgeon General's report (U.S. Public Health Service, 2001) estimated that 21% of children, ages 9 to 17, have diagnosable emotional or behavioral health disorders, yet very few receive the help they need. Put another way, 1 in 10 children and adolescents have a mental illness severe enough to cause some level of impairment, yet only about one in five of them receive mental health services in any given year. When untreated, mental health disorders can lead to school failure, family conflicts, drug abuse, violence, and even suicide.

Taken together, these statistics comprise a discouraging snapshot of today's at-risk youth. However, there is reason to be hopeful: many of these problems, if addressed without delay, improve. Moreover, when we apply effective primary prevention strategies, many problems never arise.

We wrote this text to help you prevent and solve behavior problems in classrooms and other school settings. We selected proven approaches that work with the full range of students, from those with severe and profound developmental disabilities to those with no disabilities, from preschool children to adults. General and special classroom teachers, consultants, psychologists, guidance counselors, and administrators, as well as other professionals and parents, have applied these methods.

As you will see, a critical prerequisite of successful interventions for these students is careful assessment of the student and the contexts in which problem (as well as desired) behavior occur. To intervene successfully, and with appropriate sensitivity for the student, you will want to understand each child and his needs. That's why this chapter provides an overview of the characteristics and needs of students who present behavioral challenges as well as the process of identifying those who would benefit from special education services.

Come into My Classroom: A Case Study

MEET TRACY AND RODNEY

Tracy

Tracy is at her desk coloring a map for her third-grade geography lesson. She begins to whistle a tune and tap her crayon on the desk loudly.

Teacher: "Please don't do that. If you make so much noise no one can get any work done."

Tracy stops for a few seconds, then begins whistling and tapping again.

Teacher: "Tracy, stop that. What did I just tell you?"

Tracy stops tapping but continues whistling at a lower volume.

Teacher: "Cut it out RIGHT NOW! Do you want to go to the office?"

Tracy laughs and begins singing loudly.

Teacher: "ALL RIGHT, IF YOU WANT TO SPEND THE REST OF THE DAY IN THE OFFICE, THAT'S WHAT YOU'LL DO. LET'S GO!" (starts toward Tracy's desk)

Tracy gets out of her seat and starts to run across the room. The teacher grabs Tracy's arm and takes her back to her seat. Tracy continues singing loudly. The teacher puts her hand over Tracy's mouth and whispers in her ear. Tracy resumes coloring quietly while the teacher has her arm around her.

Rodney

Rodney is sitting in a sixth-grade basic math class. He is identified as having emotional and behavioral disorders (EBD) and is being served in general education classes in accordance with his school district's policy of full inclusion. A special education teacher aide accompanies him to most of his classes, including this one. The teacher (who is not trained in special education) has given the class a work sheet of two-place multiplication problems to do independently. The aide is attempting to assist Rodney in solving the first problem.

Rodney (loudly): "I hate these stupid problems. Why do we have to do this crap?"

Aide: "It's important that you learn how to work with numbers. Here, look: 3 times 7 equals what?"

Rodney (shoves paper off his desk): "I don't need to learn this sh—. I got a calculator."

Teacher (clearly irritated, comes over to Rodney's desk): "You know you can't talk like that in here. Using swear words is against school rules and other people are trying to work."

Rodney: "You know what you can do with your school rules? You can shove them up your a—."

Teacher (to aide): "Okay, that's enough. Take him to the office. I'll write a behavior report."

Rodney: "You ain't takin' me nowhere!" (stands, toppling desk over, and moves threateningly toward aide)

Teacher starts toward Rodney, who turns and bolts out the door and into the hall.

INTRODUCTION

Students like Tracy, who is noncompliant and disruptive, and Rodney, who is aggressive and potentially violent, present a difficult problem for educators. Assuming what we have just presented represents typical and fairly frequent interactions between these two students and their teachers, what might you assume to be the problem? Is Tracy emotionally disturbed and in need of specialized services, or is she simply a "bad" child? Should Rodney be in a segregated classroom instead of a mainstream educational setting? Could these students' teachers have addressed their disruptive behavior any differently? What might they have done that would have produced a better outcome? All educators must deal with students who exhibit such challenging behavior, even though they constitute a small portion of the student population in our schools. Among the many questions raised in reference to pupils exhibiting behavior disorders are the following:

- Should these pupils be formally identified as having an emotional or behavioral disorder (EBD)[1] and served in special education programs, or should they remain in regular programs and be treated as disciplinary problems?
- Are students with EBD or those with patterns of acting out behavior threats to school safety?
- Can the needs of students with challenging behavior or emotional problems be addressed in general education settings, or do they require services in self-contained special classes or even more restrictive settings?
- Regardless of their educational placements, what approaches to addressing these pupils' behavior problems are most effective? What skills and resources are needed to accomplish desired behavior changes?

The needs of many children and youth with EBD greatly exceed the service delivery capacity of the educational system (or any single human services system). The poor performance of these students while they are in school and their dismal postschool outcomes support the conclusion that a single agency or system alone cannot meet their needs. Findings that document this status include those presented on the Companion Website. Click on Chapter 1 to view these and the citations in which they are documented.

As schools address public concerns regarding school safety and effectiveness and simultaneously face the challenges of dealing with an increasingly complex and diverse student population, educational leaders are calling for systemic changes in the way in which student behavior is viewed and addressed. For example, it is acknowledged that schools can no longer afford to ignore the behavioral needs of students until they reach the point that special education identification is considered or that potential threats to school safety exist. In the past, schools have adopted a relatively passive attitude toward student behavior (i.e., expecting that students will enter school with the knowledge and skills necessary to meet expectations for behavioral decorum), relying on punishment and school exclusion when behavior exceeds these often poorly defined limits. Today this stance is being replaced with the recognition that schools must be prepared to address the full range of student behavior, including teaching expectations and routines to all pupils and responding proactively and constructively to misbehavior through a graduated system of positive interventions (Sugai & Horner, 2002; Sugai, Sprague, Horner, & Walker, 2000). This new approach, **positive behavior support,** is being implemented in hundreds of schools throughout the United States. Therefore, we begin this edition with an overview of positive behavior support.

POSITIVE BEHAVIOR SUPPORT

A number of years ago, professionals working with individuals with severe cognitive disabilities and challenging behavior argued that interventions based on punishment of problem behaviors do not work. The frequent use of punitive methods creates treatment and educational environments that are aversive and therefore counterproductive to facilitating educational progress. They proposed a new way of looking at problem behavior: these behaviors are functional communications in that they help persons with limited cognitive and verbal skills get what they need from other people. If the **communicative function** of their behavior could be identified, they argued, this information could be used to develop more effective interventions. Specifically, these individuals could be taught to use adaptive replacement behaviors that serve the same communicative functions as the maladaptive behaviors (LaVigna & Donnellan, 1986). Two decades of research have supported the validity of these arguments. The 1997 amendments to the **Individuals with Disabilities Education Act** (IDEA '97) established a legislative foundation for extending this approach to all students with disabilities in educational settings.

> Think back to the vignettes involving Tracy and Rodney. What might their behavior be communicating?

The cornerstones of positive behavior support are the following:

- **Functional behavioral assessments** (FBAs) of problem behavior
- Positive behavioral intervention planning

The 2004 amendments to IDEA '97 (The Individuals with Disabilities Education Improvement Act of 2004) mandate that teams who develop and monitor **individualized education plans** (IEPs) for students with disabilities use the FBA and positive behavior intervention planning processes for all students with disabilities whose problem behavior provokes a change in educational placement, including suspension and expulsion. Recent applied research with children and youth in public school settings with so-called mild disabilities (e.g., EBD, **attention-deficit hyperactivity disorder** [ADHD], learning disabilities, mild mental retardation) or even no identified disabilities has demonstrated the effectiveness of interventions based on positive behavior support (also referred to as **effective behavioral support**).

The 2004 amendments to IDEA require that FBAs be conducted and **behavior intervention plans** be developed or reviewed only when a change in educational placement has been made. However, the strategy of waiting for a student to demonstrate problem behavior, particularly if it poses a threat to the student or to others, obviously has some drawbacks. First, the intervention can be applied only if the problem behavior is observed by someone with the authority to do something. Second, such interventions are reactionary; that is, they are applied after the behavior has occurred (sometimes well after). Public concerns regarding school safety have promoted researchers and practitioners to think more preventatively, and one outcome of this thinking is that the concept of positive behavior support has been broadened to an approach that may be applied to entire schools. Professionals have begun to think about schools as "host environments" and of improving the capacity of the school setting to support the use of effective practices (Sugai & Horner, 1999). Effective host environments include policies, structures, and routines that promote the use of **research-validated practices** (Sugai et al., 2000). It has been demonstrated that the application of strategies that promote positive behavior support across the total school environment (e.g., school-wide discipline plans) dramatically reduce discipline referral rates (Lewis-Palmer, Sugai, & Larson, 1999; Nelson, Martella, & Galand, 1998; Scott, 2001; Skiba, Peterson, & Williams, 1998; Sugai et al., 2000). Accordingly, educators have had to think in terms of providing positive behavior support across the entire range of student behavior. This has been elaborated into school-wide integrated systems of intervention (Sugai et al., 2000) that emphasize multiple levels of prevention, a model that has been widely used in public health but only recently has been applied by other human service agencies, including social services, education, mental health, social work, and crime prevention. The model is described in terms of primary, secondary, and tertiary prevention (see Figure 1–1).

Primary prevention strategies (**universal intervention**) focus on enhancing protective factors in schools and communities and are intended to prevent students from falling into risk. Primary prevention is universal, that is, applied through the efforts of all school staff and across all students. An example of a universal intervention is inoculations to prevent such diseases as polio and measles. A school-based example of a universal intervention is a school-wide plan for addressing student discipline that includes consistent expectations for desired behavior that are taught to all students. One expectation is to "show respect." Students are taught that on the playground, showing respect toward others means to share play equipment. In the music room, showing respect toward property means to keep hands off the instruments that they don't use.

Secondary prevention (targeted intervention) involves activities that provide support (such as mentoring, skill development, and other types of specialized assistance) to students who are identified as at risk so that they will not develop patterns of problematic coping (e.g., antisocial behavior, substance abuse) or other behavioral manifestations that contribute to even more serious problems. Secondary prevention strategies include efforts targeted at specific problems or individuals for whom primary prevention strategies have not been effective. For example, children with thin tooth enamel may receive specialized dental care. A school-based example of secondary prevention is implementation of systematic instruction in social skills for students with poor or inappropriate interactions with peers or adults.

Tertiary prevention (intensive intervention) targets individuals with serious problems that constitute a chronic condition and attempts to ameliorate the effects of their condition on their daily functioning. These strategies are delivered through highly specialized services that are orchestrated by a team. For example, children with

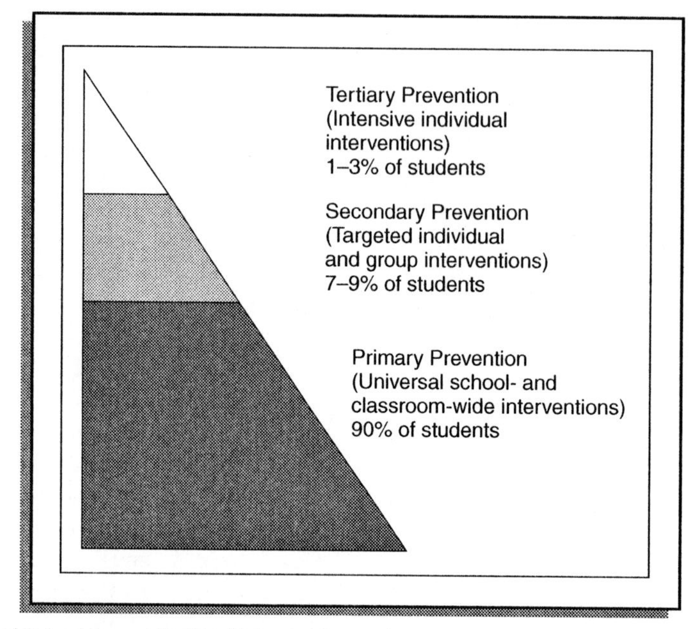

FIGURE 1–1 Model of School-Based Positive Behavior Support

chronic health conditions may receive highly specialized and ongoing treatment, and their families may be shown how to manage and support their child as well as how to meet their own continuing needs. A school-based example of tertiary prevention is the implementation of a **wraparound plan** for a student who also is being served by the mental health or juvenile justice system. This plan would coordinate services across school, home, and community life domains.

> What level of positive behavior support do you think would be most appropriate to address Tracy and Rodney's behaviors?

Implementing Positive Behavior Support

Obviously, the process of developing comprehensive interventions that address all three levels of prevention require significant changes in the way schools operate. As documented previously, this level of change can—and has—been accomplished. The process begins by building the capacity of the school as a host environment by developing school-wide systems that focus on decreasing the number of new cases of problem behavior or situations by ensuring and maintaining the use of effective practices for all students (Sugai & Horner, 2002). In other words, the foundation of positive behavior support is a set of universal interventions, implemented for all students by all school staff. Effective school-wide systems have four salient characteristics: shared vision, leadership, collaborative effort, and data-based evaluation. These four characteristics, when present in conjunction with academic and social strategies and instructional practices that are research validated, increase the likelihood that the school will provide an appropriate, proactive, and preventative learning environment for all students (Liaupsin, Jolivette, & Scott, 2004; Nelson, Martella, & Marchand-Martella, 2002).

Shared Vision. Having a shared vision means that the majority of school staff (at least 80%, according to Sugai and Horner, 1999) agree on the existence of predictable barriers and patterns that impede appropriate student academic and social growth

(Scott & Hunter, 2001). A shared vision regarding these issues is achieved through a meeting of the entire staff (including instructional, administrative, and noninstructional personnel) to achieve consensus regarding where, when, and under what conditions students are most likely to engage in problematic behaviors or to fail academically or socially. This is accomplished by sharing experiences, looking at existing data (e.g., office disciplinary referrals), and talking about current school practices, such as how students are supervised in commons areas or how the staff respond to students who violate school rules. Next, the staff agree on strategies to address problems identified and formulate a set of objectives and time frame for their accomplishment (e.g., a 50% reduction in office disciplinary referrals from the cafeteria in 2 months). Finally, the staff agree on a time frame for making these system changes and evaluating their outcomes.

Leadership. The characteristic of leadership involves both the support and commitment of the school administration and leadership from nonadministrative staff in terms of day-to-day implementation, monitoring, and evaluation of the plan. This may be performed by a school-wide team (Liaupsin et al., 2004).

Collaborative Effort. As this term suggests, the staff must next agree on how the school-wide system will be implemented. The first step is to decide how agreed-on academic and social expectations will be taught, modeled, and reinforced by all staff. Personnel with specific skills, training, or experience may be designated to perform a specific function (e.g., evaluate an academic curriculum, provide staff training in the implementation of a specific procedure). It is important that all staff collaborate in making decisions regarding changes in school practices (Liaupsin et al., 2004).

Data-Based Evaluation. To achieve and maintain an effective school-wide system, it is important that staff use data to make informed decisions regarding the changes made within the school. Data that are directly related to the goals and objectives of the plan should be collected and shared. Data should come from a variety of sources, including office referrals, student academic achievement, and student behavioral incidents. These data should be summarized and regularly presented to all staff (through straightforward visual displays) so that decisions can be made objectively and consensually (Liaupsin et al., 2004).

Behavior Intervention Planning

This process may sound daunting, but hundreds of schools throughout the United States and Canada are successfully implementing universal prevention based on positive behavior support. Consult the Website of the National Technical Assistance Center on Positive Behavioral Interventions and Supports for an extensive array of resources and links to individuals and agencies that can provide training and technical assistance. Specific procedures for implementing universal school- and classroom-wide strategies are described in Chapter 2.

Targeted interventions may be designed for individual students or for a small group having similar needs.[2] Important elements of targeted interventions are functional assessments of problem behavior; identification, instruction, and reinforcement of a desired replacement behavior; effective (direct) instruction of both academic and social skills; the use of errorless learning strategies; and systematic plans for responding to problem behavior. For individual students, a behavior intervention plan (BIP; see Chapter 4) is developed from a functional assessment of problem behaviors and their environmental contexts. Appropriate skills are identified that can serve as functional replacement behaviors, and students are taught, prompted, and reinforced in their use. At the same time, strategies are created to facilitate success in settings where problem behaviors are likely to occur and to respond to targeted problem behaviors if and when they occur. Finally, a plan for collecting data to monitor occurrences of targeted and replacement behaviors is developed, and decision

BOX 1–1 Criteria for an Effective Intervention Plan

1. The plan must be written so that all aspects will be clear to everyone involved in its implementation.
2. The plan must be implemented as written.
3. The plan must be evaluated regularly and systematically against data decision rules (see Chapter 6).
4. The plan must be revised as often as needed. If the plan isn't working, *change the plan!*

rules are created for determining when parts of the plan need to be revised or replaced (Scott & Nelson, 1999). Box 1-1 presents four important criteria that must be met if a BIP is to be effective.

Again, interventions at this level are best planned, implemented, and monitored by a team. This team, which we refer to as the **Behavior Support Team,** may be a subset of the team that provides support to staff in addressing school-wide, specific setting, or classroom behavioral issues (Todd, Horner, Sugai, & Colvin, 1999). The team supports all persons who are working with the student (as well as the student himself) through regular meetings and consultation. Todd et al. (1999) recommend that the Behavior Support Team include at least one member who is competent in designing and providing positive behavior support, the staff member who requested assistance, a family member, a representative of the school-wide team, other school staff who have a good relationship with the student, and, when appropriate, the student. The team conducts the functional behavioral assessment, designs the BIP (which may be referred to as a behavior support or positive behavior support plan) and strategies for its implementation, and provides direct and consultative assistance with regard to ongoing implementation and evaluation.

> Have you been in schools where Behavior Support Teams are in place? How do they work? How do staff and students regard them?

Experience with secondary prevention strategies indicates that they are effective for approximately 7% to 9% of the student population. Thus, schools should anticipate that tertiary prevention will be needed for the remaining 1% to 3% of students.

Tertiary prevention is accomplished through intensive interventions, which are individualized and based on multiple assessments of student, provider, and family needs as well as their strengths. A fundamental distinction of intensive interventions is that they frequently involve providers from other human service agencies (e.g., juvenile court, child welfare, mental health) and that the intervention plan extends beyond the school day. However, these intervention plans should incorporate features of other formal plans, such as IEPs and 504 accommodation plans (see p. 13). If educational programs and interventions for this most needy group of students are to succeed, they must occur in the context of an integrated system of services offered by numerous agencies that support the child and his family. Children and youth experiencing significant emotional and behavioral problems require many services that flexibly "wrap around" their needs at home, in the community, in the workplace, and in school (Eber & Keenan, 2004). Such integrated **systems of care** (Stroul & Friedman, 1986) have been established in many communities and several states (Epstein, Quinn, Nelson, Polsgrove, & Cumblad, 1993; Illback, Nelson, & Sanders, 1998). Integration of service

delivery is characteristic of wraparound planning, which is described in Chapter 10. Thus, wraparound plans consider such life domains as employment, food, clothing, transportation, and recreation. Naturally, such plans also are developed, implemented, and evaluated by a team, consisting of providers, the family, and others who know and care about the child. The wraparound planning format and strategy developed out of systems of care initiatives that attempt to deliver intensive levels of service in natural home, school, and community settings. Consult the Website of the National Technical Assistance Center for Positive Behavioral Interventions and Support for more information. You will find a summary of the major characteristics and actions needed to implement all three levels of positive behavior support on the Companion Website.

LEGISLATION AFFECTING STUDENT BEHAVIOR

IDEA 2004 Disciplinary Regulations[3]

The Education of the Handicapped Act of 1975 (PL 94-142) and its subsequent amendments have constituted a major accomplishment in terms of guaranteeing appropriate educational experiences for children and youth with disabilities. However, as the poor outcomes for students with EBD suggest, pupils whose educational performance is impaired by their emotional or behavior problems have not benefited greatly from this legislation; compared with a very conservative prevalence estimate of 2% of the school-age population, less than 1% are receiving special education across the nation (U.S. Department of Education, 2002). In contrast, Roberts, Attkisson, and Rosenblatt's (1998) review of epidemiology studies of children with emotional or behavioral disorders suggests that the average prevalence of children with such conditions is 10.2% for preschool, 13.2% for elementary, and 16.5% for secondary students. The movement toward school-wide positive behavior support notwithstanding, few schools are dealing effectively with the emotional and behavior problems of the large numbers of students *not* identified as having EBD.

As we noted earlier, the most recent amendments to IDEA have had a dramatic impact on schools' disciplinary practices regarding students with disabilities. Specifically, these amendments require that an FBA be conducted for those students with disabilities who violate a code of student conduct through behaviors that result in a change in educational placement (§615 [K]). Specifically, IDEA 2004 states the following:

1. School personnel may consider any unique circumstances on a case-by-case basis when determining whether to order a change in placement for a child with a disability who violates a code of student conduct. School personnel may remove a child with a disability who violates a code of student conduct from his current placement to an appropriate alternative educational setting, another setting, or suspension, for not more than 10 school days (to the extent such alternatives are applied to children without disabilities) (§ 615 [k] (1) (A) (B)).
2. If school personnel seek to order a change in placement that would exceed 10 school days and the behavior that gave rise to the violation of the school code is determined not to be a manifestation of the child's disability, the relevant disciplinary procedures applicable to children without disabilities may be applied to the child in the same manner and for the same duration in which the procedures would be applied to children without disabilities, except as provided in section 612 (a) (1) although it may be provided in an **interim alternative educational setting** (§ 615 [k] (1) (C)).
3. A child with a disability who is removed from his current placement (irrespective of whether the behavior is determined to be a

manifestation of the child's disability) shall continue to receive educational services, as provided in section 612 (a) (1), so as to enable him to continue to participate in the general education curriculum, although in another setting, and to progress toward meeting the goals set out in his IEP; and receive, as appropriate, a functional behavioral assessment, behavioral intervention services and modifications, that are designed to address the behavior violation so that it does not recur (§ 615 [k] (1) (D)).

4. Except as provided in subparagraph (B), within 10 school days of any decision to change the placement of a child with a disability because of a violation of a code of student conduct, the **local educational agency** (LEA), the parent, and relevant members of the **Individualized Education Program Team,** or IEP Team (as determined by the parent and the local educational agency), shall review all relevant information in the child's file, including his IEP, any teacher observations, and any relevant information provided by the parents to determine if the conduct in question was caused by, or had a direct and substantial relationship to, the child's disability; or if the conduct in question was the direct result of the local educational agency's failure to implement the IEP (§ 615 [k] (1) (E)).

The process of deciding whether the student's behavior may be attributed to his disability is known as a **manifestation determination.** If, on the basis of the information mentioned in the previous paragraph, it is determined that the behavior was a manifestation of the student's disability, the IEP Team is required to conduct a functional behavioral assessment and implement a BIP, or review a BIP that already has been developed and modify it, as necessary, to address the behavior. The law also states that the student must be returned to the placement from which he was removed, unless the parent and the LEA agree to a change in placement as part of the modification of the BIP (§ 615 [k] (1) (F)). However, if the student has brought a weapon on school premises or to a school function, or knowingly possesses or uses illegal drugs or sells or solicits the sale of a controlled substance either on school premises or at a school function, school personnel may remove him to an interim alternative educational setting for no more than 45 school days without regard to whether the behavior is determined to be a manifestation of the student's disability (§ 615 [k] (1) (G)). As previously noted, if the IEP Team determines that the behavior is not a manifestation of the student's disability, disciplinary procedures applied to students without disabilities may be used.

However, a word of caution is in order. As noted by the Council for Exceptional Children (CEC, 2004, November 30), professionals should exercise caution with regard to interpreting what these new requirements mean until final federal regulations that govern the implementation of these provisions are issued. You should attend training and/or read the upcoming regulations carefully before individually taking any action or as a member of a school team. As soon as these new regulations receive approval, you will find them on the Companion Website.

These "discipline regulations" have a potentially enormous impact on how schools address students with a problem behavior. First, as noted previously, if a student has been (or could be) identified as having a disability, he may not be disciplined through long-term suspension or expulsion unless it can be proven that the behavior that occasioned the disciplinary action was not a manifestation of the disability. Second, the emphasis placed on developing a BIP that is based on an FBA means that, in effect, problem behavior is officially viewed as an opportunity to provide positive behavioral intervention (Katsiyannis & Maag, 1998). These mandated practices are a dramatic contrast to policies that include zero tolerance for even minor student misbehavior and "get tough" disciplinary measures that include harsh punishment and school exclusion (Nelson, 2000).

However, as with many such policies, the IDEA discipline regulations have been misinterpreted and misapplied. Katsiyannis and Smith (2003) reported that placement on homebound instruction is almost routinely used as an interim alternative educational setting for disciplinary purposes. Moreover, Witt, VanDerHyden, and Gilbertson (2004) observed that an unfortunate side effect of the primary emphasis on FBA as a tool for managing undesired behavior in the classroom is that attention is directed away from less specific causes of student misbehavior (e.g., inadequate instruction, absence of feedback or praise for desired behavior). In this text, we have attempted to balance assessment-based intervention strategies with preventative strategies that are based on sound instructional and behavior management procedures.

A new feature of IDEA 2004 is a focus on preventing the mis-identification or over-identification of students with disabilities through prereferral interventions. Three strategies are described in the legislation:

1. The law provides funds for training school personnel in effective teaching strategies and positive behavioral interventions and supports to prevent over-identification and mis-identification of students with disabilities.
2. Local education agencies may use up to 15% of IDEA funds for supportive services to help students not yet identified as having a disability but who require additional academic and behavioral supports to succeed in general education.
3. School districts with significant over-identification of minority students as students with disabilities must operate prereferral programs that work to reduce over-identification.

This focus is timely, given that recent statistics show a trend toward increasing numbers of school-age children at risk for or identified as having EBD (U.S. Department of Education, 2001b). As Kauffman, Brigham, and Mock (2004) observe, prevention, in the form of early intervention, has been demonstrated to be the most promising strategy for diverting at-risk children from trajectories of school and life failure. However, referrals for EBD identification peak in the range of ages 14 to 15 years (Walker, Nishioka, Zeller, Severson, & Feil, 2000), suggesting that "late identification—the opposite of prevention—seems to be the norm" (Kauffman et al., 2004, p. 18). The U.S. Department of Education's Office of Special Education Program Website, as well as the website of the **Council for Exceptional Children** (CEC), provide up-to-date information on IDEA.

Section 504 and the Americans with Disabilities Act

Other federal laws provide protection to individuals with disabilities, including conditions not covered under IDEA. For example, **Section 504** of the Vocational Rehabilitation Act of 1973 requires that all individuals with a disability that substantially limits one or more life activities receive an education comparable to that of their typical peers through an **accommodation plan.** Students with ADHD, as well as other students with disabilities who are not considered eligible under IDEA, should be provided with services under this regulation. The Americans with Disabilities Act of 1990 (ADA; PL 101-336) addresses all types of discrimination against persons with physical or mental disabilities, primarily with regard to employment. While these laws do not afford protection from school suspension or expulsion for students with disabilities to the same extent as does IDEA, court decisions and Office of Civil Rights rulings indicate that IDEA and 504 safeguards may be applicable to students who were excluded from school before their disabilities had been verified (Katsiyannis & Maag, 1998).

No Child Left Behind Act

Finally, the **No Child Left Behind Act** (NCLB; U.S. Department of Education, 2001a) is an ambitious effort by the federal government to improve educational outcomes for all students through targeting improvements in the accountability of schools, better instruction (particularly for students who are economically disadvantaged and culturally diverse), the training and recruitment of high-quality teachers and administrators, promoting school safety, and giving parents greater choice in determining where their children will attend school. Three platforms of NCLB are particularly relevant to the education of students with disability: the law mandates that students make adequate annual progress as measured by standardized assessment of academic performance, it seeks to ensure that all students are taught by "highly qualified" teachers (i.e., teachers who have obtained full state certification or passed the state teacher licensing exam and hold a license to teach in that state), and it emphasizes the use of research-validated practices to improve academic outcomes. Many states have enacted education reform legislation that pre-dates NCLB and includes similar emphasis on schools' accountability to standards of student academic proficiency. However, most existing state standards, as well as those of NCLB, apply to *all* students, and are based on norm-referenced assessments of academic performance. As special education practitioners are well aware, norm-referenced standards do not match the characteristics, needs, and educational results of many children and youth with disabilities. Special educators have voiced concerns that this legislation works against the spirit of individualized educational planning that is the core of IDEA (Council for Exceptional Children, 2003). Furthermore, although an expectation that practices be supported by standards derived from scientific evidence of their effectiveness is a laudable goal, there has been little evidence to date that most educators are aware of or employ evidence-based practices (Landrum, Tankersley, & Kauffman, 2003). More information about this legislation can be obtained from the NCLB Website.

Provisions in both IDEA and NCLB support community-based collaboration in designing appropriate educational services for students with special needs (Eber & Keenan, 2004). These provisions address financial responsibility for services, the provision of services not available in schools, and funds to support interdisciplinary staff training. We hope that the availability of such resources will encourage schools to develop more collaborative approaches for addressing the needs of students with challenging behavior, and their families.

BEHAVIOR DISORDERS OR PROBLEM BEHAVIORS?

As we suggested earlier, the public education system has not embraced the challenge of working with students with difficult behavior. Historically, schools have excluded these pupils or have placed them in segregated schools and classrooms (e.g., alternative education programs, self-contained special education classes) for most or all of the school day. Now that students with disabilities are spending more time in general education settings, *all* educators can expect to work with students with emotional and behavioral problems (whether they are labeled as having this disability or not).

Children and youth with problem behaviors may be assigned a variety of diagnostic or descriptive labels, including emotionally disturbed or behaviorally disordered, juvenile delinquent or socially maladjusted, and ADHD or disruptive behavior disorder. Labels tend to have little relationship to the behaviors that children exhibit. Instead, the characteristics of the setting and teachers' standards and expectations are more predictive of students' behavior than their labels. Nevertheless, IDEA requires that pupils who are provided special education services because of their behavior deviations be defined so that the programs serving them can receive state and federal funds. This law defines students with emotional disorders (ED) as those who exhibit one or more of the following characteristics that adversely affect educational performance over a long period of time and to a marked degree:

1. An inability to learn that cannot be explained by intellectual, sensory, or health factors
2. An inability to build or maintain satisfactory interpersonal relationships with peers and teachers
3. Inappropriate types of behavior or feelings under normal circumstances
4. A general pervasive mood of unhappiness or depression
5. A tendency to develop physical symptoms or fears associated with personal or school problems

(Students with "social maladjustment" are specifically excluded from eligibility under this definition.)

Although this definition has been modified slightly over the years, essentially it is the same as when PL 94-142 was first passed. The definition has been widely criticized by the professional community (Forness & Kavale, 2000). Issues of contention include the vagueness and ambiguity of such criteria as "inability to learn," which results in confusion regarding the distinction between the ED and the learning disabilities definition. The criterion of "inability to build or maintain satisfactory interpersonal relationships" would seem to define social maladjustment, yet students with this condition are specifically excluded from eligibility. Similar problems exist with regard to the remaining three criteria. An alternate definition has been drafted and was circulated for public reaction and comment in the *Federal Register* (1993). Two thirds of more than 1,200 respondents were in favor of the new definition.

Find the alternative definition on the Companion Website and compare this definition to the one in the federal law. Which definition do you think is more appropriate? Why? Read on and see what experts in the field thought.

The report analyzing responses to this definition (McIntyre & Forness, 1997) was never submitted to Congress for action. However, the definition contains statements that highlight "best practices" with respect to identifying and serving students whose EBD dictates a need for special education and related services. First, it emphasizes that EBD is more than a temporary response to stress and is not responsive to **prereferral interventions.** Second, it requires that the determination of eligibility be based on multiple sources of data that are gathered in more than one school setting. Third, it indicates the **comorbidity** of EBD with other conditions, which appears to be the norm in children referred for mental health services, including special education (Forness, 2004). Fourth, it lists some of the mental health diagnoses that could make a student eligible for services if educational performance also is impaired, which allows for coordination of services with other agencies that provide services (Forness & Kavale, 2000).

If you have worked around pupils with EBD, you know that they are no more homogeneous than are children classified any other way. Furthermore, as indicated previously, students who are classified as having another disability or even those who are labeled "gifted" does not rule out the existence of serious emotional and behavior problems. Therefore, in this text we focus on strategies for preventing initial problem behavior, minimizing problems with students who are "at risk" of developing chronic patterns of maladaptive emotions or behavior, and reducing the impact of EBD on the educational outcomes of students so identified. We believe that such a focus will better serve your pupils' interests and will make you a better practitioner.

Obviously, this work is not easy! Attrition rates of educators, especially special educators, are high, and working with students who exhibit challenging emotional and behavioral problems can be highly stressful. Skill in using the strategies presented in this book may be your best protection against this stress. Other considerations and tactics for dealing with stress are presented in the epilogue to this text.

We now turn to assessment procedures used to identify and classify those students whose behavior interferes with their educational progress as well as the early intervention strategies designed to avoid the necessity of special education labels and classification. Here we address the issue of which students should be considered, for educational purposes, as having EBD. We also give you an overview of special education for students with EBD—who they are, how they are identified, and what services are available to them in school.

IDENTIFYING STUDENTS WITH BEHAVIORAL DISORDERS

Serving students through all levels of positive behavior support will lead to the identification of some whose emotional, behavioral, and academic needs dictate that special education and related services be provided so that they can benefit from their school experience. Thus, responsiveness to intervention (or lack thereof) may serve as a **screening** tool to identify students eligible for special education (Barnett, Daly, Jones, & Lentz, 2004; Gresham, 1999). In fact, the President's Commission on Excellence in Special Education (U.S. Department of Education, 2002) recommended that response to intervention be used in place of traditional assessment procedures to determine students' eligibility for special education services. This approach would replace the practice of waiting until a student's problems become sufficiently intense to warrant a referral for special education eligibility assessment (Barnett, et al., 2004). However, current federal law establishes a process for determining eligibility based on referral and assessment. Figure 1-2 depicts how school-wide pos-

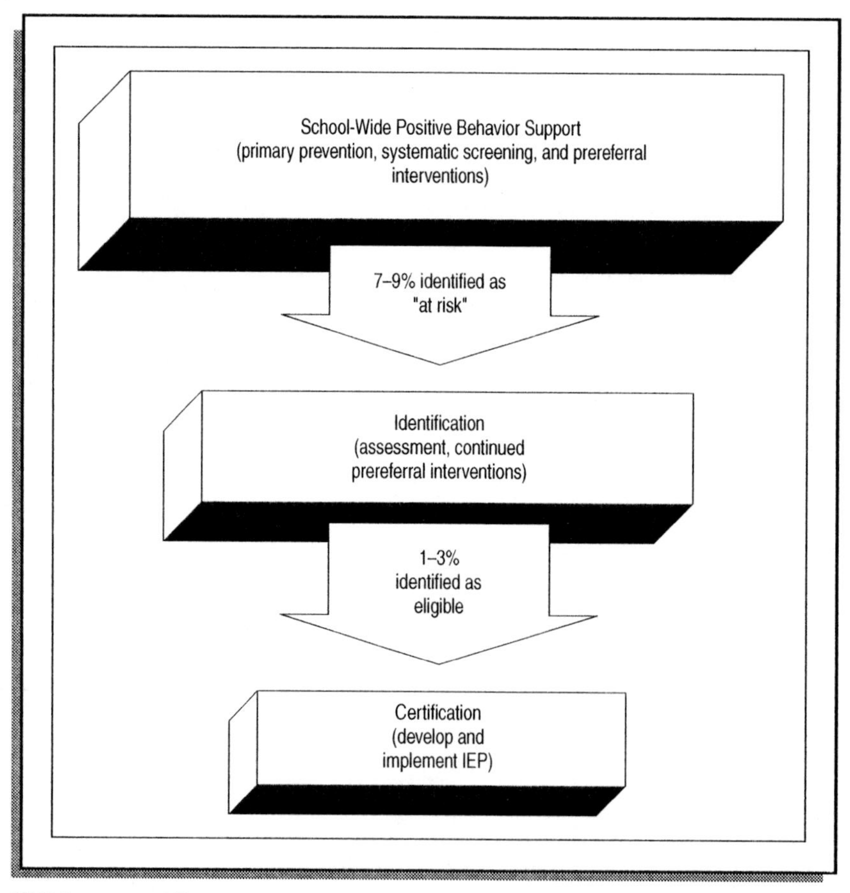

FIGURE 1–2 EBD Assessment Process

itive behavior support and the identification process work together in screening, assessing, and certifying students as eligible for special education services as EBD.

According to IDEA 2004, the determination of whether a student is a child with a disability must be made by a team of qualified professionals and the parent of the child (§ 614 [b] (4) (A)). This group of individuals supervises a series of comprehensive assessments administered by trained and knowledgeable personnel, using a variety of tools and strategies that are appropriate, ensuring that evaluation materials are not discriminatory on a racial or cultural basis and that provide relevant information that assist in determining the student's educational needs (§ 614 [b] (2) (3)). Following the assessment process, this group must decide (within 60 days of the initial referral for evaluation) whether to classify the student as having a disability. They also are responsible for determining the nature and extent of the services to be provided. This group may then become the student's IEP Team which then supervises the implementation of the student's IEP and conducts evaluations of his progress at least once every 3 years, and not more frequently than once a year, unless the parent and the LEA agree otherwise (§ 614 [d] (2) (B)). Box 1-2 lists the individuals that IDEA defines as members of the IEP Team.

Systematic Screening

Procedures commonly used to identify students with EBD include finding those students at risk for EBD through screening, implementing prereferral intervention strategies within the general education program (with appropriate documentation of the effects of these modifications on student performance), and conducting more intensive assessments to determine whether the student should be certified as eligible for special education services because of EBD (Algozzine, Serna, & Patton, 2001). The purpose of prereferral interventions is to address the student's (and the teacher's) issues in the context of the general education environment, thereby preventing a referral for determination of special education eligibility. If your school has implemented positive behavior support, a prereferral intervention corresponds to secondary prevention,

BOX 1–2 Members of the IEP Team

- the parents of the child
- not less than one regular education teacher of the student (if the student is, or may be, participating in the regular education environment)
- not less than one special education teacher, or where appropriate, not less than one special education provider of the student
- a representative of the LEA who: is qualified to provide, or supervise the provision of, specially designed instruction to meet the unique needs of students with disabilities; is knowledgeable about the general education curriculum; and is knowledgeable about the availability of resources of the LEA
- an individual who can interpret the instructional implications of evaluation results
- at the discretion of the parent or the agency, other individuals who have knowledge or special expertise regarding the student, including related services personnel as appropriate
- whenever appropriate, the student (§ 614 [d] (1) (B))

which may involve developing a BIP. However, interventions at this level do not need to be extremely complex: ideally, they consist of program modifications that are relatively easy to implement by the regular education teacher. Some of the most effective interventions are also the most straightforward. Clearly explaining expectations, modifying instruction, providing peer assistance, changing seating arrangements, removing obstacles to desired behavior, having students monitor their own behavior, and providing feedback or praise for desired performances are strategies familiar to most regular educators. Visit the Companion Website to see a form used to document prereferral intervention strategies and their effects. Note that this form suggests only some of the potential interventions that may be attempted singly or in combination.

Whereas systematic school-wide screening procedures routinely are applied to detect other disabilities (e.g., sensory, psychomotor, physical, learning, and cognitive disabilities), screening for EBD typically amounts to a referral to a special education program administrator from the general education classroom teacher. Once referred, teacher-nominated students are very likely to be certified as having EBD, especially if they exhibit **externalizing** (overt, acting-out) behavior patterns. In contrast, students manifesting **internalizing** (withdrawn, depressed) behavior patterns tend not to be referred and therefore are not identified because they are less bothersome to classroom teachers (Walker & Fabre, 1987). However, recent studies have suggested that students with EBD tend to display characteristics across both categories (Cullinan, Evans, Epstein, & Ryser, 2003), which again indicates that comorbidity may be the rule rather than the exception for students with EBD (Cullinan & Epstein, 2001; Kauffman, 2001).

Systematic screening tools have been developed to facilitate the identification of students who may need intervention for emotional or behavioral problems. For example, systematic screening techniques to identify children who are at risk have been developed for use in the elementary schools (McConaughy & Achenbach, 1989; Walker & Severson, 1990). Screening procedures also have been developed to identify children of preschool age at risk of school failure because of emotional and behavioral problems (Feil & Becker, 1993; Feil, Severson, & Walker, 1994; Sinclair, Del'Homme, & Gonzalez, 1993). Students' school records are a rich source of screening information. Walker and his colleagues (Walker, Block-Pedego, Todis, & Severson, 1991) developed a systematic protocol for compiling and analyzing such school records data as attendance and grade promotion patterns, office referrals, health history, and anecdotal comments.

These systematic screening tools are useful and effective; however, staff should receive training and support in administering such instruments as checklists, rating scales, and direct observation protocols. It also is important to be aware of legal and ethical issues involved in singling out individual students for intensive levels of screening. Before implementing school-wide screening procedures, you should consult with your school district's due process experts.

Although such procedures make identifying students with EBD more objective and accountable, they do not remove the bias that exists when identification is based on teacher referral. Referral-driven identification procedures place the regular education teacher in the role of a gatekeeper who determines which students will be considered for special education services. Some pupils are referred because their teachers simply are less tolerant of disruptive behavior. Systematic screening, coupled with early intervention that impacts the child and his home, presents a significant opportunity to prevent the development of intractable EBD.

Assessment for Identification

Once screening has identified a student as at risk, educators should begin the process of assessment.

As we stress throughout this text, assessment is an ongoing process that is integrally tied to intervention. That is, what we *do* about a student's behavior problem is based on what we *know* about the student, his academic and behavioral functioning, and the circumstances surrounding his behavior. As we have just seen, the process begins with making some adjustments in the environment and seeing how the student responds. However, at this level, interventions are likely to be more systematic and intensive, such as a BIP.

The difference between an informal tactic and a targeted intervention strategy, such as a BIP, is that the latter should be applied and evaluated systematically. To ensure this, it is desirable to create a building-based Behavior Support Team as a resource for teachers experiencing difficulty with specific pupils (Todd et al., 1999). Although these teams may develop a plan for any student, the implementation and evaluation of prereferral interventions should be ongoing throughout the process of evaluating students to determine their eligibility for special education and related services.

There are no hard-and-fast rules concerning the duration of prereferral interventions, but 20 to 40 school days (i.e., 1 to 2 months) constitutes an adequate period for determining whether the problem can be managed without more formal procedures. To avoid the tendency to turn prereferral interventions over to special services personnel, ownership of both the problem and the intervention plans should be vested in the general education program. Therefore, staff identified with the general education program are fundamental members of Behavior Support Teams. Specialized staff (e.g., special education teachers, school psychologists) may serve as ancillary team members on specific cases.

Prereferral interventions are important for two reasons. First, they emphasize making attempts to solve students' behavior problems using resources available in the general education program before considering special education referrals. Second, the results of such interventions provide assessment information useful for those making decisions about pupils' eligibility for services and determining what services are needed. Again, the processes of screening and providing prereferral interventions can be managed more effectively in a system of school-wide positive behavior support. Screening is accomplished by noting which students fail to benefit from primary prevention strategies (universal interventions). Secondary prevention for these students consists of the implementation of BIPs or more informal strategies. The need for special education and related services may be considered for students who do not benefit from these targeted interventions.

Certification

The next stage initiates formal consideration of the student's eligibility for special education services. The question of whether a student is manifesting a condition that constitutes a disability is a serious matter. Therefore, IDEA requires that the student's parents be notified of the school's intent to assess the child and give their approval. Parents also should be active participants throughout the assessment and decision-making processes, including making decisions regarding the child's educational placement and development and implementation of the IEP. These due process safeguards protect students' and parents' rights, including the right to have an independent assessment of their child and to request a hearing in the event that they disagree with the decision of the LEA.

In addition to medical and sociological screening or evaluations, traditional assessment for identifying students with EBD usually consists of a battery of psychoeducational instruments, including an individual intelligence scale, norm- and criterion-referenced measures of achievement, instruments that assess perceptual-motor skills, and, less frequently, measures of personality characteristics, although their poor reliability and validity render them suspect for diagnosing EBD (Salvia & Ysseldyke, 2001). Data from these instruments may be supplemented with teacher or parent interviews, direct observation of the pupil, and anecdotal information from school records. Responsibility for this stage of the classification process often falls on school psychologists. However, as Gresham (1999) observes, school psychologists are more comfortable and competent in assessing mental retardation and learning disabilities than EBD.

Walker and Fabre (1987) offer support for this observation, noting that research suggests the behavioral characteristics and performance deficits of referred and nonreferred pupils are quite similar and that assessment data typically have little impact on certification decisions.

Recent improvements in screening and identification procedures have made this process more objective and systematic. Several states (e.g., Kentucky, Iowa, Oregon) have developed systematic procedures for screening and identifying such pupils and providing services for them. The **Council for Children with Behavioral Disorders** (1987) recommends using multiple sources of data for identifying and documenting efforts to modify the student's behavior in general education settings. Figure 1-3 shows a checklist that teams conducting initial evaluations can use in making eligibility determinations.

Mental Health Assessment. Many school districts rely on other agencies or professionals (e.g., mental health clinics, psychologists or psychiatrists in private practice) to conduct eligibility evaluations. Mental health professionals typically use an assessment model that is considerably different from models used for educational purposes. One of the chief differences is that the mental health assessment model is based on identifying emotional or cognitive pathology that is presumed to underlie the student's behavior problems. Until recently, this medical model dominated other approaches to the assessment of emotional and behavioral problems. It is still widely used by mental health practitioners and school districts in some states.

The classification decisions resulting from mental health assessment often result in diagnostic labels that come from the ***Diagnostic and Statistical Manual of Mental Disorders, 4th Edition*** (*DSM-IV*), published by the American Psychiatric Association (2000). The *DSM-IV* classifies psychological disorders along five axes, or dimensions. Axis I consists of the major pattern of symptoms, or clinical disorders, that the student exhibits; Axis II describes personality disorders; Axis III addresses general medical conditions; Axis IV describes psychosocial factors that impose stress on the individual; and Axis V considers the pupil's level of adaptive functioning over the past year. A diagnosis may or may not be made on every axis, depending on the student and how much information the evaluator has about the case. However, a principal diagnosis, using the categories and accompanying diagnostic codes for Axis I and/or II, is always made. The Axis I or II categories for disorders usually first diagnosed in infancy, childhood, and adolescence are grouped into 10 classes, as shown in Table 1-1. More specific diagnoses are made within these categories and subcategories for individual cases. For example, the diagnostic criteria for ADHD are presented on the Companion Website.

Children may also be assigned an Axis I or II diagnosis from one of the other categories included in the system (e.g., school phobia, classified as one of the anxiety disorders; anorexia nervosa, which is one of the eating disorders). As the diagnostic criteria for ADHD suggest, the *DSM-IV* approach to assessment is descriptive in that the diagnosis is based on a pattern, or **syndrome,** of behavior. It also is clinical because portions of the diagnosis are based on judgments and inferences made from the presenting symptoms (e.g., "failure to develop peer relationships appropriate to developmental level"). Moreover, traditional diagnostic procedures usually occur in the clinician's office where the verbal reports of the child and others (e.g., parents) must be used instead of direct behavioral

Enter District Name Here
Emotional-Behavioral Disability (EBD)
Eligibility Determination Form
(Attachment to Evaluation Team Action Form)

Student's Full Name:	
Date of Birth:	Date of Team Meeting:
School:	

The Evaluation Team determines a student to have an emotional behavior disability and is eligible for specially designed instruction and related services when:

Complete During Team Meeting		
☐ Y ☐ N ☐ Insufficient	1.	When provided with interventions to meet instructional and social-emotional needs, the student continues to exhibit one or more of the following, when compared to the child's peer and cultural reference groups, across settings, over a long period of time and to a marked degree: ☐ Severe deficits in social competence or appropriate behavior which cause an inability to build or maintain satisfactory interpersonal relationships with adults or peers. ☐ Severe deficits in academic performance which are not commensurate with the student's ability level and are not solely a result of intellectual, sensory, or other health factors but are related to the child's social-emotional problems. ☐ A general pervasive mood of unhappiness or depression. ☐ A tendency to develop physical symptoms or fears associated with personal or school problems.
☐ Y ☐ N ☐ Insufficient	2.	The severe deficit in social competence, appropriate behavior, and academic performance is not the result of isolated inappropriate behaviors that are the result of willful, intentional, or wanton actions.
☐ Y ☐ N ☐ Insufficient	3.	Evaluation information confirms there is an adverse effect on educational performance.
Supporting Evidence:		
☐ Y ☐ N		Evaluation information confirms that lack of instruction in reading and/or math was not a determinant factor in the eligibility decision.
☐ Y ☐ N ☐ NA		Evaluation information confirms that limited English proficiency was not a determinant factor in the eligibility decision.

Actions Regarding Eligibility Determination for Special Education and Related Services
The Evaluation Team used the above interpretation of the evaluation data to determine:

☐ The student has an emotional–behavior disability and is eligible for specially designed instruction and related services.
☐ The student does not have an emotional-behavior disability.
☐ Evaluation data were insufficient to determine eligibility. Additional assessments and/or data in the area(s) of:_____ will be obtained/collected. The Evaluation Team will reconvene by _____ to review and determine eligibility.

FIGURE 1–3 Eligibility Determination Checklist

TABLE 1–1 *DSM-IV* Diagnostic Classifications

Mental Retardation	Predominantly Inattentive Type
Mild Mental Retardation	Predominantly Hyperactive-Impulsive Type
Moderate Mental Retardation	Attention Deficit/Hyperactivity Disorder NOS
Severe Mental Retardation	Conduct Disorder
Profound Mental Retardation	Oppositional Defiant Disorder
Mental Retardation: Severity Unspecified	Disruptive Behavior Disorder NOS
Learning Disorders	**Feeding and Eating Disorders of Infancy or Early Childhood**
Reading Disorder	Pica
Mathematics Disorder	Rumination Disorder
Disorder of Written Expression	Feeding Disorder of Infancy or Early Childhood
Learning Disorder Not Otherwise Specified (NOS)	
Motor Skill Disorder	**Tic Disorders**
Developmental Coordination Disorder	Tourette's Disorder
Communication Disorders	Chronic Motor or Vocal Tic Disorder
Expressive Language Disorder	Transient Tic Disorder
Mixed Receptive-Expressive Language Disorder	Tic Disorder NOS
Phonological Disorder	**Elimination Disorders**
Stuttering	Encopresis
Communication Disorder NOS	With Constipation and Overflow Incontinence
Pervasive Developmental Disorders	Without Constipation and Overflow Incontinence
Autistic Disorder	Enuresis (Not Due to a General Medical Condition)
Rett's Disorder	**Other Disorders of Infancy, Childhood, or Adolescence**
Childhood Disintegrative Disorder	Separation Anxiety Disorder
Asperger's Disorder	Selective Mutism
Pervasive Developmental Disorder NOS	Reactive Attachment Disorder of Infancy or Early
Attention Deficit and Disruptive Behavior Disorders	Stereotypic Movement Disorder
Attention Deficit/Hyperactivity Disorder	Disorder of Infancy, Childhood, or Adolescence NOS
Combined Type	

Source: *American Psychiatric Association (2000, pp. 13–14).*

observation. This affects the reliability of the diagnosis (i.e., two clinicians may not arrive at the same diagnostic assessment because each receives a different report or interprets the same information differently). *DSM-IV* notes that the categories are not mutually exclusive, that children often have problems not subsumed within a single diagnostic category, and that many behavior problems do not warrant diagnostic classification. This observation is consistent with evidence that EBD and other conditions exhibit substantial comorbidity (Forness, 2004).

The limitations of the mental health diagnostic and classification system have been widely discussed (Algozzine et al., 2001; Kauffman, 2001). However, Forness and Kavale (2000) suggest that *DSM-IV* diagnoses could be used to qualify a student for special education if school functioning also is impaired.

The assessment procedures followed depend on the discipline of the evaluator (e.g., psychiatrist, psychologist, social worker), the evaluator's skills, and the diagnostic tools available. Many diagnosticians conduct structured or unstructured interviews with the student, the student's parents, or others (e.g., classroom teachers). In some cases, standardized assessment procedures or instruments also may be used. These may include individually administered intelligence tests, personality tests, tests of interest or preference, language assessment instruments, behavior rating scales, or self-concept inventories. It is important to recognize that many of the instruments used, especially **projective techniques** (in which the client "projects" his personality through responses to ambiguous stimuli, such as ink blots or pictures), offer poor reliability and validity as well as inadequate norms (Salvia & Ysseldyke, 2001). The inadequacy and educational irrelevance of personality tests, as well as the threat of legal sanction arising from decisions based on their results, have led to increasing reliance on more objective procedures (Salvia & Ysseldyke, 2001).

Despite their weaknesses, clinical assessment procedures still are widely used in assessments of children and youth. A good diagnostic evaluation can be helpful, especially if the outcomes include multidisciplinary planning and follow-up activities. We have chosen to organize this text in terms of educationally relevant behavioral categories rather than those found in *DSM-IV;* therefore, you may need to translate psychiatric diagnoses into more useful terms. The term ED or EBD is sufficient to identify pupils for special education. Once more, we stress that is not necessary to formally classify students in order to work with them.

School-Based Assessment. The process used in schools for determining whether students should be considered as exhibiting EBD consists of compiling the information gathered from systematic screening and prereferral or targeted intervention procedures and the results of comprehensive assessments directed by school personnel. This process begins with a referral for formal evaluation and involves gathering information from attempts to manage the problem at the secondary prevention level as well as systematic assessments by school staff and other professionals. Table 1-2 summarizes the process. The compilation of prereferral screening and intervention data should demonstrate that (a) problem behaviors are perceived as extreme by more than one observer across more than one setting; (b) prereferral interventions have been attempted and have failed; (c) the problem has existed over a reasonably long period of time (except in the case of behavior that poses a hazard to life or safety); (d) the problem cannot be explained by factors such as temporary stress, medical problems, inappropriate educational programming, or cultural differences; (e) the pupil has deficits in academic performance or social skills; and (f) the problem behaviors occur at a high rate or deviate markedly from acceptable norms.

Intellectual Assessment. Intelligence tests have very limited utility for assessing emotional or behavior problems. However, an intellectual assessment can document that the problem is not due to cognitive impairment. (If the student has some degree of cognitive disability, it should be documented that specific programming related to this condition has not solved the student's behavior problems.) It is important to realize that students may exhibit both cognitive disabilities and behavior problems or EBD. Therefore, schools should be able to bring the needed services to the pupil in the current school placement rather than moving the student to another program unless it is decided that the latter is more appropriate. Changes in school placement require invoking due process, which includes reassessment and decision making by the IEP Team established to supervise the pupil's educational program, and thus cannot be made quickly or easily. Taking services to the student is more expedient and less disruptive and so is the preferred strategy.

Assessment of Educational Progress. The academic assessment may be accomplished through a variety of procedures, including individually administered norm-referenced achievement tests, curriculum-based assessments, analysis of classroom work samples and data regarding academic progress, and direct observation of time on task. Several sources of academic data should be provided to rule out the possibility that conclusions are based on inadequate samples of student performance. Academic assessment is important for two reasons. First, in most states, students can be

TABLE 1–2 Pupil Identification Assessment Process

I. Compilation of Screening and Prereferral Data
Documentation that student's problem behaviors occur more frequently or more intensely than nonreferred peers, that such behaviors have occurred for a long period of time, and that they have not been solved through systematic management in the general education setting

Acceptable procedures
- Standardized behavior ratings completed by two or more teachers or by teachers and parents
- Direct observation data (including data on nondeviant peer)
- Evidence that problems have occurred for a prolonged period
- Evidence that problems are not due to temporary stress or to curriculum or cultural factors
- Evidence that interventions in regular program have been systematically implemented and have not been effective
- Verification by school personnel that behavior is dangerous to student or to others

II. Intellectual Assessment
Documentation that behavior is not due to impaired cognitive functioning or, if cognitive deficits are present, that appropriate programming has not solved behavior problems

Acceptable procedures
- Acceptable individual measure of intelligence or aptitude, administered by qualified examiner

III. Academic Assessment
Documentation that academic performance or progress has not been satisfactory for a period of time

Acceptable procedures
- Individually administered norm-referenced measures of academic achievement
- Group-administered achievement tests *and* written analysis of classroom products and documentation of classroom academic progress
- Curriculum-based or criterion-referenced assessments documenting progress across curriculum
- Direct observation of academic time on task
- Samples of classroom work across time and tasks

IV. Social and Language Competence Assessment
Documentation that student is deficient in social skills or that social status is seriously affected

Acceptable procedures
- Administration of approved standardized social skills inventories or checklists
- Administration of acceptable assessments of expressive and receptive language functioning
- Administration of adaptive behavior scales
- Administration of sociometric scales or procedures
- Direct observation in unstructured social setting (include peer comparison data)

V. Social, Developmental, and School History
Documentation that problem is not due to any previously undiscovered factors or cultural differences

Acceptable procedures
- Culturally sensitive assessments and interviews with parents or guardians, referring teacher, other teachers, student
- Review of student's cumulative school records

VI. Medical evaluation
Documentation that problem is not due to health factors

Acceptable procedures
- Medical screening by physician, school nurse, or physician's assistant
- Comprehensive medical evaluation if student fails to pass screening

certified as eligible for special education under the EBD category only if their educational performance is adversely affected. Second, behavior problems and academic difficulties often are functionally related. Students with EBD have substantial deficits in academic achievement (Reid, Gonzalez, Nordness, Trout, & Epstein, 2004). It stands to reason that a pupil who is frustrated by academic tasks and expectations that are beyond his current skill levels may act out or withdraw to avoid such tasks or to express his feelings. Conversely, problem behaviors may interfere with academic learning because they are incompatible with academic performance or because they result in disciplinary actions that cause the student to be removed from the instructional setting.

Assessment of Social and Linguistic Functioning. The social and language competence assessment is likely to reveal social skills deficits in students considered for EBD classification because failure to establish satisfactory social relationships is a defining characteristic. Therefore, it is important that skills related to social interactions with peers and adults be assessed. **Social competence** is a general domain referring to summative evaluative judgments regarding the adequacy of a student's performance on social tasks by an informed social agent (Walker & McConnell, 1988). Gresham and Reschly (1987) demonstrated that social competence is composed of two subdomains: adaptive behavior and specific social skills. Measures of adaptive behavior typically assess general independent functioning, including physical development, self-direction, personal responsibility, economic or vocational skills, and functional academic skills (Walker & McConnell, 1988). The American Association of Mental Deficiency (AAMD) *Adaptive Behavior Scale, School Edition* (Lambert, Windmiller, Tharinger, & Cole, 1981) or the *Vineland Adaptive Behavior Scale* (Sparrow, Balla, & Cicchetti, 1985) are typically used to measure adaptive behavior. The format of these scales consists of ratings completed through interviews with persons familiar with the pupil's functioning or development in relevant settings. Social skills are the specific strategies one uses to respond to social living tasks (Walker & McConnell, 1988). Standardized measures of social skills typically consist of rating scale items completed by persons who are familiar with the student's functioning. A recommended alternate procedure for assessing social skills consists of conducting direct observations of the pupil's behavior in unstructured social situations.

The direct observation of behavior is an important assessment tool for pupils being considered for special education services. It provides an opportunity to evaluate the student's behavior in the immediate social context, enabling the assessor to identify excess and deficit problem behaviors and adaptive behavior patterns, as well as the antecedents and consequences of specific behaviors. Potential biases associated with personal judgment are reduced when using direct observation procedures. Behavioral observation strategies are described in Chapter 5.

Research consistently shows that the language proficiency of students with EBD, as a group, falls significantly below that of typical peers (Rodgers-Adkinson & Hooper, 2003). **Pragmatic language skills,** or the functional use of language to express social intentions in ways that are culturally acceptable, seem to be particularly affected (Rinaldi, 2003). Therefore, assessment should address pragmatics as well as language skills more typically assessed, such as syntax, semantics, and phonology. Both receptive and expressive language areas should be addressed, of course.

Archival Student Data. Additional data may be collected about social, developmental, and school history through interviews with the student's caregivers, the referring teacher, other teachers, and the student. A thorough search of the pupil's cumulative school records should be conducted to assess such variables as attendance, health history, discipline reports, and previous screenings or referrals for special education evaluation. Tools such as the *School Archival Records Search* (Walker et al., 1991) are available to systematize this process.

Assessment also must take into account the potential contribution of cultural factors. Although membership in a racially or ethnically different cultural group is not a reason to overlook a student's maladaptive behavior, school personnel must be sensitive to the effects that cultural attitudes and customs may have on behavior. Students from families with low income and those who belong to a racial minority, especially African American males, are more often referred for special education evaluation than Caucasian students (Hosp & Reschly, 2003) and are overrepresented in special education programs for pupils with EBD (Bradley, Henderson, & Monfore, 2004; Coutinho, Oswald, Best, & Forness, 2002). Culturally different students may exhibit patterns of language and social behavior that conflict with the normative standards and expectations of the school. Moreover, pupils' awareness of their deviation from school norms regarding dress, extracurricular activities, and financial status may cause them to withdraw from or rebel against persons exemplifying these norms. Cultural stereotypes also may affect the expectations and reactions of other pupils and school staff, which can intensify difficulties involving cultural issues. Therefore, in assessing students with cultural differences, evaluators should attempt to determine the function that "deviant" behaviors may serve for the student (e.g., "playing the dozens," avoiding direct eye contact) with reference to his cultural group before concluding that such behavior patterns are maladaptive. When culturally appropriate behaviors conflict with staff or peer expectations, assessors should be open to the conclusions that the expectations are in error and that intervention should address adult standards for behavior in addition to (or instead of) the student's behavior.

McIntyre (1995) developed an instrument to assist in evaluating the influence of culture on behavior and learning. Intended for use in the prereferral and referral processes, the *McIntyre Assessment of Culture* contains a student information form, a parent/home information form, and a behavior checklist. The information derived from these sources is analyzed to determine whether the behaviors of concern to educators have a cultural bias.

Medical Assessment. Finally, most states require that a medical evaluation be performed to rule out possible health factors. Generally, this may be accomplished through a routine screening by a school nurse or health practitioner. Students who do not pass this screening should be referred for a comprehensive medical examination.

Summary. An adequate assessment of students referred for possible classification as EBD is comprehensive and takes considerable time. The seriousness of the decision being considered justifies this detailed evaluation process. Also, this process is multidisciplinary; no single professional is qualified to perform all these assessments. It is appropriate and desirable to involve professionals in other roles within the school as well as outside the schools in gathering and analyzing assessment data. However, it is important that a staff member or a team of staff from the pupil's school compile and analyze the assessment data and present it to the persons who will make the certification decision.

The decision to certify a pupil as having EBD is too important to be made on the basis of limited information or by persons not familiar with all facets of the student's personality and environment. That is why IDEA requires that eligibility decisions be made by a team of professionals and the student's parent. The team determines whether the assessment information supports the need for special education certification, makes decisions regarding the most appropriate educational program and placement, and evaluates the student's progress and the effectiveness of the educational services provided.

The validity of the decisions made by evaluation teams has been questioned, however. Potter, Ysseldyke, and Regan (1983) gave a large group of school professionals assessment information on a hypothetical student that reflected performance in the average range for the student's age and grade placement. They indicated that the student had been referred for special education and asked the professionals whether they believed the pupil was eligible for it. Of these professionals, 51% declared the student eligible for special education services. This study verifies that assessment data often are not used in making certification decisions (Walker & Fabre, 1987). The procedures we described in the previous sections should help to remedy this problem; however, decisions involving the judgments of persons inescapably are subjective. Careful analysis and review are needed to make these decisions.

Behavior Support in General Education Settings

Determining that a student has EBD actually consists of a set of decisions. If the evaluation team decides that the pupil is eligible for services, it must determine which services are needed and in what settings they should be provided. In the past, these decisions were guided by the limited range of services available in schools. Often the only alternatives were special academic instruction and behavioral intervention in a self-contained special classroom or resource room. The availability of an increased range of special education and support services reduces the team's dependency on placing students in restrictive educational settings to provide them with needed services. Thus, the team may determine that a pupil needs systematic behavior management, highly structured academic instruction, and social skills training. Because the school has adopted a policy of inclusion supported by such staff resources as Behavior Support Teams or services from a **behavior specialist** or **consulting teacher,** these services can be provided without changing the student's current educational placement. Even in schools without a wide range of services, decisions regarding what services pupils need should precede and be separate from decisions about where students will access them (i.e., where they will be placed).

When students are found to be eligible for special education, the IEP Team also should consider the criteria by which their continued eligibility will be determined. Too often, students with troubling behavior are given a "life sentence" in segregated special education settings. The IEP Team should be diligent in monitoring students' progress and should hold as many IEP team meetings during a given year as are necessary to ensure that students are making progress toward their goals and objectives. (The decision to retain the pupil in special education also should be justified through a comprehensive reevaluation and should be made by the IEP Team.) It is important to realize that there always will be some students whose needs require the orchestration of services from multiple agencies over extended periods of time, perhaps throughout their lives. These students and their families should receive this support through team-based systems of care, which are characterized by bringing the resources they need to home, school, and community settings, rather than relegating the child to institutional treatment.

Table 1-3 summarizes the eligibility decision-making process from screening through decertifying and returning pupils to the general education program. Contact your state's department of education for assessment guidelines in determining students' eligibility for services under the EBD label.

Summary. The issue is not whether a pupil should be identified as having EBD and served through special education but whether an intervention plan needs to be designed. Unfortunately, in many cases, students not identified as having EBD receive no services or inadequate services because schools tend to lack effective strategies for helping pupils without disabilities who exhibit behavior problems. The effectiveness of such traditional disciplinary practices as corporal punishment, suspension, and expulsion has not been proven for the majority of students with whom they are used. Therefore, the dilemma is whether to identify the student as having EBD, which has potentially negative social and educational consequences (i.e., stigmatization, separation from behaviorally typical peers and from the general

TABLE 1–3 Eligibility Decisions

Question	Action
I. Screening	
A. Is student "at risk"?	A. Administer screening procedure, activate Behavior Support Team
B. Can student be helped through regular program?	B. Modify or adapt regular program
II. Identification	
A. Has student benefited from adaptations made in regular program?	A. Evaluate effects of regular education interventions
B. Is additional support or service needed?	B. Implement consultative intervention
C. Should student be identified as EBD?	C. Conduct assessment; hold staffing
III. Certification	
A. Should student be referred for EBD services?	A. Conduct evaluation team meeting
B. What services are needed?	B. Develop IEP
C. Where should services be provided?	C. Identify least restrictive settings for pupil
D. What expectations must the pupil meet to return to the regular classroom?	D. Specify criteria for decertification
IV. Program Evaluation	
A. Is the program working?	A. Ongoing formative and summative evaluation procedures
V. Decertification	
A. Is special education no longer needed?	A. Evaluate progress against exit criteria, conduct exit IEP Team meeting

academic program), or not to identify in the hope that the student's problem behaviors can be remediated by using resources available in the general education program.

BEHAVIOR PROBLEMS AND EDUCATIONAL PLACEMENT

The range of problem behaviors encountered in schools can be described in many ways. For practical reasons, this range generally is matched to a continuum of special education interventions: the more severe the problem behavior, the more intensive the level of intervention. As we noted previously, special education interventions in the past have been "place oriented," that is, confined to special places such as self-contained classrooms or resource rooms. This orientation has created an expectation that pupils who are referred for special education will be removed from the general education program and treated in some "special" place with a "special" set of methods. Nowhere is this expectation more prevalent than in the area of EBD. Students who are unruly, aggressive, disrespectful, threatening, or just "weird" are aversive to regular education teachers; many such teachers report that they are unable to manage such students effectively (Lloyd & Kauffman, 1995). Others use punishment and coercive tactics in attempting to cope with undesired student behavior (Shores, Gunter, & Jack, 1993). For years, special education has served these students in segregated pull-out programs, thereby reinforcing the expectations that pupils with behavior problems cannot be taught in the mainstream and that regular educators are not responsible for their management.

Unfortunately, this refer-and-remove pattern reinforces the assumption that it is the referred pupil who "owns" the problem. Seldom is it acknowledged that inappropriate expectations, curriculum, or teaching methods may contribute to the behavior disorder. Thus, the referring teacher emerges from this process without any new skills and with a reinforced attitude that "only a specialist can handle these students." The referred child, however, may come out of this process with a stigmatizing label and segregated in a "special" environment, perhaps never to be returned to the educational mainstream.

> Consider the "ownership" of Tracy's and Rodney's problem behavior. Where should their problems be addressed?

In recent years, this pattern of placing students with disabilities in special classrooms away from the educational mainstream has given way to policies that emphasize the provision of services in inclusive settings. The IDEA specifically requires that students with disabilities be educated, to the maximum extent possible, with peers who are not disabled. The IEP Team must carefully justify educational placements in more restrictive settings. The larger number of students in general education classrooms, teachers' lack of sophisticated training in behavior management procedures, and the unavailability of adequate technical assistance to classroom teachers make the full inclusion of many pupils with behavioral disabilities implausible (Kauffman & Hallahan, 1995). Furthermore, as Polsgrove and Ochoa (2003) observe, "the placement of increasing numbers of children in regular education classrooms—inclusion—has occurred largely without evidence supporting the effects of this practice or considering the 'voices' of parents, teachers, or students" (p. 163). Meadows, Neel, Scott, and Parker (1994) compared the educational programming for students with EBD who were placed in mainstream versus segregated programs. They found that "placement in general education settings represented a major reduction, if not complete cessation, of [individually differentiated] programming" (p. 170). A more recent study by Mamlin (1999) corroborated this observation.

To compound these problems, children with serious behavioral disorders do not interact well with their peers, who do not accept them (Walker, Ramsey, & Gresham, 2004). Moreover, the general education curriculum often falls short of meeting the needs of pupils who are behind their age-mates both academically and socially. Many students with mild disabilities (those who are closest to typical peers in terms of functional levels), especially those with EBD, drop out or are "elbowed out" of school by the time they reach adolescence.

The basic dilemma is whether to redouble efforts to integrate these pupils into general academic programs (which may not meet their needs) or to educate them in segregated environments (in which they miss many of the curricular and extracurricular opportunities available in the mainstream and in which they are likely to remain throughout their school years). Unfortunately, the dilemma has no ready solution. Zigmond (2003) observed that research has not supported the superiority of one service delivery model over another. Rather, the effectiveness of a special education program for individual students depends on the characteristics and needs of the student as well as the quality of the program's implementation. Therefore, it is not "place" that makes special education special or effective but, rather, effective and individualized teaching (Zigmond, 2003). In schools that have adopted systemic changes based on positive behavior support, resources (e.g., Behavior Support Teams) are available to support and assist staff who serve students with challenging academic and behavioral problems. This model of **supported inclusion** may improve the educational status and outcomes of both students who are at risk and those with EBD.

Zigmond (2003) succinctly summarized what we know from 35 years of efficacy research on the settings in which special education is delivered. Her findings are presented in Box 1–3.

BOX 1-3 What We Know About Educational Placement

We know that:

✓ what goes on in a place, not the place itself, is what makes a difference
✓ you learn what you spend time on, and most students with disabilities will not learn if they are not explicitly taught
✓ some instructional practices are easier to implement and more likely to occur in some settings than in others (Zigmond, 2003)

In keeping with Zigmond's observations, some school districts are attempting to redesign the concept of **least restrictive environment** from a focus on placements to a focus on a continuum of services that are brought to pupils and their teachers, according to their needs. An outgrowth of the emerging policy of moving services to the student instead of moving the student to the services is an effort to design services that address the pupil's needs in the least restrictive settings and also providing adequate support to the staff who serve the student in these settings.

For students with challenging behavior, we advocate a philosophy of supported inclusion instead of **full inclusion.** While we described wraparound planning with regard to the most intensive level of intervention (i.e., tertiary prevention), the goal of intervention at any level of prevention should be to provide supports and services that effectively meet students' and caregivers' needs. Teacher and student support teams plan and implement interventions that are brought to the student rather than moving the student to settings where these services presumably are provided. Consistent with the philosophy we have just advocated, intervention planning should be based on the identification and assessment of strengths in both the student and settings rather than on the mere elimination of identified deficits. Thus, administrators should view behavior problems as indicating a need for services, not a need to change a student's educational placement. The latter requires considerably more elaborate and time-consuming activities, which are likely to disrupt the student's program, with no guarantee that the new placement will benefit the pupil more than did the old one.

Again, the least restrictive placement depends on the individual student, and we urge that special education be conceptualized as a continuum of services, with consideration given to more restrictive educational placements only after interventions have been tried unsuccessfully in less restrictive settings. We also recommend that the behavioral requirements of educational settings be assessed and that those competencies be targeted for instruction in more restrictive placements so that the curriculum is functional and promotes student progress to less restrictive educational settings. Procedures for assessing the behavioral expectations of less restrictive environments are described in Chapter 12.

Finally, to change problem behavior, that is, to teach pupils and their caregivers to use new and better skills in their total environment, you must systematically implement strategies to ensure that these skills are generalized and maintained in other settings (Rutherford & Nelson, 1988). What has been accomplished when you have taught a student to accept your correction of his behavior if the student blows up when corrected in algebra class? Working with pupils exhibiting behavioral disorders requires that you spend a good deal of time outside your classroom. In Chapter 12, we offer techniques and suggestions for working effectively with persons in other settings.

The concepts and strategies presented in this chapter are not in widespread use in many school programs. In addition, their implementation may depend on school policies developed by boards of education and administrators. You may feel powerless to use these models in your school. However, in an effort to make public education more responsive to local needs and issues, schools are moving toward management by school councils, consisting of staff, parents, and community members. These councils afford frontline staff an opportunity to participate actively in school-based decision making. Far from being futuristic ideals, the concepts and strategies we have presented are part of a currently developing technology for serving pupils who have behavior problems. In the following chapters, you will learn some of this technology as well as guidelines for judging when and where to apply it. We hope that the skills you acquire will help you function more effectively in your professional role and advocate on behalf of more effective services for students whose behavior reduces their chances of succeeding in the educational system.

SUMMARY

- Schools today are being challenged to meet increasingly higher standards of student achievement, to create safe and effective learning environments, and to meet the needs of an increasingly diverse student population.
- To address this challenge, school staff are joining other professionals, parents, and representatives of local communities in developing innovative strategies for supporting students across the full range of potential behavior.
- Federal regulations, including the "discipline regulations" of IDEA 2004, are compelling educators to view students with behavioral problems differently and to make fundamental changes in the way interventions are planned and delivered.
- These events provide a dramatic new context for thinking differently about identifying and serving students with EBD, including such evidence-based practices as school-wide positive behavior support, systematic screening for students at risk of EBD, prereferral interventions, functional behavioral assessments, and behavior intervention plans.
- The expectation that students with disabilities should be educated with their typical peers has increased the need for strategies that provide effective support for them and their teachers in inclusive educational settings.

DISCUSSION/APPLICATION IDEAS

1. How can the poor educational status of, and outcomes for, students with EBD be remedied?
2. Arrange to visit a school where school-wide positive behavior support is being implemented. Observe and talk with administrative, teaching, and support staff (as well as students, if you have permission). Answer the following questions:
   A. Are there school-wide expectations? What are they? Are they posted, and do students and staff know them?
   B. Are students acknowledged for meeting expectations?
   C. Does the school appear organized and productive?
   D. If you observed any incident of student misbehavior, how was it handled? Who handled it (teacher, other staff member, administrator)?
   E. How did your impression of this school compare with schools you have visited

where positive behavior support is not implemented?

3. Think back about the scenario involving Tracy at the beginning of this chapter. Would you advocate identifying and certifying Tracy as having EBD in order to provide her with special education services, or would you favor serving her through systematic interventions in the regular program? Support your position with information you have read in this chapter. Now consider Rodney. What special education services might be helpful to him (and his classroom teacher)? Would you advocate that he remain in a general education classroom or be placed in a special education setting? Again, support your position.
4. Children and youth with EBD continue to be served in residential treatment programs outside of local school districts. How does this affect the likelihood that students can successfully reintegrate into the educational mainstream?

NOTES

1. The 2004 amendments to the Individuals with Disability Education Act uses the label "emotionally disturbed" for this population. However, many professionals and professional organizations (e.g., the Council for Children with Behavioral Disorders) prefer the label EBD because it places equal emphasis on students' behavioral and emotional characteristics and needs.

2. However, we caution against assembling groups of students who share a common deficit (e.g., poor social skills) for treatment, as appropriate peer role models are important factors in social skill instruction. Furthermore, social skills are best taught in natural social contexts (Scott & Nelson, 1998).

3. On December 3, 2004, President George W. Bush signed H.R. 1350, the Individuals with Disabilities Education Improvement Act of 2004, which reauthorizes IDEA. IDEA 2004 contains a number of changes in addition to those we describe in this text. To learn more about the new law, consult the IDEA Practices Website, or the Website of the Council for Exceptional Children.

REFERENCES

Algozzine, R., Serna, L., & Patton, J. R. (2001). *Childhood behavior disorders: Applied research and educational practices* (2nd ed.). Austin, TX: PRO-ED.

American Psychiatric Association. (2000). *Diagnostic and statistical manual of mental disorders* (4th ed.). Washington, DC: Author.

Barnett, D. W., Daly, E. J., III, Jones, E. J., & Lentz, F. E., Jr. (2004). Response to intervention: Empirically based special education service decisions from single case designs of increasing and decreasing intensity. *Journal of Special Education, 38,* 66–79.

Bradley, R., Henderson, K., & Monfore, D. A. (2004). A national perspective on children with emotional disorders. *Behavioral Disorders, 29,* 211–223.

Council for Children with Behavioral Disorders. (1987). Position paper on definition and identification of students with behavioral disorders. *Behavioral Disorders, 13,* 9–19.

Council for Exceptional Children. (2003). CEC members speak out against No Child Left Behind. *CEC Today, 10*(4), 4, 7.

Council for Exceptional Children. (2004, November 30). The new IDEA: CEC's summary of significant issues, Retrived December 1, 2004, from http://www.sec.sped.org/pp/IDEA_112304.pdf.

Coutinho, M. J., Oswald, D. P., Best, A. M., & Forness, S. R. (2002). Gender and sociodemographic factors and the disproportionate identification of culturally and linguistically diverse students with emotional disturbance. *Behavioral Disorders, 27,* 109–125.

Cullinan, D., & Epstein, M. H. (2001). Comorbidity among students with emotional disturbance. *Behavioral Disorders, 26,* 200–213.

Cullinan, D., Evans, C., Epstein, M. H., & Ryser, G. (2003). Characteristics of emotional disturbance of elementary school students. *Behavioral Disorders, 28,* 94–110.

Eber, L., & Keenan, S. (2004). Collaboration with other agencies: Wraparound and systems of care for children and youths with emotional and behavioral disorders. In R. B. Rutherford, M. M. Quinn, & S. R. Mathur (Eds.),

Handbook of research in emotional and behavioral disorders (pp. 502–516). New York: Guilford.

Epstein, M. H., Quinn, K., Nelson, C. M., Polsgrove, L., & Cumblad, C. (1993). Serving students with emotional and behavioral disorders through a comprehensive community-based approach. *OSERS News in Print, 5*(3), 19–23.

Federal Register, February 10, 1993, p. 7938.

Feil, E. G., & Becker, W. C. (1993). Investigation of a multiple-gated screening system for preschool behavior problems. *Behavioral Disorders, 19,* 44–53.

Feil, E. G., Severson, H. H., & Walker, H. M. (1994). *Early screening project (ESP): Identifying preschool children with adjustment problems.* The Oregon Conference Monograph, 6, 177–183.

Forness, S. R. (2004). Part III introduction. In R. B. Rutherford, M. M. Quinn, & S. R. Mathur (Eds.), *Handbook of research in emotional and behavioral disorders* (pp. 235–241). New York: Guilford.

Forness, S. R., & Kavale, K. A. (2000). Emotional or behavioral disorders: Background and current status of the E/BD terminology and definition. *Behavioral Disorders, 25,* 264–269.

Gresham, F. M. (1999). Noncategorical approaches to K-12 emotional and behavioral difficulties. In D. Reschly, W. D. Tilly, & J. Grimes (Eds.), *Special education in transition: Functional assessment and noncategorical programming* (pp. 107–138). Longmont, CO: Sopris West.

Gresham, F. M., & Reschly, D. (1987). Issues in the conceptualization, classification, and assessment of social skills in the mildly handicapped. In T. Kratchowill (Ed.), *Advances in school psychology* (Vol. 6, pp. 203–264). Hillsdale, NJ: Lawrence Erlbaum Associates.

Hosp, J. L., & Reschly, D. J. (2003). Referral rates for intervention or assessment: A meta-analysis of racial differences. *Journal of Special Education, 37,* 67–80.

Illback, R. J., Nelson, C. M., & Sanders, D. (1998). Community-based services in Kentucky: Description and 5-year evaluation of Kentucky IMPACT. In M. H. Epstein, K. Kutash, & A. Duchnowski (Eds.), *Outcomes for children and youth with emotional and behavioral disorders and their families: Programs and evaluation best practices* (pp. 141–172). Austin, TX: PRO-ED.

Katsiyannis, A., & Maag, J. W. (1998). Disciplining students with disabilities: Issues and considerations for implementing IDEA '97. *Behavioral Disorders, 23,* 276–289.

Katsiyannis, A., & Smith, C. R. (2003). Disciplining students with disabilities: Legal trends and the issue of interim alternative education settings. *Behavioral Disorders, 28,* 410–418.

Kauffman, J. M. (2001). *Characteristics of emotional and behavioral disorders of children and youth* (7th ed.). Upper Saddle River, NJ: Merrill/Prentice Hall.

Kauffman, J. M., Brigham, F. J., & Mock, D. R. (2004). Historical to contemporary perspectives on the field of emotional and behavioral disorders. In R. B. Rutherford, M. M. Quinn, & S. R. Mathur (Eds.), *Handbook of research in emotional and behavioral disorders* (pp. 15–31). New York: Guilford.

Kauffman, J. M., & Hallahan, D. P. (Eds.). (1995). *The illusion of full inclusion: A comprehensive critique of a current special education bandwagon.* Austin, TX: PRO-ED.

Lambert, N., Windmiller, M., Tharinger, D., & Cole, L. (1981). *AAMD adaptive behavior scale* (school ed.). Monterey, CA: Publishers Test Service.

Landrum, T. J., Tankersley, M., & Kauffman, J. M. (2003). What is special about special education for students with emotional or behavioral disorders? *Journal of Special Education, 37,* 148–156.

LaVigna, G. W., & Donnellan, A. M. (1986). *Alternatives to punishment: Solving behavior problems through non-aversive strategies.* New York: Irvington.

Lewis-Palmer, T., Sugai, G., & Larson, S. (1999). Using data to guide decisions about program implementation and effectiveness: An overview and applied example. *Effective School Practices, 17*(4), 47–53.

Liaupsin, C. J., Jolivette, K., & Scott, T. M. (2004). School-wide systems of behavior support: Maximizing student success in schools. In R. B. Rutherford, M. M. Quinn, & S. R. Mathur (Eds.), *Handbook of research in emotional and behavioral disorders* (pp. 487–501). New York: Guilford.

Lloyd, J. W., & Kauffman, J. M. (1995). What less restrictive placements require of teachers. In J. M. Kauffman, J. W. Lloyd, D. P. Hallahan, & T. A. Astuto (Eds.), *Issues in educational placement: Students with emotional and behavioral disorders* (pp. 317–334). Hillsdale, NJ: Lawrence Erlbaum Associates.

Mamlin, N. (1999). Despite best intentions: When inclusion fails. *Journal of Special Education, 33,* 36–49.

McConaughy, S. M., & Achenbach, T. M. (1989). Empirically based assessment of severe emotional disturbance. *Journal of School Psychology, 27,* 91–117.

McIntyre, T. (1995). *The McIntyre assessment of culture.* Columbia, MO: Hawthorne Educational Services.

McIntyre, T., & Forness, S. R. (1997). Is there a new definition yet, or are our kids still seriously emotionally disturbed? *Beyond Behavior, 7*(3), 4–10.

Meadows, N. B., Neel, R. S., Scott, C. M., & Parker, G. (1994). Academic performance, social competence, and mainstream accommodations: A look at mainstreamed and non-mainstreamed students with serious behavioral disorders. *Behavioral Disorders, 19,* 170–180.

Nelson, C. M. (2000) Educating students with emotional and behavioral disorders in the 21st century: Looking through windows, opening doors. *Education and Treatment of Children, 23,* 204–222.

Nelson, J. R., Martella, R., & Galand, B. (1998). The effects of teaching school expectations and establishing a consistent consequence on formal office disciplinary actions. *Journal of Emotional and Behavioral Disorders, 6,* 153–161.

Nelson, J. R., Martella, R. M., & Marchand-Martella, N. (2002). Maximizing student learning: The effects of a comprehensive school-based program for preventing problem behaviors. *Journal of Emotional and Behavioral Disorders, 10*(3), 136–148.

Polsgrove, L., & Ochoa, T. (2003). Trends and issues in behavioral interventions. In A. M. Sorrells, H. J. Rieth, & P. T. Sindelar (Eds.), *Current and emerging issues in special education* (pp. 154–179). Boston: Allyn & Bacon.

Potter, M. L., Ysseldyke, J. E., & Regan, R. R. (1983). Eligibility and classification decisions in educational settings: Issuing "passports" in a state of confusion. *Contemporary Educational Psychology, 8,* 146–157.

Reid, R., Gonzalez, J. E., Nordness, P. D., Trout, A., & Epstein, M. H. (2004). A meta-analysis of the academic status of students with emotional/behavioral disturbance. *Journal of Special Education, 38,* 130–143.

Rinaldi, C. (2003). Language competence and social behavior of students with emotional or behavioral disorders. *Behavioral Disorders, 29,* 34–42.

Roberts, R. E., Attkisson, C. A., & Rosenblatt, A. (1998). Prevalence of psychopathology among children and adolescents. *American Journal of Psychiatry, 155,* 715–725.

Rodgers-Adkinson, D. L., & Hooper, S. R. (2003). The relationship of language and behavior: Introduction to the special issue. *Behavioral Disorders, 29,* 5–9.

Ruhl, K. L., Hughes, C. A., & Camarata, S. M. (1992). Analysis of the expressive and receptive characteristics of emotionally handicapped students served in public school settings. *Journal of Childhood Communication Disorders, 14,* 165–176.

Rutherford, R. B., Jr., & Nelson, C. M. (1988). Generalization and maintenance of treatment effects. In J. C. Witt, E. N. Elliott, & F. M. Gresham (Eds.), *Handbook of behavior therapy in education* (pp. 227–324). New York: Plenum.

Salvia, J., & Ysseldyke, J. E. (2001). *Assessment in special and remedial education* (8th ed.). Boston: Houghton Mifflin.

Scott, T. M. (2001). A school-wide example of positive behavioral support. *Journal of Positive Behavior Interventions, 3,* 88–94.

Scott, T. M., & Hunter, J. (2001) Initiating school-wide support systems: An administrator's guide to the process. *Beyond Behavior, 11,* 13–15.

Scott, T. M., & Nelson, C. M. (1998). Confusion and failure in facilitating generalized social responding in the school setting: Sometimes 2 + 2 = 5. *Behavioral Disorders, 23,* 264–275.

Scott, T. M., & Nelson, C. M. (1999). Using functional behavioral assessment to develop effective behavioral intervention plans: Practical classroom applications. *Journal of Positive Behavioral Interventions, 1,* 242–251.

Shores, R. E., Gunter, P. L., & Jack, S. L. (1993). Classroom management strategies: Are they setting events for coercion? *Behavioral Disorders, 18,* 92–102.

Sinclair, E., Del'Homme, M., & Gonzalez, M. (1993). Systematic screening for preschool behavioral disorders. *Behavioral Disorders, 18,* 177–188.

Skiba, R. J., Peterson, R. L., & Williams, T. (1998). Office referrals and suspension: Disciplinary intervention in middle schools. *Education and Treatment of Children, 20*(3), 1–21.

Sparrow, S. S., Balla, D. A., & Cicchetti, D. V. (1985). *Vineland Adaptive Behavior Scale.* Circle Pines, MN: American Guidance Service.

Stroul, B. A., & Friedman, R. A. (1986). *A system of care for severely emotionally disturbed children and youth.* Washington, DC: CASSP Technical Assistance Center, Georgetown University Child Development Center.

Sugai, G., & Horner, R. H. (1999). Discipline and behavioral support: Practices, pitfalls, and promises. *Effective School Practices, 17*(4), 10-22.

Sugai, G., & Horner, R. (2002). The evolution of discipline practices: School-wide behavior supports. *Child and Family Behavior Therapy, 24*(1/2), 23-50.

Sugai, G., Horner, R. H., Dunlap, G., Hieneman, M., Lewis, T. J., Nelson, C. M., Scott, T., Liaupsin, C., Sailor, W., Turnbull, A. P., Turnbull, H. R., III, Wickham, D., Wilcox, B., & Ruef, M. (2000). Applying positive behavior support and functional behavioral assessment in schools. *Journal of Positive Behavior Interventions, 2,* 131-143.

Sugai, G., Sprague, J. R., Horner, R. H., & Walker, H. M. (2000). Preventing school violence: The use of office discipline referrals to assess and monitor school-wide discipline interventions. *Journal of Emotional and Behavioral Disorders, 8,* 94-101.

Todd, A. W., Horner, R. H., Sugai, G., & Colvin, G. (1999). Individualizing school-wide discipline for students with chronic problem behaviors: A team approach. *Effective School Practices, 17*(4), 72-82.

U.S. Department of Education. (2000). *21st annual report to Congress on the implementation of the Individuals with Disability Education Act.* Washington, DC: U.S. Government Printing Office.

U.S. Department of Education. (2001a). *P.L. 107-110 the No Child Left Behind Act of 2001.* Washington, DC: Author.

U.S. Department of Education. (2001b). *23rd annual report to Congress on the implementation of the Individuals with Disability Education Act.* Washington, DC: U.S. Government Printing Office.

U.S. Department of Education. (2002). *24th annual report to Congress on the implementation of the Individuals with Disability Education Act.* Washington, DC: U.S. Government Printing Office.

U.S. Department of Education, Office of Special Education and Rehabilitation Services. (2002). *A new era: Revitalizing special education for children and their families.* Washington, DC: Author.

U.S. Public Health Service. (2001). *Report of the surgeon general's Conference on Children's Mental Health: A national action agenda.* Washington, DC: Department of Health and Human Services.

Walker, H. M., Block-Pedego, A., Todis, B., & Severson, H. (1991). *The school archival records search.* Longmont, CO: Sopris West.

Walker, H. M., & Fabre, T. R. (1987). Assessment of behavior disorders in the school setting: Issues, problems and strategies revisited. In N. Haring (Ed.), *Measuring and managing behavior disorders* (pp. 198-243). Seattle: University of Washington Press.

Walker, H. M., & McConnell, S. R. (1988). *The Walker-McConnell scale of social competence and school adjustment: A social skills rating scale for teachers.* Austin, TX: PRO-ED.

Walker, H. M., Nishioka, V. M., Zeller, R., Severson, H. H., & Feil, E. G. (2000). Causal factors and potential solutions for the persistent underidentification of students having emotional or behavioral disorders in the context of schooling. *Assessment for Effective Intervention, 26*(1), 29-39.

Walker, H. M., Ramsey, E., & Gresham, F. M. (2004). *Antisocial behavior in school: Evidence-based practices* (2nd ed.). Belmont, CA: Wadsworth/Thomson.

Walker, H. M., & Severson, H. (1990). *Systematic screening for behavioral disorders.* Longmont, CO: Sopris West.

Witt, J. C., VanDerHyden, A. M., & Gilbertson, D. (2004). Instruction and classroom management: Prevention and intervention research. In R. B. Rutherford, M. M. Quinn, & S. R. Mathur (Eds.), *Handbook of research in emotional and behavioral disorders* (pp. 426-445). New York: Guilford.

Zigmond, N. (2003). Where should students with disabilities receive special education services? Is one place better than another? *Journal of Special Education, 37,* 193-199.

CHAPTER 2 SCHOOL- AND CLASSROOM-WIDE POSITIVE BEHAVIOR SUPPORT

OUTLINE

Introduction
Why Emphasize Prevention?
Implementing School-Wide Positive Behavior Support
Implementing Positive Behavior Support in the Classroom

OBJECTIVES

After completing this chapter, you should be able to

- Explain the concept of early identification and intervention from the perspective of universal prevention.
- Describe the components and procedures involved in a school-wide prevention system.
- Describe how to identify predictable problems across various school settings.
- Give examples of how rules, routines, and physical arrangements are used to prevent predictable problem behaviors.
- Describe how school-wide and classroom rules should correspond—when they should be the same and when they can vary.
- Indicate which aspects of classroom settings are likely to predict the occurrence of undesired pupil behavior and how they may be altered to increase the probability of desired behavior.
- Describe the advantages and disadvantages of level systems and their application in classroom management programs.

KEY TERMS (refer to the Glossary on the Companion Website for definitions)

behavior report
conditioned reinforcer
differential reinforcement
discriminative stimulus
edible reinforcers
extinction
levels system
office discipline referral
opportunities to respond
pre-correction
psychotropic medication
setting events
social reinforcement
stimulus control
tangible reinforcers
tokens

The focus of this chapter is on primary prevention, accomplished through the implementation of universal interventions that are applied consistently to benefit all students. Primary prevention is important to consider in two educational contexts: the total school environment, which includes common areas (e.g., hallways, cafeteria, auditorium, bus waiting areas, playgrounds) where students congregate, and individual classrooms. We begin with a case study illustrating how one school addresses student discipline problems through school-wide planning. Next, we discuss the importance of developing strategies to prevent problem behavior, as opposed to waiting for it to occur and reacting with punitive interventions. We then describe specific procedures for implementing school-wide positive behavior support. Finally, we describe procedures for implementing primary prevention in the classroom.

Come into My Classroom: A Case Study

PROBLEMS AT HAPPY VALLEY ELEMENTARY SCHOOL

by Terrance M. Scott

Happy Valley Elementary is an inner-city school of approximately 450 students, 92% of whom qualify for free or reduced lunch. With a 10-year pattern of decreasing statewide achievement scores, the district's highest rate of suspension, and an escalating number of students being referred to the office for disciplinary action, Happy Valley Elementary is identified by the state as a school in crisis. Principal Ruth Jones is determined to make a difference. She brings the faculty and staff together and asks for their input and ideas regarding possible solutions. There is general agreement among all that something needs to be done—but suggestions for change are varied, fragmented among cliques, and often contradictory. Principal Jones is aware that any change efforts that are not agreed on and adopted by the entire school are unlikely to be implemented widely or consistently enough to have an effect on the school as a whole. She determines that the school must come together and generate a school-wide plan that is acceptable to all and calculated to prevent the school's predictable problems.

Principal Jones again calls all faculty and staff together and proposes a school-wide solution. As a group, they identify the conditions in the school that best predict problem behaviors and then brainstorm simple preventative solutions to those problems. Next, the group votes to establish consensus regarding which of the strategies will be adopted on a school-wide basis. Principal Jones assures everyone that decisions are to be made by the group, with no one individual having any more say than any other. She then reminds everyone that, once they have come to consensus and agreed on an expectation or strategy, that expectation or strategy becomes the school policy on which all faculty and staff will be expected to abide. She makes clear, "Once you agree upon a solution, I'm going to make sure you follow through." The staff agree that decisions need to be made on a school-wide basis and decide that 80% staff approval will be the criterion for consensus regarding school-wide decisions. Further, all agree that, regardless of their individual feelings about any particular expectation or strategy, once consensus is reached, all will abide by that decision and will teach the

---

This chapter was coauthored by Terrance M. Scott.

expectations to the students, consistently enforce the rules, and follow through with strategies for responding to student behavior.

Determining School-Wide Rules and Strategies

The first task in determining school-wide rules and strategies is to identify the areas, times, and conditions in which problem behaviors are most likely to occur. Ideally, the staff at Happy Valley Elementary would go to their school-wide data to make these determinations. However, although **office discipline referral** (ODR) and suspension data exist, those data often identify only the student and the behavior. Identifying predictable locations and times across the school would require a search of every student file in an attempt to recall each incident and the conditions surrounding it. Obviously, this is too large a chore to be realistic for Happy Valley Elementary. In the absence of such data, at a school-wide meeting, the staff identify the areas and times that they see as most predictive of problems across the school based on their experiences in the school over the past year. Principal Jones divides the entire faculty and staff into several small groups by common role in the school. For example, she asks that the instructional assistants, primary grade teachers, intermediate grade teachers, specialists, secretaries, custodians, and additional adults (including involved parents) form small groups. Each of these groups is then asked to create a list of predictable problems, times, and locations across the school. After a 20-minute period, Ms. Jones calls the entire group back together to list the identified problems by area. As each area of the school is listed on a flip chart, small-group spokespersons relate the problems and the locations and times they see these. When each physical area of the school has been covered and all staff have had an opportunity to give their impressions, the outcome is a comprehensive list of the school's predictable problems, and when and where they occur.

Principal Jones then asks each small group to reconvene to brainstorm the strategies and rules that might be developed as a method of preventing the identified problems. This time, she asks each group to spend 10 minutes focusing on each specific area of the school. She reminds them to spend their time concentrating on prevention, sets the timer, and asks the groups to begin with a specific setting. When the timer goes off at the end of 10 minutes, Principal Jones prompts the groups to move to the next setting and continue. Once all the settings have been covered, Principal Jones reconvenes the large group and again records the responses of the smaller groups on a flip chart. She reminds the large group that these responses represent only brainstorming and that there should be no critique of the proposed strategies until they are all recorded. Then, for each area of the school, Principal Jones goes through the list of possible solutions and asks the group as a whole to decide (a) whether each solution would solve the problem if it were consistently put into effect and (b) whether those that would be effective could realistically be adopted and implemented by all as part of a daily school-wide procedure. Only those solutions that are deemed to be *both* effective and realistic by at least 50% of the group move forward for a vote.

One last time, Principal Jones goes back through the locations of the school, this time asking for the group as a whole to vote on each. She reminds them that a "yes" vote signifies a willingness to adopt the rule or strategy by every staff member and for the entire school day. The criterion set for accepting a rule or strategy on a school-wide basis is 80% consensus by the staff. If 80% consensus is not achieved, additional solutions are generated, or some compromise is reached through group discussion. For example, when student pushing and shoving on the stairway after school dismissal was identified as a problem, several solutions were suggested, including releasing the students individually, 10 seconds apart. Although all agreed that sending the students individually would likely be effective, less than 50% agreed that this was a realistic solution because of the time required to implement and monitor it. Therefore, this strategy was removed from consideration. However, another potential solution was to teach the students to go to the right side of the stairs and always hold the railing with their right hands. This rule would encourage the students to maintain some distance from one another as they ascended and descended the stairs. In addition, by keeping their right hands on the rail, the students would have to move in single file. The majority agreed that this was both logical and reasonable. A vote was taken, and 85% of the group agreed that this should be a rule that is taught to the students and consistently modeled and enforced by all staff. This same process was repeated for each identified problem and area.

Developing a School-Wide Data Collection System

The staff of Happy Valley Elementary now has decided what steps they will take to decrease predictable problem behaviors across the school. The next step is to determine what outcomes they wish to measure and the simplest way to measure them. Because the school is considered to be in crisis in several areas, several potential goals could be adopted by the group. However, Principal Jones has persuaded the group to focus on larger outcomes for measurement rather than developing a longer set of more specific goals. That is, the rule about keeping to the right on stairways may decrease problems here, but what effect will this have on suspensions or ODRs? Still, there must be some way of measuring whether stairway problems are decreasing so that the staff will know if their strategy is effective. The staff agree that their major goals will be to decrease student suspensions or expulsions and to decrease ODRs. They will do this not by changing the way they use those disciplinary procedures but by preventing the problem behaviors that lead to them. Next, the staff rewrite their ODR form to include more information, including the time, location, and outcome of problem behaviors. This information is then summarized weekly in a spreadsheet, allowing the staff to monitor the effectiveness of the strategies they implemented as a school.

Monitoring and Evaluation

Each month, the staff look at the data reported from the ODR forms. Because the forms include disciplinary outcomes as a category, suspensions/expulsions can be monitored using the ODR-generated database. The school can assess the agreed-on strategies across each identified time and location. This information is used to evaluate the effectiveness of rules and strategies and to determine new times and locations that may become predictors of problems. In this way, the school stays on top of problems, providing new solutions for situations before these issues bring themselves to staff attention in a more painful manner. Principal Jones shares the data with staff monthly, and the staff make new decisions depending on what the data show.

Sustaining the School-Wide Program

As time goes by, staff and student changeover, new problems, and changing cultures or conditions will likely affect every school. Although it is not necessary to repeat this process every year, Principal Jones realizes the importance of formative evaluation of the school-wide agreements. In addition to the monthly data meetings, the staff meet at the beginning of each year to revisit their plans, making certain that all new staff are aware of the school-wide agreements and prompting a new round of teaching the expectations, rules, and routines associated with these agreements for the new students.

Principal Jones knows that the system her school has created will not prevent all problem behaviors. The behavior of some students will require more intensive and individualized intervention. However, her staff understand that when they design a system to prevent problems for all students, the number of students who present ongoing problems will decrease, which will free up the time and resources needed to design and implement the specific interventions necessary to facilitate the success of these more challenging students.

INTRODUCTION

The situation at Happy Valley Elementary is not unlike that experienced by many elementary, middle, and secondary schools throughout the country. Perhaps you have visited or worked in a school where student behavior problems were an issue. If so, how did these affect your impression of the school or your attitude about coming to work? How did these problems affect staff morale? Have you been in a school where school-wide positive behavior support was implemented? How was the climate there?

Although the focus on accountability in the No Child Left Behind Act (NCLB) and state educational reform legislation emphasizes student academic performance, substantial evidence indicates that student behavioral issues are closely related to levels of academic achievement (Darch & Kame'enui, 2004; Scott, Nelson, & Liaupsin, 2001). Moreover, states increasingly are including student disciplinary data (e.g., rates of suspension and expulsion) in accountability reporting, and schools are being expected to develop strategies to reduce the use of disciplinary strategies that remove students from educational settings. Teachers who leave the field because of dissatisfaction with teaching as a career report that student discipline problems were their number one reason for leaving (National Center for Education Statistics, 1997). As you read this chapter, you will see how effective instruction and primary prevention of student behavior problems fit together.

WHY EMPHASIZE PREVENTION?

School problems involving weapons, violence, and student safety have garnered increasing media attention in the past few years (Lichter, Lichter, & Amundson, 1999), promoting a community perception of ever-present danger in schools (Brooks, Schiraldi, & Ziedenberg, 2000; Leone, Mayer, Malmgren, & Meisel, 2000). However, the vast majority of problems in schools do not involve violence, and, in fact, children are less likely to be victims of violence when they are in school than when they are anywhere else, including their own homes (Elliott, Hamburg, & Williams, 1998; Snyder & Sickmund, 1999). Teachers' concerns about student discipline tend to be about simple, repetitive, and annoying problems such as "disrespect," "noncompliance," and "lack of responsibility for work completion" (Scott, 2001). Still, these concerns may reflect a perceived increase in the rate of problem behaviors rather than in their intensity. Because small problems tend to become larger when not dealt with immediately, repeated minor problems sometimes become overwhelming simply because they occur in a significant proportion of the student population. The most obvious solution is to prevent these frequent but minor behavioral infractions and to react more effectively when they do occur.

As the case study at the beginning of this chapter illustrates, effective prevention requires forethought about the reasons for common behavior problems as well as insight into the factors that seem to predict these. If we can predict when, where, and why problems occur across the school and in the classroom, we can design strategies to prevent them. While these strategies likely will not prevent all problems, they will decrease their frequency. As you will see later, reducing the number of students who exhibit minor behavioral incidents will help identify those students who need more individualized and intensive intervention.

Universal Interventions

This chapter presents examples of a variety of assessment and intervention strategies for the prevention of problem behaviors across the school and in the classroom. These strategies represent *universal interventions* as defined by Walker, Ramsey, and Gresham (2004): they are applied to all students in a group and address the "margins" in which the boundaries between acceptable and unacceptable student behavior typically are not clear. The objective of preventative behavior management is to analyze and structure social environments in such a way as to minimize the occurrence of behaviors requiring more complex and intensive interventions. While you may think that primary prevention strategies benefit only those students at low risk, studies have demonstrated that those students at the highest risk are those who benefit the most from universal interventions (Brown, 2003; Robertson, Greenberg, Kam, & Kusche, 2003).

Many potentially difficult situations can be prevented through careful assessment, effective academic instruction and support of desired student behavior, and appropriate group behavior management. Thus, universal behavior management should be viewed as a set of proactive strategies that reduce the need for targeted interventions for the majority of pupils. (Management procedures and systems intended for specific behavior problems are emphasized in subsequent chapters.)

Who Owns the Problem?

The typical focus of strategies for behavior management is on acting-out (externalizing) behavior problems. This focus may appear to overlook behavioral deficits, that is, the absence of socially desirable behaviors. However, many students whose behavioral excesses create management problems also are deficient in academic skills and appropriate social behaviors (Kauffman, 2001; Lane, 2004; Reid, Gonzalez, Nordness, Trout, & Epstein, 2004; Walker & Gresham, 2003). Behavior management aimed at preventing or reducing the occurrence of behaviors that interfere with productivity and learning will be more effective if the curriculum simultaneously addresses pupils' social skill deficits. Students who consistently break rules of conduct, whose inappropriate behaviors repeatedly disrupt order in the school, or who fail to correct their undesired behavior when exposed to the school's available disciplinary measures should be assessed with respect to desired academic, social, and school survival skills, and their deficits in these areas should be addressed through appropriate school-wide and classroom curricular interventions.

It would be simple to assume that every problem behavior is "owned" by the student (i.e., that behavior problems are attributable to students' personal characteristics and histories). The assertion that students are responsible for their own behavior is inarguable, and many students do have physical and psychological disabilities that affect their behavior. To be certain, we must attempt to identify and provide support for these students' special needs. However, it is a mistake to assume that all student misbehaviors are the product of permanent physical characteristics or personality traits. In the first place, this perspective suggests that educators can do nothing to prevent problem behavior.

The attitude that the cause of the student's problem behavior is centered within the child relegates intervention to a reactive mode only in which educators wait for problem behavior to occur and then attempt to alter the student's motivation to exhibit the behavior, often by using punishment. Assuming that misbehavior is an unavoidable trait also encourages the use of more intrusive treatment options (e.g., medications or prosthetics) without first assessing the effects of less intrusive options. Providing students with effective instruction in the necessary skills to manage their own behavior surely is more empowering than simply giving them a pill. Furthermore, while there obviously are students whose behaviors are the result of physical or personality traits, even these pupils can benefit from environmental arrangements that predict success as well as effective instruction in self-management. For example, research indicates that students with attention-deficit hyperactive disorder respond best to low dosages of **psychotropic medication** in conjunction with effective behavioral interventions (Forness, Kavale, Sweeney, & Crenshaw, 1999). An instructional approach in addressing problem behavior focuses on external environmental variables that can be altered much more effectively and efficiently. This approach also assumes that desired student behavior can be learned, reinforced, and maintained.

What is your opinion regarding the use of medications to control children's behavior?

Prevention and Early Intervention

Aside from being annoying, time consuming, and distracting, minor problem behaviors are predictive of more chronic and pervasive problem behaviors in the future (Kauffman, 2001; Walker et al., 2004). For this reason, systematic screening to identify students who are at risk for displaying patterns of maladaptive behavior, as well as early intervention practices, have been widely advocated as a preferred practice in the effort to prevent student failure (Kauffman, 1994; Scott & Nelson, 1999; Walker, Severson, & Feil, 1994). However, we suggest another interpretation of early intervention, one that focuses on the prevention of problem behaviors throughout the school as opposed to the more familiar method of identifying individuals at risk for failure. While traditional early identification and intervention are effective practices, evidence suggests that the number of children identified as at risk for school failure because of their patterns of undesired behavior can be reduced significantly if prevention focuses first on the larger environment (Horner, Sugai, Todd, & Lewis-Palmer, in press; Scott, 2001). These prevention strategies are universal because they involve assessment, analysis, and action taken by all staff and affecting all students, locations, times, and problems. The goal of this chapter is to help you create productive learning environments in which the occurrences of challenging student behavior are minimized.

In the average school, a sizable portion of the student population can be expected to display problem behaviors at some time (Horner & Sugai, 2000; Sugai et al., 2000). However, not all of these students require targeted intervention strategies (including behavior intervention plans). Some pupil misbehavior occurs because the environment sets the occasion for problem behavior. Environmental variables that may contribute to such behavior include the absence of clear and consistent rules and consequences, problematic routines, or providing inadequate supervision of common areas (e.g., halls, playground, lunchroom). While 80% to 90% of students probably can function adequately even under such circumstances, some students (as many as 10%) will experience failure (manifested as recurring behavior problems) if these environmental deficits prevail. These are the students who are likely to receive multiple behavior reports or ODRs, who spend large amounts of time in the principal's office or in suspension, or who are excluded from school altogether because of their behavior. Studies consistently report that 5% to 7% of students account for 50% of the behavioral challenges in the school (Horner & Sugai, 2000).

Such punishment exacerbates the academic skill deficits exhibited by many students in this group (Gunter, Hummel, & Venn, 1998; Scott et al., 2001) because they spend so much time out of the learning environment. When they return to the classroom, their lack of skill makes academic work aversive, increasing the likelihood that they will engage in behavior that leads to escape and avoidance (e.g., disruption, noncompliance). If these students continue to fail, they will develop patterns of antisocial behavior or maladaptive coping mechanisms that contribute to lifelong failure. And their failure is our failure because individuals who exhibit such patterns become lifetime consumers of the most expensive programs and services that we support as taxpayers—institutionalization, incarceration, and the like (Centers for Disease Control and Prevention, 1995). Thus, universal prevention strategies promote success among a group of students for whom small failures accumulate to become large failures. In this sense, universal systems of prevention can be conceptualized as early intervention because not only do these strategies prevent many students from exhibiting the types of failures that annoy, distract, and burden educators, but they also help more students be successful in school. Without universal strategies, the number of students whose behaviors require targeted intervention often outpaces available services and supports.

The task is to determine which students are, in fact, candidates for specialized intervention systems and which are having problems because the school environment is not consistent in supporting appropriate and desired student behavior. When school staff can reliably predict the times, places, and contexts in which problem behaviors are likely to occur, they have the information necessary to effectively prevent these failures. When the environment is arranged to prevent predictable minor behavior problems for the majority of students, the 7% to 10% who truly are in need of more intensive intervention will be identified as a distinct group because they continue to exhibit problem behavior even when universal supports are in place. Universal prevention strategies reduce the number of students who might otherwise be unnecessarily exposed to these more labor-intensive interventions. Thus, the implementation of universal strategies is the first step in an early intervention process. Universal assessment and intervention strategies may be applied across the entire school as well as at the classroom level.

Typically, students whose behavior problems have been frequent or intense enough to come to our attention are students who repeatedly have failed in a variety of academic and social contexts (Kauffman, 2001; Kendziora, 2004). As explained previously, every new failure strengthens a pattern of failure that, over time, greatly decreases the likelihood that the student in question will ever experience success (Walker et al., 2004). Operating under the principle that what can be predicted can be prevented, we must determine the contexts and conditions under which problem behaviors are most likely to occur.

> Based on schools you have attended, worked in, or visited, can you identify environmental factors (times of day, events, or settings) that predicted problem student behavior?

IMPLEMENTING SCHOOL-WIDE POSITIVE BEHAVIOR SUPPORT

Descriptions and analyses of school-wide systems of prevention are appearing more frequently in the professional literature (Horner et al., in press; Lane & Menzies, 2003). Chapter 1 presented a model of positive behavior support in which prevention and intervention strategies are organized into three levels that address the full range of student behavior (Sugai et al., 2000). You will recall that this model involves three levels of systemic prevention: (a) universal systems—prevention strategies applied across the school for all students, (b) targeted systems—school-wide and individualized prevention and response strategies aimed at approximately 10% of the school population for whom universal systems were not sufficient, and (c) intensive systems—individualized prevention and response strategies aimed at the approximately 1% to 3% of students for whom both universal and targeted systems have been insufficient. Each level can be characterized in terms of strategies that are unique and increasingly intensive and by the specific portion of the school population on which it is focused.

The foremost concern at all three levels is prevention. However, whereas targeted and intensive interventions are much more prescriptive and individualized, the focus of universal systems is on the identification and amelioration of environmental factors that predict failure across the total student population. Research has demonstrated that systems of positive behavior support have been successful in decreasing problem behaviors across a range of elementary, middle, and high schools of varying sizes (e.g., Chapman & Hofweber, 2000; Horner et al., in press; Lohrmann-O'Rourke et al., 2000; Scott, 2001). Because positive behavior support has only recently been used systemically in schools, its effectiveness has not been replicated in a sufficient number of studies to qualify it as a research-based practice according to NCLB. However, many of the individual practices advocated within systems of positive behavior support have been empirically validated (Lewis, Hudson, Richter, & Johnson, 2004). Targeted and intensive strategies are described in detail as individual interventions in Chapters 7 through 12.

Using Behavior Incident Data

The best predictor of when, where, and under what conditions problem behavior will occur in the future is the history of when, where, and under what conditions it has occurred in the past (Scott, 2001; Scott & Nelson, 1999). When available, such school data as Office Discipline Referrals (ODRs) generally provide the simplest method of evaluating the predictors of past problem behaviors. As we pointed out in Chapter 1, many schools summarize data on behavior problems, collecting data on ODRs or other behavioral incidents. This information can be used as a basis for making decisions about where and when prevention strategies are needed as well as the types of strategies likely to be effective (e.g., Nakasato, 2000). Of course, this information is useful only if it provides sufficient data on the environmental conditions that were associated with each problem. For example, if behavior referral forms include information on when and where behavioral incidents or disciplinary infractions occur, these data may be summarized over time and used to answer questions about settings or times of the day where problem behaviors are most likely to occur across the school or to identify students who are receiving multiple behavioral reports.

This level of information is critical to the development of effective prevention strategies. For example, if ODR data indicate that problems frequently occur in the hallways, a logical prevention strategy may be to improve supervision in the halls. However, continuous hallway monitoring throughout the day would require a substantial effort on the part of the staff. If the ODR or **behavior report** form also includes the time that the behavior incident occurs, analysis of data collected over several days may suggest that supervision needs to be increased only for a specific time (e.g., during the lunch hour). Thus, the use of behavior incident data can facilitate strategic planning to create procedures that are more effective and more efficiently delivered, as staff are not being asked to exert extra effort that results in small, if any, gains in prevention. The content and complexity of a school-wide data collection form is completely dependent on the types and amount of information desired. That is, if a school wishes to assess the predictability of problem behaviors by time and location, this information must be included on the data collection form. Similarly, if a school is interested in determining whether staff respond differently to problem behaviors of special versus general education students, information regarding student characteristics and outcomes must be included on the form. Each school should develop its own data collection form to answer its own unique questions and fit its own unique needs. Typically, data forms that are small, easily carried, and formatted as a checklist (as opposed to requiring a written report) are the easiest to use and promote the greatest level of staff consistency in use. An example of an ODR form is presented in Figure 2-1. A somewhat more elaborate behavior report form is described on the Companion Website.

Once behavior incident data have been collected, they must be summarized so that analyses can be performed regularly and with ease. A simple method of summarizing data is to enter it on a spreadsheet. To accomplish this, a school might design a procedure in which all ODR forms are placed into a box in the office. Each Friday, an office worker can transfer data from the forms onto the spreadsheet—generating a weekly summary of all behavior problems. Figure 2-2 presents an example of a weekly ODR summary. Note that the information summarized for Acme Elementary allows school staff to quickly see who had problems, what those problems were, where they occurred, and who observed them. Additional characterizing information (e.g., educational placement, student gender, or minority status) also can be summarized as necessary to answer questions that are pertinent to a particular school. In Acme Elementary, the staff might determine from their analysis of weekly data summaries that behavior problems are predictable in the cafeteria during the lunch hour. Additionally, it appears that Sally Jones is having multiple problems and that fighting seems to be a recurring problem. Collecting and summarizing this information is the first step in school-wide decision making.

DATE 2-5-05						***NAME*** Sally Jones	***STAFF*** Ms. Shank
TIME		***LOCATION***		***BEHAVIOR***			
8–9	___	classroom	___	fighting	___	***SPECIAL ED.***	(Yes) / No
9–10	___	hallway	___	disrespect	✓		
10–11	___	lunchroom	✓	stealing	___	***GENDER***	Male / (Female)
11–12	___	gym	___	vandalism	___		
12–1	✓	playground	___	noncompliance	___		
1–2	___	bus stop	___	out of bounds	___	***MINORITY***	(Yes) / No
2–3	___	library	___	safety violation	___		

FIGURE 2–1 Sample ODR Form

Acme Elementary—Office Referral Summary
February 1–5

Student	***Date***	***Time***	***Location***	***Problem***	***Referred By***
Smith, Jeff	2–1	12:15	lunchroom	fight	Mr. Otis
Jones, Sally	2–2	3:10	field	vandalism	Ms. Hawkins
Blake, Eddy	2–4	7:30	bus stop	fight	Mr. Hanks
Orr, Jenny	2–4	12:10	lunchroom	stealing	Ms. Shank
Jones, Sally	2–5	12:20	lunchroom	disrespect	Ms. Shank

FIGURE 2–2 Weekly ODR Summary

In effect, behavior report or ODR data serve as a compass, directing staff to where more information should be gathered. For instance, the data from Acme Elementary may suggest that Ms. Otis and Ms. Shank should be asked about the exact nature of problems in the lunchroom and what they see as potential solutions. Furthermore, staff would likely want to look further into Sally Jones's problems. Appropriate questions to ask about Sally include what seems to predict her behavior problems and which teachers are most likely to have more in-depth information. The staff at Acme Elementary would continue to collect data and summarize it weekly throughout the year, while at the same time they would analyze the entire database for emerging trends across months.

While data collection and analysis across the school is the most effective and efficient way to identify the predictors of behavioral failure, many schools do not collect behavior incident data or do not routinely summarize it in a manner that allows access to the level of information necessary for designing effective prevention systems. In such cases, the next-best strategy is to do as Principal Jones did in the case study—survey the school staff to identify problem behaviors they see most often in the school as well as when and where these problems are observed (Scott, 2001; Scott & Hunter, 2001). This process offers the advantage of engaging all staff and encouraging their input regarding problem behaviors to which they most often respond. This staff engagement also may encourage them to be more involved in the process of developing strategies to prevent these predictable problems.

Designing School-Wide Systems

Whether by collecting behavior incident data or by surveying staff, identified predictable problems should be addressed by prevention strategies that are agreed on by the entire school staff. A rule of thumb is that for every identified problem, staff should determine whether the problem could be prevented by (a) a simple rule that students could be taught, (b) adapting an existing routine or creating a new routine, or (c) changing the physical structure of the environment or the presence of adults in the environment. As mentioned in Chapter 1, a specific team may be created to oversee the implementation of school-wide universal interventions. However, the same staff who fill out the behavior reports or who respond to school-wide problem surveys should participate in designing prevention strategies. Regardless of which strategy (rule, routine, physical arrangement) or combination of strategies is determined to be the best solution, it must be adopted by the entire school staff. If more than one strategy is identified as a viable solution, the staff must then decide which strategy or combination is the easiest and least expensive method of affecting the desired change. Again, once a strategy or set of strategies has been agreed on, it must be put into place and applied consistently throughout the school. At this point, if it doesn't already exist, a data collection procedure should be developed to monitor the identified problems and evaluate the effectiveness of the adopted solutions. When data determine that selected strategies are not successful, staff must convene and adjust or design alternate strategies.

Teaching "Big Ideas". Adapting school rules is most easily accomplished when the initial set of school-wide rules are developed under a set of "big ideas," which are school-wide expectations for appropriate student behavior throughout the school rather than a laundry list of specific rules that vary by location and context. Horner et al. (in press) recommend that three to five school-wide expectations be defined. For example, Finster Elementary School has removed their lists of "don'ts" that had served as the school-wide rules. In its place, staff have taught all students three basic school expectations: respect yourself, respect others, and respect property. On the first day of school, all faculty took time to teach each of the expectations. *Respect yourself* was defined as "keep yourself safe and learning," *respect others* was defined as "treat others the way you want them to treat you," and *respect property* was defined as "treat property that does not belong to you as you would like others to treat your property." Once students understood these big ideas, faculty and staff urged them to come up with examples of rules that would help them meet each expectation. On the playground, students determined that allowing the first person in line to have the final word in judging play would help keep the game moving and thus would demonstrate respect for self and others. In the classroom, students felt that calling out was not respectful to those with their hands raised and so decided that the rule should be to raise your hand when you wish to speak.

The concept of big ideas to teach school-wide rules has several advantages. First, students are actively involved in establishing the rules across all locations and contexts in the school. Second, all rules are tied into a school-wide rationale that helps students (and staff) remember them. Third, when students do not live up to any of the expectations, correction can be accomplished simply by asking the student, "Were you being respectful of others?" Follow-up can then involve instruction and the question "What would be a better way?" Finally, when school-wide data reveal unanticipated problem behavior, the same expectations can be used to create new rules aimed at preventing those predictable problems. Thus, school rules are never rewritten, only expanded.

The following sections present more concrete examples of how predictable problem information is used to develop or adapt rules, routines, and physical arrangements in the school. Look at the map of a portion of a school building presented in Figure 2-3. Assume that summaries of ODR data indicate that hallway A outside the music room is an area in which pushing and shoving, arguments, and even some vandalism have occurred. A closer inspection of these data indicates that these problems tend to be evenly distributed through the day, except during the noon hour, when no music classes are held. Knowledge of when and where problems are occurring can lead staff to develop hypotheses regarding why these problems take place. For example, suppose that many students are using this hallway at the same time (i.e., leaving and entering the music room). In addition, students are going in both directions throughout the hallway and are not under the immediate supervision of their teachers. Given this information, here are some simple rules, routines, and physical arrangements that could be introduced or adapted to prevent these problems.

Rules. A pertinent question is, Could students be taught a simple rule that might prevent this problem? One explanation for the problem is that students are milling about through the hallway in a haphazard manner. Therefore, a strategy might be to teach all students the rule "Keep to the right when in the hallway." It is reasonable to assume that, if students stay to the right, much of the pushing and shoving will be eliminated because students no longer will be crossing paths going in opposite directions. In addition to the potential effectiveness of a strategy, staff also must consider how realistic it would be to put in place. At face value, there seems to be no reason to believe that this strategy would be difficult to implement, and thus it appears to be an effective and realistic solution. However, it is up to the staff to decide whether the strategy will be adopted.

Routines. Is there a simple routine that can be implemented or an existing routine that can be adapted that might prevent this problem? Again, staff must think back to the identified problem and why it is occurring. Recall that many students were in the small hallway area at one time. One change in routine that might be considered is to arrange for students in the music room to completely vacate the room prior to the next group entering. Another possible change in routine is to allow the students in the music room to exit by the other door to the room rather than through the door to the hallway. By using one door as an entrance and another door as an exit, contact between students going different directions in the hallway can be avoided. Again, whether either of these strategies is adopted will be determined by the staff after considering all possible solutions.

Physical Arrangements. Is there a simple physical arrangement that could be introduced to prevent

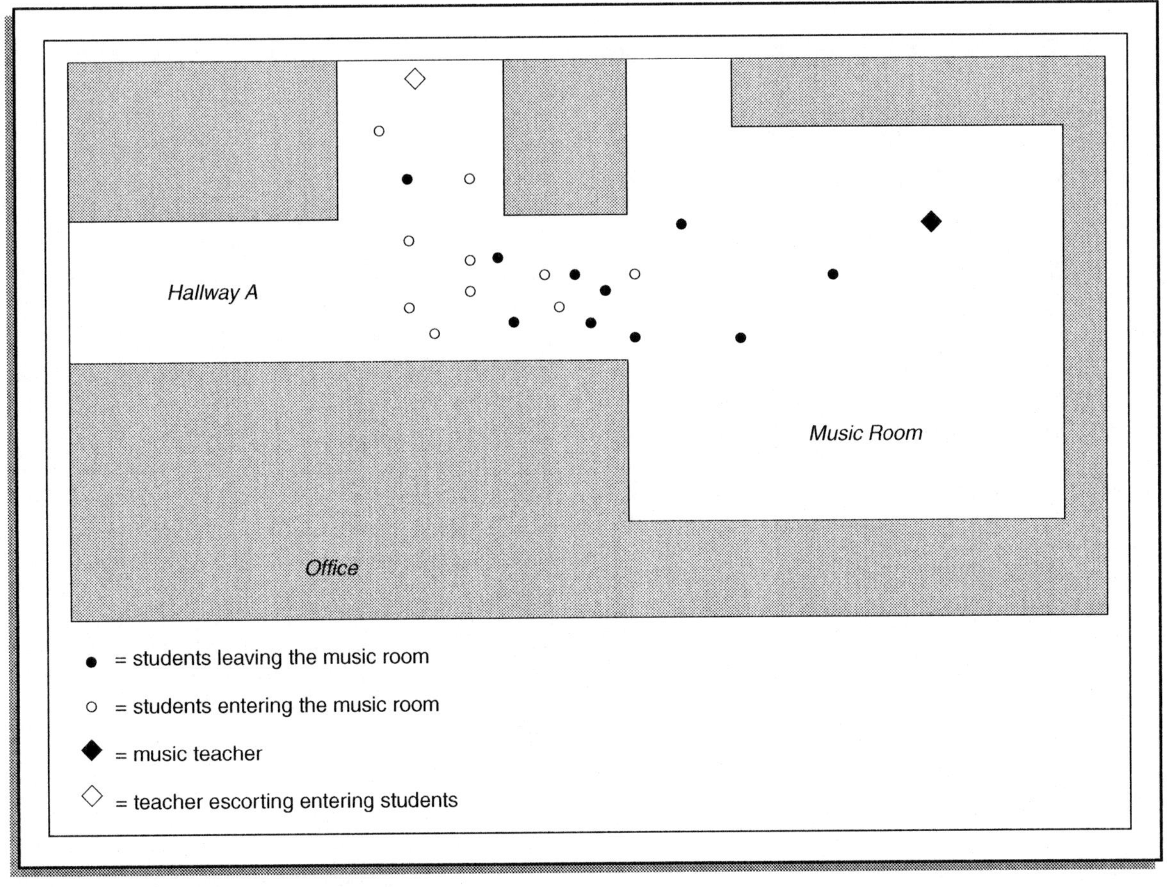

FIGURE 2–3 Conditions Predicting Student Problems

the problem? Recall that lack of immediate supervision was identified as a possible reason for behavior problems in that hallway. One strategy might be to ask the music teacher to stand in the music room doorway when dismissing and admitting students. In addition, the teacher escorting the students entering the room could be asked to lead the group through the hall, making certain that the line is orderly and that students are following the rules established for this transition. As with the other alternative strategies, this one has face validity. A bigger issue with regard to changing student supervision patterns is the degree of effort required to implement them. The more difficult the change, the less realistic it is and the more likely that it will be abandoned over time. In this case, the staff changes appear to be fairly simple, although this again will be the decision of the staff. Once each of these strategies has been considered, the staff must determine which one or combination might realistically be implemented and be effective in preventing the problem.

Again, when school-wide prevention strategies are adopted by all staff, implemented consistently and fairly, monitored to evaluate their effects on student behavior, and adjusted as needed according to school-wide data collection, significant reductions have been observed in rates of ODRs and behavior incidents. Responding to these incidents ordinarily requires large amounts of time by some school staff (e.g., discipline dean, assistant principal), but more often than not, the results are less than desired in terms of serving as a deterrent to student misbehavior. In one study, Scott and Barrett (2004) documented substantial reductions in the time administrators spend processing ODRs following the implementation of school-wide positive behavior support (averaging over 11 days per year for 2 years) in an elementary school as well as an increase of almost 30 days in student instructional time (because students were spending more time in classrooms) per year over the same period.

School-wide prevention strategies must be owned by the entire school, meaning that general education personnel (teachers and noninstructional staff) must take the major role in their implementation. Table 2–1 summarizes the seven key features of school-wide positive behavior support identified by Horner et al. (in press). Note that building- and district-level administrative support and leadership are essential features. These authors also have developed an instrument, the School-Wide Evaluation Tool (SET), to assist schools in assessing the need for and implementation of school-wide positive behavior support. If you think your school staff may be interested in pursuing this approach to school discipline, the resources listed on the Companion Website may be useful. You also will find information, tools, and links to contact persons on the Website of the National Center for Positive Behavioral Interventions and Supports. Click the Online Library button.

TABLE 2–1 The Seven Key Features of School-Wide Positive Behavior Support

School-Wide Positive Behavior Support Practices and Systems
1. Define three to five school-wide expectations for appropriate behavior.
2. Actively teach the school-wide behavioral expectations to all students.
3. Monitor and acknowledge students for engaging in behavioral expectations.
4. Correct problem behaviors using a consistently administered continuum of behavioral consequences.
5. Gather and use information about student behavior to evaluate and guide decision making.
6. Obtain leadership of school-wide practices from an administrator who a. establishes a team to develop, implement, and manage the school-wide behavior support effort in a school; b. serves as a member of the team; c. allocates sufficient time to implement behavior support procedures; and d. allocates school-wide behavior as one of the top three improvement goals for the school.
7. Obtain district-level support in the form of a. training in school-wide behavior support practices, b. policies emphasizing the expectations that schools are safe and organized for effective learning, and c. expectation that information on problem behavior patterns be gathered and reported.

IMPLEMENTING POSITIVE BEHAVIOR SUPPORT IN THE CLASSROOM

A wide range of universal interventions have been developed for use in classrooms in dealing with both students exhibiting disabilities and those who are typical. As emphasized at the beginning of this chapter, the appropriate context for a classroom behavior management program is a school-wide disciplinary plan that connects the teacher's strategy with expectations and consequences that exist throughout the school building.

Extending School-Wide Strategies

School-wide systems of positive behavior support typically include only the commons areas of the school, such as hallways, playground, cafeteria, and restrooms. School staff vote on the expectations that they'd like to see in place and agree to carry out the strategies on which consensus has been reached. These strategies normally do not translate directly to the classroom. That is, even when school-wide strategies are in place, teachers maintain their autonomy regarding the management structure and style within the confines of their own classrooms. Despite this autonomy, teachers must be careful that classroom structures do not contradict school-wide expectations or set students up to fail in the larger school environment. For example, if all school staff agree that no gum is allowed, no teachers should allow gum in their classrooms. To do so would set students up for failure if they forget to dispose of their gum before moving into the hallway or are seen carrying gum on campus. Similarly, if the school decides to use conflict managers to mediate disputes between students, every teacher should support that strategy in her classroom. The goal is to establish consistent expectations and procedures, thereby encouraging students to engage in behaviors that will promote their success.

Aside from considering the school-wide rules that logically should be applied to the classroom, teachers must evaluate their own classrooms in much the same manner as the entire staff considered circumstances that appeared to predict student failures throughout the school. Teachers can think back and identify the times, places, and conditions under which problem behaviors have most often occurred in their classrooms. Then they can use the same procedure as followed in school-wide planning (i.e., developing classroom rules, routines, and physical arrangements). But in this case, the teacher has autonomy in deciding which strategies to adopt. As before, strategies should be considered in terms of expected effectiveness and the effort required to implement them. In the end, classroom teachers develop their own classroom management structure that both fits within the school system and provides the most efficient and effective strategies for preventing student failure.

> Reflect on the classrooms in which you have observed. Can you think of circumstances that tended to predict problem student behavior?

Promoting Success in the Classroom

Recall that behavior management in the school involves facilitating student success in group settings. This focus also should be maintained in the classroom. Strategies to facilitate success in this setting involve organizing the curriculum, arranging and individualizing instruction, evaluating students' acquisition of skills and information, and adjusting instructional and behavior management procedures according to their progress. Managing student behavior is a necessary if not sufficient condition for accomplishing the teacher's major task—facilitating pupils' learning. The teacher who cannot maintain behavior within reasonable limits through positive management procedures will face constant frustration and personal dissatisfaction and is likely to find those same feelings expressed by students and their parents.

In the classroom, the specific management goals expressed by teachers are likely to include increasing such desired student behaviors as attending to tasks, remaining in seat, following teacher directions, using time productively, and giving correct academic responses (Gresham & Reschly, 1987). These behaviors correspond to a "model behavioral profile" (Hersh & Walker, 1983), but note that they have little to do with developing students' peer relationship skills (Gresham & Reschly, 1987). Teachers are also concerned about decreasing behaviors that are dangerous, disruptive, or incompatible with the completion of academic tasks. The majority of pupils also would like to achieve these goals. That is, they want to be academically and socially successful in school. Therefore, it is important to negotiate with students when setting expectations for classroom behavior. Your expectations will more likely be accepted if you consider those of your students. Again, the majority of students want to be successful in school both with other students and with adults. It is necessary to look to the problems that inhibit this success and assess to determine why students fail. The key is to facilitate success for all students.

The following discussion of classroom behavior management focuses on decisions and strategies aimed at the prevention of occasions in which one or more students exhibit behaviors that disrupt the learning environment or are potentially dangerous. A classroom management system should be a flexible, operating framework, not a rigid, intolerant set of rules and consequences. As a matter of principle, use the system most natural (i.e., that involves the fewest number of contrived or "extra" factors, such as points or **tangible reinforcers**) and easy to operate. Artificial systems usually must be phased out if student behavior learned in the setting where they are implemented is to generalize to classroom environments where such procedures are not in use. In the following sections, we describe strategies that have been shown to have a positive impact on the classroom environment: effective instruction and classroom-wide and individual behavior management strategies. For descriptions of how to implement 12 evidence-based classroom management systems, see Cipani (2004).

Effective Instruction and Student Behavior

There are four important reasons why teachers of students with behavior problems (especially those with emotional and behavioral disorders [EBD]) should pay careful attention to the content and delivery of the academic curriculum. First, research clearly links curriculum (what is taught) and instruction (how curriculum is taught) variables to challenging behavior (Darch & Kame'enui, 2004; Lane, 2004; Scott et al., 2001). Second, students with challenging behavior often perform at lower academic levels than their peers, and students with EBD make even slower progress in special education programs than students with learning disabilities (Anderson, Kutash, & Duchnowski, 2001). Third, there is growing evidence that improving the academic performance of these students also results in improved classroom behavior (Jolivette, Wehby, & Hirsch, 1999; Kern, Choutka, & Sokol, 2002; Nelson, Johnson, & Marchand-Martella, 1996; Scott & Shearer-Lingo, 2002). Finally, if students are working at a frustration level and are unable to successfully acquire new skills, attempts to manage their behavior without addressing their academic instruction will be futile (Witt, VanDerHayden, & Gilbertson, 2004). However, researchers also have found that interventions for students with well-established EBD must address *both* their academic and their behavioral needs (Lane & Menzies, 2003; Wehby, Falk, Barton-Arwood, Lane, & Cooley, 2003).

Another impetus for emphasizing effective instruction is provided by federal law. As mentioned in Chapter 1, NCLB promotes the use of educational practices that have been validated by empirical research. A number of instructional strategies have been evaluated against rigorous criteria and have been identified as evidence based by national experts. The literature on effective teaching indicates that such strategies as using brisk instructional pacing, reviewing students' work frequently, giving systematic and constructive corrective feedback, minimizing pupil errors and providing frequent praise for correct responding, offering guided practice, modeling new behaviors, providing transitions between lessons or concepts, and monitoring student performance are strongly related to pupil achievement and attitudes toward learning (Darch & Kame'enui, 2004; Lewis, Hudson, Richter, & Johnson, 2004; Mercer & Mercer, 2001).

Although detailed description of these instructional behaviors is beyond the scope of this text, effective instruction is an essential prerequisite to classroom behavior management. Recall also that students with established patterns of challenging behavior are likely to require both academic and behavioral intervention. A number of online resources exist for addressing the instructional needs of students, such as the Center for Early Intervention for Reading and Behavior, the National Center for Learning Disabilities, and the U.S. Department of Education Sciences Institute of Education Sciences What Works Clearinghouse. Consult their Websites for more information.

Witt et al. (2004) describe three prerequisites to effective classroom behavior management. These

BOX 2–1 Prerequisites to Classroom Behavior Management

1. The teacher must be competent to teach the academic subjects to which she is assigned, the curriculum must be appropriate for the students, and instruction must include opportunities for students to learn, practice, and receive feedback.
2. Students must know what is expected of them behaviorally.
3. *If* the academic program is solid and *if* positive behavioral expectations have been taught, *then* strategies for responding to problem behavior can be successful.

are listed in Box 2-1. As the third item suggests, these prerequisites are pyramidal; that is, each one is a foundation for the next. Witt et al. (2004) advocate that, when classroom behavior problems occur, the teacher should first look at her academic curriculum and teaching strategies, then ask whether behavioral expectations have been taught successfully, and, finally, ask whether responses to undesired student behavior are consistent and accurate.

As a classroom teacher, you may not be in a position to select the curriculum. Rather, your responsibility is to implement the curriculum that has been identified for your grade level and subject matter area. However, it is important that teachers continually assess students' placement and progress in the curriculum to ensure that what is being taught is meaningful, relevant, and accomplishable for all pupils (Darch & Kame'enui, 2004). However, the delivery of the curriculum (i.e., instruction) is the classroom teacher's primary responsibility. Fortunately, the least intrusive and most natural behavior management strategies are good teaching practices.

The purpose of using effective instructional and behavior management strategies is to increase the likelihood of student success. The focus of the following discussion is on the important issue of facilitating success in students who have, or are at risk of developing, repetitive academic and social failure in the school. Sugai and Tindal (1993) developed an "effective teaching profile," presented in Figure 2-4, which is both a succinct summary of evidence-based teaching skills and a self-assessment checklist that you can use to evaluate your use of these important teaching behaviors.

One view of management is that it involves controlling student behavior. However, if we view management from an instructional perspective, the issue is predictability. That is, you want to be confident that students will behave in specific ways under specific conditions. For example, when you give the prompt "What is 2 + 2?" you want to know that the student will respond predictably with the answer "4." Similarly, when presented with an assignment, a request to pay attention, or a difficult task, you want to be confident that the student will respond appropriately. Therefore, control is simply the ability to predict that a student will respond appropriately to a given environmental condition or demand. The way to achieve this predictability is through effective instruction.

Instruction and Stimulus Control. Effective instruction demonstrates for the student that a particular response will result in success—the most important reinforcer available to you and your students. When success is predictable, students are more likely to repeat the behaviors that lead to successful outcomes in the future. As a teacher, you must demonstrate the specific conditions under which specific behaviors are appropriate (i.e., will result in success). Thus, you teach students that "4" is the correct response to a specific class of math problems (e.g., 1 + 3, 2 + 2, etc.) but not correct in response to a much larger class of problems

Effective Teaching Profile

Place an X on the scale to indicate the extent to which the teacher displayed the best teaching practices. Connect each X to display a teaching profile.

Yes_____ No 1. Brisk pacing
Yes_____ No 2. Specific explanations and instructions for new concepts
Yes_____ No 3. Allocated time for guided practice
Yes_____ No 4. Cumulative review of skills being taught
Yes_____ No 5. Regularly varied assessments of learning of new concepts
Yes_____ No 6. Regular and active interactions with individual students
Yes_____ No 7. Frequent and detailed feedback
Yes_____ No 8. Varied forms of positive reinforcement
Yes_____ No 9. Positive, predictable, and orderly learning environment
Yes_____ No 10. Maintenance of student attention within and across instructional activities and materials
Yes_____ No 11. Reinforcement for task completion
Yes_____ No 12. Appropriate selection of examples and nonexamples
Yes_____ No 13. Consistent application of contingencies for rules and expectations
Yes_____ No 14. Appropriate use of model/demonstrations
Yes_____ No 15. Appropriate use of behavior rehearsal (role-plays)
Yes_____ No 16. Smooth transition within and between lessons
Yes_____ No 17. High rates of correct student responding

FIGURE 2–4 Teaching Behaviors of Effective Teachers
Source: *Sugai, G. M., & Tindal, G. A. (1993).* Effective school consultation: An interactive approach. *Pacific Grove, CA: Brooks/Cole. Used with permission.*

(i.e., all other math problems). When students respond predictably in the presence of the relevant stimulus but not in the presence of all other stimuli, the **discriminative stimulus** is controlling (i.e., predicting) behavior. The concept of **stimulus control** is the very heart of instruction. You must teach students how to behave (academically and socially) in a variety of relevant circumstances. When stimulus control has not been established, you cannot predict a student's response, and the chances for failure are high.

The goals of classroom behavior management are to develop stimulus control over pupil behavior and to prevent problem situations from occurring. These must be accomplished in settings where you are responsible for delivering instruction to groups of students. Consequently, as discussed earlier, appropriate classroom management interventions are those that are less intrusive and restrictive; they may be implemented without significant interruption of ongoing activities and without removing students or instructional staff from the teaching setting. Remember the main premise of this chapter: ***prevention is the most effective early intervention strategy.*** Thus, your task is to use the instructional techniques required to facilitate regular predictable student success. In the following paragraphs, we describe several instructional approaches to effective classroom behavior management. Consult Cipani (2004) and Darch and Kame'enui (2004) for others.

Modifying Tasks. You may have observed that with some students, certain academic tasks are associated with the occurrence of problem behavior, while other tasks are associated with acceptable behaviors. Therefore, one instructional strategy for addressing problem behaviors is to modify the tasks that predict these. Researchers have demonstrated that problem behaviors that are associated with task difficulty or demand may be reduced in two ways (Witt et al., 2004). The first involves reducing the amount of effort needed to perform the task through altering the task requirements, changing ways to fulfill the task, providing breaks during the task, and scheduling briefer task time periods (Kern et al., 2002). The second approach is to make the task less aversive by modifying task difficulty (Umbreit, Lane, & Dejud, 2004) or by giving students a choice of task (Blair, Umbreit, & Bos, 1999; Dunlap, Kern, & Worchester, 2001). For example, it has been demonstrated that increasing the difficulty of tasks that were too easy (Umbreit et al., 2004) and allowing students to choose tasks and instructional materials resulted in increased academic engagement and reduced disruptive behavior of students with EBD (Dunlap et al., 2001; Jolivette, Wehby, Canale, & Massey, 2001). As Witt et al. (2004) observe, the effectiveness of modifying tasks most likely is due to the fact that this strategy increases reinforcement through reducing student errors and increasing rates of teacher praise or diminishes aversive nature of the task through shorter task duration.

Pre-correction. The least intrusive prevention strategy is to teach students the rules and routines that will facilitate their success. **Pre-correction** originated as a strategy for making adjustments in academic instruction before a student had an opportunity to make errors (Colvin, Sugai, Good, & Lee, 1997; Colvin, Sugai, & Patching, 1993). Academic pre-correction focuses on instructional areas in which the teacher anticipates the student will make errors. Using pre-correction involves thinking ahead to the problems, conditions, or contexts in which stimulus control is not yet firmly established. Applying this strategy to prevent student failure in social behavioral areas is a matter of teaching rules and routines for students to follow, usually during times or routines that typically are less highly structured than academic lessons, such as transitions between lessons or classes. One pre-correction strategy is to simply provide a verbal reminder of the stimulus-response relationship (e.g., "Remember that when the bell rings we need to put our work away before we can be dismissed" or "If someone calls you a name during this activity what would be a good thing to do?"). Walker et al. (2004) list seven steps for implementing pre-correction for social behavior. Figure 2-5 presents a pre-correction checklist and plan that was developed around these steps for a student who has experienced difficulty entering the classroom following recess.

Using Prompts and Cues. Pre-correction involves using a verbal prompt that is delivered prior to behavior. But prompts and cues can be verbal, tangible, and even sensory and may be used prior to behavior, along with the behavior, or as part of a corrective sequence after a behavior. The rule of thumb for prompts and cues is to use the least amount or least intrusive prompt necessary to facilitate a successful response. Because prompts typically are not naturally occurring, be careful not to allow them to become the only stimulus that sets the occasion for appropriate behavior.

Prompts should be used only to draw a student's attention to the natural discriminative stimuli that should control behavior and then be systematically faded so that the desired behavior occurs reliably in the presence of the naturally occurring discriminative stimulus. For example, the dismissal bell, rather than the teacher's verbal reminder, should be the discriminative stimulus for students to put away materials, straighten their desks, and leave the classroom in an orderly manner.

Prompts and cues may take the form of gestures, sounds, signals, notes, signs, modeling, or any other physical display that will increase the probability of success. Prompts and cues can be used in the same circumstances as pre-correction, namely, to remind students to use appropriate behaviors prior to the occurrence of a condition that predicts high failure rates. Once students begin the behavior or routine, you can provide hints, suggestions, reminders, and questions designed to facilitate

Pre-Correction Checklist and Plan

Teacher Sarah Enlow
Student Dominic Smith
Date 11/15/05

Context	*Students entering classroom immediately after recess.*
☐ 1. Predictable behavior	*Enter shouting, laughing, and pushing before complying with teacher direction.*
☐ 2. Expected behavior	*Enter the room quietly, go to desks, begin task, keep hands to self.*
☐ 3. Context modification	*Teacher meets students at door, has them wait and then go to desk to begin entry tasks.*
☐ 4. Behavior rehearsal	*Teacher reminds students just before recess of expected behaviors. Asks Dominic to tell what are expected behaviors.*
☐ 5. Strong reinforcement	*Students are told that if they cooperate with teacher requests, they will have additional breaks and 5 extra minutes for recess.*
☐ 6. Prompts	*Teacher gives signals at the door to be quiet and points to activity on chalkboard. Teacher says "hush" to noisy students and praises students who are beginning work.*
☐ 7. Monitoring plan	*Teacher uses a watch to measure how long it takes for all students to get on task and counts how many students begin their tasks immediately (within 10 seconds).*

FIGURE 2–5 Example of Pre-correction Checklist and Plan for Dominic.
Source: *Colvin, G., Sugai, G., & Patching, B. (1993). Pre-correction: An instructional approach for managing predictable problem behaviors.* Intervention in School and Clinic, *28(3), 143–150. Copyright PRO-ED. Used with permission.*

success (e.g., "Remember to wait for the student who is at my desk to return to her seat before coming up"). Finally, if a student has failed to demonstrate the appropriate behavior, prompts and cues can be used to help lead her back through the situation and see the stimuli that should have signaled the appropriate behavior (e.g., "When you approached me, Johnny was at my desk so I didn't have time to help you—when I'm working with someone else when you need me what should you do?"). Even when applying a negative consequence for misbehavior under these conditions, it is advisable to use corrective prompts and cues to decrease the likelihood of repeated failure in the future. When misbehaviors are regarded as errors rather than intentions to be "bad," it is more logical to apply a correction procedure than punishment. However, exercise caution in using prompts. Walker et al. (2004) point out that teachers are prone to escalate their use of prompts with behaviorally difficult students to the point that these become negative and even threatening.

Increasing students' **opportunities to respond** also has been shown to positively affect the academic and social behavior of students with EBD. Specifically, it has been demonstrated that increasing students' rates of academic responding is associated with increased correct responses and increased task engagement as well as with decreased disruptive behavior (Sutherland, Alder, & Gunter, 2003; Sutherland & Wehby, 2001).

Using Attention and Praise Effectively. Unfortunately, the typical behavior management practices of teachers who work with students exhibiting problematic behaviors are not conducive to pupil achievement or desired social behavior. In fact, many educators appear to find punishment a more acceptable approach to managing student behavior than positive reinforcement (Maag, 2001). This attitude is supported by professionals such as Kohen (2001) who argue (without any scientific evidence) that praise is counterproductive, manipulative, and reduces reinforcement intrinsic in the completion of tasks (Strain & Joseph, 2004). On the contrary, "one of the most effective practices described in the literature is the application of contingent positive reinforcement following desired appropriate social behavior" (Lewis et al., 2004, p. 250).

One of the most regrettable by-products of displaying undesired behavior in the classroom is that teachers tend to avoid students who do this. Studies have documented that instructional interactions between teachers and students who exhibit challenging behavior are infrequent (Carr, Taylor, & Robinson, 1991; Gunter, Jack, DePaepe, Reed, & Harrison, 1994) and aversive (Gunter, Denny, Jack, Shores, & Nelson, 1993; Shores, Gunter, & Jack, 1993).

Teacher-administered **social reinforcement** includes three kinds of teacher behavior: feedback, attention, and approval. Feedback typically occurs as a consequence of particular behaviors (finishing a task, following a rule). However, by itself, the effects of feedback are weak (Madsen, Becker, & Thomas, 1968; O'Leary, Becker, Evans, & Sudargas, 1969). However, contingent teacher attention has been shown to strongly influence behavior. Attention differs from approval in two ways: it need not involve any verbal behavior, and it is not necessarily positive.

Using teacher attention involves applying **differential reinforcement**. When appropriate behavior occurs, provide natural reinforcement such as attending, standing near, touching, looking at, or interacting with the student. Inappropriate behavior is placed on **extinction** by withholding attention through looking away, moving to another part of the room, or calling attention to another child. Early applied behavior analysis researchers demonstrated that simply providing such differential attention is a powerful strategy: it has been used to eliminate regressive crawling (Harris, Johnston, Kelly, & Wolf, 1964), reduce aggression (Brown & Elliott, 1965), increase following instructions (Schutte & Hopkins, 1970), and accelerate correct academic performance (Zimmerman & Zimmerman, 1962). However, keep in mind that withholding attention will be effective in reducing undesired student behavior *only* when the behavior is motivated by a desire to obtain teacher attention. In addition, when using social extinction, you should be prepared for an initial increase in the behavior (see Chapter 3).

As you know, attention is a potent natural reinforcer for most students. However, in cases where it is not, teacher attention must be established as a **conditioned reinforcer** (a consequence that has acquired reinforcing properties through association with previously established reinforcers). If your attention does not appear to function as a reinforcer for a student (i.e., if the student does not engage in behaviors—appropriate or inappropriate—that result in your attending to her), you should repeatedly pair it with the presentation of a stimulus that already has been demonstrated to be reinforcing, such as points or tangibles. Gradually and systematically fade the artificial reinforcer until attention alone produces the desired effect. This process may take time for many pupils with severe problem behaviors. Other students may reveal an extensive repertoire of inappropriate attention-getting behaviors (e.g., raising a hand and saying, "Hey teacher!," getting up to ask a question). Clearly stated rules governing how teacher attention may be solicited are helpful, but they serve little purpose if you even occasionally respond to the inappropriate activity. Using your attention as a behavior management tool requires a high degree of self-monitoring and self-control.

Teacher approval or praise involves the same contingencies as attention and may be verbal or nonverbal. However, in using approval the teacher usually specifies the desired behavior verbally, such as "I like the way you are working" or "You really did a good job on your algebra assignment." Nonverbal approval (smiles, pats on the back) also may be effective. The contingent use of approval is more critical than the amount of approval per se, but use contingent praise four times as often as verbal aversives (Alberto & Troutman, 2003).

> Can you think of some strategies to increase your use of praise for appropriate student behavior? In conjunction with increasing students' rates of correct responding, doing this can have a dramatic positive impact on classroom climate.

Used systematically and consistently, these "good teacher skills" will strengthen the behaviors that most teachers desire in their pupils: compliance with teacher requests and instructions, on-task behaviors, cooperative interactions with others, and low rates of noise and disruption. Most teachers prefer to use the least intrusive management strategies that produce these results. Again, the most appropriate group behavior management procedures are those that are more natural and easier to implement. For example, praise and attention are more natural and easier to administer than **tokens**, and tokens are easier to deliver than **edible reinforcers.** Effective classroom teachers use a range of strategies to influence student behavior, and they develop the ability to "read" situations and behaviors on the spot and apply interventions appropriately and in a timely fashion. You should strive to develop proficiency with a range of interventions so that you can use each of them effectively. To learn more about evidence-based practices with students who exhibit serious behavior disorders, consult the Website of the National Center for Students with Intensive Social, Emotional, and Behavioral Needs.

Group Management Systems in the Classroom

As we have emphasized throughout this chapter, the best behavior management systems are focused on teaching students appropriate expected behaviors and reinforcing them for compliance. In keeping with this orientation, we recommend that you plan your behavior management repertoire around the use of effective instruction, contingent praise and attention, and the reinforcement that comes from student success to facilitate appropriate student classroom behavior. However, in both general and special education classrooms, a number of pupils may be found who require more elaborate intervention, which suggests that a group behavior management plan may be needed.

Specific classroom behavior management systems are described in detail in Chapter 7. The following discussion addresses behavior management considerations and strategies for students with significantly challenging behavior. Such educational settings as resource rooms, self-contained classrooms, or even segregated special schools may be the least restrictive environment for students identified as EBD. The greater need of these students for individualized behavior support, including direct instruction in academic and social skills provided by educators who are well trained in these strategies in addition to behavior management procedures, is not easily met in general education classrooms (Kauffman, Bantz, & McCullough, 2002; Kauffman, Lloyd, Astuto, & Hallahan, 1995).

Day-to-day classroom behavior management can be one of the most complex and demanding tasks faced by educators who work with groups of students who exhibit serious problem behavior. Pupils who are chronically disruptive, defiant, withdrawn, or aggressive or who engage in nonfunctional stereotypic behaviors and who possess minimal social or functional communication skills often are difficult to manage even in one-to-one situations. Fortunately, like other students, these pupils respond to proactive and preventative behavior management strategies. Systematically teaching and rewarding desired academic and social behaviors are fundamental to effective behavior management in alternative education programs as well as in self-contained or resource classrooms. With universal classroom management strategies in place, individual student problem behaviors will be minimized. However, *they will not be eliminated.* Therefore, it is important to have a repertoire of effective techniques for managing individual student behavior.

When you encounter students who, despite your best efforts at prevention, continue to exhibit challenging behavior, it may be tempting to blame their behavior problems on the underlying "pathology" supposedly inherent in students who have been identified as "behaviorally disordered" or "emotionally disturbed." As pointed out earlier, we regard this attitude as inappropriate. However, neither can all classroom misbehavior be attributed to inept behavior management. Nevertheless, pupils with histories of exhibiting tantrums, defiance of authority, aggressive acts against others, or noncompliance will tend to exhibit such behavior in situations where rules are vague or inconsistently applied, teachers are less observant, and learning tasks are unpleasant. The key to effective management of these behaviors lies in the teacher's ability to analyze and adjust variables in the immediate environment—specifically, the antecedents and consequences that predict both maladaptive and desired behavior.

Think about students you have known who were behaviorally challenging. Were their behavior patterns different with some teachers than with others? Try to identify some differences in the behavior of their teachers that may have accounted for these observations.

In addition to not providing positive reinforcement for desired behavior, there are a number of other negative behavior management practices that you should try to avoid. Johns and Carr (1995) identified several techniques that effective teachers seldom exhibit. These are summarized in Box 2-2. Engaging in these practices greatly increases the chances that students with established patterns of challenging behavior, as well as those on the "margins" with respect to classroom behavior, will act out. They provide fertile soil for the cultivation of crisis situations. To the extent that you can avoid these practices and instead use the practices listed in Figure 2-4, you and your students will experience a much more productive classroom climate.

Using Antecedents and Consequences Systematically. In addition to the *types* of antecedents and consequences you can use, it also is important to attend to *how* you use them. Here are some variables to consider: the specific antecedents you will use as discriminative stimuli for student behavior, the contingencies of reinforcement or punishment you will establish, how you will arrange the delivery of reinforcement or punishment, and who will administer consequences.

BOX 2-2 Negative Behavior Management Strategies

- Forcing a student to do something she doesn't want to do
- Forcing students to admit to lies
- Demanding confession from students
- Using confrontational techniques
- Asking students why they act out
- Punishing students
- Making disapproving comments
- Comparing a student's behavior with other students' behavior
- Yelling at students
- Engaging in verbal battles
- Making unrealistic threats
- Ridiculing students

Antecedent stimuli include a range of **setting events** that may influence student behavior, some of which are beyond your control (e.g., students' sleep schedules, nutrition, events occurring at home). However, if you can identify patterns in your students' behavior that apparently are not related to school or classroom factors, you may be able to establish links with parents or other professionals who can give you information to functionally assess the relationship of these setting events to student behaviors. Perhaps you can then have input on collaborative interventions to alter their influence on behavior. Within the classroom, such setting events as the physical arrangement, schedule of events, instructional materials, and teacher proximity have been shown to affect student behavior. These variables can be managed through establishing a predictable classroom structure.

A predictable classroom structure establishes clear rules, routines, and physical arrangements for students and staff. Whether because of an absence of rules, inconsistent application of consequences for behavior, or ability to outmanipulate the adults who control these consequences, some students enter education programs with the expectation that the social world is a chaotic place where nothing can be predicted. Structure involves providing clear directions, prompts, and cues; following student behavior with predictable, consistent, and appropriate consequences; and planning of physical space, daily schedule, rules, and teacher movement patterns. These strategies are explained in detail in Chapter 7.

Levels Systems. A **levels system** is a comprehensive behavior management strategy that establishes a hierarchy of increasing expectations for behavioral improvement with increasing student reinforcement and decreasing behavioral structure. Levels systems are used to help students progress from the academic and social skills they exhibit on entry into the system to performance levels that enable them to make successful transitions to less restrictive settings. Typically, students advance through a sequence of four or five levels, each associated with higher expectations for academic performance and social behavior, as well as with greater student autonomy and access to more naturalistic reinforcers. For example, at the first level, a student may be expected to follow basic classroom rules, attempt all academic assignments, and work in a one-to-one relationship with the classroom teacher or paraprofessional. At more advanced levels, expectations may include fulfilling the terms of individual contingency contracts, completing assignments with a high degree of accuracy, and working independently in group settings, which may include participation in mainstream classes. Advancement through the levels is based on periodic assessments of student progress against specific criteria for academic and social behaviors. Questions to consider in developing a levels system are listed in Box 2–3 (Reisberg, Brodigan, & Williams, 1991). You can find more information on levels systems in Chapter 12, and an example is on the Companion Website.

Although levels systems have been popular in more restrictive educational programs for students with behavioral problems, their efficacy in promoting successful transitions to less restrictive environments has not been demonstrated (Scheuermann, Webber, Partin, & Knies, 1994; Smith & Farrell, 1993). Scheuermann et al. (1994) suggested that levels systems might, in fact, violate some legal requirements associated with the due process and the least restrictive environment regulations of IDEA. Specifically, the right to an education in the least restrictive environment may be abridged in that access to general education classrooms is treated as a privilege and is not based on whether the student can benefit from such participation. In addition, to the extent that criteria for placement in a given level and movement among levels are the same for all students, levels systems are not consistent with the individualized program requirement of the law. Even the placement of students in mainstream school settings based on their status in the levels system (e.g., lunch in the cafeteria) violates their right to have decisions regarding their participation in such settings made by their IEP Teams. Scheuermann et al. (1994) proposed a

BOX 2–3 Levels System Considerations

1. Are the levels or steps in the system clearly defined?
2. Do students understand the desired behaviors they must exhibit to progress through the system?
3. Do students understand the inappropriate behaviors (and their consequences) that prohibit student advancement or will cause students to regress at each level?
4. Are the reinforcers students may earn at each level explicit?
5. Do students know the criteria for placement in each level and movement within the system?
6. Are there procedures for continuous evaluation and measurement of student performance?
7. Are there procedures to facilitate frequent communication between everyone who comes into contact with the system (students, parents, other staff)?

model for designing individualized levels systems based on the curriculum for a given student.

SUMMARY

- Planning and operating positive and productive school and classroom environments are important elements of success in teaching any group of students at any level.
- Primary prevention is based on univeral interventions, whether school-wide or in the classroom, and involves assessing environments and developing strategies to prevent student failure.
- The best strategy for preventing student behavior problems is effective instruction. Instruction isn't a consideration only for imparting academic skills; it also is a critical element of strategies for addressing student social behavior. If you think of undesired student behavior as a mistake rather than as a conscious decision to misbehave, you will be more likely to respond with an error correction procedure than with punishment.
- Prevention is the most effective form of behavior management. Think about the times, places, and conditions under which student behavioral failures are most likely to occur and develop consistent strategies involving rules, routines, and physical arrangements to prevent those problems.
- Collect and use data on student behavior to assess school environments and to make decisions about student and staff needs.
- Set expectations that are specific, clear, and fair. The most effective expectations for behavior are stated behaviorally and include clear criterion statements. This enables both staff and students to clearly evaluate progress. In your own classroom, base your expectations on those for the entire school and have your students participate in translating these into specific classroom rules.

DISCUSSION/APPLICATION IDEAS

1. Finster Elementary has determined that several students are wandering to the far end of the field during recess and are playing behind a group of trees. This is a very popular location because there is a play structure in that location, but it is far from the playground, where the vast majority of students play. Many problem behavior referrals have been made from this location. Because of a staff shortage and scheduling difficulties, only one teacher supervises the playground during recess. What could Finster Elementary do to prevent these predictable problems? Think of some simple rules, routines, and physical arrangements.

2. When Ms. Peters says to her students, "Please line up quietly to go to the lunch room," her first-grade pupils immediately line up in single file with no disruptive behavior. When Ms. Thomas issues the same request to her class, there is a great deal of running, shouting, and fighting among her first-grade students to be first in line. How did Ms. Peters establish stimulus control over the behavior of lining up?
3. Ms. Thomas often uses a loud voice, threats, and spankings to attempt to control her class, but her pupils are among the most unruly in the building. Why has this happened?
4. What strategies would you recommend that Ms. Thomas use to improve her stimulus control over student behavior during these transition times?
5. If you were to set up a resource room for elementary-age pupils with EBD, how would you structure it? How would you structure a resource room differently for junior high school students?

REFERENCES

Alberto, P. A., & Troutman, A. C. (2003). *Applied behavior analysis for teachers* (6th ed.). Upper Saddle River, NJ: Merrill/Prentice Hall.

Anderson, J. A., Kutash, K., & Duchnowski, A. J. (2001). A comparison of the academic progress of students with EBD and students with LD. *Journal of Emotional and Behavioral Disorders, 9,* 106-115.

Blair, K., Umbreit, J., & Bos, C. (1999). Using functional assessment and children's preferences to improve the behavior of young children with behavioral disorders. *Behavioral Disorders, 24,* 151-166.

Brooks, K., Schiraldi, V., & Ziedenberg, J. (2000). *Schoolhouse hype: Two years later.* Washington, DC: Justice Policy Institute.

Brown, C. H. (2003, June). *Methodologic issues in variation in impact among universal prevention programs.* Paper presented at the 11th Annual Meeting of the Society for Prevention Research, Washington, DC.

Brown, P., & Elliott, R. (1965). Control of aggression in a nursery school class. *Journal of Experimental Child Psychology, 2,* 103-107.

Carr, E. G., Taylor, J. C., & Robinson, S. (1991). The effects of severe behavior problems in children on the teaching behavior of adults. *Journal of Applied Behavior Analysis, 24,* 523-535.

Centers for Disease Control and Prevention. (1995). Youth risk behavior surveillance—United States, 1993. *Morbidity and Mortality Weekly Report, 44,* 6-7.

Chapman, D., & Hofweber, C. (2000). Effective behavior support in British Columbia. *Journal of Positive Behavior Interventions, 2,* 235-237.

Cipani, E. (2004). *Classroom management for all teachers: 12 plans for evidence-based practice* (2nd ed). Upper Saddle River, NJ: Merrill/Prentice Hall.

Colvin, G., Sugai, G., & Patching, B. (1993). Pre-correction: An instructional approach for managing predictable problem behaviors. *Intervention in School and Clinic, 28*(3), 143-150.

Colvin, G., Sugai, G., Good, R. H., III, & Lee, Y. (1997). Using active supervision and pre-correction to improve transition behaviors in an elementary school. *School Psychology Quarterly, 12,* 344-363.

Darch, C. B., & Kame'enui, E. J. (2004). *Instructional classroom management: A proactive approach to behavior management* (2nd ed.). Upper Saddle River, NJ: Merrill/Prentice Hall.

Dunlap, G., Kern, L., & Worchester, J. (2001). ABA and academic instruction. *Focus on Autism and Other Developmental Disabilities, 16,* 129.

Elliott, D., Hamburg, B., & Williams, K. (Eds.). (1998). *Violence in American schools.* New York: Cambridge.

Forness, S. R., Kavale, K. A., Sweeney, D. P., & Crenshaw, T. M. (1999). The future of research and practice in behavioral disorders: Psychopharmacology and its school implications. *Behavioral Disorders, 24,* 305-318.

Gresham, F. M., & Reschly, D. J. (1987). Issues in the conceptualization, classification, and assessment of social skills in the mildly handicapped. In T. R. Kratochwill (Ed.), *Advances in school psychology* (Vol. 6, pp. 203-264). Hillsdale, NJ: Lawrence Erlbaum Associates.

Gunter, P. L., Denny, R. K., Jack, S. L., Shores, R. E., & Nelson, C. M. (1993). Aversive stimuli in academic interactions between students with serious emotional disturbance and their teachers. *Behavioral Disorders, 19,* 265-274.

Gunter, P. L., Hummel, J. H., & Venn, M. L. (1998). Are effective academic instructional practices used to teach students with behavior disorders? *Beyond Behavior, 9,* 5-11.

Gunter, P. L., Jack, S. L., DePaepe, P., Reed, T. M., & Harrison, J. (1994). Effects of challenging behaviors of students with EBD on teacher instructional behavior. *Preventing School Failure, 38,* 35-46.

Harris, F. R., Johnston, M. K., Kelly, C. S., & Wolf, M. M. (1964). Effects of positive social reinforcement on regressed crawling of a nursery school child. *Journal of Educational Psychology, 55,* 35-41.

Hersh, R. H., & Walker, H. M. (1983). Great expectations: Making schools effective for all students. *Policy Studies Review, 2,* 147-188.

Horner, R. H., & Sugai, G. (2000). School-wide behavior support: An emerging initiative. *Journal of Positive Behavior Interventions, 2,* 231-232.

Horner, R. H., Sugai, G., Todd, A. W., & Lewis-Palmer, T. (in press). School-wide positive behavior support: An alternative approach to discipline in schools. In L. Bambara & L. Kern (Eds.), *Individualized supports for students with problem behaviors: Positive behavior plans.* New York: Guilford.

Johns, B. H., & Carr, V. G. (1995). *Techniques for managing verbally and physically aggressive students.* Denver: Love.

Jolivette, K., Wehby, J. H., Canale, J., & Massey, N. G. (2001). Effects of choice making opportunities on the behavior of students with emotional and behavioral disorders. *Behavioral Disorders, 26,* 131-146.

Jolivette, K., Wehby, J. H., & Hirsch, L. (1999). Academic strategy identification for students exhibiting inappropriate classroom behaviors. *Behavioral Disorders, 24,* 210-221.

Kauffman, J. M. (1994). Taming aggression in the young: A call to action. *Education Week, 13,* 43.

Kauffman, J. M. (2001). *Characteristics of emotional and behavioral disorders of children and youth* (7th ed.). Upper Saddle River, NJ: Merrill/Prentice Hall.

Kauffman, J. M., Bantz, J., & McCullough, J. (2002). Separate and better: A special public school class for students with emotional and behavoiral disorders. *Exceptionality, 10,* 149-170.

Kauffman, J. M., Lloyd, J. W., Astuto, T. A., & Hallahan, D. P. (1995). *Issues in the educational placement of students with emotional or behavioral disorders.* Hillsdale, NJ: Lawrence Erlbaum Associates.

Kendziora, K. (2004). Early intervention for emotional and behavioral disorders. In R. B. Rutherford, M. M. Quinn, & S. R. Mathur (Eds.), *Handbook of research in emotional and behavioral disorders* (pp. 327-351). New York: Guilford.

Kern, L., Choutka, C. M., & Sokol, N. G. (2002). Assessment-based antecedent interventions used in natural settings to reduce challenging behavior: An analysis of the literature. *Education and Treatment of Children, 25,* 113-130.

Kohen, A. (2001). Five reasons to stop saying "good job!" *Young Children, 56*(5), 24-30.

Lane, K. L. (2004). Academic instruction and tutoring interventions for students with emotional and behavioral disorders: 1990 to the present. In R. B. Rutherford, M. M. Quinn, & S. R. Mathur (Eds.), *Handbook of research in emotional and behavioral disorders* (pp. 462-486). New York: Guilford.

Lane, K. L., & Menzies, H. M. (2003). A school-wide intervention with primary and secondary levels of support for elementary students: Outcomes and considerations. *Education and Treatment of Children, 26,* 431-451.

Leone, P. E., Mayer, M. J., Malmgren, K., & Meisel, S. M. (2000). School violence and disruption: Rhetoric, reality, and reasonable balance. *Focus on Exceptional Children, 33*(1), 1-20.

Lewis, T. J., Hudson, S., Richter, M., & Johnson, N. (2004). Scientifically supported practices in emotional and behavioral disorders: A proposed approach and brief review of current practices. *Behavioral Disorders, 29,* 247-259.

Lichter, S. R., Lichter, L. S., & Amundson, D. (1999). *Merchandizing mayhem: Violence in popular culture.* Washington, DC: Center for Media and Public Affairs.

Lohrmann-O'Rourke, S., Knoster, T., Sabatine, K., Smith, D., Harvath, B., & Llewellyn, G. (2000). School-wide application of PBS in the Bangor area school district. *Journal of Positive Behavior Interventions, 2,* 238-240.

Maag, J. W. (2001). Rewarded by punishment: Reflections on the disuse of positive reinforcement in schools. *Exceptional Children, 67,* 173-186.

Madsen, C. H., Jr., Becker, W. C., & Thomas, D. R. (1968). Rules, praise, and ignoring: Elements of elementary classroom control. *Journal of Applied Behavior Analysis, 1,* 139-150.

Mercer, C. D., & Mercer, A. R. (2001). *Teaching students with learning problems* (6th ed.). Upper Saddle River, NJ: Merrill/Prentice Hall.

Nakasato, J. (2000). Data-based decision making in Hawaii's behavior support effort. *Journal of Positive Behavior Interventions, 2,* 247-251.

National Center for Education Statistics. (1997). *Schools and staffing survey. Characteristics of stayers, movers, and leavers: Results from the teacher follow-up survey, 1994-95.* Washington, DC: U.S. Department of Education, Office of Educational Research and Improvement. Document #NCES 97-450. Retreived November 10, 2003, from http://nces.ed.gov/pubs97/97450.pdf.

Nelson, J. R., Johnson, A., & Marchand-Martella, N. (1996). Effects of direction instruction, cooperative learning, and independent learning practices on the classroom behavior of students with behavioral disorders: A comparative analysis. *Journal of Emotional and Behavioral Disorders, 4,* 53-62.

O'Leary, K. D., Becker, W. C., Evans, M. B., & Sudargas, R. A. (1969). A token reinforcement program in a public school: A replication and systematic analysis. *Journal of Applied Behavior Analysis, 2,* 3-13.

Reid, R., Gonzalez, J. E., Nordness, P. D., Trout, A., & Epstein, M. H. (2004). A meta-analysis of the academic status of students with emotional/behavioral disturbance. *Journal of Special Education, 38,* 130-143.

Reisberg, L., Brodigan, D., & Williams, G. (1991). Classroom management: Implementing a system for students with BD. *Intervention in School and Clinic, 27,* 31-38.

Robertson, E., Greenberg, M., Kam, C. M., & Kusche, C. (2003, June). *Who is likely to be impacted by universal prevention: Findings from the PATHS curriculum.* Paper presented at the 11th Annual Meeting of the Society for Prevention Research, Washington, DC.

Scheuermann, B., Webber, J., Partin, M., & Knies, W. C. (1994). Level systems and the law: Are they compatible? *Behavioral Disorders, 19,* 205-220.

Schutte, R. C., & Hopkins, B. L. (1970). The effects of teacher attention on following instructions in a kindergarten class. *Journal of Applied Behavior Analysis, 3,* 117-122.

Scott, T. M. (2001). A school-wide example of positive behavioral support. *Journal of Positive Behavioral Interventions, 3,* 88-94.

Scott, T. M., & Barrett, S. B. (2004). Using staff and student time engaged in disciplinary procedures to evaluate the impact of school-wide PBS. *Journal of Positive Behavior Interventions, 6,* 21-28.

Scott, T. M., & Hunter, J. (2001). Initiating school-wide support systems: An administrator's guide to the process. *Beyond Behavior, 11,* 13-15.

Scott, T. M., & Nelson, C. M. (1999). Universal school discipline strategies: Facilitating learning environments. *Effective School Practices, 17,* 54-64.

Scott, T. M., Nelson, C. M., & Liaupsin, C. J. (2001). Effective instruction: The forgotten component in preventing school violence. *Education and Treatment of Children, 24,* 309-322.

Scott, T. M., & Shearer-Lingo, A. (2002). The effects of reading fluency instruction on the academic and behavioral success of middle school students in a self-contained EBD classroom. *Preventing School Failure, 46,* 167-173.

Shores, R. E., Gunter, P. L., & Jack, S. L. (1993). Classroom management strategies: Are they setting events for coercion? *Behavioral Disorders, 18,* 92-102.

Smith, S. W., & Farrell, D. T. (1993). Level system use in special education: Classroom intervention with prima facie appeal. *Behavioral Disorders, 18,* 251-264.

Snyder, H. N., & Sickmund, M. (1999). *Juvenile offenders and victims: 1999 national report.* Washington, DC: Office of Juvenile Justice and Delinquency Prevention.

Strain, P. S., & Joseph, G. E. (2004). A not so good job with "good job": A response to Kohen 2001. *Journal of Positive Behavior Interventions, 6,* 55-59.

Sugai, G., Horner, R. H., Dunlap, G., Hieneman, M., Lewis, T. J., Nelson, C. M., Scott, T., Liaupsin, C. J., Sailor, W., Turnbull, A. P., Turnbull, H. R., III, Wickham, D., Ruef, M., & Wilcox, B. (2000). Applying positive behavioral support and functional assessment in schools. *Journal of Positive Behavioral Interventions, 2,* 131-143.

Sugai, G. M., & Tindal, G. A. (1993). *Effective school consultation: An interactive approach.* Pacific Grove, CA: Brooks/Cole.

Sutherland, K. S., Alder, N., & Gunter, P. L. (2003). The effect of varying rates of opportunities to respond to academic requests on the classroom behavior of students with EBD. *Journal of Emotional and Behavioral Disorders, 11,* 239-248.

Sutherland, K. S., & Wehby, J. H. (2001). Exploring the relation between increased oportunities to respond to academic requests and the academic and behavioral outcomes of students with emotional and behavioral disorders: A review. *Remedial and Special Education, 22,* 113-121.

Umbreit, J., Lane, K. L., & Dejud, C. (2004). Improving classroom behavior by modifying task difficulty: Effects of increasing the difficulty of too-easy tasks. *Journal of Positive Behavior Interventions, 6,* 13-20.

Walker, H. M., & Gresham, F. M. (2003). School-related behavior disorders. In W. M. Reynolds & G. Miller (Eds.), *Handbook of Psychology (Vol. 7): Educational Psychology* (pp. 511–530). New York: Wiley.

Walker, H. M., Ramsey, E., & Gresham, F. M. (2004). *Antisocial behavior in school: Evidence-based practices* (2nd ed.). Pacific Grove, CA: Brooks/Cole.

Walker, H. M., Severson, H. H., & Feil, E. G. (1994). *The Early Screening Project: A proven child-find process.* Longmont, CO: Sopris West.

Wehby, J. H., Falk, K. B., Barton-Arwood, S., Lane, K. L., & Cooley, C. (2003). The impact of comprehensive reading instruction on the academic and social behavior of students with emotional and behavioral disorders. *Journal of Emotional and Behavioral Disorders, 11,* 225–238.

Witt, J. C., VanDerHayden, A. M., & Gilbertson, D. (2004). Instruction and classroom management: Prevention and intervention research. In R. B. Rutherford, M. M. Quinn, & S. R. Mathur (Eds.), *Handbook of research in emotional and behavioral disorders* (pp. 426–445). New York: Guilford.

Zimmerman, E. H., & Zimmerman, J. (1962). The alteration of behavior in a special classroom situation. *Journal of the Experimental Analysis of Behavior,* 5, 59–60.

3 CHAPTER PRINCIPLES OF INTERVENTION PLANNING

OUTLINE

Introduction
Principles of Applied Behavior Analysis
Systematic Procedures for Influencing Behavior
Legal and Ethical Guidelines
Effective Practices

OBJECTIVES

After completing this chapter, you should be able to

- Describe six principles of applied behavior analysis and give examples from school situations.
- Describe professional, legal, and ethical guidelines affecting the use of behavioral interventions.
- Locate and use information systems and Internet services that provide intervention planning resources.
- Describe criteria for identifying effective (research-based) practices and list examples and nonexamples.
- Identify appropriate and inappropriate intervention alternatives for given behaviors and circumstances and provide a rationale for each decision.

KEY TERMS (refer to the Glossary on the Companion Website for definitions)

activity reinforcement
antecedent stimuli
applied behavior analysis
aversive stimulus
behavior or contingency contract
behavior-specific praise
consequent stimuli
contingency
contingent observation
differential reinforcement of alternate behaviors
differential reinforcement of incompatible behaviors
differential reinforcement of low rates of behavior
differential reinforcement of other behaviors
enhancement procedures
escape and avoidance behaviors
exclusionary time-out
fair pair rule
high-probability behavior
intrusiveness
low-probability behavior
modeling
negative reinforcement
overcorrection
physical aversive
planned ignoring
positive practice overcorrection
positive reinforcement
punishment
reductive procedures
reinforcement
reinforcer sampling
reinforcing event menu
replacement behavior
response cost
restitutional overcorrection
restrictiveness
seclusionary time-out
self-evaluation
self-injurious behavior
self-monitoring
self-regulation
self-reinforcement
self-stimulatory behavior
sensory extinction
shaping
social reinforcement
subsequent event
tactile and sensory reinforcement
tangible reinforcement
time-out
token economy
verbal aversives

In the preceding chapters, we described procedures for screening and identifying students who require intervention for their behavior problems and for designing school- and classroom-wide systems of positive behavior support. You are now ready to consider the principles that underlie effective intervention planning for students who exhibit emotional and behavioral challenges. This chapter describes the principles on which effective behavioral interventions are based and suggests legal and ethical guidelines that affect intervention decisions. Finally, we review criteria for identifying research-based practices, present examples from the professional literature, and suggest sources of current information regarding effective practice.

COME INTO MY CLASSROOM: A CASE STUDY

MARCIA VERSUS MS. HILL

Marcia is a sixth-grade student who has been identified as having emotional and behavioral disorders (EBD). Currently, she is being served in a full inclusion classroom. However, she is experiencing increasing difficulties in this setting. Her regular classroom teacher, Ms. Hill, reports that Marcia is failing academically and refuses to comply with teacher directions. She is not popular with other students and has become increasingly aggressive toward them. She has been referred to the assistant principal for discipline on 15 occasions so far this year and has had three out-of-school suspensions, for a total of 9 days of suspension. Her individualized education program (IEP) team realizes that if she receives another 3-day suspension, the school will be out of compliance with regard to the stay-put provisions of the Individuals with Disabilities Education Act (IDEA). The school district's behavior specialist has been called in to assess the behavioral and academic interventions that are being used with Marcia and to revise these if needed.

Dr. Jolivette (the behavior specialist) has met with Ms. Hill, Mr. Frey (her resource teacher), and Marcia and has reviewed Marcia's IEP and conducted several classroom observations. She has found that, although Marcia is receiving the same instruction as the other students, she is not participating actively in lessons. Her test scores indicate that she is performing at the mid-third-grade level in reading and at the upper-fourth-grade level in math. Marcia says that the work is "too hard," that Ms. Hill won't give her assistance when she needs it, and that she hates school. Mr. Frey provides individual assistance in these subject matter areas twice a week in the regular classroom and has provided Ms. Hill with supplementary instructional materials. In addition, he has helped Ms. Hill design an in-seat time-out intervention to address Marcia's noncompliance and peer aggression. When Marcia refuses to comply with a teacher direction or is verbally aggressive toward another student, she is instructed to put her work aside and lay her head down on her desk between her arms. Ms. Hill is not sure how many times she has had to use this intervention, but she is certain that it isn't working: Marcia now refuses to comply with the time-out direction and, when pressed, is openly defiant. This has resulted in Ms. Hill referring Marcia to the office for disciplinary action.

INTRODUCTION

If you were Dr. Jolivette, how would you approach the problems that Ms. Hill and Mr. Frey are experiencing with Marcia? Can you identify some potential reasons that Marcia is acting out in the classroom? Why isn't the time-out intervention working? What strategies would you suggest as alternatives? In this and subsequent chapters, we describe principles and strategies derived from research on behavioral interventions with students who present a variety of behavioral challenges, from extreme acting-out behavior to extreme social withdrawal. This chapter lays the groundwork for intervention planning by presenting an overview of the principles of behavior, behavioral interventions, and guidelines from the perspective of the law, professional ethics, and best practice.

Behavioral interventions are based on a set of principles that explain the relationship of human behavior to immediate environmental events that occur before (**antecedent stimuli**) or after (**consequent stimuli**) the behavior being studied. As you have seen, learning about the relationships between these antecedent and consequent stimuli enables us to identify events that predict where and when certain behaviors will occur. Mastering the principles of **applied behavior analysis** will help you understand the way behavior functions, the environmental factors that influence it, and how this knowledge may be used in designing interventions. We begin with a brief explanation of these principles, followed by a description of systematic procedures used by behavior analysts to influence behavior. Next, we present guidelines that affect the choice of procedure, followed by a discussion of effective practices.

PRINCIPLES OF APPLIED BEHAVIOR ANALYSIS

Applied behavior analysis implies that the practitioner is interested in more than the simple behavior management. It implies an interest in understanding behavior and its functional relationship to environmental events (Baer, Wolf, & Risley, 1968). The behavior analyst therefore studies behavior in the context of the immediate situation. This involves examining stimuli that precede and follow the behavior. Diagrammatically, the model may be represented as A-B-C: (A) antecedent stimuli, which precede behavior (B), and those stimuli that occur predictably as outcomes or consequences (C) of the behavior.

The following principles describe how this model operates. A word of caution before proceeding: *Under no circumstances should specific behavior analysis techniques be used by practitioners who do not thoroughly understand the principles on which they are based.* These techniques are a powerful set of tools, but they are easily misapplied. Therefore, you should master them through reviewing basic texts on applied behavior analysis and behavior management—such as Alberto and Troutman (2003); Cooper, Heron, and Heward (1987); Kazdin (2001); Malott, Malott, and Trojan (2000); or Zirpoli and Melloy (2001)—as well as through competent supervised practice in the implementation and evaluation of behavior intervention procedures.

Principle I

Behavior is controlled by its consequences, that is, the stimuli that immediately follow it. This principle is the heart of behavior analysis, yet it is also the least understood. Most persons assume that behavior is controlled by preceding, or antecedent, stimuli. Consider the teacher who wants a pupil to sit down. He might say, "Sit down." This clearly is an antecedent (A) to the student sitting (B). If the child sits, it is obvious that the antecedent controlled (i.e., predicted) his behavior. But what if the pupil does not sit down after receiving the instruction? The normal tendency is to repeat the command until it is followed, varying voice intensity and adding gestures or possibly even threats. Antecedent stimuli effectively control behavior when they enable the student to discriminate that certain consequent stimuli will follow that behavior. Thus, the pupil is more likely to sit if he knows there is a predictable relationship between sitting (or remaining standing) and consequent events. Repeated association with consequences enables the student to learn that sitting when asked will likely be followed with positive consequences or that being out of seat is likely to result in different consequences. As explained in Chapter 2, if this occurs, the student has acquired a discrimination. If he consistently sits on request, we can assert that this behavior is under antecedent stimulus control. This means that pupils respond appropriately to antecedent stimuli (A) without always having to experience direct consequences (C) for their behavior. Using a nonacademic behavior as an example, stimulus control has occurred when students respond to the request "Take out your science books" by getting out the appropriate text and not by leaving their seats, shouting, or daydreaming. The teacher who has stimulus control over pupil behavior experiences a minimum of crisis situations, and both teacher and pupils work in an orderly and productive atmosphere. Unfortunately, some teachers fail to provide predictable consequences for students who do not follow their instructions, with the result that pupils learn to rely on other discriminative stimuli: how often the command has been repeated, how loudly it is given, or how red is the teacher's face.

The behavior of most children is at least partially under stimulus control by the time they begin school. However, some pupils (both those with disabilities and typical students) do not respond appropriately to antecedent stimuli. Getting antecedents such as teacher directions and instructional materials to function as discriminative stimuli for desired behavior is accomplished by systematically applying positive consequences to appropriate responses made in the presence of those stimuli. For example, if you want pupils' desks to be the stimulus that predicts in-seat behavior, apply positive consequences (attention, praise, points) for students who sit at their desks and apply different consequences (ignoring, verbal reprimands, loss of points or privileges) for students who are not at their desks when they are expected to be.

Developing stimulus control with students with challenging behavior may require many systematic applications of consequences. Begin by reinforcing approximations of the desired behavior (e.g., praising a student for only a few seconds of in-seat behavior). This process is known as **shaping.** As Horner, Sugai, Todd, and Lewis-Palmer (in press) emphasize, teachers' behavioral expectations often are considerably above students' abilities to perform. Therefore, after you have identified the behavior you *expect,* decide what behavior you can *settle for* and build up to your behavioral expectation through shaping. It is important to begin with the behavior the student gives you rather than the behavior you demand. If you expect too much initially, the student will fail, and so will the intervention. The process of reinforcing closer and closer approximations to desired behavior must be carried out slowly and systematically, and the hierarchy of steps must be adjusted according to the behavior of individual students. This again emphasizes the importance of behavior analysis and underscores the need for a thorough understanding of behavior principles and their application.

> What are some behaviors that could be successive approximations of the following desired student behavior: completing assignments on time with at least 80% accuracy?

Consequences can affect behavior in three ways. Some consequences *strengthen* or increase the frequency of the behavior they follow, others *weaken* or decrease behavior, whereas other consequences *maintain* preceding behavior at its current level. However, neutral consequences have no effect on the behavior they follow. Only consequences that strengthen, weaken, or maintain behavior have a functional relationship to that behavior. Actually, because it does not influence the behavior it follows, a stimulus or event that is neutral is not a consequence. It is merely a **sub-**

sequent event. Consequences are always defined by their effects: strengthening consequences increase behavior, weakening consequences decrease it, and maintaining consequences keep behavior at the current level.

Principle II

Behavior is strengthened or maintained by **reinforcement.** Reinforcement functions in two ways. **Positive reinforcement** occurs when the presentation of a consequence maintains or strengthens behavior over time. Remember that procedures as well as consequences are defined by their effects. For example, a classic study (Madsen, Becker, Thomas, Koser, & Plager, 1968) demonstrated that when first-grade teachers told their pupils to sit down, higher rates of out-of-seat behavior occurred. Thus, the direction to sit down (or, more precisely, the teacher attention that accompanied it), given when students were out-of-seat, actually served as positive reinforcement for out-of-seat. In other words, out-of-seat behavior functioned to access teacher attention. As we suggested in the previous chapter, the behavior management procedures used by teachers may, in fact, predict problem situations. This has been documented in a number of studies. For example, the failure to praise desired student behavior when it occurs both reduces the likelihood of its future occurrences and increases the chances that students will engage in undesired behavior, which more predictably results in teacher attention (Sutherland, Wehby, & Copeland, 2000; Van Acker & Talbott, 1999; Walker, Ramsey, & Gresham, 2004).

It is important to keep in mind that what is a reinforcer for one student may not be for another. One way to determine whether a given stimulus may be an effective reinforcer is to observe whether it results in an increase in behavior when the opportunity to obtain it depends on the display of that behavior.

Behavior also may be strengthened or maintained if it functions to avoid or escape an **aversive stimulus.** This is called **negative reinforcement.** Aversive stimuli are those that people choose not to encounter. Just as reinforcers vary from student to student, what is aversive to one person may not be to another. However, most of us avoid stimuli that involve the threat of physical pain or discomfort, the loss of something that is reinforcing (e.g., money), or personal embarrassment. Look at the aversive stimuli table on the Companion Website. Consider how each affects the behavior described before it. These are examples of behaviors that are influenced by negative reinforcement. Because negative reinforcement emphasizes aversive stimuli, it may promote **escape and avoidance behaviors** other than those the teacher intends to strengthen. For example, a child may learn to avoid reprimands by not coming to school. Therefore, the most effective strategies for increasing desired behavior are based on positive reinforcement.

> Referring back to the case study at the beginning of this chapter, what principle do you think accounts for Marcia's noncompliance?

Principle III

Behavior is weakened by withholding the consequences (usually social) that have maintained it. As explained in Chapter 2, this process is called extinction. For example, if your attention has consistently followed a pupil's out-of-seat behavior and you withhold attention each time the student is out-of-seat, over time you can expect this behavior to occur less frequently. However, for extinction to work, you must know which consequences have been supporting the behavior, and these must be under your control (i.e., your ability to provide or withhold). Therefore, extinction is likely to be ineffective in reducing behaviors for which you cannot identify or control the reinforcer (e.g., social interactions between pupils, bullying, or **self-stimulatory behavior** [SSB]) or in reducing a behavior that has been maintained by intermittent positive reinforcement. Out-of-seat behavior, for example, may be maintained by reinforcement from the student's peer group instead of (or in addition to) teacher attention. If so, the teacher's ignoring out-of-seat behavior will have little effect. Once again, such examples emphasize the analysis component of applied behavior analysis, for only by studying antecedents, behaviors, and consequences can you understand their interrelationships and apply appropriate procedures. Extinction has been used with success in reducing mild behavior problems (e.g., disruptive classroom behavior, off-task, and tantrums) and, in combination with differential reinforcement of appropriate behavior, in reducing more serious problems such as aggression (Alberto & Troutman, 2003).

Attempting to weaken behavior through extinction takes time. At first, you will likely see an immediate but temporary increase in the undesired behavior. Hold your ground when this occurs and give the procedure time to work. For example, if you consistently have attended to a student's problem behavior and you initiate an extinction procedure, be prepared for a temporary increase in rate and intensity.

Thus, the student who repeatedly calls out to get your attention may increase his calling out and perhaps add standing up, yelling, or coming to you for several days after you first apply extinction. Alberto and Troutman (2003) suggest some strategies to help you control your attention under such circumstances: become involved with another student, read or write something, recite something to yourself, or leave the room (if possible). If you cannot tolerate a temporary increase in the behavior, extinction is not a good choice. Should using extinction not achieve the desired effect after a fair trial (depending on the student's past history of reinforcement for the behavior), conduct a functional behavioral assessment (FBA). Also consider alternative strategies if you cannot control other sources of reinforcement (e.g., peer reactions) for the target behavior, if the target behavior is likely to be imitated by other pupils, if you are not able to withhold your attention consistently, or if alternative behaviors that you can teach and reinforce have not been identified (Alberto & Troutman, 2003; Zirpoli & Melloy, 2001).

Principle IV

Behavior is also weakened by **punishment.** There are two classes of punishment. The first involves presenting an aversive consequence immediately after a response has occurred (e.g., a verbal reprimand for inappropriate use of hands). The second involves removing a positive consequence following a response (e.g., taking away a minute of recess time or a point for making noises). This type of punishment differs from extinction because a consequent stimulus being removed is arbitrarily chosen rather than the stimulus that has been maintaining the undesired behavior. In addition, something is actually taken away rather than merely being withheld. Just as with reinforcement or extinction, punishment is defined by its effects (i.e., the behavior must decrease in frequency when the consequence is applied). Therefore, to know whether punishment is effective, you must analyze its effects over a period of time. For example, if your verbal reprimands result in an increase in the undesired behavior, punishment has not been implemented. Keep in mind that whether a given stimulus is reinforcing or aversive is not determined by the practitioner's judgment of their value to the student. For example, if standing in the corner for talking out results in an increase in this behavior, the consequence functions as a reinforcer.

> If Marcia's rate of office disciplinary referrals is increasing over time, is this punishment?

Whenever the use of punishment is considered, always identify a desired **replacement behavior** (ideally, one that will serve the same function as the undesired behavior) to teach and reinforce. This is known as the **fair pair rule** (White & Haring, 1980). Overreliance on punishment creates educational environments that are unpleasant and sets the occasion for coercive exchanges between you and the student. Therefore, we urge you to administer positive reinforcers (e.g., attention, praise, points) at least four times more than reductive procedures. When students are accustomed to receiving positive reinforcement and know which behaviors are likely to earn reductive consequences, withholding of reinforcement is more effective in reducing undesired behavior, thereby lowering the necessity for more intrusive and aversive procedures (Kazdin, 2001).

Principle V

To effectively influence behavior, consequences must consistently and immediately follow the behaviors they are meant to control. A planned, systematic relationship between a behavior and a consequence is referred to as a **contingency.** Although some contingencies in the environment are naturally systematic and predictable (failing to adjust cold water to warm before stepping into the shower results in an unpleasant sensation), many are not. A teacher sometimes may allow pupils to leave their seats without permission and at other times reprimand them. To the extent that such practices diminish the predictability of a contingency, so too is the teacher's stimulus control over behavior weakened. For example, if teacher praise is not consistently connected to desired student behavior, it will be less effective. Consistency is one of the most taxing requirements of effective behavior management, but in the long run, effort here will save a great deal of frustration and suffering.

Principle VI

Behavior is also strengthened, weakened, or maintained by **modeling** (Bandura, 1969). Modeling involves the alteration of one's behavior through imitating the performance of that behavior by a model. Models may be live or vicarious, adults or children, and the behavior imitated may be appropriate or inappropriate. Children more readily imitate the behavior of models who are similar to them in some way, who have high status, and who have been reinforced. If a model's behavior is punished, the same behavior is more likely to be suppressed by the imitator (Bandura, 1969). It is important to apply planned consequences consistently to all students who serve as models for others.

Although these principles have been described separately, they seldom operate in isolation. For example, teachers often apply positive reinforcement to desired behavior (e.g., in-seat) and extinction to incompatible undesired behavior (e.g., out-of-seat). In this and the following chapters, we present a number of strategies based on these principles. First, however, remember that the complexity of behavior analysis and of behavioral interventions requires that practitioners be well versed in these principles as well as in data collection and evaluation procedures (presented in Chapters 5 and 6). An alternative is to have access to a consultant with demonstrated competence in the principles and techniques of behavior analysis.

SYSTEMATIC PROCEDURES FOR INFLUENCING BEHAVIOR

The principles just described explain the effects of environmental events on behavior and how these effects may be enhanced or weakened. Using their knowledge of these principles, behavior analysts have designed procedures to strengthen or weaken behavior. These are summarized in Table 3-1. Note that we have arranged them in two groups according to their influence on behavior: those that maintain or increase behavior (**enhancement procedures**) and those that decrease behavior (**reductive procedures**). You also may have heard these sets of procedures referred to as those that *accelerate* or *decelerate* behavior. Within each category, we have listed procedures from those that are least intrusive or restrictive to those that are most intrusive or restrictive. **Intrusiveness** refers to the extent to which interventions impinge or encroach on students' bodies or personal rights (Wolery, Bailey, & Sugai, 1988) as well as the degree to which they interrupt regular educational activities. Thus, more

TABLE 3–1 Enhancement and Reductive Procedures

Enhancement Procedures	Reductive Procedures
Self-regulation	Differential reinforcement
Social reinforcement	Extinction
Modeling	Verbal aversives
Contracting	Response cost
Activity reinforcement	Time-out
Token reinforcement	Overcorrection
Tangible reinforcement	Physical aversives
Edible reinforcement	
Tactile and sensory reinforcement	

intrusive interventions potentially involve the risk of interfering with students' rights (e.g., to freedom of movement, bodily integrity), of exposing them to physical risks (e.g., through restraint or aversive stimuli), or of interrupting their normal educational programs. (Those interventions that pull the teacher away from normal instructional routines are also intrusive because such an interruption affects the educational program for other students.) **Restrictiveness** involves the extent to which an intervention inhibits students' freedom to be treated like all other pupils (Barton, Brulle, & Repp, 1983).

We describe each of the major enhancement and reductive procedures briefly here. More detailed descriptions appear in Chapters 7 through 10 along with examples of how these are applied singly and in combination with other methods. In reviewing these, it is important to keep in mind that this hierarchy is based on our own beliefs regarding which interventions are more or less intrusive or restrictive. Other authorities may place the same interventions in a different hierarchy, although there is growing consensus about the relative intrusiveness/restrictiveness of alternate reductive procedures in particular (Alberto & Troutman, 2003; Kazdin, 2001; Zirpoli & Melloy, 2001). Also note that although we describe these procedures separately, in practice they usually are combined as intervention packages that are applied together to increase their effects on behavior. Consult the online library at the National Center for Positive Behavioral Interventions and Support's Website to see examples of intervention packages.

As you read about specific intervention strategies in the following sections, keep in mind that the best approach to addressing behavior problems is to prevent them. The most effective prevention strategy is to actively engage students in academic instruction that is appropriately matched to their abilities. Students who are interested, involved, and successful in their academic work are far less likely to engage in undesired behavior. Until recently, neither researchers nor practitioners have devoted much attention to the need for effective instruction with students who exhibit problem behavior (Gunter & Denny, 1998; Gunter, Hummel, & Venn, 2000). In fact, Shores, Gunter, and Jack (1993) observed high rates of negative exchanges between students with EBD and their teachers, and other studies have found that teachers give easier tasks to students with problem behavior (Carr, Taylor, & Robinson, 1991) or have significantly fewer instructional interactions with them than with less disruptive students (Gunter, Jack, DePaepe, Reed, & Harrison, 1994; Wehby, 1997). Fortunately, the need for greater attention to the academic deficits of students with behavior problems is being recognized. Consult Darch and Kame'enui (2004) or Witt, VanDerHayden, and Gilbertson (2004) for strategies that specifically address the prevention of classroom behavior problems through effective instruction. Another approach to preventing behavior problems is to teach and reinforce desired nonacademic behaviors in students (Scott & Nelson, 1999). This includes teaching students both school- and classroom-wide rules and routines, providing reinforcement to students who comply with these, as well as teaching appropriate social skills and strategies for resolving conflicts. These strategies are emphasized throughout this text.

What are some suggestions that Dr. Jolivette might make to help Ms. Hill prevent Marcia's noncompliance?

Behavioral Enhancement Procedures

Self-Regulation. **Self-regulation** actually includes three procedures: **self-monitoring, self-evaluation,** and **self-reinforcement.** We consider these the least intrusive and least restrictive of the enhancement procedures because after students have been taught to use these strategies, they may do so across a wide range of situations without interrupting ongoing activities. Most students learn to monitor their own performance ("Am I doing this right?"), evaluate it ("Yes, that's right"), and administer reinforcement or corrective feedback ("So far, so good") without systematic training. However, pupils with behavior problems often appear deficient in these skills. Although self-regulation procedures have shown much promise in terms of changing behavior (Polsgrove & Smith, 2004), because they are usually private events, it is difficult to objectively establish the degree to which students use them. However, changes in overt behaviors that result from self-regulation procedures (e.g., self-recording, verbal reports, the frequency of targeted behaviors) may be monitored to evaluate the extent to which these strategies are used. One factor in its success appears to be training in self-regulation prior to allowing students to control reinforcing events (i.e., to decide when they have earned reinforcement) (Polsgrove & Smith, 2004; Zirpoli & Melloy, 2001). A number of self-regulation strategies are described in the self-mediated interventions sections of Chapters 7 through 10.

Social Reinforcement. Like self-regulation, **social reinforcement** consists of several operations: feedback, attention, and approval. However, social consequences are mediated by another person. Social reinforcement may be delivered easily and nonintrusively. Three types of social consequences have been studied: verbal feedback, social attention, and social approval (i.e., praise). Used by itself, contingent verbal feedback has been shown to have only weak effects, but attention and approval have been found to be powerful reinforcers for both typical learners and students with disabilities, particularly those who are developmentally younger (Nelson, Scott, & Polsgrove, 1999). Teacher attention, even when paired with frowns, warnings, and reprimands, may be a potent reinforcer, especially with students who tend to be ignored except when they misbehave (Van Acker & Talbott, 1999). Furthermore, it has been shown that such students receive proportionately more teacher attention than pupils who are not deviant (Walker, 1995), which may strengthen their undesired behaviors. However, when teacher attention and approval (e.g., praise) is made contingent on desired student behavior, it is very effective in strengthening or maintaining these behaviors.

Unfortunately, as we discussed in the previous chapter, teachers do not appear to use praise frequently, especially in classrooms for students with EBD. Descriptive studies report praise rates of from 1.2 to 4.5 times per hour per student (Sutherland et al., 2000; Van Acker, Grant, & Henry, 1996; Wehby, Symons, & Shores, 1995). The ratio of praise to reprimands is more critical than rates of praise per se. Authorities suggest that this ratio should be 3:1 to 4:1 in favor of praise (Alberto & Troutman, 2003; Walker et al., 2004). But research indicates that teachers use reprimands two to four times as much as praise! As these data suggest, a major problem with attention and approval is getting teachers to use the technique. Consult the Companion Website for a strategy that you can use to monitor your use of praise and reprimands.

Aside from being used more frequently than reprimands, in order for attention and praise to control student behavior successfully, they must have been established as conditioned reinforcers through repeated pairings with previously established reinforcers. Their effectiveness also depends on whether strong competing reinforcers exist for undesired behavior and whether the teacher uses them contingently and delivers them immediately following desired behavior (Nelson et al., 1999; Shores, Gunter, Denny, & Jack, 1993). Praise is more effective when it is genuine and is applied consistently. However, it should not disrupt the behavior being emitted and should not involve the same phrase (e.g., "Good") time after time (Alberto &

Troutman, 2003). In addition, **behavior-specific praise** is more effective than praise that does not indicate the behavior that has resulted in reinforcement. Box 3-1 illustrates behavior-specific praise statments suggested by Sutherland et al. (2000). With older pupils or those with more severe disabilities, social consequences tend to work better in combination with other behavior enhancement procedures.

Modeling. Having another person demonstrate desired behavior has been used successfully to accelerate these behaviors in students of all ages and levels of disability (Kazdin, 2001). In addition, vicarious modeling through films or printed materials has been effective with students who do not have severe cognitive impairments. Modeling is especially useful for teaching complex behaviors, such as social skills. Modeling is most effective if the model is highly regarded by the student (e.g., a school athlete), the model is like the student in some way (e.g., age or sex), the student observes the model receive reinforcement for the desired behavior, the modeled behavior is something the student can do, and the target student is reinforced on other occasions when he displays the desired behavior (Bandura, 1969, 1977). Undesired behaviors also may be reduced if students observe that a model receives aversive consequences as a result of engaging in the target behavior. As with social reinforcement, modeling is likely to be used in conjunction with other procedures and is a component of behavioral rehearsal and role-playing, both of which are used in several social skills training packages. Strain, Shores, and Kerr (1976) observed positive behavior changes in some nontarget children when positive consequences were applied to a target pupil's behavior. Kazdin (2001) suggests that reinforcement becomes a discriminative stimulus for nonreinforced peers because it signals the probability that similar behavior on their part will be reinforced. If students have a history of positive reinforcement for appropriate behavior, a statement such as "I like the way Tommy is waiting his turn" increases the probability that other pupils will imitate this behavior. However, to be effective with more disruptive children, modeling should be accompanied by the contingent use of positive consequences for appropriate behavior.

Behavioral Contracting. A **behavior or contingency contract** is a formal, written agreement

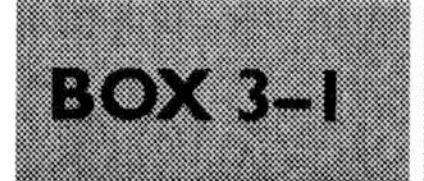

Examples of Student Behavior and Corresponding Behavior-Specific Praise Statement

Behavior	BSPS
Mark has been sitting quietly, listening to the teacher.	"Mark, I like the way you are looking at me."
Lisa gives an example of how she would approach a group of children to join a game.	"Lisa, that is a wonderful example of how to enter a group."
Louis and Jameel come to a consensus on a topic for their poster assignment.	"I really like the way you two are working together."
Christine completes her independent practice.	"You did a super job completing your work today, Christine."
The class is sitting quietly.	"Wow, you all are doing a great job sitting quietly."

negotiated between the student and other persons. A contract usually specifies the behavior(s) to be increased (or decreased), the consequences to be delivered contingent on satisfaction of the contract's terms, and the criterion for determining whether the terms of the contract have been fulfilled. Contracts may be written so that the student's access to a **high-probability behavior** (one that has a high probability of occurrence) is made contingent on the performance of a **low-probability behavior.** Although contracts are more intrusive in terms of the time required to negotiate, write, monitor, and fulfill, they do not restrict the student's freedom to participate in normal educational activities. Contingency contracts have been used effectively to increase desired replacement behaviors as well as to reduce undesired behaviors (Walker et al., 2004; Zirpoli & Melloy, 2001). However, they must be carefully monitored and adjusted according to students' progress. Behavioral contracts may be used as a group contingency. The teacher negotiates individual contracts with students, but access to high-probability behaviors may be arranged on a group basis by setting aside a special area for such activities. Pupils also may select a variety of reinforcing events from a **reinforcing event menu** (RE menu). Contracting is low cost and effective (Zirpoli & Melloy, 2001), but the process takes time. Procedures for developing contingency contracts are explained in Chapters 7 and 9.

Activity Reinforcement. Providing the opportunity to engage in preferred or high-probability behaviors contingent on completion of less preferred or low-probability behaviors (Premack, 1959), or **activity reinforcement,** is an effective reinforcement procedure with both typical students and those with disabilities. It is a relatively intrusive procedure because the reinforcing activity must be identified and access to it made contingent on the occurrence of desired target behaviors. However, high-probability behaviors do not necessarily have to be such major events as a class party or an extra recess; the opportunity to engage in a preferred academic task (e.g., reading, tutoring a peer) can be used as a reinforcer for a less desired academic activity (e.g., working on a composition). Activities are often used as backup reinforcers in token systems or behavioral contracts. As indicated previously, access to activity reinforcement may be scheduled for a group of students at specific times of the day. Students may select their preferred activity from a menu of reinforcers, or they simply may earn "free time" in an area that contains a variety of interesting things to do. Students may even bring items from home (games, CDs, models to build), but make sure that items they bring to school are appropriate! When free time is used as a reinforcer, the teacher typically awards tickets representing a certain amount of free time (e.g., 1 minute, 5 minutes). When free time is scheduled, all students with tickets are allowed to "cash in" one ticket to enter the free time area. Then a timer is set, and when it goes off, students must cash in another ticket to remain in the area. To ensure compliance with this arrangement, be sure to teach students the routine for returning from the free time area and provide occasional "surprise" reinforcement for prompt return (e.g., another ticket that can be spent to return immediately to the free time area). Also make sure that students do not have access to free time activities outside the specified area or other than during specified free time.

Token Reinforcement. A **token economy** is a behavior management system involving nonsocial conditioned reinforcers (e.g., points, chips, paper clips) earned for exhibiting desired academic or social behaviors that may be exchanged for backup reinforcers of predetermined token value. Token systems have been used in regular and special classrooms, with children exhibiting mild to severe disabilities, with preschoolers and adults, and with social and academic behaviors (Kazdin, 2001). Token economies may be used with students individually, but they are more often applied with groups. They also may be adapted to fit any situation, or they may be combined with a variety of other management strategies (Walker, 1995). The essential ingredients of a token system include tokens, backup reinforcers (tangibles or activities) for which tokens may be exchanged, contingencies specifying the conditions under which tokens may be obtained or lost, and the exchange rate of tokens for backup reinforcers.

A variety of backup reinforcers is possible: classroom or school privileges, activities, trinkets, clothes, costume jewelry, toys, or even such large items as bicycles. Some community agencies (e.g., the Chamber of Commerce, Volunteers of America, church groups, labor unions) may be willing to conduct drives or donate items. Cast-off items from your basement or attic may prove valuable in a token system. However, remember that preferred activities are also effective reinforcers, and they are much less expensive and present no storage problems. Therefore, consider using such activities as listening to music, talking with a peer, using a computer, or playing a game as backup reinforcers.

Because tokens are conditioned reinforcers, their value derives from association with previously established consequences. Teach students to value tokens by pairing their presentation with an existing social or tangible reinforcer or by **reinforcer sampling,** that is, giving pupils a number of tokens and letting them purchase backups immediately. Over a period of days, fade out the paired reinforcer or delay token exchange and make receipt of tokens contingent on desired behaviors. As your system evolves, increase the length of intervals between token exchanges. This teaches pupils to delay gratification and encourages saving for larger items, which, of course, are desirable skills in our economic system.

Token systems offer a number of advantages. Because each student can select from a variety of backup reinforcers, pupil satiation and loss of reinforcer power are not likely problems. In addition, tokens can be delivered more easily than individualized tangibles, and simply by announcing that a student has earned a token, your praise and approval develops as a conditioned reinforcer. If tokens are awarded contingent on academic performance, incompatible social behaviors are reduced in most cases, and with such contingencies, little time is lost from teaching as a result of behavior management. In addition, the requirement that tokens be awarded influences teachers to interact frequently with pupils. With activities as backups, the cost of the system is minimal. Specific guidelines for setting up a classroom token system are presented in Chapter 7. Although tokens may be delivered quickly and easily, the time required to develop a token system makes this a more intrusive intervention. A major problem with token systems is teachers' failure to phase out tokens in preparation for moving pupils to less restrictive environments where token systems are not in effect.

Tangible Reinforcement. Nonedible items (e.g., stickers) that are reinforcing for particular students represent **tangible reinforcement.** Often they are used as backup reinforcers in token economies, but they may also be used as immediate reinforcers for desired student behavior. Many types of tangible reinforcers are inexpensive, but because the same item may not be reinforcing to every student, delivering the correct reinforcer to each student immediately contingent on desired behavior makes this an intrusive procedure. One effective use of tangible reinforcers is to award them only on occasion (e.g., placing a sticker on a particularly good student paper) or as a surprise. This application provides some variety in routine so that the effectiveness of usual reinforcers (e.g., praise, points) doesn't diminish.

Edible Reinforcement. Suffering the same drawbacks as tangibles, edible reinforcers also involve several additional disadvantages. First, the student must be in a state of relative deprivation for the edible item. Thus, pretzels, popcorn, or even M&Ms® may be ineffective immediately after breakfast or lunch. Second, students have varying food preferences, which again makes delivering the right reinforcer to every student immediately contingent on desired behavior rather difficult. Third, because these are consumable items, health factors (such as food allergies) and parental preferences must be taken into account. Finally, many public schools have policies restricting the use of edible items in classrooms. Edibles have been widely effective, especially with developmentally younger pupils. Fortunately, behavior analysis technology has advanced to the point where teachers seldom have to rely exclusively on edible reinforcement.

Tactile and Sensory Reinforcement. The application of tactile or sensory consequences (**tactile and sensory reinforcement**) that are reinforcing has been used almost exclusively with students exhibiting severe disabilities, especially in attempts to control SSB (Stainback, Stainback, & Dedrick, 1979). The teacher must first identify sensory consequences that appear to be reinforcing (e.g., vibration, movement, touch) and then arrange for these consequences to follow desired behavior. For example, if the student self-stimulates by rubbing his palm, the teacher can rub the pupil's palm immediately contingent on a desired behavior. Alternately, the teacher can allow the student to rub his own palm when the desired behavior occurs. Among the risks of such a procedure is that of strengthening SSB even further. Before considering tactile or sensory reinforcement, evaluate such possibilities and consider parental wishes and whether the SSB interferes with the acquisition of more adaptive behaviors, or select toys or other devices for the student to use that provide sensory stimulation or feedback like that received through SSB (Wolery et al., 1988).

The Website of the National Center for Students with Intensive Social, Emotional, and Behavioral Needs (Project REACH) contains descriptions of several behavior enhancement strategies, including self-management, choice, contingent access to preferred activities, behavioral momentum, task interspersal, and social skills instruction. Visit this site to learn about implementation steps, considerations, and troubleshooting procedures and to see examples of these strategies.

Behavior Reduction Procedures

Although behavior enhancement procedures should dominate intervention strategies at all levels, many students (and adults!) are adept at manipulating situations so that their inappropriate behavior results in positive reinforcement. Also remember that teacher attention, even when accompanied by reprimands or other negative reactions, may be positively reinforcing to some pupils. Students who are constantly punished may develop a tolerance for aversive consequences, and the accompanying attention may be a powerful reinforcer, especially if the pupils' appropriate behaviors are largely ignored. In a study of family interactions involving children with high rates of antisocial behavior, Strauss and Field (2000) found that the use of harsh physical (e.g., spanking) and psychological (e.g., shouting, threatening) discipline by parents was so prevalent that they referred to it as an "implicit cultural norm" independent of social or ethnic factors.

Used by itself, positive reinforcement of appropriate behavior is generally thought to be effective in encouraging low rates of undesired behavior of pupils with relatively mild behavior problems, but even with these students it should not be assumed that positive reinforcement alone will be effective. For example, Pfiffner and O'Leary (1987) found that increasing the density of positive reinforcement alone was ineffective in maintaining acceptable levels of on-task behavior and academic accuracy in first- through third-grade students with academic or behavioral problems, unless they had previously experienced negative consequences. Research with individuals exhibiting more severe behavior disorders consistently indicates that a combination of positive reinforcement and punishment procedures is superior to either reinforcement or punishment alone (Shores et al., 1993). Unfortunately, as the findings of Strauss and Field's (2000) study suggest, this likely is because these children have become habituated to negative consequences.

This discussion of reductive procedures will help you establish a repertoire of interventions that should be used before behavior gets out of control. For example, what should you do if a pupil breaks a rule, ignores a direct request, or persistently engages in off-task or disruptive behavior? Having command of a range of reductive interventions can help you quickly resolve such problems before they become crisis situations. Later in this chapter, you will find guidelines and policies regarding the use of aversive consequences. Subsequent chapters present intervention procedures for dealing with inappropriate behavior and problem or crisis situations.

Remember that the range of reductive procedures is limited by the need for strategies that are less intrusive and restrictive. Nevertheless, several procedures can be applied with minimal interruption of instructional interactions: differential reinforcement, extinction, verbal reprimands, response cost, and some forms of time-out. In the following discussion, keep in mind that such techniques should be used only in the context of systematic positive reinforcement of desired behaviors occurring at least four times as often as the delivery of aversive stimuli.

Procedures for reducing undesired student behavior have received an enormous amount of attention from professionals who deal with children and adults exhibiting challenging behavior. Consequently, the research literature on the topic of reductive strategies and techniques is extensive. It is matched by the tradition in our schools of attempting to control unwanted pupil behavior through reactive management strategies involving the administration of aversive consequences. Fortunately, this thinking is giving way to more proactive procedures, such as a recognition of the influence of a sound and relevant curriculum, interesting instructional activities, appropriate stimulus control, and positive classroom structure on increasing desired student behaviors (Darch, Miller, & Shippen, 1999; Rutherford & Nelson, 1995). These antecedent events, which were described at greater length in the preceding chapter, are clearly prerequisite to the effective management of maladaptive behavior.

In addition, research on FBA is leading to the identification of antecedents and consequences that are functionally related to undesired pupil behavior (Fox & Gable, 2004; Shores, Wehby, & Jack, 1999) and to strategies for encouraging the use of desired replacement behaviors (Meadows & Stevens, 2004). However, keep in mind that behavioral enhancement procedures alone are not sufficient to decelerate undesired behavior in pupils who exhibit moderate to severe behavioral disorders. The following continuum of reductive procedures is arranged from least to most intrusive and restrictive. It is likely that the more intrusive and restrictive procedures we describe will be aversive to both students and teachers. Note that federal law requires that behavior intervention plans (BIPs) be based on FBAs. It is important that BIPs include direct instruction of replacement behaviors and the systematic use of behavior enhancement strategies. Also remember that changing antecedent events that predict problem behavior may be an effective intervention.

Differential Reinforcement. The strategy of differential reinforcement was described in our discussion of stimulus control. The procedure involves increasing reinforcement for replacement behaviors while attempting to reduce or eliminate reinforcement for undesired target behaviors (Meadows & Stevens, 2004). Accordingly, differential reinforcement is a fundamental component of BIPs. Four strategies are involved in differential reinforcement. **Differential reinforcement of low rates of behavior** (DRL) is applied by providing reinforcement when the targeted behavior occurs no more than a specified amount in a given period of time (e.g., if fewer than three talk-outs are observed in a 1-hour period, the student earns 5 bonus points). **Differential reinforcement of other behaviors** (DRO), which Dietz and Repp (1983) appropriately renamed differential reinforcement of the *omission* of behavior, requires that the target behavior be suppressed either for an entire interval of time (whole interval DRO) or only at the end of a time interval (momentary DRO). For example, a student may receive a reinforcer for zero instances of noise making in a 1-hour period (whole interval DRO) or if he is not engaged in making noises when observed at the end of a 30-second interval (momentary DRO). **Differential reinforcement of incompatible behaviors** (DRI) and **differential reinforcement of alternate behaviors** (DRA) involve reinforcing behaviors that are functionally incompatible with (i.e., cannot occur at the same time) or that are simply alternatives to the target behavior (Meadows & Stevens, 2004). A DRL contingency is appropriate for relatively minor behavior problems that can be tolerated at low rates, whereas DRO, DRI, and DRA may be used with severe behavior disorders. However, because direct consequences (i.e., loss of reinforcement) are not provided for target behaviors under DRI and DRA, they may take longer to work than DRL or DRO, and they may be ineffective if the target behavior has a long history of reinforcement or has been maintained by other sources of reinforcement.

> If a differential reinforcement procedure were implemented with Marcia, what are some potential behaviors that could serve as replacements for noncompliance?

Extinction. As we explained earlier in this chapter, withholding social reinforcers (e.g., attention) will result in a reduction of undesired behavior if the reinforcer being withheld is the one that maintained the target behavior and is consistently and contingently withheld. However, this is a relatively weak procedure for controlling severe maladaptive behavior and is inappropriate for behaviors reinforced by consequences that are not controlled by the teacher (e.g., talking-out, aggression, SSB) or that cannot be tolerated during the time required for extinction to work, such as **self-injurious behavior** (SIB) or physical aggression. Nevertheless, many pupil behaviors are maintained because they result in peer or teacher attention, and therefore extinction can be effective, particularly when combined with differential reinforcement. **Sensory extinction** (Rincover, 1981) is an intrusive procedure in which the sensory consequences of SSB or SIB are masked so that reinforcement is effectively withheld (e.g., covering a tabletop with felt to eliminate the auditory feedback produced by spinning objects). The need to monitor student behavior carefully and to use special equipment limits the usefulness of sensory extinction beyond very specific circumstances.

Verbal Aversives. Of the range of **verbal aversives** used by adults to influence children's behavior (i.e., warnings, sarcasm, ridicule, threats), reprimands are the most effective and ethical. Other types are usually not applied immediately or consistently following undesired behavior; they imply consequences that are not likely to be carried out (e.g., "If you do that one more time, I'll kick you out of class for a week!"), or they involve evaluations that are personally demeaning to students (e.g., "You're the worst student I've ever had"). Appropriate reprimands provide immediate feedback to students that their behavior is unacceptable, and they serve as discriminative stimuli that punishment contingencies are in effect. Verbal reprimands have been used effectively with many mild and moderate behavior problems but by themselves are less successful with severe behavior disorders. However, they should be used with caution because one provides attention when delivering a reprimand, and this can be a potent reinforcer. Therefore, reprimands should be brief and to the point (e.g., "No hitting") rather than accompanied by lectures or explanations. Obviously, the student should know in advance which behaviors are not allowed so that a reprimand is not an occasion for a discussion (e.g., the pupil says, "What did I do?"). O'Leary, Kaufman, Kass, and Drabman (1970) found that soft, private reprimands were more effective than those given loudly and in public. Van Houten, Nau, MacKenzie-Keating, Sameoto, and Colavecchia (1982) demonstrated that reprimands are more effective when accompanied by eye contact and when delivered in close proximity to the target pupil. In addition, they found that reprimanding one student for behavior that another student was also exhibiting reduced the problem behavior of both students. If the student fails to correct his behavior, provide a more intrusive backup consequence (e.g., response cost) instead of another reprimand or a threat. Note: Never ask a pupil whether he "wants" to go to time-out, the principal's office, and so forth. Such verbalizations merely invite the student to challenge your statement (e.g., "No, and you can't make me!"). When reprimands are associated with other aversive backup consequences (e.g., response cost, time-out), they acquire conditioned aversive properties and subsequently are more effective when used alone.

Response Cost. **Response cost** involves the loss of a reinforcer, contingent on an undesired behavior (Kazdin, 2001). It differs from extinction in that the reinforcer is taken away rather than withheld and is not the reinforcer that has maintained the target behavior. The consequence lost may be an activity, such as a privilege or a portion of recess time, or an item, such as a token. Variables that influence the success of response cost include the type of behavior on which it is used, the ratio of fines to reinforcers, and the amount of cost imposed (Polsgrove & Reith, 1983). Response cost has been used successfully with various children in different settings without the undesirable side effects (escape, avoidance, aggression) sometimes observed with other forms of punishment (Kazdin, 2001). It is easily used in conjunction with a token system and compares favorably with positive reinforcement in controlling behavior (Hundert, 1976; Iwata & Bailey, 1974). However, McLaughlin and Malaby (1972) found positive reinforcement to be more effective, presumably because the teacher had to attend to disruptive students when taking away points.

> In addition to the teacher attention that may be associated with response cost, physically taking something away from a resistant student can lead to greater difficulties than the student's behavior in the first place. Therefore, it may be preferable to use an alternative strategy with some students.

Response cost contingencies can be arranged so as to limit this kind of attention. For example, you can post the number of points or minutes of an activity that can be lost for given rule violations and simply give the pupil a nonverbal signal (raising a finger, pointing) indicating what has been lost. (Examples of cost penalties are given in Chapter 7.) It is important to maintain a balance between cost penalties and reinforcers earned so that a pupil does not get "in the hole" with no chance of obtaining any positive reinforcers. Once all opportunity to earn reinforcers has been lost, you hold no contingencies over undesired behavior; that is, there's no reason for the student to behave appropriately (Zirpoli & Melloy, 2001). As with any aversive system, you should negotiate systematic response cost penalties with your pupils before they are used. Strategies involving response cost are described in Chapter 9.

Time-Out. Like differential reinforcement, **time-out** from positive reinforcement involves several possible strategies, ranging from planned ignoring to putting the student in a secluded place for a period of time. Three levels of time-out may be used in the instructional setting. **Planned ignoring** involves the systematic withholding of social attention for the length of the time-out period. Like extinction, it will be effective if teacher attention during time-in is associated with positive reinforcement, and other sources of reinforcement can be controlled during time-out. The effectiveness of planned ignoring may be increased by the addition of a discriminative stimulus to aid staff in identifying which students are eligible for reinforcement and which are not. For example, Foxx and Shapiro (1978) gave disruptive students a "time-out ribbon" to wear while they were exhibiting appropriate behavior. The ribbons were discriminative stimuli for staff to deliver high levels of reinforcement. When a student misbehaved, his ribbon was removed, and reinforcement was withheld for 3 minutes. Salend and Gordon (1987) used a group contingency time-out ribbon procedure to reduce inappropriate verbalizations in students with mild disabilities. **Contingent observation** requires the student to remain in a position to observe the group without participating or receiving reinforcement for a specified period. Having the pupil take time-out without leaving the setting offers the advantage of being able to observe his behavior during the time-out condition.

Exclusionary levels of time-out (i.e., when the pupil is removed from the immediate instructional setting) are intrusive and restrictive. Therefore, these should only be used as backup consequences when less intrusive interventions have not been effective and only with school district approval and written parental consent. **Exclusionary time-out** involves the student being physically excluded from an ongoing activity. In **seclusionary time-out,** the student is removed from the instructional setting, generally to a specified area, such as a time-out room. As discussed later in this chapter, there are a number of legal and ethical concerns when using these levels of time-out.

The levels of time-out and procedures to follow should be carefully planned when using this intervention. In addition, time-out periods should be brief (1 to 5 minutes), and students should be taught how to take time-out appropriately before it is used. Time-out has been effective in reducing severe maladaptive behaviors when combined with procedures to enhance desired behavior (Kazdin, 2001; Nelson & Rutherford, 1988; Zirpoli & Melloy, 2001). However, effectiveness has been shown to vary depending on the level used and its duration, whether a warning signal precedes placement in time-out, how it is applied, the schedule under which it is administered, and procedures for removing pupils from time-out (Gast & Nelson, 1977; Nelson & Rutherford, 1983; Polsgrove & Reith, 1983; Rutherford & Nelson, 1982; Twyman, Johnson, Buie, & Nelson, 1993). Perhaps the most important variable affecting the success of time-out is whether the time-in setting is more reinforcing. When students may escape or avoid unpleasant demands or persons or when they may engage in more reinforcing behavior (e.g., SSB) while in time-out, this clearly is *not* a good intervention to choose. It is also an inappropriate option when the student is likely to harm himself while in time-out. One state (Maine) has passed legislation requiring that time-out rooms be unlocked, well ventilated, and sufficiently lighted and that safe supervision be provided to students in time-out (Lohrmann-O'Rourke & Zirkel, 1998). Go to the Companion Website to view a statement from Kentucky's commissioner of education regarding the use of seclusionary time-out. Kentucky's specific guidelines for using time-out may be found on the Behavior Homepage Website.

> Recall that the work Marcia is asked to do in Ms. Hill's classroom is too difficult for her. How might this contribute to the ineffectiveness of time-out as an intervention?

Overcorrection. There are two types of **overcorrection** procedures. **Positive practice overcorrection** involves having the student repeat an arbitrarily selected behavior (e.g., arm movements) contingent on the occurrence of an undesired target behavior (e.g., stereotypic hand wringing). **Restitutional overcorrection** requires the student to overcorrect the effects of his behavior on the environment (e.g., returning stolen items and giving one of his possessions to the victim). Overcorrection has been used primarily with students who exhibit stereotypic behaviors, including SSB and SIB. In general, both types of overcorrection have been effective, but the procedures are time consuming and often aversive to both students and staff. In addition, while overcorrection has been touted as teaching the student appropriate replacement behaviors (primarily through positive practice), research has not supported such claims (Luiselli, 1981).

Physical Aversives. Substances having aversive tastes and odors, sprays of cold water, electric shock, slaps, pinches, and spankings illustrate the range of physically aversive stimuli that have been used. Such procedures have been shown to be an efficient and effective means of reducing severe maladaptive behaviors (Rutherford, 1983;

Stainback et al., 1979). However, the frequency with which the use of **physical aversives** are abused, the occurrence of undesired side effects, and the objections by parents, educators, and community groups have limited the application of these most intrusive and restrictive procedures. A policy statement regarding the use of physical interventions prepared by the Council for Exceptional Children (1993) is on the Companion Website. Behavior management procedures that are not consistent with this policy are indefensible.

Even less defensibly, many school districts sanction the use of corporal punishment with students despite the absence of empirical studies demonstrating its effectiveness (Zirpoli & Melloy, 2001) and policy statements of professional organizations that specifically prohibit its use. The general trend has been away from using aversives and toward greater use of procedures to decrease undesired behaviors by increasing functional and desired replacement behaviors through behavior enhancement strategies.

Other Procedures. Other reductive procedures, such as in-school suspension and temporary exclusion from school, are also available. These procedures are quite disruptive to students' educational programs, and their use with pupils who have been certified as having disabilities is carefully regulated by federal and state laws. The development of strategies based on positive behavior support fortunately has opened up numerous options to educators concerned with reducing maladaptive student behaviors. It is important that you learn to use such strategies effectively in your daily work with students. The "front line" of school discipline is the immediate context (classroom, hallway, cafeteria), *not* the principal's office.

No matter how mild, use procedures that involve aversive stimuli systematically in conjunction with positive reinforcement and monitor their effects carefully. Master a hierarchy of such consequences and plan specific techniques for each level in the hierarchy so you will have alternate intervention strategies for any given behavior or situation. Then when you apply a selected consequence, use it at maximum intensity (e.g., a firm "No" instead of a plaintive "It hurts my feelings when you do that"). Give students choices when applying consequences (e.g., "You may go back to work or you will lose 5 minutes of recess time"). This indicates to pupils that they have control over the consequences they receive. If the student returns to work, give positive reinforcement (e.g., praise, a point). If undesired behavior persists, apply the stated consequence. Reinforce student decisions to take point or time-out penalties by praise and attention after the penalty has been paid (e.g., "I appreciate the way you took your time-out"). Note, however, that reinforcement for accepting consequences appropriately should not be equal to or greater than the reinforcement the student would receive for exhibiting appropriate behavior in the first place. If pupils can obtain strong reinforcers by engaging in undesired behaviors and then taking a mild penalty, they will learn to use such behaviors to initiate the chain of events leading to reinforcement. Reserve more restrictive procedures (e.g., overcorrection) for situations in which it is documented that the previously mentioned procedures have been ineffective and pay careful attention to due process and to other procedural considerations discussed later in this chapter. Avoid using strategies that reduce students' academic engaged time or that remove them from the instructional setting. The large number of existing intervention alternatives has placed greater demands on practitioners to make appropriate choices. This decision-making process has been made easier through the emergence of professional guidelines and validated effective practices, which are discussed next.

Now that you have reviewed a range of behavior enhancement and reductive procedures, what intervention procedures would you recommend in place of those attempted with Marcia?

LEGAL AND ETHICAL GUIDELINES

As we have pointed out, the tradition of relying on the application of aversive consequences to reduce undesired behaviors in schools continues. However, interventions based on positive behavior support are beginning to provide viable alternatives to this practice. Best practices for children and youth who exhibit chronic and severe acting-out behavior typically include procedures for teaching and reinforcing appropriate replacement behaviors as well as planned reductive strategies (Walker et al., 2004). Verbal reprimands, response cost, time-out, and overcorrection are all considered punishment procedures if they result in the deceleration of behaviors on which they are contingent. (Based on observations of its side effects, extinction also is perceived as an aversive event by some students.) The excessive and inappropriate use of aversive procedures constitutes one of the most difficult practices to change in professional educators, especially those who work with behaviorally challenging students. Concerns regarding the potential and real abuse of aversives have led some professional organizations to adopt policies severely limiting the use of procedures that involve aversive stimuli (e.g., American Association on Mental Retardation, Association for Retarded Citizens, Association for Persons with Severe Handicaps, Council for Exceptional Children, National Association of School Psychologists).

Other professional groups (e.g., the Council for Children with Behavioral Disorders [CCBD], 1990) have prepared detailed position statements addressing the use of punishment procedures. Like the Council for Exceptional Children (CEC), the National Education Association (NEA), and the National Association of School Psychologists (NASP) have adopted positions against the use of corporal punishment with all students. The CEC has drafted specific professional policies for the use of school exemption, exclusion, suspension, or expulsion as well as physical intervention for students with disabilities. Consult CEC's Website to review these, especially in light of the recent reauthorization of IDEA.

The position statements cited previously were adopted for the purpose of guiding professional practice. However, they clearly do not prohibit all use of aversive procedures, nor are practitioners, especially those not belonging to the respective professional organizations, legally bound to follow these policies. Educators are legally required to follow federal and state laws that regulate the use of disciplinary procedures. As Yell and Peterson (1995) pointed out, a dual standard exists for disciplining nondisabled students and those with disabilities. The latter group includes those protected under IDEA and Section 504 of the Rehabilitation Act of 1973. In addition, the U.S. Supreme Court's *Honig v. Doe* (1988) decision established that normal disciplinary procedures customarily used for dealing with schoolchildren (e.g., restriction of privileges, detention, removal of students to study carrels) may be used with students exhibiting disabilities.

However, as we pointed out in Chapter 1, IDEA severely limits disciplinary procedures that constitute a unilateral decision to change the placement of students with disabilities, except in cases where the student brings a weapon to school or commits a drug offense or has inflicted serious harm to another person during school, on school premises, or at a school function. In such cases, the student may be placed in an interim alternative educational setting (IAES) for up to 45 school days. However, students placed in an IAES must have access to the general education curriculum and continuation of IEP-specific activities, and an FBA and BIP should be implemented to address behavior. The law also requires that, as of 1998–1999, states provide annual reports to the secretary of education on the number of students with disabilities who are placed in these alternative settings, the acts that precipitated their removal, and the number of these students who are subject to long-term suspension or expulsion (U.S. Department of Education, 2000).

Studies of the use of long-term suspension or expulsion indicate that students with disabilities are disproportionately exposed to these disciplinary measures (Skiba, Peterson, & Williams, 1997). Mellard and Seybert (1996) reported that students with disabilities were twice as likely to be suspended than students without disabilities and that students identified as having an emotional or behavioral disability were 11 times more likely to be suspended. It is hoped that these federal reporting requirements will establish whether students with disabilities are disproportionately represented in terms of their commission of weapons or drug violations, their placement in IAES, or both. Whatever the outcome, it is certain that school disciplinary practices, especially for students with or suspected of having disabilities under IDEA, Section 504, or the Americans with Disabilities Act will be carefully scrutinized in the foreseeable future.

Yell and Peterson (1995) have grouped school disciplinary policies into three categories. *Permitted procedures* include those that are part of a school district's disciplinary plan and are used with all students (e.g., verbal reprimands, warnings, contingent observation time-out, response cost, temporary delay or withdrawal of goods, services, or activities). Physical restraint or immediate suspension are permissible in emergency situations; however, recall that IEP teams are held strictly accountable to state and federal regulations on the use of suspension for students with disabilities. No legal restrictions exist regarding the involvement of the police if a law has been violated (Maloney, 1994). *Controlled procedures* include interventions the courts have held to be permissible if they are used appropriately, are not abused, and are not used in a discriminatory manner. These include exclusionary time-out, seclusion/isolation time-out, in-school suspension, and out-of-school suspension. Suspensions up to 10 days are permitted. *Prohibited procedures* are those that involve unilateral decisions (i.e., decisions not made by the student's IEP Team) affecting educational placement and include expulsions and indefinite suspensions. This applies even if the student's behavior is dangerous to himself or to others. The only exception allowed is when it can be proven that the behavior resulting in suspension or expulsion is not a manifestation of the student's disability, and courts have tended not to agree with IEP committees who have ruled that such is the case, especially with regard to students with EBD (Yell & Peterson, 1995).

> Twenty years of case law has defined suspensions or expulsions of more than 10 days in a school year as a change of educational placement subject to the stay-put provision of IDEA (U.S. Department of Education, 2000).

Educators are also obligated to follow local school district policies regulating the use of aversives, but many districts do not have such policies, so your best source of guidance is case law. Lohrmann-O'Rourke and Zirkel (1998) reviewed judicial rulings since 1990 concerning the use of aversive techniques. They found that few court cases have involved the use of electric shock or noxious substances, but case law does support these procedures under narrowly defined circumstances and with careful attention to statutory due process procedures. However, courts have provided wide constitutional boundaries on corporal punishment but have stressed that appropriate administrative process be followed when parents file grievances against schools and educators. Conversely, parents must present sufficient evidence of disparate treatment based on disabilities when corporal punishment is used with their children. The courts have also offered qualified support for the use of restraints and time-out.

The absence of clear legal guidelines for many reductive procedures and the observation that corporal punishment is used in many schools despite rulings against it may cause you to wonder whether to be concerned with these issues. A precaution offered by Barton et al. (1983) should clear up this ambiguity: "Any person who provides aversive behavioral therapies for persons [with disabilities] without knowledge of the current legislative and litigative mandates governing such provision and concern for the rights of the individual invites both professional and personal disaster" (p. 5). In fact, the Supreme Court has ruled that if punishment is found to be excessive, the teacher or school officials who are responsible may be held liable for damages to the student (Singer & Irvin, 1987). Thus, you may avoid using punishment procedures altogether or use them carefully and with proper attention to student and parental rights. Reductive procedures may be necessary with highly disruptive and aggressive pupils, but they should be used in combination with procedures for teaching desired replacement behaviors. Further, as Wood and Braaten (1983) stated, corporal punishment "has no place in special education programs" (p. 71).

The possibility of legal sanctions is a compelling reason for school districts to adopt policies regulating the use of reductive procedures. Singer and Irvin (1987) suggested that students' and teachers' rights concerning intrusive or restrictive procedures should be safeguarded through establishing school district procedures. These safeguards are still valid today and are listed in Box 3–2.

Wood and Braaten (1983) suggested that school district policies regarding the use of punishment procedures include definitions and descriptions of procedures that are permitted and those that are not allowed; references to relevant laws, regulations, court decisions, and professional standards; and procedural guidelines that contain the following elements:

- Information concerning the use and abuse of punishment procedures
- Staff training requirements for the proper use of approved procedures
- Approved punishment procedures
- Procedures for maintaining records of the use of punishment procedures
- Complaint and appeal procedures
- Punishment issues and cautions
- Procedures for periodic review of procedures used with individual students

Resources that can be used in drafting such policies include guidelines in the professional literature

BOX 3–2 Recommended School District Human Rights Safeguards

- Obtaining informed consent, including a detailed description of the problem behavior, previously attempted interventions, proposed intervention risks and expected outcomes, data collection procedures, and alternative interventions, and a statement of consent from the parents, including the right to withdraw consent at any time.
- Review by a school district human rights committee. (Such review procedures are not found in most school districts, but they should be developed.)
- Due process procedures to regulate school district actions when intrusive behavior management techniques are used. (Again, few school districts have developed such procedures. However, "formal IEP processes must be used if disciplinary methods for any [student] are a regular part of a child's [with disabilities] educational program" [p. 50]. Intrusive interventions require a level of review beyond regular IEP procedures [e.g., human rights committee review].)
- Use the least restrictive alternative. Restrictive interventions must be aimed at educational objectives, and those proposing an intervention must prove that less intrusive methods are not the best approach and that the proposed intervention is the least restrictive alternative (Singer & Irvin, 1987).

BOX 3–3 Questions to Ask Regarding the Acceptability of an Intervention

1. Is it suitable for general education classrooms?
2. Does it present unnecessary risks to pupils?
3. Does it require too much teacher time?
4. Does it have negative side effects on other pupils?
5. Does the teacher have the skill to implement it (Witt & Martens, 1983)?

for specific interventions (consult the references cited in the earlier sections of this chapter). As noted earlier, parent and professional organizations, such as the Association for Retarded Citizens, the NEA, and the CCBD, have developed policies and guidelines regarding intervention procedures. The CCBD guidelines are particularly useful for practitioners.

This discussion has considered the impact on and acceptability by persons directly affected by behavioral interventions. The IEP team format provides a means of socially validating the goals, the appropriateness, and the acceptability of intervention procedures, that is, the extent to which caregivers and significant others agree with the objectives and methods of intervention programs (Wolf, 1978). In planning interventions for typical students, take care to ensure that intervention objectives and procedures are seen as appropriate and necessary by those persons who are involved and concerned with pupils' well-being and educational progress. School policies regulating the use of behavior reduction procedures should apply to all students, not just to those with disabilities.

The acceptability of interventions to practitioners is especially relevant because some procedures will be recommended to general educators working with pupils having disabilities in mainstream settings. Research on this issue has revealed that, in general, more restrictive interventions (e.g., time-out, psychoactive medications) are viewed as less acceptable than such interventions as positive reinforcement of desired behavior, although more restrictive procedures are seen as more acceptable with students exhibiting highly deviant behavior (Kazdin, 1981; Witt, Elliott, & Martens, 1984). Student and teacher ethnicity also have been suggested as factors affecting treatment acceptability (Pearson & Argulewicz, 1987). Witt and Martens (1983) recommended that professionals ask five questions regarding the acceptability of an intervention (even one whose effectiveness has been documented in the literature) before implementing it (see Box 3–3).

EFFECTIVE PRACTICES

In Chapter 1, we introduced the term "research-validated practices" to designate educational practices that have been documented as effective through empirical research. We also mentioned that the federal No Child Left Behind Act stresses that research-validated practices be used to improve academic outcomes for all students. Actually, efforts to establish standards for evidence-based practice and to identify strategies and programs that meet these standards have been in development for some time. A number of professional groups (e.g., American Federation of Teachers; Center for the Study and Prevention of Violence; CEC; Division 12 Task Force of the American Psychological Association; Office of the Surgeon General; Safe, Disciplined, and Drug-Free Expert Panel; Task Force on Evidence-Based Interventions in School Psychology; U.S.

Department of Education's Institute of Education Sciences) have been engaged in sorting the knowledge base of practices into categories variously labeled "best practice," "promising practice," "blueprint programs," "promising programs," "empirically supported," and "well established and probably efficacious." While the criteria used to identify and classify practices vary among these initiatives, they contain several common elements: (a) the use of a sound experimental or evaluation design and appropriate analytical procedures, (b) empirical validation of effects, (c) clear implementation procedures, (d) replication of outcomes across implementation sites, and (e) evidence of sustainability.

Over the years, a number of interventions used in American schools, including those employed with students with EBD, have been shown to meet these criteria, among them contingent praise, pre-correction, precision requests, self-monitoring, direct instruction, curriculum-based measurement, class-wide peer tutoring, group contingencies, response cost, token economies, time-out, overcorrection, and some psychopharmacological interventions. Landrum, Tankersley, and Kauffman (2003) have summarized a set of "promising interventions" that address the basic characteristics of students with EBD, and they provide examples of potential intervention targets and effective practices. Their findings are presented in Table 3-2.

Researchers have documented a number of intervention programs and practices that have demonstrated positive outcomes for students who exhibit behavioral challenges, including modifying academic instruction and curricular materials (Kern, Bambara, & Fogt, 2002; Miller, Gunter, Venn, Hummel, & Wiley, 2003; Penno, Frank, & Wacker, 2000), social skill instruction (Hune & Nelson,

TABLE 3-2 Promising Interventions for Students with Emotional and Behavioral Disorders (EBD)

Characteristics of Students with EBD	Potential Targets of Intervention	Examples of Effective Practices
Inappropriate behavior	Excesses • Aggression • Disruptive classroom behavior	• Reinforcement (positive, differential, negative) • Precision requests • Behavioral momentum
	Deficits • Social withdrawal • Noncompliance	• Time-out • Response cost • Group-oriented contingencies (e.g., the Good Behavior Game) • Continuous monitoring of student performance (e.g., single-subject research evaluation methods)
Academic learning problems	• Achievement • Attention to task • Academic responding • Reciprocal Peer Tutoring	• Direct instruction • Self-monitoring • Class-wide Peer Tutoring • Continuous monitoring of student performance (e.g., curriculum-based measurement, single-subject research evaluation methods)
Unsatisfactory interpersonal relationships	• Social skills • Language skills	• Direct instruction of individually targeted behaviors • Modifying antecedents and consequences • Opportunity to practice in natural settings

2002; Kamps, Tankersley, & Ellis, 2000; Lo, Loe, & Cartledge, 2002), anger management (Kellner, Bry, & Colletti, 2002), First Steps to Success (Golly, Sprague, Walker, Beard, & Gorham, 2000; Overton, McKenzie, King, & Osborne, 2002), Second Step (Frey, Hirschstein, & Guzzo, 2000), and school-wide positive behavior support (Carr et al., 2002; Lewis, Hudson, Richter, & Johnson, 2004; Putnam, Handler, Ramirez-Platt, & Luiselli, 2003; Scott, Payne, & Jolivette, 2003; Skiba & Peterson, 2003; Todd, Haugen, Anderson, & Spriggs, 2002).

Because research is constantly adding to the list of practices that have been empirically validated (as well as those that are not), it is important to keep abreast of the research literature. The Institute of Education Sciences has established a "What Works Clearinghouse" to assist in this regard. You can find it on the U.S. Department of Education's Website. In addition, CEC's Division of Learning Disabilities and the Division for Research have teamed up to publish periodic *Current Practice Alerts,* which are user-friendly summaries of research on specific practices. An interesting feature of these bulletins is that they alert readers to practices that are clearly effective ("Go for it") and those whose effectiveness is more doubtful ("Use caution").

Research evidence notwithstanding, it is not possible to simply adopt a practice that has been proven effective in the past and assume that it will work in any given context. On the contrary, it is necessary to carefully assess the student with whom the practice is to be applied, adjust the intervention accordingly, and ensure that the person who delivers the intervention is properly trained in its application. Finally, it is necessary to ascertain that the intervention is applied consistently and with fidelity to the plan. These are not small issues, and failing to take them into account can render a research-validated practice ineffective or even harmful. Therefore, we urge that you develop written intervention plans, carefully monitor both their implementation and effects on students, and evaluate outcomes using the data decision rules or single subject research designs described in Chapter 6.

SUMMARY

- Effective interventions for addressing problem behavior in all students, including those with EBD, involve careful assessment of the student and the context in which the behavior occurs. This context includes the antecedents and consequences to the behavior as well as the behavior itself.
- Decades of research have established recognized principles of behavior that describe how behavior works and environmental variables that affect its occurrence. These principles include the application of procedures that may increase or decrease the frequency of a given behavior.
- A continuum of strategies to increase behavior exists and may be arranged from those that are most natural and straightforward to implement to those that are highly contrived. A similar continuum of strategies to decrease behavior may be arranged according to their aversiveness or intrusiveness. The effective practitioner is able to select interventions from these continua to match the needs of the student, the behavior being addressed, and the setting in which the intervention is applied.
- Effective practitioners also are aware of legal and ethical guidelines and constraints on the use of behavioral interventions, particularly those that involve aversive stimuli and are subject to misapplication or abuse.
- Criteria are being developed for identifying practices that are validated by empirical research. It is important to keep abreast of the literature to be knowledgable regarding these "best practices." It also is important to apply these practices appropriately and to carefully evaluate their effects on individual students.

DISCUSSION/APPLICATION IDEAS

1. Give an example showing how each of the following principles affects behavior in classroom situations: positive reinforcement, negative reinforcement, extinction, punishment, modeling.
2. Why is the concept of a contingency important in determining the effectiveness of behavioral change procedures? Give examples of both planned and unplanned contingencies.
3. What procedures and policies should be addressed in developing guidelines for behavioral interventions in schools? Develop a model set of guidelines.
4. A student engages in disruptive behavior almost every day in math class. This results in his being placed in time-out for the remainder of the math class. Comment on the effectiveness and appropriateness of this intervention.
5. What suggestions would you offer to Dr. Jolivette as guidelines for developing an intervention that Ms. Hill can use with Marcia? What strategies are likely to be less intrusive, less restrictive, and acceptable to Ms. Hill but at the same time effective?

REFERENCES

Alberto, P. A., & Troutman, A. C. (2003). *Applied behavior analysis for teachers* (6th ed.). Upper Saddle River, NJ: Merrill/Prentice Hall.

Baer, D. M., Wolf, M. M., & Risley, T. R. (1968). Some current dimensions of applied behavior analysis. *Journal of Applied Behavior Analysis, 1,* 91–97.

Bandura, A. (1969). *Principles of behavior modification.* New York: Holt, Rinehart and Winston.

Bandura, A. (1977). *Social learning theory.* Upper Saddle River, NJ: Merrill/Prentice Hall.

Barton, L. E., Brulle, A. R., & Repp, A. C. (1983). Aversive techniques and the doctrine of least restrictive alternative. *Exceptional Education Quarterly, 3,* 1–8.

Carr, E. G., Taylor, J. C., & Robinson, S. (1991). The effects of severe behavior problems in children on the teaching behavior of adults. *Journal of Applied Behavior Analysis, 24,* 523–535.

Carr, R. G., Dunlap, G., Horner, R. H., Koegel, R. L., Turnbull, A. P., Sailor, W., et al. (2002). Positive behavior support: Evolution of an applied science. *Journal of Positive Behavior Interventions, 4,* 4–16.

Cooper, J. O., Heron, T. E., & Heward, W. L. (1987). *Applied behavior analysis.* Upper Saddle River, NJ: Merrill/Prentice Hall.

Council for Children with Behavioral Disorders. (1990). Position paper on use of behavior reduction strategies with children with behavioral disorders. *Behavioral Disorders, 15,* 243–260.

Council for Exceptional Children. (1993). CEC policy on physical intervention. Adopted by the CEC Delegate Assembly, San Antonio, TX.

Darch, C. B., & Kame'enui, E. J. (2004). *Instructional classroom management: A proactive approach to behavior management* (2nd ed.). Upper Saddle River, NJ: Merrill/Prentice Hall.

Darch, C., Miller, A., & Shippen, P. (1999). Instructional classroom management: A proactive model for managing student behavior. *Beyond Behavior, 9*(3), 18–27.

Dietz, D. E., & Repp, A. C. (1983). Reducing behavior through reinforcement. *Exceptional Education Quarterly, 3,* 34–46.

Fox, J., & Gable, R. A. (2004). Functional behavioral assessment. In R. B. Rutherford, M. M. Quinn, & S. R. Mathur (Eds.), *Handbook of research in emotional and behavioral disorders* (pp. 143–162). New York: Guilford.

Foxx, R. M., & Shapiro, S. T. (1978). The timeout ribbon: A non-exclusionary timeout procedure. *Journal of Applied Behavior Analysis, 11,* 125–143.

Frey, K. S., Hirschstein, M. K., & Guzzo, B. A. (2000). Second step: Preventing aggression by promoting social competence. *Journal of Emotional and Behavioral Disorders, 8,* 102–112.

Gast, D. L., & Nelson, C. M. (1977). Legal and ethical considerations for the use of timeout in special education settings. *Journal of Special Education, 11,* 457–467.

Golly, A., Sprague, J., Walker, H., Beard, K., & Gorham, G. (2000). The First Steps to Success program: An analysis of outcomes with identical twins across multiple baselines. *Behavioral Disorders, 25,* 170–182.

Gunter, P. L., & Denny, R. K. (1998). Trends, issues, and research needs regarding academic instruction of students with emotional and behavioral disorders. *Behavioral Disorders, 24,* 44–50.

Gunter, P. L., Hummel, J. H., & Venn, M. L. (2000). Are effective academic instructional practices used to teach students with behavior disorders? *Beyond Behavior, 9*(3), 5–11.

Gunter, P. L., Jack, S. L., DePaepe, P., Reed, T. M., & Harrison, J. (1994). Effects of challenging behavior of students with E/BD on teacher instructional behavior. *Preventing School Failure, 38,* 35–46.

Honig v. Doe, 479 U.S. 1084 (1988).

Horner, R. H., Sugai, G., Todd, A. W., & Lewis-Palmer, T. (in press). School-wide positive behavior support: An alternative approach to discipline in schools. In L. Bambara & L. Kern (Eds.), *Positive behavior support.* New York: Guilford.

Hundert, J. (1976). The effectiveness of reinforcement, response cost, and mixed programs on classroom behaviors. *Journal of Applied Behavior Analysis, 9,* 197.

Hune, J. B., & Nelson, C. M. (2002). Effects of teaching a problem-solving strategy on preschool children with problem behavior. *Behavioral Disorders, 27,* 185–207.

Iwata, B. A., & Bailey, J. S. (1974). Reward versus cost token systems: An analysis of the effects on students and teacher. *Journal of Applied Behavior Analysis, 7,* 567–576.

Kamps, D. M., Tankersley, M., & Ellis, C. (2000). Social skills interventions for young at-risk students: A 2-year follow-up study. *Behavioral Disorders, 25,* 310–324.

Kazdin, A. E. (1981). Acceptability of child treatment techniques: The influence of treatment efficacy and adverse side effects. *Behavior Therapy, 12,* 493–506.

Kazdin, A. E. (2001). *Behavior modification in applied settings* (6th ed.). Belmont, CA: Wadsworth.

Kellner, M. H., Bry, B. H., & Colletti, L. (2002). Teaching anger management skills to students with severe emotional or behavioral disorders. *Behavioral Disorders, 27,* 400–407.

Kern, L., Bambara, L., & Fogt, J. (2002). Class-wide curricular modification to improve the behavior of students with emotional or behavioral disorders. *Behavioral Disorders, 27,* 317–326.

Landrum, T. J., Tankersley, M., & Kauffman, J. M. (2003). What is special about special education for students with emotional or behavioral disorders? *Journal of Special Education, 37,* 148–156.

Lewis, T. J., Hudson, S., Richter, M., & Johnson, N. (2004). Scientifically supported practices in emotional and behavioral disorders: A proposed approach and brief review of current practices. *Behavioral Disorders, 29,* 247–259.

Lo, Y., Loe, S. A., & Cartledge, G. (2002). The effects of social skills instruction on the social behaviors of students at risk for emotional or behavioral disorders. *Behavioral Disorders, 27,* 371–385.

Lohrmann-O'Rourke, S., & Zirkel, P. A. (1998). The case law on aversive interventions for students with disabilities. *Exceptional Children, 65,* 101–123.

Luiselli, J. K. (1981). Behavioral treatment of self-stimulation: Review and recommendations. *Education and Treatment of Children, 4,* 375–392.

Madsen, C. H., Jr., Becker, W. C., Thomas, D. R., Koser, L., & Plager, E. (1968). An analysis of the reinforcing function of "sit down" commands. In R. K. Parker (Ed.), *Readings in educational psychology* (pp. 265–278). Boston: Allyn & Bacon.

Maloney, M. (1994). How to avoid the discipline trap. *The Special Educator,* Winter Index, 1–4.

Malott, R. W., Malott, M. E., & Trojan, E. A. (2000). *Elementary principles of behavior* (4th ed.). Upper Saddle River, NJ: Merrill/Prentice Hall.

McLaughlin, T. F., & Malaby, J. (1972). Intrinsic reinforcers in a classroom token economy. *Journal of Applied Behavior Analysis, 5,* 263–270.

Meadows, N. B., & Stevens, K. B. (2004). Teaching alternative behavior to students with emotional/behavioral disorders. In R. B. Rutherford, M. M. Quinn, & S. R. Mathur (Eds.), *Handbook of research in emotional and behavioral disorders* (pp. 385–398). New York: Guilford.

Mellard, D., & Seybert, L. (1996). *Voices about school suspension, expulsion, and safety.* Lawrence, KS: Center for Research on Learning. (ERIC Document Reproduction Service No. ED403639)

Miller, K. A., Gunter, P. L., Venn, M. L., Hummel, J., & Wiley, L. P. (2003). Effects of curricular and materials modifications on academic performance and task engagement of three students with emotional or behavioral disorders. *Behavioral Disorders, 28,* 130–149.

Nelson, C. M., & Rutherford, R. B., Jr. (1983). Timeout revisited: Guidelines for its use in special education. *Exceptional Education Quarterly, 3,* 56–67.

Nelson, C. M., & Rutherford, R. B., Jr. (1988). Behavioral interventions with behaviorally disordered students.

In M. Wang, M. C. Reynolds, & H. J. Walberg (Eds.), *The handbook of special education: Research and practice* (Vol. 2, pp. 125–153). Oxford, England: Pergamon Press.

Nelson, C. M., Scott, T. M., & Polsgrove, L. (1999). *Perspective on emotional/behavioral disorders: Assumptions and their implications for education and treatment.* Reston, VA: Council for Exceptional Children.

O'Leary, K. D., Kaufman, K. F., Kass, R. E., & Drabman, R. S. (1970). The effects of loud and soft reprimands on the behavior of disruptive students. *Exceptional Children, 37,* 145–155.

Overton, S., McKenzie, L., King, K., & Osborne, J. (2002). Replication of the First Step to Success model: A multiple-case study of implementation effectiveness. *Behavioral Disorders, 28,* 40–56.

Pearson, C. A., & Argulewicz, E. N. (1987). Ethnicity as a factor in teachers' acceptance of classroom interventions. *Psychology in the Schools, 24,* 385–389.

Penno, D. A., Frank, A. R., & Wacker, D. P. (2000). Instructional accommodations for adolescent students with severe emotional or behavioral disorders. *Behavioral Disorders, 25,* 325–343.

Pfiffner, L. J., & O'Leary, K. D. (1987). The efficacy of all-positive management as a function of the prior use of negative consequences. *Journal of Applied Behavior Analysis, 20,* 265–271.

Polsgrove, L., & Reith, H. J. (1983). Procedures for reducing children's inappropriate behavior in special education settings. *Exceptional Education Quarterly, 3,* 20–33.

Polsgrove, L., & Smith, S. W. (2004). Informed practice in teaching self-control to children with emotional and behavioral disorders. In R. B. Rutherford, M. M. Quinn, & S. R. Mathur (Eds.), *Handbook of research in emotional and behavioral disorders* (pp. 399–425). New York: Guilford.

Premack, D. (1959). Toward empirical behavior laws: I. Positive reinforcement. *Psychological Review, 66,* 219–233.

Putnam, R. F., Handler, M. W., Ramirez-Platt, C. M., & Luiselli, J. K. (2003). Improving student bus-riding behavior through a whole-school intervention. *Journal of Applied Behavior Analysis, 36,* 583–590.

Rincover, A. (1981). *How to use sensory extinction: A non-aversive treatment for self-stimulation and other behavior problems.* Lawrence, KS: H & H Enterprises.

Rutherford, R. B., Jr. (1983). Theory and research on the use of aversive procedures in the education of moderately behaviorally disordered and emotionally disturbed children and youth. In F. H. Wood & K. C. Lakin (Eds.), *Punishment and aversive stimulation in special education* (pp. 41–64). Reston, VA: Council for Exceptional Children.

Rutherford, R. B., Jr., & Nelson, C. M. (1982). Analysis of the response-contingent timeout literature with behaviorally disordered students in classroom settings. In R. B. Rutherford, Jr. (Ed.), *Severe behavior disorders of children and youth* (Vol. 5, pp. 79–105). Reston, VA: Council for Children with Behavioral Disorders.

Rutherford, R. B., Jr., & Nelson, C. M. (1995). Management of aggressive and violent behavior in the schools. *Focus on Exceptional Children, 27*(6), 1–15.

Salend, S. J., & Gordon, B. D. (1987). A group-oriented timeout ribbon procedure. *Behavioral Disorders, 12,* 131–137.

Scott, T. M., & Nelson, C. M. (1999). Universal school discipline strategies: Facilitating positive learning environments. *Effective School Practices, 17*(4), 54–64.

Scott, T. M., Payne, L. D., & Jolivette, K. (2003). Preventing predictable problem behaviors using positive behavior support. *Beyond Behavior, 13*(1), 3–11.

Shores, R. E., Gunter, P. L., Denny, R. K., & Jack, S. L. (1993). Classroom influences on aggressive and disruptive behavior of students with emotional and behavioral disorders. *Focus on Exceptional Children, 26*(2), 1–10.

Shores, R. E., Gunter, P. L., & Jack, S. L. (1993). Classroom management strategies: Are they setting events for coercion? *Behavioral Disorders, 18,* 92–102.

Shores, R. E., Wehby, J. H., & Jack, S. L. (1999). Analyzing behavior in classrooms. In A. C. Repp & R. H. Horner (Eds.), *Functional analysis of problem behavior: From effective assessment to effective support* (pp. 219–237). Baltimore: Paul H. Brookes.

Singer, G. S., & Irvin, L. K. (1987). Human rights review of intrusive behavioral treatments for students with severe handicaps. *Exceptional Children, 54,* 46–52.

Skiba, R., & Peterson, R. (2003). Teaching the social curriculum: School discipline as instruction. *Preventing School Failure, 47,* 66–73.

Skiba, R., Peterson, R. L., & Williams, T. (1997). Office referrals and suspension: Disciplinary intervention in middle schools. *Education and Treatment of Children, 20*(3), 295–316.

Stainback, W., Stainback, S., & Dedrick, C. (1979). Controlling severe maladaptive behaviors. *Behavioral Disorders, 4,* 99–115.

Strain, P. S., Shores, R. E., & Kerr, M. M. (1976). An experimental analysis of "spillover" effects on the social interaction of behaviorally handicapped preschool children. *Journal of Applied Behavior Analysis, 9,* 31–40.

Strauss, M. A., & Field, C. (2000, August). *Psychological aggression by American parents: National data of prevalence, chronicity, and severity.* Paper presented at the meeting of the American Sociological Association, Washington, DC.

Sutherland, K. S., Wehby, J. H., & Copeland, S. R. (2000). Effect of varying rates of behavior-specific praise on the on-task behavior of students with EBD. *Journal of Emotional and Behavioral Disorders, 8,* 2–8.

Todd, A., Haugen, L., Anderson, K., & Spriggs, M. (2002). Teaching recess: Low-cost efforts producing effective results. *Journal of Positive Behavior Interventions, 4,* 46–52.

Twyman, J. S., Johnson, H., Buie, J. D., & Nelson, C. M. (1993). The use of a warning procedure to signal a more intrusive timeout contingency. *Behavioral Disorders, 19,* 243–253.

U.S. Department of Education. (2000). *21st annual report to Congress on the implementation of the Individuals with Disability Education Act.* Washington, DC: U.S. Department of Education, Office of Special Education and Rehabilitative Services.

Van Acker, R., Grant, S. H., & Henry, D. (1996). Teacher and student behavior as a function of risk for aggression. *Education and Treatment of Children, 19,* 316–334.

Van Acker, R., & Talbott, E. (1999). The school context and risk for aggression: Implications for school-based prevention and intervention efforts. *Preventing School Failure, 44,* 12–20.

Van Houten, R., Nau, P. A., MacKenzie-Keating, S. E., Sameoto, D., & Colavecchia, B. (1982). An analysis of some variables influencing the effectiveness of reprimands. *Journal of Applied Behavior Analysis, 15,* 65–83.

Walker, H. M. (1995). *The acting-out child: Coping with classroom disruption* (2nd ed.). Longmont, CO: Sopris West.

Walker, H. M., Ramsey, E., & Gresham, F. M. (2004). *Antisocial behavior in school: Evidence-based practices* (2nd ed.). Belmont, CA: Wadsworth/Thomson Learning.

Wehby, J. H. (1997, November). *Teacher interactions in SED classrooms: Implications for academic and social behavior.* Paper presented at the 21st Annual Conference on Severe Behavior Disorders of Children and Youth, Tempe, AZ.

Wehby, J. H., Symons, F. J., & Shores, R. E. (1995). A descriptive analysis of aggressive behavior in classrooms for children with emotional and behavioral disorders. *Behavioral Disorders, 24,* 51–56.

White, O. R., & Haring, N. G. (1980). *Exceptional teaching* (2nd ed.). Upper Saddle River, NJ: Merrill/Prentice Hall.

Witt, J. C., Elliott, S. N., & Martens, B. K. (1984). Acceptability of behavioral interventions used in classrooms: The influence of amount of teacher time, severity of behavior problem, and type of intervention. *Behavioral Disorders, 9,* 95–104.

Witt, J. C., VanDerHayden, A. M., & Gilbertson, D. (2004). Instruction and classroom management: Prevention and intervention research. In R. B. Rutherford, M. M. Quinn, & S. R. Mathur (Eds.), *Handbook of research in emotional and behavioral disorders* (pp. 426–445). New York: Guilford.

Witt, W. C., & Martens, B. K. (1983). Assessing the acceptability of behavioral interventions used in classrooms. *Psychology in the Schools, 20,* 510–517.

Wolery, M., Bailey, D. B., & Sugai, G. M. (1988). *Effective teaching: Principles and procedures of applied behavior analysis with exceptional students.* Boston: Allyn & Bacon.

Wolf, M. M. (1978). Social validity: The case for subjective measurement or how applied behavior analysis is finding its heart. *Journal of Applied Behavior Analysis, 11,* 203–214.

Wood, F. H., & Braaten, S. (1983). Developing guidelines for the use of punishing interventions in the schools. *Exceptional Education Quarterly, 3,* 68–75.

Yell, M. L., & Peterson, R. L. (1995). Disciplining students with disabilities and those at risk for school failure: Legal issues. *Preventing School Failure, 39*(2), 39–44.

Zirpoli, T. J., & Melloy, K. J. (2001). *Behavior management: Applications for teachers and parents* (3rd ed.). Upper Saddle River, NJ: Merrill/Prentice Hall.

CHAPTER 4 ASSESSMENT-BASED INTERVENTION PLANNING

OUTLINE

Introduction
The Assessment Process
Identifying Problem Behavior
Assessment-Based Intervention Planning

OBJECTIVES

After completing this chapter, you should be able to

- Describe the process and procedures for conducting behavioral assessments.
- Describe issues that should be considered when identifying behaviors for intervention.
- Explain the steps for conducting a functional behavioral assessment.
- Given descriptions of recurring sequences of behavior in specific contexts, develop hypotheses describing functional relationships.
- Given the function of behavior and other assessment data, identify components of a behavior intervention plan.
- Given descriptions of target behaviors, write terminal intervention objectives and analyze these objectives by breaking them down into three to five task steps.

KEY TERMS (refer to the Glossary on the Companion Website for definitions)

antecedent-behavior-consequence (A-B-C) assessment
behavioral contexts
behavioral interviews
behavioral objectives
checklists
direct assessment of behavior
functional analysis
indirect behavioral assessment
long-term objective
operational definition
problem behavior pathway
rating scales
replacement behavior
response efficiency
response equivalency
response topography
scatter plot
self-report
short-term objective
social skills
social validation
sociometric procedures
successive approximations
target behaviors
task analysis
teacher expectations
teacher rankings

In Chapter 1, we described the assessment decisions involved in determining students' eligibility for special education services. This chapter deals with the process of conducting specific assessments of student behavior and using this information to design interventions directed at pupils' social behaviors. The assessment and intervention decisions discussed here are those you make as an intervention agent, whether you are a classroom teacher, a school counselor or psychologist, or some other support person in the school setting. The following case study illustrates how this process is carried out.

COME INTO MY CLASSROOM: A CASE STUDY

A BEHAVIOR PLAN FOR RODNEY

You may recall that Rodney (one of the students in the case study presented in Chapter 1) is a sixth-grade student identified as having emotional and behavioral disorders (EBD) who participates in general education classes throughout the day. He has presented a number of behavior problems (noncompliance, swearing, leaving the classroom without permission) in his general math class. Although he is not performing at grade level in any of his subjects, he is not a behavior problem in any of his other classes. He is not socially popular with other students, but he is tolerated by his peers. As a result of his behavior in math class, Rodney has been given several in-school suspensions and recently received an out-of-school suspension. The school district is aware of the requirement that the services specified on Rodney's individualized education plan (IEP) not be interrupted because of a change in placement, and the building's Behavior Support Team has been called to perform a functional behavioral assessment (FBA) and develop a behavior intervention plan (BIP). Members of the team (including the special education teacher, school psychologist, assistant principal, and physical education teacher) have met with Mr. Kauffman (Rodney's math teacher), Rodney's mother, and Rodney himself. They also have observed on several occasions in the math class and completed an **antecedent-behavior-consequence (A-B-C) assessment** based on these observations.

From this information, the team and Mr. Kauffman defined Rodney's problem behavior as noncompliance (refusals to work on math assignments) and hypothesized that the function of this behavior (which escalates into progressively more disruptive and aggressive behavior if he is pressed to comply) is avoidance of math work. Rodney is performing well below grade level in math and, in fact, knows fewer than 50% of the multiplication facts through 10. To test the hypothesis of function, for 3 days Ms. Shearer (the special education teacher aide) gave Rodney brief (10 problem) worksheets containing only math facts that Rodney has mastered. Rodney refused to comply only once (when the first worksheet was presented), but when Ms. Shearer pointed out that he knew all the answers to the problems, he worked them quickly and accurately and continued to do so for the next 3 days.

Having demonstrated that Rodney could comply with the instruction to complete his math worksheets, the Behavior Support Team defined compliance (working on math assignments) as his primary replacement behavior. Because of his typical reactions when he became frustrated, the team decided that two additional behaviors should be targeted in the

Student: Rodney

School: Washington

Teacher: Mr. Kauffman

Date: 2/1

Step	Action	Outcomes
1	Identify the function of the behavior. • Describe the behavior in measurable terms. • How does the behavior meet the student's needs?	Noncompliance (refusal to attempt seat work) to avoid math assignments.
2	Select a replacement behavior. • What should the student do instead? • What do successful students do? • Will the behavior help students meet their needs?	1. Complete math seat work. 2. Raise hand to get assistance. 3. Use appropriate language (e.g., "stuff").
3	Design a teaching plan. The expected behavior includes: • Conditions • Behavior	Expected behavior When you are given math seat work, complete them without disruptions. Raise your hand if you need help.
	Teaching examples should: • Describe when to use the behavior • Be realistic	Teaching examples Look at all the problems before you begin working. Raise your hand and ask Ms. Shearer to help you with the ones you don't know how to solve.
	Nonexamples should: • Describe when not to use the behavior • Be realistic	Nonexamples When out of the classroom.
		Models and/or demonstrations Rodney can demonstrate appropriate hand raising and language.
4	Arrange the environment to facilitate success. Consider changes to: • Physical environment • Classroom procedures • Task requirements • Teacher–student interactions	Prevent failure 1. Present one row of problems (10 facts) at a time. 2. Intersperse two known math facts for every one not known.
		Promote success Ms. Shearer drills Rodney with flash cards on unknown facts before Rodney attempts independent seat work.

(Continued)

FIGURE 4–1 Rodney's Behavior Intervention Plan

Step	Action	Outcomes
5	Develop consequences for desired and undesired behavior.	Natural positive consequences Immediate praise for requesting assistance.
		Withholding access to natural positive consequences Do not remove task when Rodney is noncompliant or disruptive.
		Prompts Corrective prompts: 1. Remember to raise your hand when you need help. 2. Use good language.
	• If the replacement behavior is not exhibited despite natural positive consequences and prompts.	Artificial positive consequences One point for each hand raise or use of good language, exchanged for computer time at end of class.
	• If the problem behavior continues despite natural consequences and prompts.	Negative consequences Loss of points/computer time for each instance of noncompliance.
6	• Develop procedures for monitoring/measuring behavior.	Target behavior Count instances of noncompliance (failure to begin work within 5 seconds of being given worksheet). Replacement behavior Record number of multiplication facts attempted and percentage correctly solved.
7	Write behavioral objectives. • Conditions • Learner • Behavior • Criteria	Rodney will complete five out of five multiplication fact worksheets per day with 90% accuracy and zero instances of noncompliance for 3 consecutive days.

Date for implementation: 2/2

Date for review: 3/29

Notes:

FIGURE 4–1 (Continued)

BIP: using appropriate language (e.g., "stuff" instead of "sh—t") and raising his hand when he needed help.

The next step was to design a plan for teaching these replacement behaviors. Rodney has shown that he can raise his hand to get help and that he can use appropriate language. Therefore, it was decided that, whenever math worksheets were handed out, Mr. Kauffman (or Ms. Shearer) would remind Rodney to look at all the problems and identify those that he knew how to solve, work on those first, and ask Ms. Shearer for help with the rest. He also was prompted to use appropriate language. To increase Rodney's success in complying with the plan, Ms. Shearer tutored him for 10 minutes prior to worksheets being handed out. These sessions consisted of flash card drills on facts that Rodney had mastered previously as well as a limited number of unknown facts. In addition, Ms. Shearer created new math worksheets. Initially, she interspersed two math facts that Rodney had mastered for every one he had not. She also divided his worksheets so that he was only given one row of 10 problems at a time (each day, Rodney was expected to work five rows of problems).

As Rodney worked independently on math worksheets, Ms. Shearer remained nearby. If she saw that he was struggling with a fact, she prompted him to raise his hand. If he looked frustrated (e.g., began to fidget or mutter under his breath), she prompted him to use good language. Hand raising and use of good language were praised immediately. Early in the intervention, Ms. Shearer also awarded Rodney a point each time he raised his hand or used appropriate language. He could exchange these points for minutes of computer time at the end of class. Failure to raise his hand or to use good language resulted in a loss of 1 point for each instance. Mr. Kauffman agreed that, unless Rodney's behavior escalated to crisis proportions, he would not remove him from class.

The Behavior Support Team agreed that a reasonable objective for this intervention plan would be that he complete five out of five 10-problem worksheets per day with 90% accuracy and no instances of noncompliance for 3 consecutive days. To monitor Rodney's progress toward this objective, Ms. Shearer agreed to keep track of the number of occasions in each math class period when he failed to begin working on a math task within 5 seconds of being given a worksheet. She also kept a record of the number of multiplication facts attempted and the percentage that Rodney solved correctly every day. The BIP that was developed for Rodney is presented in Figure 4-1 on pages 99-100.

INTRODUCTION

As you can see from the BIP developed for Rodney, intervention planning does not need to involve elaborate changes in classroom procedures. There are three major differences between a BIP and more conventional attempts to solve students' behavior problems. The first is that the intervention is based on the function of the problem behavior. What might have been the effect on Rodney's disruptive behavior if Ms. Shearer had sent him from the classroom when he used inappropriate language or refused to work? The second difference between traditional interventions and BIPs is that the plans are developed by a team that works in support of the student and the teacher. How would you feel if you had to deal with a student like Rodney every day with no consultative assistance? The third difference is that BIPs are formalized in writing and implemented as written so that they can be fully evaluated. *The main reason that interventions fail is because they are not implemented as planned.* Another example of a BIP may be found on the Companion Website.

Intervention planning requires data from various levels of assessment in order to tailor strategies to the characteristics of the students with whom they will be applied, the persons applying them, and the settings in which they are used. The purposes of these assessments are (a) to identify problem behavior(s) and determine whether intervention is warranted, (b) to analyze the problem in terms of the context(s) in which it occurs (i.e., where it occurs, characteristics of the settings in which it is seen, stimuli and events occurring before or after the behavior that seem to predict its occurrence), and (c) to develop hypotheses about the factors that may cause or contribute to the problem as well as about the potential intervention strategies that address the relevant characteristics. Hypotheses are then tested by systematically altering predictor variables and observing the effects on the target behavior. The process illustrated in the case study is explained in detail in the following sections. As you read, consider how each step of the assessment-based intervention planning process was applied with Rodney.

We begin this chapter with an overview of assessment for intervention planning. Then we describe the process of conducting FBAs. Next, we explain how to develop a BIP based on the FBA and knowledge of intervention strategies. We conclude with a discussion of intervention goals and objectives—as well as how to task-analyze terminal objectives for intervention.

THE ASSESSMENT PROCESS

Behavioral assessment involves the evaluation of observable student behaviors across the range of environmental settings in which they occur. As indicated in Chapter 1, traditional mental health assessment focuses on internal processes that are assumed to underlie overt behavior patterns. In contrast, the focus of behavioral assessment is on objective analysis of the overt behavior itself, which minimizes inferences about underlying conditions. Tests that measure personality constructs, attitudes, and feelings typically are not used in behavioral assessment. Because behaviors occur in a variety of settings (e.g., home, school, community) and because the behaviors that take place in one setting may not happen in others, it is important to assess student behaviors across various settings. A single environmental setting actually is comprised of many subsettings. For example, the school setting consists of classrooms, offices, a lunchroom, a gymnasium, hallways, a bus waiting area, a playground, and so forth. Settings are also referred to as **behavioral contexts** because they include an abundance of events that occur before and after a given behavior. Even a single classroom includes a variety of behavioral contexts (e.g., reading group, science class, recess, lunch period, dismissal time). These contexts often differ in terms of other persons, behavioral expectations, the degree of structure, and the interactions likely to occur. It is important to assess a student's behavior in all settings that are relevant to planning and implementing interventions, including those in which problem behavior occurs and does not occur. Polsgrove (1987) articulated the goals of behavioral assessment as identifying specific interpersonal and environmental variables within each setting that influence behavior, analyzing the behavioral expectations of various settings, and comparing expectations and the pupil's behavior across settings. These analyses provide a comprehensive picture of the student's behavior in a range of places and among a variety of persons. They also reveal differences in expectations, structure, and social interaction patterns that characterize these settings. Differences among settings and of the student's behavior in these settings may provide valuable clues for intervention planning. Table 4-1 presents guidelines for assessing behavior across the settings in which the student functions.

Review the case of Rodney. What differences were there between settings in which he did and did not exhibit disruptive behavior?

TABLE 4–1 Guidelines for Behavioral Assessment

Information to Be Obtained	Potential Sources of Information
1. What are the pupil's major environmental settings and reference groups?	1. Pupil, parents, other teachers, peers
2. Who are the significant persons in these settings?	2. Pupil, parents, other teachers, peers, direct observation
3. What behaviors occur in these settings? (List both desired and undesired behaviors.)	3. Parents, other teachers, peers, direct observation
4. (For settings in which problem behavior occurs) Who sees the behavior as a problem?	4. Significant others in the setting
5. What behaviors are expected in the setting?	5. Significant others in the setting
6. How does the pupil's behavior differ from these expectations?	6. Significant others in the setting

Thus, behavioral assessment procedures address the range of behaviors and settings that characterize each student's total environment. Such broad assessments are particularly useful in identifying potential **target behaviors** where they occur, both immediate and remote environmental factors that influence their occurrence and other variables that potentially may contribute to intervention planning. Within and across these environmental settings, increasingly specific and precise assessments are conducted to identify, analyze, and monitor the behaviors targeted for intervention. The assessment process is guided by the decisions intervention agents make based on evaluations of the student's behavior in each relevant behavioral context.

IDENTIFYING PROBLEM BEHAVIOR

In the following paragraphs, we describe procedures for initial problem identification. This includes procedures used to determine whether a given behavior constitutes a problem that warrants an intervention. Next, we describe the procedures used in developing an assessment-based intervention plan. As pointed out in Chapter 1, this process must be followed when a student with a disability violates a code of student conduct that results in a change in educational placement.[1] We recommend it as the best practice for intervention planning at any point in time regardless of the situation or whether the student has a disability.

Standards for Social Behavior

Behavioral assessment often begins with the assumption that there is a problem. That is, the student is doing too much of something that she is not supposed to be doing or too little of something that she is supposed to be doing. However, the decision that too much or too little behavior is occurring requires that we evaluate the behavior in question relative to the expectations for social behavior in specific settings. Therefore, it is prudent to ask whether a problem really exists or whether our perceptions are out of line. As Howell, Fox, and Morehead (1993) point out, a problem exists if there is a discrepancy between student behavior and a standard. In other words, someone must use his or her own judgment and decide that there is a discrepancy and that it is serious enough to justify intervention. In the case of academic behaviors, making judgments about discrepancies between standards and behaviors is relatively straightforward and objective (e.g., the student is getting less than 50% correct on her assignments in language arts). However, standards for social behavior are based on the expectations of other persons, and such expectations are both personal and subjective. For example, Mr. Smith believes that pupils should not talk to each other while working; therefore, he expects students to speak only when called on. But Ms. Peterson believes that pupils should talk to each other while working; therefore, she expects some level of noise in her classroom.

Ruling Out Medical Explanations for Problem Behavior

As in the case of assessment to determine a student's eligibility for special education services, it is important to rule out medical explanations for the presence of specific problem behavior. A student who lacks functional communicative skills may be unable to tell you that she is striking her head because she has an earache. Or a pupil whose listlessness, lethargy, and inattention to tasks interfere with her educational performance may be unaware that she has diabetes. Mild or potentially serious medical problems may underlie student behavior problems, and educators should not assume that managing the environment is the only effective way to influence behavior. Particularly if an undesired behavior pattern has a sudden onset and if behavioral assessment procedures reveal no apparent environmental factors that affect its occurrence, you should ask the parents if they have observed any recent changes in their child's behavior and whether the child has had a recent physical examination. In any case, it may be wise to ask the school nurse or health practitioner to conduct a brief medical screening (with parental permission). If the screening reveals any indicators of potential health problems, ask the parents to obtain a medical examination and indicate the suspected medical cause of the problem. With parental permission (in writing), you may contact the examining physician to explain the behaviors of concern.

If there is an underlying health problem, the next step is appropriate medical intervention. While the pupil is receiving treatment, continue to observe the behaviors of concern and note any changes. Be aware that in cases of long-standing medical problems, successful medical treatment may not solve the problem immediately. For example, if the student has missed out on instruction in important skills or if the undesired behavior originally caused by her health problem has been reinforced (e.g., she has been able to avoid undesired tasks), solving her physical problem may not alleviate the corresponding behavior pattern.

Social Validation of Problem Behaviors

Social validation (Wolf, 1978) is a strategy for evaluating whether significant persons agree that a problem is serious enough to require intervention. Several procedures can be used to validate the existence and severity of a behavior problem. The most obvious is simply to ask other persons who have daily contact with the student whether the identified target behaviors are major problems. In the case of a serious behavior problem (e.g., aggression, stereotypic behavior), discrepancies between standards and behavior are more obvious. Students with severe disabilities or those who display bizarre or extremely deviant behaviors clearly depart from expectations for "normal" behavior. However, judgments about the seriousness of less extreme behavior problems are more difficult because of the absence of instruments and procedures for accurately setting behavioral standards and assessing student performance relative to these standards. One way to establish that a problem exists is to directly observe the identified student in settings where problem behaviors are occurring. Direct observation data will tell you little about the need for intervention, however, unless the problem behavior is dangerous or intolerable at any level or unless you have some indication of what level of the behavior persons in the setting will tolerate. For example, even a single instance of physical aggression during a classroom work period is likely to be intolerable, but what about off-task, out-of-seat, or noncompliant behavior? Almost all students display some undesirable social behaviors as well as some deficits in appropriate social skills. Pupils who are identified as having EBD usually are distinguished from those who are not by *excesses or deficits* in the frequency or rate at which they exhibit such behaviors rather than by differences in the *kinds* of behaviors they exhibit. It is possible that the teacher simply notices the designated student's disruptive behavior more than she notices the same behavior in others. One way to assess the discrepancy between the identified student's behavior and the standard for that behavior in the classroom is to simultaneously observe the target pupil and a peer whom the teacher designates as typical with respect to how much of the problem behavior she displays. Comparing the frequencies of the behavior exhibited by the two students will help you assess the relative severity of the target behavior. Figure 4–2 displays a sheet of interval data

Behavior Observation Record

Recorder B. Hogg
Date 2/16
Child Frances
Circumstance Study Period
Length of time observed 15 min.

+ = Behavior observed at least once during interval.
− = Behavior not observed during interval.

Target Child

Behavior	1	2	3	4	5	6	7	8	9	10	11	12	13	14	15	TOTAL
Noise	−	+	+	−	−	−	+	+	−	+	−	+	−	+	+	8
Out of place	−	−	+	+	−	−	+	+	−	+	−	−	−	−	−	5
Off-task	−	+	+	+	+	−	+	+	+	−	+	+	+	+	+	12
Physical contact	−	−	+	−	−	−	−	−	−	+	−	−	−	−	−	2
Other: Calling out for teacher	−	−	−	+	−	−	+	−	−	−	+	−	−	−	+	4

Peer

Behavior	1	2	3	4	5	6	7	8	9	10	11	12	13	14	15	TOTAL
Noise	+	−	+	−	−	+	+	−	+	−	+	+	−	+	+	9
Out of place	−	−	−	−	−	−	−	−	−	−	−	−	−	−	−	0
Off-task	−	−	+	−	−	+	−	−	+	−	−	−	−	+	+	5
Physical contact	−	−	−	−	−	−	−	−	−	−	−	−	−	−	−	0
Other	−	−	−	−	−	−	−	−	−	−	−	−	−	−	−	0

Note: Each square represents one minute of observation.

FIGURE 4–2 Target Student and Peer Comparison Observational Data

Source: *Deno, S., & Mirkin, P. (1978).* Data-based program modification. *Reston, VA: Council for Exceptional Children. Used with permission.*

collected on a target student and a selected peer (see Chapter 5 to learn how to use this direct observation tool). Note that on some behaviors, the target student was much like her behaviorally acceptable peer.

Assessing differences between the student's behavior and that of behaviorally typical peers also will help you decide whether intervention is warranted. For example, one teacher may regard students who are noisy and boisterous or who violate her standards for order and routine as having serious problems that require intervention, but other staff members may view the same behavior in other settings as typical. We are not suggesting that students who act out in only one classroom should not be considered candidates for intervention; we mean only that persons' standards and tolerance for pupil behavior are subjective and vary from setting to setting or from one occasion to another. In addition, because students with behavioral problems seldom display only one undesired behavior or lack only one appropriate social skill, it is necessary to decide which behaviors to act on first. Social validation and direct observation procedures will help you evaluate the discrepancy between pupil behavior and standards. With this information, you can determine whether intervention is justified and which behaviors should receive priority for intervention. Checklists and rating scales also may be administered across persons and settings to socially validate the perception of a problem.

Another facet of social validation is consideration of whether the student's behavior is deviant with respect to the standards of her cultural reference group. The overrepresentation of culturally different learners in classes for children with disabilities, including programs for students with EBD, may be partially explained by the teachers' lack of sensitivity to culturally based behavior (McIntyre, 1996). Therefore, it should be determined that the problem behavior is not typical for the student's cultural group. Assessment procedures that may provide this information include interviews with the target student or her caregivers, in combination with rating scales, checklists, and direct observation of behavior across settings.

A variety of tools and procedures are available for conducting behavioral assessments. These may be used at any stage in the assessment process, from determining whether a problem exists to conducting an FBA and monitoring student behaviors that are targeted for intervention. For example, a review of school archival records (described in Chapter 1) can help identify patterns of behavior over time as well as events in students' lives that may influence their behavior. Interviews and direct observation procedures can be used to determine whether a problem behavior warrants intervention and to gather information across persons and settings as part of an FBA or to evaluate the effects of a BIP. Here we describe some procedures and tools that are useful in screening, the first step in problem identification. In the following section, we describe procedures for more precise assessments of targeted behaviors during the FBA process. In Chapter 5, we expand the topic of assessment to include strategies for ongoing monitoring of student progress. Chapter 6 presents strategies for making intervention decisions from this information.

Screening

The screening procedures we described in Chapter 1 for identifying students with behavioral problems also should clarify whether a significant discrepancy exists between behavior and expectations regardless of whether the student is being considered for special education services. The specific procedures used should be relatively brief and efficient so that persons in each relevant setting will be inclined to cooperate. Alternately, screening assessments may be conducted by persons who are familiar with the student's performance across most or all of the relevant behavioral contexts. Systematic school-wide screening procedures serve the purpose of establishing whether a problem exists, but, as we pointed out earlier, these are not widely used. The traditional method of screening students for behavioral problems is through teacher referral. You will recall that referral-driven identification procedures are unreliable and tend to identify only students who exhibit externalizing, or acting-out, behavior. Screening for intervention planning addresses the following questions: *Is intervention needed?* If so, *in which settings should it be applied?* The assessment procedures used to answer these questions are likely to involve more time and more sophisticated procedures across more settings than those required for general screening to identify pupils at risk. However, this level of screening focuses on a limited number of students, and the importance of the decisions to be made justifies the greater expenditure of time and resources needed for these assessments. In addition, recall from Chapter 2 that this type of screening may be accomplished through systematic analysis of office discipline referrals.

As we emphasize repeatedly throughout this text, **direct assessment of behavior** through direct observation is the most precise strategy and provides the most precise and accurate data on which to base intervention decisions. However, **indirect behavioral assessment** procedures are less time consuming and simpler to use. Furthermore, many instruments are available. In this section, we describe several procedures: checklists and rating scales, teacher rankings, self-report measures, and sociometric procedures. In addition, we describe procedures designed to measure teacher expectations and pupil social skills. The great weakness of indirect assessment tools and procedures is that they really are assessing the evaluator's opinion regarding the student's behavior rather than the behavior itself. Thus, assessment information may be distorted by the biases and expectations of the person conducting the assessment. Examples of the indirect behavioral assessment tools described here are on the Companion Website.

Checklists and **rating scales** generally use information supplied by a significant other (e.g., teacher, parent, sibling, or peer) to produce a picture of a target child's behavior. A checklist merely asks the responder to indicate whether she has observed specific behaviors at any time. These behaviors are selected from a list of behaviors. A rating scale gives the rater a set of items and asks her to evaluate these items with respect to a particular student in terms of how frequently behaviors occur. Less commonly, the rater responds to each item in terms of how much it characterizes the student's behavior (e.g., is very characteristic of the student, is not at all characteristic). Typically, ratings are presented in a Likert or similar numeric scale format.

Sometimes the rater may be instructed to rate how often a student engages in a particular behavior (never, rarely, occasionally, often, very frequently). If you are asked to complete a rating scale as part of a formal screening program, be sure that you have had enough experience with the student to provide valid responses. Remember, behavior ratings are only standardized ways of representing opinions regarding the presence or strength of students' behaviors. Thus, they should not be the only assessment tool used, nor are they appropriate as a basis for making intervention decisions.

Behavior rating scales may be *standardized,* meaning that tests were administered to a number of persons and that, on the basis of their responses, norms and criteria for discriminating between groups were established (e.g., a conduct problem/not a conduct problem). A sample of items contained in the *Walker Problem Behavior Identification Checklist* (Walker, 1983) is presented on the Companion Website. Rating scales also may be informal and nonstandardized, such as the next instrument shown on the Website. The format used here has the advantage of rating a group of students on the same sheet, thereby permitting comparisons. Rating scales may contain items that assess undesired or maladaptive behaviors, desired or adaptive behaviors, or both. Many rating scales are available commercially, and we suggest that you study their items, reliability, validity, norms, and recommended uses in order to identify those that are likely to be most appropriate and useful for your purposes (see Fox & Gable, 2004).

To make the assessment of **teacher expectations** less subjective, Walker and Rankin (1980) developed a standardized rating scale format, the *SBS*

Inventory of Teacher Social Behavior Standards and Expectations. It asks teachers to rate the importance of adaptive behaviors (e.g., child takes turns, uses free time appropriately) and their own tolerance for maladaptive pupil behaviors (e.g., child whines, has tantrums, uses obscene language) in terms of how these affect their willingness to work with the students in their classrooms. This instrument is also a component of the *Assessments for Integration into Mainstream Settings* (AIMS) system (Walker, 1986), which is used to identify the minimal skill requirements of mainstream settings, to prepare the student to meet these requirements, and to assess the pupil's adjustment following mainstream placement. We describe the AIMS system in greater detail in Chapter 12.

Teacher rankings on the basis of social criteria (e.g., frequency of peer verbal interactions) have been shown to be a reliable and valid method of identifying pupils who are not socially responsive (Walker, Severson, & Haring, 1986). Figure 4-3 illustrates one such ranking procedure. The teacher initially ranks all students in the class, divides them into two groups according to the behavior pattern being considered (e.g., most and least disruptive), and finally ranks all pupils according to the criterion (Hops & Greenwood, 1981). The systematic schoolwide screening procedure (Walker & Severson, 1990) mentioned in Chapter 1 includes this ranking procedure. Teacher rankings offer a quick way to establish the relative standing of pupils in the group with respect to a criterion.

Another format is a **self-report.** As the name implies, this type of instrument requires that students describe their own behavior in response to a number of questions or statements. For young students or nonreaders, the questions may be read orally with subsequent directions for students to color in a response area, to circle a happy or sad face, or to sort pictures into groups. Self-report instruments have been designed to assess a variety of general (e.g., locus of control) and specific (e.g., anger, depression) constructs. Self-reports provide useful information, but they should be supplemented with data from other sources, such as behavioral ratings and direct observations.

Although **sociometric procedures** may not be considered traditional behavioral assessment devices, they nevertheless can play a role in identifying students at risk for social behavior problems (Hops & Lewin, 1984). Before using a sociometric procedure in your classroom, check to see what, if any, parental permissions are required in order for students to participate in this process. In general, a sociometric procedure requires that students describe one another according to a predesignated set of criteria. For example, students might be asked to name their best friends or to list classmates they do not like. In this type of peer nomination, a student makes an acceptance or rejection choice about a selected number of peers. Because peer acceptance and rejection appear to be independent dimensions, both positive (e.g., "With whom would you most like to go to a movie?") and negative (e.g., "With whom would you least like to go to a movie?") social preferences should be obtained from peers (Hops & Lewin, 1984). Asking students to make negative nominations raises ethical questions that should be weighed before using this procedure. Students' sociometric ratings of peers should be kept confidential.

A variety of instruments have been developed to measure student **social skills.** Remember that these instruments ask for the evaluator's opinion regarding the student's social skills; they are not direct measures of social behavior. Evaluations are more likely to be valid if they come from a variety of sources (e.g., teachers, parents, peers, and students themselves) and if they address multiple social domains (i.e., interactions across environmental settings). The instruments and procedures just described may be used to conduct general assessments of students' social behaviors. Remember that it is important to assess student behavior across several settings and to obtain data from multiple sources in order to get a valid and comprehensive picture of pupils' behavioral assets and liabilities. While some procedures may be useful in gathering data for an FBA, they (with the exception of

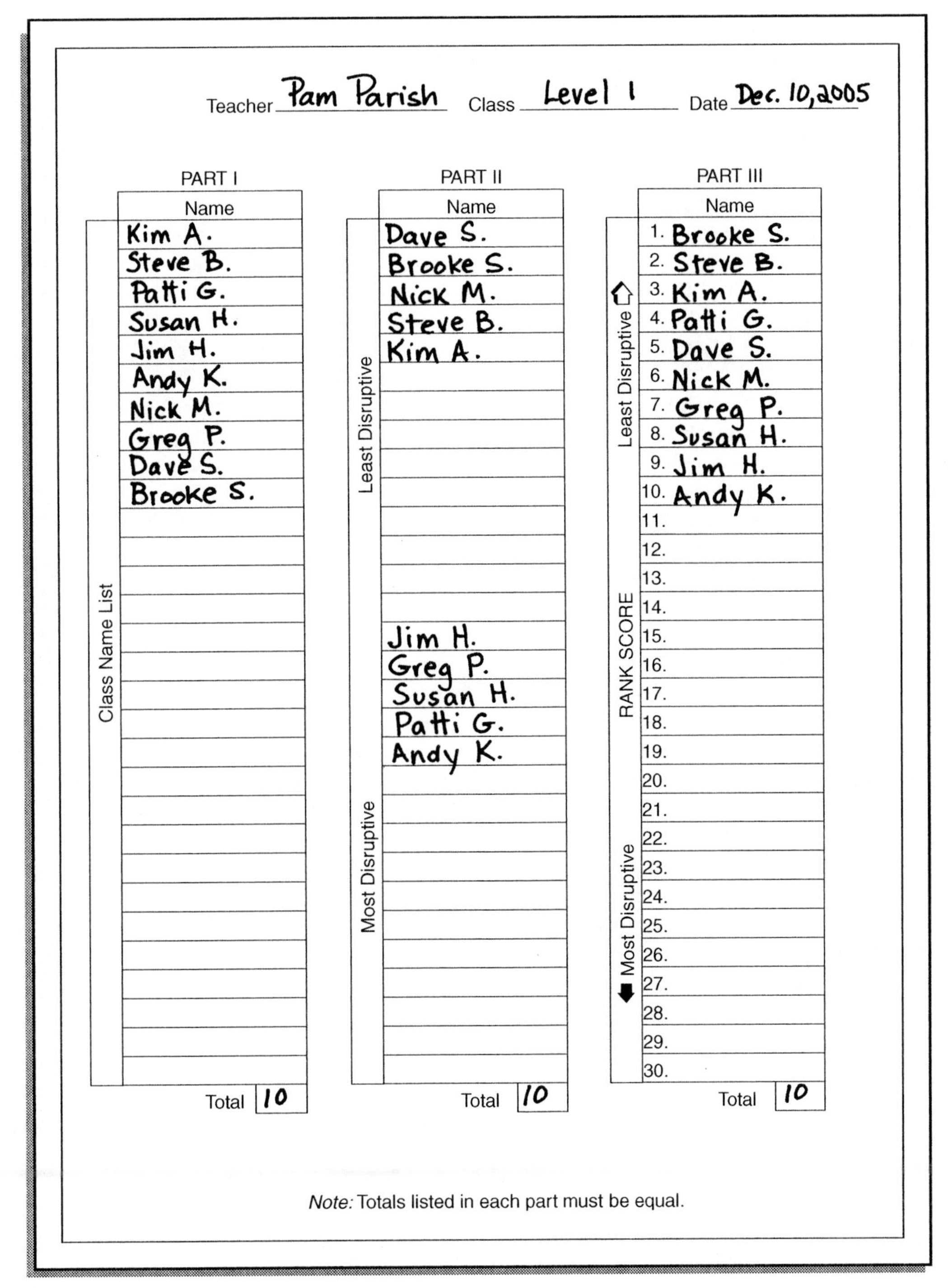

Teacher Pam Parish Class Level 1 Date Dec. 10, 2005

PART I — Class Name List

Name
Kim A.
Steve B.
Patti G.
Susan H.
Jim H.
Andy K.
Nick M.
Greg P.
Dave S.
Brooke S.

Total 10

PART II

Least Disruptive — Name
Dave S.
Brooke S.
Nick M.
Steve B.
Kim A.

Most Disruptive — Name
Jim H.
Greg P.
Susan H.
Patti G.
Andy K.

Total 10

PART III — RANK SCORE (↑ Least Disruptive / Most Disruptive ↓)

	Name
1.	Brooke S.
2.	Steve B.
3.	Kim A.
4.	Patti G.
5.	Dave S.
6.	Nick M.
7.	Greg P.
8.	Susan H.
9.	Jim H.
10.	Andy K.
11.	
12.	
13.	
14.	
15.	
16.	
17.	
18.	
19.	
20.	
21.	
22.	
23.	
24.	
25.	
26.	
27.	
28.	
29.	
30.	

Total 10

Note: Totals listed in each part must be equal.

FIGURE 4–3 Student Ranking Form

direct observation and measurement) are indirect measures of behavior and should not be used by themselves as assessments of student behavior, evaluations of intervention effectiveness, or FBAs. Direct observation and interviews also frequently are used to assess student behavior. We describe these in the following section, which includes developing a BIP from assessment data.

ASSESSMENT-BASED INTERVENTION PLANNING

As discussed in Chapter 1, The Individuals with Disabilities Education Improvement Act (IDEA 2004) stipulates that schools must conduct FBAs of students with disabilities whose behavior prompts a change in educational placement, including suspension and expulsion. An intervention plan addressing the student's problem behavior then must be developed based on the information obtained from the FBA. Because this process requires the collection of fairly large amounts of assessment data from multiple sources and over extended periods of time, we recommend that FBAs be coordinated by Behavior Support Teams.

Assessment-based intervention planning has a relatively lengthy history with individuals who have severe cognitive impairments and who also exhibit challenging behavior. Research with students with or at risk for mild disabilities has only begun recently and is considerably more limited. Systematic reviews of this research suggest that assessment-based interventions may not produce any better results than interventions that are not based on evaluations of the functions of challenging student behavior (Fox & Gable, 2004; Gresham, 2003; Reid & Nelson, 2002; Sasso, Conroy, Stichter, & Fox, 2001). Naturally, this raises the question, "Why do it?" There are two answers. First, it is required by law. Unfortunately, this requirement does little to guarantee the adequacy of the process or the accuracy of the outcomes. Many school districts have responded to the legislation by creating simplistic one-shot FBA checklists that simply document compliance with state and federal special education regulations and contribute nothing to intervention planning. Gresham (2003) concludes his review of the research by stating, "There is virtually no evidence that school personnel charged with implementing FBA procedures can reliably determine behavioral function" (p. 293).

However, we believe there is a second, more compelling reason for conducting FBAs as a basis for intervention planning. As we pointed out in Chapter 1, assessment is fundamental to the technology of applied behavior analysis. Whether the specific function of a student's challenging behavior is correctly identified or not, it is important to evaluate behavior in environmental contexts and to adjust contextual variables as part of the intervention process. Moreover, a basic concept underlying positive behavior support is that there is indeed *positive support for desired student behavior.* This represents a major shift from the intervention philosophy of creating disincentives for undesired behavior through the application of aversive consequences when such behavior occurs but providing no opportunity to teach the student appropriate behaviors to use instead, or to receive positive reinforcement engaging in these behaviors. In addition, as we have documented in previous chapters, there is ample evidence that interventions based solely on punitive consequences are ineffective. Assessment-based intervention planning is predicated on the fact that misbehavior happens for a reason; that is, it serves a function, or "works," for the student (though this does not necessarily imply a conscious intent). Knowledge of the reason for this behavior can lead to designing an intervention that includes not only disincentives for engaging in the problem behavior but also a plan for teaching and reinforcing occurrences of desired behavior. We also believe that researchers will continue to develop and evaluate more effective assessment tools and procedures as well as strategies for training professionals to conduct efficient and accurate FBAs (Scott et al., 2004). A tutorial, "Understanding Problem Behavior," that explains how behavior functions to produce desired outcomes or to escape/avoid undesired outcomes is on the Companion Website.

We describe the process of developing an assessment-based intervention plan, or BIP, in terms of six steps, adapted from Scott and Nelson (1999). These steps are interrelated and include a number of subordinate components. For example, assessing the student's behavior includes identifying and describing the target behavior, determining the contexts in which it occurs and those in which it does not occur, identifying potential predictable relationships between the behavior and these contexts, and testing these relationships to establish their validity.

You will note that the behavior intervention for Rodney at the beginning of this chapter included seven steps. The number of specific steps and the sequence in which they are implemented in a BIP are not important; what is important is the process. For the sake of convenience, we have combined certain steps in describing the process.

Step 1: Assess the Student's Behavior

The three primary outcomes of an FBA include (a) a concrete definition of the problem behavior(s), (b) identifying environmental variables reliably associated with the behavior and formulating hypotheses regarding which factors appear to predict its occurrence, and (c) identifying the function that the behavior appears to serve in meeting the needs of the individual (O'Neill, Horner, Albin, Storey, & Sprague, 1997). Initial assessments of behavior for the purpose of developing intervention plans are likely to involve informal conversations and the use of indirect assessment tools, such as questionnaires, checklists, and structured interviews, with individuals (e.g., classroom teachers and parents) who have frequent contact with the student and who may be able to offer insights regarding what factors seem to predict problem behaviors (Scott & Nelson, 1999).

What Does the Problem Behavior Look Like? The task here is to develop a definition of the behavior or behaviors that will be the primary target(s) of intervention. Target behaviors should be defined or described in terms that are measurable, observable, and objectively defined so that two or more persons can agree on their occurrence or nonoccurrence. These characteristics constitute an **operational definition** of target behaviors (i.e., what the behavior looks like). Sometimes you will be working from the verbal descriptions of behavior provided by others or from statements contained in behavior checklists. In addition, you will be writing **behavioral objectives** based on definitions of behaviors. For these reasons, it is important that your definitions be observable and precise. Table 4–2 provides examples of target behavior definitions

TABLE 4–2 Examples of Target Behavior Definitions

General Statement	Target Behavior
1. Kim does not comply with teacher requests.	1. When given a direction by the teacher, Kim fails to initiate the behavior requested within 5 seconds.
2. Andy is hyperactive.	2. Andy is out of his seat more than one time in 10 minutes.
3. Fred cannot ride the school bus appropriately.	3. Fred is out of his assigned seat on the bus.
4. Betsy is aggressive.	4. Betsy hits, kicks, pushes, and calls other children names during recess.
5. Billy is withdrawn.	5. Billy initiates less than one interaction with a peer in any given 10-minute free play period.

derived from general statements. Study these operational definitions and practice writing some of your own in order to gain competency in this skill. While target behaviors may include those to be decreased (e.g., refusal to complete assignments, tantrums, self-injurious behavior) or increased (e.g., completion of assignments, making appropriate requests of peers, keeping hands to self), the focus of most behavior intervention plans is on behaviors to be decreased.

Under What General Conditions Do Problem Behaviors Tend to Occur? Under What General Conditions Do Desired Behaviors Tend to Occur? Several indirect assessment instruments can help answer these questions. For example, the *Motivation Assessment Scale* (Durand & Crimmins, 1992) and the *Problem Behavior Questionnaire* (Lewis, Scott, & Sugai, 1994) are simple paper-and-pencil tools for assessing the likelihood of problem behavior under a variety of circumstances. A direct descriptive assessment tool is a **scatter plot** (Touchette, MacDonald, & Langer, 1985), which enables practitioners to estimate rates of targeted behaviors across time and settings. One scatter plot format is presented in Figure 4-4. Each day is represented by a vertical column divided into 30-minute blocks of time. The observer notes the activity taking place during each time interval and marks the interval for a given day according to whether the target behavior occurred. Alternately, different symbols can be used to indicate whether the behavior occurred at a high rate (e.g., a completely filled cell) or at a low rate (e.g., a slash). A blank grid indicates that the behavior did not occur. Although a scatter plot does not indicate the actual frequency with which a target behavior occurs, it does reveal patterns over time and settings. Therefore, this procedure may be used to identify relationships between problem behaviors and time of day, the presence or absence of certain persons, a physical or social setting, a particular activity, and so forth.

Behavioral interviews are another useful indirect assessment strategy for obtaining assessment data from both children and adults. The interview should be structured to obtain specific information about the behaviors that occur, the settings in which they take place, and the antecedent and consequent conditions associated with these behaviors, including the social behavior of other persons (Conroy & Fox, 1994). An interview may be used to gather information about concerns and goals, identify factors that maintain or occasion problem behaviors, obtain historical information, and identify reinforcers. Information from two or more sources can be compared to evaluate the reliability of informants or to obtain individual perceptions of behaviors and environmental events across settings. For example, Kern, Childs, Dunlap, Clarke, and Falk (1994) developed a student-assisted functional assessment interview that provides information from the student's perspective regarding expectations, curricula, and other variables in the school setting as well as her perceptions about the target behaviors. The *Problem Behavior Questionnaire* (Lewis et al., 1994) is a teacher-based interview format that provides information from the teacher's perspective regarding the student's problem behaviors and the circumstances under which they occur as well as those under which they do not occur.

A general interview format for identifying and analyzing target behaviors appears on the Companion Website. Note that the questions are open ended (they do not limit answers by requiring only one-word responses) but are structured to focus on observable events. The format also includes probes for following up on previous answers. Additional interview formats are presented in subsequent chapters.

Interviews and scatter plot ratings furnish information that may be used to identify times and locations where more direct assessments can be performed (Scott & Nelson, 1999). In addition, they may help identify stimuli or events that affect pupil behavior but that take place outside the settings where the problem behavior occurs, or they may be concurrent events, such as a change in seating arrangement. As indicated in Chapter 2, these influential antecedents are known as setting events and may include such variables as the student's

Student: John

Observer: Ms. Lewis (teacher)

Dates: 3/2 through 3/13

Target Behavior:

Leaving seat without permission

Using a scatter plot involves recording the times of the day (and/or activities) in which the behavior does occur and does not occur to identify patterns that occur over days or weeks.

		Dates									
Time	Activity	3/2	3/3	3/4	3/5	3/6	3/9	3/10	3/11	3/12	3/13
7:30	Arrival		■								
8:00	Writing	■	■	■	■		■	■	■	■	■
8:30	Social Skills		■				■				
9:00	Reading		■	■		■	■	■		■	■
9:30	P.E.	NA	NA	NA	NA	NA	NA	NA	NA	NA	NA
10:00	Science			■				NA			
10:30	Crafts					■		NA			
11:00	Mathematics	■			■			NA	■		
11:30	Lunch							NA			
12:00	Recess	NA	NA	NA	NA	NA	NA	NA	NA	NA	NA
12:30	Projects						■				
1:00	Music		■				■				
1:30	Reading	■	■	■		■	■	■		■	■
2:00	Mathematics		■		■			■		■	
2:30	Dismissal	NA	NA	NA	NA	NA	NA	NA	NA	NA	NA

□ Behavior did not occur

■ Behavior occurred

NA Did not observe

FIGURE 4–4 Scatter Plot

Source: "Facilitator's Guide: Positive Behavioral Support" by the Positive Behavioral Support Project, p. 30. Copyright 1999 by the Department of State, State of Florida. Reproduced with permission.

experiences over a weekend, the time of day, a particular classroom environment, or transition periods. Setting events can set the occasion for some behaviors; that is, when they have taken place or when they are present, the target behavior is more likely to occur.

School records often contain information that may be useful in identifying patterns of behavior or variables that may have some bearing on the student's target behavior(s). Systematic tools, such as the *School Archival Records Search* (Walker, Block-Pedego, Todis, & Severson, 1991), are quick and reliable methods for summarizing the sometimes large amount of data found in students' cumulative records. Pay particular attention to previous disciplinary records, anecdotal notes from meeting with caregivers, IEP Team minutes, and health records.

Although it may be possible to form a hypothesis regarding the variables that predict problem behavior from the previously described assessments, more information generally is required. At this point, it is useful to observe directly in settings where the target behavior occurs. Human behavior occurs in environmental contexts that contain a variety of stimuli. Some of these stimuli influence behavior either directly or indirectly. It is helpful to know precisely which stimuli affect behavior and which do not. Direct observation may enable you to identify the variables that affect student behavior. An A-B-C assessment is a direct observation format that organizes events into those that are present or take place immediately before a behavioral event and those that occur immediately afterward. We just pointed out that setting events can influence behavior, even when they take place some time before the target behavior occurs. However, more immediate antecedent events, such as the task the student is expected to perform, the other persons present, or the instructions provided to the student, may be important "triggers" for problem behavior. In addition, stimuli that occur subsequent to the pupil's behavior often exert a powerful influence on that behavior. For example, does the student receive social attention, praise, or criticism following specific behaviors? Does her behavior result in avoiding or escaping task demands?

An A-B-C assessment involves carefully observing and recording events that occur immediately before the target pupil's behavior, the behavior itself, and the events that take place immediately afterward. Figure 4-5 illustrates a portion of an A-B-C assessment. Note that the observer logs the time and describes the immediate antecedents, the student's behavior, and the consequences in the sequence in which they occur. An analysis of recurring antecedent and consequent events provides some clues as to which of these stimuli potentially influence behavior. Can you identify some of these events in the example?

An A-B-C assessment is only useful for observing students individually; it would become too unwieldy to use with several pupils at the same time. In addition, it typically is not something you can do while teaching; therefore, you may need to enlist the aid of another person (e.g., a paraprofessional) to provide instruction while you do the assessment and vice versa. It is important to conduct A-B-C observations for sufficient lengths of time to capture a range of behavioral sequences (both those that include instances of the target behavior and those that do not). In addition, conduct observations across several days to ensure that typical ranges of student performance are observed (you can ask persons in the setting to verify that such is the case). We have found it useful also to perform A-B-C assessments in settings and at times of the day when the target behavior does not occur, as this information can uncover events that predict when more desirable behavior is likely to take place (which is important for developing the BIP). By doing these assessments over a period of time and analyzing the results in conjunction with data from other sources (e.g., interviews, school records searches), it may be possible to identify setting events that influence the behavior. For example, if the problem behavior occurs more often during the first period of the day, there may be something that happens in the morning (e.g., the student doesn't eat breakfast or is teased or bullied on the school bus).

Although the procedure is not complex, it is neither quick nor simple. We recommend 30- to 40-minute observation periods over several days to get representative samples of student behavior (remember to validate your findings against the judgments of adults in the setting, such as the classroom teacher). The A-B-C assessment routine can be confusing to persons who are not experienced. Therefore, such assessments should be performed by persons with specific training in this

Student Raymond Date Oct. 29

Observer Dionne McInerney Time 2:15 - 2:25

Behavior Talking out during class discussion, off task Activity Social Studies

Antecedent	Behavior	Consequence
Teacher says, "Everyone please get out your Social Studies notebook and pencil."	Raymond asks student next to him, "What did she say?"	Teacher says, "No talking."
Teacher asks Tommy to name the capital of Alabama.	Raymond shouts out, "Montgomery."	Tommy yells, "Shut up, Raymond."
Teacher says, "Please, Raymond, sit quietly until it is your turn."	Raymond yells, "What did I do?"	Teacher says, "Raymond, be quiet."
Teacher asks, "Which state has the largest population? Raymond, can you answer?"	Raymond says, "Uh? I didn't do anything!"	Class laughs.
Teacher asks, "Alice, which state is nicknamed the Keystone State?"	Raymond calls out, "I know. It's Pennsylvania."	Teacher says, "Raymond, I've had enough. Put your head down on your desk."

FIGURE 4–5 Sample A-B-C Record
Source: *McInerney, D. (1986). Personal communication.*

procedure. The purpose of an FBA is to generate hypotheses regarding which variables may influence the student's behavior. As Wehby (1994) pointed out, up to 10 hours of assessment time may be needed to evaluate functioning in all the areas required for an FBA of a given student's behavior. However, the process can be conducted much more efficiently when A-B-C assessments focus on settings and events that historically have predicted desired and undesired behavior.

While direct observation of behavior is by far the preferred strategy, alternate procedures may be used in situations where trained personnel are not available. For example, persons who are present when problem behaviors occur can be given behavior incident logs to complete as soon as possible following a behavioral incident. Data from several such logs can be summarized in a three-column format (antecedents to the behavior, a description of the behavior occurring in each incident, and events that took place immediately following the behavior). See an example of a behavior incident report format on the Companion Website. A completed report may be found in Chapter 9. The disadvantage of recording only events surrounding occurrences of problem behavior is that no insight is gained about events that predict occurrences of desired behavior.

Figure 4–6 displays a format for documenting the methods used in the FBA process. This information should be updated by the Behavior Support Team as information is collected from their assessments.

> What methods were used to assess the function of Rodney's behavior? What tools would you recommend that his Behavior Support Team use to improve their effectiveness and efficiency?

Step 2: Propose a Hypothesis

Analysis of the data gathered through the assessment process leads to the identification of recurrent patterns involving setting events, antecedents, or consequences (or all of these) associated with occurrences of the target behavior as well as events that are not associated with it. This analysis should enable the Behavior Support Team to answer questions about the antecedent contexts in which the behavior occurs, such as those posed in Box 4–1.

While the contexts in which problem behaviors occur often are the primary focus of assessment procedures, as we pointed out earlier, it also is important to know the variables that seem to predict instances of *desired* behavior. Therefore, remember to look at settings in which the student's behavior is appropriate and identify setting events, antecedents, and consequences that are associated with these behavior patterns. From answers to these questions, we can form hypotheses about antecedent or consequent events that predict both desired and undesired behavior. For example, the hypothesis "When Lewis is disruptive, his teacher attends to him" predicts a relationship between Lewis's behavior and a specific consequent event: attention from the teacher. However, the hypothesis "Toya engages in self-stimulatory behavior when approached by peers" suggests a predictable relationship between antecedents and behavior.

BOX 4–1 Questions Addressed Through an FBA

- In what settings does the behavior occur?
- During what times of the day does the behavior occur?
- Does the behavior occur in the presence of certain persons?
- During what activities is the behavior more likely to occur?
- During what activities is the behavior less likely to occur?

Answers to questions regarding events following the target behavior suggest what functions it may serve for the student:

- What happens to the student following the behavior?
- Does the surrounding environment change in any way following the behavior?
- What does the student gain or lose?
- How do others respond to the behavior (Positive Behavioral Support Project, 1999)?

Records: What records were reviewed? Conducted by:	_____ academic records (cumulative) _____ discipline records _____ previous interventions _____ other:	_____ child study notes _____ anecdotals/home notes _____ evaluations (e.g., social work, psychological)	What relevant information was obtained? _____ see attached summary/notes
Interviews: What interviews were conducted? Tools used: Conducted by:	_____ student _____ special education teacher _____ general education teacher _____ other _____ see attached interviews	_____ parent(s) _____ administrator _____ related services	What relevant information was obtained? _____ see attached interviews
Observations: What direct observations occurred? Tools used: Conducted by:	Location	Date/Time	What relevant information was obtained? _____ see attached observations
Other Assessments: What, if any, other assessments were conducted (e.g., ecological or classroom management inventories, reinforcer surveys, academic assessments)?			

FIGURE 4–6 Functional Assessment Methods

Source: *"Facilitator's Guide: Positive Behavioral Support" by the Positive Behavioral Support Project, p. 30. Copyright 1999 by the Department of State, State of Florida. Reproduced with permission.*

However, keep in mind that antecedent or consequent events are not likely to be identical every time. The key is to identify events that have some common elements (Scott & Nelson, 1999). Thus, sometimes Lewis's teacher responds to his outbursts with a verbal reprimand, and sometimes she takes him aside to calm him down. The common element, however, is that she consistently gives him her attention when he behaves this way. By looking at sequences in which he is not disruptive, we may be able to strengthen our hypothesis. For example, if we observe that Lewis is not disruptive when he is engaged in one-to-one interactions with the teacher, we have a better basis for hypothesizing that teacher attention is the variable that supports Lewis's disruptive behavior (i.e., he exhibits the target behavior only when he is not receiving the teacher's personal attention).

Although, as we have emphasized, human behavior is complex and influenced by many variables, all behavior can be classified into one of two broad functions: to *gain access* to something (e.g., peer or teacher attention, a desired item, sensory stimulation from stereotypic behavior) or to *escape or avoid* something (e.g., an unpleasant task, a specific person or situation) (Scott & Nelson, 1999). Thus, Lewis's disruptive behavior gains attention from his teacher and peers; Toya's self-stimulatory behavior may persist because it results in other persons leaving her alone (i.e., escape/avoidance) or because it produces pleasant sensory consequences (access reinforcement). On the Companion Website, you will find a format that may be used to analyze patterns of behavior and propose a function served by the behavior. This information will guide the formulation of hypothesis statements.

We have pointed out that the FBA process was developed in working with individuals who display challenging behavior but lack cognitive and expressive language skills. As recent research demonstrates (Shores, Wehby, & Jack, 1999), the undesired behavior of students with more extensive behavioral repertoires than those with severe disabilities also serve functions. For example, the observation that a student predictably displays disruptive behavior during certain classroom activities resulting in her being removed from the classroom may suggest that disruptive behavior serves the function of helping her escape or avoid these task demands. In this case, providing remedial instruction or adjusting the level of task difficulty is a more appropriate response than punishing her undesired behavior (or reinforcing it by removing her from the classroom). Thus, knowledge about recurring setting-event-antecedent-response-consequence relationships is important for intervention planning. However, the extensive social behavior repertoires of many students who exhibit behavioral disorders, as well as the complexity of their social interactions with peers and adults, renders the task of establishing functional relationships between their behavior and environmental variables extremely difficult, as the same target behavior may serve different functions in different settings (Shores et al., 1999).

Step 3: Assess the Validity of the Hypothesis

Our hypothesis about the relationship between Lewis's disruptive behavior and his teacher attending to it basically is an informed guess: when Lewis engages in disruptive behavior, we predict that his teacher is likely to attend. To the extent that such attention consistently follows his behavior, we can say that the function of Lewis's disruptive behavior is to gain teacher attention. However, at this point we have not *proven* that these events are functionally related. To demonstrate such proof (i.e., establish a causal relationship), it is necessary to change some of the variables involved and observe the effect on Lewis's behavior. We have observed that Lewis does not display disruptive behavior when he has the teacher's undivided attention. Therefore, one way to demonstrate a causal relationship is to assess Lewis's disruptions in situations where the teacher already is attending to him and when she is not. Another way is for the teacher not to respond to Lewis's disruptions and observe what happens to their frequency of occurrence.

However, if Lewis's behavior functions to gain access to teacher attention, under the latter circumstance we would expect to see an immediate increase in disruptive behavior (see the discussion of extinction in Chapter 3). While this would validate our hypothesis, it also may create a situation that would be undesirable to the teacher.

Fortunately, it isn't necessary to go through prolonged periods in which these conditions are in effect to validate a hypothesis. But keep in mind that behavior is strongly influenced by contextual variables and other setting events. Thus, Lewis may be quite a bit more disruptive in a loosely structured language arts class than during a science lesson. In addition, the same behavior may serve different functions in different settings, and very different behaviors (e.g., making barking noises, hand raising) may be equally effective in gaining attention. Therefore, it is often important to use a variety of methods to assess behavior and conduct assessments across multiple settings and sources to form a reasonable hypothesis.

Researchers refer to the process of changing conditions while observing their effects on the target behavior as **functional analysis** because repeated demonstrations that the systematic alteration of certain events reliably increase or decrease a specific behavior indicate a predictable, functional relationship. Go to the Companion Website to see how the functional analysis process was completed for Fred.

From a research perspective, a functional relationship cannot be scientifically proven without this level of functional analysis. However, Steege and Northup (1998) identified a range of functional assessment procedures and evaluated the extent to which each strategy was useful in forming or confirming hypotheses regarding functional relationships. *Indirect assessment* procedures rely mainly on interviews with persons who observe the behavior (archival records searches also would be classified as indirect). *Descriptive assessment* involves naturalistic observations of behavior, including scatter plot ratings and A-B-C observations. *Brief functional analysis* entails observing target behavior in briefly alternating conditions (e.g., Lewis and Sugai, 1996). *Extended functional analysis* involves more prolonged exposure to each condition, usually across several sessions or days.

Which type of functional analysis procedure was used to test the hypothesis the Behavior Support Team generated regarding Rodney's problem behavior?

Naturally, briefer and more indirect strategies are much simpler to implement but at the expense of greater confidence in the validity of the hypotheses that are formed. Sugai (personal communication, 1999) offered practical advice for evaluating the validity of hypotheses. If, after using indirect and descriptive procedures to generate a hypothesis, the team has a high level of confidence in the hypothesis, a BIP based on the hypothesis (see step 4) can be implemented. The team should then monitor the target and behavior systematically for a sufficient period of time to evaluate the intervention. If behavior changes that are consistent with the hypothesis are observed, it is reasonable to assume that the hypothesis is valid, and the intervention can be continued. If, however, the team does not feel confident in the hypothesis or if after the BIP has been implemented for several days the behavior does not change in the direction that would be predicted based on the hypothesis, the FBA process should be continued. In any case, the target behavior should be directly monitored to evaluate the effects of the BIP. Data decision rules should be used as a basis for determining whether the plan or the hypothesis needs to be revised (see Chapter 6).

If you have followed the steps to this point, you will have completed an FBA. Training in the FBA process is available in a variety of formats, including printed manuals (e.g., Crone & Horner, 2003; Gable, Quinn, Rutherford, Howell, & Hoffman, 1998; Nelson, Roberts, & Smith, 1999; O'Neill et al., 1997; Witt, Daly, & Noell, 2000) and CD-ROM (e.g., Liaupsin, Scott, & Nelson, 2001). Some state departments of education (e.g., Florida and Virginia) and agencies (e.g., Center for Effective Collaboration and Practice) have developed training packages.

Consult the Center for Effective Collaboration and Practice Website for training manuals that you can download.

Step 4: Design an Intervention

If the FBA has been successful, the Behavior Support Team will have identified the function(s) served by the target behavior, that is, how the behavior "works" for the student. They also will have gathered additional information that is critical to the development of a BIP, including (a) any setting events that increase the likelihood of the behavior, (b) specific antecedents that reliably predict the behavior, and (c) the outcome(s) or consequences that usually follow the target behavior. For example, social studies class appears to be a setting event for Lewis's disruptive behavior. The recurring antecedent event appears to be the teacher posing a question to the entire class, and the consequence is teacher attention. This information constitutes a **problem behavior pathway,** and it is useful to write down this sequence for analysis by the Behavior Support Team. Figure 4–7 shows a problem behavior pathway for a student who runs from peers who taunt her on the playground.

Simultaneous to the identification and functional assessment of problem behavior, the team may identify the *desired* or expected behavior that should occur instead as well as its typical outcome or consequence. These events can be identified by looking at what the other students do. The desired behavior for Lewis is to raise his hand and wait to be called on before speaking. The consequence for this behavior is being called on occasionally and sometimes being praised for having the correct answer. In this case, hand raising and waiting to be called on before speaking is a **replacement behavior**—a socially valid, effective, and efficient behavior that Lewis may use instead of blurting out. Identifying, teaching, and supporting replacement behaviors are critical features of BIPs. Replacement behaviors should be selected carefully. Fox and Gable (2004) suggest that teams should ensure that the replacement behavior can serve the same function as the problem behavior. This is known as **response equivalency.** They also recommend that the replacement behavior should achieve the functional outcome at least as quickly, as consistently, and with the same quality of maintaining consequence as the problem behavior. This is referred to as **response efficiency.** These concepts offer a more specific prescription for implementing the fair pair rule mentioned in Chapter 1. Table 4–3 illustrates functional replacement behaviors and their benefits.

What might be an appropriate replacement behavior for Jamey in Figure 4–7?

The BIP must address two parallel intervention strategies: one to teach and support the replacement behavior and one to correct or reduce the target behavior. The plan should ensure that the target (undesired) behavior is *ineffective, inefficient,* and *irrelevant* with regard to producing the outcomes it once did. However, the replacement

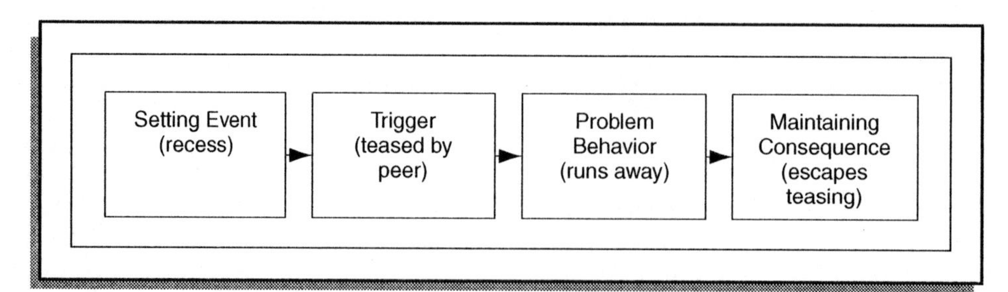

FIGURE 4–7 Problem Behavior Pathway for Jamey

TABLE 4–3 Functional Replacement Behaviors and Their Benefit

Predictor	Undesirable Behavior	Replacement Behavior and Contingency	Function of Both Behaviors	Benefit of Replacement Behavior
Addition problems with regrouping	Scream until thrown out of class	Raise hand to get assistance	Escape frustration	More math completed & less screaming
Line-up	Pushes peers and ends up at front of line	Don't touch anyone and is allowed to be the first one in line	Access first spot in line	No physical aggression in line
Reading groups	Refuses directions to read and ends up playing alone at desk	Is allowed to sit and play at desk after reading a predetermined number of pages	Escape from reading/access playing at desk	Student now gets some reading instruction
Robert	When Robert is near, student will engage in off-task behavior to get Robert's attention	Complete all assigned tasks and earn time to play alone with Robert	Access to Robert's attention	Student remains on-task and completes assigned tasks

Source: *Scott, T. M. & Nelson, C. M. (1999). Using functional behavioral assessment to develop effective intervention plans: Practical classroom applications,* Journal of Positive Behavioral Interventions, I, *242–251, copyright 1999 by PRO-ED, Inc. Reprinted with permission.*

behavior should be consistently *effective, efficient,* and *relevant* in terms of serving this function. To accomplish these goals, the BIP must address two issues: (a) where the student is with respect to the criterion (terminal skill level) and (b) what changes must be made in the environment to increase the student's fluency of performance and the likelihood that the replacement behavior will be used repeatedly and the target behavior will not.

Increasing the Replacement Behavior. It is important to know whether the target behavior reflects a deficit in the skills needed to perform as expected or a lack of incentive to perform as desired (Howell et al., 1993). For example, if a student lacks the skills necessary to gain peer attention appropriately, she may use undesired behavior to produce this effect. However, she may have the skills to perform as desired, but the problem behavior is more successful in producing outcomes that are rewarding to her. If the desired behavior is one the pupil *cannot* do (i.e., she lacks the necessary information or component skills), the appropriate intervention is instruction in the skill. Attempting to change the student's motivation to perform the skill through arranging positive or aversive consequences will be ineffective unless accompanied by relevant skill instruction. It is important to be sensitive to the possibility that pupils may be deficient in social skills. Often, teachers assume that undesired student behavior reflects the pupil's decision to misbehave. However, the student who lacks appropriate social behavior does not have a choice because alternative social behaviors are missing from her repertoire. As Howell et al. (1993) emphasize, students should be taught the social skills they lack rather than just receiving behavior management interventions to control their maladaptive behavior.

However, if the skill is something the student *can* perform (i.e., she has done it before or performs it in other settings), the problem behavior may be maintained by its consequences (i.e., accessing something desirable or avoiding something undesirable). In this case, the appropriate intervention consists of providing opportunities for the replacement behavior to occur or removing obstacles to desired performance and reinforcing the desired behavior when it occurs. At the same time, strategies are developed to reduce undesired behaviors by withholding or removing reinforcing consequences or by applying consequences designed to weaken the behavior.

Behavioral interventions would be simple if the only requirement were to tell the student what she should do and then reinforce her for doing it. But often, students either lack the skill to perform the replacement behavior or have long histories of being reinforced for using the target behavior. Therefore, you must begin where the student is now and work up to where you want her to be. Using the replacement behavior at rates typical of other students and with consequences that are naturally available to support it is a **long-term objective:** we want Lewis to raise his hand and wait to be called on before speaking, which will be followed by intermittent teacher attention and praise. To get from the student's current level of performance to the long-term objective, we must think in terms of some intermediate steps or **short-term objectives.** This entails identifying some approximations to this objective as well as strategies for addressing the consequences of both target and replacement behaviors. Regarding where to begin, a good rule of thumb is to *start with the behavior the student gives you.* For example, if Lewis has never raised his hand in social studies class (and that is an expectation the other students understand and meet), practice it with him in a direct instruction format (i.e., model the behavior, lead the student through its performance, test for acquisition, reward correct performance or correct errors). If Lewis can comply with the rule but doesn't do it reliably, we look at his typical performance and set our first approximation (expectation) there. Thus, if he typically raises his hand and waits 5 seconds before speaking, we make sure to catch him as soon as he raises his hand and provide attention (praise for hand raising). When we see an increase in compliance, we can increase the criterion to the next level (expecting him to wait a few more seconds).

As Scott and Nelson (1999) observe, it may be necessary to modify immediate goals so that the replacement behavior will serve the same function as the target behavior. For example, if the function of the target behavior is to escape or avoid an undesired academic task, it may be necessary to teach the student to use a replacement behavior that temporarily will serve the same function (e.g., asking to take a break, as opposed to creating a disruption). While this behavior is being taught, tasks can be simplified and reinforcement provided for **successive approximations** to the long-term objective.

Even though the student may have the skill to perform the desired replacement behavior, she isn't likely to do so without being directly taught. This is because the student has a history of using the target behavior successfully to produce a desired outcome. Introduction of the replacement behavior should be accompanied by a general rule and a rationale (Scott & Nelson, 1999). The rule explains when the behavior is appropriate, and the rationale describes what the consequences will be for using it. Thus, we teach Lewis the rule ("Raise your hand when you want to speak and wait for my permission before you do") and explain the rationale for following it ("Each time you follow the rule, I will come and talk to you"). Following this introduction, the replacement behavior should be taught or practiced, using strategies that minimize failure and maximize success.

Again, replacement behaviors should serve the same function as target behaviors, but they must do so more effectively and efficiently. Therefore, identify a signal that will indicate to the student when she should use the behavior. This may be a naturally occurring stimulus or time (e.g., be in your seat when the tardy bell rings) or a specific prompt (e.g., "Remember to ask for my help if you get stuck"). When the replacement behavior occurs in the presence of the stimulus, be sure to reinforce it immediately. Be prepared to prompt and guide the student to perform the replacement behavior. Remember that ensuring the student's success is the key.

It also is necessary to consider conditions in the environment that may either facilitate or inhibit the student's acquisition and use of the replacement behavior. If FBA data suggest times of the day, settings, or specific antecedent events that increase the likelihood that the replacement behavior will be used, incorporate this information into the BIP. For example, if one student is a particularly good role model for following the hand-raising rule, we could seat this student by Lewis. We may even teach this student to prompt Lewis at intervals throughout the class period ("Remember the rule about hand raising"). Conversely, if there are circumstances that increase the likelihood of failure, the BIP should include strategies for avoiding these. For example, we could move peers who are likely to respond to Lewis's blurting out farther away and place him next to students who are better at ignoring his inappropriate behavior (in addition, peers can be taught to ignore and be reinforced for doing so).

> What are some skills you could teach a student like Jamey to help her avoid being teased? What cues or prompts could you use to signal her when to use these skills?

Reducing the Target Behavior. The BIP also must address the issue of managing the target behavior. It is unrealistic to expect students to discard behaviors that have been successful in meeting their needs for some time. However, the focus of the plan is on teaching and reinforcement of the desired replacement behavior. Sugai (1995) suggests that instances of the target behavior be regarded as errors rather than intentional misbehaviors. The appropriate response to a mistake is to provide an error correction procedure ("No, remember the rule about hand raising"), not punishment. However, reductive procedures may be required if the target behavior poses a risk to the safety of the student herself or to others or if it interferes with learning. A review of alternative strategies for reducing undesired behavior is provided in Chapter 3, and Chapters 7 through 10 provide examples of methods for reducing problem behavior. At this point, we reiterate that the plan should ensure that the target behavior is no longer effective, efficient, or relevant to serving the functions that it once did, whereas the replacement behavior is highly effective, efficient, and relevant (Sugai, 1995). The *difference* between what happens when the target and the replacement behaviors occur is more important than the magnitude of punishment that can be delivered.

> Bear in mind that the target behavior will have a history of being effective and efficient in terms of the function it has performed. Therefore, just using a correction procedure may not be sufficient (particularly when paired with a powerful reinforcer such as teacher attention). Under these circumstances, the BIP should include planned reductive consequences.

Just as you should assess the environment for conditions that make the student's success (use of the replacement behavior) more or less likely and adjust these to increase the likelihood of success and reduce failure, you should also look for conditions that support or discourage use of the target behavior and modify these. By anticipating and correcting these circumstances before the target behavior has a chance to occur, we again minimize the need for punishment.

Nevertheless, if the target behavior poses a danger to the student or to others, the BIP must include strategies for crisis management. The Positive Behavioral Support Project (1999, p. 60) defines a crisis as an "unforeseen combination of circumstances posing continuous risk that calls for immediate action." Procedures for dealing with such situations should include strategies that will ensure safety and rapid deescalation of the crisis. Emergency procedures are not part of regular programmatic intervention but rather are reactive strategies to prevent students who are engaging in self-injurious, aggressive, or destructive behavior from harming themselves or others. *Use of emergency procedures should be regarded as evidence that the BIP is in need of revision.* Crisis intervention plans should be monitored carefully, and if it cannot be documented that their use is decreasing over time or if implementation of emergency procedures provokes emotional reactions from the student, the plan should be revised immediately. If emergency procedures are to be considered in conjunction with a BIP, consult your school district or agency's policies and obtain the necessary permissions from your agency and the student's caregivers (see Chapter 3). You also may need to obtain training or consultation from persons who are skilled in safe physical management procedures (Positive Behavioral Support Project, 1999).

Finally, the Behavior Support Team should obtain input from the student's educational management team (e.g., IEP Team), and BIPs should be integrated into her overall program and daily routines. For example, plan goals should be written into IEPs or accommodation plans. At a minimum, BIPs should include descriptions of the target and replacement behaviors; intervention goals; strategies to prevent, replace, and manage target behavior(s); and mechanisms for ensuring implementation and progress. Particularly if the BIP was developed in response to an incident that invoked placement in an interim alternative educational setting, the team should carefully document the procedures used throughout the process (Positive Behavioral Support Project, 1999).

Step 5: Collect Data on Intervention Effectiveness and Adjust the Plan as Needed

On the Companion Website, you will find a flowchart that will guide decision making as the BIP is being implemented. Careful and continuous monitoring of the effects of the BIP on the target and replacement behaviors is critical to ensuring that the plan is working. Moreover, the team needs to be accountable to the school district or agency and to the student's caregivers. At a minimum, data should be collected on rates of occurrence of the target behavior. We strongly recommend that occurrences of the replacement behavior be documented with equal rigor, given the BIP's focus on promoting the latter. Informal, subjective evaluations of progress are not a sufficient basis for making the kinds of sensitive intervention decisions required for adjusting BIPs. The data collected provide the basis for making decisions regarding the need for adjustments in the plan. Therefore, the team should not only gather direct observation data on the behaviors of concern but also use these data in making intervention decisions. The process of formulating and following data decision rules is presented in Chapter 6.

The long-term and intermediate objectives established for BIPs provide a framework for data collection and evaluation of the plan. Thus, the objective "During social studies class, Lewis will raise his hand and wait to be called on before speaking on 100% of opportunities for 5 consecutive days" suggests that we should monitor hand raising and blurting out. The intermediate or short-term objective "Given a prompt at the beginning of social studies class to remember to raise his hand, Lewis will raise his hand on 80% of the opportunities" indicates a progress marker after the intervention has been in place for a while. If short-term objectives are not met, the Behavior Support Team should reassess the intervention by looking at the data patterns, reanalyzing FBA data, or conducting additional assessments. Based on these analyses, several adjustments to the BIP may be made. The plan may be continued, but with an abbreviated time line for evaluating outcomes. Alternately, it may be changed in some way (e.g., adding or deleting prompts, changing criteria for performance, changing consequences, redefining the behavior, or teaching a prerequisite skill that has not been mastered). Finally, the plan may be replaced entirely (Scott & Nelson, 1999). Again, *if the plan isn't working, change the plan;* don't eject the student from the program.

Step 6: Write Long- and Short-Term Intervention Objectives

Although we list this as the last step, the beginning point of intervention, whether it consists of skill instruction or behavior management, is to write behavioral objectives that describe the behavioral outcome to be achieved following intervention. A well-written behavioral objective specifies in observable and measurable terms the terminal behavior the student is to demonstrate, the conditions under which the behavior should occur, and the criteria for acceptable performance (Mager, 1962). Table 4–4 contains examples of acceptable and unacceptable terminal instructional objectives.

Maheady, Harper, Mallette, and Sacca (1989) analyzed the IEP objectives of students who exhibit social behavior problems. They determined that the objectives for these students, who were certified as having EBD, reflected a preponderance of academic targets and few social behavioral objectives. The written social objectives tended to target behaviors related to the completion of academic tasks, such as staying on task, completing work, and turning in assignments on time. It has been our experience that many written objectives for social behaviors are inappropriate not because the teacher failed to specify the behavior in observable and measurable terms but for the following reasons. First, the conditions or criteria for the objective sometimes are meaningless (e.g., "90% of the time" suggests that the teacher will be observing the student constantly). Second, objectives often are not matched to the behavior that is desired (e.g., "Sandra will demonstrate that she understands the classroom rules by coming to class on time").

TABLE 4–4 Acceptable and Unacceptable Instructional Objectives

Instructional Objectives	Acceptable?	Reason (if unacceptable)
1. Arnold will behave in gym class.	No	Behavior and criteria not specified
2. Given a 45-minute study hall, Sally will remain on task 90% of the time.	No	On-task behavior not specified; impossible to assess "90% of the time"
3. Yen-Su will interact with her peers with no hitting, kicking, biting, pushing, or verbal taunting for 30-minute lunch periods for 5 consecutive days.	Yes	
4. Washington will be punctual in arriving at school for 15 consecutive days.	No	"Punctual" not defined; conditions not specified
5. When given a task request. Tanya will begin the task within 10 seconds without stating "I can't."	Yes	
6. Karen will refrain from biting or scratching herself for any given 1-hour period.	No	Conditions not specified (i.e., instruction, prompts, or supervision to be provided during the hour)
7. Yolonda will not take any drugs during school for 20 consecutive days.	No	Impossible to monitor drug intake accurately
8. When approached by a peer, Philip will emit an appropriate greeting response (make eye contact, smile, and say "hello") on 10 of 10 trials.	Yes	

Finally, objectives may not be matched to the intervention strategy used (e.g., "Given immediate positive consequences for completing her math assignments, Renee will remain on task for 80% of five consecutive math periods"). Less frequently, objectives are beyond the student's ability to reach or expect performance well above that of typical peers (e.g., "Linda will be on task 100% of the period"). With practice and feedback, you will become proficient at writing good instructional objectives for social skills.

> See if you can improve the objectives just presented so they are more appropriate.

Long-term behavioral objectives indicate relatively long-range desired outcomes of intervention strategies. The student may have none or some of the skills she needs to perform the desired behavior. Once you have written the objective, it is important to know whether she can perform all necessary components of the terminal behavior because this information will affect the strategies you will use to get her there. The best way to assess the skills pupils need in order to perform a particular task (or to engage in a desired social behavior) is to observe their attempts to perform it. This establishes a starting point. Next you should conduct a **task analysis.** Essentially, task analysis is a fine-grained assessment of a task; that is, the task is broken down into sequential component steps. The number of components depends on the complexity of the task and the entry skills of the pupil (the skills the student brings to the task). A task analysis can be done by performing the task oneself, by observing someone who is proficient do it, or by outlining a logical sequence of steps (Wolery, Ault, & Doyle, 1992).

Analyzing academic or motor tasks is relatively simple. For example, most teachers are familiar with the component steps involved in solving two-place addition problems. Social skills are more difficult to analyze by task, however. One reason is that many social behaviors are performed without obvious, discrete steps. Another reason is that most persons are not accustomed to analyzing social skills systematically. Box 4-2 suggests three strategies for organizing a task sequence.

Once you have constructed a task sequence, assess the pupil with respect to the component steps. The evaluation will help you determine where to begin instruction and how to revise your sequence if needed. The steps included in your program can be written as instructional objectives and matched to teaching methods and materials. This, then, constitutes your intervention plan for a target behavior. Describe it in general terms on the student's IEP and develop it more specifically in your weekly and daily lesson plans. Your plan is not inflexible; it should be adjusted and revised as indicated by your continued assessment of the student's progress. Chapter 6 describes this phase of monitoring progress.

Figure 4-8 illustrates the process of sequencing short-term objectives to approximate a replacement

BOX 4-2 Using One or More Strategies to Organize Task Steps

1. A change in response criterion (e.g., a systematic increase in length of time engaged in desired play behavior across days or trials)
2. A progression through a sequence of discrete skills (e.g., learning social greeting responses)
3. A change in **response topography** (e.g., controlling one's temper by substituting verbal for physical reactions, such as counting to 10 silently)

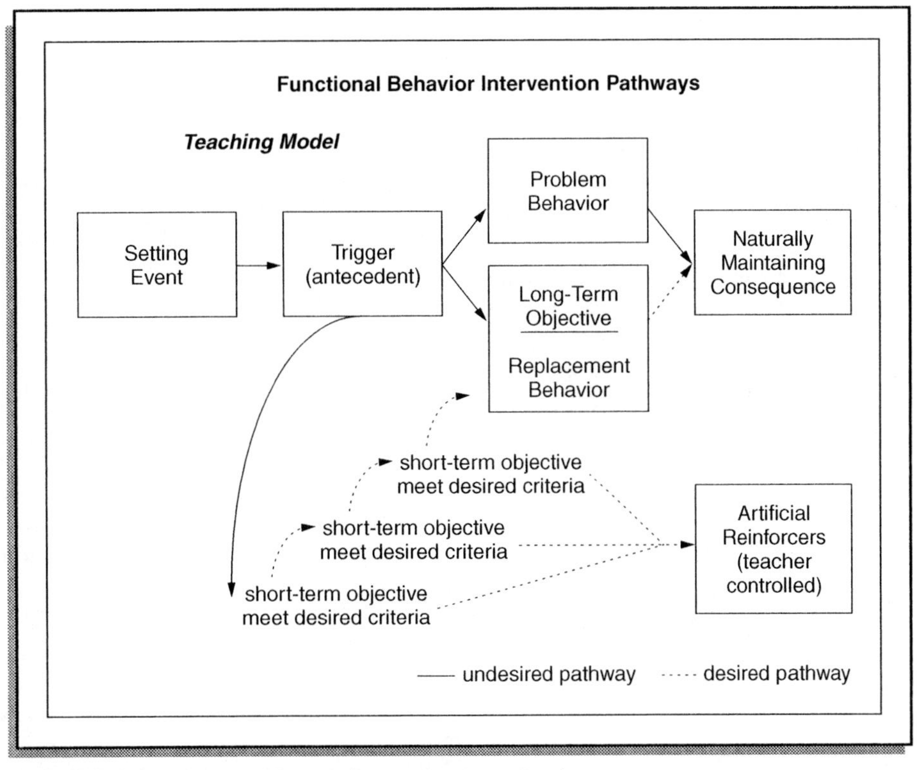

FIGURE 4–8 Teaching Through Successive Approximations
Source: *Copyright 1997 by T. M. Scott. Used with permission.*

behavior specified in a long-term objective. Note that each occurrence of short-term approximations to the replacement behavior should be followed by reinforcing consequences. Because it often is not possible to arrange for these approximations to result in the outcome (function) produced by the target behavior (e.g., avoidance of difficult or undesired tasks), it may be necessary to use artificial reinforcers that are controlled by the teacher (e.g., points that can be exchanged for free time). Once the replacement behavior (e.g., asking for assistance with difficult tasks) has become established, the natural consequence (avoidance of difficult work) will be effective (e.g., the student uses the replacement behavior successfully to get assistance, thereby reducing task difficulty). For example, an early short-term objective for Lewis may be "Given a reminder at the beginning of social studies class to raise his hand before he speaks, Lewis will raise his hand and wait to be called on before speaking on 50% of opportunities for 2 consecutive days." Each time he remembers to raise his hand, he earns a point. When he raises his hand at least half the opportunities, he can cash in his points for time with the teacher at the end of class. Each time he meets the criterion, the standard is increased slightly. His teacher also praises his hand raising and tries to respond to this behavior immediately and frequently. Ultimately, the function served by the target behavior (getting the teacher's attention) is better served by the replacement behavior, and the artificial consequence can be faded out. A blank functional behavioral intervention pathway is located on the Companion Website.

Download a copy and practice task-analyzing long-term objectives for replacement behaviors into short-term approximations.

Additional training in developing, implementing, and evaluating BIPs is available, again in several different formats (e.g., Gable, Quinn, Rutherford, Howell, & Hoffman, 2000; Positive Behavioral Support Project, 1999; Scott, Liaupsin, & Nelson, 2001). You also may consult the Websites for the Florida and Virginia departments of education or the Center for Effective Collaboration and Practice to obtain copies of their behavior intervention planning materials. A list of resources is compiled on the Companion Website.

SUMMARY

- Conducting behavioral assessments involves gathering data from multiple sources of information and assessment strategies.
- Functional behavioral assessment is a specific example of behavioral assessment. The outcome of an FBA is a hypothesis regarding the function, or purpose, of the target behavior, that is, how it works for the student.
- All behavior, whether desired or undesired by others, serves one of two functions: to gain access to something desired or to escape or avoid something aversive.
- Data gathered from the FBA process guide the development, implementation, and evaluation of a BIP, which includes strategies for teaching and supporting desired replacement behaviors as well as for preventing and responding to instances of targeted undesired behavior.
- The focus of assessment-based intervention planning is on the student's success. The BIP emphasizes strategies that strengthen replacement behaviors while seeking to prevent the occurrence of target behaviors, thereby minimizing the use of punishment.
- This is an important process that should be directed by a Behavior Support Team that includes persons with expertise in designing and evaluating behavioral interventions.
- Long-term and intermediate behavioral objectives are used to evaluate the student's progress.

DISCUSSION/APPLICATION IDEAS

1. A student with a disability has demonstrated a pattern of aggressive behavior. What steps should the IEP team take before considering placement in an interim alternative educational setting?
2. For the situation described in question 1, indicate several alternate instruments and procedures you could use to conduct an FBA. What questions would you attempt to answer through this process?
3. What are the components of a BIP? How should it be developed, implemented, and evaluated?
4. Assuming that the function of a student's physical aggression is to obtain items from peers, what are some replacement behaviors that the student can use to achieve this goal more appropriately?
5. Using the format presented in Figure 4-8, transcribe the information presented in the case study of Rodney into the appropriate boxes (a blank copy can be downloaded from the Companion Website). Then task-analyze the long-term objective into three to five short-term objectives. Don't forget to include criteria for each step and to indicate the reinforcement to be provided for meeting each. When you are finished, compare your work with the completed pathway on the Website.

NOTES

1. The 2004 reauthorization of IDEA states that a student with a disability must remain in her current educational

placement until proceedings relative to disciplinary action are completed, except under specific circumstances. However, the law also permits school personnel to consider any unique circumstances on a case-by-case basis when determining whether to order a change in placement for a student with a disability (§ 615[j], [k]). Obviously, this wording leaves room for a great deal of interpretation. The administrative regulations for IDEA 2004 hopefully will clear up this ambiguity.

REFERENCES

Conroy, M. A., & Fox, J. J. (1994). Setting events and challenging behaviors in the classroom: Incorporating contextual factors into effective intervention plans. *Preventing School Failure, 38*(3), 29–34.

Crone, D. A., & Horner, R. H. (2003). *Building positive behavior support systems in schools: Functional behavioral assessment.* New York: Guilford.

Deno, S., & Mirkin, P. (1978). *Data-based program modification.* Reston, VA: Council for Exceptional Children.

Durand, V. M., & Crimmins, D. B. (1992). *The motivation assessment scale.* Topeka, KS: Monaco.

Fox, J., & Gable, R. A. (2004). Functional behavioral assessment. In R. B. Rutherford, M. M. Quinn, & S. R. Mathur (Eds.), *Handbook of research in emotional and behavioral disorders* (pp. 143–162). New York: Guilford.

Gable, R. A., Quinn, M. M., Rutherford, R. B., Howell, K. W., & Hoffman, C. C. (1998, May). *Addressing student problem behavior—Part II: Conducting a functional behavioral assessment.* Washington, DC: Center for Effective Collaboration and Practice.

Gable, R. A., Quinn, M. M., Rutherford, R. B., Howell, K. W., & Hoffman, C. C. (2000, June). *Addressing student problem behavior—Part III: Creating positive behavioral intervention plans and supports.* Washington, DC: Center for Effective Collaboration and Practice.

Gresham, F. M. (2003). Establishing the technical adequacy of functional behavioral assessment: Conceptual and measurement challenges. *Behavioral Disorders, 28,* 282–298.

Hops, H., & Greenwood, C. R. (1981). Social skills deficits. In E. J. Mash & L. G. Terdal (Eds.), *Behavioral assessment of childhood disorders* (pp. 347–396). New York: Guilford.

Hops, H., & Lewin, L. (1984). Peer sociometric forms. In T. H. Ollendick & M. Hersen (Eds.), *Child behavioral assessment: Principles and procedures* (pp. 124–147). New York: Pergamon.

Howell, K. W., Fox, S. L., & Morehead, M. K. (1993). *Curriculum-based evaluation: Teaching and decision making* (2nd ed.). Pacific Grove, CA: Brooks/Cole.

Kern, L., Childs, K. E., Dunlap, G., Clarke, S., & Falk, G. D. (1994). Using assessment-based curricular intervention to improve the classroom behavior of a student with emotional and behavioral challenges. *Journal of Applied Behavior Analysis, 27,* 7–19.

Lewis, T., Scott, T., & Sugai, G. (1994). The problem behavior questionnaire: A teacher based instrument to develop functional hypotheses of problem behavior in general education classrooms. *Diagnostique, 19*(2–3), 59–78.

Lewis, T. J., & Sugai, G. (1996). Functional assessment of problem behavior: A pilot investigation of the comparative and interactive effects of teacher and peer social attention on students in general education settings. *School Psychology Quarterly, 11,* 1–19.

Liaupsin, C. J., Scott, T. M., & Nelson, C. M. (2001). *Functional behavioral assessment: An interactive training module* [CD-ROM]. Longmont, CO: Sopris West.

Mager, R. F. (1962). *Preparing instructional objectives.* Palo Alto, CA: Fearon Press.

Maheady, L., Harper, G. F., Mallette, B., & Sacca, M. K. (1989, September). *Opportunity to learn prosocial behavior: Its potential role in the assessment and instruction of behavior disordered students.* Paper presented at the CEC/CCBD Topical Conference on Behaviorally Disordered Youth, Charlotte, NC.

McIntyre, T. (1996). Guidelines for providing appropriate services to culturally diverse students with emotional and behavioral disorders. *Behavioral Disorders, 21,* 137–144.

Nelson, J. R., Roberts, M., & Smith, D. (1999). *Conducting functional behavioral assessments: A practical guide.* Longmont, CO: Sopris West.

O'Neill, R. E., Horner, R. H., Albin, R. W., Storey, K., & Sprague, J. R. (1997). *Functional assessment and program development for problem behavior: A practical assessment handbook* (2nd ed.). Pacific Grove, CA: Brooks/Cole.

Polsgrove, L. (1987). Assessment of children's social and behavioral problems. In W. H. Berdine & S. A. Meyer (Eds.), *Assessment in special education* (pp. 141-180). Boston: Little, Brown.

Positive Behavioral Support Project. (1999, November). *Facilitator's guide: Positive behavioral support.* Tallahassee: Florida Department of Education.

Reid, R., & Nelson, J. R. (2002). The utility, acceptability, and practicality of functional behavioral assessment for students with high-incidence problem behaviors. *Remedial and Special Education, 23*(1), 15-23.

Sasso, G. M., Conroy, M. A., Stichter, J. P., & Fox, J. J. (2001). Slowing down the bandwagon: The misapplication of functional assessment for students with emotional and behavioral disorders. *Behavioral Disorders, 26,* 282-296.

Scott, T. M., Bucalos, A., Nelson, C. M., Liaupsin, C., Jolivette, K., & Deshea, L. (2004). Using functional assessment in general education settings: Making a case for effectiveness and efficiency. *Behavioral Disorders, 29,* 189-201.

Scott, T. M., Liaupsin, C. J., & Nelson, C. M. (2001). *Behavior interventions planning: A CD training module.* Longmont, CO: Sopris West.

Scott, T. M., & Nelson, C. M. (1999). Using functional behavioral assessment to develop effective intervention plans: Practical classroom applications. *Journal of Positive Behavioral Interventions, 1,* 242-251.

Shores, R. E., Wehby, J. H., & Jack, S. L. (1999). Analyzing behavior in classrooms. In A. C. Repp & R. H. Horner (Eds.), *Functional analysis of problem behavior: From effective assessment to effective support* (pp. 219-237). Baltimore: Paul H. Brookes.

Steege, M. W., & Northup, J. (1998). Functional analysis of problem behavior: A practical approach for school psychologists. *Proven Practice, 1*(1), 4-11.

Sugai, G. (1995, June). *Proactive classroom management.* Workshop presented at the Springfield School Improvement Conference, Springfield, OR.

Touchette, P. E., MacDonald, R. F., & Langer, S. N. (1985). A scatter plot for identifying stimulus control of problem behavior. *Journal of Applied Behavior Analysis, 18,* 343-351.

Walker, H. M. (1983). *Walker problem behavior identification checklist.* Los Angeles: Western Psychological Services.

Walker, H. M. (1986). The AIMS (Assessments for Integration into Mainstream Settings) assessment system: Rationale, instruments, procedures, and outcomes. *Journal of Clinical Child Psychology, 15*(1), 55-63.

Walker, H. M., Block-Pedego, A., Todis, B., & Severson, H. (1991). *The school archival records search.* Longmont, CO: Sopris West.

Walker, H. M., & Rankin, R. (1980). *The SBS inventory of teacher social behavior standards and expectations.* Eugene: University of Oregon, SBS Project.

Walker, H. M., & Severson, H. (1990). *Systematic screening for behavioral disorders.* Longmont, CO: Sopris West.

Walker, H. M., Severson, H., & Haring, N. (1986). *Standardized screening and identification of behavior disordered pupils in the elementary age range: Rationale, procedures and guidelines.* Eugene: University of Oregon.

Wehby, J. H. (1994). Issues in the assessment of aggressive behavior. *Preventing School Failure, 38*(3), 24-28.

Witt, J. C., Daly, E. J., & Noell, G. H. (2000). *Functional assessments: A step-by-step guide to solving academic and behavior problems.* Longmont, CO: Sopris West.

Wolery, M., Ault, M. J., & Doyle, P. M. (1992). *Teaching students with moderate and severe disabilities: Use of response prompting strategies.* White Plains, NY: Longman.

Wolf, M. M. (1978). Social validity: The case for subjective measurement or how applied behavior analysis is finding its heart. *Journal of Applied Behavior Analysis, 11,* 203-214.

CHAPTER 5 MONITORING STUDENT PROGRESS

OUTLINE

Introduction
Overview of Classroom Measurement
Measuring Student Progress

OBJECTIVES

After completing this chapter, you should be able to

- Select alternate ways to measure targeted behaviors that take into consideration the characteristics of the behavior, the setting, constraints on data collection, and the person collecting the data.
- Explain and illustrate the following measurement strategies so that a parent or paraprofessional could use them: permanent product recording, event recording, trials-to-criterion recording, duration and response latency recording, interval recording, and time sampling.
- Design an appropriate recording strategy for two or more target behaviors or for monitoring multiple students who are exhibiting similar behaviors.
- Given event or interval data collected simultaneously by two observers, select the appropriate formula for calculating interobserver agreement and calculate interobserver agreement correctly.

KEY TERMS (refer to the Glossary on the Companion Website for definitions)

continuous behavior
curriculum-based measurement
data decision rules
dependent measures
discrete behavior
discrete learning trials
distributed trials
duration recording
formative evaluation
frequency recording
interobserver agreement
interval recording
massed trials
measurement probes
momentary time sampling
permanent products
portfolios
rate per minute
response latency recording
summative evaluation
time sampling

As Reschly, Kicklighter, and McGee (1988) point out, there are three educative purposes for conducting assessments of student performance: (a) to identify those students who are eligible for services, (b) as a basis for intervention planning, and (c) to evaluate program effectiveness. In previous chapters, we discussed assessment strategies and procedures that guide screening, identification, and intervention planning. If you follow the assessment sequence that we have been describing, you should be able to determine which students are in need of interventions that address their academic and social behavior and which behaviors you are going to target for specific interventions. You also should know how to develop an assessment-based behavior intervention plan. This chapter and the one that follows address the important area of assessment (or data collection) for the purpose of program evaluation. In this chapter, you will learn strategies and techniques for monitoring the progress of students for whom you have developed intervention plans that address either academic or social behaviors. Precise and systematic monitoring of student progress provides data on which to base decisions regarding instructional and behavior management interventions. In Chapter 6, we explain various formats for the visual display of data that facilitate clear and accurate analysis of student performance. Chapter 6 also describes strategies for evaluating interventions on the basis of your measures of student performance.

COME INTO MY CLASSROOM: A CASE STUDY

HOW TO MONITOR THE RATE OF STUDENT CORRECT ACADEMIC RESPONDING

by Phillip L. Gunter and Marti L. Venn

Ms. Christle was teaching math to a group of students in a third-grade classroom. The group was comprised primarily of students without disabilities; however, some students with emotional and behavioral disorders (EBD) were in the group. Ms. Christle wanted to be sure that she was instructing her students effectively since her training program had not prepared her to teach students with EBD. However, because she was also a first-year teacher, she seemed to have little time for self-reflection of her instruction, and she knew that her principal would observe her teaching only twice that year.

She was reading a copy of *Beyond Behavior* (Vol. 9, No. 4) in the faculty lounge. This is a professional magazine with information for those teaching students with behavior disorders. She found an article by Gunter, Hummel, and Venn (1998) that provided a protocol for determining whether classroom instruction was effective based on the number of correct responses students in the classroom gave (see Figure 5-1). One of the primary aspects of the use of this protocol was its simplicity. Therefore, she decided that she would attempt to use the protocol to determine if her classroom instruction was effective.

To do this, Ms. Christle placed a video camera at the back of her room during instruction of the math class and videotaped her instruction. She waited until the end of the school day to review the recorded lesson. She rewound the tape to the first part of the class period in which new information was presented. She used the self-evaluation protocol from the Gunter et al. article and her digital watch. When she began reviewing the tape, she entered the time in

Teacher Ms. Smith Observer Ms Smith

Date 10/30/00 Starting time 10:00:00 Ending time 10:19:30

Length of observation in minutes 19 and seconds 30

X60

1140 plus 30 = 1170 seconds

/60

= 19.5 time

Frequency of Correct Responses

𝍸 𝍸 𝍸 𝍸 𝍸 𝍸 𝍸 𝍸 𝍸
𝍸 𝍸 𝍸 𝍸 𝍸 ///

Frequency of correct responses 73

Divided by

Time 19.5

= Rate of correct responding 3.74

For instruction of new material, the rate of correct responses should be at least 3 per minute.
For drill and practice instruction, the rate of correct responses should be at least 8 per minute.

FIGURE 5–1 Calculating the Rate of Correct Responding

hours, minutes, and seconds (10:00:00) on the protocol sheet for starting time, and when she came to the end of the period in which she provided instruction on new information, she entered the time again in hours, minutes, and seconds (10:19:30) in the space for ending time. While watching the lesson for the total time of 19 minutes and 30 seconds, Ms. Christle recorded the number of correct responses that were given by each student she called on or the correct response of the group if she had asked for all the students to respond simultaneously. She used her best teacher intuition for group responses to determine if at least 80% of the students responded correctly.

To record the correct responses, Ms. Christle simply made a tally mark in the box on the form for frequency of correct responses. Examples of correct responses included Jimmy's response of "6" when asked, "What is 2 times 3?" Additionally, a correct response was marked when 80% of the class responded, "In the ones column." When asked, "Where do we put the 2 from the number 12 when we multiply 2 times 6?" She did not mark a correct response when Frank answered "sum" when asked, "What is the term used to define the answer of multiplying two numbers?" since "product" would have been the correct answer. During the 19 minutes and 30 seconds, she recorded 73 correct responses made by students in the classroom during math instruction.

To make the calculations on the protocol, Ms. Christle first subtracted the starting time from the ending time of the observation and entered 19 minutes and 30 seconds in the spaces for length of observation. The 19 minutes were multiplied by 60, and that product (1,140) was added to the remaining seconds (30) of the observation. The total seconds (1,170) were then divided by 60 to result in a whole number and a decimal (19.5 minutes). She then counted the number of tally marks she made (73) and divided that number by the time (19.5). The result is the rate of correct responses per minute (3.74).

Next, Ms. Christle compared the rate of correct responses she observed to that rate recommended in the effective instruction literature as presented on the bottom of the protocol. She noted that the rate of correct responses she observed (3.74) was greater than the minimum number recommended (3) for instruction of new material to be effective (Gunter & Denny, 1998).

The entire process took less than an hour for Ms. Christle to complete, and she had a description of her academic instruction that had at least some foundation in empirically validated procedures. Had Ms. Christle found that the level of correct responses from students was lower than that recommended, she could use a different protocol like the one developed by Gunter and Reed (1997) to help determine the cause for student failure to reach the number of correct responses required for instruction to be effective. This more elaborate self-evaluation procedure requires the observation of several teacher and student behaviors but allows the development of a functional behavioral hypothesis for both academic and social behaviors of students.

For drill and practice independent work, the process might be modified to determine the effectiveness of the instructional session. The same protocol can be used to evaluate only correct academic responding, but instead of observing videotaped instruction, the teacher can simply count the number of problems or tasks completed correctly on permanent product samples and divide the number correct by the amount of time needed to complete the work. In this aspect of academic instruction, the rate of correct responses expected would be at least 8 per minute (Gunter & Denny, 1998).

INTRODUCTION

In the previous case study, Drs. Gunter, Callicott, Denny, and Gerber (2003) wryly describe the attitude of many educators toward this component of assessment: "If we were to ask most teachers about data collection, a grimace would be a predictable response" (p. 4). However, they also observe that the National Council for Accreditation of Teacher Education (NCATE, 2000) has articulated the expectation that teachers are to assess and analyze student learning, make appropriate adjustments to instruction, monitor student learning, and have a positive effect on the learning of all students. In the previous case study, Drs. Gunter and Venn described how a teacher used data she collected on students' rates of correct academic responding to evaluate the effectiveness of her instruction.

In this chapter, we provide an overview of measurement procedures, including common objections to student performance measurement, frequently asked questions about monitoring student performance, and the use of measurement in individualized education plans (IEPs). Next, we present measurement considerations, followed by step-by-step procedures for data collection, and/or assessing the accuracy of behavioral measurement. A number of alternate strategies are described and illustrated.

OVERVIEW OF CLASSROOM MEASUREMENT

Reflecting on the steps that Ms. Christle went through to evaluate the effectiveness of her reading instruction, do you find yourself wondering whether it is worth this much effort? We think it is. Evaluating academic instruction and behavior intervention programs involves many complex decisions. Should you continue with a strategy, discard it, or modify it? Is the pupil ready to move on to more complex skills or to less restrictive settings, or does he need more training at his current skill level and in the present setting? To make good decisions, you must have useful information. In behavior change programs involving powerful methods that can be misapplied, student progress must not be evaluated subjectively or casually. As White (1986) explained, "To be responsive to the pupil's needs the teacher must be a student of the pupil's behavior, carefully analyzing how that behavior changes from day to day and adjusting the instructional plan as necessary to facilitate continued learning" (p. 522). Careful monitoring is a critical element of your role as an intervention agent.

To be an effective teacher—that is, to ensure that your students are progressing as rapidly as their capacities and present educational technology allow—you need a system for monitoring their progress on a frequent and regular basis. The process of ongoing assessment with frequent (at least weekly) and repeated measurement of student performance is **formative evaluation**, which is distinct from **summative evaluation**, which occurs at static points in time (Tawney & Gast, 1984). Because your daily planning depends on the information you obtain from such monitoring, data collection is, in effect, a matter of conducting ongoing assessments of students throughout the school year. The data you obtain serve as a basis for evaluating pupil growth, for locating flaws or deficiencies in your instructional programs or behavior intervention plans (BIPS), and for evaluating the effects of program modifications.

Research has demonstrated that pupil performance is enhanced when teachers use formative evaluation (Fuchs & Fuchs, 1986). When teachers employ **data decision rules** (teacher-determined guidelines for responding to patterns in student performance) as a basis for deciding when an educational program should be changed, student performance tends to improve even more. Finally, when data are graphed instead of simply being recorded, even greater progress has been noted in desired student outcomes (Fuchs & Fuchs, 1986). Data decision rules based on visual analyses of graphed data facilitate the efficient and effective evaluation of instructional and behavior management programs. These features of program evaluation are described in the next chapter.

> Why would it not be advisable for Ms. Christle to use standardized achievement test scores as a standard for determining whether students were making adequate progress under her reading instruction?

Some educators may be able to function adequately without using systematic procedures such as those described in this text. Continuous monitoring and evaluation of student progress is one of the most time consuming of these procedures. Because most public school and educational agencies do not require teachers to monitor student progress continuously, it is the first set of skills lost from a beginning teacher's repertoire (Gunter et al., 2003). Nevertheless, effective teachers, such as Ms. Christle in the preceding case study, constantly monitor, evaluate, and revise their instructional programs and intervention plans. Consequently, they are more sensitive to the instructional needs of their pupils, and they are accountable to students, supervisors, and parents for the methods they use. If you want to be an effective teacher, you must expect to spend much time and effort collecting student performance data and planning and implementing systematic interventions. The result will be greater pride in your own skill as a teacher, the recognition of fellow professionals, and more rapid progress by your students. Again, Fuchs and

Fuchs (1986) found that students whose programs are systematically monitored and adjusted through ongoing data-based evaluation procedures make greater gains than students whose programs are not systematically monitored or formatively evaluated.

Teacher Objections to Systematic Measurement of Student Progress

Educators and supervisors lament the tendency of classroom teachers to avoid data collection despite the emphasis placed on this function in preservice training. The most common objections are presented next, and strategies for addressing these concerns are mentioned. You will find examples of how these strategies may be applied later in this chapter.

1. "I don't have enough time to monitor their behavior—I have to teach." Walton (1985) surveyed general and special education teachers regarding their data collection practices. Approximately 76% reported not having enough time during the day to carry out data collection. This objection suggests a basic misunderstanding of the role of data collection. Frequently, it is seen as impractical or as a useless activity required by an administrator or bureaucrat. We understand why many teachers hold this attitude. School districts require teachers to gather and report such data as daily attendance, which students will be eating the school's hot lunch, and who will be taking the early (or late) bus home, in addition to periodic surveys, questionnaires, and lists. Because these data have little application to what the teacher does, it is no wonder that practitioners develop an aversion to data collection in general.

Still, teachers are notorious data collectors. Their grade books are full of check marks showing assignments turned in, scores on daily or weekly tests, counts of disciplinary actions, and so forth. Unfortunately, these data are used infrequently as a basis for evaluating pupils or programs. One solution to the problem of time constraints on data collection is to make sure the data you keep are data you will use. This *does not* include IQ scores, test profiles, and the like. It *does* include daily reading or math performance rates, spelling test scores, frequencies of social behaviors targeted for intervention, number of disciplinary actions, and student progress toward individual behavioral objectives. As a rule of thumb, you should carefully decide what to measure, then measure it as precisely as you can.

Another solution is to reduce the amount of time spent on data collection. Gunter et al. (2003) suggest three ways to simplify data collection: (a) reduce the number of variables on which to gather data, (b) reduce the amount of time required for data collection, and (c) teach students to self-record and graph data on their own performance.

2. "Measuring behavior doesn't help me teach." Nearly 45% of teachers surveyed by Walton (1985) reported that data collection procedures were of little help or only somewhat helpful to their teaching responsibilities. This objection also suggests that the teacher is not gathering useful data, that is, data that can be used to make educational decisions and on which to base program adjustments. In response to this objection, we offer this guideline: if you do not use the data frequently, do not collect it. (Note: This guideline does not apply to data you are required to collect by your agency.) However, failure to gather data you should use is inexcusable. See what James M. Kauffman has to say about the role of data collection in teaching in Box 5-1.

If your data are not useful to you, perhaps you need to select measures that are more sensitive to what you are trying to accomplish. A common mistake is to measure the results of behavior instead of the behavior itself. For example, if you are trying to increase a pupil's use of specific social skills, do not record the number of points he earns for appropriate social behaviors each day. Instead, directly record the frequency with which these skills are exhibited.

Systematic data collection can help you accomplish many things, including (a) making instructional

BOX 5–1 The Importance of Measuring Student Progress

The teaching profession is dedicated to the task of altering student behavior—changing it demonstrably for the better. What can one say, then, of educational practice that does not include reliable measurement of the behavior change induced by the teacher's methodology? *It is indefensible.* (Kauffman, 2001, p. 532)

decisions; (b) providing feedback for the student, yourself, and others regarding the effectiveness of instructional and behavior intervention programs; (c) ensuring accountability; (d) giving you a common basis for discussion among parents, teachers, other professionals, and students; (e) giving support and reinforcement to parents, teachers, and students; and (f) increasing student performance (Cooke, Heward, Test, Spooner, & Courson, 1991; Fuchs & Fuchs, 1986; Lund, Schnaps, & Bijou, 1983). We hope you will appreciate the value of data collection by the time you complete this text.

3. "I don't get any support or reinforcement for monitoring student progress." Obviously, if teachers don't gather data, they shouldn't expect to be reinforced for completing this task! However, many teachers enter their profession with an earnest desire to use systematic teaching and measurement procedures, and a year later their teaching is guided by guesses and hunches. Earlier we noted that the expectation has been stated that educators assess and analyze student learning and modify their instruction so that their students all make positive gains (NCATE, 2000). In addition, state and federal legislation (e.g., the No Child Left Behind Act) now require that schools document student learning through standardized testing. However, there are no explicit reinforcement contingencies for data-based instruction in most schools. Therefore, to persevere at such a complex and sometimes difficult task, you will need to "recruit" reinforcement (Stokes & Baer, 1977). One way is to share your data with those to whom you report student progress. Parents are likely to be more receptive to graphs or charts detailing their child's progress in, for example, learning a functional speaking vocabulary than to a letter grade in language arts. Administrators too can learn to view your performance in the school by progress made toward individual student objectives. So share your student data with everyone with whom you communicate. Show them what you are trying to do and how you are trying to measure and evaluate progress. Solicit their assistance in solving your measurement problems. In addition to getting valuable feedback and support, you are more likely to gain other teachers' cooperation with data collection activities such as beginning to record student performances in their own classrooms.

Frequently Asked Questions About Monitoring Student Behavior

In addition to recruiting reinforcement for data-based interventions from others, you also must minimize the cost to yourself in terms of time and effort. Here are some responses to teachers' questions that may help make data collection more relevant and less aversive.

1. "Do I need to monitor everything?" Without question, the most important behavior to monitor is student performance in academic subjects. In previous chapters, we stressed not only that educators are increasingly being held accountable for student learning but also that effective instruction is associated with reductions in classroom behavior problems. While standardized achievement test scores are required by law, these summative evaluation data are not useful for developing more effective interventions or for evaluating the effectiveness of a specific intervention (Deno, 2000). Thus, you should measure students' performance in the curriculum on a frequent and regular basis and evaluate this against the goals and objectives of the curriculum and student IEPs (i.e., **curriculum-based measurement**; Hosp & Hosp, 2003). In addition, periodic monitoring of students' rate of correct academic responding and opportunities to respond are good ways to keep track of your teaching effectiveness (Gunter & Denny, 2004; Sutherland & Morgan, 2003).

You also should monitor pupils' social behaviors that are identified in their IEPs, accommodation plans, or BIPs. Keep in mind that you can measure the target behavior or, if the goal is to reduce it, a replacement behavior. We have found that even young students can learn to record and graph their own behavior. If you periodically record the same behavior independently and reinforce students for being accurate, they will perform accordingly.

As students make progress toward academic and behavioral goals, you may shift to intermittent recording strategies. For example, once an IEP goal has been reached for a targeted behavior, you may conduct periodic **measurement probes** (see page 145) instead of daily recording to verify that the goal is being maintained.

If you follow the rule of collecting only those data you can use in decision making, you also may find that you can consolidate some data. For example, if you are concerned with general classroom disruptions and don't need to respond differently to specific behaviors in this category, such as out-of-seat or talking out, count the number of disruptions rather than the number of times out-of-seat and the number of talk-outs.

2. "What is most important for me to measure?" Sometimes teachers waste a lot of time and energy collecting data on nonessential behaviors. The points we mentioned previously will also help you avoid this pitfall. If you focus on identified objectives and target behaviors, if you consolidate measures of behaviors, and if you gather only those data to which you will respond, you should be able to cut down on this problem significantly. It does not hurt to ask, "Do I use this?" every time you review data sheets and summaries. Our emphasis on using data to make frequent program adjustments applies to your monitoring procedures as well. Remember that your monitoring strategy is also part of the instructional or intervention plan.

3. "Isn't it simpler to measure the results of students' behavior?" With regard to behaviors that result in an academic product, the answer to this question is definitely yes. However, while academic performances result in a permanent product that is a reasonably sensitive measure of the behaviors that produced it, many other behaviors leave no such record. For example, many persons monitor their eating by measuring their weight. They are dismayed if decreases in eating are not accompanied by immediate reductions in their weight. This may occur because weight is also affected by other factors, such as fluid retention or muscle mass. Likewise, behavioral indexes such as teacher rating or point earnings are affected by variables other than the pupil's behavior (e.g., the teacher's mood) and therefore are less accurate measures of actual behavior. These data are convenient, and they may give a rough estimate of student progress, but they do not provide a sufficient basis for making specific educational decisions. Further, the time and effort used in obtaining and summarizing these data can be spent more productively in recording more sensitive measures.

Therefore, instead of counting the number of points earned, it is preferable to count the behaviors that earn points (e.g., assignments completed, directions followed). Finally, if your students are interested in such information as their daily point earnings, teach *them* to record and chart these data. Indirect measures such as rating scale scores and point earnings may help an IEP or Behavior Support Team gain a more complete perspective on a student's current status and rate of progress. When these are the *only* measures of performance, however, they are not sufficient. Therefore, if you do use indirect measures of social behaviors, get data from several sources and perspectives. Always remember to verify the accuracy of the impressions you are getting by comparing this information with data obtained from direct observation and measurement.

Teachers are not always present to observe and record student behavior when it occurs. Further, some behaviors (e.g., stealing, verbal threats) are less frequent when an authority figure is around. However, sometimes these behaviors do have measurable effects on the environment. For example, the number of items stolen, papers torn, marks made on furniture, or objects damaged represent **permanent products** that can be counted with reasonable accuracy. These results of behavior are not based on teachers' subjective evaluations of pupils' responses, so they are more reliable indicators of the behaviors that produced them.

The increased use of alternative assessment procedures, particularly student **portfolios,** has led many practitioners to incorporate data from such procedures as rating scales, informal criterion-referenced assessments, and curriculum-based measurement of progress in social skills curricula. We will describe some of the uses of portfolios in monitoring student progress in a later section.

4. *"How do I use student performance data once I collect it?"* If you follow our suggestions thus far, there is little danger that you will wind up gathering information that you will not use. Still, it is wise to review periodically all student programs with your supervisor or colleagues to ensure that you are gathering important data, that your data collection procedures are appropriate, and that you are making the best use of these data. Other teachers may be interested in informal biweekly group meetings to talk about programs and review data.

A major reason teachers fail to use the data they collect is that the data are not summarized graphically. This process takes time and frequently is put off until it is too dated to be useful. Teachers' grade books or plan books often are full of data regarding academic performances and social behaviors. However, these data typically are not arranged so that they allow clear interpretation of changes in student behavior over time. Graphing or charting organizes these data to show such changes and is critical to making program adjustments based on student performance. More efficient techniques have been devised, some of which combine the functions of data recording and graphing or charting. Alternative graphing and charting formats are presented in the next chapter.

> List some student behaviors you are measuring in the classroom or want to measure. As you read further, identify some recording strategies to use with each behavior.

The following sections present a number of measurement principles and techniques. Because the focus of this text is on students' social behavior (and because recording social behavior presents more challenges than recording academic responses), most of the examples we present are of nonacademic behaviors. As you read, you may find yourself thinking, "I can't do all this!" You will be quite right. Our goal is for you to understand recording principles and procedures well enough to make intelligent compromises about fitting these methods to your teaching situation. For example, if you are a beginning teacher, we suggest that you attempt *some* systematic monitoring of your students' performance (e.g., progress through an academic curriculum, top-priority social behavior targets). As you gain skill and confidence, you can increase the amount and sophistication of your measurement of behavior. Furthermore, it is not necessary to do everything we suggest in order to be an effective teacher. Experienced educators develop their own decision-making strategies. (You will notice that the chapter case studies do not follow all our guidelines regarding data collection.) As you gain more experience, you will develop your own strategies, many of them perhaps less formal than those we describe. Nevertheless, we hope you will strive for the principles presented here and will find our suggestions to be useful in your efforts to be an effective teacher.

MEASURING STUDENT PROGRESS

Progress monitoring involves four basic steps, several of which we already have highlighted: selecting a monitoring format and procedures, recording data, assessing the accuracy of data, and summarizing the data for analysis. In this section, we describe and illustrate procedures for accomplishing the first three of these steps. Strategies for summarizing data are presented in the following chapter on evaluating student performance.

Selecting a Monitoring Format and Procedures

This step includes several components: determining what aspects of student behavior to measure, selecting an appropriate recording procedure, and deciding what data to collect. We describe these separately, but in practice, you probably will evaluate these components simultaneously.

Deciding what to measure requires that you first know what properties or aspects of behavior can be measured. Obviously, human behavior does not have the dimensions of a physical object; therefore, it cannot be measured in terms of height, weight, volume, or mass. However, behavior does have features that can be observed and accurately assessed. The first of these is *frequency* or *rate,* which refers to how often a behavior occurs in a period of time. For example, you can measure the number of times a student hits, asks a question, or raises his hand in an hour. Second, behavior may be described or measured in terms of its *duration:* the length of a verbal interchange, the duration of temper tantrums, and so forth. Third, the *latency,* or lag time between the presentation of a prompt or verbal instruction and the initiation of an appropriate response (i.e., compliance), may be observed. Behavior also may be measured in terms of *intensity,* which includes its frequency and its duration, for example, recording the number and the length of a pupil's temper tantrums. *Locus* refers to the location where a behavior occurs, such as the library, cafeteria, or third period classroom. Finally, behavior sometimes is measured in terms of its *magnitude,* or force, although this is difficult to do objectively without laboratory apparatus. The decision of which of these properties to measure depends on which is best suited to the pupil, the situation, and the changes you want. For example, if your target involves a student's compliance with adult requests, you may consider whether compliance is best characterized in terms of frequency or latency and then whether your goal is to increase rate, decrease latency, or both.

The selection of a monitoring format, therefore, is partly based on the characteristics of the behavior being observed and how you want it to change. If you want to increase the speed of student responding (i.e., fluency), measure rate. If your goal is to reduce the amount of time a student spends on an activity, measure duration. However, another important consideration is convenience. Although you may want to increase the duration of on-task behavior, for example, keeping track of it with a stopwatch is highly inconvenient unless you have nothing else to do. We suggest alternative strategies for such circumstances later.

Thus, you have several decisions to make regarding the choice of the behaviors you will measure and attempt to change. The range of these **dependent measures,** or variables to be monitored, is described in a table that you will find on the Companion Website. Study it carefully to determine which option best suits your purposes and situation.

If you are not accustomed to observing behavior systematically, it is easy to make mistakes that may adversely affect the data you collect. Because unreliable data increase the probability of bad decisions, it is imperative that your procedures be as sensitive and precise as possible. To help you accomplish this goal, we offer the following guidelines.

1. Select a direct and sensitive monitoring format. Consider several factors before deciding on a format: What constraints do the observation setting place on observation and recording? What is it about the behavior observed that you want to change? How do you want the behavior to change? Remember to measure behavior directly (i.e., measure the behavior itself, not the results of the behavior).

Direct measures of behavior are more sensitive to the effects of your instructional programs and BIPs. Therefore, the data are more useful to you in analyzing and "fine-tuning" your intervention. The more experience you acquire with observation and recording techniques, the easier it will become to tailor monitoring formats to the behaviors you want to measure. The major exception to monitoring behavior directly is permanent products. Written responses on worksheets, number of objects stolen, and so forth are indirect measures of the behaviors contributing to an outcome, but they are also more convenient to measure, and unless it is possible for students to cheat on every written assignment or items reported as stolen were simply misplaced, there generally is only one way to produce the outcome that is measured.

2. Observe and record long enough to "capture" the typical rates of the target behavior. Unless the behaviors you want to monitor occur fairly often across all settings and times, you should plan to observe or have others record the events long enough to obtain an adequate sample. This is important particularly with regard to social behaviors that occur only in certain settings (such as the playground) or in the presence of very specific stimuli (such as a particular person). You can use a scatter plot (see Chapter 4) to estimate the rates of behaviors across various times of the day and activities. This assessment will help you identify when and where a target behavior occurs so that you can design your monitoring format accordingly.

Longer observation and recording periods yield more accurate records of behavior and provide a better check of your BIP. In addition, you will be able to check for generalization of behavior changes across settings or time. With **discrete behavior** (which has a definite beginning and ending, does not take place constantly, and is apparent when it occurs, e.g., hand raising and taking things from other students), you should be able to observe and record it several times during the day. However, with more subtle, **continuous behavior** (no definite starting or stopping point between episodes, such as some forms of stereotypic or on-task behavior), you may be able to use one of the internal or time-sampling techniques described later in this chapter that permit you to sample behaviors across the day.

There are no hard-and-fast guidelines for determining the optimal length for observation periods. Generally, you should adjust the interval to the "typical" rate at which the behavior occurs; that is, you should ensure that the data are representative of natural rates of occurrence. If the target behavior is infrequent, longer observation periods are required. However, brief time samples are possible for more frequent behaviors, provided they represent the rate of occurrence accurately. Ask yourself, "Do these data reflect the behavior as I evaluate it?" If the answer is no, adjust your recording period (or reevaluate your subjective assessment of the behavior).

Although daily measurement provides the best basis for making intervention decisions, research supports the conclusion that twice-weekly monitoring of student academic performance is as adequate as daily monitoring in terms of promoting academic achievement (Fuchs, 1986). However, priority social behaviors should be monitored daily during the initial phases of intervention (i.e., when strategies are being tested and revised). Less frequent measurement probes may be taken when students have advanced to maintenance or generalization phases.

3. Observe and record behavior where it occurs. Obviously, measures of behavior will not be valid if the observation periods do not coincide with the times or activities during which the behavior occurs. Thus, if fighting occurs only during lunch or recess, observe in the lunchroom or playground instead of the study hall. In addition, as we stated earlier, if the behavior does not occur in your presence, find someone who is present when it happens and train him to monitor it. Consider asking other school staff to monitor behavior: custodians, cafeteria workers, aides, and so forth. Given proper training and supervision, other students can be reliable observers of behavior.

However, be cautious when using this tactic; peers may have a vested interest in the target student's behavioral performance. Consult the Companion Website to find guidelines for training others to observe behavior systematically and reliably. It is very important that you train observers well if you are going to base decisions on the data they collect.

Unless there are no predictable differences in the level of the behavior across settings or activities, observations and recording should take place in the same setting, activity, or time period each day. Not only will this result in more comparable performance data, but it will also be easier remember to monitor specific performances.

4. Keep observation time relatively constant. If you are maintaining a numerical count of behavior, your data will be affected by the length of time you observe. For example, there is twice as much opportunity to make appropriate verbal comments in 60 minutes as in 30 minutes. If your observation period is not controlled, your data may reflect variations in the opportunity to respond rather than in the response itself. If you are unable to observe for the same amount of time each session or day, use a rate (frequency divided by time) or a percentage-of-time recording procedure (discussed later) to control for these variations. Rate data are particularly useful because they permit comparison of measures taken across different settings or for varying lengths of time.

5. Once a behavior is defined, observe and record only responses meeting that definition. One of us supervised a teacher who was working on a preschool child's self-injurious behavior. The teacher was counting the number of times the child slapped himself in the head or bit his fingers. The teacher reported that intervention was successful, and our observations in the classroom confirmed this. However, we could see very little change in the data. Our questioning revealed that the teacher's definition of self-injurious behavior had gradually shifted from slaps and bites to touches to the face and mouthing of fingers. The solution to this problem is to establish a clear, written definition of the target behavior (see Chapter 4) that includes both instances and noninstances. Thus, self-injurious behavior could be defined as slaps to the face or head and bites to the fingers or hands that result in an audible sound and perhaps skin reddening. Noninstances would include covering the face with the hands, twisting the hair with the fingers, and so forth. The latter would not be counted as instances of self-injurious behavior. The best way to discriminate instances from noninstances when developing behavioral definitions is to observe the child continuously for a period of time, writing down every response as well as antecedents and consequences. As you will recall from Chapter 4, this initial A-B-C assessment will help you not only establish all the forms of the behavior you will be observing but also identify environmental factors that may predict occurrences. It is also desirable to conduct periodic assessments of **interobserver agreement.** These are especially useful if after each session the observers discuss their agreements and disagreements.

Go back to the list you developed of student behaviors you wish to measure. Write down as many examples as you can of what you would consider to be instances and noninstances of these behaviors.

6. Monitor only as many behaviors in as many settings as you can manage. There is little purpose in observing and recording so many behaviors that you have no time left for instruction or you confuse yourself and your students. Likewise, the purpose of monitoring behavior is lost if you have more data than you can act on. One suggestion is that the more severe the pupil's educational problem, the more behaviors should be monitored (Cooper, 1981). Teachers of students with mild disabilities should monitor all responses to direct (planned academic) instruction, whereas teachers of students with severe and profound disabilities should monitor all student responses to planned academic instruction and those during social activities.

Cooper (1981) also provides several suggestions for practitioners who are just beginning to monitor student behavior. These are listed in Box 5-2.

You will find it possible to monitor a larger number of behaviors if you adjust your data collection procedures to the behavior you are recording. All behavior does not need to be monitored constantly, such as when you are evaluating the maintenance or generalization of a previously taught skill. In such cases, you might employ periodic (weekly or biweekly) measurement probes. For example, you may observe a student once a week to see whether he continues to play appropriately with others during recess. Data probes are also useful for general monitoring (e.g., spot-checking pupils' on-task behavior) and for monitoring programs in which student progress is slow. Table 5-1 summarizes

BOX 5-2 Suggestions for Novice Observers

- Begin observing one or two behaviors of one student. Gradually expand observations of the same behavior to include another student, a third, and so on. Experiment with different measurement strategies (duration, time sample, interval) to find those that are most useful, sensitive, and direct for a particular setting.
- Monitor behavior for the shortest time possible to get an adequate sample (i.e., without occurrences of behavior "escaping" measurement).
- Use other persons (classroom aides, other students) to observe, to record, and to collect observer agreement information.
- Ask persons who are skilled in recording and graphing behavior to help you analyze your measurement strategies (Cooper, 1981).

TABLE 5-1 Guidelines for Adjusting the Frequency of Monitoring

Student or Program Characteristics	Monitoring Strategy
Rapid student progress or progress through small-step sequence	Session-by-session recording (one or more per day)
Daily progress or fluctuation in student behavior, daily program adjustments	Daily recording
Slow rate of student progress	Data probes (biweekly, weekly)
General monitoring of behavior, less frequent program adjustments	Data probes (biweekly, weekly)
Evaluating maintenance or generalization of previously mastered programs or steps	Data probes (biweekly, weekly, monthly)

guidelines for adjusting the frequency of measurement to student and program characteristics.

7. If you are observing in a setting other than your own classroom or school building, follow established procedures. Each institution, residential treatment program, or school district has its own policies regarding visitors. Although we cannot prepare you for every situation, we have summarized general guidelines that can be found on the Companion Website. These procedures are important if you are to obtain accurate data without offending anyone.

Recording Strategies

Advances in the technology of behavior measurement have resulted in a variety of alternatives for recording. The alternatives you select depend on a number of factors, some of which are presented in Table 5-2. Your answers to the questions posed in this table will help determine which recording procedure you should use. For example, if you must observe while you are involved in direct instruction with pupils other than or in addition to the target student, you would likely choose a sampling technique or train someone other than yourself to observe and record. Following is a discussion of alternative approaches for recording behavior. You will find additional guidelines and suggestions on Dr. Mac's Amazing Behavior Management Advice site and the Center for Effective Collaboration and Practice's Functional Behavior Assessment home page.

Counting Permanent Products. If your measurement strategy is based on permanent products, your choices of recording techniques are fairly straightforward. You may obtain numerical counts, rate, or percentage or record the number of instructional trials required for the student to reach the criterion (see pp. 147–148). Your choice will be based on some of the considerations listed in Table 5-2. For example, does the student not attempt any of the work assigned, or is his work inaccurate? Will you be recording student responses in a one-to-one instructional situation, in which you are presenting discrete instructional trials? Do you want to increase the pupil's response speed, accuracy, or both? Will you be giving daily or weekly probes over the objective you are attempting to reach? Will the student monitor and record the target behavior himself? Will you use a peer observer? Permanent product recording is useful primarily for monitoring academic behaviors that result in written student responses, although, as we suggested earlier, some social behaviors may have results that can be measured as permanent products. In addition, you can use audio or video recordings as permanent products of social behaviors. Permanent products are useful documents to include in student portfolios.

TABLE 5-2 Considerations in Selecting a Measurement Strategy

1. Definition of the behavior target	Topography/function or both?
2. Characteristics of target behavior	Frequency/duration/latency/intensity? Individual/group? High rate/low rate?
3. Goal of intervention	Change rate/duration/latency/intensity?
4. Observation situation	Your class/another class? Group/one-to-one? Teacher giving lesson/individual seat work/recess or free time/lunch/other?
5. Person doing observation	Trained observer/untrained observer? Adult/child?
6. Time available for observation	All day/one period/portion of several periods/portion of one period?
7. Equipment available for measurement	Automatic recorder/cumulative recorder/multiple-event recorder/wrist counter/timing device/pad and pencil?
8. Accuracy	High/medium/low? Interobserver agreement critical/not critical? Reliability observers trained/untrained?
9. Audience for whom data are intended	Professionals/parents/students?

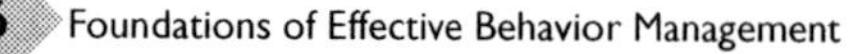

To measure behaviors that do not result in a permanent product (e.g., most human social behavior), you must rely on observational recording techniques. A variety of these are available, or you may adapt or design a recording procedure suited to your own situation. We briefly describe and illustrate several approaches, and other examples appear in subsequent chapters.

Frequency or Tally Method. If you have defined target behaviors specifically and objectively, recording their frequency is relatively easy. **Frequency recording** is the method of choice for most behaviors that are brief and discrete (i.e., have a definite beginning and end and are best characterized in terms of their frequency, such as hand raising, talking out, or social initiations to peers). In some cases, a simple numerical count will be sufficient, but it generally is better to record the time period in which the behavior occurred or keep observation time constant to permit comparison across observation sessions. If observation sessions vary in length, you may convert event data to **rate per minute** by dividing the numerical count by the time observed (e.g., Katie initiated a verbal interaction with a peer seven times in 30 minutes—rate = 7/30, or 0.23 times per minute). This will permit comparison of your data across unequal observation periods. The case study at the beginning of this chapter illustrates a procedure for collecting data on the rate per minute of students' correct academic responding.

Frequency recording may be accomplished with a paper and pencil, or you may use other devices. For example, you can attach a piece of masking tape to a clipboard, watchband, or your wrist and mark on it whenever a target behavior occurs. Transfer coins or paper clips from one pocket to another or to a container whenever a target behavior occurs. Inexpensive golf counters, knitting counters, and even digital stopwatches or wristwatches can be purchased at variety stores.

Counting Number of Trials to a Performance Criterion. When you are providing skill instruction through **discrete learning trials** (i.e., presenting a fixed number of trials that consist of a specific instruction or model, the pupil's response, and a subsequent teacher response) or otherwise controlling the student's opportunities to respond (e.g., through teacher-paced instructions), it is useful to monitor performance on each trial. Figure 5–2 shows a discrete trial recording format (also referred to as controlled presentation recording) for teaching a pupil to ask for teacher assistance appropriately. Note that the teacher records whether the desired response occurred following each verbal instruction and whether a verbal prompt was needed to occasion the correct performance. Note also that the teacher has set 10 trials per instructional session and that the criterion for moving to the next level of delay between when the student first requests attention and the teacher responds is specified on the recording sheet. Trials-to-criterion data sheets may be attached to a separate clipboard for each student. Trials may spread out (**distributed trials**) over the course of a class period or a day rather than being presented together (**massed trials**). Counting the number of trials needed for the student to reach the criterion is an appropriate measurement strategy for monitoring progress through a task-analysis sequence, as in Figure 5–2.

Recording Duration. If the length or the latency of a response is its major characteristic or the one you most want to change, **duration recording** may be the best method. For example, a student may have a low frequency of in-seat behavior, but each episode may last several minutes, or a student may be extremely slow in following directions or in joining group activities.

Response duration or latency may be monitored by any watch or clock with a second hand or second counter, but a stopwatch or digital timer is best. By starting and stopping a stopwatch without resetting it, you may record the cumulative time out-of-seat or on-task across several instances. Although a *total duration* recording procedure is more convenient, it is less descriptive than *duration per occurrence* because the latter keeps track of each event and its

Objective: When instructed to "show me how you ask for my help," Robert will raise his hand and sit quietly for 15 seconds. *Criterion:* 8 of 10 consecutive correct trials for two consecutive sessions.

Duration	Session	Trials 1	2	3	4	5	6	7	8	9	10
5 seconds	1	O	XP	XP	O	XP	XP	X	X	X	X
	2	XP	O	XP	XP	X	X	X	X	X	X
	3	XP	XP	X	X	X	X	X	X	X	X
	4	X	X	X	X	X	X	X	X	X	X
10 seconds	1	O	O	OP	OP	XP	XP	OP	OP	XP	XP
	2	XP	XP	OP	OP	X	X	O	O	XP	XP
	3	X	X	X	O	XP	XP	X	X	X	X
	4	O	XP	X	X	X	X	X	X	X	X
	5	X	X	X	X	X	X	X	X	X	X
15 seconds	1	XP	XP	O	XP	X	X	X	X	X	X
	2	O	O	XP	X	X	X	X	X	X	X
	3	X	X	X	X	X	X	X	X	X	X
	4	X	X	X	X	X	X	X	X	X	X

Scoring Key: X = correct
O = incorrect
XP = correct prompted (verbal)
OP = incorrect prompted (verbal)

FIGURE 5–2 Trials-to-Criterion Data Sheet

duration. Both of these procedures are easier to use if the observer is not occupied with direct instruction or classroom management.

Response latency recording is accomplished by starting a timer when a cue (verbal instruction or visual signal) is presented and stopping the timer when the pupil complies with the request (e.g., "Take your seat"). Although teachers generally want to decrease latency, as when a student does not comply with teacher requests or instructions, sometimes it is desirable to increase latencies, as when students respond impulsively and thereby make more errors.

Using Interval Recording. **Interval recording** is a versatile technique for recording both discrete and continuous behaviors. It requires your full attention for observing and recording, but you can observe several behaviors or pupils simultaneously. Interval recording also may be the most practical strategy if a response occurs too frequently for each instance to be counted (e.g., hand flapping or other stereotypic behaviors). When using this technique, break the observation period down into small intervals of equal length (10, 15, or 30 seconds) and observe whether the behavior occurs or does not occur in any given interval. The size of the interval should be at least as long as the average duration of a single response but short enough so that two complete responses normally cannot occur in the same interval. For example, if the duration of an instance of out-of-seat typically is 20 seconds, 30-second observation intervals would be appropriate, but 1-minute intervals would be too long.

You may define the occurrence of a behavior according to a proportion of the interval during which it took place (e.g., 50% or more of the interval) or score an occurrence if the behavior occurred at all during the interval. The latter procedure is easier and lends itself to higher levels of interobserver agreement. When monitoring several behaviors simultaneously, it may be easier to observe for one interval and use the next to record your observations (10 seconds to observe, 10 seconds to record, and so on). It is also possible to arrange your recording sheet to allow more time for observing than for recording (e.g., 15 seconds to observe followed by 5 seconds to record or three observation and recording intervals per minute). Figure 5-3 shows interval data collected in 15-second blocks. Another option for coding more than one behavior is to preprint recording sheets with the behavior codes written in each interval, as in Figure 5-4. The observer indicates a behavior's occurrence by drawing a slash through the appropriate code. Subsequent chapters contain other examples of interval recording.

In addition to being versatile, interval recording does not require sophisticated equipment. A clipboard and a digital timer or watch with a second hand are all you need. Because interval recording does not provide a measure of absolute frequency, it is not appropriate to report the total number of target behaviors that occurred in a given observation period. Instead, report the percentage of the intervals in which you observed the behavior. Calculate this by the following formula:

$$\frac{\text{Number of intervals in which the behavior occurred}}{\text{Total number of intervals}} \times 100$$

With a little practice, you will become proficient in collecting interval data.

The scatter plot (Touchette, MacDonald, & Langer, 1985) described in Chapter 4 is a compromise between rating and interval scale measurement. Once each interval (e.g., 30 minutes) or instructional period, the practitioner enters a code indicating his estimation of the frequency of the target behavior for that interval. However, convenience comes at the price of accuracy because the scatter plot yields a summary estimate of the behavior rather than an indication of whether it occurred in a much briefer time period.

Time Sampling. If you do not have a block of time to devote to observing and recording, if you want to sample behaviors across an extended time period or across settings, or if you are monitoring a number of pupils or behaviors, a **time sampling** technique may suit your needs. Time sampling is similar to interval recording, but the intervals are much longer (e.g., 1 to 20 minutes), are less frequent, and may be variable. There are many variations to this approach. For example, you may take a 5-minute sample out of every hour, take one momentary sample every 5 minutes, or sample behavior on a variable interval schedule. If you employ a **momentary time sampling** procedure, rate the occurrence or nonoccurrence of the target behavior immediately following a specified interval of time. In this case, it is advisable to use a wristwatch timer to signal when to observe. Set the timer for the desired interval, and when it signals, record whether the behavior is occurring. A drawback to

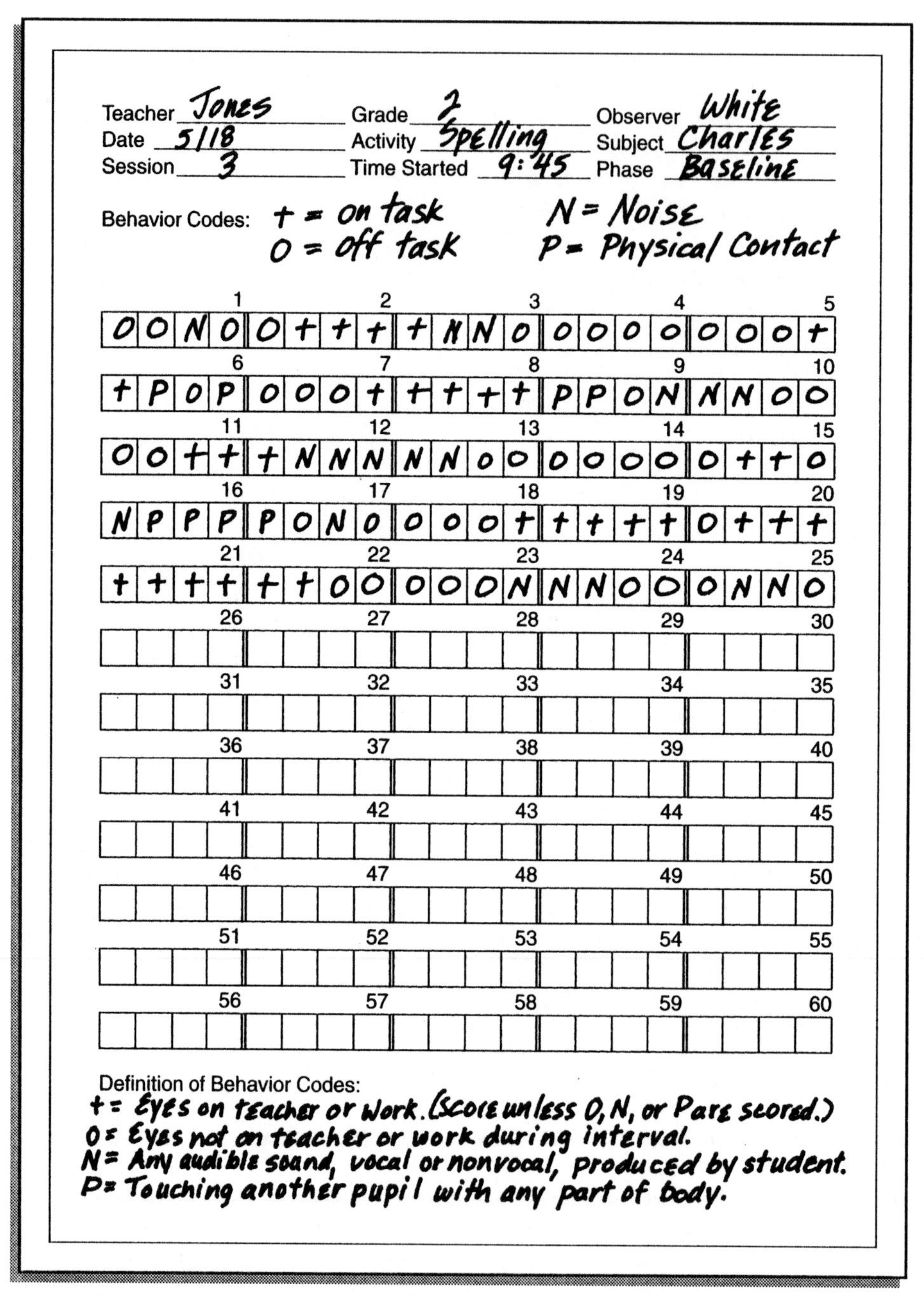

Teacher *Jones* Grade *2* Observer *White*
Date *5/18* Activity *Spelling* Subject *Charles*
Session *3* Time Started *9:45* Phase *Baseline*

Behavior Codes: *+ = on task* *N = Noise*
O = off task *P = Physical Contact*

Intervals					
1–5	O O N O	O + + +	+ N N O	O O O O	O O O +
6–10	+ P O P	O O O +	+ + + +	P P O N	N N O O
11–15	O O + +	+ N N N	N N O O	O O O O	O + + O
16–20	N P P P	P O N O	O O O +	+ + + +	O + + +
21–25	+ + + +	+ + O O	O O O N	N N O O	O N N O
26–30					
31–35					
36–40					
41–45					
46–50					
51–55					
56–60					

Definition of Behavior Codes:
+ = Eyes on teacher or work. (Score unless O, N, or P are scored.)
O = Eyes not on teacher or work during interval.
N = Any audible sound, vocal or nonvocal, produced by student.
P = Touching another pupil with any part of body.

FIGURE 5–3 Sample Interval Recording Form

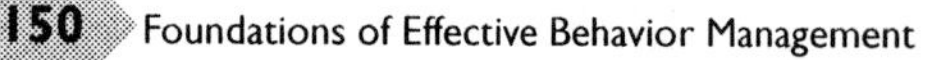

Observer Dianne McInerney Student(s) John

Date Oct. 29 Activity Science

Behavior Code(s) T= Touching, O= out of seat N= Noises Time 10:45– 10:50

	10 secs.	20 secs.	30 secs.	40 secs.	50 secs.	60 secs.
1	T O N	T O N	T O ~~N~~	T O ~~N~~	T O ~~N~~	T O ~~N~~
2	T ~~O~~ N	T ~~O~~ N	~~T~~ O N	T O ~~N~~	T O ~~N~~	T O N
3	~~T~~ ~~O~~ N	T O N	T O N	T O N	T O ~~N~~	T O ~~N~~
4	T O N	T O N	T O N	T O N	T O N	~~T~~ O N
5	T O N	~~T~~ O N	T O N	~~T~~ ~~O~~ N	T O N	T O N

Definition of Behavior Codes

T= Touching other students with hands

N= Noises: grunts, whistles, burping sounds, or other vocalization

O = Leaving seat or seated position during lesson without permission

Total % of Intervals

T= 16.6%

N= 26.6%

O= 13.3%

FIGURE 5–4 Interval Recording Form

any time sampling procedure is that it is unlikely to capture infrequent behaviors.

Kubany and Slogett (1973) developed a recording form to use in conjunction with a timer set for variable schedules averaging 4, 8, or 16 minutes (see Figure 5-5). The numerals in the columns indicate the number of minutes to set the timer according to each variable interval schedule. The advantage of a variable observation schedule is the unpredictability of each interval, particularly if the timer announcement is audible to students (e.g., if a kitchen timer is used). Students may be aware of the behavior being observed but cannot predict each interval and change their behavior only when the timer is due to ring. This strategy is particularly useful for measuring the behavior of a group of pupils relative to classroom rules, for example. When the timer sounds, you can check which pupils are on

Target Behavior On task (✓)

Schedule VI 4 min.

Date 5/18

Student Rob

Teacher Jones

Starting time 8:40

Activity Language Arts

VI Schedule (in minutes)

Comments		Four		Eight		Sixteen
	2	✓	12		12	
	5	—	2		8	
	7	✓	10		28	
	1	✓	4		2	
	3	✓	6		24	
	6	—	14		6	
	4	✓	8		24	
	6	—	2		6	
	4	—	10		30	
	1	✓	14		12	
	2	✓	8		16	
	5	✓	10		4	
came in from fire drill	3	—	6		8	
	7	—	4		30	
	2	—	12		28	
	1	✓	4		6	
	7	—	12		24	
	3	✓	14		16	
	4	—	2		12	
	5	✓	6		2	

Scoring Key: ✓ = on-task

— = off-task

FIGURE 5–5 Variable-Interval Recording Form

Source: *Kubany, E. S., & Slogett, B. B. (1973). Coding procedure for teachers.* Journal of Applied Behavior Analysis, 6, *339–344. Used with permission.*

task, in-seat, and so forth. A similar procedure is PLACHECK (Hall, 1973), which involves recording which students are engaged in a particular activity at the end of specified intervals. Pupils also may be trained to take momentary time sample data.

> In the table on the Companion Website, write the list you developed earlier of student behaviors you want to measure. For each behavior, identify a recording strategy you would use with each and justify your choices. Share these with others and discuss.

Observing and Recording Multiple Behaviors of Students

As some of the examples we have presented indicate, event, interval, and time sampling formats can be adapted to monitor several behaviors simultaneously. Sometimes researchers measure a number of behaviors at the same time, but we do not recommend that you attempt such complex recording systems without appropriate training. Teachers usually can observe and record up to four behaviors accurately by using appropriately constructed interval recording formats.

There are occasions when you may want to monitor two students who are exhibiting the same behaviors or when you may want to collect simultaneous data on the target pupil's behavior and that of selected peers, either as a basis for validating that the behavior warrants intervention or for setting a criterion level for a behavioral objective (see Chapter 4). One way to accomplish this using an interval format is to observe and record one student's behavior for 10 seconds. Then observe and record the second pupil's and so on until you have sampled the behavior of all pupils you wish to observe. Observe pupils in the same sequence (Jim, then Vernon, then Carol, then Yvonne, and so on) during any single observation session but vary the sequence from session to session to avoid unintentional bias. Kubany and Slogett's (1973) variable-interval procedure or Hall's (1973) PLACHECK strategy may be used if you are observing the same behavior for each student. Figure 5-6 shows an interval recording form developed for this purpose. When recording more than one behavior or the behavior of more than one student, be careful not to make your data collection task too great. The advantages of having more data may be erased by the problem of low accuracy. When attempting new or complex recording procedures, practice collecting data with an experienced observer until you reach 80% to 90% agreement. Remember to recheck observer agreement frequently.

Student Portfolios

Educational reform efforts that call for increasing literacy and academic achievement among school-age children have posed a dilemma for professionals who serve students with disabilities. Should these pupils be required to take standardized tests along with their typical peers, and should their scores be averaged in with those of their school or district? One response that does not place students or schools at a disadvantage is to develop alternative assessment and reporting strategies. Student portfolios are a viable alternative. A student portfolio contains information systematically compiled from relevant curricular domains that document his change and growth over time (Swicegood, 1994). Therefore, portfolios offer a means of monitoring student progress across curricula and settings. Table 5-3 suggests the types of information you may enter into student portfolios. Portfolios are developed through a team process, involving all who participate in delivering services listed on the student's IEP.

A portfolio is a collection of a student's work over time. Together, a student and his teacher systematically choose, collect, evaluate, and display papers, projects, tapes, artwork, compositions, and other items that accurately reflect the student's progress in one or more courses. In this way, portfolios use students' strengths and diverse learning styles. The student should assume increasing responsibility for managing his portfolio, and it should be reviewed and updated frequently by the

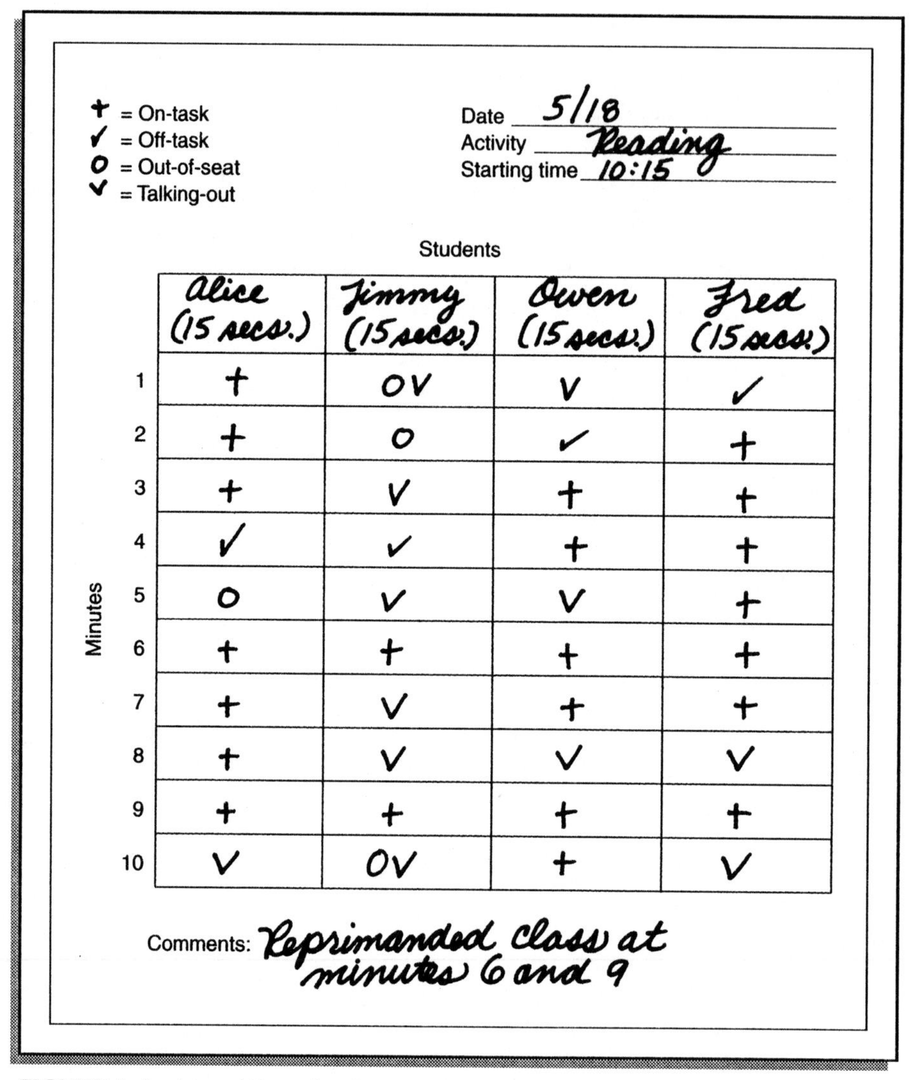

+ = On-task
✓ = Off-task
O = Out-of-seat
V = Talking-out

Date 5/18
Activity Reading
Starting time 10:15

Students

Minutes	Alice (15 secs.)	Jimmy (15 secs.)	Owen (15 secs.)	Fred (15 secs.)
1	+	OV	V	✓
2	+	O	✓	+
3	+	V	+	+
4	✓	✓	+	+
5	O	V	V	+
6	+	+	+	+
7	+	V	+	+
8	+	V	V	V
9	+	+	+	+
10	V	OV	+	V

Comments: Reprimanded class at minutes 6 and 9

FIGURE 5–6 Interval Recording Form for Monitoring Four Students

student, his parents, and relevant professionals. Make the shift to portfolio assessment carefully and allow sufficient time for students, parents, and staff to learn to use them properly (Swicegood, 1994). Often portfolios link classroom experiences to district or state standards. The basic steps in student portfolio development are presented in Box 5–3.

Many teachers take advantage of technology to create electronic or digitized portfolios (Barrett, 2000). Computer software assists in storing, displaying, comparing, and retrieving student work. For other practical tips on portfolio assessment, see Belanoff and Dickson (1991) or Rolheiser, Bower, and Stevahn (2000). Smith, Brewer, and Heffner (2003) describe portfolio assessment for younger students.

TABLE 5–3 Possible Information to Include in Student Portfolios

Measures of behavior and adaptive functioning
Anecdotal records or critical incident logs
Observations of behavior across settings and conditions
Behavior checklists
Interviews about interests, motivation, and attributions
Videotapes of student behaviors
Social skills ratings and checklists
Peer ratings and sociometric measures

Measures of academic and literacy growth
Criterion-referenced tests
Curriculum-based assessments
Teacher-made tests in selected literacy or content-area domains
Analysis of oral reading such as informal reading inventories
Writing samples collected over time
Photographs of student projects
Running records in reading, writing, or math, such as "stories read and completed"
Classroom tests in spelling, math, etc.

Measures of strategic learning and self-regulation
Ratings and checklists of skills or strategies a student is using
Student self-evaluations of task performance
Miscue analysis procedure in oral reading
Interviews and questions about how a student performs in literacy and classroom tasks
Student thinks aloud: Verbal descriptions of strategies and operations used in different academic situations
Excerpts from teacher-student dialogue journals
Observations and ratings of study skills

Measures of language and cultural aspects
Cultural interviews with students and parents
Primary language sample
Observations of student responses to changing social and classroom situations
Simulations and role-plays

Source: Swicegood, P. (1994). *Portfolio-based assessment practices: The uses of portfolio assessment for students with behavioral disorders or learning disabilities.* Intervention in School and Clinic, 30(1), 9. Copyright 1994 PRO-ED. Used with permission.

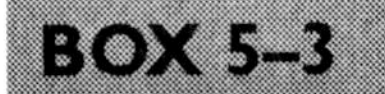

Procedures for Portfolio Development

1. Collect the permanent products that accurately reflect the student's performance.
2. Select permanent products, or artifacts, that illustrate specific skills or knowledge (standards).
3. Evaluate each product, using written reflections, or rubrics. Students and teachers complete this task together.
4. Compare the work products against standards, IEP objectives, or other measures.
5. Present the portfolio to others through a parent-student-teacher conference or in-class activities. Student-led conferences are a great forum for sharing portfolios with parents.

Using Technology to Observe and Record Behaviors

Technology has affected nearly every aspect of education, and observing and recording student behavior is no exception. A variety of computer software and hardware is available for observing behavior and for recording and plotting data from direct observations. Laptop computers and personal digital assistants are capable of recording and storing data on a number of coded behaviors, or the data can be fed simultaneously into a monitor that displays a graphic record of the data as they are recorded. Flexible software programs are available that allow the observer to design an observation system to suit almost any circumstance (e.g., Martin, 2002; Reynolds & Kamphaus, 2004).

Some researchers (e.g., Hausafus & Torrie, 1995; Tapp & Wehby, 2000) have used bar code scanners (like those used to inventory stock in commercial establishments) and handheld computers to record occurrences of behaviors. New tools and programs are appearing almost daily. Investigate these labor-saving data collection and analysis systems with your school's technology specialist.

Assessing Observer Agreement

If all human behavior could be observed and recorded automatically by machines (as the disk pecks or lever presses of laboratory animals are recorded), the accuracy of measurement would be a minor concern. However, we must rely on our own powers of observation, and this raises the question of the accuracy of the observer's estimates. In the classroom, if the target behaviors result in a permanent product (e.g., math worksheet, spelling test, carburetor assembled), measurement accuracy is relatively certain. But most social behaviors are ephemeral; they leave no trace. Unless you are able to obtain an audio or a video recording of the student's performance, your accuracy in observing and recording behavioral occurrences is a concern. Human observers are biased rather easily, and their measures may be influenced by many subjective factors. In addition, documented changes in observed behaviors may be due to errors of measurement rather than to actual changes in behavior resulting from intervention procedures. Therefore, some procedures for improving and evaluating the accuracy of observational measures of behavior are necessary.

One way to improve the accuracy of observational measures is to specifically and objectively define the behaviors to be observed, meaning that observations must be confined to what the student actually does rather than reflecting a generalization or impression. Consider the difficulty you might have in measuring "hostile" remarks or "pesky" noises. Human behaviors are objectively defined if two or more persons agree on whether they occurred. It is unlikely that high interobserver agreement could be obtained for either of the behaviors we just mentioned. What is hostile or pesky to one person may not be to another. To make these behavioral definitions specific and objective, we would ask, What does the pupil do that makes you interpret his remarks as hostile or his noises as pesky? To answer this question, we might prepare a list of specific behaviors, the occurrence or nonoccurrence of which two independent persons could agree on: for example, he says to others, "Go to hell," "I don't like you," "Your momma," and so forth; he taps his pencil against his desk; he squeaks his chair; or he belches.

It is not sufficient to develop definitions of target behavior about which two observers *could* agree, however. The primary criterion for evaluating the adequacy of a behavioral definition is the extent to which independent observers actually *do* agree that they have observed the same levels of behavior during the same observation period. Only then can we feel relatively confident that the data reflect what the pupil is actually doing and not measurement error. Several methods are used to assess agreement between observers. The simplest method is to calculate the percentage of interobserver agreement by dividing the smaller observed frequency by the larger and multiplying by 100. This method is appropriate for event, frequency, or rate data. For example, if one observer counted seven and a second observer counted eight episodes of self-stimulation in a 30-minute period, their reliability would be $7/8 \times 100 = 88\%$. Another procedure must be used when discrete units of observation, such as time intervals, problems solved, or trials, are being compared. For each time interval or opportunity to observe the behavior, two observers may agree or disagree as to its occurrence or nonoccurrence (i.e., both may "see" the behavior as defined, or both may not see it, or one may see it although the other does not). Thus, agreement is calculated by

$$\frac{\text{Number of agreements}}{\text{Number of agreements} + \text{disagreements}} \times 100 = \text{Percentage agreement}$$

If, for example, on-task behavior is being observed in 10-second blocks for 30 minutes, there would be six observations per minute, or 180 observations for the 30-minute period. If two observers agreed (that on-task behavior occurred or did not occur) on 150 of these observations and disagreed on 30, their reliability would be

$$\frac{150}{150 + 30} \times 100 = 83\%$$

This approach is more useful when several behaviors are being observed and recorded simultaneously, when interval data are recorded, or when pupil responses to discrete learning trials are being measured. If you are unsure of the approach to use, consult someone more experienced in behavioral measurement.

There are no hard-and-fast rules for determining how much agreement is enough. When observing low levels of behavior, a single disagreement may make a difference of several percentage points when the total reliability method is used. Generally, 80% agreement is considered satisfactory, but 90% or better is preferred (Tawney & Gast, 1984). Use periodic assessments of interobserver agreement to rule out gradual changes in the observers' interpretation regarding the occurrence or nonoccurrence of a behavior. Conduct these assessments at least once during each program phase and otherwise once a week, unless you are measuring permanent products. If interobserver agreement is below 80%, check with the other observer regarding how he or she is scoring instances and noninstances of the behaviors observed before resuming formal data collection. If agreement is below 90%, follow the same procedure without interrupting formal data collection. However, in both cases, you should conduct additional assessments to ensure that disagreements have been resolved.

SUMMARY

- The range of procedures for measuring human behavior is expanding rapidly.
- Although there are no tangible incentives to encourage data-based instruction or intervention, research indicates that pupils whose teachers monitor their performance make greater progress than those who do not.
- Practice in data collection will increase your fluency and confidence.
- A variety of alternate recording formats and strategies are available, and these should be selected based on the behavior being observed and the practical circumstances of the situation.
- Interobserver agreement should be assessed regularly to ensure that direct observation data are accurate and objective.

DISCUSSION/APPLICATION IDEAS

1. What are some of the factors that contribute to teachers' unwillingness to collect behavioral data? Suggest strategies for overcoming these resistances.
2. Suggest alternate recording strategies for the following behaviors and situations: a behavior that occurs infrequently on the playground, a behavior that occurs at a high rate across a

number of settings, a behavior that is characterized by its duration, a behavior that is continuous, and several behaviors exhibited by more than one pupil.

3. With a colleague, develop a strategy for assessing delivery of instruction in the classroom. Use this strategy to determine how effectively both of you are instructing your students.
4. Talk with a teacher who has used portfolios to document students' progress over time. What are some of the advantages and limitations of portfolio assessments compared with more traditional approaches?
5. If your school or program has access to a computer-based observational system, obtain a copy and experiment with different types of data collection. How does it compare with "hard copy" observational data collection procedures?
6. Why is interobserver agreement an important consideration in measuring social behavior? How can it be influenced by such factors as low or high rates of targeted behaviors?

REFERENCES

Barrett, H. C. (2000). *Electronic portfolios = multimedia development + portfolio development.* Paper presented at the STE 2000 and NECC 2000 Conferences. Available at http://transition.alaska.edu/www/ portfolios/twoframeworks.html.

Belanoff, P., & Dickson, M. (Eds.). (1991). *Portfolios: Process and product.* Portsmouth, NH: Heinemann.

Cooke, N. L., Heward, W. L., Test, D. W., Spooner, F., & Courson, F. H. (1991). Student performance data in the classroom: Measurement and evaluation of student progress. *Teacher Education and Special Education, 14,* 155-161.

Cooper, J. O. (1981). *Measuring behavior* (2nd ed.). Upper Saddle River, NJ: Merrill/Prentice Hall.

Deno, S. L. (2000). Academic progress and incompatible behavior: Curriculum-based measurement (CBM) as intervention. *Beyond Behavior, 9*(3), 12-16.

Fuchs, L. S. (1986). Monitoring progress among mildly handicapped pupils: Review of current practice and research. *Remedial and Special Education, 7*(5), 5-12.

Fuchs, L. S., & Fuchs, D. (1986). Effects of systematic formative evaluation: A meta-analysis. *Exceptional Children, 53,* 199-208.

Gunter, P. L., Callicott, K., Denny, R. K., & Gerber, B. L. (2003). Finding a place for data collection in classrooms for students with emotional/behavioral disorders. *Preventing School Failure, 48,* 4-8.

Gunter, P. L., & Denny, R. K. (1998). Trends, issues, and research needs regarding academic instruction of students with emotional and behavioral disorders. *Behavioral Disorders, 24,* 44-60.

Gunter, P. L., & Denny, R. K. (2004). Data collection in research and applications involving students with emotional and behavioral disorders. In R. B. Rutherford, M. M. Quinn, & S. R. Mather (Eds.), *Handbook of research in emotional and behavioral disorders* (pp. 582-595). New York: Guilford.

Gunter, P. L., Hummel, J. H., & Venn, M. L. (1998). Are effective academic instructional practices used to teach students with behavioral disorders? *Beyond Behavior, 9*(3), 5-11.

Gunter, P. L., & Reed, T. M. (1997). Academic instruction of children with emotional and behavioral disorders using scripted lessons. *Preventing School Failure, 42,* 33-37.

Hall, R. V. (1973). *Managing behavior—Behavior modification: The measurement of behavior* (Part 1). Lawrence, KS: H & H Enterprises.

Hausafus, C. O., & Torrie, M. (1995). Scanning to the beep: A teacher-tested computer-based observational assessment tool for the distance education classroom. *Tech Trends, 40*(5), 26-27.

Hosp, M. K., & Hosp, J. L. (2003). Curriculum-based measurement for reading, spelling, and math: How to do it and why. *Preventing School Failure, 48,* 10-17.

Kauffman, J. M. (2001). *Characteristics of emotional and behavioral disorders of children and youth* (5th ed.). Upper Saddle River, NJ: Merrill/Prentice Hall.

Kubany, E. S., & Slogett, B. B. (1973). Coding procedure for teachers. *Journal of Applied Behavior Analysis, 6,* 339-344.

Lund, K., Schnaps, L., & Bijou, S. (1983). Let's take another look at record keeping. *Teaching Exceptional Children, 15,* 155-159.

Martin, S. (2002). *!Observe desktop CD-ROM and instruction manual.* Longmont, CO: Sopris West.

National Council for Accreditation of Teacher Education. (2000). *Professional standards for the accreditation of schools, colleges, and departments of education.* Washington, DC: Author.

Reschly, D. J., Kicklighter, R. H., & McGee, P. (1988). Recent placement litigation, Part III: Analysis of differences in Larry P. Marshall, and S-1 and implications for future practices. *School Psychology Review, 17,* 37-48.

Reynolds, C. R., & Kamphaus, R. W. (2004). *Behavior assessment system for children: Portable observation program.* Circle Pines, MN: American Guidance Services.

Rolheiser, C., Bower, B., & Stevahn, L. (2000). *The portfolio organizer: Succeeding with portfolios in your classroom.* Alexandria, VA: Association for Supervision and Curriculum Development.

Smith, J., Brewer, D. M., & Heffner, T. (2003). Using portfolio assessment with young children who are at risk for school failure. *Preventing School Failure, 48,* 38-40.

Stokes, T. F., & Baer, D. M. (1977). An implicit technology of generalization. *Journal of Applied Behavior Analysis, 10,* 349-367.

Sutherland, K. S., & Morgan, P. L. (2003). Implications of transactional processes in classrooms for students with emotional/behavioral disorders. *Preventing School Failure, 48,* 32-37.

Swicegood, P. (1994). Portfolio-based assessment practices: The uses of portfolio assessment for students with behavioral disorders or learning disabilities. *Intervention in School and Clinic, 30*(1), 6-15.

Tapp, J. T., & Wehby, J. H. (2000). Observational software for laptop computers and optical bar code time wands. In T. Thompson, D. Felece, & F. Symonds (Eds.), *Behavioral observation: Computer assisted innovations and applications in developmental disabilities* (pp. 71-81). Baltimore: Paul H. Brookes.

Tawney, J. W., & Gast, D. L. (1984). *Single subject research in special education.* Upper Saddle River, NJ: Merrill/Prentice Hall.

Touchette, P. E., MacDonald, R. F., & Langer, S. N. (1985). A scatter plot for identifying stimulus control of problem behavior. *Journal of Applied Behavior Analysis, 18,* 343-351.

Walton, T. W. (1985). Educators' responses to methods of collecting, storing, and analyzing behavioral data. *Journal of Special Education Technology,* 7(2), 50-55.

White, O. R. (1986). Precision teaching—Precision learning. *Exceptional Children, 52,* 522-534.

CHAPTER 6 EVALUATING INTERVENTION EFFECTS

OUTLINE

Introduction
Graphing and Charting Student Performance
Data-Based Decision Making
Single-Subject Research Designs

OBJECTIVES

After completing this chapter, you should be able to

- Summarize and graph or chart data using techniques appropriate for the data.
- Visually analyze graphed data and write data decision rules.
- Identify the major types of single-subject research designs and give the uses and limitations of each.

KEY TERMS (refer to the Glossary on the Companion Website for definitions)

aim line
alternating treatments design
bar graph
baseline
baseline data
changing criterion design
chart
competing explanations
condition lines
conditions
cumulative graph
data-based decision making
dependent variable
ecological ceiling
equal interval graph
equal ratio graph
experimental control
external validity
frequency polygon
functional relationships
graph
independent variable
internal validity
intervention
level
line of desired progress
multiple baseline designs
multiple probe design
performance graph
phase change lines
progress graph
reversal designs
single-subject research design
split-middle line of progress
static measures
trend lines
trends
withdrawal designs

In the preceding chapter, we discussed the advantages of formative evaluation over summative evaluation for evaluating student progress in academic or behavior intervention programs. Three types of procedures are useful in conducting formative evaluations of student programs. The first is to visually display student performance in a **graph** or **chart,** which permits rapid and efficient analysis of the pupil's status at various points in time. The second is **data-based decision making.** This process involves comparing student performance or progress to a desired level and making adjustments based on this comparison (Deno, 2000). The third procedure is to apply a **single-subject research design** to identify and isolate specific variables that have a direct cause-and-effect relationship to target behavior. We discuss these procedures separately, although they have much in common. Graphing or charting of student performance data is essential to both data-based decision making and the use of single-subject research designs because they rely on the visual analysis of data. In addition, both procedures may be used simultaneously. The case study that follows shows a continuous visual record of student progress in a classroom intervention procedure and illustrates how a single-subject research design was used to evaluate it.

COME INTO MY CLASSROOM: A CASE STUDY

HELP FOR AMANDA

Ms. Wong has been teaching in the primary grades at Hindman Elementary School for 12 years. This year, she has a group of 25 third graders. Among them are several students with disabilities. Ms. Wong is very comfortable working with special needs students; in fact, she is pursuing a master's degree in special education. However, one student, Amanda, has been a handful. Amanda is identified as a student with Asperger's syndrome. While she is capable of doing work at this grade level, she has displayed several very troubling behaviors since the first day of school. Specifically, Amanda has been highly aggressive to other children and adults. When she is asked to perform a task or to participate in an activity, she hits, spits, or throws objects. These behaviors have resulted in Amanda being placed in time-out in the principal's office and on several occasions in calling her mother to take her home. These procedures have had no beneficial effect on Amanda's aggressive behavior; in fact, it seems to have increased. The school district's behavior specialist, Dr. Lingo, has been called in to assess the problem and help develop a behavior intervention plan.

Dr. Lingo observed Amanda in the classroom on several occasions, talked with Amanda's parents, and interviewed Ms. Wong and Mr. Brighton, the teaching assistant assigned to work with Amanda in Ms. Wong's classroom. During her classroom observations, Dr. Lingo performed an A-B-C assessment of Amanda's aggressive behavior. Amanda's Behavior Support Team (consisting of Ms. Wong, Mr. Brighton, Amanda's mother, and Dr. Lingo) agreed that the problem behavior should be defined as aggression: specifically, hitting (striking another person with an open hand or closed fist), spitting (expelling saliva from between her lips), and kicking (striking a person or object with her foot). Based on Dr. Lingo's observations and their familiarity with Amanda, the team hypothesized that the function of her aggressive behavior was to avoid task demands and social contact. Because of the severity of her behaviors, it was agreed that this hypothesis would be tested by implementing an intervention and observing the effects on Amanda's aggressive behavior. The team further agreed that, since hitting, spitting, and kicking were discrete and topographically dissimilar behaviors, they could be monitored separately. Mr. Brighton was assigned the task of recording daily frequencies of each behavior.

After further discussion, the team agreed to use overcorrection procedures to address Amanda's aggressive behavior. Specifically, she would be required to apologize to the person to whom her aggressive behavior had been directed and also to all other persons in the particular setting in which the behavior occurred. She also would be taught to say "Not right now, thank you" to indicate refusal to comply with task requests or to participate in activities. (However, she would not be allowed to avoid the task or activity for very long—after several minutes, Mr. Brighton would redirect Amanda to comply.) If Amanda started to hit, spit, or kick, Mr. Brighton would physically interrupt her and prompt her to perform the overcorrection routine.

Amanda's mother was concerned that the procedure may be no more effective than anything used previously. The school district superintendent also insists that all intervention procedures for behaviors that may cause harm to anyone be carefully evaluated for effectiveness. Therefore, the team decided to use a single-subject research design to evaluate the effects of the overcorrection plan. Because Amanda's aggression involved three discrete behaviors, Dr. Lingo suggested that a multiple baseline across behaviors design be used. An advantage of this design is that the intervention can be tested on a single behavior. It was agreed that, if the procedure proved to be effective, it would be repeated across the remaining target behaviors. However, if it was not effective with the first behavior, the procedure would be modified or replaced.

The intervention began with a baseline phase. Mr. Brighton recorded the frequency of all three of Amanda's aggressive behaviors. After 3 days, it was determined to implement the overcorrection procedure on Amanda's throwing because both Ms. Wong and Mr. Brighton felt this behavior was the most potentially dangerous. As demonstrated in Figure 6–1, the overcorrection procedure, combined with teaching Amanda to use her replacement behavior, was effective in decreasing the frequency of Amanda's throwing objects. However, her frequency of hitting and kicking remained at previous levels. Furthermore, because Ms. Wong and Mr. Brighton provided immediate assistance with tasks and reinforcement for joining in activities with her peers, Amanda was observed to be using her replacement behavior less often. After reviewing these data, the team agreed that their hypothesis regarding the function of Amanda's aggressive behavior was correct, and they determined to implement overcorrection with the next most serious problem, hitting. For the next 5 days, the procedure was implemented with both throwing and hitting, while spitting was monitored but no intervention was attempted. After the effectiveness of the overcorrection procedure on throwing and hitting had been demonstrated, intervention was begun with spitting, with similar results. Several weeks later, Amanda continued to participate appropriately in both academic and social activities.

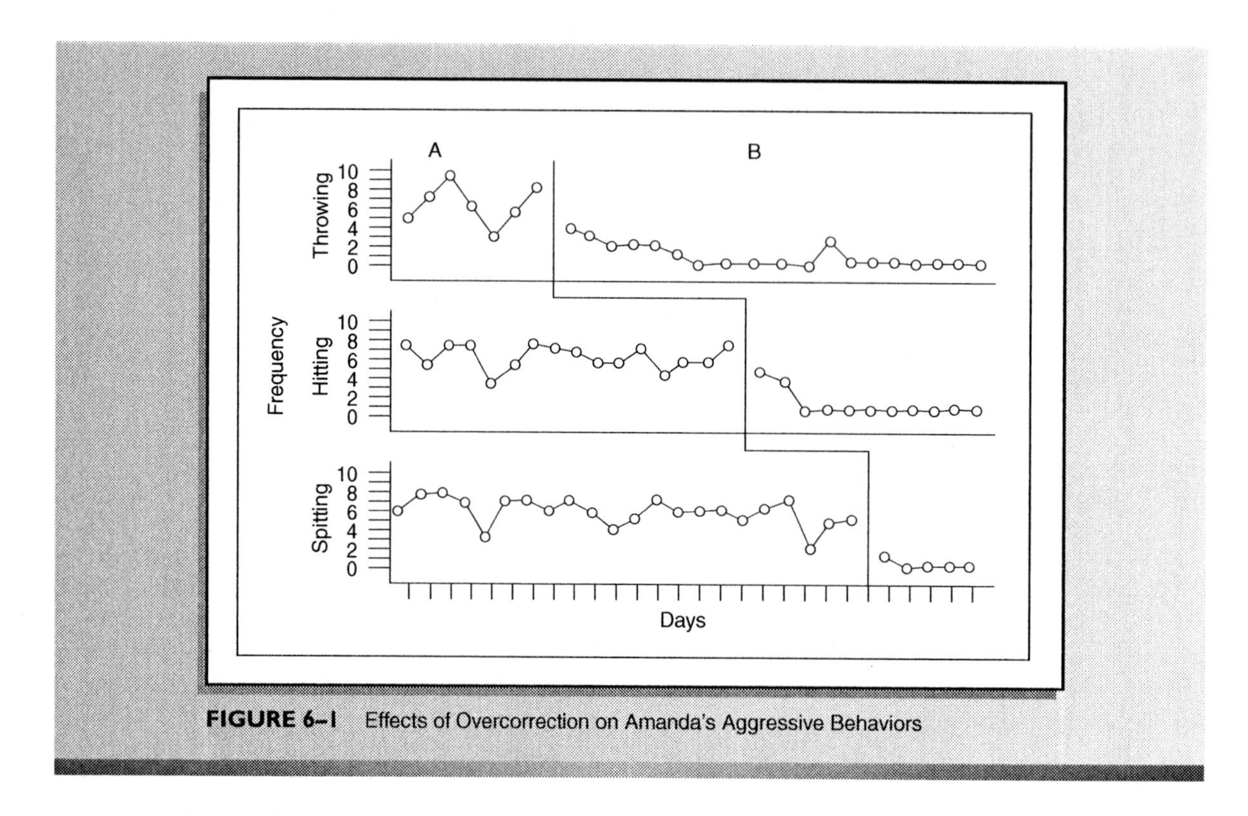

FIGURE 6–1 Effects of Overcorrection on Amanda's Aggressive Behaviors

INTRODUCTION

Do Amanda's behavior problems seem too extreme for her to be placed in a general education classroom? Is it unfair to ask a teacher with 25 other students to implement an intensive and complex intervention? Regardless of your response to these questions, the reality is that more students with more severe disabilities (including those involving challenging behavior) are being educated in mainstream education settings. Moreover, federal and state laws require that schools be as accountable for the educational performance of these students as any other. And, as we have seen in previous chapters, state and school district policies increasingly are insisting that powerful and potentially aversive interventions be carefully documented and thoroughly evaluated. As the case of Amanda illustrates, the implementation and evaluation of such procedures is best supervised by a team of professionals and caregivers.

GRAPHING AND CHARTING STUDENT PERFORMANCE

Obviously, if your observations are recorded with a wrist counter, on scraps of paper, or on an interval data sheet, you will want to transfer the data to a central form, both for convenience and for safekeeping. Such forms need not be elaborate, but they should contain all relevant information: dates, sessions, observation time, data taken, and program phase. Software spreadsheet programs can be used to quickly generate data summary forms. Figure 6–2 is a data summary sheet for rate data measured in terms of responses per minute. Such forms centralize your data for easy reference and for transfer to a chart or graph.

Teacher Swenson Margaret
(last) (first)

Student Issacs Jean
(last) (first)

Target Offers to share with peers

Phase	Session	Number of responses	Time (minutes)	Rate (number of responses per minute)	Consequence
baseline	1	0	30	0	
	2	0	30	0	
	3	10	30	.33	
	4	0	30	0	
	5	0	30	0	
Intervention	6	9	30	.30	1 min. free
1	7	11	30	.35	time if .33
	8	5	30	.18	per min.
	9	9	30	.30	
	10	13	30	.42	
	11	8	30	.27	
	12	5	30	.18	
Intervention	13	16	30	.52	Sit by
2	14	13	30	.42	preferred
	15	18	30	.58	peer if
	16	11	30	.35	.42 per min.
	17	16	30	.52	
	18	20	30	.62	
	19	17	30	.55	
	20	20	30	.64	
	21	17	30	.55	Lunch with
	22	20	30	.64	preferred
	23	20	30	.64	peer if
	24	18	30	.58	.52 per min.
	25	20	30	.64	
	26	20	30	.64	
	27	20	30	.64	
	28				
	29				
	30				

FIGURE 6–2 Rate Data Summary Sheet for Jean

Autographing Formats

Data summaries can be organized to include graphing or charting in a one-step process. For example, Nelson, Gast, and Trout (1979) developed an individualized education plan (IEP) performance chart to monitor progress on task steps or short-term objectives. Figure 6–3 shows how the system can be used to summarize performance regarding several targeted social behaviors. In this figure, an X indicates that a criterion was met for a particular behavior, a / (forward slash) indicates that a criterion was not met, and the daily total indicates whether the short-term objective was met for that day.

Fabry and Cone (1980) developed a procedure that combines data collection and creating a visual display for discrete trial recording. In this procedure, an X indicates a correct response, and an O designates an error response. Figure 6–4 illustrates three uses of this procedure. The left-hand portion displays a summary of pupil responses to each trial across

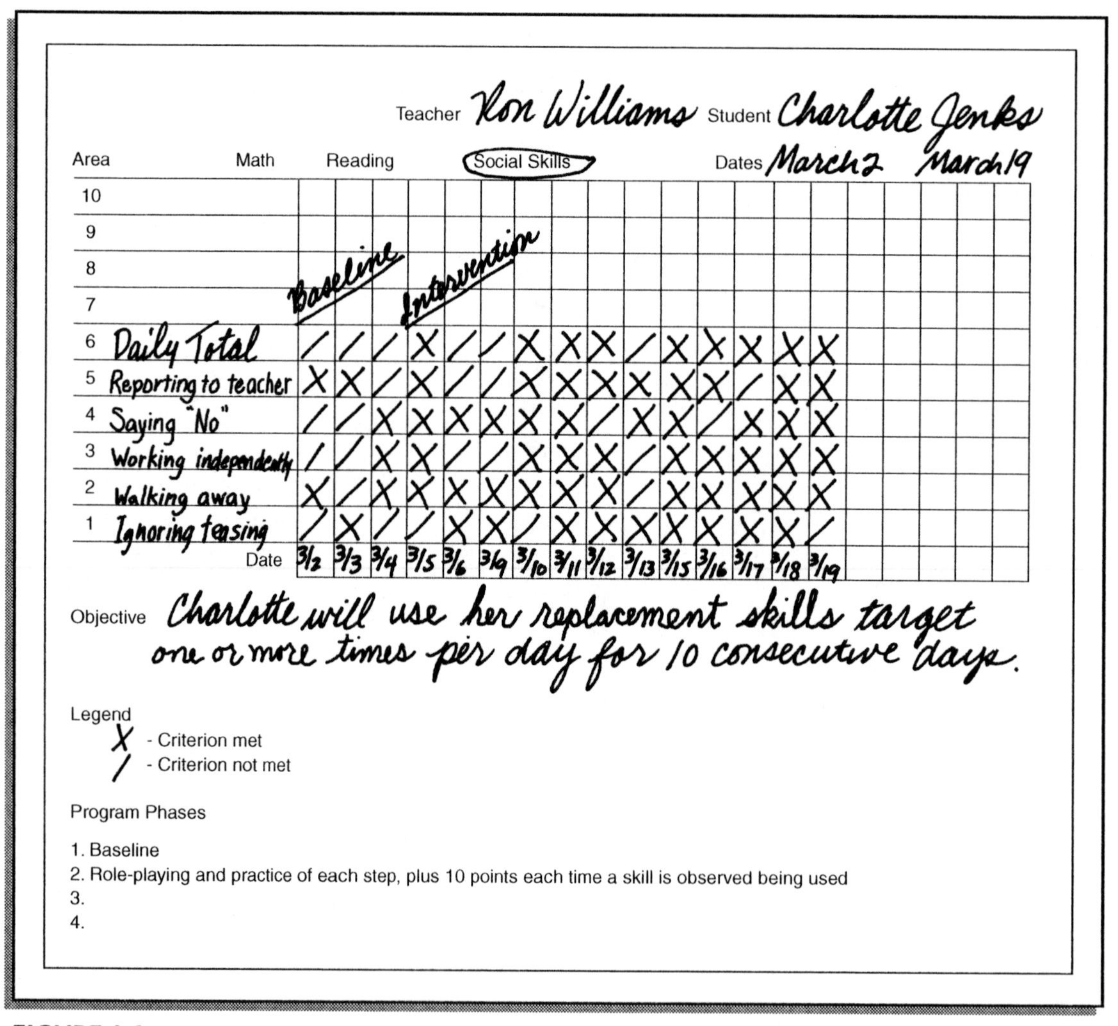

Teacher Ron Williams Student Charlotte Jenks

Area Math Reading (Social Skills) Dates March 2 March 19

Baseline / Intervention

		3/2	3/3	3/4	3/5	3/6	3/9	3/10	3/11	3/12	3/13	3/15	3/16	3/17	3/18	3/19
10																
9																
8																
7																
6	Daily Total	/	/	/	X	/	/	X	X	X	/	X	X	X	X	X
5	Reporting to teacher	X	X	/	X	/	/	X	X	X	X	X	X	/	X	X
4	Saying "No"	/	/	X	X	X	X	X	X	/	X	X	/	X	X	X
3	Working independently	/	/	X	X	/	/	X	X	X	/	X	X	X	X	X
2	Walking away	X	/	X	X	X	X	X	X	X	/	X	X	X	X	X
1	Ignoring teasing	/	X	/	/	X	X	/	X	X	X	X	X	X	X	/

Objective Charlotte will use her replacement skills target one or more times per day for 10 consecutive days.

Legend
X - Criterion met
/ - Criterion not met

Program Phases

1. Baseline
2. Role-playing and practice of each step, plus 10 points each time a skill is observed being used
3.
4.

FIGURE 6–3 Charlotte's IEP Performance Chart

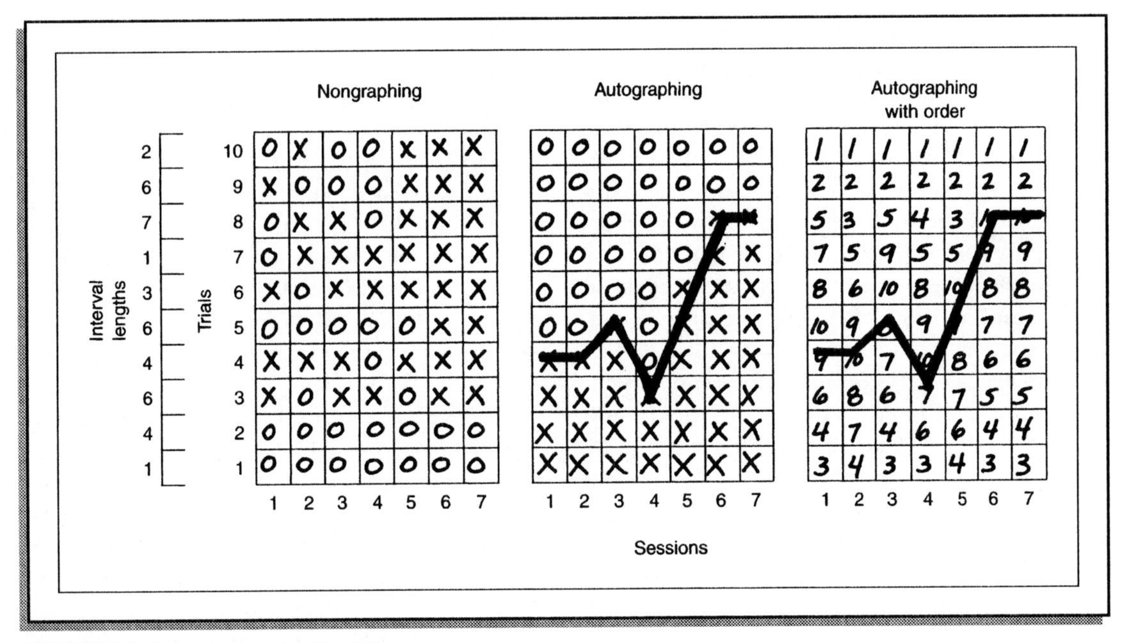

FIGURE 6–4 Autographing Data Forms

Source: *Fabry, B. D., & Cone, J. D. (1980). Auto-graphing: A one-step approach to collecting and graphing data.* Education and Treatment of Children, 3, *361–368. Used with permission.*

sessions. Here the teacher has recorded the student's performance for each instructional trial in the order that trials were presented. The middle portion shows these same data, but the teacher entered each correct student response from the bottom of the chart and each error from the top down. You can see that the student had 4 correct trials out of 10 during session 1. An autograph of these data was produced by connecting the Xs representing the cumulative total of correct responses for each session. The right-hand portion summarizes the same student's performance, but this time the teacher also wrote the number of each trial according to whether the response was correct or incorrect. Trials 3, 4, 6, and 9 in session 1 were correct; the first correct trial was 3, and the last was 9. These data also have been transformed into a graph by connecting the cells representing the last correct trial per session. The advantage of this procedure is that the teacher can collect, summarize, and graph student performance while administering instructional trials.

A final variation of Fabry and Cone's (1980) system is to substitute time intervals for trials. Interval lengths are set according to a predetermined variable interval schedule (see the left side of Figure 6–4). The teacher sets a timer for the designated interval lengths and, when it signals the end of an interval, she enters the appropriate symbol for the pupil's behavior. These data may be arranged to create an autograph, just as when trial-by-trial data are recorded.

Graph or Chart?

If you employ either of the charting systems just presented, you will already have a useful visual display. However, there are other meaningful ways to present data visually. Remember that most teachers can get a variety of data pertaining to student performance. Much of it is work samples, weekly test scores, or results of standardized achievement tests. Such data are used infrequently for program decision making because these samples are not organized to be useful for this purpose: they do not show trends in student performance or compare performance to predetermined criteria. Nongraphic data summaries, such as the one depicted in Figure 6–2, do organize the data, but they fail to display trends or communicate clearly to anyone who is not familiar with the program or student they represent. However, graphs and charts meet these goals. A graph typically uses only one or two symbols to represent data (e.g., a dot or a triangle). A chart, however, displays from several to many symbols to represent the data. All types of graphs and charts serve three important purposes: (a) they summarize data in a manner convenient for precise, daily decision making; (b) they communicate information that is helpful in evaluating the effects of an intervention or program on a frequent basis; and (c) they provide reinforcement and feedback to those persons involved with the program.

> Have you used or seen visual displays of students' classroom performance? As you read the following section, consider how these formats could be used to summarize and display the performance of students. Do you see any advantages over simply posting student work on a bulletin board?

Types of Graphs and Charts

There are as many types of charts and graphs as there are behaviors to monitor. However, these can be grouped into a few categories. The selection of any particular type depends on the considerations described in Chapter 5 as well as on the type of data to be presented. A **bar graph** may be used to show progress toward a specific goal or objective. For example, Figure 6–5 shows a student's progress toward earning a class party through appropriate classroom behavior. This type of graph is useful for presenting data to be used by students because it is easily interpreted and because being able to see daily progress may be reinforcing. Allowing a pupil to fill in the data also may be a reinforcer.

Other variations of bar graphs and charts are illustrated on the Companion Website. For example, the graph depicting Linda's daily percentage of assignment completion provides an informative display of fluctuations in her daily performance. Bar graphs may be used to plot any kind of data, and they are easily understood by pupils, parents, and other laypersons. An even simpler presentation is a star chart, also illustrated on the Companion Website. Charts such as these can be sent home to parents as daily or weekly reports. Charts that report the results of behavior (points earned, stars) instead of the behavior itself are reinforcing and do communicate readily, but they do not provide the kind of data useful to teachers for decision-making purposes.

The graph pictured in Figure 6–5 is a **cumulative graph;** each day's total is added to the previous day's earnings. Line graphs may also be cumulative, as shown in Figure 6–6. Although you may plot cumulative time, percentages, frequencies, or rates of either appropriate or inappropriate behavior, if the graph is to be used by the student, plot desired behavior (e.g., time in-seat instead of time out-of-seat) so that increases in level will be associated with improvement, not regression.

A noncumulative frequency graph, or **frequency polygon,** is the most common type used in behavioral research and is the type most useful in data-based decision making (see the next section). It may be used to report frequency, rate, or percentage data. Frequency polygons are illustrated in Figures 6–7 (p. 171) and 6–8 (p. 172). Numerical frequency is plotted in Figure 6–7, and rate (frequency divided by time) is graphed in Figure 6–8.

Figure 6–7 illustrates plotting on **equal interval graph** paper (i.e., the difference between a frequency of 15 and 16 is equal to the difference between that of 19 and 20). Figure 6–8 shows data plotted on **equal ratio** (or semilogarithmic) **graph** paper, on which equal changes in rate show up as identical changes in the slope of the data path regardless of their absolute rate. For example, a change in rate from 0.1 to 0.2 responses (movements) per minute or from 5 to 10 movements per minute (an acceleration in rate of times 2) shows up as identical slopes on the graph. Although equal

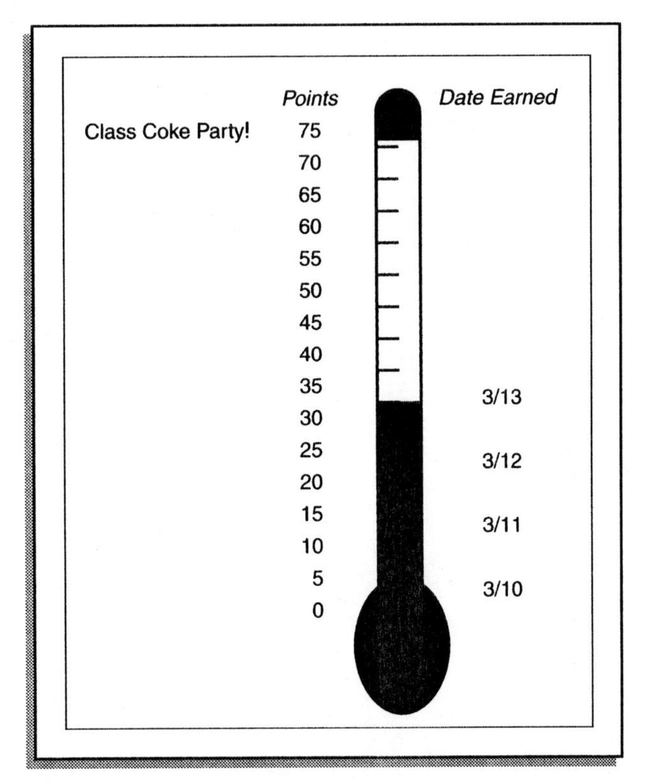

FIGURE 6–5 Susan's Progress Toward a Class Party

ratio graph paper may be confusing to those who are not accustomed to it, the rules for plotting data are learned quickly. Also, this standard semilogarithmic charting paper offers several advantages: (a) it saves time in drawing and scaling graphs, (b) it allows behaviors occurring anywhere between 1 time in 24 hours and 1,000 times per minute to be plotted on the same graph, (c) it permits comparison across different times and activities when the amount of time or number of opportunities to respond varies, and (d) once persons become familiar with the ratio scale, time is saved in reading and interpreting the plotted data (White, 1986).

The major disadvantage of equal ratio graphing is that it is cumbersome to collect data on students' responses per minute when each response is controlled by the teacher's instruction (e.g., "Do this." . . . "Now do this". . .) because, in order to measure only the pupil's rate of response, the teacher would have to subtract the time required to give each instruction from the time period in which response rate was measured (Tawney & Gast, 1984).

Graphs and charts may be designed to display either student progress or performance. A **progress graph** or chart shows the time it takes a student to master a set of objectives, for example, weekly progress in a curriculum (Fuchs & Deno, 1991). Figure 6–9 (p. 173) is a chart of Donnie's progress toward mastery of a set of sight words. A **performance graph** or chart, in contrast, reports a change on a single task or behavior (Fuchs & Deno, 1991). The same type of data may be plotted either way. Look at the performance chart on the Companion Website. It shows Donnie's daily performance on the same set of sight words. Whether you elect to use progress or performance graphing depends on the kind of data you will be using to

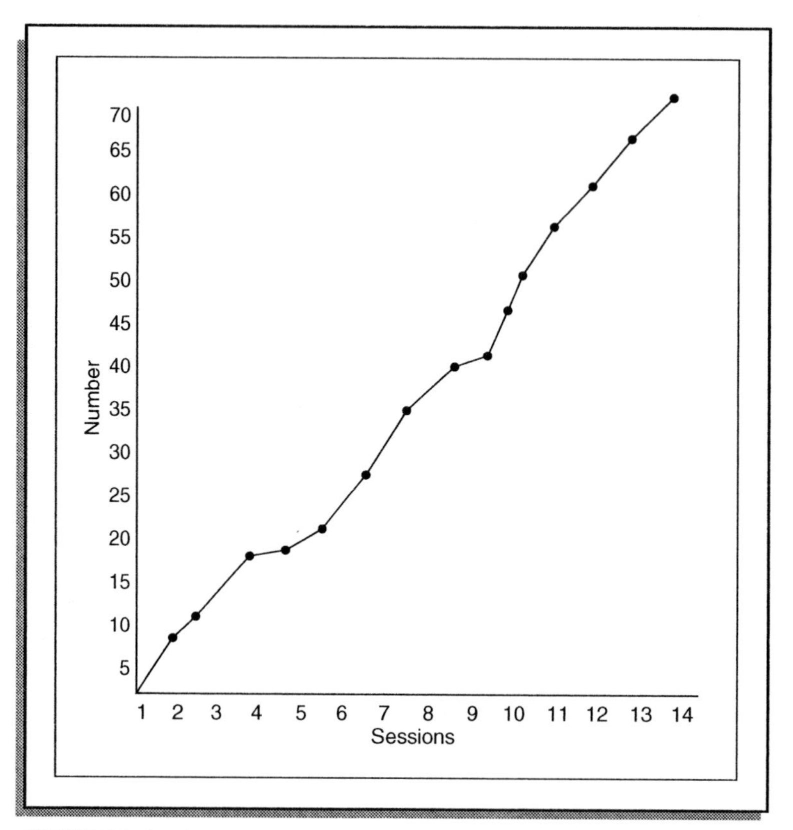

FIGURE 6–6 David: Math Facts Learned

make decisions: daily performance or sequential progress (Fuchs & Deno, 1991). The choice will also be influenced by your instructional strategy. If you have task-analyzed your terminal objective, for example, progress charting will be more suitable. Performance graphs or charts are better suited for monitoring most social behaviors, unless you are using direct teaching procedures to shape a particular skill or behavior.

> If you are not sure whether to monitor and evaluate students' academic performance or social behavior, remember that effective instruction and academic progress are deterrents to many common behavior problems. Progress in the academic curriculum may be incompatible with problem behavior (Darch & Kame'enui, 2004; Deno, 2000).

Guidelines for Graph or Chart Construction

The communication function of charts and graphs is not fulfilled if they are cluttered or inconsistent or if the reader cannot follow what is being reported. Tawney and Gast (1984) indicate that graphic presentations of data should communicate to the reader the sequence of conditions, the time spent in each condition, the independent and dependent variables, the type of design used (if any), and the relationships among variables. Figure 6–10 (p. 174) identifies the major components of a frequency polygon or simple line graph. Because charts use a variety of symbols to represent the data, they require more elaborate legends, but the basic parts are the same. **Condition lines** are used to

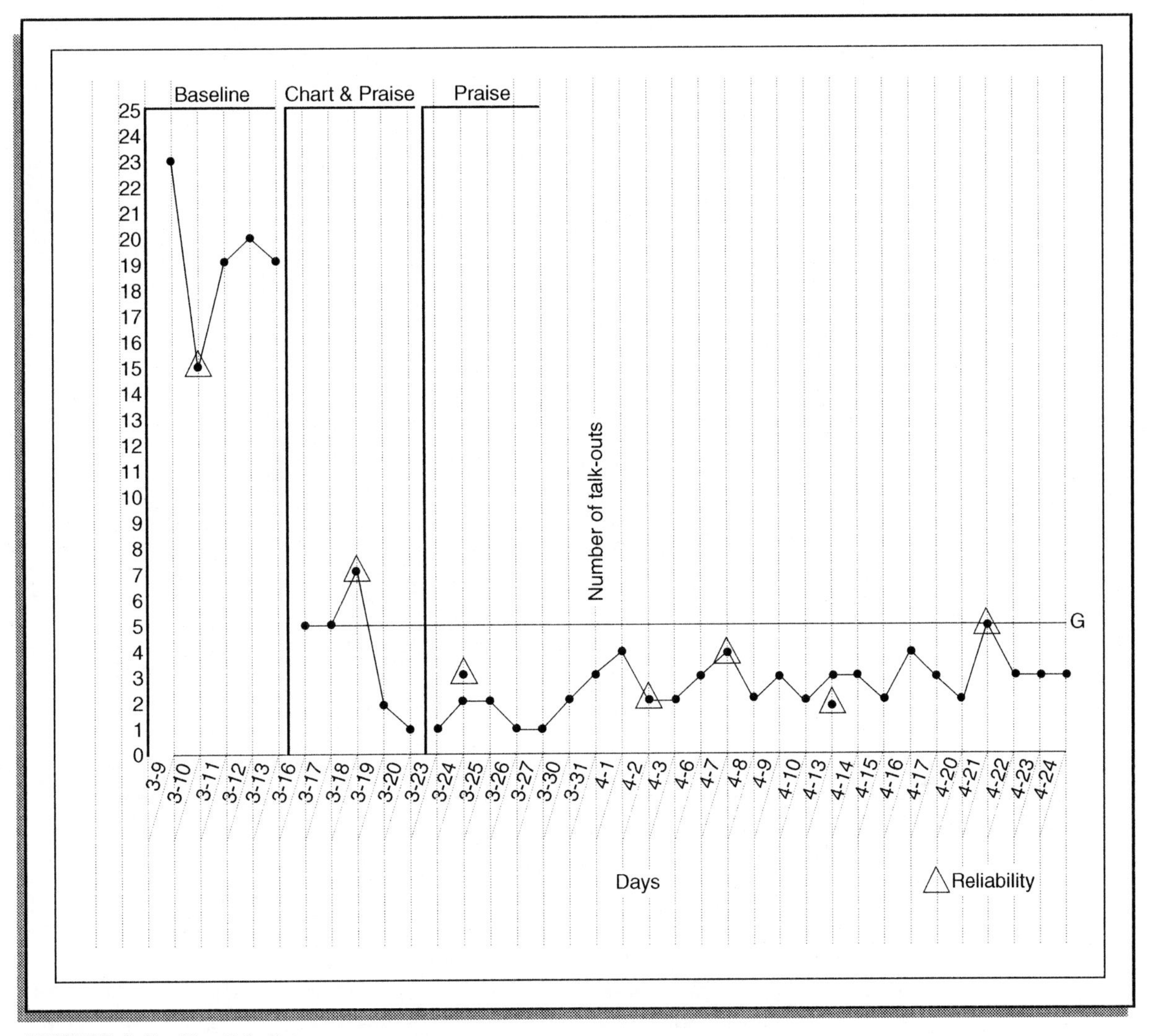

FIGURE 6–7 Kay: Talk-Outs

designate where changes in **conditions** (e.g., implementation of a new instructional program) are made. Generally, behavior graphs begin with a **baseline** condition, followed by **intervention** conditions that may include phase changes (adjustments in the intervention, such as a change in the schedule of reinforcement, which are indicated by **phase change lines**). Intervention conditions and phases should be labeled descriptively but briefly so that the reader knows what conditions are in effect at any given time. The examples we have provided in this chapter illustrate the range of options possible without grossly violating these guidelines. With practice, you will be able to construct useful graphs quickly and efficiently. Your pupils also can learn to construct graphs and plot data (self-graphing may be reinforcing for students interested in their own progress). A number of software programs are available for creating charts and graphs.

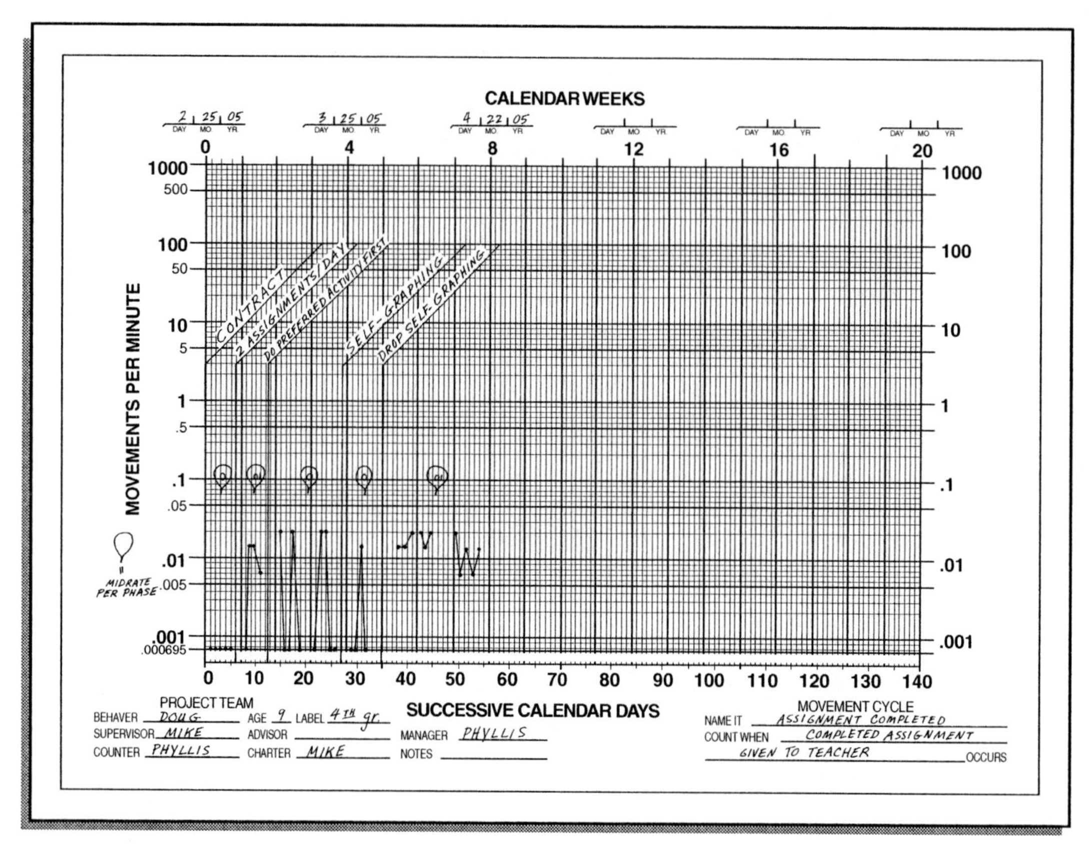

FIGURE 6–8 Doug: Rate of Assignment Completion

The Role of Program Monitoring and Evaluation in IEPs

As we mentioned at the beginning of this section, one of the principal uses of charts and graphs is to facilitate decision making by educators and intervention planners. While displaying data in these formats helps us understand how target behaviors are being affected by intervention procedures, decisions can be made more precisely and expediently if the data are visually analyzed and objective rules are developed. This process is described in the following section. Single-subject research designs, which are overviewed in the final section of this chapter, may be used to identify functional relationships between instructional or intervention procedures and targeted student behavior. Both of these procedures facilitate your ability to make appropriate and timely decisions regarding instructional or intervention strategies.

The 2004 amendment to the Individuals with Disabilities in Education Act (IDEA) state that a reevaluation of each student with a disability should be conducted whenever the local education agency (LEA) determines that the student's performance warrants a reevaluation, or if the student's parents or teacher requests a reevaluation. This reevaluation must occur at least once every 3 years, unless the LEA and the parents agree that it is unnecessary, but no more than once a year, again unless the parents and the LEA agree otherwise (§614[a](2)(A)). Even an annual review of goals and objectives is far too infrequent for any child, especially one who has a great deal of catching up to do. Annual,

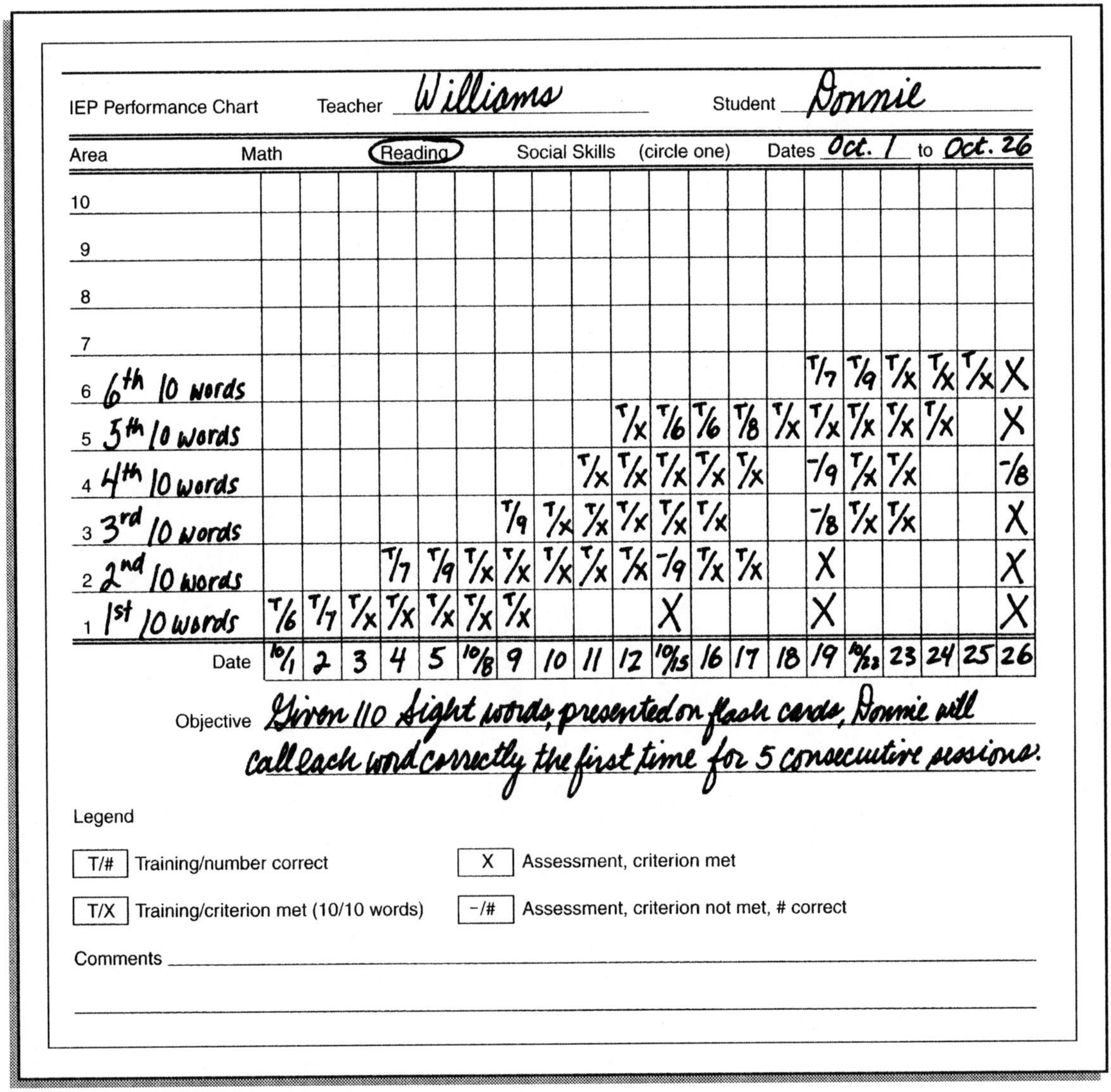

IEP Performance Chart Teacher *Williams* Student *Donnie*

Area Math **(Reading)** Social Skills (circle one) Dates *Oct. 1* to *Oct. 26*

10																				
9																				
8																				
7																				
6 *6th 10 words*															T/7	T/9	T/X	T/X	T/X	X
5 *5th 10 words*										T/X	T/6	T/6	T/8	T/X	T/X	T/X	T/X	T/X		X
4 *4th 10 words*									T/X	T/X	T/X	T/X	T/X		-/9	T/X	T/X			-/8
3 *3rd 10 words*							T/9	T/X	T/X	T/X	T/X	T/X			-/8	T/X	T/X			X
2 *2nd 10 words*				T/7	T/9	T/X	T/X	T/X	T/X	T/X	-/9	T/X	T/X		X					X
1 *1st 10 words*	T/6	T/7	T/X	T/X	T/X	T/X	T/X				X				X					X
Date	10/1	2	3	4	5	10/8	9	10	11	12	10/15	16	17	18	19	10/22	23	24	25	26

Objective *Given 110 sight words, presented on flash cards, Donnie will call each word correctly the first time for 5 consecutive sessions.*

Legend

T/#	Training/number correct	X	Assessment, criterion met
T/X	Training/criterion met (10/10 words)	-/#	Assessment, criterion not met, # correct

Comments

FIGURE 6–9 Progress Chart: Donnie's Sight Words

semiannual, or even quarterly reassessments relative to the goals and objectives stated in a pupil's IEP are **static measures;** that is, they provide a report of progress at a single point in time. They also represent an evaluation process that is summative, meaning that measurement occurs after teaching and learning have taken place. In addition to the potential inaccuracy or unreliability of static measures, they are not made often enough to allow the teacher to make timely program decisions or precise program adjustments. Deno (1986) observed that summative evaluation data (e.g., annual achievement test scores) are not useful for developing more effective interventions, nor can they be used to evaluate the effectiveness of an intervention. In this context, it is unfortunate that

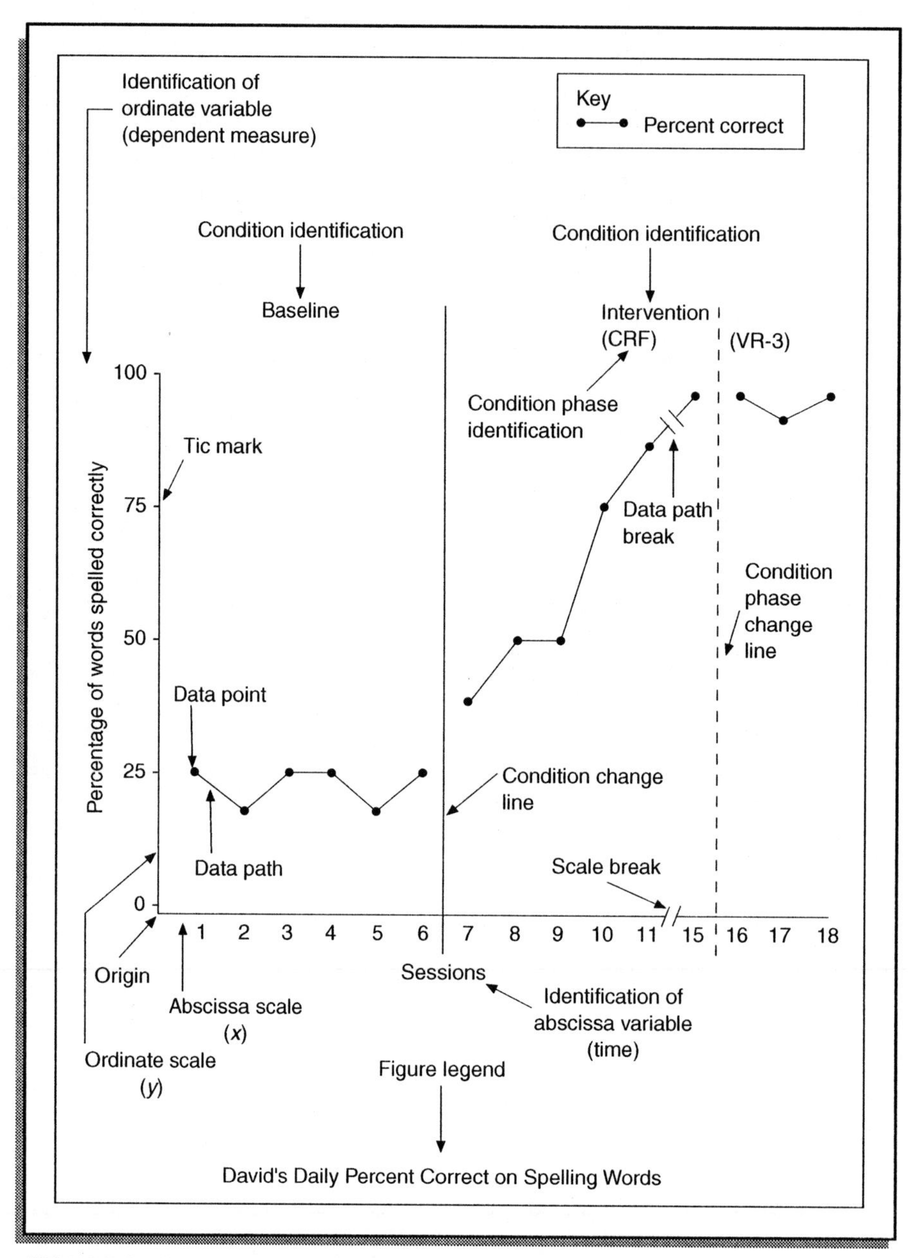

FIGURE 6–10 Basic Components of a Simple Line Graph

Source: *Tawney, J.W., & Gast, D. L. (1984).* Single subject research in special education. *Upper Saddle River, NJ: Merrill/Prentice Hall. Used with permission.*

Note: Draw condition lines between sessions; do not connect data points in adjacent conditions: set 0 on the ordinate scale above the abscissa.

federal and state educational accountability legislation mandates static annual testing as a means of evaluating schools' effectiveness. Gunter, Calicott, Denny, and Gerber (2003) point out that the danger of being driven by summative evaluation in the absence of formative evaluation procedures is that the gap will widen between empirically validated procedures and actual classroom practices.

Figures 6–11 and 6–12 illustrate the difference between infrequent and frequent measures of student progress. The set of panels in Figure 6–11 depict measures of six students' performances, relative to the criterion, or desired level of performance, taken at 6-week intervals.

> The panels in Figure 6–12 represent performance measures of the same students at 1-week intervals. What decisions would you make regarding each of the six students' instruction based on the data presented in Figure 6–11 versus Figure 6–12? Compare your responses to the following paragraph.

As we indicated in Chapter 5, the data presented in Figure 6–12 constitutes formative evaluation; that is, it occurs while skills are being developed. Notice how much more information is available for making instructional decisions. For example, we can see that Cal reached the criterion after only 3 weeks of instruction; he was ready to move on to another skill well before the other students. In contrast, Minnie and Georgia did not profit from the instruction offered for some time; their time (and the teacher's) was wasted on instruction that was not beneficial. Finally, Virginia, Tex, and Washington performed inconsistently and would have benefited from some adjustments in their daily instruction. As Gast and Gast (1981) pointed out,

> The pretest/posttest methods of determining pupil performance are only the peripheral ends of a continuum of evaluating and monitoring individual education plans. Systematic procedures that result in formative data, from which decisions of program maintenance and modification can be made, are imperative if the IEP is to be a truly functional tool for assuring appropriate education for exceptional children. (p. 3)

In the following section, you will learn how to develop and apply systematic data decision rules that will help you determine whether and when to make changes in instructional or intervention procedures.

DATA-BASED DECISION MAKING

In Chapter 2, we described how disciplinary referral data, when collected and reviewed systematically, can be used to make decisions relative to school-wide disciplinary strategies (Lewis-Palmer, Sugai, & Larson, 1999). This process extends also to making decisions about ongoing interventions and instructional programs at the individual student level. Professionals who are directly responsible for serving the students in settings where behaviors targeted for intervention occur must be able to evaluate these interventions continuously and make or recommend adjustments to intervention procedures on the basis of these evaluations. Data-based decision making is based on data that are collected systematically to monitor targeted academic and social behaviors. This technology facilitates ongoing formative evaluations of student performance.

One of the first skills required for data-based decision making is determining what the collected data are telling you. In other words, you must know how to analyze data. There are two approaches to behavioral data analysis: statistical and visual. The debate between proponents of both approaches has been long standing and lively. We advocate the visual method because visual analysis is more conservative and because most statistical analysis procedures are not useful in evaluating the performance of one or a small group of students. In addition, visual inspection is more realistic for practitioners.

Formative evaluation, then, is based on ongoing data collection. These data are used to decide when to change an instructional or behavior

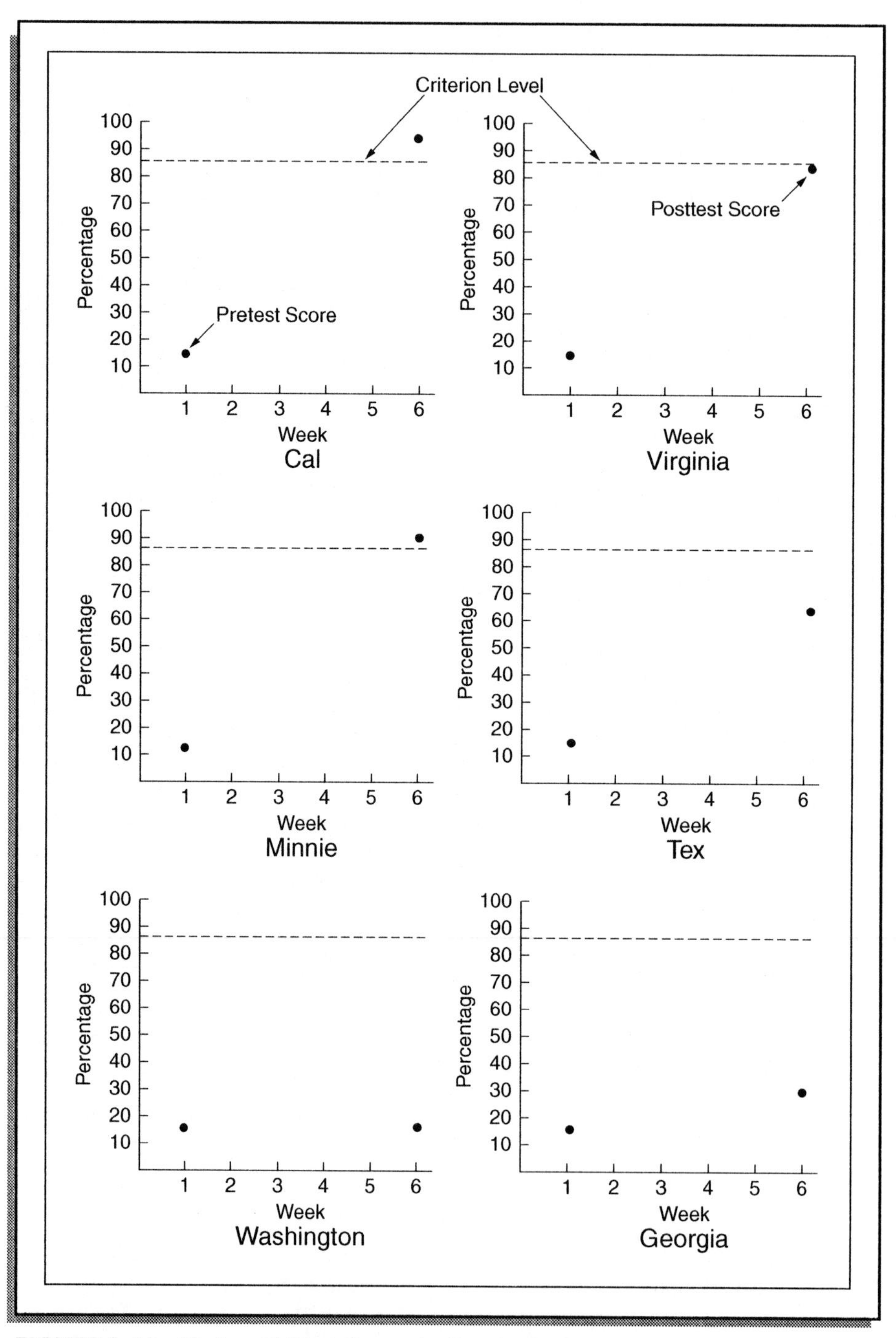

FIGURE 6–11 Display of 6-Week Summative Data for Six Students

Source: *Sugai, G. M., & Tindal, G.A. (1993).* Effective school consultation: An interactive approach, *p. 59. Pacific Grove, CA: Brooks/Cole. Used with permission.*

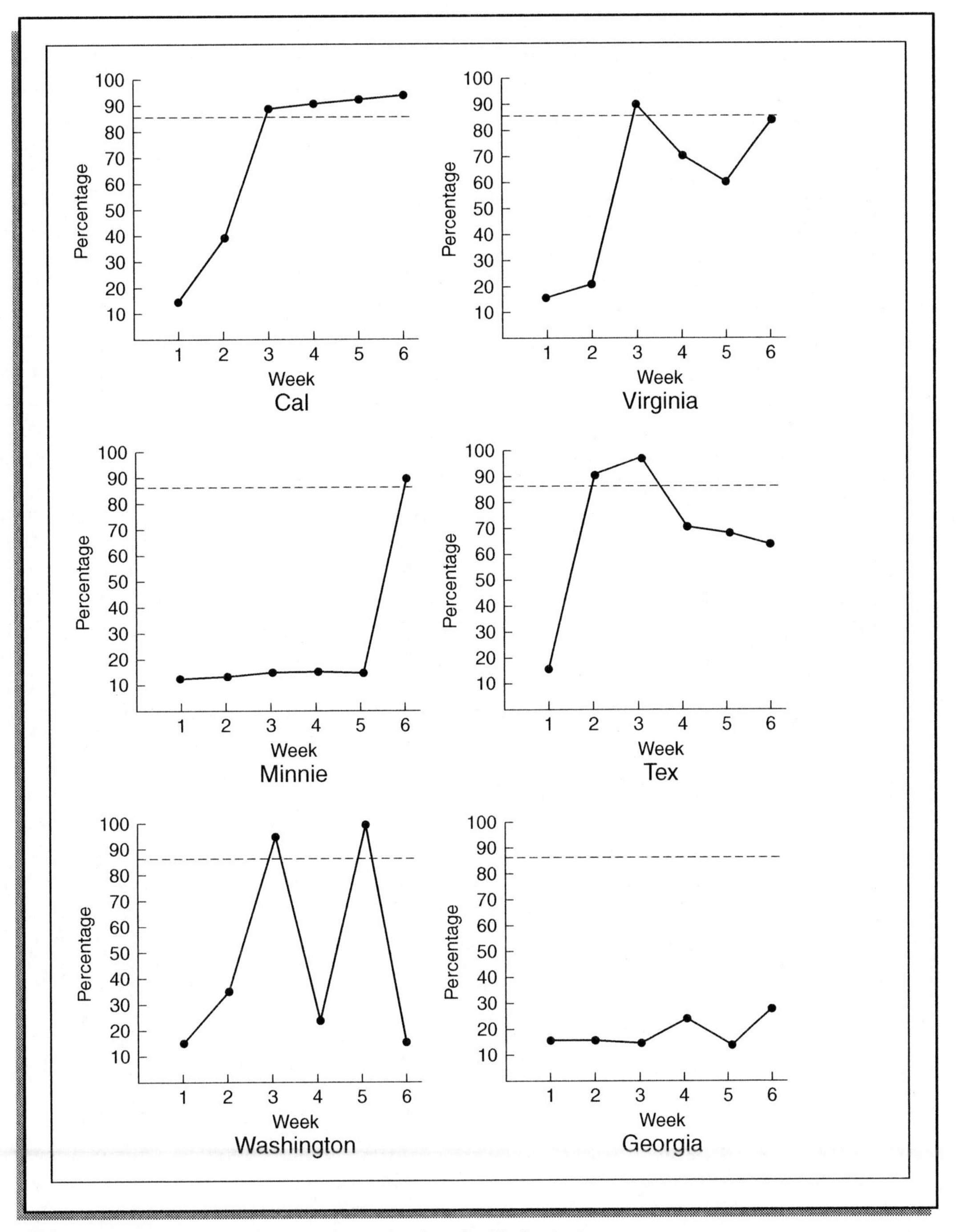

FIGURE 6–12 Display of 6-Week Formative Data for Six Students

Source: *Sugai, G. M., & Tindal, G. A. (1993).* Effective school consultation: An interactive approach, *p. 60. Pacific Grove, CA: Brooks/Cole. Used with permission.*

intervention program as well as which components of a student's program to alter, remove, or replace. Obviously, this task cannot be accomplished without data that are sensitive to variations in students' daily performances and that are reliable measures of those performances. If your data are sensitive and reliable, you can make good program evaluation decisions from visual analysis.

Formative evaluation based on visual data analysis (data-based decision making) amounts to identifying **functional relationships** between environmental variables and the target behavior being measured. This is accomplished by systematically manipulating certain environmental variables (e.g., curriculum, reinforcement, instructions) one at a time while keeping other variables as constant as possible. (You may recall that this is the same process used to verify hypotheses generated through functional behavioral assessments.)

Before implementing an academic or social intervention, assess the student's current performance. Instead of a static pretest approach, which may not represent the pupil's typical performance, measure target behavior across several sessions or days. Your intervention data then can be compared to this preintervention or **baseline data** to determine whether your program is effective. Thus, the purpose of collecting baseline data is twofold (Alberto & Troutman, 2003). First, these data serve a *descriptive function* in that they describe current levels and trends in student behavior. Second, baseline data serve a *predictive function* in that they serve as a basis for predicting the student's level of performance in the immediate future if an intervention is not implemented.

There are no hard-and-fast rules for determining the length of a baseline condition. Length depends on the level of the behavior, its variability, and whether it shows a trend toward the desired criterion level for the student's performance as well as such factors as the effects of the student's behavior on others and the amount of time left in the school term. Box 6-1 presents recommended guidelines for determining the length of baseline conditions.

Not only do baseline data provide a measure of student performance over time before intervention or instruction is begun, but they also supply a relative standard against which subsequent program changes may be evaluated. Because important decisions may be based on comparisons of data collected during baseline and subsequent intervention conditions, it is essential to analyze these data as carefully as those gathered during intervention conditions. Baseline data should be stable or display a trend that is counter to the direction desired during intervention (see the following discussion of analyzing data level and trends).

The visual display of data via graphs and charts provides a convenient summary across baseline and intervention conditions. Within these conditions, the data may be characterized in terms of level, trend, and stability. Straightforward and useful procedures

BOX 6-1 Guidelines for Determining Length of Baseline Conditions

- If baseline data are highly variable or show a trend in the direction of the desired criterion level, consider extending the baseline condition while looking for sources of variation or factors contributing to trends.
- A minimum of three baseline data points generally are recommended for academic target behaviors (e.g., White & Haring, 1980), although White (1971) demonstrated that a minimum of seven data points is needed to project a reliable performance trend.
- Collect five to seven baseline data points on social behavior targets, unless circumstances prohibit it.

for analyzing data about these characteristics on simple line graphs have been developed.

Analyzing Level

The magnitude of the data in terms of the scale value on the ordinate, or vertical axis, of the graph is its **level.** Tawney and Gast (1984) describe two characteristics of level that are important in data analysis. Within a given condition, level may be analyzed with regard to stability and change. *Level stability* refers to the variability of the data points around their middle value. Having baseline data that are relatively stable is particularly important because these data provide a comparison for evaluating the effects of an intervention. During intervention conditions, however, a change in level in a therapeutic direction is desired. Alberto and Troutman (2003) suggest that for classroom purposes, data may be considered stable if no single data point in a condition varies more than 50% from the mean of all data points in that condition. Data that vary widely from session to session or from day to day impair your ability to assess the impact of an instructional or intervention procedure on the target behavior. For example, unstable data following the introduction of an intervention suggest that the other variables may be influencing the behavior as much as the intervention procedures (Tawney & Gast, 1984).

Level change refers to the amount of relative change in the data within or between conditions. To determine the amount of level change within a condition, find the ordinate values of the first and last data points in the condition, subtract the smallest from the largest, and note whether the change is occurring in a therapeutic (improving) or contratherapeutic direction based on the intervention objective. Knowledge of the amount of level change within a condition is useful for deciding whether it is appropriate to change conditions. For example, if a level change is occurring in a therapeutic direction during baseline conditions, it may be unnecessary to begin an intervention. To find the amount of *level change between adjacent conditions* (e.g., baseline and intervention), identify the ordinate values of the last data point of the first condition and the value of the first data point of the second condition. Then subtract the smaller from the larger and note whether the change is in an improving or decaying direction. The amount of level change between baseline and intervention conditions is an indication of the immediate impact of the intervention on the target behavior (Tawney & Gast, 1984).

Another important characteristic to consider when evaluating changes in data between conditions is the amount of *overlapping data points.* This is determined by noting the proportion of data points in adjacent conditions that fall within the same range. For example, if more than 50% of the data points during an intervention condition fall within the range of baseline data points, it is reasonable to conclude that the intervention has only weak effects. However, the trend of the intervention data must also be considered.

Analyzing Data Trends

Data paths seldom follow straight lines, nor do they increase or decrease in even increments. This can create difficulty in making reliable judgments about whether rates of behavior are accelerating, decelerating, or remaining relatively stable. A relatively simple way to analyze data **trends** is to draw **trend lines** (also called lines of progress) that depict the general path of the data within a condition. This can be done by the freehand method, which involves drawing a line of "best fit" that bisects the data points. This method takes very little time, but the trend lines produced are likely to be inaccurate. A more reliable procedure is to draw a **split-middle line of progress** (White & Haring, 1980) explained in Box 6-2. This method may be used to analyze trends in data plotted on either equal interval or equal ratio (semilogarithmic) graph paper, and with a little practice you can do it quickly.

Data trends often reveal important and useful information. For example, an *increasing (accelerating) trend* indicates that the target behavior

BOX 6–2 Drawing a Line of Progress (Trend Line)

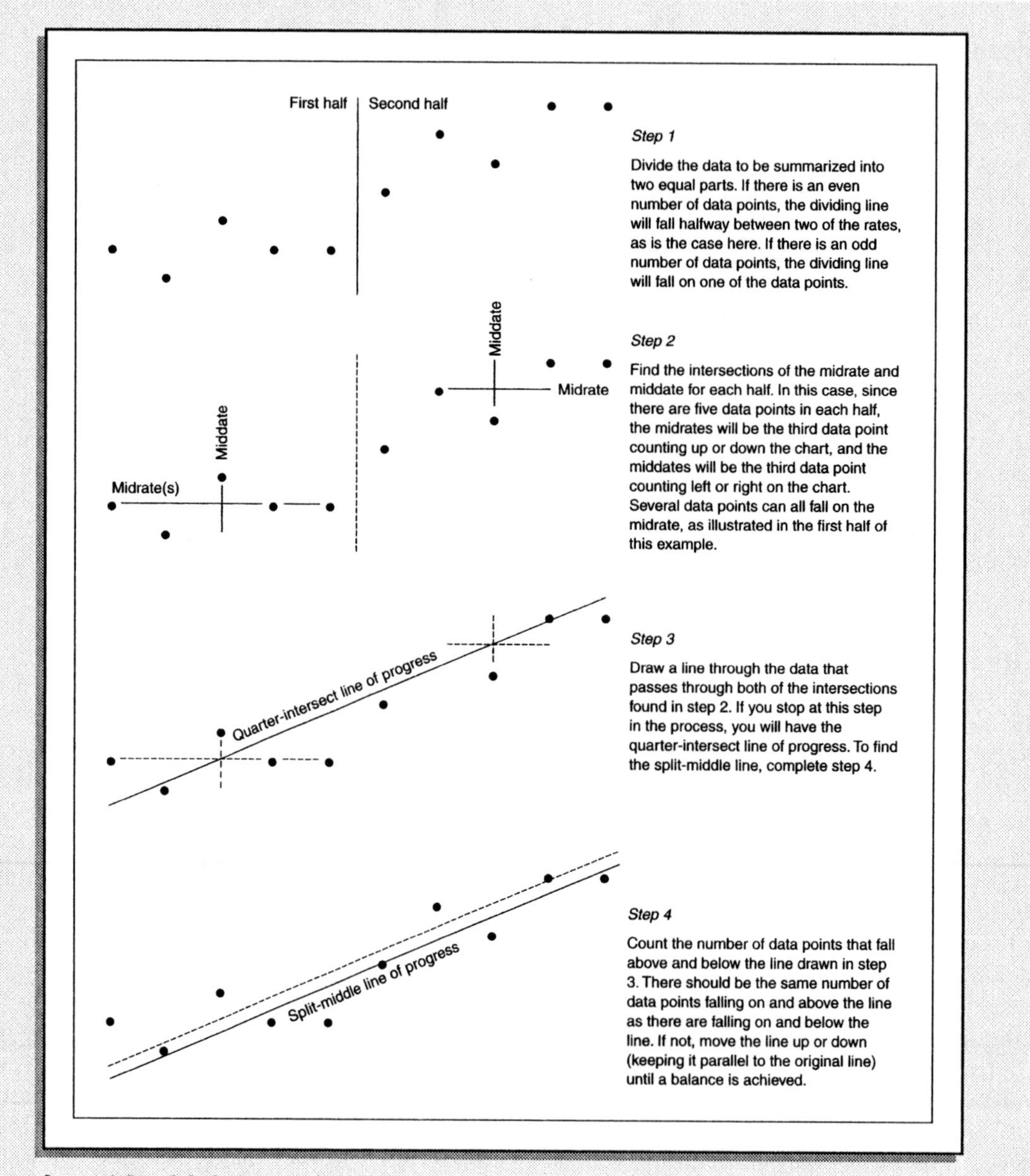

Source: *White, O. R., & Haring, N. G. (1980).* Exceptional teaching *(2nd ed.). Upper Saddle River, NJ: Merrill/Prentice Hall. Used with permission.*

probably is being reinforced. A *level trend* suggests that reinforcement is serving to maintain the behavior at its current rate. A *decreasing (decelerating) trend* indicates that extinction or punishment contingencies are in effect. Such trends may show that contingencies unknown to or unplanned by intervention agents are operating. For example, if a baseline trend is in the direction of your intervention goal and you implement an intervention, it would be difficult to attribute a continued change in a therapeutic direction (were this to occur) to the intervention because the behavior was changing in the desired direction anyway. However, if the baseline trend is stable or in a direction opposite the intervention criterion, you could justifiably hypothesize that therapeutic changes following the initiation of an intervention condition were the result of your procedure.

Determining data trends during intervention also may help you assess functional relationships and troubleshoot your program. Tawney and Gast (1984) provided several guidelines. For example, stable intervention data following a variable baseline indicates that recurring baseline variables perhaps are the treatment variables (e.g., differential teacher attention that was not controlled systematically during baseline). Weak program effects are suggested by variable intervention data or by considerable overlap between data points in baseline and intervention conditions. This problem is less critical if the overlap diminishes later during the intervention phase. A delayed therapeutic trend in the intervention data (i.e., no positive change for a number of sessions, followed by a change in the desired direction) may indicate the presence of initial training steps that are redundant or a waste of time. Figure 6–13 presents stylized graphs illustrating several intervention trends and their interpretation. As you become more proficient in analyzing data visually, you also will be able to interpret trends more accurately.

Data trend analysis tells you whether an instructional program or intervention is working and can prompt you to remove or revise an ineffective strategy, but waiting for a trend to emerge may take too long. Practitioners who must make day-to-day program decisions need rules to expedite their decision making. Fortunately, empirical data decision rules have been developed for academic targets (Deno, 2000; White & Haring, 1980). To implement these rules, follow the steps outlined in Box 6–3. A more detailed step-by step tutorial is presented on the Companion Website.

Figure 6–14 illustrates a data decision graph for an academic target. The teacher's decision rule was to change the intervention if three consecutive data points fell below the line of desired progress. Data decision rules for social behaviors are not as clear-cut because student performance, rather than sequential progress, generally is measured. Therefore, it is more difficult to establish a line of desired progress. You may, however, set your criterion in terms of a *daily level of desired performance* and base your decisions on the steps presented in Box 6–4. Actually, data decision rules are guidelines rather than rules; thus, they should be applied flexibly. Different behaviors and circumstances will require different data decision guidelines.

When setting criterion levels for targeted social behaviors, keep in mind an **ecological ceiling** (Howell, Fox, & Morehead, 1993). This means simply to acknowledge that it is unrealistic (and unfair) to expect students to demonstrate rates of targeted behaviors at levels that are not typical of peers in the same settings. Thus, expecting a student to exhibit zero talk-outs per hour is unreasonable if the usual rate of peer talk-outs is five per hour. By assessing peers who are exhibiting rates of the target behavior that are acceptable to adults in the setting, you can establish reasonable criterion levels. Lines of desired progress or performance should reflect an appropriate ecological ceiling rather than an arbitrarily chosen rate.

As we have emphasized in this chapter and the preceding chapter, powerful intervention strategies, especially those that are restrictive or intrusive, require precise and sensitive evaluation procedures to ensure that students do not spend unnecessary

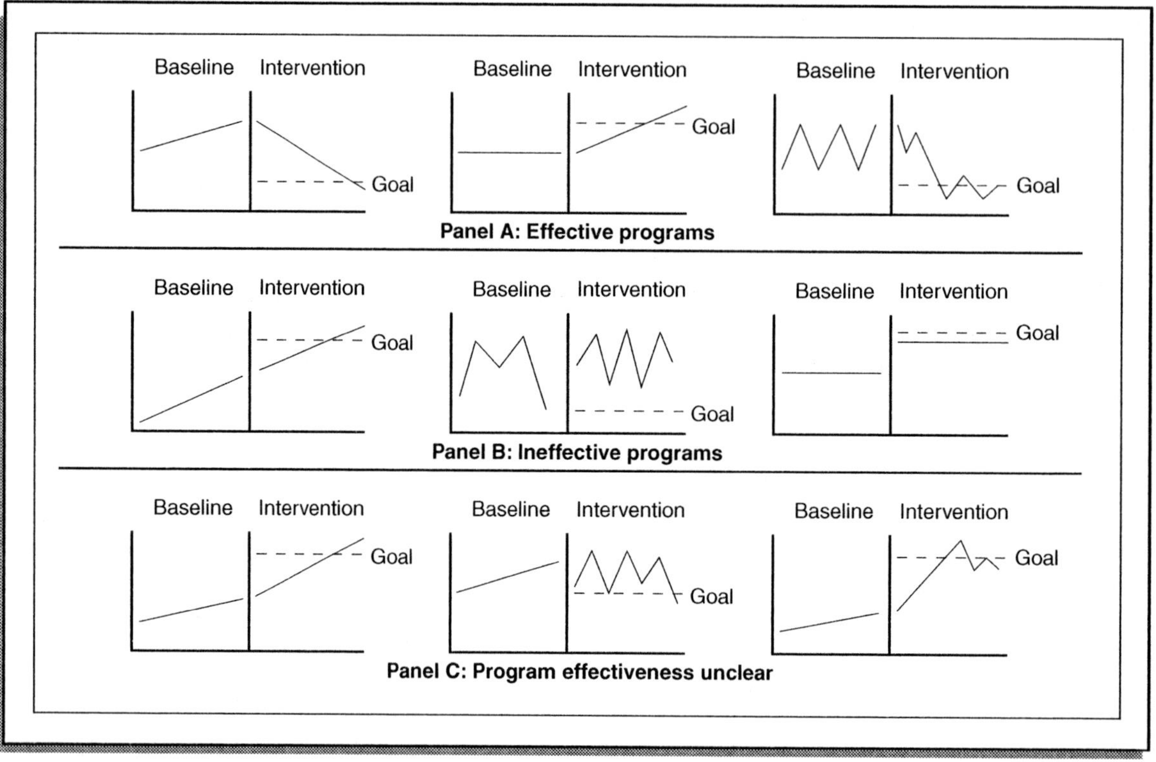

FIGURE 6–13 Interpretation of Data Trends

BOX 6–3 Steps for Implementing Data Decision Rules

1. Obtain and plot baseline assessment data for at least 3 days (or sessions) if more than one instructional session takes place each day.
2. Determine a desired terminal criterion level. This may be established arbitrarily by the curriculum, by assessing peers, from data obtained in previous programs with the student, from normative data on the target behavior if available, or by comparing the performance of peers who are fluent in the skill being measured. Plot this on the graph at a location corresponding to when you expect the criterion to be reached (see step 3).
3. Set a date when you want to meet the criterion. Also plot this on the graph. (Use an "A" [for aim] to designate the goal level and date. For an acceleration goal, draw an A at the appropriate location on the graph or chart. To designate a deceleration goal, invert the A.)
4. Draw a **line of desired progress,** or **aim line,** from the median (middle value) of the last three baseline data points to the criterion level and date.
5. Change the program if the student's progress fails to meet or exceed the line of desired progress for 3 consecutive days or sessions (White & Haring, 1980).

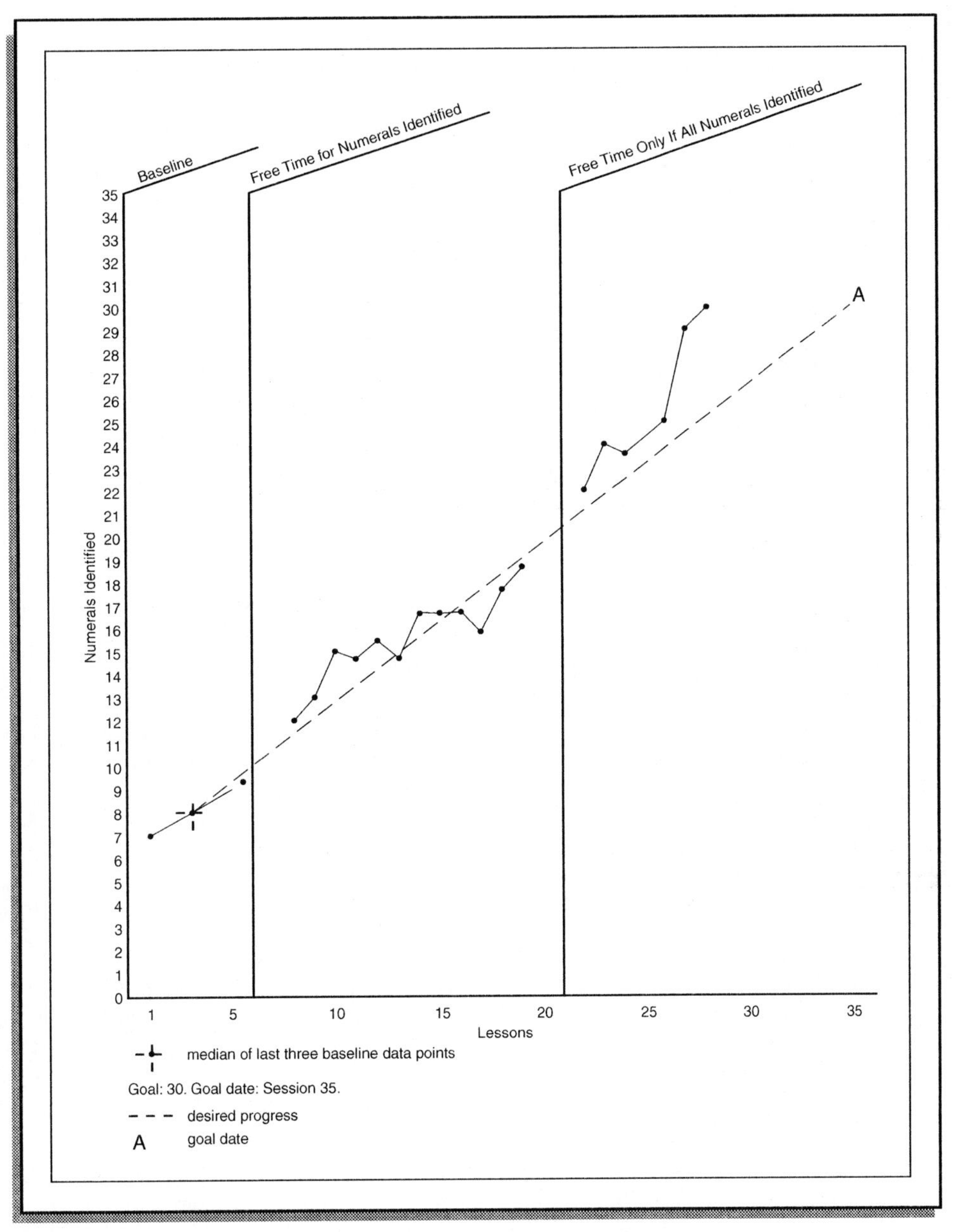

FIGURE 6–14 Data Decision Graph: Identifying Math Numerals

amounts of time in ineffective programs. Good evaluation procedures also protect those who carry out interventions in that they provide feedback that may be used to adjust or change procedures that are inappropriate, incorrectly applied, or simply do not work as planned. Unlike assessment, which yields information regarding the current status of a student, evaluation involves assessing the impact

BOX 6–4 **Data-Based Decision Making for Social Target Behaviors**

1. Obtain 5 to 7 days (or sessions) of baseline data (more if the data are extremely variable or a therapeutic trend is apparent).
2. Select and plot the terminal criterion level and date, just as for academic targets.
3. Write a data decision rule for the program (e.g., change the program if data collected on the student's performance for 3 consecutive intervention days or sessions falls on the wrong side of the aim line).
4. Collect intervention data and adjust the program according to your rule.

of a program on a pupil's current status. Recall from our earlier discussion that evaluation may be *summative,* occurring after teaching and learning have taken place, or *formative,* which means it occurs as skills are being formed. Traditionally, most educational programs are evaluated summatively (e.g., once or twice a year) when it is too late to make any program changes based on the data obtained. Formative evaluation, therefore, is an integral part of the teaching process, especially for students who are struggling academically or socially.

SINGLE-SUBJECT RESEARCH DESIGNS

By using data decision rules and by learning to visually analyze data, you should become skilled at systematically evaluating interventions and making appropriate decisions. Although data-based decision-making procedures are extremely useful in determining whether an intervention is working, they do not provide a convincing demonstration that the intervention is responsible for changes in target behaviors. Other uncontrolled factors may influence the behavior simultaneously with the intervention, and these offer **competing explanations** for observed changes (e.g., something else in the setting was altered; the student became more mature or gained insight, her parents established a contingency at home). Single-subject research designs control for the effects of such extraneous variables through systematic manipulation of intervention variables over time while the target behavior is monitored. These designs establish the **internal validity** of the intervention; that is, they demonstrate that the intervention is responsible for observed changes in the target behavior(s). However, to establish high levels of **external validity** (meaning that the intervention is effective across a variety of individuals, situations, and implementers) through single-subject research, many replications of intervention effects are necessary (Tawney & Gast, 1984).

Box 6–5 lists the required features of single-subject research designs. If the rate of target behavior changes in a therapeutic direction only when the intervention is introduced and otherwise remains at baseline levels, a functional relationship has been demonstrated (researchers also refer to this as demonstrating **experimental control**).

At this point, many teachers say they do not care whether these variables are uncontrolled as long as something works to change behavior. The problem with this attitude is that it may lead to using nonfunctional procedures or complex interventions that place extensive demands on the teacher. For example, a teacher designed a group contingency to reduce a disruptive behavior of a fourth-grade class. The game involved points, backup consequences, and much of the teacher's time. It was, however, very effective, and the teacher used the game with subsequent groups for several years. Unfortunately, the effects weren't

BOX 6–5 Requirements of Single-Subject Research Designs

1. Repeated measurement of the **dependent variable** (target behavior) over time
2. Following a baseline condition, introduction of one or more **independent variables** while measurement of the dependent variable continues
3. At least one replication of the implementation of the independent variable to rule out competing explanations and demonstrate a functional relationship between the independent variable and changes in the dependent variable (Alberto & Troutman, 2003)

always as dramatic as the first time. Had the teacher been able to determine which components of the intervention were responsible for its effectiveness, the group contingency could have been adjusted to the demands of each new situation. Further, some components could have been dropped, thereby simplifying the procedure and reducing the teacher's effort. The point is that you should use the simplest procedures that also are effective. If praise is an effective reinforcer, why develop an elaborate token economy?

Single-subject research designs not only are useful in controlling for the effects of unsystematic variables and for isolating the essential components of intervention "packages" that incorporate more than one intervention (e.g., Amanda's intervention included both overcorrection and teaching her to use a replacement behavior) but also in helping understand studies reported in the research literature. While you may not be interested in conducting such research yourself, knowledge of these research designs will help you interpret the research reports that you read as part of your professional growth plan. The reference lists for each chapter in this text will give you an idea of the journals reporting research in areas of interest or concern to you. You also may visit the Online Library at the Website of the National Technical Assistance Center for Positive Behavioral Interventions and Supports to see examples of how single-subject research designs are used in the center's research.

Now we briefly describe four single-subject research designs. For more comprehensive explanations, you may wish to consult a single-subject design book (e.g., Richards, Taylor, Ramasamy, & Richards, 1999). The information in our discussion of data-based decision making regarding the length of baseline phases and the determination of stability or trends in data through visual analysis applies here as well. You also may apply data decision rules within phases of a single-subject design.

As you read about each of the following single-subject research designs, try to identify each of the required features presented in Box 6–5.

Withdrawal and Reversal Designs

These designs, also referred to as A-B-A-B designs, involve collecting preintervention (baseline) data (A), followed by an intervention condition (B), a withdrawal or reversal of intervention procedures (A), and finally reinstatement of the intervention (B). If the target behavior, continuously measured during all conditions, changes in accordance with the condition in effect, it may be concluded that the intervention is effective. Although A-B-A-B designs are commonly referred to as **reversal designs,** a "true" reversal design involves a reversal of intervention contingencies in which the intervention is withdrawn from one behavior (e.g., in-seat) and simultaneously applied to an incompatible behavior (e.g., out-of-seat). The purpose of this manipulation is to demonstrate that the intervention procedure (e.g., teacher attention delivered contingent on a behavior) has a functional relationship to the behaviors to which it is applied. Reversal designs are uncommon in the applied research literature because of the understandable reluctance of researchers and practitioners to directly reinforce undesired behavior once it has been reduced (Tawney & Gast, 1984). **Withdrawal designs,** however, involve simply removing the intervention during the second A condition. In other words, baseline conditions are reinstated.

> If you collect baseline data and then implement an intervention condition, you have implemented an A–B design. However, because there is not at least one replication of the use of the intervention, this design cannot demonstrate a functional relationship between dependent and independent variables (Alberto & Troutman, 2003).

Figure 6–15 shows a withdrawal design used to evaluate the effects of time-out contingent on a student's temper tantrums. It may be concluded that time-out was effective in this case because the frequency of Ralph's tantrums decreased when the intervention was applied. The second replication of baseline and intervention conditions establishes time-out as the variable that was responsible for the observed effects. Without this replication, we could not be sure that time-out was responsible for changes in the target behavior because other uncontrolled events may have been introduced at the same time as the time-out contingency, leading to the possibility of competing explanations for the observed outcome. Changes in levels and trends of the target behavior in accordance with repeated introduction and withdrawal of the intervention demonstrates that manipulation of the time-out contingency controlled the student's tantrums regardless of any uncontrolled events that may have taken place.

Multiple baseline designs provide a means of evaluating an intervention without a return to baseline conditions. The effectiveness of a program is demonstrated by applying it sequentially across different students, across different behaviors in the same student (as in the case of Amanda, see Figure 6–1), or across different conditions or settings with the same student and behavior. If the measured behaviors change in the desired direction only when the intervention is applied, it may be concluded that the intervention is effective. See the Companion Website for examples of multiple baseline designs across students and settings. Note that in each case, rates of target behavior changed only when the intervention was applied to each behavior, to each student, or in each setting.

Multiple baseline designs are applicable to a variety of situations. However, they require two or more replications (two or more students, settings, or behaviors), prolonged baselines, and target behaviors that can be separately altered without changing the rate of the behavior still in baseline (Alberto & Troutman, 2003).

A variation on the multiple baseline is the **multiple probe design.** It differs from the former in that data probes, or periodic assessments, rather than continuous data are recorded for the settings, behaviors, or students to which the intervention has not yet been applied. This variation is useful particularly if you are unable to monitor all target behaviors each day (Tawney & Gast, 1984). See an example on the Companion Website.

Changing Criterion Design

The **changing criterion design** (Hartmann & Hall, 1976) actually is a variation on the multiple baseline design, but it may be used with only one student, with only one behavior, or in only one setting. Following the baseline phase, an intervention program is applied through a series of increments in criterion levels. If the rate of the target behavior changes as the criterion is altered, it may be concluded that the intervention was responsible (Alberto & Troutman, 2003). For example, Figure 6–16 shows a changing criterion design used to evaluate a response cost procedure (loss of recess time) to decrease Kristine's use of swear words. As the figure shows, the criterion was

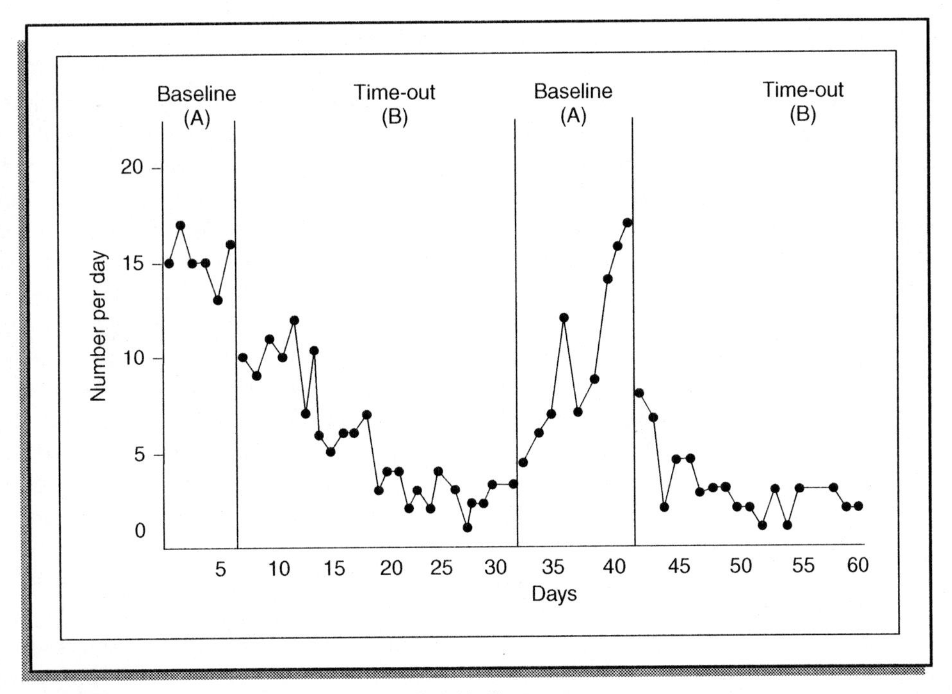

FIGURE 6–15 Effects of Time-Out on Ralph's Tantrums

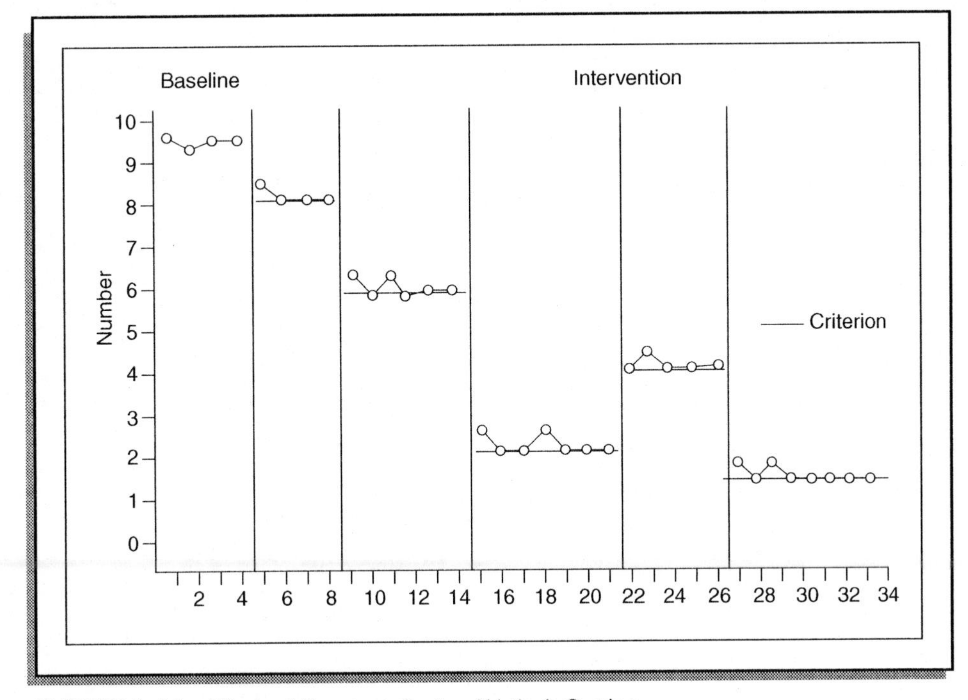

FIGURE 6–16 Effects of Response Cost on Kristine's Cursing

changed every few days. Kristine's performance changed according to the criterion in effect. Note that the pattern of criterion changes was varied so that phases were not the same length and the criterion actually was increased in one phase. This was done to document that changes in Kristine's behavior were due to the specific response cost contingency in effect and not to extraneous variables. A functional relationship is demonstrated when changes in the target behavior occur only in response to the specific criterion in place. This design is especially appropriate for evaluating programs in which a stepwise progression is desired, such as when a new skill is being acquired (Alberto & Troutman, 2003).

Alternating Treatments Design

In contrast to the previous designs, in which a single independent variable is applied in any one condition, an **alternating treatments design** is used for comparing the effects of two interventions within a condition. This design is the preferred choice if the teacher or researcher wishes to compare two or more interventions (e.g., instructional curricula). These interventions are presented on alternating sessions or days according to a schedule worked out in advance (e.g., random or counterbalanced). The student should receive the same number of exposures to each treatment until it is established that one treatment is superior, and tasks (or behaviors) should be equivalent in difficulty. The superiority of one treatment over others is demonstrated when its data path clearly departs (in a therapeutic direction) from the others. One advantage of an alternating treatment design is that a baseline condition prior to intervention is not required. This same feature also permits the immediate introduction of treatment variables. Still another advantage is that target behaviors do not have to be reversible, as there is no requirement to return to baseline conditions. Thus, alternating treatment designs are ideally suited to investigating the relative merits of instructional procedures. However, because this design does not include a replication

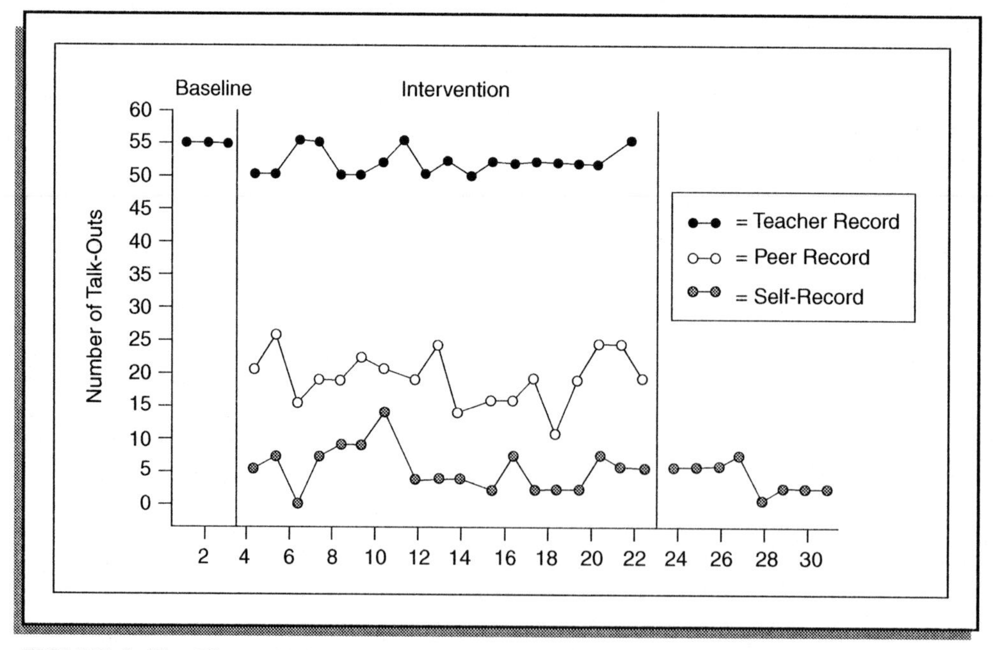

FIGURE 6–17 Effects of Self, Peer, and Teacher Recording on Carl's Daily Talk-Outs

phase (second intervention condition), it does not provide a strong case for a functional relationship (Alberto & Troutman, 2003; Tawney & Gast, 1984). Figure 6–17 shows how Carl's teacher used an alternating treatments design to compare three strategies for reducing the number of his talk-outs. The separation of the data paths established that self-recording was superior to peer or teacher recording of talk-outs. Therefore, in the last condition, the teacher just had Carl self-record his talking-out.

SUMMARY

- Visual presentation of data through graphs and charts facilitates communication and evaluation of student progress. There are many different formats for presenting data visually.
- Formative evaluation procedures based on continuous and precise measurement of target behaviors are needed for studying and for adjusting interventions.
- Formative evaluation reduces the chances that students will be subjected to ineffective or unnecessarily aversive procedures.
- Data-based decision making involves visual analysis of graphic data depicting student performance and evaluating daily student progress compared with the desired rate of progress.
- Single-subject research designs are used to document functional relationships between targeted student behaviors and instructional or behavioral interventions.

DISCUSSION/APPLICATION IDEAS

1. Describe the features of well-constructed graphs and charts and how these contribute to clear communication.
2. Differentiate between equal interval and equal ratio graphs and between performance or progress charts. What circumstances influence decisions about which to use?
3. How do data levels, trends, and stability affect decisions about changing intervention conditions?
4. Use the graph in Figure 6–1 to explain how a functional relationship (experimental control) was demonstrated between the independent and dependent variables in this intervention. Identify the dependent and independent variables.
5. Follow the procedures described in Chapters 5 and 6 to monitor and evaluate an academic or behavioral program for one of your students. Be sure to collect and graph data across baseline and intervention conditions and describe changes in data trend and level within and across conditions. Write a data decision rule and use it to evaluate and adjust your procedures.
6. For what behaviors and circumstances are the following designs appropriate: withdrawal, reversal, multiple baseline, multiple probe, changing criterion, and alternating treatments?

REFERENCES

Alberto, P. A., & Troutman, A. C. (2003). *Applied behavior analysis for teachers* (6th ed.). Upper Saddle River, NJ: Merrill/Prentice Hall.

Darch, C. B., & Kame'enui, E. J. (2004). *Instructional classroom management: A proactive approach to behavior management* (2nd ed.). Upper Saddle River, NJ: Merrill/Prentice Hall.

Deno, S. L. (1986). Formative evaluation of individual student programs: A new role for school psychologists. *School Psychology Review, 15,* 358–374.

Deno, S. L. (2000). Academic progress as incompatible behavior: Curriculum-based measurement (CBM) as intervention. *Beyond Behavior, 9*(3), 12–16.

Fabry, B. D., & Cone, J. D. (1980). Auto-graphing: A one-step approach to collecting and graphing data. *Education and Treatment of Children, 3,* 361–368.

Fuchs, L. S., & Deno, S. L. (1991). Paradigmatic distinctions between instructionally relevant measurement models. *Exceptional Children, 57,* 488–500.

Gast, D. L., & Gast, K. B. (1981). Educational program evaluation: An overview of data-based instruction for classroom teachers. In *Toward a research base for the least restrictive environment: A collection of papers* (pp. 1-30). Lexington, KY: College of Education Dean's Grant Project.

Gunter, P. L., Calicott, K., Denny, R. K., & Gerber, B. L. (2003). Finding a place for data collection in classrooms for students with emotional/behavioral disorders. *Preventing School Failure, 48,* 4-8.

Hartmann, D. P., & Hall, R. V. (1976). The changing criterion design. *Journal of Applied Behavior Analysis, 9,* 527-532.

Howell, K. W., Fox S. L., & Morehead, M. K. (1993). *Curriculum-based evaluation: Teaching and decision-making* (2nd ed). Pacific Grove, CA: Brooks/Cole.

Lewis-Palmer, T., Sugai, G., & Larson, S. (1999). Using data to guide decisions about program implementation and effectiveness: An overview and applied example. *Effective School Practices, 17*(4), 47-53.

Nelson, C. M., Gast, D. L., & Trout, D. D. (1979). A charting system for monitoring student progress in instructional programs. *Journal of Special Education Technology, 3,* 43-49.

Richards, S., Taylor, R., Ramasamy, R., & Richards, R. (1999). *Single subject research: Applications in educational and clinical settings.* San Diego: Singular Publications.

Sugai, G. M., & Tindal, G. A. (1993). *Effective school consultation: An interactive approach.* Pacific Grove, CA: Brooks/Cole.

Tawney, J. W., & Gast, D. L. (1984). *Single subject research in special education.* Upper Saddle River, NJ: Merrill/Prentice Hall.

White, O. R. (1971). *A pragmatic approach to the description of progress in the single case.* Unpublished doctoral dissertation, University of Oregon, Eugene.

White, O. R. (1986). Precision teaching—precision learning. *Exceptional Children, 52,* 522-524.

White, O. R., & Haring, N. G. (1980). *Exceptional teaching* (2nd ed.). Upper Saddle River, NJ: Merrill/Prentice Hall.

STRATEGIES FOR SPECIFIC BEHAVIOR PROBLEMS

Chapter 7 **Addressing Disruptive Behaviors**

Chapter 8 **Improving School Survival Skills and Social Skills**

Chapter 9 **Addressing Aggressive Behaviors**

Chapter 10 **Developing Alternatives to Self-Stimulatory and Self-Injurious Behavior**

CHAPTER 7 ADDRESSING DISRUPTIVE BEHAVIORS

OUTLINE

Introduction
Environmentally Mediated Interventions
Teacher-Mediated Interventions
Peer-Mediated Interventions
Self-Mediated Interventions

OBJECTIVES

After completing this chapter, you should be able to

- Explain the four types of behavioral interventions and give examples of each.
- Select the best intervention for a student's disruptive behavior.
- Design and implement a token economy.
- Design and carry out a group contingency.
- Design and carry out a self-monitoring procedure.

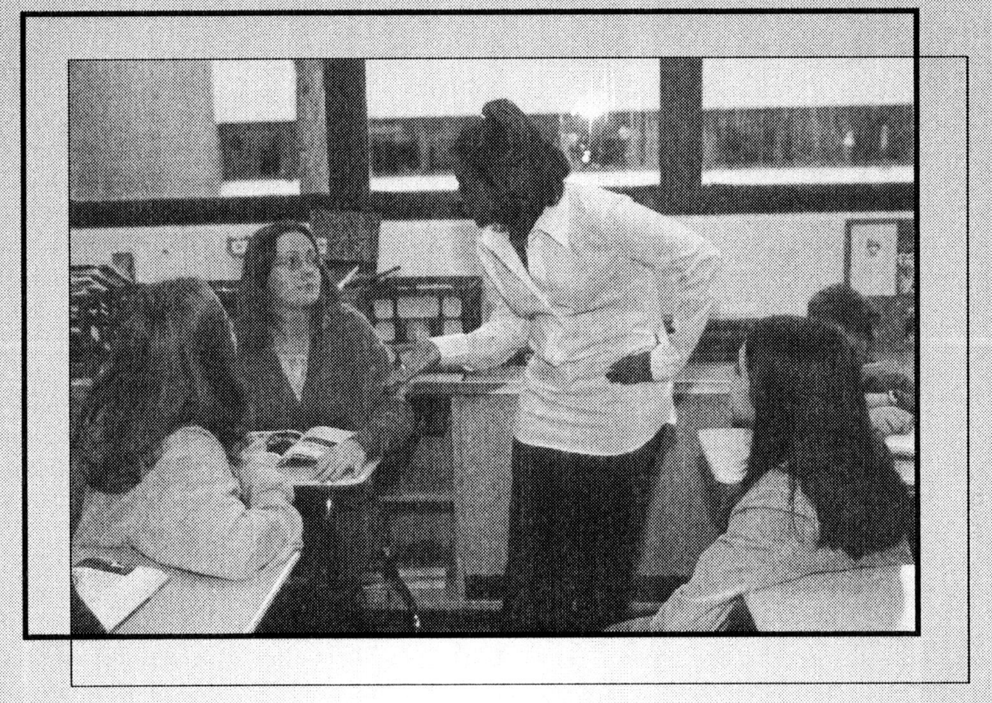

KEY TERMS (refer to the Glossary on the Companion Website for definitions)

communicative function
dependent group contingency
environmentally mediated interventions
group goal setting and feedback
high-probability requests
home-based contract
independent group contingency
interdependent group contingency
peer manager strategy
peer-mediated interventions
peer-monitoring procedure
public posting
reprimands
self-evaluation
self-instruction
self-mediated interventions
self-monitoring
self-recording
teacher-mediated interventions

As our opening case study illustrates, we have no single precise description of disruptive behavior because youngsters can misbehave in a variety of ways. Students can climb on furniture, grab classmates' materials, make obscene noises or gestures, verbally or physically defy the teacher, touch their classmates, or run through the hallways.

How many different disruptive behaviors can you find in the case study? Given what you've been learning about assessment in previous chapters, how would you measure each problem behavior?

INTRODUCTION

In this chapter, you will discover new options for addressing disruptive behaviors. To begin, let's decide whether to intervene to change a disruptive behavior. First, ask yourself whether the behaviors interfere with the personal freedom and learning of others. Many behaviors will annoy and irritate you. However, as a veteran middle school teacher once advised, "In this classroom, you must pick your battles carefully; you can't take on everything." Next, consider the purpose, or **communicative function,** of the behavior. Here are some possible reasons why students disrupt classroom activities:

COME INTO MY CLASSROOM: A CASE STUDY

No wonder Dr. Covaleski, the principal, sounded so frustrated when she called me to consult with the sixth-grade team! I had been in the building only minutes when I was almost trampled by a group of kids changing classes. In the background, I could hear their teacher screaming to them, "Slow down! Stop running this minute!"

Hoping that the problem was limited to transitions, I stepped out of their way and watched as they entered their next classes. That's when I realized that we were facing more than mere hallway bedlam. Miss Perrone, an exasperated young teacher, marched over to the lockers and began to reprimand the students who were hanging around outside her classroom:

"How many times do I have to tell you to get to this class on time? If you don't get into this classroom by the time I count to 10, I will send you all to the office. And I mean it!"

I winced as one of the teens baited Miss Perrone into a prolonged verbal tug-of-war while most of the class waited inside with bored expressions. With no assignments on their desks or on the board, they were left to entertain themselves. Soon, three girls began to look through papers on Miss Perrone's desk, confident that she would not return to the classroom from the heat of battle with her tardy students. Another student sat in front of Miss Perrone's computer, reading e-mail and laughing out loud. At the back of the classroom, giggling classmates watched their classmate gesture obscenely to a physical education class outdoors.

Confronted with these behaviors, teachers like Miss Perrone may react emotionally, use ineffective approaches, and ultimately burn out. Imagine that you were using an antecedent–behavior–consequence form to understand the problems of this middle school. Can you envision how that form might appear? What role does Miss Perrone play in her students' misbehavior?

* To gain your attention (positive or negative)
* To get the attention or approval of classmates
* To avoid doing work
* To gather information, for example, to test the limits of your authority or to find out whether the rules will be enforced
* To make a boring class more interesting

> Consider the case study again. What motivated the students in Miss Perrone's class to act as they did? Which behaviors warranted teacher attention?

When you are really clear about the behavior you want to change, you narrow the scope of the problem. This makes it easier to interpret the behavior and find just the right intervention. We present four categories of interventions: environmentally mediated, teacher mediated, peer mediated, and self-mediated. In each section, you will find examples of strategies to use in your classroom. Check out the Companion Website for additional resources on planning effective strategies, such as the Behavior Advisor Website.

ENVIRONMENTALLY MEDIATED INTERVENTIONS

In **environmentally mediated interventions,** we alter some aspect of the classroom environment to prevent or to address behavioral problems. For example, you might modify your rules, curricula, schedules, seating, and the general physical layout of your room. (For good information on classroom planning to prevent problems, see Wong & Wong, 2004.)

Two important ideas may help you when considering environmental strategies. First, merely altering the environment is not a powerful intervention strategy. Environmental modifications should be combined with other strategies. Second, those other strategies depend on a sound environment that discourages disruptive behavior and that supports the other, more powerful interventions. In other words, environmental modifications are necessary if other strategies are to be successful but not sufficient alone to change misbehavior. For ideas about preschool environments, check out the University of Minnesota's link on the Companion Website.

Here's an example of an effective environmentally mediated strategy that might solve the problems raised in our opening case study. To reduce hallway noise in a middle school, Kartub, Taylor-Greene, March, and Horner (2000) selected a small blinking light to help students remember the motto, "When you see the light, lips tight." This environmental approach was successful in combination with adult supervision, verbal reprimands, and assigned detention for excessive noise.

Rules

Even experienced teachers occasionally make two mistakes. The first is to assume that students know what is expected of them. An indication of this problem is the absence of clear rules for classroom behavior. Either rules are nonexistent or they are worded too generally (e.g., show respect for other persons, use good manners). Vague rules may be explained so that pupils understand them (e.g., showing respect means keep hands and feet to yourself, do not interrupt when others are talking, take turns), but often they are not. The second mistake is to punish students for their failure to exhibit a behavior that they do not know how to perform (e.g., following directions, remaining in seat). This problem relates to the failure to discriminate correctly the difference between a skill deficit and a performance deficit. Look at Table 7-1, which gives examples not only of student rules but also of student and teacher responsibilities.

Consider these guidelines for establishing rules:

1. Select the fewest possible number of rules. Too many rules are difficult to remember and

TABLE 7–1 List of Rules

Recommended Rules	Student Expectations	Teacher Responsibilities
Enter the classroom quietly.	Walk in and speak softly. Put away belongings. Take assigned seats.	Stand at the door. Wait to share conversations with students. Establish areas for putting away coats, turning in assignments, and so on. Create a permanent seating arrangement. Recognize appropriate behaviors.
Begin work on time.	Listen to/read instructions carefully. Begin to work immediately.	Prepare practice assignments in advance. Expect students to begin work promptly. Monitor student behavior. Recognize appropriate behaviors.
Stay on task.	Ignore distractions from others. Continue to work without interruptions.	Assign developmentally appropriate tasks. Check for student understanding. Provide positive and corrective feedback. Monitor student behavior and assignment completion progress. Prevent/end distracting behaviors. Recognize appropriate behaviors.
Complete work on time.	Check assignment completion requirements. Ask questions for understanding. Set goals for assignment completion.	State complete assignment information, including a grading criteria. Provide appropriate models and demonstrations. Teach goal setting. Allow sufficient class time to work. Recognize appropriate behaviors.
Follow directions at all times.	Listen carefully. Ask questions for understanding. Do as all teachers request.	Gain student attention. Give clear directions for particular situations. Check for student understanding. Provide examples and/or demonstrations. Monitor student behavior. Recognize appropriate behaviors.
Listen while others speak.	Maintain a positive body posture. Look at the person. Note important information. Signal for more information.	Teach listening skills. Model good listening skills. Encourage verbal elaboration. Encourage "risk free" active participation.
Use appropriate language.	Avoid angry and foul words. Use kind words to tell how you feel.	Teach appropriate statements for avoiding conflicts. Teach techniques for self-control. Model respect toward students and peers. Recognize appropriate behaviors.
Keep hands, feet, objects to self.	Avoid hitting, kicking, or throwing things.	Teach safety habits and procedures. Teach techniques for self-control. Recognize appropriate behaviors.

Source: *Rademacher, J. A., Callahan, K., & Pederson-Seelye, V. A. (1998). How do your classroom rules measure up?* Intervention in School and Clinic, 33, *284–289. Reprinted with permission.*

frequently are so specific that pupils easily can find exceptions to them. For example, one teacher who was concerned about fighting in the classroom developed a long list of rules: no hitting, no shoving, no biting, no name-calling, and so forth. She later substituted just one rule—"Remain in your seat during our quiet seat work"—because in-seat behavior was incompatible with behaviors leading to and involving fighting.

2. Use different rules for different situations. Obviously, rules for classroom activities should be different from playground, lunch line, or bus-waiting-area rules. Some pupils need to be taught that different situations call for different behavior. Clearly stated rules can help them make this discrimination.
3. Rules should be stated behaviorally and be enforceable. Thus, the rule "Show respect toward others" invites differing interpretations of what constitutes respect or disrespect and is not easily enforceable. The rule "No talking when my back is turned" is behaviorally stated but would be difficult to enforce. Rules that are not enforceable invite tattling as well as limit testing, both of which can lead to disruptions.
4. Rules should be stated positively; that is, they should describe appropriate and desired student behaviors rather than those to avoid. This focuses attention on positive replacement behaviors rather than on inappropriate pupil activity. For example, the rule "Wait to be called on before speaking" is preferable to "No talking."
5. Rules should be reasonable. The most common response to an unreasonable rule is to challenge it, which may lead to a serious power struggle. Another option is to give up rather than try to meet the expectation. Thus, the rule "All homework must be in before first period" is reasonable only if all students are capable of meeting it; that is, no student has a night job, and the homework is within all pupils' ability to complete. The best way to ensure that rules are reasonable is to develop them with students.
6. There must be consistent consequences for rule fulfillment or infraction. This does not mean the use of threats or lectures. Rule consequences should be posted with the rules themselves or taught until all pupils know them thoroughly. Posted rules and consequences, incidentally, are a tremendous help to substitute teachers or new classroom paraprofessionals. Without consequences, rules have little effect on behavior. Therefore, consistent teacher follow-through is critical, including praise or points for following rules and systematic withdrawal of attention or other reinforcers (or presentation of aversive consequences) for their infraction. Avoid bending the rules for specific pupils or situations unless you have planned it with students in advance.

Teacher Movement Patterns

Gunter, Shores, and Susan (1995) observed that increasing the amount of time teachers spend away from their desks during independent activities increases student academic engagement. Teacher movement also increases proximity to students. In turn, closer proximity is associated with the increased power of both social reinforcement and punishment (Shores, Gunter, Denny, & Jack, 1993) and can increase academic engagement (Conroy, Asmus, Ladwig, Sellers, & Valcante, 2004).

As you travel around your classroom, you may notice that some pupils are overly dependent on your attention, flagging you down or chronically approaching your desk. Help students to design and use a signaling device (see Figure 7-1) to show whether teacher assistance is needed. This procedure reduces the need for students to be out-of-seat to get teacher attention and may help them stop to think before calling on you.

> Take a hard look at your classroom. Are the rules well-written? Does the physical layout support your students' appropriate behavior, or does the physical plan set the occasion for problems? How do students get your attention?

FIGURE 7–1 Signaling Device for a Child's Desk

TEACHER-MEDIATED INTERVENTIONS

Once you have adopted good environmentally mediated interventions, you can select from among many **teacher-mediated strategies** proven to improve students' behavior. This section tells how to increase your effectiveness as you help your students learn new behaviors.

Monitoring Teacher Verbal and Nonverbal Behavior

What you say or do not say may be your most powerful strategy for remedying disruptive behavior. We know that teacher praise can have positive effects on the academic and behavioral outcomes of students with emotional and behavioral disorders (EBD). Yet teachers of students with challenging behaviors make infrequent use of this effective strategy (Sutherland & Wehby, 2001b). In contrast to what you might expect, your negative comments can actually increase misbehavior. As illustrated in our opening case study, students may act out just to "get the teacher." Teacher attention to undesired behavior, though negative, seems to function as positive reinforcement. Furthermore, both of these studies demonstrated that peer attention to inappropriate responses exerted more powerful control over child behavior than did the adult reactions.

Shores et al. (1993) conducted numerous studies of the interactions between general and special education teachers and students with EBD. Teachers responded less than half the time to students raising hands and requesting assistance with tasks. Such teacher neutrality creates an unpleasant classroom environment, encouraging pupil escape and avoidance behaviors.

As Walker (1995) found, the cumulative effect of disproportionate teacher attention (in addition to peer support and attention) to acting-out children's misbehavior is to strengthen undesired behavior patterns. The unfortunate result of this combination of events is a classroom situation in which the teacher relies on progressively more aversive management practices (public reprimands, sending children to the principal's office, suspensions, and so on). These measures may have temporary suppressive effects for some students, but they have no effect or, worse still, a strengthening effect on undesired behaviors of other pupils. In summary, patterns of unintentional teacher reinforcement of problem behaviors lead to cycles characterized by high levels of student misbehavior and aversive teacher countercontrol (Shores et al., 1993).

Recent research has examined opportunities to respond (OTR) and teacher talk. It appears that teachers who veer off the academic topic often provide fewer explanations about the lesson. This pattern in turn leads to fewer opportunities for students to respond (Sutherland, Wehby, & Yoder, 2002).

A common side effect of aversive teacher control is power struggles between the teacher and some or all pupils. Like adults, children react negatively to aversive management. If they sense that the teacher is reacting from frustration or feels out of control of the situation, they may respond with even more intensive misbehavior. We all know teachers who are "naturals" at disciplining students. These individuals have distinctive speaking voices that command students' attention without screaming. You, too, can have an authoritative but courteous voice. First, ask a colleague to role-play some situations with you. Pretend that you are stopping a rambunctious student in the corridor. Ask your colleague to tell you honestly how you sound. Do you sound angry and out of control? Do you convey authority without losing your "cool"? Are you meek or apologetic? Now practice again. This activity might seem silly at first, but it makes you more aware of your verbal reactions, especially in stressful situations.

Next, concentrate on your facial expressions, gestures, and posture. Ask a colleague for feedback on how you look. Research has shown that 80% of the message received by a person in a stressful situation is nonverbal. **Self-monitoring** is a great (and even fun) way to gain control of your verbal and nonverbal messages. Here is a simple activity to help you monitor your verbalizations (e.g., praise, reprimands, nags, repeated requests) and body language (e.g., hands on hips, tightened fists, clenched jaw, pointing a finger, standing too close, arms folded across chest):

1. Obtain at least 50 pennies or paper clips.
2. Place the pennies or paper clips in one pocket.
3. Each time you find yourself saying something negative or using a gesture you'd like to avoid (e.g., pointing at students), move a penny or a paper clip to the other pocket.
4. At the end of the day, count the items in each pocket.
5. Record your scores on an individual chart and try to improve your record the next day.
6. For more fun, challenge a friend to track her statements and gestures, too.

Reprimands

Sutherland and Wehby (2001a) found that teachers who self-evaluated their classroom statements reduced the level of their **reprimands.** You can use the strategy mentioned in the previous section to monitor your reprimands. Here are some guidelines for making necessary corrections more effective:

- Make your reprimand privately, not publicly. Humiliating or embarrassing a student is likely to increase that student's resentment and may create an unsafe situation. Raising your voice repeatedly merely desensitizes students to your reprimands. Students may be more inclined to listen to what you are saying when you use a normal speaking voice.
- Be sure you have the student's attention. Do not insist that the student give you eye contact, however, as this may violate a student's cultural traditions or humiliate him or her.
- Do not point your finger at the student. This habit, shared by many educators, can be very difficult to break. Try self-monitoring your gestures or ask students to help you.
- Do not insist on having the last word, especially with teenagers.

Physical Interactions with Students

Most of your interactions with problem students will be—and certainly should be—verbal, not physical. We advise that you not engage in any physical interactions that you would deem inappropriate with an unfamiliar adult. Whereas a handshake may be appropriate and courteous, touching a student in any other way may lead to problems, especially with students who have a history of acting-out behaviors or who have been victims of abuse. Naturally, there will be good exceptions to this rule, but a conservative stance is usually best. Adolescents who are developing their own sexual identities are often confused about physical affection. Hypersensitive to your initiations, they may misunderstand your intentions. This likelihood increases when teenagers are under stress, angered, or embarrassed.

Physical interventions for aggressive students create their own problems. Avoid physical confrontations whenever possible, taking precautions to protect yourself and others. Maintaining a 3-foot distance is one way to develop the habit of honoring students' personal space needs.

> Reread the opening case study, asking yourself these questions: How did Miss Perrone invite a power struggle with her students? What suggestions might you offer her?

High-Probability Request Sequences

High-probability request sequences have improved appropriate behavior in a number of studies (Davis, Reichle, & Southard, 2000). Typically, during a high-probability request sequence, you would deliver three to five easy requests to which the student has a history of responding (**high-probability requests**) immediately before you ask the student to do something that she typically refuses (low-probability request). The high-probability requests can be an effective strategy for students who engage in escape-motivated challenging behavior.

The Praise-and-Ignore Approach

Sometimes we ignore problem behaviors, only to be disappointed in the results. Our failure to control behavior may be due to a misunderstanding of the basic principles that underlie this intervention. Here are five guidelines for an effective praise-and-ignore approach:

1. Remember that ignoring will not work unless the reason for the student's behavior is to gain your attention. Use an A-B-C analysis to determine this.
2. Remember that when an ignoring intervention is successful, disruptive behavior will increase before decreasing. Do not give up when students test to see if you will give in and pay attention to their antics.
3. Develop ways in which other adults can distract you from the student who is being disruptive so that you do not find yourself giving the student attention. Let others present know to ignore the student's disruptive behavior.
4. Be sure to praise the student for appropriate behaviors. Ignoring without praise will not work; it's merely "going cold turkey." Consider this advice:

   > Catching students being good is one of the easiest and most effective ways for dealing with students with challenging behaviors (Maag, 1999). It is not used more often because many teachers believe students "should" behave well and, consequently, only give them attention for displaying inappropriate behaviors. These students have learned very early in their school career that the only way they get attention from teachers is to misbehave. As a general rule, the second time a teacher gives a student a verbal warning should be a cue for that teacher to catch the student being good. (Maag, 2001, p. 173)

5. Consider the "peak" of the extinction curve before you begin this strategy. If you will not be able to tolerate (ignore) the behavior as it accelerates, select a different strategy. Remember that the problem behavior almost always worsens (e.g., swearing may escalate to hitting) before it gets better as the ignored child tries to get your attention.

Differential Reinforcement of Other Behaviors

Differential reinforcement of other behaviors (DRO) is a strategy whereby you reinforce the nondisruptive behaviors when they occur during a specified time interval. To help you get started in planning a DRO approach, take a look at the Case Illustration on DRO, a link on the Companion Website.

Differential Reinforcement of Low Rates of Behavior

Differential reinforcement of low rates of behavior (DRL) has been applied to swearing, inappropriate questioning, and negative verbal statements. Zwald and Gresham (1982) targeted teasing and name-calling. Here are the steps they took:

1. The teacher posted and discussed class rules, telling the group the maximum number of teasing/name-calling occurrences allowed to still obtain reinforcement for that day.
2. The teacher made a mark on the blackboard for every teasing/name-calling verbalization. These verbalizations were not discussed or reprimanded.
3. Each boy selected positive reinforcement from a reinforcement menu mutually decided on by the teacher and class members. The reinforcement menu for each day consisted of a hot drink (hot chocolate, tea, or coffee), free reading, or listening to the radio.
4. To prevent the number of teasing remarks from getting out of hand if the students went beyond the limit set for the day (thereby losing that day's reinforcement), the teacher gave a larger reward at the end of the week if the group had five or fewer "extra" recorded teasing remarks for the week. The large reinforcer was 20 minutes of free time on Friday.
5. A line graph was posted so that class members could graphically see their progress. The extra teasing remarks (the number of remarks that exceeded the imposed limit) were recorded on a bar graph so that the students could observe whether they would obtain free time at the end of the week (p. 430).

Trice and Parker (1983) reduced obscene words in a resource room by using DRL and a response cost. Specific words were targeted, and each time a student said one of the six targeted words, he or she got a colored marker. At the end of the period, the markers were tallied, and the students' behavior was posted on a graph. A 5-minute detention (the response cost) was required for each marker. Under the DRL condition, students received praise each time the tally fell below the mean tally for the day before; students whose tallies were higher received no comment. The authors cited the response cost procedure as more immediately effective than the DRL procedure.

> Reflect on the DRL interventions. What were the targeted behaviors (i.e., the behaviors that were "lowered")? Why might DRL have been more effective than a praise-and-ignore approach in these two cases?

Public Posting

Public posting is a successful, relatively simple strategy that combines an environmental intervention with a teacher-directed approach. In public posting, students receive visual feedback about their performance (e.g., a poster telling them how well they have performed a given behavior). Two studies illustrate the versatility of this intervention. Both were conducted with secondary school students, but there is no reason why the public posting strategy would not be effective with younger students as long as they understand the contents of the poster.

Jones and Van Houten (1985) used public posting to change seventh graders' disruptive behavior (i.e., noises, pushing, teasing, "showing off," leaving seats) during science and English classes. Before trying the posting, the authors instituted pop quizzes to see whether these would remediate the misbehavior, but they were not entirely successful, so the authors turned to the public posting of each student's daily quiz score. The public posting resulted in decreased disruptive behaviors as well as in similar or improved quiz scores for the seventh graders. Caution: post students' grades with their student numbers to protect confidentiality.

In a second study of public posting, Staub (1987) sought to improve the rambunctious hall behavior of middle school students during change of classes. Large posters at each end of a very busy corridor gave students the following information: the percentage change in the daily occurrence of disruptive behavior (as compared with the day before) and the "best record to date" of decreasing disruptive behaviors. To enhance the public posting strategy, the dean gave verbal feedback and praise matching the posters to each classroom during the first minute of classes. This simple and inexpensive intervention proved successful in reducing the disruptive behaviors of the middle school students.

Contingency Contracting

We call a written explanation of contingencies a contingency contract (Downing, 2002). General guidelines for implementing a contingency contract would include the following:

- Explain to the student what a contract is. Your explanation will depend on the conversational level of the child, but it may be helpful to use examples of contracts that the student will encounter.
- Share examples of contracts with the student.
- Ask the student to suggest tasks that might be included in a contract between student and teacher. Write these down.
- Suggest tasks that you would like to see the student accomplish and write these down.
- Decide on mutually agreeable tasks. If a third party is to be involved in the contract, be sure that the party also agrees on the tasks that you have selected.
- Discuss with the student possible activities, items, or privileges that the student would like to earn. Write these down.
- Negotiate how the student will earn the reinforcers by accomplishing portions or all of the tasks.
- Identify the criteria for mastery of each task (time allotted, achievement level, how the task is to be evaluated).
- Determine when the student will receive the reinforcers for completing tasks.
- Determine when the contract will be reviewed to make necessary revisions or to note progress.
- Make an extra copy of the contract. Give this copy to the student and any third party involved.
- Sign the contract, get the student to sign the contract, and if there is a third party involved, ask the third party to sign the contract.

Figure 7-2 provides an example of a contract for a disruptive child. Notice that it is a **home-based contract** in which the parents have agreed to participate. Involving parents (or other persons important to the child) is an excellent way to strengthen a contingency contract. At the bottom of the home-based contract is an important feature: the review date. This frequent review allows everyone involved to offer suggestions for how the procedure can be improved before major problems arise. Did you also note that the reinforcers within the contract tend to be educational activities? By selecting special privileges that enhance your academic program, you move away from the tendency to "bribe" students into improved performance. For more information on contingency contracts, see the Companion Website.

Next, let's turn to another powerful contingency management tool: the token economy.

Token Economy Programs

You learned the underlying assumptions and general guidelines for token economy and levels systems in Chapter 2. Now let's examine some examples you might want to adapt for your classroom or school. Warren et al. (in press) implemented a school-wide token system, referred to as "Gotcha" coupons, to reinforce appropriate behavior. Overall, there was a decrease in all in-school aversive methods used. (Interestingly, 72% of the "Gotcha" coupons were given by only 25% of the teachers, suggesting that results may have been greater if the entire staff had consistently "bought in" to this intervention.)

I, Randy (student), agree to do the following at school:

1. Try not to interrupt the teacher

on this schedule: during social studies class

2. Try to work without disturbing other kids

on this schedule: during math

I, Mr. Jameson (teacher), agree to provide assistance as follows:

Arrange for Randy to take part in the social studies discussion, by calling on him daily.
Move Randy away from the gerbils.

We, the Bergers (parents), agree to provide privileges as follows:

provide Randy with ✓ marks on the chart posted in the kitchen. When Randy earns 50 ✓s, he can buy a gerbil. We will also try to have conversations about the news at home.

We have read and discussed this contract in an after-school meeting on 2/16.
and we hereby sign as a way of making our commitment to this arrangement.

We will all meet on 2/28 to reevaluate the contract.

Signed Randy Berger (student)
JJ Jameson (teacher)
Anita Berger (parent)
George Berger (parent)

Date 2/16

FIGURE 7–2 Home-Based Report

To improve rule following and encourage teachers to catch students who were following the rules, McCurdy, Mannella, and Eldridge (2003) tried a school-wide token economy based on "keys" or tickets that could be exchanged weekly for a variety of low-priced backup rewards. Students who always earned tickets for basic rule compliance earned membership in the Gold Key Club, entitling them to participate in movies, trips, and other special events.

Following are the resources you will need for initiating a token economy program:

- Backup reinforcers appropriate for your classroom group.
- Tokens appropriate for your group.
- A kitchen timer if you plan to reinforce behaviors by measuring their duration.
- A monitoring sheet on which to record the tokens or points earned.
- Token dispensers, containers, or devices to denote the gain or loss of tokens.

You will need a couple of hours to get materials together and to get the monitoring sheets duplicated. Then plan to spend about 30 minutes per day for the first week of the program introducing the tokens and orienting students to the program. After the first week, the program should require no more than 20 minutes per day in addition to the time spent delivering tokens. (Note: Programs may differ in the amount of time required.)

To begin the program, select target behaviors for your class. Some of the behaviors you list should be ones you presently take for granted. Select easy behaviors to ensure that all students can earn a few tokens from the beginning of the program. Select target behaviors that are compatible with your classroom rules. Include behavioral targets from your students' individualized education plans (IEPs). Sample target behaviors developed for a primary classroom token economy could include the following:

- Say hello to teachers when you arrive at school.
- Hang up your coat when you come to school.
- Put your lunch away when you arrive at school.
- Pick up your work for the day and take your seat.
- Eat lunch within the allotted time.
- Line up for activities outside the room.

To ensure that the selected target behaviors are appropriate, ask yourself the following questions:

1. How can I describe this behavior in words the student(s) can understand?
2. How can I measure this behavior when it occurs? If the behavior is measured in terms of time (on task for 10 minutes, no outburst during a 15-minute period, solving a certain number of math problems within a specified amount of time), assign the tokens or points on the basis of a token-to-time ratio. If the behavior is measured in terms of frequency (percentage correct on a worksheet, number of positive verbal comments to a peer, number of independent steps in a self-care task), award tokens or points on the basis of a token-to-frequency ratio.
3. How will I know when this behavior is exhibited?
4. How important is this behavior? You will not be able to initiate the program with all the behaviors you identify, so you may have to rank them. Start with some behaviors that you can alter successfully.
5. Is the behavior one that you wish to reduce or eliminate? You can handle this behavior in two ways. The first approach is to reward a behavior that is incompatible with the problem behavior. For example, reward in-seat behavior to reduce classroom wandering. The second approach is to fine the student. We call this a response cost. If the student wanders around the room, he or she loses a privilege.
6. Does this behavior occur in other settings? If so, you may want to extend the token economy program to include other classes or the home. You will need to monitor the behavior in those settings, so include space on your monitoring form or develop a different form for those settings.

As you present these target behaviors or rules to your students, incorporate a daily review of the rules to strengthen the effectiveness of the token. Selecting reinforcers and fines is the next step. If your students can help, let them develop a list of reinforcers. Think of items or events that will be enjoyable and that can be obtained within the school. Some ideas for involving students in identifying their own reinforcers might include the following:

- Ask students to draw, write, or select from a set of pictures those items or events that appeal to them.
- Allow students some free time and observe what they choose to do.
- Allow students to "sample" reinforcers by placing them in an accessible place and recording which items the students select frequently.

Selecting tokens is the next step. These may take the form of check marks, stamps, or other marks on a form. However, you may want to use tangible items, especially with young children. In considering the types of tokens to use, you must consider the following variables:

- The age of the students.
- The skill level of the students.
- The likelihood that students will destroy, eat, or cheat with respect to the tokens.
- The expense of the tokens.
- The durability of the tokens.
- The convenience of using the tokens.
- Tokens that are being used in other programs within the same setting (Do not use these!).

Once you have chosen tokens for your program, select an appropriate container or form for them. Counterfeiting may be prevented by using a special color marking pen, by awarding tokens at specified times, or by awarding bonus points for honesty and deducting points for cheating.

As students learn to manage their behavior, their reinforcers should reflect their increasing ability to handle classroom freedom. Moreover, their reinforcers should provide them with a smooth transition to the less restrictive mainstream environment where frequent and tangible reinforcers are not common. After all, we cannot expect any child to leave a special education classroom willingly if that classroom resembles a toy department.

Another component of your token economy will facilitate the development of new—and unexpected—skills. Issue "bonus points" for spontaneous behaviors that you would like to recognize but did not include in your monitoring forms.

> Imagine that you teach in a general education subject where your students change each period. You want to address only four or five behaviors, using checks instead of tokens. You'd like class privileges such as homework credits or extra points for your reinforcers. Sketch a chart to show how you might design this simple application of token economy principles.

Finally, be sure that you review your token economy program with your students at least once a month. Remember that you will have students at different levels at the same time, so you will need to examine how each student is functioning. If you find that a student is not moving from one level to another, make the higher level a bit easier to reach or reexamine your lower level to see why the student is not succeeding. This review is similar to assessing students' progress in academic curricula or materials. Through careful initial planning and regular monitoring of students' progress, your token economy will be a success.

Here are some tips for making your token economy successful (Bicanich, 1986).

Do

- Include your students, whenever possible, in planning your token program.
- Deliver the reinforcement only as a consequence of the desired behavior.
- Let the student know why a reinforcer is being given.
- Give some free tokens at the beginning of your program.
- Reduce tokens gradually so that more work is done for each reinforcer.

- Review all rules frequently.
- Exchange tokens formally.
- Consider reinforcers that are controlled by the peer group.
- Change reinforcers whenever boredom sets in. (If you become bored, your students have probably been bored for some time!)
- Make the number of tokens needed consistent with the difficulty or effort required to perform the behavior.
- Keep reinforcers appropriate to your system's levels.
- Keep a record of tokens earned for everyone to see.
- Include behavior/reinforcers and response cost/fines on the same classroom poster but in separate columns.
- Combine praise with tokens so that social reinforcement can eventually be used alone.
- Withdraw material reinforcers gradually and let social reinforcement maintain the behaviors.
- Encourage students to compete with themselves to earn tokens as they improve their own behavior.

Do Not

- Use tokens that students can obtain outside your system.
- Give away the best reinforcers at the beginning; high-level reinforcers (the best ones) should cost more and be more appealing.
- Spend tokens for your students; let them choose for themselves.
- Let students stockpile tokens.
- Let students "go in the hole."

The case study at the end of this chapter illustrates token economy programs for teenagers.

PEER-MEDIATED INTERVENTIONS

What? Turn over behavioral intervention to the very class that is giving you such a hard time? It may sound completely out of the question. Yet many studies have proven that peers can be effectively trained to change their classmates' behaviors (Joseph & Strain, 2004; Strain, 2001; Strain & Hoyson, 2000; Strain & Schwartz, 2001). Here are some reasons to adopt peer-mediated strategies:

1. Peers make good behavioral managers. The research has proven this repeatedly. In fact, several studies have shown that peers teach skills as well as or better than adults do.
2. Nondisabled students from toddlers to high schoolers can model and teach their peers, making it a highly versatile tool.
3. Both those teaching and those taught have benefited in the many studies of peer tutoring, whether the targets were social or academic behaviors.
4. Carefully implemented **peer-mediated interventions** provide invaluable opportunities for appropriate social interaction among children with disabilities or within an integrated setting.
5. Through teaching others, children learn to identify what works and doesn't work in social situations. More information about the value of peer-mediated interventions awaits you on the Companion Website.

Peer-mediated interventions take advantage of a student's peer group to alter problem behaviors or to teach new ones. These interventions are especially appealing to adolescents, who prefer their contemporaries. The entire class can be involved in changing an individual's disruptive behavior or the disruptive behavior of the whole class.

Group Goal Setting and Feedback

This intervention is based on a group discussion in which peers vote on a fellow student's behavior. Each student receives a behavioral goal. Either daily or twice a week, students meet in a highly structured, 20-minute group discussion to vote and give feedback under adult direction. Here are some target goals for your consideration:

- Rob will help another student during recess.
- Mario will go from his class to the library without getting a detention slip.
- Cristina will not swear during her morning classes.
- Alexa will stay awake in classes after lunch.
- Bonifacio will attend his last class.

The goals are very specific. You may wonder why they are not more ambitious; after all, wouldn't we want Alexa awake all the time? Shouldn't Bonifacio attend all classes? Two rationales support these goals. First, the behavior may be specific to a particular class. Second, the goal should shape successive approximations. We will succeed in changing behavior if we break the goal into small, attainable target behaviors and reinforce students for mastering them.

Steps for directing **group goal setting and feedback** are outlined in Table 7-2.

Peer Monitoring

To give you an idea of the versatility of peer-mediated interventions—even with younger children—take a look at a **peer-monitoring procedure.** Carden-Smith and Fowler (1984) taught kindergarten children to issue and withdraw points from their classmates. To introduce the strategy, they initiated a teacher-directed points program. The eight children

TABLE 7–2 Strategy for Conducting Group Goal Setting and Feedback

1. For each student in the group, develop a social behavior objective written in language the student can understand. Typical goals might be to speak up in the class discussion times, to share materials with others on the playground, to play baseball without teasing classmates, or to play with at least one other child at recess.
2. Write each student's name, goal, and the date on which the goal was announced on a separate sheet in the group notebook. Record the feedback of the student's peers each day during the group session.
3. Schedule a 15- to 20-min daily session for the group goal-setting and feedback sessions.
4. Ask everyone to sit in a circle for the group session. Instruct students that this is a time when everyone will speak and that no one is to speak out of turn. Explain further that each student has some behavior that warrants improvement and that the time will be spent talking about our behavior goals.
5. Explain to each student on the first day of the group goal-setting session what her goal is for the next week or two. It is recommended that individual goals be maintained for at least 10 school days.
6. On subsequent days of the group goal-setting session, turn to the first student sitting next to you in the group, announce that student's goal, and state either "I think you made your goal today" or "I don't think you made your goal today." Then provide limited feedback in the form of a statement to support your evaluation. A typical evaluation statement might be, "I like the way you cooperated with Charlie on the playground" or "I don't like the way you took the baseball away from Jane."
7. Request that the student sitting next to the target individual now evaluate that individual's progress toward the goal. Reinforce eye contact with the target student and other constructive feedback. Be certain that each student in the group provides both an evaluation and a feedback statement. Repeat this process until each student in the group has provided the target individual with an opinion and a feedback statement.
8. Tally the votes of making or not making the goal and announce the result. If the student has made the goal, invite others in the group to give her a handclap or other reinforcement you have chosen. If the student has not made the goal, the group makes no response.
9. Repeat this process until all members of the group have received feedback on their goals.
10. If the group has developed a consistently productive performance, you may decide to allow one of the students to be the group leader. This student then reads each student's goals and requests feedback from members of the group. These goals could still be teacher assigned, or in the case of an advanced group, the goals could be self- or peer assigned.

Source: *Kerr, M. M., & Ragland, E. U. (1979). PowWow: A group procedure for reducing classroom behavior problems.* The Pointer, 24, 92–96. *Reprinted with permission of the Helen Dwight Reid Educational Foundation. Published by Heldref Publications, 4000 Albemarie St., N.W., Washington, DC 20016. Copyright 1986.*

received or lost a point for obeying or disobeying each of these rules: cleaning up after play, waiting appropriately, and going to and from the bathroom appropriately. After a few training sessions, the class was divided into two teams that changed membership each day. Each child on each team then earned (or lost) teacher-distributed points for the designated behaviors. In this system, the token exchange was simple: children with 3 points each day could vote on and participate in play activities children with 2 points could participate but not vote, and children with 1 point were required to remain inside and complete cleanup chores.

The peer-mediated feature of the program built on the introductory teacher-directed program. During the peer-mediated intervention, the teacher appointed a team captain who issued and withdrew points from classmates. (The privilege of team captain was awarded students who had earned 3 points the previous day.) The program showed that even young children with learning and behavior problems could manage a basic token economy. Remember to get approval through the IEP process before using this procedure.

Peer Management

Students can learn to reinforce and ignore their classmates' misbehavior through a **peer manager strategy:** peer confrontation. Peer confrontation is a combined teacher-directed and peer-mediated intervention in which elementary school students alter one another's problem behaviors (Salend, Jantzen, & Giek, 1992). The peer confrontation works this way: The teacher calls on the group with questions such as "Who can tell Jake what problem he is having with his behavior?" or "Who can help Sarina figure out a different way to be acting right now?" The teacher then selects a volunteer who explains the problem behavior and offers an alternative. Students learn this strategy through teacher-led practice and role-playing. Here are some guidelines for using peer confrontation effectively:

1. To minimize embarrassment, consider calling on the entire group for a quick assessment of the class members' behavior: "How are we doing? Does anyone notice a problem we need to correct?"
2. Watch for signs that students are avoiding the activity or the approach or are trying to "gang up on one another." These effects of punishment were observed only initially in two studies (Salend et al., 1992), but you may find that your group responds differently.
3. Emphasize positive responses when you teach the system to your students. Role-play correct responses.
4. Don't use this approach unless you have a good relationship with your students, as they may feel that you are singling out their behavior publicly. Encourage students to offer behavioral alternatives and to deemphasize comments regarding the problem behaviors. One of the advantages of peer interventions such as this one is that it gives students an opportunity to solve behavioral problems and to express alternatives in words that make sense to their peers.
5. Be sure children's participation is cleared through their IEP Teams if applicable.

Group Contingencies

Contingencies related to group characteristics take advantage of social reinforcers controlled by the peer group and are adaptable to a variety of situations. Moreover, some have reported these approaches to be more effective than any other intervention (Popkin & Skinner, 2003). A group contingency also reduces the number of individual consequences the teacher must deliver, saving time from behavior intervention duties.

The basic characteristic of group contingencies is group reinforcement. Whether the target is an individual student or the entire class, the group shares in the consequences of the behavior. In many cases, group-oriented contingencies are devised to deal with specific problem behaviors. Nevertheless, they can be used to establish appropriate behaviors and to prevent problems. There are three categories of group-oriented contingencies: dependent, independent, and interdependent.

In a **dependent group contingency,** the peer performance of certain group members determines the consequence received by the entire group (Popkin & Skinner, 2003). Because the focus is on the performance of a few students, this arrangement works best when (a) the behavior of the large group is better than that of the target student or students, (b) the group does not exhibit antisocial behavior, and (c) the students do not engage in bullying and teasing. For example, pick this approach for silly, off-task behaviors or to improve homework completion in a classroom where more serious conduct problems are not in evidence. Safeguards described here will assist you in preventing scapegoating.

The primary characteristic of an **independent group contingency** is that the same consequence is applied to individual group members. Contingency contracting is an independent group-oriented contingency. Because this represents an "every person for herself" arrangement, adults and students generally view these as fair. However, students with academic and behavioral problems may not perceive them as equitable given the barriers to achievement that they perceive as outside of their control.

In an **interdependent group contingency,** each student must reach a prescribed level of behavior before the entire group receives a consequence. If designed and managed effectively, these arrangements are not only powerful but also efficient, as you will be handling one contingency. The well-designed interdependent group contingency is a "win-win" for the group. Because an individual benefits from the efforts of others, you can reduce the risk of scapegoating, teasing, and resentment of those who earned rewards by those who did not.

Despite these potential advantages, any group contingency can turn sour. Pay close attention to the following safeguards. Some of them help make the contingencies less apparent to the students, thereby protecting those who might be blamed. Other guidelines offer "wriggle room" to the teacher who needs to make adjustments for situations as they arise. Finally, by following these tips, you'll design a contingency that is inclusive of students of different abilities:

- Consider having a random criterion so that students never reach the point of "I've already blown it. I've got nothing to lose, so I might as well undermine this deal." This also protects those students whose performance is being scrutinized by their classmates.
- Consider several "winner" behaviors that earn rewards or recognition. This offers students more chances to succeed (Popkin & Skinner, 2003).
- Use group reinforcement rather than a response cost.
- Be sure that the behavior target and criteria are within the students' reach.
- Include "language loopholes" that make the contingency easier to master and harder to sabotage (e.g., As soon as . . . , Whenever . . . , If . . .).
- Use the principle of successive approximations to make the contingency easy to achieve.
- Avoid language that implies an ultimatum, such as "If you don't do . . . , then I will do . . . " or "Unless you do . . . , we will not do . . . ."
- Get a colleague to help you as you write your contingencies. Consider together the worst-case scenario for your proposed group-oriented contingency and alter your contingency accordingly.

Table 7–3 illustrates the three types of group contingencies. Pay special attention to each example. Can you identify the loophole in each one? How was an ultimatum avoided?

TABLE 7–3 Group Contingency Arrangements

Type of Group Contingency	Examples
Interdependent	If all students turn in homework on a given day, I will put two marbles in the jar. If, on Friday, there are at least eight marbles in the jar, I will add a shooter (large) marble. When the jar is full, the class will have a pizza party—teacher's treat!
	Each table of students has a can with six Popsicle sticks. I take away a Popsicle stick when a student breaks a rule. If the group still has five sticks on Friday, they get to pick out a treat from the treat bag.
	If everyone remembers to bring his math books to class for four consecutive days, you will not be assigned homework for the fifth day of class.
Independent	Each student with fewer than one tardy per grading period will receive a free homework pass.
	Each student who finishes his research project on time will receive a "dog ate my homework" pass.
Dependent	If a student who returns to the classroom from the in-school suspension room has a good day (i.e., no warnings and classwork completed), all students will get to drop their lowest daily classwork grade. (This recognizes the supportive role of classmates.)
	Three students in this class served detention last week for pushing in the hall. If these three students do not get detention for 2 weeks, the entire class will get to play their favorite music during indoor recess.
	As soon as a group of students completes their science project, the class wins a free homework pass.

One nice variation of a group contingency is the "hero procedure," in which one student earns reinforcers for the rest of the group. Here is an example of a group-oriented procedure that incorporates a hero procedure:

> This will be a three-week mathematics estimation contest. If anyone in your class guesses the correct number of cubes in the container, everyone in the class will receive a prize. If more than one person (within or across classes) guesses the correct number, more than one class will receive prizes. If no one guesses the correct answer, then the person guessing closest to the correct number during week 3 will be the winner and his/her class will receive prizes. Each week you will receive written information about whether you guessed correctly or were too high or too low in your estimation. (Williamson, Williamson, Watkins, & Hughes, 1992, p. 418)

Good Behavior Game

The Good Behavior Game (Ialongo, Poduska, Werthamer, & Kellam, 2001) is yet another variation on a group contingency. This intervention involves teams of students competing on the basis of their behavior in the classroom (Salend, Reynolds, & Coyle, 1989). While the name of this intervention might not sound sophisticated, it has been shown to reduce disruptive behavior in diverse classroom settings. Salend et al. (1989) used the Good Behavior Game in an individualized format to improve the behaviors of high school students in a special education classroom. Students joined a team according to their target behaviors (e.g., inappropriate verbalizations, cursing, drumming/tapping). Each team, therefore, had a common goal. Salend et al. (1989) reported that the teams created positive peer pressure and that students enjoyed being rewarded for their behavioral improvements. This individualized approach (basing the team target behaviors on identified needs of students) is a good way to comply with the requirements of your students' IEPs. On the Companion Website, you'll find more information about the Good Behavior Game.

SELF-MEDIATED INTERVENTIONS

One of our goals with students who are disruptive is to promote self-control of their problem behaviors. For example, students whose behavior has responded to a token economy can become gradually more independent of external control when they use **self-mediated interventions.** In recent years, we have learned more about such valuable tools as self-instruction and self-evaluation. (For a review of self-management research with students who have behavioral disorders, see Nelson, Smith, Young, & Dodd, 1991.) In this section, we focus on four procedures: self-monitoring, self-evaluation, self-graphing, and self-instruction.

Self-monitoring

Self-monitoring, or **self-recording,** allows the student to record his or her own behaviors. Perhaps you have tried self-monitoring for dieting, smoking cessation, or tracking your physical fitness goals. Before you begin a self-monitoring program, consider the suggestions in Table 7-4.

One of your decisions in designing this intervention is to select a practical monitoring form. Figure 7-3 shows the monitoring form used by Keith.

Space is provided for tallies each day and period, although you might find that your student will at first need to monitor in only one or two periods a day. Printing the target behavior definition at the bottom of the form is a good idea; it helps the child remember what he or she is monitoring. The form could be modified for an older or more sophisticated student.

Once you have trained a student to self-record, you can move to a behavioral intervention program. During the first few days of the program (at least 3 days), ask the student to self-record disruptive behaviors without additional intervention. The

TABLE 7–4 Guidelines for Self-Management Strategies

1. Consult the section on token economy programs for ideas about selecting appropriate target behaviors.
2. Decide how this behavior might be measured most easily by the student.
3. Some studies have shown that students perform better when they record an academic behavior rather than merely recording whether they are on task (Lam, Cole, Shapiro, & Bambara, 1994). Students may use a self-correction aid to see if they have completed a math problem right, for example. Even though this procedure takes a bit of time, the results indicate that it is a preferable approach.
4. Be sure your students can correctly identify the target behaviors, through explanation, discussion, and practice.
5. Consider using a question format. For example, the student's form might read: "Did I get this problem right?" YES _____ NO _____
6. Reinforce students not only for improvements in their performance but also for not cheating! Unannounced teacher monitoring of the student's target behaviors will allow you to see if the student is recording his behavior honestly.
7. If a student is oppositional to the procedure, supplement it with a positive contingency for cooperation or with another strategy (Lam et al., 1994).
8. Try to make the self-monitoring as minimally intrusive as possible (Reid & Harris, 1993).
9. Choose a behavior that is relevant to the student (Reid & Harris, 1993).
10. Work with the student to develop a procedure that is enjoyable, not a chore (Reid & Harris, 1993).

	Reading	Math	Language Arts	Science	Social Studies	Total
Monday	//		/	//	/	6
Tuesday	/	/	/		/	4
Wednesday	//		//		///	7
Thursday		/	///	/	//	7
Friday	/	/	///			5

I will put a tally mark in the box each time I get out of my seat without asking permission during class. I know I am out of my seat when my backside is not touching my chair and I have not asked permission to leave my seat.

Name KEITH Date Begun 2-22 Teacher COVALASKI

FIGURE 7–3 Self-Monitoring Form

data from these sessions will provide you with a baseline assessment of the student's performance. The next step in this program is to establish contingencies under which the student receives a reinforcer for reducing the number of disruptions per session. A student might use a contract form to record a self-management plan. Martin et al. (2003) used self-determination contracts with four sections: (a) plan, (b) work, (c) evaluate, and (d) adjust. In still another approach, the student might self-reinforce without using tokens or contracts. For some students, self-recording alone may reduce disruptions.

Whether you use self-monitoring alone or as part of a larger behavioral intervention system, encourage students to reduce disruptions and increase appropriate behavior relative to their own baseline performance. For example, a student whose baseline assessment indicates that he is off task 80% of the period could be encouraged to improve his performance little by little until he reaches a mutually agreed-on goal (e.g., on task 80% of the period). By setting small but reasonable goals for students and gradually increasing expectations for their behavior, you help ensure that the self-monitoring program will be successful. This strategy is called shaping successive approximations (see Chapter 3).

Self-Evaluation

Self-evaluation requires a student to assess the quality of his or her behavior, while in self-monitoring the student simply counts his or her behavior. Even very young children can learn to self-evaluate their behaviors. Miller, Strain, Boyd, Jarzynka, and McFetridge (1993) taught four preschoolers with disabilities to self-evaluate their behaviors with a "thumbs-up" or "thumbs-down" signal as the teacher pointed to visual depictions of appropriate behaviors on a poster. Behaviors included cleaning up the play area, following teacher instructions, and interacting with peers appropriately.

Self-Graphing

Self-graphing is a strategy whereby students plot their own performance, perhaps their efforts during a self-management project. Showing students the graphed results of their performance can improve outcomes, according to one study (Noell, Duhon, Gatti, & Connell, 2002).

Self-Instruction

In a **self-instruction** program, the student is trained to whisper statements that will help accomplish the task. Be sure to analyze the self-instructional task before attempting to use this procedure with a student.

SUMMARY

- Environmentally mediated interventions are necessary if other strategies are to be successful but not sufficient alone to change misbehavior.
- Teacher-mediated interventions include self-monitoring of your interactions as well as more complex interventions, such as token economies.
- Peer-mediated interventions such as group contingencies can be very powerful but require careful preparation and worst-case-scenario planning.
- Finally, the self-management strategies promote generalization of new behaviors to other settings.

COME INTO MY CLASSROOM: A CASE STUDY

TOKEN ECONOMY

Wyllie Keefer

My classroom is a part-time resource room with the students coming on various schedules. My 13 students are in sixth, seventh, and eighth grades, with the majority of students in eighth. The age group is between 11 and 14 years old. There is such a diversity of abilities among the students that grade-level curriculum is difficult to assess on a general basis. Some students are nonreaders, some do not know their multiplication tables, while others are on grade level but behavior problems have deterred them from academic success.

When needed, the students who are the readers or mathematicians are the classroom peer tutors. Their special abilities come in handy when other students are having difficulties in their mainstream classes or particular assignments in the resource room. Two of my students are extremely talented in art and are always excited and interested in any lesson or project dealing with art.

Our school day begins at 7:40 A.M. and ends at 2:33 P.M. There are eight periods a day; each period is 42 min. long. Most of my students spend first period in my room (directly after first period is homeroom). First period usually goes very well, with a calm environment.

I bring my students to my room from study halls, for extra monitoring time, if I sense there may be trouble brewing or a potential crisis. Many days my students are sent to my room to have tests read to them, to get help with

Reprinted with author's permission.

classwork/assignments, or if their behavior is disrupting a mainstream class. I have a full-time aide so there are always two adults in our room for the kids to model. Together with our students' current IEP Teams, we designed a four-level behavior chart listing "Earners" and "Losers." To be sure that our students really understood the four levels, we made four posters. Each poster showed the "Earners" and "Losers" for that level. We placed the posters next to each other on our classroom wall. We included the values assigned to these behaviors so there was no question as to how much a behavior earns or loses (see Figure 7-4).

The selection of behaviors to be targeted is a group activity. The students are asked to contribute their ideas of expected or appropriate behaviors in school, to include along with my expectations.

I divided the chalkboard into four sections and labeled them Level I to Level IV. The students then participated and decided which behaviors would be listed at which level.

- *Level I*—Behaviors everyone can do, easy to achieve.
- *Level II*—Slightly more demanding than Level I.
- *Level III*—Bigger effort, trying to make a change.
- *Level IV*—Major effort, highest level.

Bonuses

Students can earn extra points (money) when they go "beyond the call of duty" and do something out of the ordinary. For example, a student of mine recently found a wallet filled with money, credit cards, and a driver's license. Other students were arguing over how they would split the cash. My student grabbed the wallet from them and turned it into the office. As it turned out, the wallet belonged to the art teacher. She was not only relieved but impressed that one of the "special" students had fought to do the right thing. This deed of honor earned a lot of bonus bucks! Bonuses will always be positive and awarded as surprises. Other examples would be when one student compliments another, lends a pencil, or helps another student or teacher. In my particular environment, there are many opportunities to reward behavior, however small!

The design of our checkbook money system is twofold. Each student receives his own personal checkbook. With help from the art teacher, the class creates their own checkbook covers made from heavy cardboard and wallpaper samples. I have designed checks and withdrawal slips.

For *earners,* the student receives *deposits;* for *losers, withdrawals.* Behaviors are assigned a dollar amount. Each period the student self-monitors the behaviors that were exhibited, negative or positive. At the end of the period, we schedule 5 minutes to go over their checklist and we agree on deposits or withdrawals earned. Mainstream teachers also have checklists and are familiar with our system. They have a supply of previously made deposit slips with money amounts and behaviors on them. They check each behavior earned or lost during that particular period. Each student brings back the deposit slip to enter the earned or lost amounts into their accounts.

The second advantage of using a fictitious banking system is to teach the students, for their employable future, that if they do a good job, they will get a paycheck, or perhaps a bonus/raise. If they do a bad job, argue, or forget their responsibilities, they can be fired, lose pay, and so on. They learn how to keep and balance a checking account, along with practicing basic, consumer math.

The banking system is not only a self-monitoring system but is also an interdependent contingency. Every student is responsible for her behaviors, and the class can benefit or

Earners

Level I

Behaviors	Cost
Try to follow classroom rules	$2
Be in seat when bell rings	$2
Stay in your seat	$2
Raise your hand	$2
Use kind & courteous language	$2
Write down assignments	$2
Have all teachers fill out deposit slip	$2
Greet adults and classmates	$2

Level II

Behaviors	Cost
Respect others	$3
Bring book, pen/ pencil, & worksheet to class	$3
Bring homework & worksheets to class	$3
Neat papers	$3
Appropriate behavior on bus, in hallways, or in cafeteria	$3
Remain on task 70% of the time	$3
Start and try to complete assignments 70% of the time	$3
All teachers filled out deposit slip	$3

Level III

Behaviors	Cost
Ignore other student's inappropriate behavior	$4
Participate in class	$4
Hand in completed assignments 80% of the time	$4
Work without disturbing others	$4
Keep checkbook current and correct	$4
Organize school work	$4

Level IV

Behaviors	Cost
Follow classroom rules all day	$5
Complete all assignments and turn them in on time	$5
Use appropriate behavior 90% of the time	$5
Be self-monitored 90% of the time	$5
Have no discipline offenses all week	$5

Losers

Level I

Behaviors	Cost
Break a classroom rule	$1
Use vulgarities, swearing, or inappropriate gestures	$5
Be out of seat	$1
Be tardy	$1
Receive anecdotals, DT, ISS, or OSS	$5
Have physical or verbal outbursts	$5
Fail to keep checkbook up-to-date	$1

Level II

Behaviors	Cost
Have physical or verbal outbursts	$10
Argue	$2
Not be prepared	$2
Be off-task	$2
Receive anecdotals, DT, ISS, or OSS	$10
Fail to keep checkbook up-to-date	$2

Level III

Behaviors	Cost
Fail to turn in assignments	$3
Disrupt class	$15
Cheat on checkbook	$3
Receive anecdotals, DT, ISS, or OSS	$3

Level IV

Behaviors	Cost
Receive anecdotals DT, ISS, or OSS	$20
Miss assignments	$4
Break a classroom rule	$4

Monitoring

Level I	Level II	Level III	Level IV
To be monitored at the end of each period (5 min.)	To be monitored at the end of each period (5 min.)	To be monitored at the end of each day	To be monitored at the end of each week on Fridays (1/2 hour)
Also on Fridays (1/2 hour)	Also on Fridays (1/2 hour)	Also on Fridays (1/2 hour)	

FIGURE 7–4 Level System Poster

lose out, together. My former classroom was an "every person for himself" classroom. I changed it because I believe a group plan helps students learn that together everyone achieves more. The more "money" each student "earns," the more reinforcers the group has to choose from.

The students know how often their behavior will be monitored by referring to the time frame listed at the bottom, at each level, of the chart. DT, ISS (in-school suspension), and OSS (out-of-school suspension) are included as "losers," based on our school-wide plan.

When I initially introduced the idea of a banking system for behavior, I was delighted that my students thought it would be a lot of fun and a challenge. (They did suggest that the plan include *real* money!) They helped me make a list of reinforcers that they would like to be able to earn with their "bank accounts" (see Table 7-5).

Here are my troubleshooting guidelines:

- *If a student loses the checkbook:* Student's behavior for that period goes to zero.
- *If students cannot decide on the same reinforcer for the week:* The class must resolve this problem among themselves. They may discuss the situation, vote majority rules, secret ballot, or other ways the students come up with to solve the problem, or they may vote to have alternate choices.
- *If a student does not move up to the next level:* An individual contract will be made between the teacher and student. The student will choose a particular reinforcer he or she would like to earn.
- *If a mainstream teacher will not cooperate:* For example, a student chooses to "buy" a test or homework assignment and the teacher does not agree. The mainstream teacher must then decide to offer other reinforcers that are acceptable and achievable in their room.

Including New Students

Before a new student arrives in class, we review the program within their IEP team. We figure an average balance for her initial deposit into the checking account. Depending on which level the class is on, the new student will be observed for 2 weeks and an individual adjustment will have to be made as to her needs and level.

Modifications to the System

Controlled/creative tinkering is an important factor to consider when designing and making successful any behavioral management plan. Problems may arise at any point of my banking/checkbook plan. I discuss problems with the students as a group. They have helpful suggestions, ideas, and negative comments. This plan is for them and I take their concerns or the question/problem at hand and deal with it on an individual basis. Sample modifications are to "up the ante," to increase the dollar amounts for deposits, to provide earners or losers, or to rearrange the levels or change the reinforcers.

Summary of the Steps for the Banking System

1. Discuss behavioral management plan with students. Introduce the Bank checking account system.
2. Help each student make a checkbook out of heavy cardboard and wallpaper samples.
3. Complete each checkbook with a check register, checks, and a supply of deposit slips. (The teacher designs and copies behavior deposit slips.)
4. IEP Teams, students, and teachers will decide upon behavior earners and losers (to be sorted into Levels I–IV) and the reinforcers the students want to earn.
5. Draw charts for earners, losers, and reinforcers. Post it in the classroom.
6. Each Monday, the class decides on which reinforcers the whole class will be working toward for the week.
7. Each Monday, deposit the following dollar amounts into their accounts:

Level I	$10.00
Level II	$20.00

TABLE 7–5 Reinforcers to Accompany Banking System

Reinforcers			
Level I—Minimum Balance $12	**Level II—Minimum Balance $24**	**Level III—Minimum Balance $36**	**Level IV—Minimum Balance $48**
10 min. of free time at the end of each period	Mrs. Keefer to buy new game for the room	Get a pet (hamster, rabbit, gerbil) for the classroom	Walk to bowling alley (bowl for two periods)
Skip a homework assignment	Make a treat in the home-ec room	Help work in the school store	Paint wall mural in classroom
Movie day	Go to the library for an extra period	Eat lunch at the high school	Use weight room at high school
Popcorn party	Have a free day	Walk to Taco Bell or Dairy Queen	Go to Heights Elem., read to a class
Can of pop	Have a pizza party	Use gym for free time	Hold a car wash for the faculty
Candy store coupon	Skip a test	Do a special tech-ed project	Walk to Heights Plaza
Computer time	Listen to music in room	Do a special art project	Take a field trip

8. Each period, check off behaviors on preprinted deposit slips.
9. Instruct each student to keep his or her checkbooks current.
10. Students *add* earners, *subtract* losers, and enter total deposits or withdrawals on their check register.
11. Monitor students according to the level timetables.
12. Supplementary procedures: If a student does not cooperate, consider the following consequences:

    Written assignment as to why they are having problems
    Extra assignments to earn a (+) higher balance
    Detention.

    Choose an additional *reinforcer*
    Become Bank President, monitoring some part of the system
    Offer suggestions from the students
14. If the students have saved enough money, at any time, they may write a check to "buy" the following:

Study Hall pass	$ 3.00
A homework pass	$10.00
A detention pass	$15.00
A day of In-School Suspension pass	$20.00

(I have discussed this with the administration, and they have given me their approval.)

Case Study Reflection Questions

As you read about the token economy in this case study, consider how the teacher distributed the record-keeping responsibilities involved in maintaining her token economy. How did she safeguard against students losing motivation for earning points? How did the teacher move students toward behaviors that they would need in a less restrictive environment? What life skills could students earn through their participation in this economy?

DISCUSSION/APPLICATION IDEAS

1. Which strategies are preferable for younger students? Older students?
2. When are peer-mediated strategies preferable to teacher-mediated approaches?
3. How can several strategies be combined to reduce disruptive behaviors?
4. What are some possible mistakes one might make in implementing a token economy?
5. For what disruptive behaviors is self-monitoring a good choice?
6. What is the importance of levels within a token economy?
7. How can parents be involved in interventions for disruptive behavior?

REFERENCES

Bicanich, P. (1986). *So you want to try a token economy.* Unpublished manuscript, University of Pittsburgh.

Carden-Smith, L. K., & Fowler, S. A. (1984). Positive peer pressure: The effects of peer monitoring on children's disruptive behavior. *Journal of Applied Behavior Analysis, 17*(2), 213–227.

Conroy, M. A., Asmus, J. M., Ladwig, C. N., Sellers, J. A., & Valcante, G. (2004). The effects of proximity on the classroom behaviors of students with autism in general education settings. *Behavioral Disorders 29*(2), 119–129.

Davis, C. A., Reichle, J. E., & Southard, K. L. (2000). High-probability requests and a preferred item as a distractor: Increasing successful transitions in children with behavior problems. *Education and Treatment of Children, 23*(4), 423. Retrieved June 7, 2004, from Questia database, http://www.questia.com.

Downing, J. A. (2002). Individualized behavior contracts. *Intervention in School and Clinic, 37*(3), 168. Retrieved June 7, 2004, from Questia database, http://www.questia.com.

Gunter, P. L., Shores, R. E., & Susan, J. L. (1995). On the move: Using teacher student proximity to improve student's behavior. *Teaching Exceptional Children, 28*(1), 12–14.

Jalongo, N., Poduska, J., Werthamer, L., & Kellam, S. (2001). The distal impact of two first-grade preventive interventions on conduct problems and disorder in early adolescence. *Journal of Emotional and Behavioral Disorders, 9*(3), 146. Retrieved June 7, 2004, from Questia database, http://www.questia.com.

Jones, D. B., & Van Houten, R. (1985). The use of daily quizzes and public posting to decrease the disruptive behavior of secondary school students. *Education and Treatment of Children, 8*(2), 91–106.

Joseph, G. E., & Strain, P. S. (2004). Building positive relationships with young children. The Center on the Social and Emotional Foundations for Early Learning. University of Illinois at Urbana-Champaign, pp. 1–3. Retrieved December 15, 2004, from www.csefel.uiuc.edu.

Kartub, D. T., Taylor-Greene, S., March, E. R., & Horner, R. H. (2000). Reducing hallway noise: A systems approach. *Journal of Positive Behavioral Interventions, 2*(3), 179–182.

Lam, A. L., Cole, C. L., Shapiro, E. S., & Bambara, L. M. (1994). Relative effects of self-monitoring on-task behavior, academic accuracy and disruptive behavior in students with behavior disorders. *School Psychology Review, 23*(1), 44–58.

Maag, J. W. (1999). *Behavior management: From theoretical implications to practical applications.* San Diego: Singular.

Maag, J. W. (2001). Rewarded by punishment: Reflections on the disuse of positive reinforcement in schools. *Exceptional Children, 67*(2), 173. Retrieved June 7, 2004, from Questia database, http://www.questia.com.

Martin, J. E., Mithaug, D. E., Cox, P., Peterson, L. Y., Van Dycke, J. L., & Cash, M. E. (2003). Increasing self-determination: Teaching students to plan, work, evaluate, and adjust. *Exceptional Children, 69*(4), 431. Retrieved June 13, 2004, from Questia database, http://www.questia.com.

McCurdy, B. L., Mannella, M. C., & Eldridge, N. (2003). Positive behavior support in urban schools: Can we prevent the escalation of antisocial behavior? *Journal of Positive Behavior Interventions, 5*(3), 158. Retrieved June 7, 2004, from Questia database, http://www.questia.com.

Miller, L. J., Strain, P. S., Boyd, K., Jarzynka, J., & McFetridge, M. (1993). The effects of classwide self-assessment on preschool children's engagement in transition, free play, and small group instruction. *Early Education and Development, 4*(3), 162–181.

Nelson, J. R., Smith, D. J., Young, R. K., & Dodd, J. M. (1991). A review of self-management outcome research conducted with students who exhibit behavioral disorders. *Behavioral Disorders, 16*(3), 169–179.

Noell, G. H., Duhon, G. J., Gatti, S. L., & Connell, J. E. (2002). Consultation, follow-up and implementation of behavior management interventions in general education. *School Psychology Review, 31*(2), 217. Retrieved June 13, 2004, from Questia database, http://www.questia.com.

Popkin, J., & Skinner, C. H. (2003). Enhancing academic performance in a classroom serving students with serious emotional disturbance: Interdependent group contingencies with randomly selected components. *School Psychology Review, 32*(2), 282. Retrieved June 7, 2004, from Questia database, http://www.questia.com.

Reid, R., & Harris, K. (1993). Self-monitoring of attention versus self-monitoring of performance: Effects on attention and academic performance. *Exceptional Children, 6*(1), 29–40.

Salend, J. S., Jantzen, N. R., & Giek, K. (1992). Using a peer confrontation system in a group setting. *Behavioral Disorders, 17*(3), 211–218.

Salend, S. J., Reynolds, C. J., & Coyle, E. M. (1989). Individualizing the Good Behavior Game across type and frequency of behavior with emotionally disturbed adolescents. *Behavior Modification, 13*(1), 108–126.

Shores, R. E., Gunter, P. L., Denny, R. K., & Jack, S. L. (1993). Classroom influences on aggressive and disruptive behavior of students with emotional and behavioral disorders. *Focus on Exceptional Children, 26*(2), 1–10.

Staub, R. W. (1987). *The effects of publicly posted feedback on middle school students' disruptive hallway behavior.* Unpublished doctoral dissertation, University of Pittsburgh.

Strain, P. S. (2001). Empirically-based social skill intervention. *Behavioral Disorders, 27,* 30–36.

Strain, P. S., & Hoyson, M. (2000). On the need for longitudinal, intensive social skill intervention: LEAP follow-up outcomes for children with autism as a case-in-point. *Topics in Early Childhood Special Education, 20,* 116–122.

Strain, P. S., & Schwartz, I. (2001). Applied behavior analysis and social skills intervention for young children with autism. *Focus on Autism and Other Developmental Disorders, 8,* 12–24.

Sutherland, K. S., & Wehby, J. H. (2001a). The effect of self-evaluation on teaching behavior in classrooms for students with emotional and behavioral disorders. *Journal of Special Education, 35*(3), 161. Retrieved May 28, 2004, from Questia database, http://www.questia.com.

Sutherland, K. S., & Wehby, J. H. (2001b). Exploring the relation between increased opportunities to respond to academic requests and the academic and behavioral outcomes of students with emotional/behavioral disorders: A review. *Remedial and Special Education, 22,* 113–121.

Sutherland, K. S., Wehby, J. H., & Yoder, P. J. (2002). Examination of the relationship between teacher praise and opportunities for students with EBD to respond to academic requests. *Journal of Emotional and Behavioral Disorders, 10*(1), 5. Retrieved May 28, 2004, from Questia database, http://www.questia.com.

Trice, A. D., & Parker, F. C. (1983). Decreasing adolescent swearing in an instructional setting. *Education and Treatment of Children, 6,* 29–35.

Walker, H. M. (1995). *The acting out child: Coping with classroom disruption* (2nd ed.). Longmont, CO: Sopris West.

Warren, J. S., Edmonson, H. M., Turnbull, A. P., Sailor, W., Wickham, D., & Griggs, S. E. (in press). School-wide application of positive behavior support: Implementation and preliminary evaluation of PBS in an urban middle school. *Educational Psychology Review.*

Williamson, D. A., Williamson, S. H., Watkins, P. C., & Hughes, H. H. (1992). Increasing cooperation among children using dependent group-oriented reinforcement contingencies. *Behavior Modification, 16*(3), 414–425.

Wong, H. K., & Wong, R. T. (2004). *The first days of school: How to be an effective teacher.* Mountain View, CA: Harry K. Wong Publications.

Zwald, L., & Gresham, F. (1982). Behavioral consultation in a secondary class: Using DRL to decrease negative verbal interactions. *School Psychology Review, 11*(4), 428–432.

CHAPTER 8 IMPROVING SCHOOL SURVIVAL SKILLS AND SOCIAL SKILLS

OUTLINE

How This Chapter Is Organized
Improving School Survival Skills
Assessing School Survival Skills
Teacher-Mediated Strategies
Peer-Mediated Strategies
Self-Mediated Strategies
Strategies to Improve Social Competence
Assessment Considerations
Social Withdrawal
Teacher-Mediated Strategies
Peer-Mediated Strategies
Self-Mediated Strategies

OBJECTIVES

After completing this chapter, you should be able to

- Describe three assessment approaches for problems in social skills and school survival skills.
- Identify resources to help you become more culturally sensitive when assessing and teaching social skills and school survival skills.
- Plan a teacher-mediated intervention for a student with poor social skills.
- Plan a comprehensive sequence of peer-mediated interventions for a socially withdrawn child.
- Use a group contingency procedure to modify off-task behaviors.
- Develop a self-monitoring procedure to improve students' academic productivity.

KEY TERMS (refer to the Glossary on the Companion Website for definitions)

analog measures
cooperative learning
elective mutism
peer tutoring
school survival skills
self-determination
social competence
social skills
social withdrawal

HOW THIS CHAPTER IS ORGANIZED

This chapter addresses *two* domains: **school survival skills** and **social skills.** You'll read first about strategies to improve school survival skills, including environmentally mediated, teacher-mediated, peer-mediated, and self-mediated approaches. Next, you'll learn about approaches that improve students' social skills.

IMPROVING SCHOOL SURVIVAL SKILLS

Our opening case study depicts students whose school survival skills are inadequate. The first part of this chapter addresses these behaviors that enable a student to get the most from instructional interactions.

> Take a look at Figure 8–1 to see if you can detect the skills that Andy, Yvonne, Corrado, and Lila—the students in our opening case study—needed to learn. Do you have some ideas already on how best to assist them? Can you tell that they present different needs even though they are within the same classroom?

ASSESSING SCHOOL SURVIVAL SKILLS

In order to teach such diverse learners, we must first assess their interests, learning preferences, and readiness—the three cornerstones of differentiated instruction. (For more information on differentiated instruction, see the Companion Website.)

COME INTO MY CLASSROOM: A CASE STUDY

I retired from teaching over a year ago, yet I still wonder about some of the students I simply couldn't reach. They weren't always the bad actors. On the contrary, what bugged me was that those kids had real potential. For example, Andy was never really a troublemaker, but he just didn't seem to "get his act together" at school. His projects were always incomplete, and he often showed up late for classes, resulting in repeated detentions. Sometimes he forgot he had detention and wound up having to go to the in-school suspension room for a day or two. We never seemed to find the right intervention for Andy, and he developed a reputation as a "loser."

Andy wasn't the only student I didn't figure out. I can still see Yvonne, who just didn't seem to fit into any classroom. She wasn't exactly a behavior problem, but she was no angel either. For example, she would never answer the questions I asked, and I found myself repeating questions to her just because she was daydreaming during our discussions. Sometimes I actually wondered if she had a neurological problem, but her pediatrician said she was fine. Let's face it: Yvonne was a "space cadet."

How could I ever forget Corrado? I never could put my finger on his problem. He was a nice enough kid, but he was totally disorganized. His assignments always looked like they had been run over, and his test papers were decorated with doodles. No amount of lecturing could ever change that kid.

I guess you could call Lila unmotivated or lazy. She really got under my skin because she never did what I asked the first time. Every request turned into a battle. She was fine as long as you didn't ask her to do anything.

School survival skills reflect these three dimensions yet often are overlooked in our assessment practices. The School Survival Skills Scale shown in Figure 8–1 was developed to meet this need.

Many of the problems in Figure 8–1 will be obvious to you and to other teachers. In a large secondary school, however, you may not have a chance to compare notes with a student's other teachers. Consider using a pencil-and-paper checklist for assessing a student's specific skill limitations. The School Survival Skills Scale is appropriate for middle and high school students. Consider the skills and problems that teachers viewed as most important for success in high school (Kerr, Zigmond, Schaeffer, & Brown, 1986):

Important Skills

1. Meets due dates
2. Arrives at school on time
3. Attends class every day
4. Exhibits interest in academic work
5. Accepts consequences of behavior

Problem Behaviors

1. Seldom completes assignments
2. Cannot follow written directions
3. Gives "back talk" to teacher
4. Falls asleep in class
5. Is quick to give up

Focus your intervention efforts on these skills and problems first. By the way, similar rankings have resulted from work with elementary school children (McConnell et al., 1984; Walker & Rankin, 1983). Notice the emphasis on compliance and academic productivity; as you prepare children for inclusion at any grade level, be sure to give these skills special attention.

As you identify students' weaknesses in school survival skills, be aware of your own perceptions and expectations. Studies have shown how these deeply held perceptions—sometimes stereotypes—can change what happens in a teacher–student interaction (see a review by Pigott & Cowen, 2000). For example, Taiwanese science students scored higher when they perceived their teacher as "using more challenging questions, as giving more nonverbal support, and as being more understanding and friendly" (She & Fisher, 2002). A longitudinal study of over 1,700 U.S. schools found that caring relationships and high expectations contributed to improved test scores (Hansen & Austin, 2003). One interesting strategy for getting to know your students better is through Photovoice, in which students create and share everyday photographs for personal growth and to identify their needs (Kroeger et al., 2004).

Promoting Self-Determination

Teachers play the pivotal role in assisting students who need to improve their school survival skills. Yet students may assist in this process by identifying what helps them. This is an important step in developing what we call **self-determination.** Teachers can foster self-determination in students with disabilities by (a) promoting generalization of self-determination skills and behaviors, (b) respecting students' choices and decisions, and (c) supporting students' goals (Wood, Karvonen, Test, Browder, & Algozzine, 2004). In an example of promoting self-determination, Sue Perfetti and her colleagues (personal communication, 1999) developed a self-assessment for secondary students to use in determining what adaptations and modifications they needed in the classroom. For example, students endorsed these strategies as helpful to them in taking notes:

- Provide outline of lecture
- Have student fill in the blanks of a structured outline
- Have another student carbon-copy notes
- Allow students to tape-record lessons
- Photocopy teacher or student notes
- Use graphic organizers/premade outlines
- Provide skeletal outline
- Provide word bank
- Highlight key words and important ideas
- Allow extra time for taking notes

Date ______________________

Student's Name ______________________ (please print)

Teacher's Name ______________________ (please print)

Circle the appropriate response.

Student's Grade 9 10 11 12

Student's Sex M F

Student's Special Ed Classification

SED LD EMR VH HI PH

This student is in your class for:

Homeroom Social Studies

English Science

Math Other _____

Directions: *Please read each statement and circle the corresponding letter that best describes this student's typical behavior. Be sure that you mark every item.*

This student	Never	Sometimes	Usually	Always	Not Observed
1. . . . stays awake in class.	N	S	U	A	X
2. . . . gets to class on time.	N	S	U	A	X
3. . . . complies with requests of adults in authority.	N	S	U	A	X
4. . . . stays calm and in control of emotions.	N	S	U	A	X
5. . . . brings necessary materials to class.	N	S	U	A	X
6. . . . is persistent even when faced with a difficult task.	N	S	U	A	X
7. . . . asks for help with school when necessary.	N	S	U	A	X
8. . . . responds to others when they speak.	N	S	U	A	X
9. . . . arrives at school on time.	N	S	U	A	X
10. . . . completes assigned work.	N	S	U	A	X
11. . . . behaves appropriately in a variety of settings.	N	S	U	A	X
12. . . . manages conflict through nonaggressive means.	N	S	U	A	X
13. . . . organizes study time efficiently.	N	S	U	A	X
14. . . . can concentrate on work without being distracted by peers	N	S	U	A	X
15. . . . works well independently.	N	S	U	A	X
16. . . . accepts the punishment if caught doing something wrong.	N	S	U	A	X
17. . . . turns in assignments when they are due.	N	S	U	A	X
18. . . . speaks appropriately to teachers.	N	S	U	A	X
19. . . . follows written directions.	N	S	U	A	X
20. . . . talks calmly to an adult when perceived to be unjustly accused.	N	S	U	A	X
21. . . . uses time productively while waiting for teacher.	N	S	U	A	X
22. . . . attends class.	N	S	U	A	X
23. . . . exhibits interest in improving academic performance.	N	S	U	A	X
24. . . . is good at taking tests.	N	S	U	A	X
25. . . . appropriately handles corrections on classwork.	N	S	U	A	X
26. . . . identifies the central theme of a lecture (demonstrates by stating or writing the main ideas and supporting facts).	N	S	U	A	X

Please Check to Make Sure All Items Are Marked

FIGURE 8–1 School Survival Skills Scale

Source: *Zigmond, N., Kerr, M. M., Schaeffer, A., Brown, G., & Farra, H. (1986).* The school survival skills curriculum. *Pittsburgh: University of Pittsburgh. Reprinted with permission.*

- Provide activities to practice getting the main idea
- Implement note-taking learning strategies
- One-to-one check for information with students
- Make sure students have key points
- Demonstrate abbreviated or speed-writing techniques
- Compare note-taking strategies with partner or teacher

(To obtain a copy of the Secondary Instructional Support Strategies and Intervention Lists produced by Apollo-Ridge School District, contact Dr. Susan Perfetti at ARIN Intermediate Unit, 2895 Route 422 West, Indiana, PA 15701-8300.)

Figure 8–2 shows a form used to assess school survival skills in preparation for middle school student-led parent conferences. This form allows the student to self-evaluate school survival skills and compare self-ratings with teacher ratings.

Go to the Companion Website to learn about the Self-Determination Synthesis Project Website, where you'll find lesson plans, sample individualized education plans (IEPs), and guidelines for promoting self-determination.

> See if you can write a good IEP self-determination goal for each of the students in our opening case study.

As you develop your own standards and expectations, ask yourself these questions:

- What does the student say that he or she needs in order to succeed? Are you meeting this need?
- Is there a clear expectation for an alternative, appropriate behavior in this setting? Be sure your students have clear, appropriate expectations for performance. Are the rules posted or orally reviewed for the student?
- Is the behavioral expectation developmentally appropriate for this student? Perhaps the environment or the social situation is too demanding (or too boring) for a student at this developmental level.
- Has the student received training in alternative appropriate behaviors? If you're unsure about a student's skills, review these skills as a teaching assessment. Remember that some students require regular review and practice in order to maintain their self-help and social skills.
- Has the student suddenly lost the skills? If so, then contact as many other persons involved with the student as possible. See if there is a health or family change that may be responsible for the sudden behavioral change. Remember, many problem behaviors may be the result of anxiety or depression, and this may reflect a serious but treatable problem.
- Has the problem occurred before? Can you identify any similarities between the episodes? Consider using an A-B-C analysis to determine what causes or maintains the behavior. Perhaps the behavior is being reinforced.
- Are other students engaging in the same behavior? There's a possibility that the student is imitating others. Reevaluate the contingencies for the other students. Are they being reinforced? How can you alter the contingencies for the target student and peers?

Let's turn now to specific interventions, beginning with teacher-mediated strategies, that promote school survival skills.

TEACHER-MEDIATED STRATEGIES

General Guidelines

The following guidelines include ways to prevent a child from experiencing the repeated failure or the unwarranted success that can be demoralizing to a child's sense of self-worth and achievement. The goal is to make the classroom environment challenging but predictable, allowing students a sense of control and accomplishment:

- Schedule ample time for a student working at a typical pace to complete the assignment, but if you have planned a task carefully, do

Student ______________________ Date ______________________

A = Almost Always S = Sometimes R = Rarely		Science		Social Studies		Math		Language Arts			
		Teacher	Student	Teacher	Student	Teacher	Student	Teacher	Student	Teacher	Student
I come to class prepared.	A										
	S										
	R										
I pay attention during class.	A										
	S										
	R										
I follow directions.	A										
	S										
	R										
I participate regularly in class.	A										
	S										
	R										
I stay on task during individual and group activities.	A										
	S										
	R										
I keep an organized notebook, folder, and binder.	A										
	S										
	R										
I complete my assignments accurately, neatly, and carefully, as required by teacher.	A										
	S										
	R										
I bring and use my agenda.	A										
	S										
	R										
I prepare for tests and quizzes.	A										
	S										
	R										
I spend time reviewing class notes regularly.	A										
	S										
	R										
Last Nine-Weeks Grade											

FIGURE 8–2 Subject Evaluation Form

Source: *Harrison Middle School. (2001). Baldwin-Whitehall School District, Pittsburgh. PA. Reprinted with permission.*

not give in to a student's complaints that it is too long.

- Place work materials in a designated storage area, off your desk, so that the student must take responsibility for picking up and returning work.
- Plan tasks that will challenge students but will occasionally allow them to experience some failure so that they will learn how to handle frustration. However, let students know when an assignment is difficult or encompasses new knowledge or skills.
- Let students know how they are performing. Help students develop a sense of competence by sharing your evaluations with them. Encourage self-evaluation by asking questions ("How do you think you worked in algebra today?" "Did you organize your study time well for this exam?").
- Do not assist students every time they request help. Establish guidelines for requesting help and follow these guidelines.
- Encourage students to help themselves by using the dictionary, reference books, or study guides. Even a strategy as simple as using mnemonic devices (e.g., jingles or acronyms that jog one's memory) can facilitate the learning of students with behavioral disorders (see Cade & Gunter, 2002; Kleinheksel & Summy, 2003).

Managing Routines

As Wong and Wong (1998) point out, "The number one problem in the classroom is not discipline; it is the lack of procedures and routines. . . . A procedure is simply a method or process for how things are to be done in a classroom" (pp. 167, 169). They recommend a three-step procedure for teaching classroom procedures:

1. State, explain, and demonstrate the routine
2. Rehearse and practice the procedure
3. Reteach, rehearse, practice, and reinforce the procedure until it becomes routine

Several studies offer suggestions for helping students and the teacher manage routines and transitions. For example, public posting and positive reinforcement were combined to reduce the transition time of middle school physical education students. Students who made the transitions within the designated times had their names displayed on a poster. If their names appeared nine or more times, they earned reinforcer activities they had chosen in a survey. The teachers reported an immediate and substantial decrease in transition times. Moreover, after 4 weeks, the student no longer required the public posting and reinforcers (Dawson-Rodriques, Lavay, Butt, & Lacourse, 1997).

For a comprehensive plan for improving transition behaviors in hallways, in the cafeteria, at recess, and at arrival and dismissal times, see Leedy, Bates, and Safran (2004).

Homework Strategies

Finishing homework is an essential study skill (Epstein, Polloway, Foley, & Patton, 1993). In an attempt to raise academic standards, many schools are placing special emphasis on homework completion. Consider these suggestions as you develop your own homework policy:

- Assess your students' homework difficulties, including the perceptions of their parents and other teachers.
- Present very clear and specific directions with all assignments.
- Make it relevant! Help the student understand the connection with his or her classwork. Share sample assignments from general education or less restrictive settings (Epstein et al., 1993).
- Assign homework that emphasizes proficiency, maintenance of skills already learned, or generalization of those skills and knowledge to another situation or example. Be sure that the homework is neither too novel nor too complex (Epstein et al., 1993).
- To ensure that you can provide adequate and timely feedback on homework, be as efficient as you can. Consider self-correcting

assignments, peer-monitored homework, or other assistance.

- Establish the routine early in the school year. Begin with written explanations to parents and students about the homework schedule and subjects. Collect homework after each assignment. Provide homework folders for students to take back and forth from school to home; these may help those who are likely to misplace their papers.
- Don't assume that a student will understand spoken homework assignments. Encourage the use of written assignments. (You may write them for younger students; older students may use an assignment book.)
- Pair students to work on homework.
- Involve parents. Have parents sign completed homework but do not expect parents to teach their students material that has not been learned in school. (Check out the Companion Website for parent-developed ideas for helping students with disabilities organize their schoolwork and schedules.)
- Try home-school notebooks to facilitate communication with parents. For guidelines on how to develop and successfully implement home-school notebooks, see Davern (2004) and Hall, Wolfe, and Bollig (2003).

Instructional Modifications

To assist students with attentional problems, C.H.A.D.D. and Dr. Sydney Zentall published the guidelines shown in Table 8–1.

Technology offers teachers infinite resources for modifying and enhancing instruction. For Internet resources to promote academic performance of students with disabilities, see Castellani and Jeffs (2001) and the Companion Website.

Direct Teaching of School Survival Skills

One of your best approaches to improving your students' time on task is to *teach* them the important skills they lack. Several publishers now offer study skills curricula. (Check the Companion Website for free guides to improve study strategies produced by Schwab Learning.)

One example of a school survival skill you might teach is time management. Meeting deadlines is a critical skill for school success. Even young children can begin thinking about the length of assignments and how to accomplish them. Middle and secondary school teachers may put their class assignments on a Website so that students can review them and plan their study time accordingly. It may be useful to give students some idea about how much time has elapsed during a work period and how much time remains for them to complete work. If you work with a student who seems easily upset when the school schedule changes, arrange a time to review the schedule with the student. Suggest that he or she use a highlighter pen to mark special or important dates (e.g., the date a term paper is due, the date and time for auditions for the school chorus, or the deadline for ordering class rings).

Combining Contingency Management with Other Strategies

When you develop contingency contracts, token economies, group-oriented contingencies, or other reinforcement and response-cost systems, remember to include school survival skills. Research has demonstrated the effectiveness of token reinforcement for improving academic performance (McGinnis, Friman, & Carlyon, 1999). Group contingencies are powerful peer-mediated strategies that can be especially useful for older students whose poor academic skills are the result of "goofing around" in the classroom (refer to Chapter 7 for guidelines). To illustrate how a combination of interventions might work, here are the suggestions made by a teacher who wanted to increase the productivity of eighth graders:

1. At the beginning of the class, review classroom procedures or ask an individual student to state one without looking. Give a coupon to students who can recite the procedures.

TABLE 8–1 Principles for Remediation

Principles of Remediation for Excessive Anxiety

- Do not attempt to reduce activity, but channel it into acceptable avenues.
  - Encourage directed movement in classrooms that is not disruptive.
  - Allow standing during seatwork, especially during end-of-task.
- Use activity as a reward.
  - Give activity (errand, clean board, organize teacher's desk, arrange chairs) as individual reward for improvement.
- Use active responses in instruction.
  - Use teaching activities that encourage active responding (talking, moving, organizing, working at the board).
  - Encourage diary writing, painting, etc.
  - Teach child to ask questions that are on-topic.

Principles of Remediation for Inability to Wait (Impulsivity)

- Give the child substitute verbal or motor responses to make while waiting and, where possible, do encourage daydreaming or planning in the interim.
  - Instruct the child on how to continue on easier parts of tasks (or do a substitute task) while waiting for teacher's help.
  - Have the child underline or rewrite directions before beginning or give magic markers or colored pencils for child to underline directions or relevant information.
  - Encourage doodling or play with clay, paper clips, or pipe cleaners while waiting or listening to instructions.
  - Encourage note taking (even just cue words).

Note: Dr. Barkley also suggests the teacher actively focus on and reward short intervals of waiting and gradually increase the length of the period.

- Where inability to wait becomes impatience and bossiness, encourage leadership but do not assume that impulsive statements or behavior are aggressive in intent.
  - Suggest/reinforce alternate ways (e.g., line reader, paper passer).
  - For children who interrupt, teach them to recognize pauses in conversations and how to hang onto ideas.
  - Cue child about upcoming difficult times or tasks where extra control will be needed.
  - Instruct and reinforce social routines (hellos, goodbyes, please, thank-you).

Principles of Remediation for Failure to Sustain Attention to Routine Tasks and Activities

- Decrease the length of the task.
  - Break one task into smaller parts to be completed at different times.
  - Give two tasks, with a preferred task to be completed after the less preferred task.
  - Give fewer spelling words and math problems.
  - Use fewer words in explaining tasks (concise and global verbal directions).
  - Use distributed practice for rote tasks, rather than mass practice.
- Make tasks interesting.
  - Allow work with partners, in small groups, in centers.
  - Alternate high and low interest tasks.
  - Use overhead projector when lecturing.
  - Allow child to sit closer to the teacher.
- Increase novelty, especially into later time periods of longer tasks.
  - Make a game out of checking work.
  - Use games to over-learn rote material.
  - Do not teach or reinforce "dead-man's behavior"—that is, do not assume the child is not paying attention just because s/he looks out the window or at another child. Do not make on-task behavior a goal, without changing the nature of the task or learning environment.

TABLE 8–1 (Continued)

Principles of Remediation for Noncompliance and Failure to Complete Tasks

• Generally increase the choice and specific interest of tasks for the child.
  • Allow a limited choice of tasks, topics, and activities.
  • Determine child's preferred activities and use as incentives.
  • Bring child's interests into assignments.
• Make sure tasks fit within child's learning abilities and preferred response style.
  • Allow alternate response modes (typewriter, computer, taped assignments).
  • Alter assignment difficulty level (give advanced level assignments or lower the level of difficulty).
  • Make sure disorganization is not a reason for failure to complete tasks.

Principles of Redemption for Difficulty at the Beginning of Tasks

• Generally increase the structure and salience of the relevant parts of tasks and social settings.
  • Prompt child for verbal directions (i.e., use written directions in addition to verbal ones; encourage note taking).
  • Structure written assignments and tests (i.e., use graph paper for math; state standards of acceptable work, being as specific as possible).
  • Point out overall structure of tasks (topic sentences, headings, table of contents).
  • Allow work with partners or in small groups with quiet talking.
  • Color, circle, underline, or rewrite directions, difficult letters in spelling, or math process signs.

Principles of Media for Completing Assignments on Time

• Increase the use of lists and assignment organizers (notebooks, folders).
  • Write assignments for child in a pocket notebook.
  • Write assignments on the board. Make sure the child has copied them.
• Establish object-placement routines to retrieve routinely used objects such as books, assignments, and clothes.
  • Encourage routines of pocket folders with new work on one side and completed graded work and class notes organized chronologically on the other.
  • Encourage parents to establish places for certain things at home (books, homework).
  • Organize desk or locker with labels and places for certain items.
• Use color and physical/spatial organizers.
  • Before leaving one place for another (walking out of the door) teach routine of child self-questioning—"Do I have everything I need?"
  • Tape prompt cards in desks, on books, or on assignment folders.

Increasing Planning and Sequential Organization of Thought

• Practice planning.
  • Practice planning different activities (what is needed, how to break tasks into parts).
  • Practice estimating time needed for activities.
  • Teach outlining skills.
• Practice sorting, ordering, and reordering.
  • Teach the use of a word processor to reorder ideas.
  • Teach the child to take notes on lectures or on written materials in three columns (main points, supporting points, questions).

Principles of Remediation for Poor Handwriting

• Reduce need for handwriting.
  • Do not have child recopy material. It will get progressively worse instead of better.
  • Allow student to copy a peer's notes or the teacher's notes.

TABLE 8–1 (Continued)

• Accept typed or taped assignments. • Reduce standards on some assignments and make relevant standards clearer on important assignments. • Color, circle, or underline parts of letters that children typically fail to close in cursive writing. • Allow reduced standards for acceptable handwriting. • Display particularly good samples of the child's work.
Principles of Remediation for Low Self-Esteem
• Generally recognize child's strengths and efforts. • Call attention to areas of the child's strengths by allowing for a consistent time each day or week during which child can display his/her talents. • Recognize that excessive activity can also mean increased energy and productivity. • Recognize that bossiness can also be leadership potential. • Recognize that attraction to novel stimulation can also lead to creativity. • Increase child's feelings of success by increasing child's skills. • Recognize these children's playfulness and use it to develop skills. • Mark student's correct performance, not the mistakes.

Source: *Fowler, M. (1995).* Educators manual: Children and adults with attention deficit disorders. *Plantation, FL: Children and Adults with Attention Deficit Disorder (C.H.A.D.D.), pp. 15–16. Reprinted with permission.*

2. Use a 1-inch voice; avoid yelling or publicly reprimanding students.
3. Don't disrupt students deep in concentration by stopping at their desk and talking to them.
4. Provide a reward or incentive. Put lottery tickets/coupons in the "jackpot" with the names of students who have done a thorough job with their work. When the jackpot is full, provide a classroom prize and have a drawing for individual prizes.
5. Provide choices for students. For example, "You can do 20 simple math problems worth 2 points each or 10 harder ones worth 4 points each" or "You can do this equation sheet about figuring out your car payments, or you can do this equation sheet about how many Barbies are sold each month."
6. Make sure that you monitor students as they work. After 10 minutes, say, "You should have completed at least eight problems." Save the last 10 minutes for them to check each others' work. They usually like this. They like it even better if an assignment is done well by everyone and the teacher makes it worth more points.
7. Recognize students who are doing what they are supposed to do. This can be nonverbal. Write a student a note and put it on his or her desk or worksheet for the next day. Put a sticker or a stamp on his class folder or a coupon in the jackpot. (E. Liston, personal communication, 1999).

Another example of a multifaceted intervention appears in Figure 8-3. Here you see how a combination of classroom rules, teacher movement, precision requests, and mystery motivation worked in conjunction with a token economy and response cost.

> Why do you think the teacher chose not to cue the students when the 30-minute periods began and ended? How does this intervention reflect what the research tells us about the importance of teacher–student relationships in the classroom? How did the teacher prevent students from misbehaving just to earn rewards?

Erinn Musser, Melissa Bray, Thomas Kehle, and William Jenson

Our intervention consisted of classroom rules, teacher movement, precision requests, and mystery motivators in conjunction with a token economy and response cost. Initially, we posted five classroom rules written in behavioral terms. They included "Sit in your seat unless you have permission to leave," "Do whatever Mrs. Green (the teacher) or Mrs. Doyle (the aide) asks immediately (compliance rule)," "Look at the teacher when she is talking and work when you are supposed to," "Raise your hand, wait for permission to speak," and "Do not make noises."

The teacher frequently moved around the room to detect and reinforce appropriate behavior or to reduce inappropriate behaviors. To promote student compliance, the teacher made any first request for compliance standing approximately 3 feet from the student while maintaining eye contact and using a statement rather than question format. The word "please" was the prompt, followed by the request. If the student did not comply within 5 seconds, the teacher asked again, using the prompt, "you need to." If the student did not respond to this second request within the 5-second wait time, a response-cost technique was instituted. When students did comply, they received praise.

The token economy, mystery motivator, and response cost were administered in the following manner:

- The teacher explained that students could earn stickers by following the newly publicly posted classroom rules. The teacher awarded stickers for student observance of the classroom rules during 30-minute time periods. The students were unaware of these time periods.
- Once students acquired the requisite number of stickers, they received the mystery motivator envelope containing a facsimile of a desired reward available at the end of the day.
- Students lost one sticker if there was no compliance after the second request.

To keep students from deliberately misbehaving to increase (a) teacher requests for compliance and (b) undeserved stickers, we chose verbal reinforcement for compliance rather than awarding an additional sticker. Initially, there were nine possible 30-minute time periods in which the student could earn stickers each day. Students needed to earn eight stickers within the nine time periods to redeem their first mystery motivator. This was relatively easy. We increased the criterion to gain access to the second mystery motivator to 10 stickers, then 12.

FIGURE 8–3 Multicomponent Treatment to Reduce Classroom Disruptive Behavior

PEER-MEDIATED STRATEGIES

Peer Tutoring

Peer tutoring, a successful way of structuring academic activities to involve peers, relies on the principles of peer modeling and peer teaching. Research shows that academic peer tutoring can have a positive influence on peer social interactions, although researchers cannot always document how and why (Cook, Scruggs, Mastropieri, & Casto, 1986). Another goal for peer tutoring may be a shift in attitudes toward children who are behaviorally challenged. Tutoring may allow nondisabled students to view their peers with disabilities in a different, less stereotyped role. In fact, students with behavioral disorders successfully can tutor their nondisabled peers in what we call *reverse-role tutoring* (Tournaki & Criscitiello, 2003).

The peer tutor must be a student who wants to do the tutoring, who may or may not have the content area skills but who can follow teacher directions and learn from a model. Use your judgment when pairing students for tutoring. Do not select a tutor who may embarrass or criticize the target student. When using a cross-age peer tutor (someone from another class), plan a schedule that is mutually convenient and decide how to evaluate the student tutor's involvement. Studies have shown that peer tutoring for students with disabilities in general education settings is more effective if those students are tutors for at least part of the time. Selecting the task for peer tutoring is an important step. Give first priority to the subject area in which the target student has difficulty. Choose academic tasks that are best taught through a "model or prompt plus feedback or praise" format. Good choices include spelling, vocabulary, sight words, and foreign language vocabulary; math facts; scientific formulas; and dates and names in social studies. Select academic tasks that require discrete responses and simple evaluation procedures (e.g., keeping a written tally of the number correct and errors, sorting flash cards into mastered and nonmastered piles). Plan tasks that require relatively brief 15- to 20-minute sessions. While tutor preparation should be specific to the content of the lessons, general guidelines for tutor training would include the following:

1. Pinpoint the task and analyze it before you begin
2. Collect all needed materials
3. Explain the goal of tutoring to the tutor
4. Explain the task to the tutor, as much as you think is needed
5. Instruct the tutor in the use of the materials
6. Explain how the data are to be collected
7. Role-play the actual tutoring procedures with the tutor
    a. Model the teaching and the feedback/praise with the tutor and the target student
    b. Ask the tutor to try being the student for a couple of steps
    c. Provide feedback to the tutor
    d. Role-play some problems the tutor may encounter
    e. If needed, train the tutor to use particular phrases to reinforce the student
    f. Provide the tutor with sample data and have him or her record them
    g. Meet with the tutor before the first session to review the procedures
    h. Meet daily after the tutoring session to answer questions
    i. Reinforce the tutor for his or her efforts

Wentzel and Watkins (2002) offered steps for training peer tutors of partners with attention-deficit hyperactivity disorder that included teaching prosocial skills such as reflective listening, giving positive feedback, and avoiding "put-downs." *Together We Can! ClassWide Peer Tutoring to Improve Basic Academic Skills,* developed at the University of Kansas with a federal grant, assists teachers in planning, implementing, monitoring, and troubleshooting their classroom tutoring programs (Greenwood, Delquadri, & Carta, 1997). For a detailed explanation of tutor training in elementary mathematics, see Fuchs, Fuchs, Yazdian, and Powell (2002).

Cooperative Learning

The link between social skills and school survival skills is apparent in one of our effective instructional strategies: **cooperative learning.** (For a review of effective instructional strategies, see Marzano, Pickering, & Pollock, 2001. The Companion Website has a link.) This approach holds promise for students with behavioral problems (see Rutherford, Mathur, & Quinn, 1998). Sutherland, Wehby, and Gunter (2000) warn against placing students with emotional and behavioral problems in cooperative learning situations without an adequate assessment of their prerequisite group skills (e.g., leadership, decision making, conflict resolution, and communication). In addition, try to incorporate all five of the components thought to make cooperative learning effective (i.e., positive interdependence, individual accountability, promotive interaction, group processing, development of small group social skills). For a discussion of the five components and a description of different kinds of cooperative learning groups, go to the University of Minnesota's Cooperative Learning Center through a link on the Companion Website.

SELF-MEDIATED STRATEGIES

Self-mediated strategies can be especially helpful for dependent students who are manipulative or oppositional when confronted with adult demands. Moreover, these interventions are "portable" in that the student can carry his or her self-monitoring form from class to class. Self-monitoring has the added advantage of freeing teacher time for instructional activities (Carr, 2002; Levendoski & Cartledge, 2000). Self-evaluation works even with children in preschool and first grade (Kasanen & Räty, 2002) and with students who have intellectual challenges, such as Hannah, the student in the intervention described in Figure 8-4.

> Why do you think it was so important to ensure that Hannah understood and could follow the self-evaluation procedures? How did this expenditure of time "up front" save teacher time in the long run?

Figure 8-5, a case study, describes how a 9-year-old learned to proofread her math. Proofreading, a self-mediated strategy, is essential across the content areas.

DiGangi, Maag, and Rutherford (1991) combined self-monitoring with self-graphing for two older elementary school students and found that academic performance and on-task behavior improved even more when the students graphed the results of their self-monitoring.

We now move to the second major topic of this chapter: strategies to improve social competence.

STRATEGIES TO IMPROVE SOCIAL COMPETENCE

Success in school depends in part on students' **social competence,** "the ability to respond appropriately in social contexts, and to meet the cognitive, physical, and linguistic demands of a social context as judged by significant others in that environment" (Hune & Nelson, 2002, p. 195). Yet the goal of helping students achieve social competence continues to elude researchers and practitioners (Gresham, 1997: McConnell, McEvoy, & Odom, 1992). As Smith and Travis (2001) explained,

> It may be that we have not been able to achieve more favorable outcomes from social competence research because we do not have a complete picture of its multiplicity of components and how they interrelate. Because we do not have a representation of the complete "puzzle," it is difficult to know where to fit individual pieces. (p.367)

Where does this leave a classroom teacher? Many of your students exhibit an inability to respond in social situations and to solve interpersonal problems, so their need is urgent. Recognizing that the field has not yet answered all your questions, we'll nevertheless try to explain and illustrate interventions that you should consider. (Chapter 9 describes problem-solving skills instruction for students with aggression and anger management problems.) Let's begin with an assessment of what it means to be socially skilled.

ASSESSMENT CONSIDERATIONS

As the previous quote mentioned, we do not yet understand all of the pieces in the puzzle of social competence. Researchers have identified several components:

- *Perceiving, decoding, and interpreting social cues* (Dodge, 1986). An example would be listening to the directions regarding a group project, looking around the classroom to see where groups are beginning to form, and joining a group.
- *Selecting and appropriately enacting appropriate responses* (Dodge, 1986) or *social skills.* These include discrete behaviors viewed favorably by others in one's social environment. An example would be greeting the way you initially greeted your classmates by saying hello, introducing oneself, and smiling. Naturally, what's acceptable in one age-group or situation will be different in another: we would not expect a

The intervention described for Hannah required a systematic approach for teaching the specific motor and cognitive skills required for completing the self-management routine. The self-management routine included two parts: use of a paper-and-pencil system for record keeping and the use of a tape cassette player and headphones to hear the signal to self-evaluate her behavior. Further elaboration on the design of instruction and the initial and ongoing instructional plan is provided. A review of teacher and parent interviews, Hannah's IEP and progress data, and direct observations helped define the level of complexity in the design and rate of instruction for teaching Hannah to manage her own behavior during seat work activities. The instructional design features for Hannah's plan included four specific strategies as described here. Since Hannah likes to draw/color, we added one drawing to her math and writing assignments. She was also encouraged to draw or doodle during free time activities.

Instructional Design Features

Defining task complexity. A task analysis was written to define each step in the self-management routine. For each of those steps, we identified the knowledge forms (noun, noncomparative, comparative, rule, and difficulty of the motor skill) needed for successful performance. The more knowledge forms involved in a specific step, the more complex the step.

Defining positive and negative examples. "On task" was defined as a noncomparative concept by using direct observation data. We further defined the list of examples to represent the range of positive and negative examples and the minimal difference pairs of positive and negative examples.

Sequencing simple to complex examples. Some of the discriminations needed for labeling on task or not on task have a very slight difference that makes it a positive or negative example. A simple discrimination might be throwing a pencil, while a complex discrimination involves writing versus doodling during assigned tasks. These minimal difference pairs were defined, sequenced, and overtly taught. The motor skills involved were also defined as simple or complex so that difficulty of the manipulation could be monitored.

Predictability for getting adult and peer attention. The results of the functional behavioral assessment showed that Hannah's problem behaviors were maintained by adult and peer attention. Therefore, consequences when Hannah used positive alternative behaviors included the predictability of getting brief adult attention throughout the activity. Every six checkpoints, Hannah's card had an icon of a hand that signaled Hannah to raise her hand to self-recruit adult attention. Initially, the teacher came over and gave Hannah a plus on the hand icon, but over time, Hannah learned that a thumbs-up from across the room was just enough to keep her going. Hannah had three or four opportunities to self-recruit teacher attention during seat work time. In addition, Hannah was allowed to share her homework, drawings, and just talk with several peers at the end of the activity.

Instructional Plan

Initial 30-minute instructional sessions. Hannah required 12 30-minute instructional sessions before meeting criteria for the two identified goals: (a) cassette player operation and (b) accurate self-evaluation and recording of her behavior. The defined examples were used in a model-lead-test type of format to label and discriminate the noncomparative concept "on task." In addition, situations occurring at school offered instructional opportunities. Hannah's teacher used the naturally occurring situations as teachable moments as often as possible. A task analysis was used to design the instruction of the tape recorder operation. The motor skills and discriminations needed for use of the self-management system were taught by following the task analysis to model the sequence of steps and specific manipulations (i.e., inserting a tape) followed with minimal

FIGURE 8–4 Hannah's Self-Management Intervention

assistance for success. Hannah's motivation was strong for learning this skill because of her interest in music and book tapes. Hannah received this part of instruction during the last 10 minutes of the 30-minute session. Listening to music at the end of instruction was already a natural motivator. In addition to using the tape recorder to signal the self-evaluation and recording time, Hannah gained independence for using a cassette player to listen to tapes.

Ongoing use of the system during seat work. Hannah used the self-management system every morning during seat work time in fourth grade. A behavior support person was there, collecting the research data, and was available for coaching Hannah if needed. The times when Hannah recorded her behavior inappropriately, we talked about the incident later in the day, in private. The plan was working so well that this didn't happen too often. The focus was more on the positive feedback for being on task and completing her work. At the end of the seat work session, Hannah counted her points and wrote the total number on the card (counting and writing numbers are IEP objectives as well). The behavior support person calculated the percentage of on-task behavior by dividing the total points possible by the total points earned so that seat work sessions could be compared. That percentage was graphed on a daily basis. We also kept a cumulative graph on work completion to see the effect of the use of the self-management system on independent work (an IEP objective). Hannah's on-task behavior increased to acceptable levels when she used the self-management system. In addition, her negative interactions on the playground ceased because of her learning more appropriate ways to access peer attention. When Hannah used the system, she completed her work; when she did not use the system, she reverted to problem behaviors and did not complete her work.

Using the Data for Decision Making

As designed, Hannah took her own data by rating herself on her self-management card. This was a very efficient strategy by providing a way to keep track of performance without adding teacher effort to data collection. The teacher effort shifted from nagging Hannah about getting work done to responding positively to Hannah's raised hand and work completion. Hannah's time on task and work completion data were reviewed weekly by the behavior specialist and monthly by the team.

FIGURE 8–4 (Continued)

Source: *Adapted from Brooks, A., Todd, A. W., Tofflemover, S., & Horner, R. (2003). Use of functional assessment and self-management system to increase academic engagement and work completion.* Journal of Positive Behavior Interventions, 5, *144–152.*

preschooler to introduce himself and say where he works, nor would we expect a graduate student immediately to offer her name and age!

- *Maintaining a social exchange for an appropriate length of time*. For example, a high school student who rambles during initial introductions will not be well received by her peers and will reduce the time left to work on the group task. Conversely, a 9-year-old who maintains social exchanges only fleetingly will not succeed in keeping his new friends.
- *Acknowledging the reciprocity, or give-and-take nature, of social exchanges*. The student who interrupts others' introductions or who dominates the conversation is not socially skilled (Strain, 2001).
- *Interpersonal problem solving*. This is the capacity to analyze an interpersonal conflict and find acceptable solutions. An example would be identifying the points of view of peers in a cooperative learning session and offering a compromise that would resolve their conflict.

When you analyze your students' interpersonal difficulties, consider each of these dimensions. This will require that you carefully observe your students in their social interactions and attempt to analyze where they fail. Watching socially successful

The Story of the Proofreading Card

By Cristina Carlson

When I was 10 years old, I brought home an "F" on a math pretest. Although it wasn't a grade, I was very, very upset. The week before, I got a "C" on the real test. My teacher said that I read too fast and made careless errors. (I think I am a lot better in reading than in math.)

Then one day after math class, Mrs. Carrick called me over to her desk and said, "I know you're not doing so well in math, and I think there's a solution. Let's talk about this. First, tell me what steps you use when you take a test."

"I put my name on the paper, read the question, do the work, and put down the answer."

"Aren't you proofreading?" she asked.

"What's that?" I replied.

"Proofreading. Proofreading is going over your work to make sure it's correct."

I thought, "Why didn't I do that before?"

Ms. Carrick and I made a proofreading card that I used every day to remind me. Here it is.

Step 1. Take a deep breath.
Step 2. Remember that you are a speedy reader, so slow down.
Step 3. Say the directions to yourself.
Step 4. Even if you feel confident, proofread:
- ☐ Check to be sure you didn't skip anything.
- ☐ Proofread your work.
- ☐ Proofread your answer.

I did all four steps.
Signed: _____ Date: _____

After a few days I began to catch my mistakes. On my English test, I didn't put a period. On my math homework, I skipped a step in multiplication. I left a letter out of my spelling word.

And on my next math test, I got a 96%—an A!

FIGURE 8–5 Proofreading Case Study
Source: *Reprinted with permission of the author.*

students may provide you with the naturalistic data you need to identify what's missing from their exchanges. To do less is to fall into the trap described by Strain (2001):

> When teachers write their . . . IEPs based on some mythical, self-generated metric (e.g., saying "hello" 8 out of 10 times; playing cooperatively 75% of the time), we consider that a willy-nilly nonempirical recipe for failure. (p. 32)

As stated in earlier chapters, rating scales and checklists are useful assessment and monitoring techniques for an initial look at a student's problem behaviors. For example, you might use a problem behavior checklist or the evaluation checklists taken from a social skills curriculum to get a general picture of the social skill problems experienced by one of your students. To make this assessment especially helpful, solicit the ratings from as many significant others as possible, including the parents, teachers, and other professionals who know the child. Do not overlook the student's previous teacher, who might be a valuable source of information.

The information you gather from checklists and ratings can give you a starting place for further, more finely grained assessments, including behavioral interviews and direct observations. Gresham, Sugai, and Horner (2001) offered guidelines for analyzing our observational data. First, your observations may reveal that a student does not ever exhibit the appropriate social skill. We would call this a "can't do" or *acquisition deficit.* Acquisition deficits require direct modeling and teaching of the new skill. In contrast, you may notice that the student has the skills but chooses not to use them. This is called a "won't do" or *performance deficit.* A third problem, comparable to that of a student just beginning to use a new skill, is a *fluency deficit.* Fluency deficits tell us that a student has not yet seen enough examples of when to use a new social skill, has not yet had enough practice, or has not been reinforced for using the skill. In other words, the student knows the appropriate social skill and wants to use it but uses it infrequently or ineffectively.

Interviews are especially important in the assessment of social skills because others in the child's life are apt to have strong convictions about the student's social relationships and functioning. Some questions you might ask in a social assessment interview include the following:

- Who are this student's friends?
- What social situations are difficult for this student?
- What "social mistakes" does this student make?
- Does this student initiate social interactions?
- What social skills does this student have?
- What do others say about this student's social behavior?
- What skills does this student need to be more socially successful?
- Can this student maintain a social interaction?
- In what situations is this student socially successful?
- What behavior does this student exhibit in these situations?

An **analog measure** is a role-play or behavioral rehearsal in which an individual demonstrates how he or she would respond in a given social interaction. You have probably used analog measures and not realized it. For example, you may have asked a student to describe how he would respond to a certain social situation. Analog measures may help you understand a student's social perception and the skills he needs to learn in order to respond successfully to a given social situation.

SOCIAL WITHDRAWAL

What should you do if you observe a student who *avoids* social exchange? **Social withdrawal,** a very serious problem, refers to a cluster of behaviors that result in an individual escaping or avoiding social contact. This may be intentional, as in extreme cases of **elective mutism** (an uncommon syndrome involving a refusal to speak by someone who can talk), or it may reflect a broader lack of social competence, as is often found in children or adults with retardation, psychotic behaviors, or autism. Social withdrawal may result from a lack of specific social skills, an anxiety disorder (see Chapter 12), or it may have its origins in a history of rejection and punishment associated with social interaction. In many cases, social withdrawal may be maintained by negative reinforcement: the child continues the specific form of withdrawn behavior because she escapes or avoids social contact, which apparently constitutes an aversive stimulus for her. In other cases, behaviors incompatible with social interaction, such as self-stimulatory behavior, may be maintained by self-produced reinforcement. Thus, social withdrawal covers a broad and complex range of problem behaviors.

For a long time, social withdrawal was not considered a serious problem in the field of special education or in related disciplines. Even today, an extremely quiet child, seldom enjoying the benefits of positive relationships with others but creating no observable problems for his teachers, may drift unnoticed from one school year to the next. Yet the consequences of untreated social withdrawal can be extremely serious. Unless a child can learn to interact with others at a reasonably competent level, access to less restrictive settings and subsequent learning opportunities may be seriously curtailed.

Some strategies you should always *avoid* when dealing with social withdrawal. One of these is coercion, or punishment, designed to "make the child come out of herself." Unfortunately, classmates often ridicule and tease their withdrawn peers, making initiating simple interactions even more difficult for the student. Try to help classmates recognize that social withdrawal is a problem for that student and consider using one of the peer-mediated interventions to assist her.

Another strategy to avoid is leaving the isolate individual alone. Isolate children who are left alone for long periods may develop additional serious problems rather than learning skills that improve their social interactions. Time-out procedures are thus inappropriate interventions for the socially withdrawn.

A third approach to socially withdrawn students—one that has not proven effective—is to accept their social isolation as a developmental phase and simply to await their decision to approach their classmates. Unfortunately, many withdrawn children have not learned the social skills required to develop social relationships with their classmates and cannot learn them without help. Maturation as a singular intervention on social withdrawal is not effective. Children do not simply outgrow this problem; the more they avoid people, the less opportunity they have to develop personally reinforcing situations.

Let's turn now to some of the interventions that can help students with acquisition, performance, and fluency deficits.

TEACHER-MEDIATED STRATEGIES

Social Skills Instruction

Faced with the many choices in social skills curricula, you may wonder how to make a good choice. Consider these guidelines and essential features.

Setting. Social skills instruction should take advantage of naturally occurring situations to increase the likelihood that the new skills will generalize and be reinforced by others.

Assessment. Instead of a "one size fits all" approach, carefully consider your students' individual social skills deficits and be sure that the social skills instruction meets those needs. This is an important factor in maintaining the students' participation in the intervention (sometimes referred to as treatment adherence). Check out the Companion Website for a social skills intervention for teens with learning disabilities (Court & Givon, 2003).

Cultural Sensitivity. Be sure that your social skills instruction is responsive to your students' diverse cultural and linguistic backgrounds. Social interactions by their nature are personal and values laden, so we urge you to tap other resources (e.g., Cartledge & Milburn, 1996; Franklin, 1992) before assessment and instruction begin. For example, you may teach students to maintain a firm handshake or look directly at the other person, only to discover that this is not condoned in their culture (Lee & Cartledge, 1996).

As Cartledge and her colleagues observed,

> The achievement and adjustment problems of African American students are well documented and may appear intractable to many educators. A closer analysis . . . can reveal misguided curriculum approaches and aversive school policies that do not reflect the culture or instructional needs of these students. (Cartledge, Sentelle, Loe, Lambert & Reed, 2001, p. 253)

Competing Behaviors. Analyze competing behaviors and what maintains them. For example, if a student avoids stressful social interactions by refusing to participate in student groups, then rearrange the contingencies so that the student finds it more rewarding to participate and less rewarding to withdraw.

Remember, the "old" behaviors have served the student for a long time and may be hard habits to break. Your goal is to make the new behaviors more meaningful for the student (Gresham, 1998). Again, be sure that you are not contradicting deeply held cultural beliefs.

Modeling. The first step in most social skills teaching programs is to introduce students to examples of the social skill through live, audio, or video modeling. Usually, one skill, broken down as much as possible, is the focus of each vignette or lesson. To incorporate peers, call on various students in your class to demonstrate social skills during a lesson. Use as many naturally occurring examples as possible to strengthen the new behaviors.

Role-Playing. After an initial demonstration, the social skills program may call for a role-play of the targeted skill. To facilitate this component, encourage students first to discuss the demonstration and to think of real-life situations in which they might use the skill. Following this discussion, arrange student-designed role-playing or follow a scripted role-play from the curricular materials. (Before teaching a lesson, be sure that you would feel comfortable role-playing the social skill yourself. In addition, double-check with other resources to ensure that you are not violating students' cultural beliefs and traditions. For example, many Native Americans prefer to stand 2 to 3 feet from their conversation partner, while many European Americans are comfortable within 20 to 36 inches [Lee & Cartledge, 1996]).

Performance Feedback. Letting students know how they performed the skill during the role-play is crucial. Some of the most helpful and candid feedback (e.g., approval, praise, constructive criticism) will come from the other group members. A good rule is to encourage positive, supportive feedback while indicating aspects of the behavior that the student could improve. Adult supervision is very important during this phase. A helpful strategy is to have the student immediately replay the scene so that the group can give feedback on the improved performance.

Generalization and Maintenance. By now, these terms are familiar. The chance to "overlearn" and repeatedly practice the social skills in other settings is vital to a youngster's social development. Self-monitoring can be an essential feature of this transfer-of-learning phase. Many social skills programs include "behavioral homework" and notes sent home to reinforce the skills outside the classroom. In addition, try to incorporate different "trainers." In one consultation experience, a teacher of junior high school students with moderate disabilities "primed" various faculty colleagues to enter her classroom and initiate certain social interactions, including gentle teasing for a student having trouble with this kind of interaction. She simply posted her "social skills needs list" in the teachers' lounge each Monday.

> One way to increase the generalization of social skills out of school is first to ask parents which social skills are important to them.

Figure 8-6 illustrates strategies to improve the effectiveness of social skills instruction in three key dimensions: programming generalization, facilitating treatment adherence, and increasing social validity (Hansen, Nagle, & Meyer, 1998).

Let's take a look at some of the social skills available to help you. (For a review of social-emotional curricula for preschoolers, see Joseph & Strain, 2003.)

Widely used in many countries, the *Second Step* social competence curriculum seeks to prevent violence by promoting essential social competencies (Frey, Hirschstein, & Guzzo, 2000). A Spanish-language supplement is available for bilingual learners. This program emphasizes competencies in the areas of empathy or perspective taking, prosocial problem solving, and impulse control. Within each of these three areas, pre-K through grade 8 students learn specific behavioral skills. "By applying perspective-taking, problem-solving, and anger management strategies, children decide *what* to do; in behavioral skills training children rehearse specific steps for *how* to do it" (Frey et al., 2000, p. 103). Information about this successful approach is available through the Companion Website.

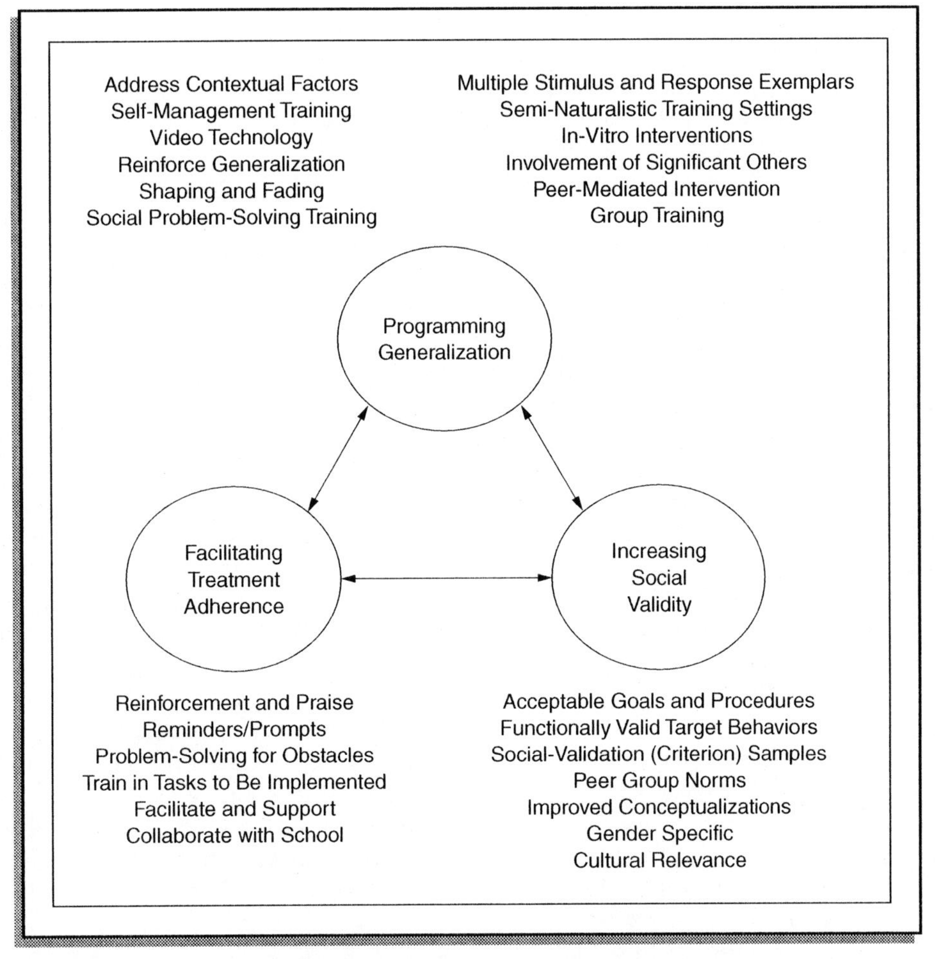

FIGURE 8–6 Enhancing the Effectiveness of Social Skills Instruction

Source: *Hansen, D. J., Nagle, D. W., & Meyer, K. A. (1998). Enhancing the effectiveness of social skills interventions with adolescents.* Education and Treatment of Children, 21, *508. Reprinted with permission.*

Think First, a promising training program for secondary school students, uses role-playing and problem-solving scenarios in combination with a reward system. Ten 50-minute classroom sessions take place over 12 weeks. With a focus on reducing aggression in school settings, its video examples show typical high school classroom and hallway encounters involving student to student and student to teacher. For more information, go to the Companion Website.

PATHS (Promoting Alternative Thinking Strategies) is a comprehensive program for teaching social competence in general education classrooms from kindergarten through grade 6. You can find more information about this approach at the Companion Website.

Another effective approach to teaching prosocial behaviors is the *Prepare Curriculum,* which includes seven components. One of these, skill-streaming, can be used in the classroom. It consists of four parts: modeling, role-playing, performance feedback, and transfer of learning (Goldstein, 1999). This program can be taught to 6 to 12 participants who are assessed as having similar skill deficits. Problem situations are task-analyzed and modeled for the students by their teacher or through audiovisual aids. Table 8–2 lists some of these psychological skill areas. After students have witnessed good ways to manage difficult situations, they role-play these skills themselves.

The next stage of training is performance feedback, in which the actors in the role-plays receive comments on how they enacted the skills. Goldstein stressed the importance of specific encouraging comments here. Finally, students experience the transfer of training, a phase in which overlearning is emphasized. Students reexperience the modeling, role-plays, and performance feedback many times in order to ensure that they have really captured the important skills they lack. For more information about this and the other six components, you might want to review Goldstein's *The Prepare Curriculum: Teaching Prosocial Competencies* (1999).

To enhance a social skills curriculum, give students "behavioral homework assignments," writing assignments for their notebooks, "cue cards," and other learning aids. Moreover, try to link the skills with real-life situations by offering relevant teaching examples, role-plays, and discussion topics. In addition, social skills training is more effective when combined with other interventions specifically targeted to aggression (e.g., anger control training) and when parents are involved.

Many teachers prefer to develop their own social skills lessons, as illustrated in our chapter-closing case study.

PEER-MEDIATED STRATEGIES

By including peers in the intervention, you increase the likelihood that they will alter their attitudes toward the socially unskilled child. Few aspects of behavioral change have experienced such growth as the peer-mediated interventions for socially challenged young children and adolescents. Entire volumes now offer suggestions for incorporating peers in social skills training (e.g., Strain, Odom, & McConnell, 1984). As you have read, peers are involved in social skills training as they role-play different situations.

Peers as Instructional Agents

For young children with significant social skills deficits, peers have been successful interventionists—in fact, peers are preferred over adults because intervention studies showed that adults actually inadvertently interrupted the natural social exchange of two children playing together (Strain, 2001). Use these three simple criteria when selecting a peer to intervene with a young socially withdrawn classmate: (a) regularly attends school, (b) shows positive social initiation during free play times, and (c) can follow adult directions reliably (Strain, 2001). Table 8–3 illustrates a peer-mediated intervention for young socially withdrawn children.

This section closes with a look at the benefits of peer-mediated interventions for *all* students. Rob, a typically developing child whose school promotes inclusion, has learned helpful ways to accommodate his classmates with special needs. You can read his suggestions in Figure 8–7.

SELF-MEDIATED STRATEGIES

Self-mediated strategies offer promise for a student who is aware of her performance or fluency deficit and wishes to have a role in remedying it. For example, this intervention might be very useful for adolescents included in a general education setting. Students should record their own performances to visibly show their progress toward meeting the goal of increased social interactions. Thus, the intervention is twofold. First, the teacher or counselor describes to students examples of social exchanges, including appropriate initiations and responses. Second, students collect data on their own interactions. A third component,

TABLE 8–2 Psychological Skill Areas for Aggressive Students

Asking for help
1. Decide what the problem is.
2. Decide whether you want help with the problem.
3. Identify the people who might help you.
4. Choose a helper.
5. Tell the helper about your problem.

Giving Instructions
1. Define what needs to be done and who should do it.
2. Tell the other person what you want him to do and why.
3. Tell the other person exactly how to do what you want done.
4. Ask for the other person's reaction.
5. Consider that reaction and change your direction if appropriate.

Expressing affection
1. Decide whether you have warm, caring feelings about another person.
2. Decide whether the other person would like to know about your feelings.
3. Decide how you might best express your feelings.
4. Choose the right time and place to express your feelings.
5. Express affection in a warm and caring manner.

Expressing a complaint
1. Define what the problem is and who is responsible.
2. Decide how the problem might be solved.
3. Tell that person what the problem is and how it might be solved.
4. Ask for a response.
5. Decide whether you want to try again.
6. If it is appropriate, try again, using your revised approach.

Responding to contradictory messages
1. Pay attention to those body signals that help you know you are feeling trapped or confused.
2. Consider the other person's words and actions that may have caused you to have these feelings.
3. Decide whether that person's words and actions are contradictory.
4. Decide whether it would be useful to point out any contradiction.
5. If appropriate, ask the other person to explain any contradiction.

Responding to anger
1. Listen openly to the other person's angry statement(s).
2. Show that you understand what the other person is feeling.
3. Ask the other person to explain anything you don't understand about what was said.
4. Show that you understand why the other person feels angry.
5. If it is appropriate, express your thoughts and feelings about the situation.

Preparing for a stressful conversation
1. Imagine yourself in the stressful situation.
2. Think about how you will feel and why you will feel that way.
3. Imagine the other person(s) in that stressful situation. Think about how that person(s) will feel and why he (they) will feel that way.
4. Imagine yourself telling the other person(s) what you want to say.
5. Imagine the response that your statement will elicit.
6. Repeat the above steps, using as many approaches as you can think of.
7. Choose the best approach.

TABLE 8–2 (Continued)

Determining responsibility
1. Decide what the problem is.
2. Consider possible causes of the problem.
3. Determine the most likely causes of the problem.
4. Take actions to test which are the actual causes of the problem.

Setting problem priorities
1. List all the problems currently pressuring you.
2. Arrange this list in order, from most to least urgent.
3. Take steps (delegate, postpone, avoid) to temporarily decrease the urgency of all but the most pressing problem.
4. Concentrate on solving the most pressing problem.

Dealing with being left out
1. Decide whether you're being left out (ignored, rejected).
2. Think about why the other people might be leaving you out of something.
3. Consider how you might deal with the problem (wait, leave, tell the other people how their behavior affects you, talk with a friend about the problem).
4. Choose the best way and do it.
5. Show that you understand the other person's feelings.
6. Come to agreement on the steps each of you will take.

Persuading others
1. Decide on your position and predict what the other person's is likely to be.
2. State your position clearly, completely, and in a way that is acceptable to the other person.
3. State what you think the other person's position is.
4. Restate your position, emphasizing why it is the better of the two.
5. Suggest that the other person consider your position for a while before making a decision.

Following instructions
1. Listen carefully while the instructions are being given.
2. Give your reactions to the instructor.
3. Repeat the instructions to yourself.
4. Imagine yourself following the instructions and then do it.

Responding to the feelings of others (empathy)
1. Observe another person's words and actions.
2. Consider what the other person might be feeling and how strong the feelings are.
3. Decide whether it would be helpful to let the other person know that you understand his feelings.
4. If appropriate, tell the other person in a warm and sincere manner how you think he is feeling.

Responding to a complaint
1. Listen openly to the complaint.
2. Ask the person to explain anything you don't understand.
3. Show that you understand the other person's thoughts and feelings.
4. Tell the other person your thoughts and feelings, accepting responsibility if appropriate.
5. Summarize the steps each of you will take.

Responding to persuasion
1. Listen openly to another person's position.
2. Consider the possible reasons for the other person's position.
3. Ask the other person to explain anything you don't understand about what was said.
4. Compare the other person's position with your own, identifying the pros and cons of each.
5. Decide what position to support, based on what will have the greatest long-term benefit.

TABLE 8–2 (Continued)

Responding to failure
1. Decide whether you have failed.
2. Think about both the personal reasons and the circumstances that have caused you to fail.
3. Decide how you might do things differently if you tried again.

Dealing with an accusation
1. Think about what the other person has accused you of (whether it is accurate, inaccurate, said in a mean way or in a constructive way).
2. Think about why the person might have accused you (Have you infringed on the person's rights or property?).
3. Think about ways to answer the person's accusations (deny, explain your behavior, correct the other person's perceptions, assert, apologize, offer to make up for what has happened).
4. Choose the best way and do it.

Dealing with group pressure
1. Think about what the other people want you to do and why (listen to the other people, decide what their real intent is, try to understand what is being said).
2. Decide what you want to do (yield, resist, delay, negotiate).
3. Consider how to tell the other people what you want to do (give reasons, talk to one person only, delay, assert).
4. If appropriate, tell the group or other person what you have decided.

Source: *Reprinted with permission from Goldstein, A. P. (1987). Teaching prosocial skills to aggressive adolescents. In C. M. Nelson, R. B. Rutherford, Jr., & B. I. Wolford (Eds.),* Special education in the criminal justice system *(pp. 223–226). Upper Saddle River, NJ: Merrill/Prentice Hall.*

TABLE 8–3 Peer-Mediated Prompting and Reinforcement Strategy

1. Select a peer as suggested in the text.
2. Plan at least four 20-minute training sessions to prepare the individual for her role as peer trainer.
3. Explain to the peer trainer that you want assistance in helping other children to learn to play. Explain further that the role of peer trainer is helping children play with each other and letting them know they are doing a good job.
4. Train the peer trainer by inviting two children into the play session and practice with the trainer prompting and reinforcing them for playing together. Unlike other peer-mediated procedures, training for peer prompting and reinforcement should take place "on the job," using the isolate students from the beginning.
5. By modeling the strategies with the isolate children present, assist the peer trainer to think of ways to prompt and reinforce the isolate children.
6. Remind the peer trainer before each intervention session to try to get the two children to play with each other rather than directly with the peer trainer.
7. Set aside the time and materials and location described in previous peer training intervention for the actual training sessions.
8. Remember to reinforce the peer trainer for efforts after each session.

self-reinforcement, may supplement the intervention, or the teacher or counselor may provide the reinforcement to the student. Here are examples of target behaviors for a student to record:

- Raising my hand in classroom discussions to say something
- Asking a question during the class meeting
- Helping another student in my class on an assignment
- Answering a question when another student asks me something
- Saying "hello" to one of my classmates
- Asking my classmate to eat lunch next to me
- Asking someone in my class to play with me at recess
- At recess, telling others they are doing a good job
- Lending someone a pencil or paper during class

Helping a Child with Disabilities
by Rob Perrone, age eight

1. Call the child by his or her name, not "the handicapped kid."
2. Be kind to the child, and remember: this involves patience.
3. When you start out, ask the teacher, "May I help this child?"
4. Wait until the teacher says you can do it.
5. After the teacher says "Yes," then you go over to the child.
6. Ask the child what they're doing, or what they're writing, or what they're interested in.
7. Then probably ask them, [not in a mean way, but nicely], "You know, I've heard that you kind of have some trouble in doing . . "
8. The child will say, "Yeah, but. . . I still have some friends."
9. Then you say, "I'm here to help you out with your disability and help you do things like your classmates."
10. Then, say it's time to line up for gym and the child is in a wheelchair, you would say, "I'm going to help you in gym, also. I'll come and help you along with your teacher to play the sport."

YO! THIS IS A NEW PART OF THE PRESENTATION!!

11. If the child has trouble in behavior . . approach them not like you're a really sweet person. But more like, "Hey, yo, Dude, What 'ya doin?" so they feel comfortable. Then, if they start acting up, just say, "Calm down, [whatever their name is. Not like "Bad kid," or "Sick Kid,"]
12. Do not say this even with a kind voice--no matter what--to this child: "I know that you're not very good at behavior and you're not well-liked."
13. SURE, SURE. I KNOW YOU WANT TO KNOW WHY? WELL:

First of all, it would seem mean to them. Second of all, it would be like telling them that just because they have a simple disability that they can't be liked. Third of all, it would just probably make them do the same thing.

(Continued)

FIGURE 8–7 Helping a Child with Disabilities

14. For a kid who just plays a little too rough, first of all, don't say, "Do you want to play this sport that he DOES like?" [Now I know it sounds kinda mean, but the sport he likes he probably plays too rough.] Your first move when you come into the room is to definitely ask the teacher. See if the teacher will give you some information on how to work well with this child. Say, "When you have gym class, I'll probably come and help you out a little bit in case you start getting a little rough. Because the school doesn't want anyone to get hurt." Whatever you do, don't start screaming at the kid. This probably isn't my best advice for the rough-housing kid. Ask the teacher if you want really good information, because mine's probably not right. My advice might not be the best.

15. And if the child is shy, invite him to take a walk with you with his mom or something or a friend. This only works in a city. When you see a pigeon, say, "I'm gonna get that bird." And then run after it. That works because it's funny and it will get the child to laugh. Believe me, I did it to my best friend, and it worked.

16. If the child does not have trouble in behavior but--say--listening, then you would use this approach. Probably try to make the activity a little more fun or humorous. Or a little more exciting, so he or she would want to look at it. Make sure that you get the message but make sure that it is still a little humorous or fun.

Approach #2: You might just tell another student to tell them, "Can you say to this kid, 'Hey Buddy! You know how I get all my good grades?' I try to listen my best, so I hear everything the teacher is saying so I get the maximum amount you are supposed to learn."

Whatever you do, don't tell them that just because you can't listen well means that you won't get good grades Because they might get good grades in one thing but not in another thing.

FIGURE 8–7 (Continued)
Source: *Reprinted with permission of the author.*

- Sitting next to one of my friends during lunch
- Bringing a toy for someone else to play with in school
- Telling someone what I did after school yesterday
- Signing up to tutor another person in my class
- Asking someone else to help me with my self-recording project

Self-monitoring is a good way to extend your social skills curriculum, as students can monitor their progress on targeted social skills.

TEACHING SOCIAL SKILLS

Li-Lin Chen

This week the goals of my social skills program are that students will initiate a conversation, make eye contact, and smile with adults (teachers). In addition, students must get at least five marks on the group contingency according to the agreement between their self-recording charts and the teacher's recording sheet. On Monday students will practice initiating a conversation with an adult or a teacher. On Tuesday they must make eye contact as well as starting a conversation with adults (teachers). On Wednesday they will initiate a conversation with eye contact as well as smile at the adults (teachers). (Naturally, our program continues throughout the year.)

Monday
Homeroom (15 min.)

00:00–00:05 (Teacher's greeting)

The teacher says, "Good morning everyone! How are you today?"

She lets students feel free and comfortable to talk.

00:06–00:15 (Introduction of today's topic)

The teacher talks about today's topic starting a conversation with the following questions:

How do you start a conversation?
What do you do when you meet someone?
What are some other ways you can start a conversation?
Why is conversation important?

(Students can respond or ask questions if they do not understand. The teacher lists what they say on the blackboard and keeps a list on paper so that she and the students can discuss it next time.)

Reprinted with author's permission.

The teacher talks about the self-recording procedures to the entire class—including when and how to record. The teacher then asks students to start a conversation with any adult (teacher) in math, art, music, English, and social skills classes, not including the homeroom period. She hands out paper to every student and explains how to use the self-recording chart by drawing a chart on the board. Then they copy the chart onto their paper. They can place a "Y" mark on their chart if they initiate a conversation with adults (teachers) before, within, or at the end of the classes. The maximum total marks that can be earned for the week is 21. Each needs to write his name, the date, and the topic of the day on his recording chart so that he can learn to be responsible for it and also to remember what he should do for the day. The chart will be like the one in Figure 8-8.

The teacher must tell students the reason why other teachers are joining them to record their behavior by starting a conversation with teachers, in class or out of class, every day. Then they will talk about the group contingency: where it will be placed (public posting in this classroom), how the group contingency will apply in starting a conversation with adults (teachers), and how the entire class or each individual will earn rewards—the teacher lets them recommend rewards and vote for the most popular for the entire class (assuming that they like free time, reading storybooks, and computer games).

The Group Contingency

When each student has earned five "Y" marks in a week on his or her self-recording chart (this must agree with the records kept by their teachers), the whole class will have a 10-min. free conversation

Name				
Date				
Purpose				
Math	Social Skills	Music	English	Art

FIGURE 8–8 Self-Recording Chart

time in the social skills class the following week. (Where there is disagreement, the teacher clarifies by talking to the student and those teachers.)

A point will be earned for each additional "Y" mark over five "Y" marks.

Each student who accumulates nine points by Friday can choose a favorite storybook to read with a friend during free time or recess time next week.

Each student who accumulates more than 10 points by Friday can play a 15-min. computer game with a friend during recess or free time next week.

3rd Period (60 min.)

00:00–00:10 (Review)

The teacher asks how they initiated a conversation with their math teacher. She lets the students respond freely. She asks how they started the conversation. How did they record for themselves? What did they say?

00:11–00:25 (Introduction to starting a conversation with adults)

The teacher mentions the morning's response list and then discusses it in depth. She explains to students what it means to start a conversation and how they can start a conversation with adults (teachers). Give good examples from the math class. (Remember to make sure that each student understands how to initiate a conversation.)

00:26–00:40 (Demonstration of the skill)

The teacher will ask a student to volunteer to role-play initiating a conversation. For example, the volunteer will act as a bookstore owner and the teacher as a customer. The teacher might say, "Good morning! I am looking for a cook-book. Can you help me?" The teacher will then give each student in the room the opportunity to initiate a conversation.

00:41–00:55 (Role-play of the skill)

The teacher pairs off students and gives them some situations to let them practice with their partners, such as in a restaurant, a clothing store, a bookstore, an ice cream store, or a flower shop. After they practice one situation, the teacher asks them how they did and asks one of the pairs to come forward to demonstrate. The teacher then begins a discussion with the class about how their example can be improved. During this discussion the pair can incorporate the improvements into their situation. So as not to embarrass the pair, the discussion should accentuate the positives as well as pointing out the areas that need improvement. If time allows, each pair should be given the opportunity to demonstrate their role-play situation in front of the class.

00:56–00:60 (Reinforcement)

Ask the students what they remember. Review the procedures of self-recording. Remind students of the rewards for the whole class or each individual.

The End of the Day (15 min.)

00:00–00:15 (Homework)

The teacher begins by collecting all of the self-recording charts. (The teacher should also collect the other teachers' charts and make sure that they agree with the students'.) Next, the teacher passes out the homework sheet to each student and explains what they need to do at home (see Figure 8–9). The sheet should be signed by their parent and returned during homeroom period the following morning.

Tuesday
Homeroom (15 min.)

00:00–00:05 (Collecting parents' slips)

The teacher collects the parents' slips from all students, and asks how they did with their assignments and if there are any questions. (Remember to call a student's parent if he or she does not turn in the slip and write down the specific student's response.)

00:06–00:15 (Review of self-recording charts)

Dear Parents,

Good evening! Thank you for taking the time to read this letter. The purpose of this letter is to ask for your help with your child's homework. The focus of this week at school is emphasis on initiating a conversation while making eye contact, and smiling with adults (teachers). This process has been divided into three steps. The first step is to initiate a conversation with adults (teachers). The second step is not only initiating a conversation but also making eye contact with adults. The third step is initiating a conversation, making eye contact and smiling while talking with adults (teachers). Today please pay attention to and encourage your child to start a conversation with you when your child wants to watch TV, to have a drink, to ask you to sign this sheet, to ask permission to play with neighbors, etc. On Tuesday, it would be helpful if you could take your child to the library or a bookstore where he or she could practice initiating a conversation while making eye contact with adults. On Wednesday, possibly you could take him or her to a friend's home where your child is able to practice initiating a conversation, making eye contact, and smiling while talking to adults. Please do not hesitate to call me if you have any questions. I will be very glad to hear from you. Have a nice evening! Please remember to detach the answer slip from this homework sheet, sign it, and remind your child to return it to me. Thank you again.

Sincerely,

Carol

08/02/00

- -

I agree to guide my child to finish his or her homework.

Signature ____________________________

Date ____________________________

FIGURE 8–9 Homework Sheet

Under each student's name on the group contingency poster, the teacher writes each student's total marks. The poster should be placed on the wall where everyone can obviously see it. If there is a disagreement about the marks, the teacher arranges time to meet with the student and teachers, encouraging those students who have only a few marks, and praising those who gained many marks. Then the teacher will hand out paper and ask the students to draw their self-recording chart. It should include each student's name, date, and the topic of the day, as defined by the teacher. The teacher announces that they can mark a "Y" when they initiate a conversation with adults (teachers) in math and social skills classes. After the social skills class, they will record a different social behavior according to today's criterion.

3rd Period (60 min.)

00:00–00:15 (Recording marks in your social skills class and introducing the new social skill)

The teacher marks a "Y" on the recording chart when any student starts a conversation with her. She praises those students who initiate a conversation, especially those 10 students with behavioral problems.

Next, the teacher introduces today's behavioral skill—initiating a conversation and also making eye contact with adults (teachers) by asking questions or showing examples:

> What do you do when you meet someone? (For example, when you saw your friend in the mall, what did you do? Did you wave your hand or call his or her name?)

> What else did you do besides talking? Did you look at your friend or did you avoid looking at him/her?

After students respond to these questions, the teacher asks them why they reacted the way they did and explains why we need eye contact when talking to people. She also discusses some exceptional situations such as when speaking to people with different cultural backgrounds.

00:16–00:30 (Demonstration of the skill)

The teacher tells them about her own story:

> I am shy; therefore, I try not to talk to people. One time, Lillian, one of my best friends, saw me and called my name, so I had to talk to her. She made direct eye contact while speaking to me, which made me very uncomfortable and I felt like going away. However, I respected her and didn't want to embarrass her, and because she was so nice, I was encouraged to look at her while talking to her. That experience helped me to make the effort to look at people when I am talking to them.

The teacher asks for a discussion about her incident with Lillian, asking what they would have done. The teacher then speaks directly to each student, making sure to make eye contact. The class should then discuss each student's reaction to this and ask the students to describe how it made each feel.

00:31–00:45 (Role-play)

The teacher should ask for four volunteers or pick four students for a role-play situation. One will be a waiter. Three of them will be friends going to have dinner at the Pizza Hut. The waiter gives them menus. They need more time to think, so they ask him to come back later. After he comes back, everyone takes a turn to order his or her own pizza. The teacher will then initiate a discussion of the role-play and ask for feedback from the class.

The teacher asks another four students to come forward, with one student acting as a children's bookstore manager and the others as customers. One at a time, the customers will request a book that they want and buy it. They need to initiate conversations and make eye contact.

Once again, the teacher asks for a discussion of this role-play situation and asks for feedback from the class.

The teacher should pair off the students and have them take turns practicing being a taxi driver or passenger. The taxi driver needs to know where to go, so his passenger needs to give him the directions. Both of them should make eye contact during their conversations. The teacher should try to monitor each pair and offer help where needed. The pair that demonstrates the best activity should replay their situation for the whole class. Their peers can give them feedback and opinions.

00:46–00:60 (Review)

The teacher should ask students to sit in a circle (the teacher sits with them). Discuss what they learned in the last 45 minutes. How did they feel when the teacher asked them to come forward to role-play? During this time they can ask questions and express their opinions. The teacher reminds them that they mark a "Y" only when they initiate a conversation and make eye contact with the adults (teachers).

The End of the Day (15 min.)

00:00–00:15 (Homework)

The teacher collects and checks students' self-recording charts to see how they are doing in math, music, English, and art classes (the teacher should also collect the teachers' recording sheet). If some students do not earn any marks today, the teacher encourages them to try again tomorrow. Explain the next homework assignment. Their mother or father should take them to a library or bookstore. Their job is to initiate a conversation with some of the people who are there, remembering to make eye contact.

Wednesday
Homeroom (15 min.)

00:00–00:10 (Talking about the homework)

The teacher will begin by asking where students' parents took them and how they initiated a conversation: "Did you make eye contact? Was it very difficult? Why or why not?" The teacher writes their responses and feelings on the board to keep as a record.

00:11–00:15 (Review of self-recording charts)

The teacher records each student's total marks on the group contingency poster under their names, discussing the marks each student earned on Monday and Tuesday. She reminds the students about the class reward and the individual student rewards and the conditions on which they are based. This can encourage those students who have not reached five marks to do better. Next, the teacher hands out paper and asks them to draw their self-recording chart, including name, date, and today's topic (the teacher will announce this to the class). Once again the teacher reminds them to mark a "Y" on their self-recording charts for their math and social skills classes according to yesterday's criterion (starting a conversation and making eye contact with adults (teachers)). After the social skills class, the self-recording chart will be based on today's criterion.

3rd Period (60 min.)

00:00–00:15 (Recording marks in your class and introducing the new social skill)

The teacher will mark a "Y" on her recording sheet when any student starts a conversation as well as makes eye contact. She praises those students verbally. Then, the teacher introduces today's social behavior: initiating a conversation, making eye contact, and adding a "smile." She gets them started by beginning the discussion as follows:

> Do you remember the role-play situation yesterday which included three friends and a waiter at the Pizza Hut? (If they do not remember ask one volunteer student to describe it.) If the waiter had said "Good evening" without smiling, how would that make you feel? (Let students discuss this question.) Then, if one of the three friends ordered pizza without a smile, how would the waiter respond? Would he smile in return? Why or why not?

These discussions among the students help them to discover how important it is to smile and make eye contact when talking to someone.

00:16–00:30 (Demonstration of the skill)

The teacher walks around the classroom and chooses students randomly asking "How are you?" and making sure to smile and make eye contact. Then the teacher asks how this made them feel and begins a discussion with the students.

00:31–00:45 (Role-play)

The teacher groups students in pairs and gives them some situations from which to choose to practice with their partners (a shoe store, a candy store, a movie theater, etc.). The teacher asks them to pay much attention to their smile when their partners start a conversation and to be sure to make eye contact with each other. If their peers do not smile while practicing, their partners should correct them right away and practice it again. (During their role-play, the teacher needs to observe their role-play and choose one of the pairs to demonstrate for the entire class.) If time permits, the teacher can invite other pairs to come forward.

00:46–00:60 (Review)

The teacher begins a discussion by asking, "Do you like it when someone talks to you with a smile on his or her face? Why or why not? Can anybody tell me what social skills we learned this week?" (The teacher may need to give them some hints.) Next, the teacher looks at the group contingency and encourages their efforts, reminding them of the class reward and individual rewards to provoke them to practice the social skills they have learned.

The End of the Day (15 min.)

00:00–00:15 (Homework)

The teacher collects and checks students' self-recording charts to see how they are doing in other classes. If any students did not receive marks since Tuesday, she arranges a time to meet with those students privately. She discusses their previous homework assignments and encourages them to practice their skills initiating conversations, making eye contact, and smiling while making conversation.

Case Study Reflection Questions

1. Why do you think the teacher in this case study chose to use self-recording as one of her interventions?
2. How do you like the group contingency used? What type is it? (Refer back to Chapter 7.)
3. How did Ms. Chen involve parents in the intervention? Why did she do so?

SUMMARY

- In order to teach diverse learners, we must first assess their interests, learning preferences, and readiness—the three cornerstones of differentiated instruction that are reflected in students' school survival skills.
- As you identify students' weaknesses in school survival skills, be aware of your own perceptions and expectations.
- You can foster self-determination in students with disabilities by (a) promoting generalization of self-determination skills and behaviors, (b) respecting students' choices and decisions, and (c) supporting students' goals
- Be sure that your social skills instruction is responsive to your students' diverse cultural and linguistic backgrounds.
- Assessing the many dimensions of social competence is essential to planning an effective intervention.
- Peers are essential in social skills interventions.

DISCUSSION/APPLICATION IDEAS

1. How can teachers help one another become more aware of their own cultural biases as they discuss students' school survival and social skills?
2. What are five ways you can increase the opportunities for your students' skills to generalize to other, less restrictive settings?
3. Discuss this statement from a leading social skills researcher: "The only consistent predictor of outcome is the fidelity with which intervention is delivered" (Strain, 2001, p. 35). How do the case studies illustrate this important conclusion?
4. What interventions and modifications can assist a student who is overly dependent on the teacher?
5. What are the do's and don'ts of social skills interventions? Discuss the rationale behind each one.
6. Will peer tutoring lead to improved social skills? Why or why not?

REFERENCES

Brooks, A., Todd, A. W., Tofflemover, S., & Horner, R. (2003). Use of functional assessment and self-management system to increase academic engagement and work completion. *Journal of Positive Behavior Interventions, 5,* 144–152.

Cade, T., & Gunter, P. (2002). Teaching students with severe emotional or behavioral disorders to use a musical mnemonic technique to solve basic division calculations. *Behavioral Disorders, 27*(3), 208–214.

Carr, S. (2002). Self-evaluation: Involving students in their own learning. *Reading and Writing Quarterly, 18,* 195–199.

Cartledge, G., & Milburn, J. F. (1996). *Cultural diversity and social skills instruction: Understanding ethnic and gender differences.* Champaign, IL: Research Press.

Cartledge, G., Sentelle, J., Loe, S., Lambert, M. C., & Reed, E. S. (2001). To be young, gifted and black?: A case study of positive interventions within an inner-city classroom of African American students. *Journal of Negro Education, 70*(4), 243–253.

Castellani, J., & Jeffs, T. (2001). Emerging reading and writing strategies using technology. *Teaching Exceptional Children, 33*(5), 60–67.

Cook, S. B., Scruggs, T. E., Mastropieri, M. A., & Casto, G. W. (1986). Handicapped students as tutors. *Journal of Special Education, 19*(4), 483–492.

Court, D., & Givon, S. (2003). Group intervention: Improving social skills of adolescents with learning disabilities. *Teaching Exceptional Children, 36*(2), 46–51.

Davern, L. (2004). School-to-home notebooks: What parents have to say. *Teaching Exceptional Children, 36*(5), 22–27.

Dawson-Rodriques, K., Lavay, B., Butt, K., & Lacourse, M. (1997). A plan to reduce transition time in physical education. *Journal of Physical Education, Recreation, and Dance, 68*(9), 30–34.

DiGangi, S. A., Maag, J. W., & Rutherford, R. B. (1991). Self-graphing of on-task behavior: Enhancing the reactive effects of self-monitoring on on-task behavior and academic performance. *Learning Disability Quarterly, 14*(3), 221–230.

Dodge, K. (1986). A social information processing model of social competence in children. In M. Perlmutter (Ed.), *Cognitive perspectives on children's social and behavioral development* (pp. 77-125). Hillsdale, NJ: Lawrence Erlbaum Associates.

Epstein, M. H., Polloway, E. A., Foley, R. M., & Patton, J. R. (1993). Homework: A comparison of teachers' and parents' perceptions of the problems experienced by students identified as having behavioral disorders, learning disabilities, or no disabilities. *Remedial and Special Education, 14*(5), 40-50.

Franklin, M. E. (1992). Culturally sensitive instructional practices for African-American learners with disabilities. *Exceptional Children, 59*(2), 115-122.

Frey, K. S., Hirschstein, M. K., & Guzzo, B. A. (2000). Second step: Preventing aggression by promoting social competence. *Journal of Emotional and Behavioral Disorders, 8*(2), 102-112.

Fowler, M. (1995). *Educators manual: Children and adults with attention deficit disorders.* Plantation, FL: Children and Adults with Attention Deficit Disorder (C.H.A.D.D.), pp. 15-16.

Fuchs, L. A., Fuchs, D., Yazdian, L., & Powell, S. R. (2002). Enhancing first-grade children's mathematical development with peer-assisted learning strategies. *School Psychology Review, 31*(4), 569-583.

Goldstein, A. P. (1999). *The prepare curriculum: Teaching prosocial competencies.* Champaign, IL: Research Press.

Goldstein, A. P. (1987). *Teaching prosocial skills to aggressive adolescents.* In C. M. Nelson, R. B. Rutherford, Jr., & B. I. Wolford (Eds.), Special Education in the criminal justice system (pp. 223-226). Upper Saddle River, NJ: Merrill/Prentice Hall.

Greenwood, C., Delquadri, J., & Carta, J. (1997). *Together we can! Classwide peer tutoring to improve basic academic skills.* Longmont, CO: Sopris West.

Gresham, F. (1997). Social competence and affective characteristics of students with mild disabilities. *Review of Educational Research, 67,* 377-415.

Gresham, F. (1998). Social skills training: Should we raze, remodel, or rebuild? *Behavioral Disorders, 24*(1), 19-25.

Gresham, F. M., Sugai, G., & Horner, R. H. (2001). Interpreting outcomes of social skills training for students with high-incidence disabilities. *Exceptional Children, 67,* 331-344.

Hall, T. E., Wolfe, P. S., & Bollig, A. A. (2003). The home-to-school notebook: An effective communication strategy for students with severe disabilities. *Teaching Exceptional Children, 26*(2), 68-73.

Hansen, D. J., & Austin, G. A. (2003). Are student health risks and low resilience assets an impediment to the academic progress of schools? *(California Healthy Kids Survey Factsheet 3).* Los Alamitos, CA: WestEd.

Hansen, D. J., Nagle, D. W., & Meyer, K. A. (1998). Enhancing the effectiveness of social skills interventions with adolescents. *Education and Treatment of Children, 21*(2), 489-513.

Harrison Middle School. (2001). Baldwin-Whitehall School District, Pittsburgh, PA.

Hune, J. B., & Nelson, C. M. (2002). Effects of teaching a problem-solving strategy on preschool children with problem behavior. *Behavioral Disorders, 27*(3), 185-207.

Joseph, G. E., & Strain, P. S. (2003). Comprehensive evidence-based social-emotional curricula for young children: An analysis of efficacious adoption potential. *Topics in Early Childhood Special Education, 23*(2), 62-73.

Kasanen, K., & Räty, H. (2002) "You be sure now to be honest in your assessment": Teaching and learning self-assessment. *Social Psychology of Education, 5,* 313-328.

Kerr, M. M., Zigmond, N., Schaeffer, A. L., & Brown, G. (1986). An observational followup study of successful and unsuccessful high school students. *High School Journal, 71,* 20-32.

Kleinheksel, K. A., & Summy, S. E. (2003). Enhancing student learning and social behavior through mnemonic strategies. *Teaching Exceptional Children, 36*(2), 30-35.

Kroeger, S., Burton, C., Comarata, A., Combs, C., Hamm, C., Hopkins, R., et al. (2004). Student voice and critical reflection: Helping students at risk. *Teaching Exceptional Children, 36*(3), 50-57.

Kuhn, T. S. (1970). *The structure of scientific revolutions* (2nd ed.). Chicago: University of Chicago Press.

Lee, J. W., & Cartledge, G. (1996). Native Americans. In G. Cartledge & J. F. Milburn, *Cultural diversity and social skills instruction* (pp. 205-243). Champaign, IL: Research Press.

Leedy, A., Bates, P., & Safran, S. P. (2004). Bridging the research-to-practice gap: Improving hallways behavior using positive behavior supports. *Behavioral Disorders, 29*(2), 130-139.

Levendoski, L. S., & Cartledge, G. (2000). Self-monitoring for elementary school children with serious emotional disturbances: Classroom applications for increased academic responding. *Behavioral Disorders, 23*(3), 211-224.

Marzano, R. J., Pickering, D. J., & Pollock, J. E. (2001). *Classroom instruction that works.* Alexandria, VA: Association for Supervision and Curriculum Development.

McConnell, S. R., McEvoy, M. A., & Odom, S. R. (1992). Implementation of social competence interventions in early childhood special education classes. In S. L. Odom, S. R. McConnell, & M. E. McEvoy (Eds.), *Social competence of young children with disabilities* (pp. 277-306). Baltimore: Paul H. Brookes.

McConnell, S. R., Strain, P. S., Kerr, M. M., Stagg, V., Lenkner, D. A., & Lambert, D. L. (1984). An empirical definition of school adjustment: Selection of target behaviors for a comprehensive treatment program. *Behavior Modification, 8,* 451-473.

McGinnis, J. C., Friman, P. C., & Carlyon, W. D. (1999). The effect of token rewards on "intrinsic" motivation for doing math. *Journal of Applied Behavior Analysis, 32*(3), 375-379.

Pigott, R. L., & Cowen, E. L. (2000). Teacher race, child race, racial congruence, and teacher ratings of children's social adjustment. *Journal of School Psychology, 38*(2), 177-195.

Rutherford, R. B., Mathur, S. R., & Quinn, M. M. (1998). Promoting social communication skills through cooperative learning and direct instruction. *Education and Treatment of Children, 21*(3), 354-369.

She, H-C., & Fisher, D. (2002). Teacher communication behavior and its association with students' cognitive and attitudinal outcomes in science in Taiwan. *Journal of Research in Science Teaching, 39*(1), 63-78.

Smith, S. W., & Travis, P. (2001). Conducting social competence research: Considering conceptual frameworks. *Behavioral Disorders, 26,* 360-369.

Strain, P. (2001). Empirically based social skill intervention: A case for quality-of-life improvement. *Behavioral Disorders, 27*(1), 30-36.

Strain, P. S., Odom, S. L., & McConnell, S. (1984). Promoting social reciprocity of exceptional children: Identification, target behavior selection, and intervention. *Remedial and Special Education, 5,* 21-28.

Sutherland, K. S., Wehby, J. H., & Gunter, P. L. (2000). The effectiveness of cooperative learning with students with emotional and behavioral disorders: A literature review. *Behavioral Disorders, 25*(3), 225-238.

Tournaki, N., & Criscitiello, E. (2003). Using peer tutoring as a successful part of behavior management. *Teaching Exceptional Children, 36*(2), 22-29.

Walker, H. M., & Rankin, R. (1983). Assessing the behavioral expectations and demands of less restrictive settings. *School Psychology Review, 12,* 274-284.

Wentzel, K. R., & Watkins, D. E. (2002). Peer relationships and collaborative learning as contexts for academic enablers. *School Psychology Review, 31*(3), 366-377.

Wong, H. K., & Wong, R. T. (1998). *The first days of school: How to be an effective teacher.* Mountain View, CA: Harry K. Wong Publications.

Wood, W. M., Karvonen, M., Test, D. W., Browder, D., & Algozzine, B. (2004). Self-determination instruction in special education: Getting SD into the IEP. *Teaching Exceptional Children 36*(3), 8-16.

CHAPTER 9 ADDRESSING AGGRESSIVE BEHAVIORS

OUTLINE

An Introduction to Antisocial Behavior
Documenting and Understanding Aggressive Behavior
Teacher-Mediated Strategies
Peer-Mediated Strategies
Self-Mediated Strategies

OBJECTIVES

After completing this chapter, you should be able to

- Offer four reasons why students engage in antisocial behavior.
- Conduct a functional analysis of aggressive behavior.
- Identify alternatives to verbal confrontations with students.
- Implement three interventions for teaching students with aggression.

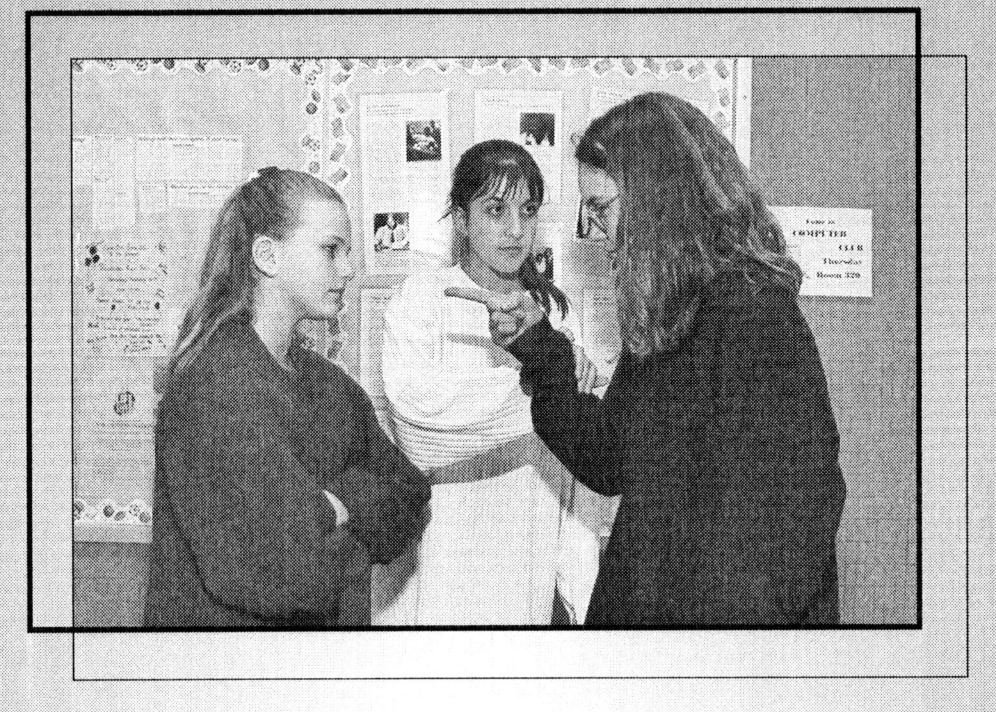

KEY TERMS (refer to the Glossary on the Companion Website for definitions)

aggression
anger management training
antecedent-behavior-consequence (ABC) analysis
antisocial behavior
conduct disorder
pinpoint
response cost

This chapter introduces you to assessment, documentation, and intervention strategies for students who exhibit aggressive behavior. Here you'll learn about what factors contribute to aggression, why early intervention is important, and what you can do to reduce aggressive behavior in your classroom. Let's begin with a case study that we'll revisit throughout the chapter.

Come into My Classroom: A Case Study

Terylyn transferred into her middle school during the late fall. That's when the problems began. Despite their best efforts to welcome her, the staff just can't seem to reach her. Their frustration emerged during a recent grade-level teachers' meeting:

First, her math teacher spoke, "It's as if she doesn't trust any adults. No matter what we do, Terylyn seems to believe that we have some ulterior motive, that we are out to get her or something. When I call on her in class, she just glares at me. When I asked her about it, she said I was picking on her. I am so frustrated that I find myself just ignoring her in class." Her physical education teacher responded, "Well, you should be glad you don't have her in physical education. Another kid accidentally bumped her the other day, and Terylyn went off. The student teacher and I had to separate her from the other kid."

Walking into the meeting with an armful of papers, the social worker explained, "Her previous school records just arrived. Check this out. This kid has been in five schools in six years. I guess her family moves to keep ahead of the landlords. Her attendance records are a disaster. It's a wonder Terylyn can even understand the work we are assigning."

Terylyn's English teacher interrupted, "Trust me, Terylyn doesn't understand the work. Her journal entries about Bearstone are way off base. She just doesn't seem to understand the characters; her analysis of the plot is really basic. I have tried pairing her with other students, but she doesn't seem to fit in. Frankly, she shuns them, and they shun her. The other day she got upset because she said another girl looked at her wrong. What an angry kid!"

Terylyn's social studies teacher commented next, "I had the same feeling about her, until the strangest thing happened last Monday. A cafeteria aide stopped by my room to drop off menus. Terylyn saw her, broke out in a big smile, and hugged her as if she were a long-lost friend. I couldn't believe my eyes! I asked the aide about it later, and she explained that she has known Terylyn since they lived in the same apartment building years ago. So there is at least one adult in this school Terylyn likes. Maybe she can help us out."

Working with students like Terylyn can be frustrating, as their behavior often eludes our best attempts to understand and explain it. As we move into our discussion of what causes **aggression,** try to form some hypotheses about factors that may contribute to Terylyn's puzzling behavior. Why do you suppose she acts out in some situations but not in others?

AN INTRODUCTION TO ANTISOCIAL BEHAVIOR

This section will offer an overview of what we know about **antisocial behavior,** or **conduct disorder.** We cannot overemphasize the importance of early intervention. As Loeber and Farrington (1998) advised, "It is never too early."

Because antisocial behavior is the result of many factors, prevention and early intervention approaches must also be multifaceted. No doubt, you will be called on to participate in the classroom aspects of a program. However, to orient you to all the components needed to prevent or intervene in antisocial behaviors, we offer this brief overview:

> Community conditions contributing to violence are those in which the social organizations (family and community standards) disintegrate and youth are not bonded to conventional norms. Socially isolated families with few resources and alternative activities for children are prone to produce violent youth.
>
> Normal transitions (home to kindergarten or elementary school to middle school) are points when children are at greater risk of disruptive behavior and make excellent points for intervention. Aggressive behavior in elementary school and lack of parental supervision in early adolescence are powerful predictors of subsequent criminal behavior. Youth who are involved in violence are likely to have witnessed it early in their lives. Aggressive youths often misjudge or misinterpret others' behaviors as threatening and are prone to strike back. Feeling threatened also leads to the possession of weapons for self-protection. The use of weaponry increases the incidence of violence for youth who are not generally antisocial by nature. Exposure to violence, in their homes and neighborhoods, can lead to symptoms similar to posttraumatic stress syndrome, like those seen in children raised in war zones. (E. Mulvey, personal communication, December 12, 2003)

Returning to our case study, Terylyn's team may want to find out more about her living situation, about how long she has exhibited aggression, and whether her family has supports and connections to their present community.

Additional research on antisocial behavior is readily available through the Internet. If you would like to find out more, check out the sites on the Companion Website, including The Safetyzone (a clearinghouse for information related to school safety), the National Association of Attorneys General/National School Boards Association, and the U.S. Department of Education's Office of Safe and Drug-Free Schools.

DOCUMENTING AND UNDERSTANDING AGGRESSIVE BEHAVIOR

Some of the direct observational and interview strategies you learned in earlier chapters will help you document aggressive behavior. One tool you can use is **antecedent-behavior-consequence (ABC) analysis.** We begin with this assessment and continue with functional explanations for aggression that the ABC may uncover. Because many aggressive acts take place suddenly and without warning, you can't really plan to observe and record systematically as you do with other behaviors. To circumvent this problem, look at Figure 9–1, an "after-the-fact" ABC form for recalling aggressive incidents.

To begin, describe the aggressive or destructive behavior in the far left column, using as many specific terms as possible. Second, write the date and time period of the aggressive incident, if known. Next, identify the location and all other participants or observers. State whether the aggressive behavior was directed toward property and/or persons and identify any personal injury or property damage. Then describe as accurately as possible what happened before and after the aggressive behavior. Note whether you directly observed the behavior or received the report of it. Finally, add any comments helpful in predicting future aggression. Those involved should complete this form independently; they may have a tendency to "color" each other's account of what actually took place. Remember, you need an objective retelling of the situation. Try to capture each person's recollection soon after each incident. By comparing facts and independent impressions, you may form useful hypotheses about the antecedents (triggers) to a student's aggressive behavior. For example, you may notice that a student is aggressive only toward younger students or only during

Directions: Complete this checklist for each aggressive behavior the student has exhibited.

Person Completing Form Mrs. Blouze Student Helen A. Date Nov. 6

Describe the behavior	When did this behavior most recently occur?	Where did this behavior take place?	Who else was in the setting?	Was the aggression directed toward anyone or toward property? Whom? What?	What was going on immediately (15 min.) before the aggressive behavior?	What happened immediately (15 min.) after the aggressive behavior?	Did you directly observe the behavior?	Comments: (Describe anything that was unusual about the schedule, setting, or student when the event took place, or anything you think would be helpful to consider.)
Came into room, threw book on desk, refused to open it. Threw book on floor. "Sassed" me. Refused to leave. Resisted, was verbally abusive, then hit me.	Yesterday	Regular Reading Class	Other Students (entire class)	More towards teacher	Was in art and came down the hall to reading class.	I told her again to open that book. Told her to pick it up. Told her to leave room. Took her hand to lead her. Buzzed the principal's office.	Yes	She seems to come to class already mad or upset.

FIGURE 9–1 ABC Form for Assessing Aggressive Behaviors

unsupervised transition activities. The form may also reveal that others inadvertently reinforce aggressive behaviors. For example, a student cursed aloud to his easily embarrassed teacher because it resulted in expulsion from history class, his most difficult subject.

In summary, use the after-the-fact ABC form to detect patterns in the aggression so that you and others can "see it coming" in the future. To predict aggression, it helps to have a good grasp of why aggression happens.

> Can you detect any clues in Figure 9–1 that might explain Helen's actions? Thinking back to the opening case study, what might an ABC analysis tell us about Terylyn's reactions to others?

TEACHER-MEDIATED STRATEGIES

To select the most effective intervention, we need to understand the individual student. After all, we know that a one-size-fits-all approach will not address a problem as serious as classroom aggression. Keller and Tapasak (1997) offer a helpful description of individual characteristics that contribute to aggression. These are shown in Table 9-1. As you review this list, consider our case study student, Terylyn. How would you characterize her aggressive behavior? What intervention would or would not be advisable for her?

In addition to the information presented in Table 9-1, be sensitive about the "fit" between an intervention and the students' cultural background (for more information, see Cartledge & Loe, 2001).

Academic Intervention

Students who struggle academically are at higher risk for antisocial behaviors, according to many studies. Too often, academic frustration leads to classroom outbursts. Therefore, your careful assessment and instruction is in itself a major intervention for antisocial behaviors. Be sure that you request a comprehensive academic assessment for any student who is exhibiting serious aggression. In addition, use the functional behavior assessment strategies described in earlier chapters to identify adaptations and accommodations that will help a student become more responsive to your instruction. Penno, Frank, and Wacker (2000) identified several accommodations based on functional analyses for their teenage students:

- Using the computer for mathematics
- Working with a peer tutor
- Shortening assignments
- Self-monitoring

By carefully selecting these accommodations based on individual student data, the teachers were able to reduce behavior problems as well as improve academic performance.

In the case of Terylyn, frequent absences from school and transfer may have disrupted her learning, leading her to avoid tasks that are too difficult. Keep in mind that you may need to modify and adapt your *interventions for aggression* as well as your *academic instruction*. For example, be sure that the student can follow the scripts for role-plays or understand the terms of your token economy.

Verbal De-escalation

A teacher may inadvertently provoke a student to react aggressively, especially if that student, like Terylyn, has a tendency to overreact to stressful situations, described in Table 9-1 as "heightened affective arousal." A verbal confrontation can escalate quickly into aggression. How can you avoid unnecessary verbal confrontations with your students? Here are a few ideas.

1. *Misbehavior or Mother Nature?* The misbehavior may be part of a normal developmental phase. All adolescents sometimes feel the need to prove their increasing autonomy and individuality. Some of these ways are not much fun for adults! For example, teenagers often engage in verbal confrontations to prove that they can "win" with an adult. Adults may be caught off guard and participate in these confrontations, making matters worse for everyone. As teenagers struggle to develop their own identities, they often reject adults' characteristics. This rejection may take the form of teasing adults. For example, we have had students say to us, "Did you really want your hair to look like that?" or "Haven't you gained an awful lot of weight since last semester?" Here is one of our favorites: "Is your mother still picking out your clothes for you, teacher?" Although you may not condone all expressions of a teenager's autonomy, you may feel better if you keep this behavior in its developmental context. One way to respond to teasing is to poke fun at yourself whenever possible. This lessens the tension and models a healthy sense of humor.
2. *Pick your battles.* An experienced middle school teacher once advised us, "You've already been a teenager. It's their turn!" Many confrontations are not worth the effort of

TABLE 9–1 Characteristics of Students Who Exhibit Aggression

Student Characteristic	Description	Targeted Interventions
Arousal-heightening interpretation of external stimuli	An event triggers anger and self-statements that arouse anger. For example, "This teacher is frowning at me. She probably hates me anyway, so I might as well make trouble for her."	• Anger management training, so the student can identify events that "set him off" • Self-instruction on coping statements and self-evaluation of behaviors • Teaching students to read accurately others' social cues
Heightened affective arousal	Individual overreacts to an event or stimulus.	• Relaxation training • Verbal de-escalation to model more appropriate behaviors for the student • Encouraging the student to talk about her feelings • Helping the student work out alternative behaviors for problem situations • Helping the student "save face" by providing privacy and alternatives
Ineffective communication	Students may lack the communication skills to negotiate a resolution, express a complaint, or share feelings.	• Conflict resolution training • Social skills training • Problem-solving skills training • Behavioral contracting (to confirm verbal resolutions)
Mismanagement of contingencies	Aggressive behaviors are being reinforced; alternatives are being punished or extinguished. For example, bullies escape consequences for their behavior, so they continue their intimidation of others.	• Functional behavior assessment to determine what motivates the behavior • Contingency management strategies such as token economy, contracting, time-out from reinforcement, Good Behavior Game
Prosocial values deficits	The student has the skills and self-control to manage his anger but chooses not to.	• Prosocial values training and/or • Problem-solving interventions, combined with other interventions to promote generalization and maintenance
Cognitive and academic skill deficits	Student is struggling with school curriculum, or student is not responding to interventions because of academic or cognitive difficulties.	• Assessment of student's cognitive and academic skills • Adapting classroom instruction • Adapting the intervention

Source: *Adopted from information contained in Keller, H. R., & Tapasak, R. C. (1998). Classroom management. In A. P. Goldstein & J. C. Conoley (Eds.),* School violence intervention: A practical handbook *(pp. 107–120). New York: Guilford.*

winning; calmly turn down the invitation to do battle. When you let students win on inconsequential issues, you avoid major power struggles. This also allows the student to save face, as recommended in Table 9–1.

3. *Later!* Suggest a later, private conference to the student who tries to create a public scene. Privacy prevents public embarrassment, and the passage of time often will reduce the student's vehemence. An absent-minded teenager may forget what was bothering him in the first place!
4. *The last word can be lethal.* Avoid needing the last word. As one principal said, "Teenagers need the last word a lot more than I do!" Many teacher assaults are the result of an adult's insistence on getting the last word rather than letting the student leave the interaction mumbling something under her breath. Statements such as "I heard what you said! Now come back here and apologize!" can worsen an already tense situation. If a student is still really angry, you cannot have a rational conversation. Take time to talk about the issues later. In so doing, you are also showing students how to get their own emotional reactions under control.
5. *Is anybody listening to me?* Listen! Students often tell us that this is really what they want. By listening to the student's complaint (just as a well-trained customer service representative would listen to your problems with a service or product), you may reduce the student's hostility and negotiate a good conclusion. Listening usually reduces affective arousal and lowers the emotional "thermometer." Active listening also models an important communication skill for students.
6. *Sarcasm isn't funny.* Sarcasm escalates tension. Adolescents may misread the intent of your communication, perceiving your comments as hostile. In other words, your well-intended wit may backfire.
7. *Save face.* Saving face is important to all of us. Embarrassing or humiliating a student never helps and could get you hurt. In fact, research by the Gun Safety Institute has shown that youth who are prone to carry guns believe that shame can be undone only through aggression (Clough, P., personal communication, February 25, 1993). For example, youth who are more likely to carry guns endorsed these beliefs: "If someone insults me or my family, it really bothers me, but if I beat them up, that makes me feel better." "If someone disrespects me, I have to fight them to get my pride back." "A kid who doesn't get even with someone who makes fun of him is a sucker" (Meador, 1992, p. 31).
8. *Don't sweat the small stuff.* Ignore minor rule infractions when you think you can: "Juan, sit down and open your book, please." [No response.] "Sarah, you're ready; why don't you get us started?"
9. *Set limits but avoid ultimatums.* Offer the student a choice or an out whenever possible. The following conversations illustrate this idea. Ultimatum: "Janice, you either get to civics class right now or go to the office. This is no time for a personal conversation!" Setting limits, with two options: "Janice, it's time for sixth period. If you can't stop your conversation with your friend now and move on to class, you will need to spend some of the afternoon break making up your work. The choice is up to you." This approach helps students learn the critical skill of interpersonal problem solving.
10. *Take charge of yourself.* Stay in control of your own emotions. Irritable, overreactive teachers will experience repeated, unsuccessful confrontations. Students can always tell which teachers they can "set off." If you are angry, then take some time, cool off, and collect your thoughts. Not every verbal challenge requires your immediate response.

We cannot overemphasize the importance of getting to know your students, their personal beliefs, and their cultural backgrounds and traditions.

You may unwittingly alienate students through your tone of voice, gestures, body language, eye contact, and choice of words. For example, an owl sticker sent home on a child's assignment may convey the wrong message: in some cultures, the owl is a symbol of death. Asking students and their families about their traditions—especially when you get an unexpected reaction—can go a long way toward minimizing these unintended signals. Resources on cultural sensitivity in the classroom are included on the Companion Website.

> You can't be expected to understand another culture entirely, but you should make every effort to find out as much as you can from colleagues, readings, and training experiences.

Anger Management Training

The goal of **anger management training** is to help students identify the antecedents to their anger, identify their own reactions, and select good behavioral choices. Figure 9-2 describes an individual anger management intervention: the anger thermometer. As you read through the case study at the end of this chapter, consider how the approach might help a student like Terylyn, whose interpretations of others lead to overreactions.

Helping youth to manage their anger was the goal of Hammond and his colleagues, who developed *Dealing with Anger* (Hammond & Gipson, 1994). Students learn a three-step approach: "Givin' it; Takin' it; Workin' it out." The training offers modeling (through a series of videotaped examples), role-plays, visual clues (e.g., flash cards), and homework assignments. Students also learn to recognize and analyze components of angry interactions. *Dealing with Anger* and *PACT* (Hammond & Yung, 1995) are available from Research Press (2612 N. Mattis Ave., Champaign, IL 61821).

Social Competence Training

As Table 9-1 indicated, aggressive classroom behavior may reflect a social skills deficit. Many students simply lack the skills to manage difficult interpersonal situations. For example, a student may not know how to express a complaint without resorting to anger and profanity. A student who has never seen adults disagree peaceably cannot be expected to resolve conflicts effectively. Students may misread the social cues of others, overlook important social signals, and have trouble solving problems in a social situation. Social competence training helps students through a curricular approach. Social competence training was described in Chapter 8.

Remember, students with antisocial behaviors need contingency management as well as direct skills training. For example, Terylyn's team not only would design interventions to help her "read" the social cues of teachers and peers more accurately but also would identify incentives to acknowledge her efforts to regulate her reactions to others. To maintain intervention gains and increase generalization or transfer of these skills across settings and persons, involve as many other persons as possible in the intervention planning and implementation. This chapter's final case study demonstrates how you can combine skills training and contingency management to improve students' self-control.

Contingency Management Strategies

Contingency management, discussed throughout this text, includes token economies, contingency contracts, and time-out from reinforcement. This section explains how to manage the contingencies that influence aggressive behavior in your classroom. For example, students may act tough because they are reinforced by the way other people react to them (see Table 9-1, "mismanagement of contingencies"). By creating a crisis, these students stop all routines, gain abundant attention from peers, and scare, embarrass, or immobilize adults in authority. Throwing work materials or swearing at the teacher may give a student a way out of a difficult lesson; avoidance of the unpleasant work is the student's reinforcer.

The first step in designing a contingency management intervention is to **pinpoint** the target behavior(s). Focus your attention on (a) identifying

The Anger Thermometer helps students increase their awareness of the signs and symptoms of anger (see Rotheram, 1986). Essential to its application is a problem-solving component. In order to use the Anger Thermometer effectively, students explore their past anger history. This includes examining the consequences of their behaviors as well as what prompted their responses.

USING THE ANGER THERMOMETER

To use the Anger Thermometer, an adult works with a student. The relationship involves a sharing of information about how we recognize that we are angry. The easiest starting point is the most obvious: extremes in behaviors. Using a scale of 100° to 0°, the adult can begin to establish a feeling range. First, establish with a student the maximum reaction: the level that is unacceptable to attain. Next, identify this as 100°. Let's use the example of a student who is referred to a school-based counselor for chronic fighting. Fighting would be a 100° or unacceptable level. After establishing the maximum level, help the student identify the 0° level. Nothing is bothersome at the 0° level. In our example, the 0° level might be "chillin'," or just "hangin' out with friends."

INCREASING SELF-AWARENESS BY ACCESSING MORE KNOWLEDGE ABOUT OURSELVES

It is usually more difficult to look inside ourselves than to describe how we appear to others. One way to begin this process is to ask, "How do you look to someone else when you have such an intense level of anger that you would fight? Say you're at 100°." The opposite question might be "What do you look like when you have absolutely no anger? You're just chillin'?" This step begins a collaborative effort to explore behavior changes that accompany anger at various levels of intensity. These behaviors might include shouting, making a fist, swearing, pointing a finger at someone, threatening, pushing, and so on. The clinician should acknowledge these behaviors and feelings as real and understandable, yet identify for the student that these behaviors are only one option and there are other behavioral choices.

It helps to provide a real example from your own experience that demonstrates your reaction to anger and how you managed it. This expression of your own struggle and positive outcome is often a motivating demonstration for the student.

RECOGNIZING THE BODY'S CUES

There are probably as many different body cues and variations of anger as there are people. Helping youth recognize these cues can, in turn, improve their awareness of their emotional states. Once they can identify their emotional states, they can begin to manage their uncomfortable feelings.

Listing behaviors that indicate anger can help students to understand that anger presents itself in many ways. Here are some examples from our students.

- I was so angry I turned as red as a beet.
- I couldn't see—my vision was blurry.
- I couldn't hear words, only my heart pounding.
- My mouth was dry as cotton.
- There was sweat on my forehead—I was soaked from sweating.
- I trembled from my head to my toes—my eyelid twitched.
- My hand was balled up into a fist.
- I bit my lip so hard that I tasted blood in my mouth.

(Continued)

FIGURE 9–2 The Anger Thermometer

EMPATHY AND TOLERANCE—NOT ACCEPTANCE

The goal of the Anger Thermometer is to increase the student's options/choices for behavior. To use this model students must grasp what made them angry and why their reaction was inappropriate and got them into trouble. This exercise can precede a program for anger control or a more comprehensive program for conflict resolution.

As you work with your students, be careful not to reinforce the inappropriate behavior. Don't say "This situation made you angry," or "That person made you mad," but instead say "You became angry," or "You got mad." In this way you acknowledge their anger, imply their responsibility for their behavior, but do not necessarily accept their angry reaction.

HELPING STUDENTS EXAMINE THEIR PERSONAL ANGER HISTORY

Recognizing the signs and symptoms of anger is the first and easiest part of the exercise. Identifying what "lit the fuse" can be more difficult. Ask the student, "The last time your anger level reached 50° or 100°, do you remember what triggered your anger?" Often, recalling the event will trigger emotional memories. Once students identify what made them angry they can assign a degree of intensity or temperature to their response. To do this it helps to list: (1) the specific event; (2) the approximate date and time; (3) what occurred before and after the event; (4) the level of anger [i.e., 20°, 50°, etc.] (This helps students evaluate their emotional response in a cognitive fashion, perhaps for the first time). Finally, students discuss what they liked or didn't like about their response to the event. (It is important for the student to identify what behaviors they want to change and why. This also gives the student the opportunity to discuss alternative behaviors.) Encourage the student to give as many details as possible. This will give the adult/helper more information to understand the student's point of view. Also, it is important to make the student feel that his or her thoughts and feelings are important to the adult/helper.

LOOKING FOR SUBTLE CUES

The cognitive exercise of rating a response allows the student to classify and create a hierarchy of intensity. When the students have rated these various levels, they can then judge from their own value structure whether their response was an appropriate level of response. This process can be the basis for establishing with the student the purpose for using the Anger Thermometer. Without the proper motivation, this can become an academic exercise with little chance of real-life application. Remember that our goal is to help our students recognize what degrees of temperature they can reach and still engage in problem solving. Often by the time they reach 100° the climate may be too "hot" to try to resolve the issues that made them angry.

USING YOUR HEAD INSTEAD OF YOUR GUT TO SOLVE PROBLEMS

Self-questioning, "What else could I do; what other choices could I make?" can begin the process of recognizing appropriate reactions to anger. The student at this point has been able to: (1) recognize signs and symptoms of anger; (2) assess the intensity of his or her anger; (3) recognize the behavior that results from these emotions; and (4) stop, think, and make an informed choice, based on the consequences of the behaviors. After this the progression to teaching problem-solving skills is a natural and logical next step.

The problem-solving steps include: (1) identifying the problem; (2) identifying the options; (3) choosing one option and following through with it; (4) evaluating the choice and the consequences; and (5) deciding if you have to make a different choice based on the current evaluation of the situation.

Once students are aware of the behavioral cues, they assess what their next move will be. Often a student is aware of the more obvious cues and gradually becomes aware of the more subtle behaviors. The overt behaviors such as making a fist or shouting might be the more obvious indicators of anger. Once they become more aware, they may notice that they are tensing their jaw muscles, feeling hot, their leg is shaking, or their eye is twitching.

FIGURE 9–2 (Continued)

ANGER THERMOMETER IN CONTEXT

For the Anger Thermometer to be useful, the participants must communicate clearly and trust each other. The student who is referred for issues of anger control has to be able to focus, to use cognitive abilities, and to be motivated to change his or her behaviors.

If the student was involved in a fight, it is important to discuss what motivated this behavior. If he has a hot temper and has been in fights before, anger management and use of the Anger Thermometer could be appropriate. However, if issues related to his ex-girlfriend's new boyfriend caused the fight, then the appropriate intervention might be mediation.

REFERENCE

Rotheram, M. J. (1986). The evaluation of imminent danger for suicide among youth. *The American Journal of Orthopsychiatry, 57,* 102–110.

FIGURE 9–2 (Continued)
Source: *Brian W. McKain, M.S.N. Reprinted with permission of the author.*

and modifying behaviors that immediately precede acts of aggression, destruction, or theft and (b) identifying and modifying the not-so-immediate setting events that precede aggression, such as situations at home that "spill over" to school. Take another look at Figure 9-1. You'll see that one column is devoted entirely to immediate antecedent events. Antecedents are good target behaviors on which to intervene (e.g., teasing remarks, initial physical contact with another student, subvocal utterances, facial flush, movement of an arm to a fighting position). For example, intervene with a student fighter not after the fight has begun but when that student first teases or picks the fight or stop and let a student "vent" verbally when you first notice that he has had a rough morning on the bus.

Aggression may be intermittently reinforced and thereby strengthened unless all adults advocate the same position: aggressive behavior will not be tolerated. Take bullying, for example. Bullies intimidate their victims so that they will not report to authorities; knowing that they won't be punished is reinforcing to bullies. For bullying to cease, adults must find out about it so that they no longer inadvertently reinforce the bully's covert behavior. (For an evidence-based bully-proofing program, see the Companion Website.)

Token Reinforcement and Response Cost

When using a token economy to reduce aggression, apply a response cost or fine to aggressive acts as well as to behaviors that predict aggression or destruction of property. The following lists display part of a teacher's classroom token economy for aggressive students.

Points may be earned for the following:

- Walking away from a fight
- Ignoring someone who teases
- Accepting teacher feedback
- Keeping hands off others
- Using an acceptable word instead of a swear word when angry

Points will be lost for the following:

- Fighting or hitting
- "Mouthing off" at a school visitor
- Teasing a classmate
- Threatening a classmate
- Blocking a classmate's free movement in class or in the halls

Note that students earn points for actions that inhibit aggression. By identifying behaviors that inhibit aggression as well as those that provoke hurtful behavior, this teacher controlled the events that might set off aggression through token reinforcement and response cost.

Here are guidelines for implementing a **response cost** (RC) contingency:

* The RC system should be carefully explained before applying it.
* RC should always be tied to a reinforcement system, preferably involving points.
* An appropriate delivery system should be developed.
* RC should be implemented immediately after the target behavior or response occurs.
* RC should be applied each time an instance of a target behavior occurs.
* The student should never be allowed to accumulate negative points (i.e., go in the hole with point totals).
* The ratio of points earned to those lost should be controlled.
* The social agent using RC should never be intimidated from using RC by the target student.
* Subtraction of points should never be punitive or personalized.
* The student's positive, appropriate behavior should be praised as frequently as opportunities permit (Walker, Colvin, & Ramsey, 1995, pp. 66–67).

Time-Out from Reinforcement

Many aggressive students, like classroom disruptors, fail to complete academic tasks because they are expelled from the instructional setting at each outburst. As a result, aggressive students may develop a "double disability" requiring remediation in both academic and social skills. When using time-out with an aggressive student, remember that it is best (and easiest) to apply it before the child loses control or becomes assaultive. For this reason, behaviors pinpointed for time-out should be antecedents to aggression (teasing, threats, lifting an arm to "deck" someone). Also provide reinforcement for incompatible, acceptable actions

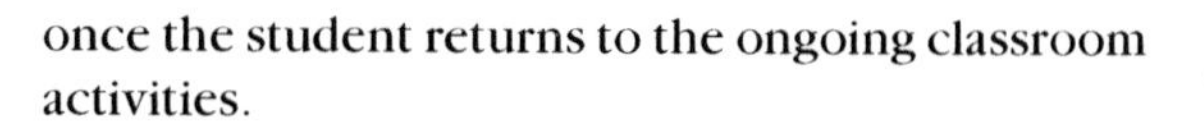

once the student returns to the ongoing classroom activities.

In the case of time-out strategies, consult with your supervisor about school policies.

Another form of time-out from reinforcement is in-school suspension. (For guidelines on how to implement an in-school suspension program, see Rhode, 1996.) If this program is implemented properly and if the student is motivated to return to his classroom, then the separation from classmates (e.g., time spent in the in-school suspension program) may reduce aggression and reinforce more appropriate classroom behavior. Unfortunately, studies of students referred for in-school suspension have uncovered frequent teacher disapproval and other aversive approaches (Hartman & Sage, 2000).

Keep in mind that overreliance on negative interventions can set into motion a vicious cycle: Perceiving the classroom teacher as biased and hostile, the student experiences heightened affective arousal, which leads to an angry outburst. Faced with the student's anger, the teacher escalates the situation by resorting to even more coercive practices. Before long, the student is experiencing only negative interactions, reaffirming his belief that "the teacher is out to get me" (Gunter, Denny, Jack, Shores, & Nelson, 1993). To break this cycle, start with many positive reinforcements in your classroom, then tailor your targeted interventions according to the guidelines outlined in Table 9–1.

Crisis Interventions

In spite of your best efforts to prevent behaviors that threaten the physical safety of an aggressive student or of others in the classroom, a situation may erupt into violence before you can intervene. We hope that these instances will be rare if you employ the strategies described in this chapter. However, when violent behavior does occur, you should know what to do. If you work with potentially aggressive students, take an annual refresher class on nonviolent crisis intervention. Local police departments or

mental health programs often offer these classes. Be sure that your class is offered by a certified professional who has time to provide concrete examples.

It helps to have a well-rehearsed crisis response plan. The guidelines in Table 9-2 will help you prepare for this situation and prevent harm. This "drill" also alleviates the anxiety of adults in the building. Just compare this drill with others we use to prepare ourselves for potentially serious (yet less frequent) events, such as a fire or tornado.

Occasionally, you may work with a student (or a student's family member) whose aggression is a result of irrational thinking, hallucinations, or another mental health challenge. Or you may want to aid a student who is living with a parent or sibling who has mental health challenges. Consider these guidelines for families affected by mental illness:

Do's

- Keep your communication simple, clear, and brief (the two-sentence rule)
- Ask only *one* question at a time.
- Stick to the current issue rather than bringing up "old issues."
- Stay calm.
- Minimize other distractions by turning off the television and radio.
- Pay attention to nonverbal behavior—both the message that you are sending with your body language and that of your family member.
- Help your loved one identify his or her feelings by suggesting several choices (e.g., are you feeling angry, sad, or worried right now?).
- Show empathy or caring for his or her feelings.
- Acknowledge what you have heard him or her express. You may wish to normalize that emotion and share a similar experience that you have had in the past.
- Decide together on a regular time for communication. Choosing a low-stress time when both of you are apt to feel at your best is important.

Don'ts

- Don't try to argue patients out of their delusional or false beliefs.
- Avoid giving advice unless asked—or if the person cannot make the decision on his or her own.
- Avoid interrupting each other.
- Don't talk down to each other (e.g., "you are acting like a child").

TABLE 9–2 Readiness Drill for Aggressive Events

1. With your principal and at least one other teacher whose room is nearby, develop a plan for getting help when the aggressive child loses control. This plan should include:
   a. transmitting a signal to the nearby adult or an alternate if that person is not available.
   b. the type of assistance you will need. For example, you might want the adult to come to your class and escort your other students out of the room so that they do not reinforce or taunt the target student.
   c. how you will notify the principal. You may want a second colleague to do this for you.
   d. how you will handle the aggressive student(s). This plan will depend in part on your school's policies. Interventions presented later in this chapter will help you.
2. Develop a "signal" that you can give to a dependable child in your classroom. This signal should be different from anything else the children may have encountered. For example, you might paint a wooden block a particular color. (If you also wish to notify the principal, you might want two such signals given to two students or their alternates.)
3. Select an alternate in the event that the designated child is absent the day you need to use your procedure.
4. Tell the students that you have an important drill for them to practice, like the fire and other drills to which they are accustomed. You do not need to declare the circumstances under which you would activate your readiness plan. If the students can read, give them a handout outlining the steps they are to take. If they are not capable readers, you might want to show an abbreviated set of steps on a poster.
5. Practice the drill, including the activities of the other adults. Begin with a weekly practice until the students and adults can complete the activities smoothly. Then have a monthly "surprise drill."
6. If at any time the drill does not proceed as you planned, revise the steps and inform everyone of the revision.

- Avoid name-calling.
- Don't generalize ("always" or "never").
- Don't yell or shout.
- Don't personalize the family member's behavior. Recognize that the symptom may be part of the mental illness and may have nothing to do with you (adapted from Sherman, 2003. Acknowledgement of funding from the Department of Veterans Affairs South Central Mental Illness Research, Education and Clinical Center [MIRECC]).

For more tips on working with hard-to-reach family members, check the Companion Website.

PEER-MEDIATED STRATEGIES

A student's peer group can play a major role in intervention programs to reduce aggressive and destructive behaviors. For example, the peers may take part in a group contingency or learn to ignore or respond in a new way to teasing or threats by the target student.

One example of an intervention that combines skills instruction with contingency management is *Linking the Interests of Families and Teachers (LIFT),* a research-based intervention program for elementary schoolers (Eddy, Reid, & Fetrow, 2000). Along with parent training and social skills instruction, this program incorporates the Good Behavior Game. During the game, children earn rewards for both positive problem-solving skills and other prosocial peer interactions as well as for avoiding negative behaviors. For more information about this program, see the U.S. Substance Abuse and Mental Health Services Agency Website available through the Companion Website.

TABLE 9–3 Guidelines for Implementation

The peer confrontation strategy is composed of six major parts. During each stage, the teacher should praise the target student(s) and peers for engaging in appropriate responses.

1. Identify the problem.
   - Identify the specific behavior(s).
   - Operationally define the target behavior(s) (e.g., verbal or gestural threats such as shaking a fist at another student; raising the middle finger; stating "I'll shoot you").
   - Teach all students to identify positive and neutral behaviors of peers.
   - Teach all students to identify negative behaviors of peers (e.g., hitting, name calling).
   - Teach all students to discriminate between acceptable and negative behaviors.
   - Teach all students to identify target behavior(s) as they are exhibited naturally.
2. Determine the effects of the problem behavior on others.
   - Teach students to recognize various types of effects. Categories might include tangible effects (e.g., "all our equipment will be broken"), intangible effects (e.g., "We'll be late for class" or "He'll lose face"), short-term effects (e.g., "We'll get detentions"), or long-term effects (e.g., "We may not get to go on the field trip at the end of the project").
   - Teach students to predict possible effects resulting from a specific behavior.
3. Conduct problem solving.
   - Teach students to precisely describe the problem behavior (e.g., "Mike's hand is in the air; he's getting ready to hit").
   - Discuss the consequences of the behavior.
   - Brainstorm alternative target student responses. Prompt students to offer a number of positive behavioral options to the target student.
4. Deliver mild punishment—as appropriate.
   - This might take the form of a verbal reprimand, presented in close proximity to the target student.
5. Provide "booster training" (e.g., periodic retraining) to ensure appropriate performance.
6. Monitor the long-term effect of behavior changes on the target student(s).

Source: *Reprinted with permission from Arllen, N. L., Gable, R. A., & Hendrickson, J. M. (1996). Using peer confrontation to reduce inappropriate student behavior.* Beyond Behavior, *7(1), 22–23.*

Peer Confrontation

In this strategy, peers confront the inappropriate behavior of a classmate, identify the effects of the behavior, and engage in joint problem solving (Arllen, Gable, & Hendrickson, 1996). Peer confrontation takes place both within a meeting format and during other times of the school day. The studies to date have taken place in small elementary schools and other self-contained settings. In these respects, the strategy is similar to group goal setting and feedback (see Chapter 6). Table 9-3 describes the steps to carry out peer confrontation.

Conflict Resolution Strategies

Many schools have established conflict resolution training, calling on peers or adults to assist students with their conflicts. *Tools for Getting Along* (Daunic & Smith, 2002) teaches fourth and fifth graders six problem-solving steps:

1. Problem recognition (recognizing anger in one's self and in others and understanding how anger can lead to or worsen problems)
2. Strategies to deescalate frustration and anger while engaging students in cognitive problem solving
3. Problem definition
4. Solution generation
5. Strategy selection
6. Outcome evaluation

For more information on the program, go to the Companion Website.

Many schools are now adopting peer mediation programs whereby students meet with classmates

TABLE 9–4 Peer Trainer Steps

Assess
1. Student will not speak aloud for at least 3 seconds in order to assess the situation. 2. Student will ask and answer aloud, "What is going on?" 3. Student will ask and answer aloud, "Why did [he/she] do or say what [he/she] did?" 4. Student will ask and answer aloud, "Did [he/she] do this on purpose or is it something that just happened?" 5. Student will ask and answer aloud, "How does [he/she] feel about the situation?" 6. Student will ask and answer aloud, "Is [he/she] upset or just kidding?"
Amend
7. Student chooses an appropriate alternative response to anger. Example: Not responding verbally or nonverbally to the situation, initiating another topic for discussion, or walking away from the situation. 8. Student tells the other person how this situation makes him or her feel. Example: "I am upset that you would not just ask me for the paper or to see my homework. I considered you my friend and thought that you considered me your friend. Therefore, I am surprised that you took my notebook without asking me." 9. Student asks the other person to tell him or her how this makes him or her feel. Example: "How do you feel just taking my notebook without asking me?"
Act
10. Student responds to the situation, using ASSESS and AMEND steps. Example: Student waits, self-instructs, and then performs alternative response. 11. Student evaluates his/her initial response to the situation and makes changes, if necessary, in his or her response by using the ASSESS and AMEND steps. Example: Student speaks aloud that he or she has not followed the steps in the ASSESS and AMEND components. Student speaks aloud the steps to assess the situation and amends it.

Source: *Presley, J. A., & Hughes, C. (2000). Peers as teachers of anger management to high school students with behavioral disorders.* Behavioral Disorders, 25*(2), 118. Reprinted with permission.*

TABLE 9–5 Examples of Antecedents, Behaviors, and Consequences for Discrimination Training

("You" and "Your" refer to the student)
Antecedents (Triggers)
1. Your friend keeps throwing paper wads at you during seatwork. 2. You're supposed to be at work by 3:30, but your friends always want you to hang out after school. 3. Your teacher gives you a book report assignment that's due in 1 week. 4. Your dad tells you that you have to babysit Friday night. 5. The girl/boy that you want to go to the dance with asks you for help with homework after school. 6. You go out to the parking lot after school and find that you have a flat tire. 7. Your teacher gives you an assignment that you don't understand. 8. One of your teachers announces that there will be a chapter test on Friday. 9. Your mom asks you to come home right after school to help her out. 10. You're walking down the hall and someone you don't get along with comes up behind you and shoves you.
Behaviors
1. You punch your friend and yell swear words at him. 2. You get to work an hour late for 5 days in a row. 3. You schedule your study time so that you work on your report a little each night and have enough time to rewrite it neatly before it is due. 4. You really want to go out, but you stay home as you've been asked to do. 5. You really want to go shopping with your friend because you'd rather do that than school work. 6. You kick in your front fender and punch the side window, cracking it. 7. You go to a teacher during seatwork time and ask for clarification of the assignment. 8. You'd rather be out partying, but you decide to study each night between now and Friday. 9. Even though your friends are going out for sodas, you go right home and help out. 10. You're really angry, but you just walk away from him/her.
Consequences
1. Your teacher sends you to the principal's office. 2. Your boss fires you and you lose the income you were using to save for a car. 3. You get a B+ on your paper. 4. Your dad lets you borrow the car Saturday night and gives you $5.00. 5. When you ask your friend to go to the dance with you, he/she says, "Forget it!" 6. Instead of just having to change a flat tire, you have to come up with $100.00 for body work. 7. You are able to complete the assignment accurately and get a good grade. 8. Even though you missed a couple of nights out, you ace the test. 9. You are able to complete the assignment accurately and get a good grade. 10. The hall monitor sends the "other guy" to detention, but you're doing fine.

Source: *Young, K. R., West, R. P., Smith, D. J., & Morgan, D. P. (1991).* Teaching self-management strategies to adolescents *(p. 35). Longmont, CO: Sopris West. Reprinted with permission.*

having a conflict and help the pair work things out. The peer mediator first learns skills, including active listening, identifying common ground, and maintaining impartiality and confidentiality. Although few peer mediation programs have undergone stringent evaluation, the results of some studies are promising (see Cartledge & Johnson, 1997).

Peers as Teachers of Anger Management

Presley and Hughes (2000) described how nondisabled teens successfully instructed their classmates with emotional and behavioral disorders to control their anger. Peer trainers received training on scripts (available from the senior author at jannpres@aol.com or at the Department of Teaching and Learning, Tennessee State University, Nashville). Using role-play situations, students practiced a three-step response adapted from the Walker Social Skills Curriculum (Walker et al., 1983). Table 9–4 depicts the steps.

SELF-MEDIATED STRATEGIES

Because aggression is an interpersonal behavior, self-management strategies alone will not remediate the problem. However, self-monitoring in combination with contingency management and the learning of alternative behaviors may succeed.

Self-recording is a good way to teach students how to anticipate situations that trigger their aggressive behavior. Young, West, Smith, and Morgan (1991) have developed an excellent student handbook for teaching the ABCs of behavior. Through an ABC analysis, students learn to discriminate between events that trigger appropriate and inappropriate responses; then students learn to self-talk about their behavioral choices (e.g., "If I do _____, then _____ will happen. But if I do _____, things will turn out better for me"). Study the examples of antecedents, behaviors, and consequences for discrimination training in Table 9–5.

We believe that you will find self-control strategies especially helpful in supplementing the direct instruction, modeling, and role-play strategies included in your skills teaching programs.

SUMMARY

- A thorough analysis of aggression attained through careful documentation early in a student's school career lays the groundwork for successful interventions.
- Early intervention, often involving multisetting components such as family intervention, is critical in cases of serious aggression.
- As part of a larger team making your school safe, you can develop policies and school-wide strategies that discourage acts of aggression, such as bullying.
- Only through a good understanding of the characteristics of students who exhibit aggression can you select an effective intervention. A one-size-fits-all model does not work.
- Most strategies are teacher mediated, requiring a high degree of control of your emotions and reactions.
- Solid management of contingencies and direct skills instruction are two of your best tools.
- Few studies have reported self-mediated strategies, but self-monitoring can contribute to a more comprehensive approach.

ANGER MANAGEMENT SKILLS LESSONS

Dawn E. Cois

Background Information

A class of sixth-grade students exhibiting behavioral problems is in need of social skills training. In particular, these 10 students need to increase their social skills in interacting with adults. The faculty at this school is extremely cooperative and resourceful and will assist in the behavioral program for these students. Students are in my classroom for homeroom (15 min.), third period (60 min.), and at the end of the day (15 min.), 5 days a week.

Behavioral Objective

When given a task request or directions from an adult, students will respond without talking back angrily or using inappropriate language (profanity).

Lesson Plan

Introduction

Students will be given an introduction on the target behavior (i.e., responding appropriately to adult requests or directions), its value to them and the consequences for noncompliance. Open discussion will follow with students' volunteering examples of good encounters and bad encounters with adults.

> ***Teacher:*** I need the class' help on a problem I have. Today Mrs. Lewis asked me to stay after school to help her finish the school newsletter. Well, I've stayed after school three times this week already to help with planning for the new weather station and the Tropicana Speech Contest, and tonight I have company coming over. Besides, I was in a hurry to get to the office to run off some copies and only had a few minutes before I had to be back in the classroom, so I really didn't have time to talk. You know what that's like, don't you? When you're in a hurry and people are bugging you for time that you don't have? Well, I paused for a second and simply told her "No way! I'm not staying after school another day. I have a life too. Find someone else or do it yourself. Why is it that I have to do everything around here anyway?" Well, she looked kind of angry and replied, "Sorry I asked you! It won't happen again."
>
> Well, I really like Mrs. Lewis and I felt sort of bad that I responded that way, but I didn't have time to apologize or explain myself so I just kept going. Anyway, remember how we talked about having an egg-drop contest next month? Well, Mrs. Lewis was going to help me with it since she's done this activity before. I really don't know much about it. Now she's mad at me and I don't know how to ask her for her assistance. What do you think she'll say if I ask her to stay after school next week to help me with this project?

What can I do to make things better so that our friendship isn't ruined?

How can I get her to still help me on this project?

Could I have avoided this problem if I had handled her request to stay after school differently?

What could I have said that would have sounded better and not made her angry?

Reprinted with permission of the author.

We all do this sometimes, just blow up on people instead of talking politely and calmly when people ask us to do things, especially when they are things we don't really want to do. But in the end we just make people mad at us and then they don't want to help us when we need them. The funny thing about this is that if we would only take a moment to think the situation through, we could make our own lives a lot easier and know that the people around us will support us.

> *First,* we need to think about what it is that the other person is asking of us. Is it a reasonable request? Is it something we can do? If not, what do we need that will better enable us to do it? Is it a fair request?
>
> *Second,* we need to think about the consequences. What will happen if we do what is being asked of us? What will happen if we do not? Is there a good reason why we can't or shouldn't do this?
>
> *Third,* we need to control our impulses to say things angrily. If we can do what is being asked of us, we should. If we can't, we need to calmly explain why we can't. Staying calm means that we don't say things that are offensive or use profanity. There's always a nice way to respond if we take the time to think about it.
>
> *Last,* we need to reward ourselves for taking the time to think the situation through and responding appropriately.

This is especially important when dealing with adults. Adults make a lot of requests on kids, especially teachers. But their job is to help you get a good education and prepare you to undertake whatever careers you may choose when you leave school. When you are all adults, you'll find you'll have a lot of responsibilities and you'll need to rely on many of the skills you've acquired in school. Parents also ask a lot of you, but they usually have your best interests in mind.

Would anyone like to share a situation they may have encountered with a teacher in the past? What was asked of you and how did you handle it? Good and bad situations are encouraged to be shared. Bad situations are discussed with suggestions on ways that it could have been handled better.

Modeling

> ***Teacher:*** Let's first review the four steps we just talked about to help us better deal with adults when they ask us to do something. (Students volunteer the four steps while the teacher writes them down.)

1. Is it a reasonable and fair request?
2. What will be the consequences of my actions?
3. I need to respond politely and calmly.
4. Reward myself for handling the situation well.

(Students are given index cards with these four steps written on them.)

> Now Mrs. B and I will demonstrate how to use these four steps in a situation that is a little worse than the one I had with Mrs. Lewis. In this situation, I'm going to play the role of a sixth grader who is being told by a teacher to take work detention for not completing an assignment that she knows she did. In this role-play I'm going to think aloud so that you can hear how I work through the four steps on your cards.
>
> ***Mrs. B.:*** Kathy, I'm really disappointed in you this week. You didn't hand in your book report even though I gave the class extra time on Monday to finish it. Here's your detention slip. You won't be allowed free time today with the rest of the class. Instead, you need to report to the detention room to finish your work. I want this

detention slip signed by one of your parents and returned to me on Monday along with your completed book report.

Teacher (sixth grader): (1) Is this fair and reasonable? No! I did the assignment and I know I handed it in. (2) What will be the consequences if I do it? Well, I'll miss free time, my parents will be angry with me, and I'll have to do the assignment all over again. What will happen if I get angry and refuse to do it? Well, I'll be sent to the principal's office and my parents will be called. That will make them even angrier at me. I'll still have to go to work detention or possibly have to sit in the office during free time, the principal will be angry with me, and I'll still have to redo the assignment. Is there another alternative? Yes, I can explain to Mrs. B. that I did the assignment and already turned it in. If I'm nice, maybe she'll listen to me. (3) Be calm and polite. Mrs. B., I worked hard on that book report and finished it on Monday when you gave us that extra time in class to work on it. I'm sure I turned it in. I remember putting it in the homework box. Maybe you misplaced it?

Mrs. B.: No, if it was in the homework box with the rest of the book reports I would have gotten it. I don't lose papers. But . . . if you say you did it, maybe you thought you turned it in and didn't. Perhaps you should check your desk and see if you still have it.

Teacher (sixth grader): I don't think so, but I'll check anyway. Look, Mrs. B., you were right. It's here in my desk.

Mrs. B.: Well, it's late, but at least I know you did it and that it was an accident that it wasn't turned in, so I won't deduct any points. I'm glad we resolved this and that you don't have to take detention. Perhaps you should keep a record of your assignments and cross them off after you've turned them in rather than when you've completed them so that this won't happen again. I'll help you organize an assignment sheet if you'd like.

Teacher (sixth grader): OK. Thanks, Mrs. B. (4) Reward myself. Wow, I handled that great and got her to listen to me. It got me out of detention and hot water with my parents.

Let's talk about that situation. (Students talk about how the four steps were used to help resolve the problem. Teacher also leads the class to discuss how that situation could have turned bad.)

Practice/Role-Play

Teacher: Now we're all going to have a chance to practice using these four steps with some practice situations that I've made up. First, we'll practice these skills as a class and then we'll pair up with partners to practice. I'll play the teacher role and let each of you respond to a situation using one of the four steps. Remember to think the steps aloud so that the rest of us know how you're working this out. When I walk next to you, it's your turn to respond. OK? If you get nervous and can't come up with something, then the person beside you can offer you some suggestions to help you out. Does anyone have any questions or comments before we begin?

Situation One Tommy is talking to Randy beside him about the football game last night while the teacher is giving instructions.

Teacher: Tommy, the rules of this classroom are that you shouldn't be talking when the teacher is talking. I want you to move your desk next to mine and stay in for 15 minutes of your recess.

(Students are each given a chance to respond to one of the four steps in responding appropriately in this situation.)

Situation Two Sam is being accused of writing on his desk when he knows he did not do it.

Teacher: Sam, why is there writing all over your desk? That's school property and you have no right to destroy or vandalize it! I want you to stay in at recess and wash not only your desk, but everyone's desk in this classroom!

Situation Three Rita is having problems understanding division problems. She put her best effort into her assignment but still did poorly.

Teacher: Rita, you missed 13 out of the 15 math problems on your homework assignment. I want you to redo this assignment for homework tonight and I want every problem done correctly. Do you understand?

Now I'd like you all to divide into pairs with the person sitting next to you. Mrs. B. and I will give you each a card with a situation. Each person will take a turn being the teacher for his or her own situation while the other person role-plays a student. Remember to talk aloud through the four steps. The person playing the teacher will be the recorder. As the recorder, you will check off each step as the student does it. At the end of each role-play, the recorder will then compliment his or her partner on one thing he or she did well and then offer one suggestion on how else the situation could have been handled.

Practice Situations

1. You stayed after class to ask your teacher a question about the assignment. Now you're late getting to your next class and running down the hall.

   Teacher: No running in the halls! Come here. I want you to go back to the end of the hall and walk this time.

2. You are Ralph. You and your grandparents flew in from California yesterday, and the family all went to a relative's for a family get-together. Your family didn't get home till after 11:00 P.M. so you didn't have time to get your spelling assignment completed.

   Teacher: Ralph, I don't have your spelling assignment. The test is tomorrow and it's important that you practice these words. I want you to stay in from recess and complete this assignment. I also want you to write each word five times tonight for homework and hand it in tomorrow.

3. Your name is Tommy, and you are anxious to get to gym class because they are playing basketball, a sport that you are real good at. Mrs. K. stops you in the hall and asks if you wouldn't mind helping her carry some boxes of books to the library. She promises you that she will write a note to your next teacher explaining why you are late.

4. You are Karen and your mother went into labor in the middle of the night. You were told this morning that she delivered a baby girl. You have not yet gone to the hospital to see your mother or your new baby sister. You're quite excited and haven't been able to pay attention in class.

   Teacher: Karen, this is the third time that I've had to ask you to look up here and pay attention. Do I need to move you up to the front of the room to keep your attention?

5. You are running to catch a football on the playground when you accidentally collide

with another student. The other student jumps up angrily and begins screaming accusations that you knocked him over on purpose. A teacher arrives promptly on the scene and hears the other student's accusations.

6. Your name is Dave and you're having a really bad day. You and your best friend are fighting, you got in trouble at home last night and are grounded for the weekend, and another student has just yelled at you for missing the ball in a volleyball game during gym class. You yell back at the student and push him.

   Teacher: Dave, report to the office. No fighting is allowed in this school. I'll be up after class to give you a detention slip. (After class:) Dave, this kind of conduct is serious. Why did you push John?

7. Larry has found that he is missing his lunch money and accuses you (Tim) of stealing it. You brought your lunch but have extra money in your pocket that you brought to buy extra cookies with. You know that you did not take Larry's lunch money.

   Teacher: Tim, Larry says that he saw you go into his desk when he went up to sharpen his pencil. He claims you have his lunch money in your pocket. Didn't you pack a lunch today? Stealing someone else's money is a crime and will have to be reported to your parents.

8. Yesterday's math assignment was really tough for you (Bob). You attempted the problems but just couldn't get it. Your mom's visiting the hospital a lot lately to see your grandma, so she wasn't around to help you, and your dad was too busy with your younger brothers. Now the teacher has asked you to put one of the problems on the board and explain it to the class.

   Teacher: Bob, I asked you to come up and put problem 4 on the board and explain to the class how you got your answer. I want you to do it now!

9. While cleaning up at the end of art class Andy accidentally bumped into you (Roy) and made you spill your paint dish all over the floor and the walls.

   Teacher: Roy, look at this mess! I want you to stay and wash the entire floor and walls until all this paint is cleaned up.

10. During reading class, Frank throws a spitball at Julie, which hits her directly in the head. The teacher has seen the direction that the spitball came from, but mistakenly thinks you (Danny) threw it.

    Teacher: Danny, that was totally uncalled for. I want you to stay in the first 15 minutes of recess and sweep the entire floor. Also, I'd like you to apologize to Julie right now!

Generalization/Transfer Activities

To ensure generalization of the new skills taught (i.e., four self-management steps) and to better enable students to respond to requests or directions from adults in an appropriate way, it is important that these skills be practiced across settings, situations, and people. Thus, the other teachers in the building have agreed to "create" situations in which the student will be required to use these skills. Students will not be forewarned about these situations, but they will be told that they are expected to self-monitor their use of these skills in their other classrooms. Additionally, they will be told that their other teachers have been informed about this self-management program and have agreed to reward each student that successfully demonstrates the use of these skills in a situation with them, if one should occur. Students

Self-Monitoring Checklist

Name ______________________ Date ______________________

Class ______________________ Teacher ______________________

	Home room	1st period	2nd period	3rd period	lunch	4th period	5th period	6th period	Home room
1. Is it a reasonable and fair request?									
2. What will be the consequences of my actions?									
3. I need to respond politely and calmly.									
4. I need to reward myself for a good job.									
Total points (1 pt/situation)									

FIGURE 9–3 Practice Session Using the Self-Monitoring Checklist

will be given a self-monitoring checklist that will be explained, modeled by the teacher, and then practiced by the students (see Figure 9-3).

Practice Session Using the Self-Monitoring Checklist

Teacher: I was told by a student from one of my other classes that someone in this classroom was given the answers to the math test yesterday. Since I don't know who it was, you will all have to retake a different math test that will be twice as hard. I'm very disappointed that someone from this class would cheat. Does anyone have any comments before we begin the test?

First Student: I don't think it's fair that we should all be punished for something that one person did. Besides, you don't know for sure whether the kid who told you that was telling the truth. How did he know?

(Students are prompted to check off the first step under third period if they have not already.)

Second Student: If we refuse to take the second test, we could get a failing grade. If we take the test, we could do poorly since it's twice as hard. If we get angry and yell, we might get in trouble plus a failing grade. But if we talk to the teacher nicely and convince her that it is wrong to punish us all, we might get out of it.

(Students are prompted to check off the second step under third period if they have not already.)

Third Student: Mrs. Cois, if someone from an earlier period gave someone in our class the answers to the test, wouldn't that be just as wrong as the person taking the answers? So why isn't that class being punished, too, since you don't know who gave the answers?

Teacher: I hadn't thought of that. You are quite right, Andy. Giving the answers is just as wrong as getting them.

Fourth Student: Couldn't you look at the tests with the same scores and see if there are any that have all the same right and wrong answers? Maybe you could talk to those kids and see if any of them did it.

Teacher: That's a good idea, too. Maybe I'd find some clues by looking at the tests.

Fifth Student: Instead of punishing all of us, why don't you just give different tests to each class from now on so that people can't cheat?

(Students are prompted to check off the third step under third period if they have not already.)

Teacher: That would certainly help to keep this from happening again. It may have happened before and I just didn't know about it. Well, you've all been pretty helpful with ways to identify the cheaters and keep this from happening again. And you're right that the other class shouldn't get off the hook if you're being punished. I guess it isn't fair to punish nine innocent people because of one student, so you won't have to take this other test. But be warned that future tests will be different for all classes.

Sixth Student: We did a great job. No one lost their cool or yelled swear words or anything nasty. We just stayed calm and came up with some good reasons why it wasn't fair and how she could find the cheaters.

(Students are prompted to check the fourth step under third period if they have not already.)

After students have been instructed on how to use the self-monitoring checklist, they will be instructed to record only situations where the teacher's request or direction makes them feel angry or upset. Students will be shown a video on "anger" so that they are more aware of the signs for anger. Discussion will follow with students talking about their own warning signals of anger. Lastly, students will be instructed to use the self-monitoring checklist during all periods.

Each of the five collaborating teachers will be instructed to set up situations with two different students a day to ensure that each student is receiving at least one practice session a day. Additionally, parents will be notified prior to implementing this behavior design and asked to sign an agreement to participate in assignments at home. The program, expectations, and monitoring system will have been explained to parents so that they can provide situations where their child(ren) can extend their practice to the home environments. Parents will be asked to monitor their child's performance utilizing these four steps and compare their evaluation with that of their child (see Figure 9-4). Parent signatures will be required on the parent's evaluation which will be returned to the school for bonus points (see Figure 9-5).

Group Contingency

Students will self-monitor their responses in all classes to adult requests and directions. Appropriate responses using the four-step strategy will earn one point for each situation.

Dear Parents,

As previously discussed, you have agreed to assist _____ in practicing a new four-step strategy to assist him or her in dealing appropriately with adult requests or directions. This means that _____ will not talk back angrily, use offensive language, or refuse to do what is asked of him or her. The attached monitoring checklist is for you to complete. Please read the directions carefully. Additionally, you should have your child go over it with you since he or she has practiced completing it in school. Your child will also be completing his or her own monitor sheet.

When finished with this homework assignment, you may compare your evaluation scores with his or her scores and talk about any discrepancies. If your child has the same score you have, you may give him or her an extra five points by writing your initials on the marked "5 bonus points."

Thank you for participating with this program. Your support is essential to the success of any program. We hope this program will provide the participating students with better skills to deal with adults appropriately by encouraging them to think about their actions.

Good luck and feel free to call me if you have any issues or concerns that you would like to discuss.

Sincerely,

Ms. D. Cois

FIGURE 9–4 Letter to Parents

Inappropriate responses (talking back angrily or using inappropriate language) will earn a zero for each situation. For every point, students will earn a penny that will be put in the coin roller. If there are no inappropriate responses (zeros) from anyone during that week, an extra 5 pennies will be earned. When the class has earned 50 pennies, the class will be allowed to play a math game of their choice during third-period math class the following day and given a free homework ticket to be used at their discretion.

Self-monitoring checklists will be randomly monitored. Any checklist found to be inaccurate will cost the individual a day without being able to earn any points.

Case Study Reflection Questions

1. Why do you think Mrs. Cois introduced the lesson with a personal situation?
2. How does the intervention package described in the case study meet the needs of some of the students described in Table 9–1?
3. As you read the case study, consider the guidelines for social competence training outlined in Chapter 8. Identify how the case study interventions follow these guidelines.

Directions: Please complete the information at the top of the checklist. You have agreed to make **two requests** of your child and monitor his or her response. You may choose one or both of the requests already provided or fill in requests of your choice in the other boxes. These requests need to be *direct* and *specific* as to what you want and when you want it completed. An example might be, "Sam, I want you to set the table right now since dinner will be ready in 5 minutes. Please don't forget the napkins."

If your child responds as requested in a calm and polite manner, you may assume that she or he thought through the four steps before responding. You may then check each box under the appropriate request column. Four checks in a column for one situation earns two points. If your child fails to respond appropriately, remind him or her to follow the four steps. If he or she still does not comply with your request, place zeros in each of the boxes under that situation and fill out the comment section as to what your child's response was.

After two requests have been made and recorded on the checklist, you can compare your checklist with that of your child. If your child has the same scores you have, you may give him or her an extra five points by writing your initials on the line marked "5 bonus points."

Monitoring Checklist

Name__________ Date ______________________

Parent's Signature__________ 5 Bonus Points ______________

Request/Direction

Four Steps	Assist with preparing dinner	Complete homework without TV on	Other	Other
1. Is it a reasonable and fair request?				
2. What will be the consequences of my actions?				
3. I need to respond politely and calmly.				
4. I need to reward myself for a good job				
Total Points (1 pt/situation)				

Comments____

____

____

FIGURE 9–5 Parent's Evaluation

DISCUSSION/APPLICATION IDEAS

1. What causes antisocial behavior? In Terylyn's case (p. 260), what do you think were the contributing factors?
2. When would you use an "after-the-fact" ABC analysis?
3. How do you select the right intervention(s) for your students with aggression? What would you suggest to Terylyn's team?
4. What can you do about bullying?
5. When should you use crisis intervention strategies?
6. Describe how self-management can help a student deal with his anger. What target behaviors might you identify for Terylyn to self-monitor?
7. Why is it important to understand a student's cultural background if you are concerned about his or her aggressive behaviors?

REFERENCES

Arllen, N. L., Gable, R. A., & Hendrickson, J. M. (1996). Using peer confrontation to reduce inappropriate student behavior. *Beyond Behavior, 7*(1), 22–23.

Cartledge, G., & Johnson, C. T. (1997). School violence and cultural sensitivity. In A. P. Goldstein & J. C. Conoley (Eds.), *School violence intervention: A practical handbook* (pp. 391–425). New York: Guilford.

Cartledge, G., & Loe, S. A. (2001). Cultural diversity and social skill instruction. *Exceptionality, 9*(1), 33–46.

Daunic, A. P., & Smith, S. W. (2002). Technical Report #1, Tools for getting along: Teaching students to problem-solve curriculum. Retrieved December 12, 2003, from http://www.coe.ufl.edu/aggression/Currtechreport%20.pdf.

Eddy, J. M., Reid, J. B., & Fetrow, R. A. (2000). An elementary school-based prevention program targeting modifiable antecedents of youth delinquency and violence: Linking the Interests of Families and Teachers (LIFT). *Journal of Emotional & Behavioral Disorders, 8*(3), 165–176.

Gunter, P. L., Denny, R. K., Jack, S. L., Shores, R. E., & Nelson, M. (1993). Aversive stimuli in academic interactions between students with serious emotional disturbance and their teachers. *Behavioral Disorders, 24,* 180–182.

Hammond, R., & Gipson, B. (1994). *Dealing with anger: Givin' it, takin' it, workin' it out* [Video]. Champaign, IL: Research Press.

Hammond, R. W., & Yung, B. R. (1995). *PACT—Positive Adolescent Choices Training: A model for violence prevention groups with African American youth* [Video]. Champaign, IL: Research Press.

Hartman, R., & Sage, S. A. (2000). The relationship between social information processing and in-school suspension for student with behavioral disorders. *Behavioral Disorders, 25*(3), 183–195.

Keller, H. R., & Tapasak, R. C. (1998). Classroom management. In A. P. Goldstein & J. C. Conoley (Eds.), *School violence intervention: A practical handbook* (pp. 107–126). New York: Guilford.

Loeber, R., & Farrington, D. P. (1998). *Serious and violent juvenile offenders: Risk factors and successful interventions.* Thousand Oaks, CA: Sage Publications.

Meador, S. A. (1992). Changing youth's attitudes about guns. *School Safety,* p. 31.

Penno, D. A., Frank, A. R., & Wacker, D. P. (2000). Instructional accommodations for adolescent students with severe emotional or behavioral disorders. *Behavioral Disorders, 25*(4), 325–343.

Presley, J. A., & Hughes, C. (2000). Peers as teachers of anger management to high school students with behavioral disorders. *Behavioral Disorders, 25*(2), 114–130.

Rhode, G. (1996). In-school suspension program. In H. K. Reavis, M. T. Sweeten, W. R. Jensen, D. P. Morgan, D. J. Andrews, & S. Fister (Eds.), *Best practices: Behavioral and educational strategies for teachers* (pp. 87–98). Longmont, CO: Sopris West.

Sherman, M. (2003). Handout H: Communicating with your loved one. Support and Family Education (SAFE) Program Manual (2nd ed.). Retrieved September 14, 2004, from http://w3.ouhsc.edu/safeprogram/index.html.

Walker, H. M., Colvin, G., & Ramsey, E. (1995). *Antisocial behavior in school: Strategies and best practices.* Pacific Grove, CA: Brooks/Cole.

Walker, H. M., McConnell, S. R., Holmes, D., Todis, B., Walker, J., & Golden, N. (1983). *The Walker social skills curriculum: The ACCEPTS program (a curriculum for children's effective peer and teacher skills).* Austin, TX: PRO-ED.

Young, K. R., West, R. P., Smith, D. J., & Morgan, D. P. (1991). *Teaching self-management strategies to adolescents.* Longmont, CO: Sopris West.

CHAPTER 10

DEVELOPING ALTERNATIVES TO SELF-STIMULATORY AND SELF-INJURIOUS BEHAVIOR

Kristina Johnson and William J. Helsel

OUTLINE

Introduction
Self-Injurious Behaviors
SSB, SIB, and Functional Relations
Motivative Operations
Assessment of SSB
Intervention Strategies for SSB
Assessment of SIB
Intervention Strategies for SIB

OBJECTIVES

After completing this chapter, you should be able to

- Define the various types of self-stimulatory and self-injurious behavior.
- Conduct a functional analysis of a self-stimulatory and self-injurious behavior.
- Discuss the theoretical concepts underlying self-stimulatory and self-injurious behavior.
- Choose an effective intervention for self-stimulatory and self-injurious behavior.
- Discuss the ethical issues in carrying out aversive and restrictive interventions.
- Assist in conducting a sensory extinction intervention.

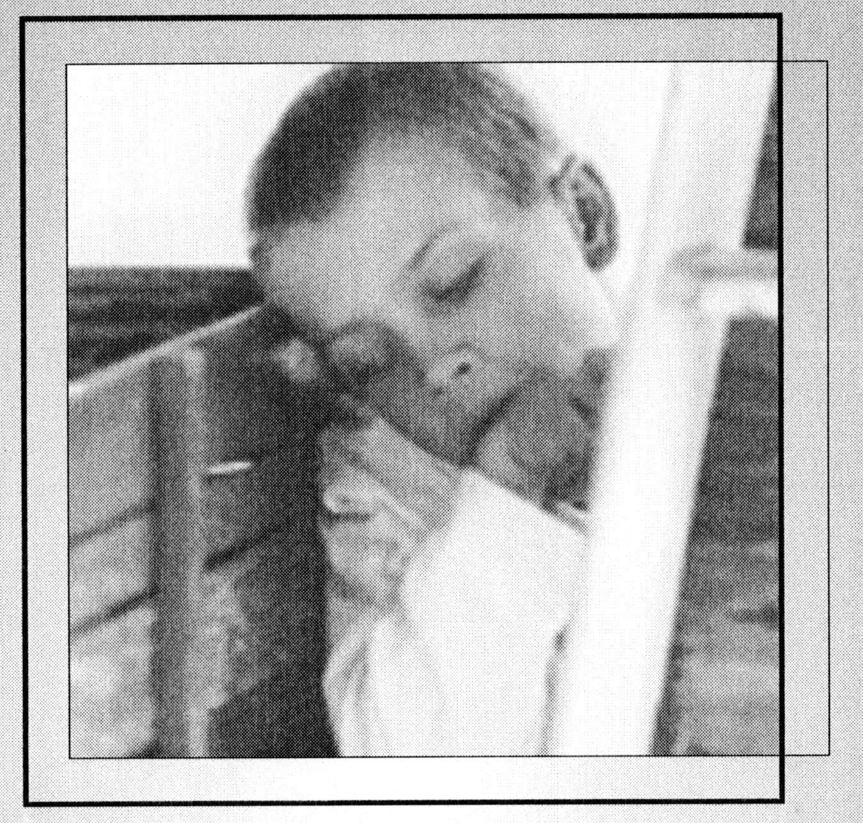

KEY TERMS (refer to the Glossary on the Companion Website for definitions)

automatic reinforcement
coprophagia
differential reinforcement of other behavior
extinction
functional analysis
functional assessment
interruption and redirection
motivative operations
movement suppression procedure
noncontingent reinforcement
perceptual reinforcement
pica
response-reinforcer procedure
ritualistic
self-injurious behavior
self-mutilating behavior
self-stimulatory behavior
sensory extinction
sensory reinforcement
stereotypic
stimulus variation

This chapter introduces you to assessment and intervention strategies for students who exhibit self-stimulatory and self-injurious behavior.[1] Here you will learn about conducting a functional analysis—an assessment where cause-and-effect relations can be established during assessment that will help you determine what factors contribute to self-stimulatory and self-injurious behaviors. You will also learn intervention strategies to help reduce self-stimulatory and self-injurious behaviors in the classroom. Let's begin with a case study as reported by a classroom teacher.

Come into My Classroom: A Case Study

Amanda is an 8-year-old girl who has been in my autistic support classroom for 2 years. She has always been a difficult child for me to handle because she engages in self-stimulatory behaviors such as hand flapping, spinning, and loud vocal humming. These behaviors are the norm for the majority of the children in my classroom; however, Amanda's parents see her self-stimulatory behaviors as a major issue. They do not want their daughter to "stick out" and want her individualized education plan (IEP) goals to address a plan for interruption redirection that will help Amanda complete task work.

To help reach everyone's goals, the behavior specialist developed a behavior plan that was successful until Amanda began to engage in severe self-injurious behaviors. She began scratching her legs and arms repeatedly until they bled, pulling out clumps of her hair, and banging her head for hours at a time. Amanda, who used to have beautiful blonde curls and big brown eyes, began to look completely different. She managed to pull clumps of hair out of her head, and her body was covered with old scars, fresh wounds, and severe bruising. Her parents' worst fear had come true; Amanda really did "stick out"!

The behavior specialist defines the motivators of Amanda's behaviors as demand related and as escape avoidance from classroom work. Her parents do not agree with this opinion and have taken Amanda to numerous specialists in an attempt to gain a different opinion. Amanda's parents also blame me for this change. They feel that I do not know how to intervene behaviorally with their daughter; *I* feel frustrated and exhausted. I do not know what to do or where to turn regarding Amanda's behaviors. The behavior specialist has designed another behavior treatment plan that I am instructed to implement. However, the parents, who are unhappy with the behavior specialist, do not want me to implement this plan. I feel trapped between the diagnosis of a professional and the wishes of the parents.

Amanda's behaviors are beginning to cause problems for others in the classroom. My aides are shying away from her. The building principal has asked me to identify what steps I am taking to follow universal precautions. And regular education teachers have stated that she is too "severe" to be included. It seems that in an attempt to "solve" Amanda's problems, we have all caused many more.

I feel as though my hands are tied. I have six other students who deserve to learn, but Amanda demands the majority of my time. I feel guilty at the end of the day because the other six children in my classroom have been neglected. I know that I cannot sit and watch Amanda hurt herself, but when I physically redirect Amanda to stop the self-injurious behaviors, I become the target of her aggression. How can I help her without understanding the cause of Amanda's self-stimulatory and self-abusive behaviors? Perhaps if I understood the motivations behind Amanda's behaviors, I would be able to design more successful behavior interventions for my classroom, thus becoming a more effective educator for Amanda and my future students.

In looking at this case study, what concerns come to your mind? What role does the teacher play in Amanda's misbehaviors? How would you as a teacher deal with Amanda's behaviors?

INTRODUCTION

The behaviors described in this chapter, like those Amanda's teacher faced in working with her, may be the most complex that you will ever confront in teaching. Sadly, they are also serious—if not life threatening to the students who exhibit them. To add to this complexity, Baer (1990) reminds us that our defining task is "to discover what behaviors need to be changed in order to solve a problem" (p. 184). He goes on to say that "behaviors are not problems. Behaviors are natural events; they occur or fail to occur because that is what must happen, given the history of the [person] and the current environment. The problem is invariably that someone complains about that necessity powerfully enough to generate behavior-change interventions by themselves, by their agents, by the [person] complained about, or by agents of those segments of society that take upon themselves interventions into complaints. The point of these interventions is to reduce the complaint" (p. 184). To begin to understand the problem and the behavior, let's look first at what is meant by **self-stimulatory behavior** and **self-injurious behavior** and the terms associated with them.

Self-Stimulatory Behavior

These actions are repetitive, frequent, and occur as highly consistent topography, but do not cause physical injury. Stereotypy can, however, move into self-injury (Kennedy, 2002). **Ritualistic** and **stereotypic** are global terms also used to describe self-stimulatory behaviors. For purposes of this chapter, however, we adopt "self-stimulatory behavior" (SSB), the term that appears to be most commonly used in schools, to describe "behaviors that are stereotyped and performed repetitiously, and that fail to produce any apparent positive environmental consequences or physical injury" (O'Brien, 1981, p. 117). Although not easily apparent, more recent research points to these behaviors being sensitive to reinforcement from social events or external reinforcers (Ahearn, Clark, Gardenier, Chung, & Dube, 2003; Kennedy, 2002). This more recent research looks carefully at the contribution of behavior momentum and its implications for difficult-to-change behavior like SSB. For instance, behavior momentum research cautions us to be aware of the relation between procedures that reduce a behavior but strengthen the persistence of the behavior. Bodfish et al. (1995) developed assessment screening instruments for stereotypy and self-injury. Findings conclude that these instruments have acceptable levels of reliability, stability, and validity for people with developmental disabilities (Bodfish et al., 1995; Lewis & Bodfish, 1998), and these psychometric findings have been independently replicated (Johnson, 1999). The assessment screening instrument Stereotypy Checklist (STY-C) (Bodfish et al., 1995) appears in Table 10–1.

Controversy exists about how we describe these repetitive, frequent, highly consistent behaviors with the term "self-stimulation" because it implies a questionable motivation for the behavior (Baumeister, 1978). Some authors prefer the term "stereotyped movements" because it is "without

TABLE 10–1 Stereotypy Checklist (STY-C)

Name: ______________________________ Date: ___________
Rated By: ______________________________

Instructions: Place a "checkmark" next to the item for any of the following list of behaviors which the subject displays repetitively (repeats the same movement or action over and over again in bouts or periods of activity). Be sure to check all that apply.

(1). WHOLE BODY:
__________ body rocking (front-to-back)
__________ body swaying (side-to-side)

(2). HEAD
__________ head rolling
__________ tilting head
__________ head turning
__________ head nod

(3). EYE/VISUAL:
__________ covering eyes
__________ looks closely/gazes at hands or objects

(4). EAR/HEARING:
__________ covering ears

(5). MOUTH:
__________ teeth grinding
__________ mouthing/chews objects
__________ hand(s) in mouth

(6). HAND/FINGER:
__________ hand flapping
__________ finger wiggling
__________ finger flicking
__________ hand clapping
__________ hand/arm wave/shake

(7). LOCOMOTOR:
__________ turning in circle(s)/whirling
__________ jumping/bouncing

(8). VOCALIZATIONS:
__________ echolalia
__________ repetitive verbalization or vocalization

(9). OBJECT MANIPULATION:
__________ spinning/twirling, twiddling objects
__________ slapping objects
__________ throws objects
__________ lets objects fall out of hands

(10). OTHER:
__________ maintaining a set body posture
__________ tip-toe walking
__________ forceful breathing
__________ smelling/sniffing
__________ rubbing surfaces
__________ tap, touch, rub body part(s)
__________ twirls hair
__________ other
(describe): __________

TABLE 10–1 (Continued)

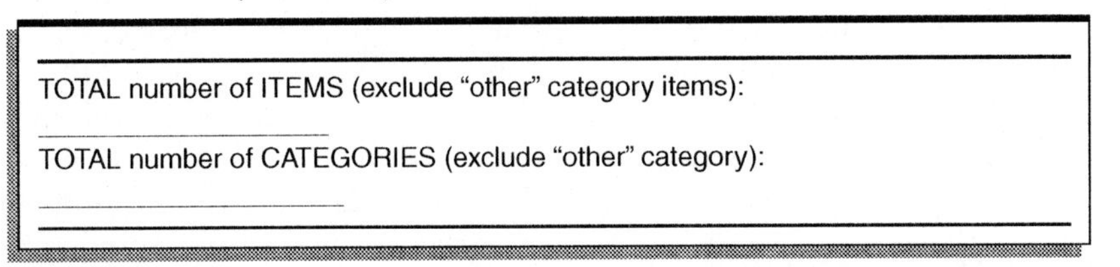

TOTAL number of ITEMS (exclude "other" category items):

____

TOTAL number of CATEGORIES (exclude "other" category):

____

Source: *Bodfish, J. W. (2004).* Stereotypy Checklist (STY-C). *Reprinted with permission.*

inference and purely descriptive" (O'Brien, 1981, p. 118). Because of its utility, however, we will stay with SSB as our descriptor, noting that it is not an attempt to go beyond a name.

Self-stimulatory behaviors are seen most often in those with severe behavioral disabilities. Research on the nature of SSB has revealed that this serious behavior problem may be maintained by the perceptual reinforcement that it provides to the self-stimulating individual (Lovaas, Newsom, & Hickman, 1987). To better understand the particular role of perceptual reinforcement in SSB, consider these points made by Lovaas et al. (1987):

1. The child controls the perceptual reinforcers; these reinforcers are not controlled by others or the environment.
2. Perceptual reinforcers are primary reinforcers. In addition, they are quite durable and not as vulnerable to satiation as other reinforcers.

When does a child begin to exhibit SSB? Research has shown that these behaviors begin in infancy in some individuals with developmental delays and, in most cases, before the age of 2 years in most cases (Berkson, McQuiston, Jacobson, Eyman, & Borthwick, 1985).

How does a child "learn" to engage in SSB? Consider this illustration (Lovaas et al., 1987):

> An autistic child initially twirls a string in a variety of different ways. Sooner or later (through trial and error) a pattern of string movements is discovered that is particularly attractive to look at (i.e., that strongly reinforces twirling the string). With practice, he or she learns to perform exactly the right manipulation of the string to achieve the preferred pattern and tends to perform only that topography and closely related topographies most of the time. Consider another example: A child will retrieve and then skillfully manipulate a variety of objects (dishes, sinkstoppers, balls, etc.) to make them rotate or spin. Once the object comes to a resting position he or she will resume the behavioral sequence. In such an example, the child's spinning of various objects may be an acquired response, an operant, whose visual consequence (the spinning object) is the perceptual reinforcer that shapes and maintains the response. In the example of the child who repeatedly arranges (lines) objects such as toys, books, or shoes in neat rows across the living room floor, "objects in a line" may constitute a positively reinforcing perceptual consequence, shaping and maintaining the lining behavior. (p. 49)

How does SSB persist? By description, SSB is highly reinforcing, and individuals engaged in SSB simply may not have other, alternative behaviors in which to engage. As the more recent research cited by Kennedy (2002) more carefully examines intricate relationships like those comprising behavior momentum (Ahearn et al., 2003), we will be able to give a more meaningful response to this question.

As you study intervention possibilities later in this chapter, you will notice an emphasis on controlling the perceptual experiences of self-stimulating individuals. In addition, you will learn how very carefully all assessments and interventions must be implemented if a program is to have any success with this difficult and durable set of behaviors. If you work with students with severe disabilities, the behaviors listed in Table 10–1 are probably familiar. Self-stimulatory behaviors are not harmful in themselves but may, in time, change to self-injurious behaviors through a slight shift in topography (Kennedy, 2002; O'Brien, 1981). It would seem then that considerable effort should be expended toward the reduction of these troublesome behaviors. Indeed, this is now the generally accepted course of treatment.

SELF-INJURIOUS BEHAVIORS

The terms "self-injurious," **self-mutilating,** and "self-destructive" describe behaviors that hurt the person exhibiting them. These terms are commonly used for chronic, repetitive acts of individuals with severe disabilities (Schroeder, Oster-Granite, & Thompson, 2002). The occurrence of self-injurious behavior (SIB) is not unique to persons with developmental disabilities, although prevalence does vary with intellectual ability, but instead co-occurs with other behaviors in developmental, neurological, psychiatric, and genetic disorders (Bodfish & Lewis, 2002). In this chapter, we use "self-injurious behavior," or "SIB," because it is the term you are most likely to hear and use.

Favell (1982) summarized into five categories the various kinds of SIB reported in research literature:

1. Striking oneself (e.g., face slapping, head banging against objects)
2. Biting or sucking various body parts (e.g., "mouthing")
3. Pinching, scratching, poking, or pulling various body parts (e.g., eye poking, hair pulling)
4. Repeatedly vomiting or vomiting and reingesting food (i.e., "rumination")
5. Consuming nonedible substances (e.g., eating objects, cigarettes: **pica;** eating feces: **coprophagia**) (p. 1).

Bodfish et al. (1995) investigated the prevalence of compulsions in adults with severe mental retardation and the phenomenology of compulsive, stereotypic, and self-injurious behavior in this group and examined comorbidity between compulsions, stereotypy, and self-injury. They developed an assessment screening instrument, Self-Injury & Self-Restraint (SIB-C), shown in Table 10-2. These descriptions not only illustrate problem behaviors but also give you and your multidisciplinary IEP Team ideas for writing target behavior descriptions (for a more current epidemiological review of SIB, see Rojahn & Esbensen, 2002).

The studies cited are attempts to treat the serious behavior of individuals who engage in SIB. Teachers must try to understand these often frightening behaviors because they can result in serious injury to a student, such as retinal detachment (Favell, 1982); loss of an appendage or of the use of a sensory modality; or a skull fracture. It is imperative that you recognize the significance of SIB and respect the highly systematic interventions designed to treat it.

A Note About SIB and SSB Assessment and Interventions

Special Note: Our guidelines on assessment and intervention of SSB and SIB are based on the assumption that an effective program to increase alternative behaviors is documented in the student's IEP and functional behavioral assessment.

We describe assessment and intervention procedures that you can implement with little supervision or outside help. Our exclusion of certain procedures will not be popular with many educators who argue that "we already have these students in our classrooms—why not go ahead and tell us how to use all of the interventions available?" We can only reiterate our concern that you may inadvertently misuse a procedure because of problems with time, support personnel, supervision, effectiveness data, and approvals.

Despite their documented effectiveness, many interventions are prohibited in school settings because they create discomfort for the target student. Therefore, a major consideration is the use of alternative, nonaversive procedures that might be suggested through a fruitful functional analysis. Lovaas and Favell (1987) stated that "if a program cannot conduct alternative interventions in a high-quality fashion, then it should not employ aversive procedures" (p. 320). Further, "The use of aversive and restrictive interventions should only

TABLE 10–2 Self-Injury and Self-Restraint Checklist (SIB-C)

Name: ____________ Date: ____________ Rated By: ____________

Instructions: Place a "checkmark" next to the item for any of the following list of behaviors which the subject displays in a repetitive manner (repeats the same movement/behavior twice or more in succession). Be sure to check all that apply.

(1) SELF-INJURY (repetitive movement/behavior which has potential to cause redness, bruising, or other injury to body part/area):

____________ hits self with body part (e.g., slaps head or face)
____________ hits self against surface or object (e.g., bangs head on floor or table)
____________ hits self with object (e.g., bangs head or face with toys)
____________ bites self (e.g., bites hand or wrist or arm)
____________ pulls (e.g., pulls hair or skin)
____________ rubs or scratches self (e.g., rubs marks on arm or leg)
____________ inserts finger or object (e.g., eye-poking)
____________ other form of self-injury (specify: ____________)

TOTAL *SELF-INJURY* ITEMS (exclude "other"): ____________

(2) SELF-RESTRAINT (self-initiated movement/behavior performed to maintain a set position and which appears to stop or prevent movement of body parts/areas):

____________ wraps self in own clothing or holds onto own clothing
____________ holds onto others or holds onto others' clothing
____________ positions self to restrain (e.g., sitting on hands, wraps arms in chair)
____________ holds hands together, holds onto self
____________ holds or squeezes objects
____________ chooses to wear item to discourage self-injury (e.g., hat, helmet)
____________ chooses mechanical restraint
____________ other form of self-restraint
(specify: ____________)

TOTAL *SELF-RESTRAINT* ITEMS (exclude "other"): ____________

Source: *Bodfish, J. W. (2004).* Self-Injury and Self-Restraint Checklist (SIB-C). *Reprinted with permission.*

be considered in the context of several issues surrounding their use. Such techniques are justified only when their effects are rigorously evaluated, caregivers are fully trained and adequately supervised in all dimensions of habilitative services, when a meaningful functional analysis of the child's problem has been conducted, alternative and benign treatments have been considered and are in place, parents and others are fully informed, and there is general agreement that the means justify the ends" (p. 324).

> Aversive procedures (always a last resort) have been replaced with more positive interventions in recent years.

It is important at the outset to remind you to review your state's rules and regulations issued by state departments of education or public instruction, offices of mental retardation, and departments of mental health and substance abuse. Since the mid-1980s those state departments overseeing mental health, mental retardation, and substance abuse services have continually refined their recommendations for practices like seclusion and restraint and, in some instances, numerous other procedures. More recently, departments overseeing educational services have also prohibited some procedures and made recommendations for the use of others. For instance, in Pennsylvania a services bulletin was issued on April

8, 2002, by the Department of Public Welfare to "provide recommended practices on the use of seclusion and restraint with adults, children, and adolescents in mental health programs and facilities. . . . The Bulletin also provides uniform definitions for restrictive procedures, and explains the conditions under which seclusion or restraint should be employed" (Commonwealth of Pennsylvania, Department of Public Welfare, 2002).

SSB, SIB, AND FUNCTIONAL RELATIONS

Let's review some explanations for why these seemingly bizarre but quite functional behaviors occur. A methodology for understanding the motivational conditions of SSB and SIB, referred to as **functional analysis** or **functional assessment** (Carr, 1977; Iwata, Pace, et al., 1994), is necessary. Functional analysis refers to techniques designed to empirically demonstrate functional or cause-and-effect relationships between what a person does (i.e., behavior) and where and when they do it (i.e., environment). Functional assessment is sometimes used to refer to techniques designed to examine functional relations without manipulation (i.e., experimentation) of conditions. These techniques include descriptive analysis and indirect assessments like rating scales. Check out the Companion Website for additional information on related workshops and conferences as well as a link to the *Journal of Applied Behavior Analysis.*

Durand and Carr (1985) cited four motivational conditions for self-injury. The first, social attention, refers to the maintenance of the behaviors through the verbal or nonverbal feedback of others (Carr & McDowell, 1980). Second, self-injury may be maintained through tangible consequences (e.g., access to play activities). Third, the student may exhibit self-injury to avoid a situation he dislikes (e.g., a difficult self-help lesson). Finally, the sensory feedback a student receives from injuring herself may be reinforcing to her.

Durand and Crimmins (1988) developed a screening tool for determining the functional significance of self-injury, the Motivation Assessment Scale (MAS). You and your supervisor might use this instrument to begin to gain a better understanding of a student's self-injurious behaviors. It is important to note that the advantage of this kind of indirect assessment is its simplicity, but that must be balanced with the knowledge that the reliability of these assessment devices has been found to be low (Sturmey, 1994). For the MAS, Zarcone, Rodgers, Iwata, Rourke, and Dorsey (1991) were unable to replicate the findings reported in original work. In 1995, Vollmer and his colleagues began to evaluate functional assessments and functional analysis to learn more about how to weigh the advantages of the various techniques (Vollmer, Marcus, Ringdahl, & Roane, 1995). Taking into consideration the serious nature of SSB and SIB and the findings published in the applied research literature to date, functional analysis is required to more precisely alter environmental determinants for efficient effective behavioral intervention.

A functional analysis suggests the purpose for the behavior, and once we understand why a student injures herself, we can better move to teaching her alternative behaviors for achieving the same goals. Carr and Durand (1985) illustrated this approach in a communication training program for children with developmental disabilities. Very carefully selected and trained phrases enabled the children to satisfy their needs without resorting to self-injury. Hagopian and his colleagues conducted further procedural analysis to more carefully examine how functional communication training has been used to reduce problem behavior (Hagopian, Fisher, Sullivan, Acquisto, & LeBlanc, 1998). What this more careful procedural analysis demonstrated was that functional communication training, when paired with other operant procedures, can be effective but in the absence of these other treatment components was ineffective.

MOTIVATIVE OPERATIONS

Assessment that goes beyond function analysis requires a look at **motivative operations** (MOs) first identified and called establishing operations by Keller and Schoenfeld (1995/1950) and further developed by Michael (1982). More recently, Michael (2002) has used MOs to better describe establishing operations and abolishing operations. An establishing operation (EO) is an environmental event, operation, or stimulus condition that increases the reinforcing effectiveness of other events as well as increases the frequency of occurrence of the type of behavior that had been consequated by those other events (Michael, 1993). An abolishing operation (AO) decreases the reinforcing effect while also decreasing the current frequency of all behavior that had been reinforced by those events. One way to come to understand what is meant by MOs is to think about the effects of food deprivation (EO) and food ingestion (AO). The behavior evoked by the MO is usually learned. There are many examples of day-to-day EOs that children with developmental disabilities or autism may experience. For instance, they may have difficulty in the afternoon as the day wears on—actions are more effortful, requiring increased reinforcement. This could be called fatigue or referred to as the buildup of too many demands, pressures, or distress of unexpected events that are not part of their usual schedule. The EO is set for behavior that gets described as "frustration" and problem behavior to occur and the "change" in situation that follows these responses being far more valuable than at other times. These same children are more likely to experience difficulty during the first 6 weeks of school, with changes in their daily schedules, for the time period between Thanksgiving and Christmas, an unexpected snow day, or the last few weeks at the end of the school year, and the first line of treatment is to increase the rate of reinforcement.

There are two main types of MOs: unconditioned and conditioned. Both of these MOs are motivational because they increase the likelihood that a behavior will occur and at the same time increase the power of the reinforcer that follows the behavior. Unconditioned motivative operations (UMOs) are events, operations, and stimulus conditions whose reinforcer establishing effects are unlearned (Michael, 1993, 2002). It is the unlearned aspect of the altered reinforcer effect that results in the MO being classified as "unconditioned." According to Michael (1993), many learned forms of reinforcement do not require learned MOs. The author states that there are variables that alter the reinforcing effectiveness of other events but only as a result of the individual organism's history. Michael (1993) refers to this definition as learned or conditioned motivative operations (CMOs). Here is an example to help you understand this concept. Teitelbaum (1977) defines thwarting (CMO) as "lack of reinforcement that are inevitable accompaniments of any reinforcement schedule" (p. 23). Thwarting is usually associated with anecdotal notes that state "he was aggressive out of the blue." For children with autism, we often recognize a statement like this is inaccurate after a functional analysis is completed. Often, what happens is the child initiates a response, we may think "they want something," and we stop the child and tell him or her to wait. After you have thwarted an autistic child, depending on the time of day (i.e., UMO), one too many times, you will increase the likelihood that he is going to hit (behavior) you and escape (i.e., negative reinforcement). Thus, that escape will be more powerful than usual in reinforcing the behavior and the occasion that it is contingent on. Brown et al. (2000) investigated the effects of functional communication training in the presence and absence of EOs. They concluded that increases in relevant manding (i.e., making requests) were observed in the EO present condition and that decreases in aberrant behavior were achieved when treatment was matched to results of functional analysis. Kennedy and Itkonen (1993) investigated the effects of setting events (another way of looking at EOs) on problem behavior of students with disabilities. The authors concluded that the occurrence of preceding setting events was related to higher frequencies of problem behaviors and that the interventions designed to eliminate preceding setting events were associated with low rates of behaviors.

ASSESSMENT OF SSB

Perhaps the first decision to be made with regard to referring a problem with SSB is whether it warrants treatment. In the event that a stereotypic behavior has become self-injurious, the decision is a quick "yes!" An SSB individual may not gain access to less restrictive environments or to training programs within the present environment until the "annoying" SSB is reduced or eliminated.

> In classroom situations, you may choose to pursue the assessment of the problem because SSB interferes with a student's ability to attend to appropriate instructional or adaptive behavior tasks.

To define an SSB problem, use the questions in Figure 10–1 to assemble information gathered from the student's teachers and the student's family. The information listed on this form will help you complete your functional analysis of the student's SSB.

Bailey and his colleagues (Pyles, Riordan, & Bailey, 1997) introduced an efficient instrument for analyzing SSB. This tool is efficient because it provides valuable information about what in the environment is associated with differential rates of SSB using brief 1-minute observations combined with ratings of occurrence or nonoccurrence of events within this same 1 minute at different times within and across days. For teachers, the brief information-gathering method of this analysis is particularly attractive because it allows you to do what you can when your schedule allows for it. (This form of analysis can be broadened beyond SSB for other high-rate behaviors of concern.)

As you read about interventions for SSB, you will understand why certain items of information are

Student ______________________ Date ______________

1. What are the precise behaviors of concern?
2. Do these behaviors occur interchangeably, simultaneously, or separately?
3. Is any kind of sensory stimulation apparent (e.g., visual flickering, repetitive auditory signal)? In other words, what kind of *perceptual reinforcement* does the SSB provide the child?
4. Does the behavior appear only in selected settings (e.g., areas where there is a hard, smooth surface, well-lit areas)?
5. Do the behaviors prevent the student from engaging in an instructional activity? How?
6. Do the behaviors gain attention for the student from adults or peers? If so, what kind of attention? (Use an ABC analysis.)
7. Does the student cease self-stimulation when asked? For how long? When asked by whom? In what tone of voice?
8. Does the student stop these behaviors when alone? In the presence of whom?
9. Does the student stop the behaviors when engaged in certain activities? Specify these activities.
10. Could the self-stimulatory behaviors be considered developmentally age appropriate for this student (e.g., masturbation)?
11. Is the student injuring himself?
12. Is the student presently involved in an intervention program? What is it? Where are the data on this program?

Name of person completing this form ______________________

FIGURE 10–1 Information-Gathering Form for SSB

Observer John M. Student Joey

Date March 19 Observation Session 1 2 3 4 5 6

Setting classroom Activity puzzles/fine motor

Others present teacher, child care worker

Time 10:49 to 10:54

(Do not observe/record behaviors that occur during a program that interrupts the behaviors.)

	10	20	30	40	50	60
Minute 1	BR	BR	BR	BR	BR Aud	BR Aud
Minute 2	BR Aud	Aud	Aud	Aud	/	/

Codes: BR = body rock. Aud = auditory SSB

Percent of intervals calculation:

Number of intervals in which behaviors occurred times 100 = _______ % Total intervals observed

FIGURE 10–2 Interval Record for Self-Stimulatory Behaviors

important to a thorough definition and analysis of SSB. For example, questions regarding the type of sensory stimulation that a student appears to gain from SSB (questions 3 and 4 in Figure 10–1) provide initial information for a sensory extinction program, whereas questions 7, 8, and 9 target information for a DRO (discussed later) or punishment program. You should also complete a health history form or ask the student's parents to do this.

You need to record specific samples of SSB in preparation for (or to monitor the effects of) an intervention program. We suggest you record SSB using an interval record such as the one in Figure 10–2. These assessment activities should provide information to facilitate the design of an appropriate intervention, although the task is still not simple.

INTERVENTION STRATEGIES FOR SSB

Research in the area of SSB has important implications for your work as a classroom teacher. Some of the following interventions are effective with SSBs, while others are not.

Enriching the Environment

No matter how interesting you make your classroom, environmental manipulation alone will not reduce self-stimulatory behaviors (Favell, McGimsey, & Schell, 1982). However, there is evidence that self-stimulating individuals prefer objects (e.g., toys) that give them their preferred mode of perceptual feedback (Favell et al., 1982), so you might want to consider this variable as you plan your classroom activities.

Social Reinforcement Approaches

Evidence has shown that self-stimulatory behavior does not extinguish with the withdrawal of social reinforcement (Lovaas et al., 1987). In other words, ignoring a self-stimulating child will not affect her problem behavior. The attention of others is simply not powerful enough to compete successfully with the perceptual reinforcement the child receives from SSB. While SSB may not respond favorably to **extinction,** a child's other behaviors may improve with this withdrawal of social reinforcement. You do not want to eliminate this strategy for a self-injurious child. (As mentioned earlier, this procedure is being analyzed more carefully for its efficacy; see Kennedy, 2002).

Reinforcing Alternative Behaviors

Differential reinforcement of other behavior (DRO) is a term frequently cited in descriptions of programs for SSB (or SIB) individuals. DRO procedures often accompany other interventions. The basic notion of a DRO program is the reinforcement of intervals at a time during which the SSB does not occur. For example, students might be reinforced initially each time they engage in 10, then 15, then 20 seconds of non-SSB behavior. The DRO approach might prove helpful in teaching the child alternative behaviors, but it does not seem fruitful as an intervention to eliminate SSB. This may be a bit confusing for you because you may notice that the stereotypic behaviors do lessen when the DRO is implemented. This problem arises when—as has been observed—the self-stimulatory behaviors return once the DRO is terminated (Lovaas et al., 1987) and, like the larger question of the role of social reinforcement, may be better answered by the research now evolving as cited by Kennedy (2002).

Noncontingent Reinforcement

Over the past 10 years, Iwata and his colleagues have built on our understanding of **noncontingent reinforcement (NCR),** or "a response-independent or time-based delivery of stimuli with known reinforcing properties," and its possible advantages over the use of differential reinforcement of other behavior (DRO) (Vollmer, Iwata, Zarcone, Smith, & Mazaleski, 1993, p. 10). Their work has led to a more careful procedural analysis examining reinforcer consumption and reinforcer magnitude, a further clarification of effect-of-treatment components (Roscoe, Iwata, & Rand, 2003). NCR removes the extinction component that is a necessary part of a differential reinforcement procedure. (Remember that extinction, or the removal of a reinforcer from a previously reinforced behavior, results in increased variability of behavior and an emotional response.) And, because it is time based, staff responsible for its implementation may find it easier to implement with the absence of an obvious contingent event.

Perceptual Reinforcement

As you will recall, the key to understanding SSB is to view it as a form of **perceptual reinforcement** to the individual. Therefore, we believe that forthcoming research will prove sensory manipulation strategies to be effective. The increased fluency of alternative behavior in skill acquisition programs will also affect the motivative analysis of SSB. Some interventions for reducing SSB require outside behavior change agents, but in many you may play a major role. (Several procedures are described in the section "Intervention Strategies for SIB," so we will only mention them here.)

Stimulus Variation

The purpose of **stimulus variation** is to increase the level of motivation and responsiveness exhibited by a student engaged in SSB. Although little research on this intervention has been conducted thus far, there is evidence to suggest that bored students may engage in SSB (Dunlap & Koegel, 1980). Early behavior analytic intervention for young children with autism supports these earlier findings (Maurice, Green, & Luce, 1996). Review carefully the sequence and length of activities you present to students. Try to intersperse two or three target tasks among other tasks rather than focusing on 15 minutes of one task followed by 15 minutes of another.

Sensory Preferences

Children engaged in SSB appear to have strong preferences for particular sensory experiences (e.g., either auditory or visual) (Lovaas et al., 1987). This finding underscores the importance of a painstaking analysis of the student's behaviors and the circumstances that maintain them. See Hanley, Iwata, Thompson, and Lindberg (2000) for an examination of using an SSB individual's "stereotypy as reinforcement" for alternative behavior.

Response-Reinforcer Procedure

In a **response-reinforcer procedure,** the immediate environment is manipulated so that the student, as a result of completing a task, has immediate access to a reinforcer physically imbedded within the task. Why might a response-reinforcer procedure result in rapid learning acquisition? Perhaps it is because the reinforcer becomes immediately available as soon as the student engages in the correct response (completes the task). In other words, "A functional response-reinforcer relationship may serve to highlight the contingency between the reinforcer and the intended target behavior" (Williams, Koegel, & Egel, 1981, p. 59). See Thompson and Iwata (2000) for a more recent examination of direct and indirect contingencies.

Sensory Reinforcement

In contrast to the response-reinforcer intervention, a **sensory reinforcement** strategy provides the child with one or more sensory experiences that are deemed desirable to the child. Rincover and Newsom (1985) found that multiple sensory reinforcers were more effective than multiple edible reinforcers in increasing correct responses. When a single sensory reinforcer was compared with a single edible reinforcer, the results were about the same. Some of the sensory reinforcers they used include tickling, hand clapping, finger tapping or drumming with sticks by the adult on a surface near the child, singing (by the adult), playing music very briefly, and caressing. To create the multiple-sensory reinforcement arrangement, the adult varied the reinforcers given for correct trials.

Automatic Reinforcement

In an **automatic reinforcement** procedure, the reinforcement is produced independently of the social environment. Behaviors that are maintained by automatic reinforcement can present treatment challenges because of the difficulty in identifying, manipulating, and controlling the specific reinforcer produced by the response (Vollmer, 1994). Additional studies have focused on developing assessment procedures to facilitate the identification of the specific source of automatic reinforcement produced by behavior. Piazza et al. (1998) described the use of functional analysis and preference assessment to identify the specific source of reinforcement for automatically reinforced pica behavior. Functional analysis results indicated that pica behavior of three subjects was maintained in part by automatic reinforcement. Piazza, Adelinis, Hanley, Goh, and Delia (2000) extended their investigation of comparing matched stimuli to aberrant behaviors. These aberrant behaviors consisted of dangerous climbing and jumping, saliva manipulation, and hand mouthing. Preference assessments were utilized to identify matched stimuli (items that provided the same or similar sensory consequence as the aberrant behavior) and unmatched stimuli (items that provided no actual sensory consequences). By integrating the results of the functional analysis, which suggested that the behavior was maintained by automatic reinforcement, and the structural observations, the authors were successfully able to develop treatment components for the aberrant behaviors of climbing, saliva play, and hand mouthing.

Sensory Extinction Procedure

A development in the alteration of SSBs, **sensory extinction**, is based on the notion that certain individuals have a strong preference for one aspect of sensory input (e.g., tactile, proprioceptive, visual, or auditory) and engage in self-stimulatory behaviors to increase this sensory input (Rincover & Devany, 1982). For example, a child may spin objects for the auditory feedback (the sound of the plate spinning), may finger-flap (for the visual feedback of watching his finger movements), or tap his fingers (for the proprioceptive stimulation).

The first step in a sensory extinction program is to determine the sensory input the student receives while engaged in the behavior. He may exhibit a behavior that provides more than one type of sensory feedback; in that case, additional sensory analyses must be completed. Rincover (1978) described such an assessment procedure and reported that "Reggie would incessantly spin objects, particularly a plate, in a stereotyped, repetitive manner. However, when he twirled the plate, he would also cock his head to the side and lean toward it, seeming to listen to the plate as it was spinning. This suggested that the auditory feedback may have been an important consequence of Reggie's self-stimulation" (p. 302). Similarly, he observed that "Robert engaged in excessive finger-flapping, in which he had one or both hands in front of his face and vigorously moved the fingers (but not the arms) back and forth. In this case, two sensory consequences were identified for testing: the visual feedback from watching the finger movements, and the proprioceptive stimulation from the finger movement itself" (p. 302). For a third person, Brenda, he noted that her "self-stimulatory behavior consisted of twirling objects such as a feather or string of beads in front of her eyes" (p. 302). From this assessment, Rincover developed his interventions. For Reggie, treatment involved the elimination of the auditory feedback from Reggie's plate spinning by installing a carpet atop the table in the classroom that muffled the sound but that was hard enough to allow for the plate to spin. Taking away the sound removed a reinforcer from a previously reinforced response (i.e., sensory extinction). For Robert and Brenda, a small vibratory mechanism was taped to the back of their hands that gave the proprioceptive feedback but did not physically restrict self-stimulatory behavior. And finally for all three children, to complete the extinction procedure, the visual consequences for each was removed by introducing a blindfold. (This latter component is restrictive and was shared for understanding but would require an alternative method of preventing the reinforcer to be found.)

Environmental Safety Considerations

In the following discussion of SIB, we mention safety precautions to take in the classroom unless an individual is to be restrained (a last resort). For ethical reasons, restraints usually are not recommended for SSB students. It is difficult to justify the deliberate restraint of an individual whose behavior is hurting no one. Nevertheless, students who engage in SSBs may incorporate some aspect of the environment as a part of their behavioral syndrome, thus creating a safety risk. Do not permit self-stimulatory students to use sharp objects, breakable items, or damaged toys as a part of a self-stimulatory sequence, for example. Toys that are safe for normal youngsters may present a hazard for a student who will use them inappropriately.

ASSESSMENT OF SIB

Now let's turn to the assessment procedures for SIB, followed by a discussion of interventions for SIB. The data you collect in performing multilevel assessments of SIB will help you do the following:

* Recognize physiological and/or biological factors in SIB
* Analyze the interaction between SIB and environment variables
* Summarize information so that you can get assistance from a behavioral consultant (Check out the Companion Website for defining characteristics of a behavioral consultant.)
* Learn procedures that will prove useful in monitoring progress of subsequent interventions

You may want assistance in conducting a comprehensive behavior analysis; certain health-related information could be provided by the school nurse or physician with help from the student's parents. Complete this step before proceeding with any intervention. Medical history is critical to determining whether the student has recently had or now needs a comprehensive physical and neuropsychiatric examination as well as comprehensive testing for syndromes thought to cause SIB (Lesch-Nyan syndrome, Cornelia de Lange's syndrome). Do not forget about UMOs. It is helpful to keep a daily log of bruises, cuts, and other injuries that may appear as well as of SIBs, such as pica, vomiting, and rumination. Be sure to record any oral or topical medications (e.g., lotion for chapped or scratched skin) administered. Iwata, Pace, Kissel, Nau, and Farber (1990) have made available the Self-Injury Trauma (SIT) scale, which allows the more careful documentation of these injuries.

An environmental analysis calls for several items of information gathered in various settings and demand situations. Figure 10–3 outlines components of an ecological approach (for a more detailed discussion of variables that contribute to SIB, see Iwata, Dorsey, et al. 1994). Because SIB varies within and across individuals, it is critical that you carry out a comprehensive individualized functional analysis (Iwata, Dorsey, et al., 1994).

Naturally, the first item on the form requests a specific definition of the problem behavior or behaviors. Since SIB is rarely confined to one environment, say, school, we have included items that reflect different settings and different times of day. These variables are combined in question 4 in Figure 10–3, which asks for information regarding possible alternative behaviors. Research on SIB individuals suggests that injurious behavior may be decreased by reinforcing alternative, noninjurious behaviors (Mulick, Hoyt, Rojahn, & Schroeder, 1978). Therefore, it is important for you to consider alternative behaviors to substitute for SIB.

Question 5 asks for demands on the individual. Again, studies have indicated that levels of SIB may be altered by the presence of demands (Iwata, Pace, et al., 1994) or by activities the student finds particularly stressful. Questions regarding consequences for SIB (7 and 8) reflect the need for a thorough understanding of what has maintained, reduced, or increased SIB in the past. Before designing and initiating a new intervention, your consultant and multidisciplinary team should examine closely the data on prior attempts at intervention (see question 9).

A completed environmental analysis should provide your intervention team with specific settings, time, and adult actions for further examination. For a more complete review of SIB research on environmental variables, see Schroeder et al. (2002).

INTERVENTION STRATEGIES FOR SIB

The following are strategies to decrease self-injurious behaviors, some of which you will be able to implement by yourself, while other programs will require outside help.

Environmental Changes

As mentioned earlier, your multidisciplinary team, treatment team, or behavioral consultant may want to alter one or more of the following antecedent circumstances in order to determine their effects on SIB:

* The demands placed on an individual during a specific part of the daily routine (or the reinforcement the student receives for compliance with that demand)

Student ______________________________ Age ______________

Date ______________________ Teacher ______________________

1. What is (are) this student's self-injurious behavior(s)? Describe specifically.

____

____

2. List all the settings in which this behavior is exhibited.

____

____

3. At what times of day does the student engage in the SIB?

____

____

4. What activities could the student engage in, throughout the day, if he were not injuring himself?

Time	Alternative Activity
7–am	
8–9	
9–10	
10–11	
11–12	
12–1 pm	
1–2	
2–3	
3–4	
4–5	
5–6	
6–7	
7–8	
8–9	
9–10	
10–11 pm	

5. What demands are made of the student immediately prior to episodes of SIB? (Use an ABC analysis to determine this.)

Demand	Setting	SIB

FIGURE 10–3 Environmental Analysis Forms for SIB

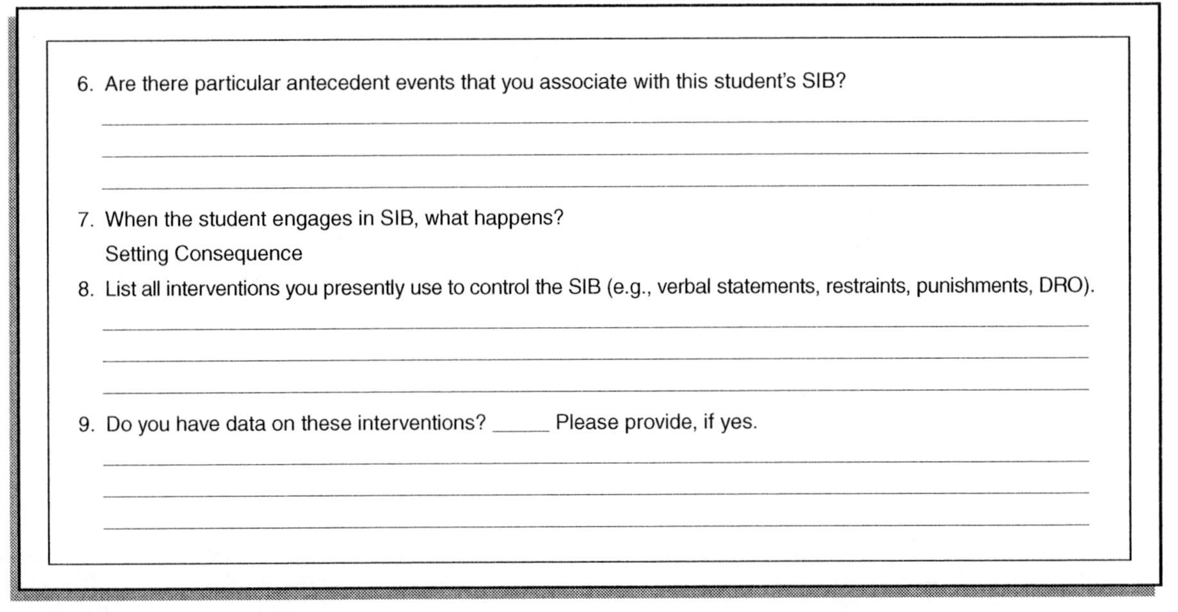
6. Are there particular antecedent events that you associate with this student's SIB?

____

____

____

7. When the student engages in SIB, what happens?
   Setting Consequence

8. List all interventions you presently use to control the SIB (e.g., verbal statements, restraints, punishments, DRO).

____

____

____

9. Do you have data on these interventions? _____ Please provide, if yes.

____

____

____

FIGURE 10–3 (Continued)

- The available, reinforced alternative activities that the student can engage in
- The physical restraints (mechanical) used with a client and the schedule for applying and removing them (see Favell, McGimsey, & Jones, 1978)
- The student's daily routine, with the possibility of rearranging stressful events

It is imperative to remember that any such alteration depends on a thorough analysis of each individual's behavior.

Environmental Safety Considerations

To prevent a self-injurious student from further harm, take safety precautions in your classroom. Remove any chemicals that may be toxic (e.g., typewriter correction fluid, cleaning supplies, medications, and paint). Remove sharp objects such as scissors, pens, needles, paper clips, and thumbtacks. It may be necessary to cushion hard surfaces if the student pounds them with head or body.

> Take the position that a self-injurious child or adolescent does not possess the judgment necessary to determine what might be dangerous.

DRO

Again, DRO is a term frequently cited in descriptions of programs for SIB (or SSB) individuals. Research has not proven DRO as successful as the "suppression interventions" in eliminating SIB (Iwata, Pace, et al., 1994), but we often rely on DRO to teach the student vitally needed alternative behaviors (Jenson, Rovner, Cameron, Peterson, & Kesler, 1985).

In some programs based on the DRO procedure, reinforcement is administered for intervals of time during which certain behaviors incompatible with SIB are exhibited (e.g., putting together a puzzle without biting one's hand). These programs are then termed DRI, or differential reinforcement of incompatible behaviors. Table 10-3 provides a step-by-step procedure for conducting a DRO or DRI program.

TABLE 10–3 Guidelines for Using a DRO or DRI Procedure

1. Set aside a block of time (e.g., 15 minutes daily or several such times per day) to conduct the training.
2. Arrange for a staff member to spend time with (or near, in later stages) the student during these sessions.
3. Record rate-per-minute baseline data on the problem behaviors and chart them. Continue recording data throughout the program.
4. Select an appropriate behavior to reinforce (preferably one that is incompatible with the problem behavior). Be sure to choose a behavior that you can count easily by the frequency or interval method. If you cannot count it, you will have difficulty knowing when to reinforce it!
5. Select a powerful reinforcer for the student. Be sure you can remove the reinforcer from the student if response cost is to be incorporated into the procedure.
6. Gather the reinforcers, a container for them (e.g., clear plastic cup), and a data record sheet and ask the student to sit across the table from you.
7. Say, "It's time to work (play)," and give the student the necessary items to engage in the appropriate (other) behavior (e.g., ballpoint pens to assemble and place in a tray, a toy car to roll toward you, a favorite stuffed animal to cuddle without self-stimulating).
8. Beginning with a "rich" schedule of reinforcement, provide the student with the reinforcer for each appropriate "other" behavior (each pen assembled) or for a brief interval of appropriate behavior (e.g., 5 to 10 seconds of play with the teacher using a toy). If you use response cost, keep the reinforcers in the container until the end of the session.
9. If you desire, you can implement a response cost procedure at the same time. For this procedure, take away one (or two) of the reinforcers at each instance of the problem behavior after saying, "NO (*problem behavior*)!"
10. As the data indicate progress (e.g., a reduction in the response per minute of problem behaviors), you can "thin" the reinforcement schedule: you reinforce less frequently and require longer and longer intervals of time spent in the appropriate "other" behavior.
11. Be sure to praise the student at each time of reinforcement and to change the reinforcer if it no longer seems effective.
12. Do not use the verbal reprimand, "NO (*problem behavior*)!" at times when you cannot remove the reinforcer until you see definite, stable behavior improvement.

NCR

As described in the SSB section earlier, NCR, or a response-independent or time-based delivery of stimuli with known reinforcing properties, avoids the extinction component that is a necessary part of a differential reinforcement procedure. For a more careful procedural analysis of NCR, see Roscoe et al. (2003).

Interruption and Redirection

There are two forms of **interruption and redirection** that have been shown to be effective in treatment of SIB. Vocal verbal interruption redirection is saying something that gets a student's attention, like her name, and then redirection to engage in a different behavior, often an incompatible response. Physical interruption paired with vocal verbal interruption and redirection is a second form of these intervention techniques. Physical interruption is a least intrusive physical contact, like placing your hand on a student's shoulder while moving toward the material the student has been redirected to.

Weakening SIB

Extinction. An outgrowth of the functional analysis work that has occurred over the past two decades has been the furthering of our understanding of procedures involving extinction. The seminal work is by Iwata, Pace, Cowdery, and Miltenberger (1994). These authors demonstrated the importance of knowing the "function" of a behavior like SIB or SSB because in the absence of knowing the functional relationship, how would you know what to reinforce or, in the case of extinction, what reinforcer to remove from a previously reinforced response? Their table on page 133

of their 1994 paper is a must for understanding any intervention designed to treat SIB. Briefly, this table shows the expected effectiveness of an extinction procedure for social positive reinforcement (i.e., attention), social negative reinforcement (i.e., escape), and automatic reinforcement (e.g., sensory) where the extinction procedures would be ignoring, maintaining demand, and removing a sensory reinforcer, respectively.

Effort. The old adage "life is hard and then you die" speaks to the natural effects effort has on our behavior. Friman and Poling (1995) shared with us the basic and applied research findings on the use of effort to weaken behavior. For instance, interruption and redirection can be paired with effort where redirection requires added effort contingent on a student's engaging in SIB. Habit reversal is an example of a technique developed originally in the early 1970s and procedurally examined more recently that relies on effort to weaken repetitive behavior (see Rapp, Miltenberger, & Long, 1998). In this technique, several procedures are combined contingent on a student's engaging in SIB or SSB to increase his or her awareness of the behavior and to learn an alternative incompatible behavior relying on effort to weaken the SIB or SSB.

Restraint Devices

SIB is sometimes treated through the application of various kinds of restraints (Irvin, Thompson, Turner, & Williams, 1998). The disadvantages associated with restraints are that (a) they do not teach new behaviors or eliminate the targeted ones, (b) they interfere with learning alternative behaviors (and may interfere with hearing and other senses), and (c) the appearance of a restraint may cause others to ostracize the child (Baumeister & Rollings, 1976).

Irvin et al. (1998) demonstrated the use of a restraint procedure that allows for systematic fading and, consequently, decreases the mobility concern. This case study illustrates utilizing increased response effort to reduce chronic hand mouthing with adjustable arm restraints. The arm restraints altered the amount of physical effort necessary to engage in hand mouthing, which successfully reduced levels of hand mouthing in children with profound disabilities. Hanley, Piazza, Keeney, Blakeley-Smith, and Worsdell (1998) also looked at the effects of effort using a different form of restraint in treating SIB and furthered their procedural analysis in a paper published in 2000 (Zhou, Goff, & Iwata, 2000).

Movement Suppression Procedure

The **movement suppression procedure** is a variation of time-out from reinforcement in which the student is punished for any movement or verbalization while in time-out (Rolider & Van Houten, 1985; Rolider, Williams, Cummings, & Van Houten, 1991). In the Rolider and Van Houten study, DRO alone (praise and candy every 15 minutes of no targeted behavior) was compared with movement suppression time-out plus DRO. The movement suppression intervention consisted of the parents or school staff placing the child in the corner, restraining his movements manually, and directing him not to move or talk. This lasted for 3 minutes. This procedure was replicated with slight modifications across cases of SIB in two other children; all reports were successful. If you are on a team that is deciding which of several related interventions to try, review the Rolider et al. studies (1985, 1991); they provide comparative information on movement suppression plus DRO versus other treatments (e.g., contingent restraint, exclusionary time-out, corner time-out, and time-out in a wheelchair, respectively).

Remember that some states have opted to prohibit selected treatment procedures based on their understanding of aversive and nonaversive procedures for protection (see Repp & Singh, 1990). To direct both the ethical and the appropriate application of behavior treatment, Van Houten et al. (1988) propose that individuals who are recipients or potential recipients of treatment designed to change their behavior have the right to a therapeutic environment, services whose overriding goal is personal welfare, treatment by a competent behavior analyst, programs that teach functional skills, behavioral assessment and ongoing evaluation, and the most effective treatment procedure available. Our case study illustrates this kind of planning.

SUMMARY

This chapter offers you many suggestions for prevention and intervention strategies when dealing with SSB and SIB.

- Be positive by emphasizing skill building with instructional design and delivery techniques that increase the likelihood of developing a happy learner.
- Be supportive by developing schedules of noncontingent and positive reinforcement sufficient to build alternative behaviors.
- Be careful in your functional analysis of SSB and SIB.
- Be sure to incorporate more complex motivative operations like physical illness or, more commonly, the effects of deprivation and satiation.
- Be accurate in your continuous monitoring of treatment effects.
- Be proactive in your implementation of prevention strategies.
- Be skilled in your implementation of intervention procedures.
- Be caring in your management of your and other staff's performance in the implementation of the procedures outlined in this chapter.

COME INTO MY CLASSROOM: A CASE STUDY

In this case study, we illustrate how a behavior plan might address behaviors. This plan was developed in a diagnostic center for use in other settings.

Amanda Sample's Behavior Treatment Plan

I PROGRAM INFORMATION

A. **Objective Statement:** A. Sample will increase her rate of practical say and do behavior acquisition by a rate of 1.25 with a fourfold decrease in any behaviors of concern.

B. **Implementation Date:** (date) or on approvals

C. **Responsible Person(s):** (must be a designated person)

II BEHAVIORAL ASSESSMENT SUMMARY

A. **Definition of Behaviors of Concern:**

1. **Self-Injurious Behavior (SIB):** Head hitting or contacting of head to object or object to head with sufficient intensity to cause skin indentation or redness.
2. **Excessive Motoric Behavior (EMB):** Away from designated area, climbing furniture, threshold crossing, quicker body movements—"higher energy"; this includes "darting" or the sudden onset of running from a designated area.
3. **Disruption (D):** Includes property destruction, slamming, throwing objects, striking, and pushing others.
4. **Thwarting (T):** Situations where A. Sample says or does something to get something she wants but has to wait or is denied immediate access.

B. **Frequency/Severity of BOCs:** Observations initiated on A. Sample's arrival in the ANY classroom showed high rates of SIB and EMB, in particular, head hitting and darting. Tallies of this movement have been initiated. Other related data being gathered by the ANY classroom staff related to the skill acquisition component of this treatment plan and A. Sample's developing IEP will be examined as part of treatment effectiveness data. A. Sample also shows counts of striking others, primarily staff, from behind, and she grasps her ears from time to time, which may be an indication of discomfort. Counts will be shared as soon as available, and the Standard Celeration Chart will be used to show a daily count of SIB and other behavior. Check out the Companion Website for more information on the chart and precision teaching.

C. **Functional Analysis:** Motivation for A. Sample's behaviors/symptoms that resulted in this intensive behavioral health service are being examined with a functional-dimensional approach that "involves organizing diagnoses according to behavioral processes (therefore functional), and these processes are seen as continual (therefore dimensional rather than categorical)" (Friman, Hayes, & Wilson, 1998). The analysis will continue until evidence for a relationship is determined or demonstrated to be multidetermined. Situations of the home and classroom were used initially for descriptive analysis as an initial phase to the more intensive functional analysis. The outcome of this analysis showed that, on average, SIB occurred in 80% of the observed intervals in the demand situation. We also examined the role of proximity of staff to the student, and similarly the demand condition resulted in the highest count of SIB, EMB, and D. With the manipulation of proximity, demand and attention condition showed higher rates when staff were within arm's reach versus 4 to 6 feet away. Rates in the demand condition were four times greater than any other condition.

For now (analysis will continue), the working best guess for what is motivating A. Sample is avoidance behavior or the moving away from a situation by her doing the movement or by making others move away. A. Sample's behavior of concern pulls people in, which is usually thought of as "attention seeking" or positive reinforcement, but a more thorough analysis suggests that A. Sample pulls people in to help her get away from a circumstance. The most obvious motivative operation occurs as the pace of instruction slows and/or as transitions are initiated. It is also likely that A. Sample is missing the opportunity to get what she wants when she wants it, which is thwarting, and a natural part of living life increases her motivation to escape a situation. Until more detailed information is made available, this will be the motivation analysis that guides A. Sample's treatment.

D. **Associated Medical or Psychiatric Factors:** (See Previous Evaluations and documentation—section to be completed)

E. **Previous Treatments:** To be listed

III BEHAVIOR TREATMENT PLAN

A. **Skill Acquisition:**

1. **Learning and Treatment Occasion:** (See IEP and specialty treatment plans, like speech and language evaluations)
   a) **Learning Skills**—Answering on signal, following along with instruction, asking for help when

needed, following instruction quickly

b) **Organization Skills**—At seat on time, has all materials, keeps work space clean, puts materials away

c) **Conduct**—Asks permission to change something, talks with appropriate voice, uses hands for task performance, stays in seat or designated area

d) **Activity Skills**—Determined by task analysis

2. **Verbal Behavior and Learning Skills**—with ongoing functional language assessment, treatment will be introduced within instructional situation and natural environment to include the following:

a) **Mand Training**—Establishing operation, verbal prompt to respond, nonverbal stimulus, and echoic stimulus.

b) **Tact with Motivation**—Establishing operation, nonverbal stimulus, verbal stimulus to respond, and echoic stimulus.

c) **Tact without Motivation**—Nonverbal stimulus, verbal prompt to respond, and echoic stimulus.

d) **Receptive Along with Tacts**—Touch the _____; or, once tact occurs place two items on table and ask, "Give me the _____."

3. **All Academic Skills Will Be Built Using the Morningside Model of Generative Instruction.** Check out the Companion Website for additional information on the model and outcome data.

B. **Prevention:**

1. Latham's "The Power of Positive Parenting" and 10 Tool Skills, from his original work on eight skills every teacher should know, paired with ongoing functional-dimensional analysis.

✓ **Staying Close:** You create a safe, positive environment and establish yourself as a source of caring, empathy, and positive consequences.

✓ **Giving Positive Consequences:** You focus primarily on building up appropriate behaviors with positive consequences.

✓ **Ignoring Junk Behavior:** You carefully ignore any age typical behavior that may be annoying but is not harmful to any person or property.

✓ **Ignoring the Junk Behavior of One Person and Giving Positive Consequences for the Appropriate Behavior of Another Person:** You carefully ignore junk behavior of one person while giving positive consequences for the appropriate behavior of another person.

✓ **Stop-Redirect-Give Positive Consequences:** You stop a person's inappropriate behavior; redirect them to a different, logically related behavior; and show you like it by giving positive consequences when the person does it.

✓ **Setting Expectations:** You let the person know what behavior is expected and what the consequences will be for meeting or not meeting the expectations.

- ✓ **Using a Contract:** You make a written agreement with the person that identifies positive expectations and consequences.
- ✓ **Time-Out:** You interrupt a person's out of control behavior to minimize consequences and allow you to attend to appropriate behaviors after the person has maintained a brief period of calm.
- ✓ **ABCs of Assessing Behavior:** You look at what happens before and right after the person's behavior to figure out why the behavior is happening and what you can do to change it.
- ✓ **Consulting Skills of Staff:** Counselors develop strategies to assist families, staff, and teachers in their homes or schools to practice positive parenting skills with regard to specific behavior problems.

2. **Noncontingent Reinforcement:** Both positive and negative reinforcement delivered based on time initially offered every 5 minutes and then faded to an average of every 10 minutes.
3. **Routine of Daily Living:** Keeping a similar daily schedule, especially for high-demand situations, will lessen distress or motivation to avoid. (An attempt will be made to use minimal prompts for schedule to better match a more typical system.)

C. **Intervention:**

1. **Extinction escape** is the procedure for unsafe behavior. For this procedure, an identified negative reinforcer that was once available is taken away. For example, if staff is in a situation where A. Sample's wants cannot be met, A. Sample begins to become disruptive; the situation needs to continue as close to unchanged as possible. Treatment is to interrupt or prevent behavior of concern while continuing to present situation until goal or part of goal is accomplished.
2. **Going too far protection** is an outcome of the approach recommended previously that is based on lots of encouragement. "Things can, of course, go too far. Sometimes preoccupied, sometimes not understanding, we make mistakes and end up having to deal with an emotional outburst that no rational treatment can possibly overcome. And then, too, emergencies arise that have to be dealt with immediately or else somebody will be hurt. Punishment [stopping behavior of concern] may indeed be necessary to put a quick halt to a dangerous situation. These are not occasions to be concerned about. In a relationship based on strong and frequent positive reinforcement, an infrequent punishment is not going to cause any long-term damage. If these mistakes or emergencies start to happen frequently, however they are danger signals, indicating a deteriorating relationship" (Sidman, 1989, p. 217). (Techniques like waiting at site of activity or protective physical intervention are to be considered when we make these mistakes.)

a) **Protective Guidance and Support:** A. Sample's SIB and EMB is rapid and intense and at times not responsive to interruption/redirection. As a result of the risk demonstrated by A. Sample's SIB and EMB, in particular, head hitting or darting, interruption/redirection will include graduated guidance as needed. *If guidance is ineffective at time of immediate episode, a protective support involving (an approved, trained, and supervised technique) will be implemented. The duration of this support is to be 30 seconds, unless A. Sample's response remains intense preventing a safe discontinuation. Support is not to exceed 2 minutes without an attempt to discontinue physical contact for at least 30 seconds while maintaining close proximity. Return immediately to extinction (escape) procedure. Hold a debriefing at the end of the school day and determine possible adjustment to schedule outlined in the Prevention section.*

b) **Documentation:** Support staff will complete ongoing assessment material for measuring behaviors of concern—most likely with a scatter plot and charts. Staff will also document events on all agency-required forms. This documentation includes a written record of the implementation of protective support. Principal and designated family member will be informed of these procedures and contacted if support goes beyond 30 seconds and after first contact, as directed by family.

OTHER INFORMATION

Preference Assessment/Reported Likes

A preference assessment will be ongoing with varied items introduced in a choose-one-from-two format with multiple presentations of each item paired with other items to determine preference of item or a select-one-from-many format. Formal sessions, if needed, are 20 to 25 minutes in length and will be conducted during each observation with A. Sample until known preferences are documented.

Tools	Library
Building things	Quiet
Music	Magazines
Foods and beverages	Movies/videos

Dislikes =

Worthy Care

A. **Parent and Staff Training:** "Talk about it," "Doing it," and "Problem solving"

B. **Performance Management:** BTP supervision who, what, and how

IV RECOMMENDATIONS

A. For a positive encouragement therapy like the one proposed in this plan, the positive effects will be cumulative—they will be small and build over time, especially in supporting someone like A. Sample who has a long history of learning to live her life by counterconditioning situations she finds coercive. As a result, the initial implementation of this plan requires 1 staff to 2 children staff support for at least 6 months. (A. Sample will ultimately determine her own level of need like we all do, but a good guess is this treatment will take effect over 2 or so years, if coercion can be avoided.)

B. A second recommendation is that all efforts be made to continuously conduct the functional-dimensional analysis alluded to previously; otherwise, we will keep working only with our best guesses for what motivates A. Sample to do the things that concern us.

Signatures

____________________ __________

Responsible Person Date

____________________ __________

Principal or Responsible Administrator Date

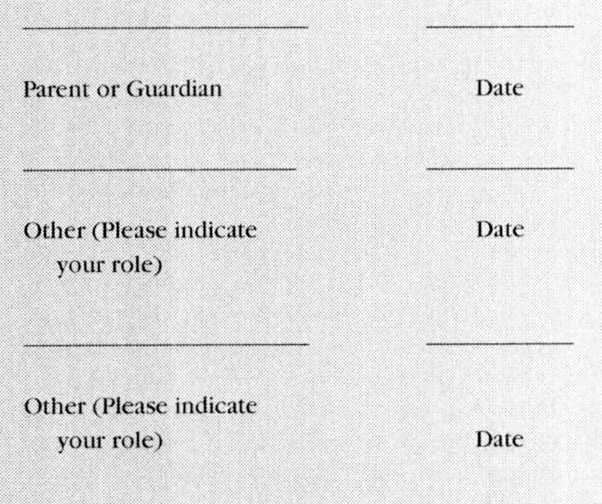

____________________ __________

Parent or Guardian Date

____________________ __________

Other (Please indicate your role) Date

____________________ __________

Other (Please indicate your role) Date

Case Study Reflection Questions

1. What makes the skill acquisition of Amanda's behavior treatment plan the primary component of the plan?
2. What is the function of Amanda's SIB and related behaviors?
3. What are the effects of adhering to a similar daily schedule and only making changes carefully?
4. What happens when things just go too far?

DISCUSSION/APPLICATION IDEAS

1. What are the steps in conducting a functional analysis for SSB and SIB?
2. What are the major concepts of a perceptual reinforcement theory of SSB and SIB?
3. How would you use sensory extinction to reduce the auditory SSB of a child with developmental delays?
4. How is DRO best used for individuals with stereotypic behaviors? Will it suppress the stereotypic behaviors?
5. How does NCR compare to DRO?
6. What criteria should you meet before trying an aversive or restrictive intervention?
7. What seems to be the most effective reinforcer for a child who engages in SSB and SIB?

NOTES

1. Check out the Companion Website for detailed information about the evolution of the science of human behavior that is the foundation of this chapter.

REFERENCES

Ahearn, W. H., Clark, K. M., Gardenier, N. C., Chung, B. I., & Dube, W. V. (2003). Persistence of stereotypic behavior: Examining the effects of external reinforcers. *Journal of Applied Behavior Analysis, 36,* 439–447.

Baer, D. M. (1990). Exploring the controlling conditions of importance. *The Behavior Analyst, 13,* 183–186.

Baumeister, A. A. (1978). Origins and control of stereotyped movements. In C. E. Meyers (Ed.), *Quality of life in severely and profoundly mentally retarded people: Research foundations for improvement* (AAMD Monograph, No. 3). Washington, DC: American Association on Mental Deficiency.

Baumeister, A. A., & Rollings, P. (1976). Self-injurious behavior. In N. R. Ellis (Ed.), *International review of research in mental retardation* (Vol. 8, pp. 1–34). New York: Academic Press.

Berkson, G., McQuiston, S., Jacobson, J. W., Eyman, R., & Borthwick, S. (1985). The relationship between age and stereotyped behaviors. *Mental Retardation, 23,* 31–33.

Bodfish, J. W., (2004). *Stereotypy Checklist (STY-C).*

Bodfish, J. W., Crawford, T. W., Powell, S. B., Parker, D. E., Golden, R. N., & Lewis, M. H. (1995). Compulsions in adults with mental retardation: Prevalence, phenomonolgy and co-morbidity with stereotypy and self-injury. *American Journal of Mental Retardation, 100,* 183–192.

Bodfish, J. W., & Lewis, M. H. (2002). Self-injury and comorbid behaviors in developmental, neurological, psychiatric, and genetic disorders. In S. R. Schroeder, M. Oster-Granite, & T. Thompson (Eds.), *Self-injurious behavior: Gene-brain-behavior relationships* (pp. 23–39). Washington, DC: American Psychological Association.

Brown, K. A., Wacker, D. P., Derby, M., Peck, S. M., Richman, D. M., Sasso, G. M., et al. (2000). Evaluating the effects of functional communication training in the presence and absence of establishing operations. *Journal of Applied Behavior Analysis, 33*(1), 53–57.

Carr, E. G. (1977). The origins of self-injurious behavior: A review of some hypotheses. *Psychological Bulletin, 84,* 800–816.

Carr, E. G., & Durand, V. M. (1985). Reducing behavior problems through functional communication training. *Journal of Applied Behavior Analysis, 18*(2), 111–126.

Carr, E. G., & McDowell, J. J. (1980). Social control of self-injurious behavior of organic etiology. *Behavior Therapy, 11,* 402–409.

Commonwealth of Pennsylvania, Department of Public Welfare. (2002). *The use of seclusion and restraint in mental health facilities and programs (OMHSAS-02-01).* Harrisburg, PA: Bureau of Policy and Program Development.

Dunlap, G., & Koegel, R. L. (1980). Motivation of autistic children through stimulus variation. *Journal of Applied Behavior Analysis, 13,* 619–627.

Durand, V. M., & Carr, E. G. (1985). Self-injurious behavior: Motivating conditions and guidelines for treatment. *School Psychology Review, 14*(2), 171–176.

Durand, V. M., & Crimmins, D. B. (1988). Identifying the variables maintaining self-injury. *Journal of Autism and Developmental Disorders, 18,* 99–117.

Favell, J. (1982). *The treatment of self-injurious behavior.* New York: American Association for Behavior Therapy.

Favell, J. E., McGimsey, J. F., & Jones, M. L. (1978). The use of physical restraint in the treatment of self-injury and as positive reinforcement. *Journal of Applied Behavior Analysis, 11,* 225–241.

Favell, J. E., McGimsey, J. F., & Schell, R. M. (1982). Treatment of self-injury by providing alternate sensory activities. *Analysis and Intervention in Developmental Disabilities, 2,* 83–104.

Friman, P. C., Hayes, S. C., & Wilson, K. G. (1998). Why behavior analysts should study emotion: The example of anxiety. *Journal of Applied Behavior Analysis, 31*(1), 137–156.

Friman, P. C., & Poling, A. (1995). Making life easier with effort: Basic findings and applied research on response effort. *Journal of Applied Behavior Analysis, 28,* 583–590.

Hagopian, L. P., Fisher, W. W., Sullivan, M. T., Acquisto, J., & LeBlanc, L. A. (1998). Effectiveness of functional communication training with and without extinction and punishment: A summary of 21 inpatient cases. *Journal of Applied Behavior Analysis, 31,* 211–235.

Hanley, G. P., Iwata, B. A., Thompson, R. H., & Lindberg, J. S. (2000). A component analysis of "stereotypy as reinforcement" for alternative behavior. *Journal of Applied Behavior Analysis, 33,* 285–297.

Hanley, G. P., Piazza, C. C., Keeney, K. M., Blakeley-Smith, A. B., & Worsdell, A. S. (1998). Effects of wrist weights on self-injurious and adaptive behavior. *Journal of Applied Behavior Analysis, 31*(2), 307–310.

Irvin, D. S., Thompson, T. J., Turner, W. D., & Williams, D. E. (1998). Utilizing increased response effort to reduce chronic hand mouthing. *Journal of Applied Behavior Analysis, 31,* 375–385.

Iwata, B. A., Dorsey, M. F., Slifer, K. J., Bauman, K. E., & Richman, G. S. (1994). Toward a functional analysis of self-injury. *Journal of Applied Behavior Analysis, 27,* 197–209. (Reprinted from *Analysis and Intervention in Developmental Disabilities, 2,* 3–20, 1982)

Iwata, B. A., Pace, G. M., Cowdery, G. E., & Miltenberger, M. G. (1994). What makes extinction work: An analysis of procedural form and function. *Journal of Applied Behavior Analysis, 27,* 131–144.

Iwata, B. A., Pace, G. M., Dorsey, M. F., Zarcone, J. R., Vollmer, T. R., Smith, R. G., et al. (1994). The functions of self-injurious behavior: An experimental-epidemiological analysis. *Journal of Applied Behavioral Analysis, 27,* 215–240.

Iwata, B. A., Pace G. M., Kissel, R. C., Nau, P. A., & Farber, J. M. (1990). The Self-Injury Trauma (SIT) scale: A method for quantifying surface tissue damage caused by self-injurious behavior. *Journal of Applied Behavior Analysis, 23,* 99–110.

Jenson, W. R., Rovner, L., Cameron, S., Peterson, B. P., & Kesler, J. (1985). Reduction of self-injurious behavior in an autistic girl using a multifaceted treatment program. *Journal of Behavior Therapy and Experimental Psychiatry, 16,* 77–80.

Johnson, K. (1999). Reliability and comorbidity measures of repetitive movement disorders in children and adolescents with severe mental retardation. *Dissertation Abstracts International, 59*(9-B), 5066.

Keller, F. S., & Schoenfeld, W. N. (1995/1950). *Principles of psychology.* Acton, MA: Copley Publishing Group for the B. F. Skinner Foundation.

Kennedy, C. H. (2002). Evolution of stereotypy into self-injury. In S. R. Schroeder, M. Oster-Granite, & T. Thompson (Eds.), *Self-injurious behavior: Gene-brain-behavior relationships* (pp. 133–143). Washington, DC: American Psychological Association.

Kennedy, C. H., & Itkonen, T. (1993). Effects of setting events on the problem behavior of students with severe disabilities. *Journal of Applied Behavior Analysis, 26*(3), 321–327.

Lewis, M. H., & Bodfish, J. B. (1998). Repetitive behavior disorders in autism. Special issue: "Autism" mental retardation. *Development Disabilities Research Review, 4,* 80–90.

Lovaas, O. I., & Favell, J. E. (1987). Protection for clients undergoing aversive/restrictive interventions. *Education and Treatment of Children, 10*(4), 311–325.

Lovaas, O. I., Newsom, C., & Hickman, C. (1987). Self-stimulatory behavior and perceptual reinforcement. *Journal of Applied Behavior Analysis, 20*(1), 45–68.

Maurice, C. (Ed.), Green, G., & Luce, S. (Co-Eds.). (1996). *Behavioral intervention for young children with autism: A manual for parents and professionals.* Austin, TX: PRO-ED.

Michael, J. L. (1982). Distinguishing between discriminative and motivational functions of stimuli. *Journal of the Experimental Analysis of Behavior, 37,* 149–155.

Michael, J. L. (1993). Concepts and principles of behavior analysis. Kalamazoo, MI: *Association for Behavior Analysis.*

Michael, J. (2002, May). *Motivation and early language training: A tutorial.* Paper presented at the meeting of the Association for Behavior Analysis, Toronto.

Mulick, J., Hoyt, R., Rojahn, J., & Schroeder, S. (1978). Reduction of a "nervous habit" in a profoundly retarded youth by increasing toy play: A case study. *Journal of Behavior Therapy and Experimental Psychiatry, 9,* 381–385.

O'Brien, F. (1981). Treating self-stimulatory behavior. In J. L. Matson & J. R. McCartney (Eds.), *Handbook of behavior modification with the mentally retarded* (pp. 117–150). New York: Plenum.

Piazza, C., Adelinis, J. D., Hanley, G. P., Goh, H. L., & Delia, M. D. (2000). An evaluation of the effects of matched stimulation on behaviors maintained by automatic reinforcement. *Journal of Applied Behavior Analysis, 33,* 13–27.

Piazza, C. C., Fisher, W. W., Hanley, G. P., LeBlanc, L. A., Worsdell, A. S., Lindauer, S. E., et al. (1998). Treatment of pica through multiple analyses of its reinforcing functions. *Journal of Applied Behavior Analysis, 31,* 165–189.

Pyles, D. A. M., Riordan, M. M., & Bailey, J. S. (1997). The stereotypy analysis: An instrument for examining environmental variables associated with differential rates of stereotypic behavior. *Research in Developmental Disabilities, 18,* 11–38.

Rapp, J. T., Miltenberger, R. G., & Long, E. S. (1998). Augmenting simplified habit reversal with an awareness enhancement device: Preliminary findings. *Journal of Applied Behavior Analysis, 31,* 665-668.

Repp, A. C., & Singh, N. N. (1990). *Perspectives on the use of nonaversive and aversive interventions for person with developmental disabilities.* Sycamore, IL: Sycamore Publishing.

Rincover, A. (1978). Sensory extinction: A procedure for eliminating self-stimulatory behavior in developmentally disabled children. *Journal of Abnormal Child Psychology, 6,* 299-310.

Rincover, A., & Devany, J. (1982). The application of sensory extinction procedures to self-injury. *Analysis and Intervention in Developmental Disabilities, 2,* 67-81.

Rincover, A., & Newsom, C. D. (1985). The relative motivational properties of sensory and edible reinforcers in teaching autistic children. *Journal of Applied Behavior Analysis, 18*(3), 237-248.

Rojahn, J., & Esbensen, A. J. (2002). Epidemiology of self-injurious behavior in mental retardation: A review. In S. R. Schroeder, M. Oster-Granite, & T. Thompson (Eds.), *Self-injurious behavior: Gene-brain-behavior relationships* (pp. 41-77). Washington, DC: American Psychological Association.

Rolider, A., & Van Houten, R. (1985). Movement suppression time-out for undesirable behavior in psychotic and severely developmentally delayed children. *Journal of Applied Behavior Analysis, 18*(4), 275-288.

Rolider, A., Williams, L., Cummings, A., & Van Houten, R. (1991). The use of a brief movement restriction procedure to eliminate severe inappropriate behavior. *Journal of Behavior Therapy and Experimental Psychiatry, 22,* 23-30.

Roscoe, E. M., Iwata, B. A., & Rand, M. S. (2003). Effects of reinforcer consumption and magnitude on response rates during noncontingent reinforcement. *Journal of Applied Behavior Analysis, 36,* 525-539.

Schroeder, S. R., Oster-Granite, M., & Thompson, T. (Eds.). (2002). *Self-injurious behavior: Gene-brain-behavior relationships.* Washington, DC: American Psychological Association.

Sidman, M. (1989). *Coercion and its fallout.* Boston: Authors Cooperative.

Sturmey, P. (1994). Assessing the functions of aberrant behaviors: A review of psychometric instruments. *Journal of Autism and Developmental Disorders, 24,* 293-304.

Teitelbaum, P. (1977). Levels of integration of the operant. In J. E. R. Staddon & W. K. Honig (Eds.), *Handbook of operant behavior* (pp. 7-27). Upper Saddle River, NJ: Merrill/Prentice Hall.

Thompson, R. H., & Iwata, B. A. (2000). Response acquisition under direct and indirect contingencies of reinforcement. *Journal of Applied Behavior Analysis, 33,* 1-11.

Van Houten, R., Axelrod, S., Bailey, J., Favell, J. E., Foxx, R. M., Iwata, B. A., et al. (1988). The right to effective behavioral treatment. *Journal of Applied Behavior Analysis, 21,* 381-384.

Vollmer, T. R. (1994). The concept of automatic reinforcement: Implications for behavioral research in developmental disabilities. *Research in Developmental Disabilities, 15,* 187-207.

Vollmer, T. R., Iwata, B. A., Zarcone, J. R., Smith, R. G., & Mazaleski, J. L. (1993). The role of attention in the treatment of attention-maintained self-injurious behavior: Noncontingent reinforcement and differential reinforcement of other behavior. *Journal of Applied Behavior Analysis, 26,* 9-21.

Vollmer, T. R., Marcus, B., Ringdahl, J. E., & Roane, H. S. (1995). Progressing from brief assessments to extended experimental analyses in the evaluation of aberrant behavior. *Journal of Applied Behavior Analysis, 28,* 561-576.

Williams, J. A., Koegel, R. L., & Egel, A. L. (1981). Response-reinforcer relationships and improved learning in autistic children. *Journal of Applied Behavior Analysis, 14,* 53-59.

Zarcone, J. R., Rodgers, T. A., Iwata, B. A., Rourke, D. A., & Dorsey, M. F. (1991). Reliability analysis of the Motivation Assessment Scale: A failure to replicate. *Research in Developmental Disabilities, 12,* 349-362.

Zhou, L., Goff, G. A., & Iwata, B. A., (2000). Effects of increased response effort on self-injury and object manipulations as competing responses. *Journal of Applied Behavior Analysis, 33,* 29-40.

PART 3 BEYOND THE CLASSROOM

Chapter 11 Supporting Students with Psychiatric Problems

Chapter 12 Extending Intervention Effects

CHAPTER 11

SUPPORTING STUDENTS WITH PSYCHIATRIC PROBLEMS

Deborah Lange Lambert

OUTLINE

Introduction
Mental Health Prevention Services
Identifying Psychological Problems
Depression
Bipolar Disorder
Suicide
Drug and Alcohol Abuse
Eating Disorders
Anxiety Disorders
Specific Phobias

OBJECTIVES

After completing this chapter, you should be able to

- Identify behaviors of a student showing signs of a psychiatric problem.
- Make an informed referral for a student showing signs of a psychiatric problem.
- Define each of the following terms: depression, bipolar disorder, suicide, drug and alcohol abuse, anorexia nervosa, bulimia nervosa, posttraumatic stress disorder, and anxiety.
- Describe the steps for interviewing a student who may have an emotional problem.

KEY TERMS (refer to the Glossary on the Companion Website for definitions)

anxiety disorders
binge drinking
bipolar disorder
bulimia
depression
drug and alcohol abuse
dysthymia
eating disorders
generalized anxiety disorder
hypersomnia
major depression
mood disorder
obsessive-compulsive disorder
posttraumatic stress disorder
school refusal
separation anxiety disorder
social anxiety disorder
specific phobia
Student Assistance Program
suicide

As our opening case study demonstrates, there are a number of psychiatric problems you may encounter in your classroom. How many identifiable features do you recognize? Are you ready to make a referral?

INTRODUCTION

Good mental health is critical to everyone—as important as physical health in determining quality of life. In an "Action Agenda," the U.S. Surgeon General (2001) declared that 1 in 10 children and adolescents suffers from a mental illness serious enough to impede development and learning. Fewer than one in five of these youngsters receives needed treatment. The Surgeon General estimates that between 2.5 million and 5 million children are not learning in school because of these problems. Clearly, the United States is experiencing a crisis in mental health for children and adolescents.

This chapter addresses psychiatric and emotional problems that require treatment outside of school. It does not attempt to cover the full range of psychiatric problems children and adolescents can experience. Instead, it provides guidance on recognizing and referring the disorders you are most likely to find in school-age children, specifically depression, suicide, drug and alcohol abuse, eating disorders, anxiety disorders, posttraumatic stress disorder, and specific phobias.

Classroom teachers spend a minimum of 6 hours per day with students. This close and consistent proximity enables educators—more than any other professional group—to distinguish between normal and abnormal child and adolescent behavior. When a student's behavior falls outside the norm,

COME INTO MY CLASSROOM: A CASE STUDY

Jeff, 17, felt an overwhelming sadness that dominated his thoughts and emotions. He hated winter because of the incessant dark and cold. Last year he was able to ski and play ice hockey with his friends. This year he couldn't imagine having the energy to exercise outdoors. Instead, he sat alone in his room playing video games.

Jeff had become obsessed with video games. He woke up and turned on his X-Box and TV. He told himself that he was only going to play for an hour. Six hours later he was still playing, having missed breakfast and lunch. He checked his cell phone and saw that three friends had been trying to reach him. He decided not to return anyone's call because he wanted to be alone. Being with his friends would require changing clothes, leaving his video game, and exerting energy.

Jeff's parents were worried because Jeff was constantly exhausted, missing school, and getting bad grades. He rarely left his room and resented his parents when they talked to him about his low energy, desire to isolate, inability to focus, feelings of sadness, and obsession with video games.

His girlfriend became worried too. She noticed Jeff's deepening malaise and urged him to see a school counselor. After months of resisting, Jeff decided to go. He was uncomfortable about opening up to anyone but found that the counselor seemed to understand what he was experiencing. After several sessions, Jeff realized that talking to an insightful adult provided some relief.

As you review this case study, consider some questions: Can you identify the symptoms of a psychological problem? As an educator, what would be your next step? As a school counselor, what would be your next step? Would you anticipate support from the parents? Why? Do you think Jeff is depressed? Why or why not? Would you recommend that Jeff first see a physician or a therapist? Why?

the teacher's job is to identify the problem and help the student receive appropriate assistance.

MENTAL HEALTH PREVENTION SERVICES

The **Student Assistance Program (SAP)** is a response to the many and varied personal problems that students bring to school. The impetus for this initiative was fundamentally educational because students with severe emotional problems are incapable of working to their academic potential.

Student Assistance Programs sprang up in response to the growing concerns about alcohol and other drug use. Now they are broader in scope and help educators identify all kinds of mental health problems. The SAP is not meant to diagnose mental illness or addiction but rather to refer students for counseling or treatment.

A 10-year retrospective study found that students who participated in SAPs increased school attendance and decreased behavior requiring disciplinary action (Fertman, Tarasevich, & Hepler, 2003). For an extensive array of SAP resources, visit the excellent Website of the National Student Assistance Association, formerly the National Association of Student Assistance Professionals, available through the Companion Website.

At the heart of the SAP is the core team—a group of trained school professionals who meet regularly to identify youngsters in need of help and to identify the factors that are inhibiting these students from learning and succeeding.

Your primary role in helping children with serious emotional or psychiatric problems is to refer them to a school counselor, social worker, or psychologist. You also may be called on to collaborate in the student's subsequent referral and treatment.

Children and adolescents receiving special education services are more likely to suffer from psychiatric disorders than students in the mainstream (Garland et al., 2001). Whether you are a regular or a special education teacher, be cognizant of these students' vulnerabilities and be prepared to take action when necessary (Forness, Walker, & Kavale, 2003).

One tool available to you is the school-based wraparound plan. This is an effective device for planning and delivering services to students with needs in multiple life domains. It is not a set of services or an intervention strategy. It is an individualized plan developed by the teachers and counselors closest to the student. It addresses the student's typical day and defines the specific mix of services that the student needs rather than relying on the services traditionally available in the school.

If one of your students receives a wraparound plan, you may be called on to collaborate with members of the student's extended support team. For example, a therapist may ask you to fill out a simple form on a weekly basis. For more information on how to develop a wraparound plan, go to the Companion Website.

IDENTIFYING PSYCHOLOGICAL PROBLEMS

While all youngsters deal with mental health problems from time to time, some issues are more significant than others. The U.S. Surgeon General (2001) identified these as the most serious barriers to learning:

- Stress and anxiety
- Worries about being bullied
- Problems with family or friends
- Loneliness or rejection
- Depression or sadness
- Thoughts of suicide or hurting others
- Concerns about sexuality
- Academic difficulties
- Dropping out
- Alcohol and substance abuse
- Fear of violence, terrorism, and war

Interview Strategy

Gather information before interviewing a student about mental or emotional problems. One tactic is to send a two-page behavioral checklist to each teacher with a list of questions pertaining to the student's academics, behavior, and attitude. Members of the SAP or counseling team can also review the student's current grades, transcript, attendance, and discipline record. This research will prepare you for your interview with the student, who may deny the problems you raise. You will have data to support or challenge the information the student offers.

> Interviewing is a good way to learn about a student's psychological problems. See the student privately and allow enough time (no less than 30 minutes). Let the student know that you are concerned and want to help.

With very young children, you will need to interview the parents. Your school social worker or guidance counselor can help by asking informal questions that address your concerns. One strategy is to share your concerns with the parents and ask if they have observed the same or other problems at home. Sometimes this approach prompts the parents to recall events that may not have seemed problematic at the time. Follow the same guidelines in talking with a parent that you follow in talking with a student. Do not badger, explain the symptom, or criticize! Instead, listen with empathy. You will be in a better position to effect positive change if you focus on building a partnership with a parent without passing judgment.

General Tips for Starting a Conversation

1. If the student hesitates, gently offer an example of the worrisome behavior:
   "You seem to have lost your interest in the track meet."
   "I've noticed that you seem more excited than usual."
   "You look as if you've dropped a lot of weight recently."
   "I notice you've been acting very tired lately."
2. Resist the urge to explain the symptom or to offer advice. You may guess incorrectly and throw the conversation off track. Refrain from comments like these:
   "I guess your track team is not doing as well this year. No wonder you're less interested."
   "Maybe you should eat more."
   "Maybe you need to . . . ."
3. Listen to the student to encourage a comfortable dialogue. Pay attention to how much you are actually listening versus counseling.
4. Do not badger! Avoid comments like these:
   "I took time to talk with you, and this is all you have to say?"
   "Why don't you face facts; something is wrong with you!"
   "If you don't want help now, then don't come to me later."
   "Stop making excuses and get your work done."
5. If the student does not want to talk, try another approach:
   "Maybe this isn't a good time. We could meet after school."
   "I know you and Dr. Robb are close. Do you feel you might want to talk with him? I could check to see when he is available."
   "If you ever want to talk, just let me know."
   "Sometimes students are more comfortable expressing their problems in writing. Would that make things any easier?"
6. Be patient! Students with problems are not always articulate. It may take a little while for them to explain how they feel. Do not interrupt. Show the student that you are interested by making eye contact and nodding your head.
7. Avoid judgments. This is no time to evaluate the student's perceptions. Don't say things like this:
   "That is nothing to worry about."
   "How did you ever get into such a mess?"
   "I hope you've learned your lesson."
8. Next, name some action that you can take with the student. If you cannot think of a plan immediately, show your acceptance and willingness to help with comments like these:

"I'm not sure how to tackle this problem, but we can think it through."
"Gee, this is a real problem. Let me give this some thought. We'll talk Wednesday, okay?"
"Now I see. How about if I share some of this with the counselor? I think she could help."
"I'd like to help you through this. How would you like to proceed?"

9. Close the conversation with reassurance (even if you cannot show genuine acceptance of the student's views). Some students need information to help them view their situations more hopefully. If this is the case, offer it:
   "I see why you were so worried about the quiz. You didn't realize that everyone did poorly. I've decided to adjust everyone's grades."
   "Suspension is serious. But no, it does not mean you fail the course."
   "I know the seniors said they could vote you off the team, but only the coach can make that decision."
10. Follow up on your commitment. Even if you have promised only to talk again, be sure you do. If you offered specific help, get it quickly.
11. Know how to help. Your work obligates you to know child and adolescent referral procedures, to understand the mental health services in your community, and to know warning signs.
12. Know how to handle confidentiality. Do not promise total confidentiality to a student; you may not be able to keep your word, especially in the case of suicidal or homicidal threats.

DEPRESSION

Depression is the most common mental illness among children and adolescents, and it is treatable. The diagnosis of depression begins with the criteria listed in the **Diagnostic and Statistical Manual of Mental Disorders (DSM-IV-TR)** (American Psychiatric Association, 2000). Depression is an illness classified as a **mood disorder.** We will discuss two types of depression: **major depression** and **dysthymia.**

In any given year, almost 10% of the U.S. population—about 18.8 million people—suffer from some form of depression. The severity of the symptoms varies, as does the duration. To meet the definition for major depression, at least five of the following symptoms must be present for more than 2 weeks, and at least one of the symptoms must be either (a) depressed mood or (b) loss of interest in activities once considered pleasurable. Symptoms of major depression include the following:

- Depressed mood (which can look like irritability among children or adolescents)
- Fatigue or loss of energy
- Disturbance in sleep patterns (insomnia or **hypersomnia**)
- Change in eating habits or appetite (weight loss or weight gain)
- Feelings of sadness or anxiety

Depressed students do not always appear sad or unhappy. Pay attention to any sudden, unexplained change in behavior, even if it is aggressive.

Depression can be mistaken for other illnesses. How does a depressed student appear in school? What warning signs will you see? When you discover that a student is fatigued, you may assume that the student is merely bored in school or suffering from a medical disorder. It is easy to overlook depression because some of the symptoms appear normal. For example, parents may overlook their child's poor grades or school attendance and chalk it up to a "bad phase." When depressed, young children pretend to be sick, cling to a parent, or worry a lot. Adolescents get in trouble at school and appear very negative, irritable, or angry. These students feel misunderstood by their peers, teachers, and family.

How does a depressed student appear at school? What should you look for? Here are some examples of teacher-reported behaviors:

1. Depressed Mood/Sadness
   "Bill has stated repeatedly that he is never happy but does not give a reason for his

unhappiness. He lays his head down in class and does not complete his work."

2. Irritability/Anger

"Rachel seems angry at everyone, including her friends. Her provocative behavior has required removal from the classroom. Any disciplinary action makes her very upset."

"Michelle is easily irritated by many things and displays her temper by slamming a locker door or throwing books down on her desk."

3. Low Self-Esteem

"After receiving a compliment about her appearance, Mary responded, 'I am not pretty at all.' She does not express pride in her academic accomplishments. Mary sees herself as unimportant and not worthy of attention."

4. Hopelessness

"During a discussion of future plans, Ellen said, 'What is the future? Who knows if we have one?' She frequently comments, 'What does it matter?' or 'What's the use?' "

5. Anhedonia

"Mark no longer seems to be interested in his favorite activities. He used to enjoy listening to music and being on the swim team but now avoids participating in those activities."

Schools are taking an active role in identifying depression in children and youth. Depression in kids is not a passing phase. When childhood depression is not identified and treated early, the prognosis for recovery is poor. Children with episodes of major depression experience a high rate of recidivism. Typically, treatment consists of therapy accompanied by medication.

> Depression interferes with everything in and out of school. When mood disorders go untreated, they get worse.

Here are some common myths about depression:

- It will go away on its own.
- Everyone feels this way.
- Having depression or seeking help is a sign of weakness.
- If a depression is mild, you don't have to worry about suicide.
- People or events "cause" depression.
- Children don't get depressed.
- Moodiness in adolescents is normal.

Because mood disorders affect intellectual functioning, depressed students often perform below their cognitive abilities. They have trouble concentrating and making decisions. Poor scholastic performance, in turn, can affect self-esteem. When children receive treatment for depression, their academic performance improves and self-esteem rises.

Another negative side effect of depression involves peer relations. Children and adolescents who are depressed tend to avoid their friends. Even with therapy, they often have more trouble repairing social relationships than school performance.

Dysthymia is a less severe type of depression. The symptoms, while chronic, do not always appear severe enough to warrant medical or psychiatric attention, so kids suffer in silence while adapting to their chronic pain. A person can be depressed for a long time without realizing it. While the symptoms of a dysthymic disorder are less severe than with those of major depression, they are longer lasting.

According to the *DSM-IV-TR* (American Psychiatric Association, 2000), a major feature of this disorder is a long-lasting depressed mood that may appear as irritability in youngsters. The symptoms extend over a majority of each day for most days for at least 1 year. They may include a disinterest in activities the student once considered pleasurable. Symptoms of dysthymia include the following:

- Depressed mood
- Change in eating habits or appetite
- Feelings of worthlessness (low self-esteem)
- Loss of energy or fatigue
- Loss of concentration or decision-making skills
- Feelings of hopelessness
- Disturbance in sleep patterns (insomnia, hypersomnia)

If you suspect a student suffers from dysthymia, identify the behaviors and make a school referral. Many youngsters with this disorder will experience major depression in their lifetime.

Every type of depression prevents children or adolescents from feeling good. The sooner you recognize the signs of depression and seek help, the sooner they can resume normal activities.

BIPOLAR DISORDER

Bipolar disorder, as defined by the *DSM-IV-TR* (American Psychiatric Association, 2000), is a mood disorder in a separate category from depression. People with this illness have dramatic mood swings from unusually happy and energized to irritable and sad. According to the *DSM-IV-TR* (American Psychiatric Association, 2000), the symptoms of this disorder include the following:

- Mood swings that are persistent or that cause functional impairment
- At least one episode of clinical depression and at least one distinct period of abnormally and persistently elevated, expansive, or irritable mood with three or more of the following symptoms:
  - Inflated self-esteem or grandiosity
  - Decreased need for sleep
  - Unusual talkativeness or pressured speech
  - Flight of ideas or racing thoughts
  - Increased distractibility
  - Increase in goal-directed activity
  - Excessive involvement in pleasurable activities with a high potential for painful consequences

With this disorder, there are episodes of mania altering with episodes of depression. In a manic episode, children and adolescents are hyperactive and function with very little sleep. Because sleep patterns change drastically, sleep deprivation can occur. A period of sleep deprivation can, in turn, trigger an episode of mania in which the student's mood appears very "up."

Because your student in a manic state feels very energized and has an inflated ego, she might not seek treatment. She likes being highly productive, as she can do a lot of schoolwork and socializing. Manic states can last a few days or a few months. Children and adolescents can demonstrate the symptoms of a manic state and of a depressive state simultaneously. The symptoms of a depressive episode in bipolar disorder are similar to the previously described symptoms of depression.

The National Depressive and Manic Depression Association maintains a Website to educate students, families, and professionals about depressive and bipolar illness. See the Companion Website for a link.

SUICIDE

Suicide is the leading cause of death for young people ages 15 to 24 (Anderson & Smith, 2003). The incidence of suicide attempts reaches a peak during the adolescent years; suicide completion, which increases steadily through the teens, is the third leading cause of death at that age (Anderson & Smith, 2003). Completed suicide is rare in children under the age of 10. Children at that age may not have the knowledge, the understanding, or the means to complete the act.

What are the risk factors for suicide? To understand suicidal behavior, let us look at some of the factors that put children and adolescents at risk. We will review how youth suicide occurs and how precipitating events factor into the equation.

> A myth about suicide that must be dispelled is, "*Students who talk about suicide are not going to do it.*" Listen to what your students say and how they say it. Seek professional help immediately for any student who talks about suicide or makes an attempt regardless of how "serious" you think the student is.

About 90% of teen suicide completers had psychiatric problems, often in combination. This finding underscores the importance of your early recognition of the signs of depression (U.S. Surgeon General, 2001) and other mood disorders. Children and youth may suffer from other psychiatric problems, such as bipolar disorder, anxiety/mood disorder, or disruptive or conduct disorder. These disorders are often associated with hopelessness and previous suicide attempts.

The most common precipitant for suicidal behavior and suicide is parent–child discord or hostile family interaction. Other family variables in suicide include a history of family psychiatric problems (including alcoholism) and a family history of suicidal behavior. Children of substance-abusing parents appear to be at risk for completed suicide. Children of depressed parents appear to have an increased risk for suicide completion (Brent, Baugher, Kolko, & Bridge, 2000). Students have more misunderstandings and poor communication with their parents (Gould, Greenberg, & Velting, 2003).

Firearms are often involved in a suicide. Children at risk should not be allowed access to their parents' or relatives' firearms. Under the influence of a substance, a student may be less inhibited than usual and engage in risk-taking behaviors that he or she would otherwise avoid. Access to firearms greatly increases the likelihood of suicide in vulnerable adolescents (Brent et al., 2000).

Exposure to a suicide or suicide attempt is another risk factor, sometimes referred to as contagion (Gould et al., 2003). This contagion effect has prompted schools to adopt carefully planned postvention efforts when a suicide takes place among the student body. Postvention (as compared to prevention) refers to a set of actions that we take to prevent contagion after a suicide.

These are some things you can do to prevent suicide. First, increase your understanding of each risk factor. Try to learn about the families of your students. Second, know how to use your community mental health resources and drug rehabilitation agencies. See the Companion Website for a link to the STAR-Center.

In summary, the risk factors for suicide are the following:

- Depression, bipolar disorders, or other mood disorders
- Feelings of hopelessness and helplessness
- Drug or alcohol abuse (personal or familial)
- Availability of firearms
- High suicidal intent
- Previous attempt
- Coexisting conditions
- Self-injurious behavior
- Behavior problems
- Current or past abuse
- Legal or disciplinary crisis
- Lack of treatment
- Family history of suicidal behavior

Reinforce the teenager's support network, family members, friends, and adults whom the student views as supportive. "Help in strengthening the [individual's] support system will be beneficial, as it is with all other problems: with suicidal [individuals] it may be lifesaving" (Gould et al., 2003). At the STAR Center at the University of Pittsburgh, you can order manuals on depression, suicide prevention, postvention, and other topics.

Following are specific steps to take with a teenager who discusses or threatens suicide:

1. Listen
2. Help the student reach a mental health service, even if you must accompany the student there
3. Contact the student's family
4. Do not leave the student alone
5. Do not underestimate the student's situation or expressed intent to end his or her life or hurt oneself

DRUG AND ALCOHOL ABUSE

Educators and parents consistently identify drug use as a paramount problem confronting our schools. When children and adolescents are asked to name the biggest problem facing them today, drug use is usually number one on their list. Educators and parents do not always agree on how schools should go about educating students about alcohol and drugs, but both groups may see value in open discussion in the classroom and at home.

Almost 11% of youth ages 12 to 17 are current drug users—defined as having used at least once in the previous month (National Household Survey on Drug Abuse, 2001). Recognizing this widespread problem, most school districts have undertaken in-service training on **drug and alcohol abuse** prevention for their faculty and staff. School and community task forces have joined hands in drug prevention.

There is no one way of disseminating drug and alcohol material. School districts across the country respond differently to the dilemma of drug and alcohol abuse. Following are some important aspects of identifying and referring students at risk for drug and alcohol abuse. We begin with a review of the behaviors you might see in students who are engaged in substance abuse (see Table 11-1).

Alcohol and Other Depressants

Children and youth receive very mixed messages about alcohol at home, through the media, and from their friends. Because many kids do not view alcohol as a drug, they start drinking with little concern about consequences. The earlier in life someone starts drinking, the more likely he or she is to develop a problem (National Household Survey on Drug Abuse, 2001). On average, U.S. children begin drinking at age 13. Peer pressure begins early. One third of fourth graders and half of sixth graders have been pressured by friends to drink. Among youth who are heavy drinkers, 65% also use illicit drugs. Among nondrinkers, 5% are using drugs (National Household Survey on Drug Abuse, 2001).

TABLE 11-1 Abused Drugs: Appeal and Risks

Substance and Slang Terms	Drug Appeal	Risks
Alcohol, booze	Relaxation Sociability Peer pressure Cheap high	Decreases the response of the central nervous system As little as two beers can impair coordination and thinking Often used by substance abusers to enhance the effects of other drugs Excessive drinking can cause psychotic behavior and liver damage
Cocaine, coke, blow	Carefree feeling Euphoria Relaxation In control	A high lasts about 5 to 20 minutes May cause severe "mood swings" and irritability You need more cocaine each time you want a "high" Increases your blood pressure Can cause death
Crack, crack cocaine, crank	Quick high Power Euphoria	Instantly addictive One use can cause a fatal heart attack Euphoria lasts only a few days More hospitalizations per year from crack and cocaine use than any other drug
Heroin, smack, H	Slows down the way you think Slows down reaction time Slows down memory	Highly addictive Can be smoked, injected, or sniffed Scars (tracks) caused by injections Can be fatal
Inhalants, glue, huff, poppers, whippets	Cheap high Immediate buzz	Can be fatal after the first use Loss of muscle control

TABLE 11–1 (Continued)

Substance and Slang Terms	Drug Appeal	Risks
	Fun Easy access	Loss of sense of smell Slurred speech Drowsiness, loss of consciousness Excessive secretions from the nose and watery eyes Brain and lung damage
Hallucinogens, lysergic acid diethylamide (LSD): acid, blotter; psilocybin: shrooms; phencyclidine: (PCP): angel dust, wack; Ecxtasy: E, X, XTC, beans	Relatively inexpensive Experimentation Difficult to detect	Hallucinations can occur weeks, months, or years after use Cannot detect if you will have a "bad trip" Long-term effects include prolonged depression, anxiety, delusions, and central nervous system damage
Club drugs	Fun Sociability Stimulation Euphoric effects	Depressant Mixing with alcohol is extremely dangerous You can't "dance" off the effects Impossible to know what chemicals are used Sedatives that can immobilize you
Stimulants	Increases alertness Relieves fatigue Euphoric effects Feel stronger Can counteract the down "feeling" of tranquilizers or alcohol Mind and mood changes	Increased blood pressure or pulse rate Overdose can cause hallucinations, convulsions, death Easily obtainable Highly addictive Can kill
Depressants	Relieves anxiety Relieves tension Relieves irritability Produces state similar to alcohol	Can impair thinking High potential for abuse Combined with alcohol creates multiple risks Large amounts cause slurred speech, impaired judgment, loss of coordination Very large doses may cause respiration, depression, coma, death
Steroids	Boosts athletic performance Increases muscle mass Helps muscles recover	Aggression, "roid rages" Long-term effects: cholesterol increases, heart disease, cancer, cataracts, and death Heart attacks Liver cancer

Source: *Lambert, D. L. (2004).* Abused drugs: Appeal and risks. *Unpublished manuscript. Reprinted with permission.*

Another high school phenomena is **binge drinking,** which is defined as drinking repeatedly on the same occasion (i.e., within a few hours) on at least 1 day in the past 30 days. Approximately 21% of students ages 12 or older participated in binge drinking at least once in 30 days prior to a national survey (National Household Survey on Drug Abuse, 2002). Warning signs of alcohol use include odor of alcohol on the breath, confusion, disorientation, staggering, drowsiness, slurred speech, and loss of coordination.

Marijuana

School personnel are responsible for providing competent supervision to prevent marijuana use during school hours. Teachers, counselors, and school psychologists—all the individuals who have regular direct personal contact with the student—share this responsibility. To identify an acute marijuana episode, observe student behavior closely.

In approaching young people you suspect of a marijuana problem, demonstrate that you are concerned with their academic and social success and are not trying to control them unreasonably or limit their freedom in any other way. Information presented in textbooks or by the media may be inconsistent, fueling student debate and justification of usage. In addition, students may seek knowledge to provide them with a means to "get high." In a nonjudgmental way, ask students about their curiosity.

> Pay attention to students who are extremely interested in obtaining specific information about marijuana and other drugs.

Marijuana can be laced with PCP, cocaine, arsenic, or other chemicals. These are warning signs of marijuana use: dilated pupils and bloodshot eyes, animated behavior, loud talking followed by sleepiness, apathy, distortion in perception, odor of cigarettes (to mask the distinct odor of marijuana), a sudden uncharacteristic change in appearance (sloppiness), and change in appetite.

Heroin

Heroin is an illegal Schedule 1 drug, meaning it is in the group of the most highly addictive drugs. Heroin enters the brain very quickly. It slows down reaction time and affects the way people act and make decisions. Recent studies suggest that users are switching from injecting to snorting or smoking. However, snorting or smoking heroin is just as dangerous as injecting. There is a misconception that these forms of use will not lead to addiction. Because the strength of heroin varies and its impact is more unpredictable when used with alcohol or other drugs, the user never knows what might happen with the next dose. The vast majority of teens are not using heroin, but the ones who are do so at great risk. The warning signs are euphoria, drowsiness, impaired mental functioning, slowed respiration, constricted pupils, and nausea.

Hallucinogens

These chemicals severely disorganize behaviors so that medical or law enforcement intervention is necessary. LSD is almost considered a mainstream drug because of the rates of experimentation. Typically, the drug is sold on small, saturated squares of paper. LSD is easy to hide and to use and difficult to detect. Behaviors you might see include bizarre behavior, distorted thoughts, and delusions of invincibility.

Inhalants

Inhalant abuse is the deliberate misuse of chemicals to attain an intoxicated state and is becoming more popular with young children. Inhalants include a broad array of cheap and accessible household products, such as aerosols, glue, paint thinner, gasoline, and nitrates (poppers). Chemicals in the inhalants can be dangerous, particularly when the user is unaware of their harmful effects. Using inhalants even once can be fatal. Behaviors you might observe include confusion, memory loss, drowsiness, irritability, headaches, and loss of consciousness.

Narcotics

In 2003, Vicodin became the second-ranking illicit drug used by seniors (National Institute on Drug Abuse, 2004). Vicodin and Oxycodin are popular synthetic narcotics that are highly addictive and dangerous. Youngsters ingest or snort these drugs after chopping them into a fine powder. As a teacher, you might observe the following:

- Overt intoxication or narcotic withdrawal
- Drowsiness and slurred speech
- Constricted pupils

Some of the symptoms look like simple fatigue except that the person cannot become fully alert when confronted. Agitation and impulsiveness are likely to accompany narcotic withdrawal. Significant withdrawal episodes require medical management. Do not rule out such an intervention.

Club Drugs

The term "club drugs" refers to a wide variety of drugs often found at all-night parties ("raves"), nightclubs, and concerts. Kids can find out the location of raves by talking to their friends or turning to the Internet. Club drugs like GHB ("liquid ecstasy" or "Georgia Homeboy") and Rohypnol ("roofies") are used in "date rape" and other assaults because they are sedatives that can immobilize a person and cause a kind of amnesia. If someone slipped GHB or Rohypnol into your drink, you would not realize it immediately because the drugs are tasteless and odorless.

MDMA ("ecstasy" or "X") and Ketamine ("K" or "Special K") are other drugs on the rave scene. Children and adolescents who experiment with these drugs are often attracted to the low cost and the intoxicating high.

Research supported by the National Institute on Drug Abuse demonstrates that club-drug use can cause serious health problems and occasionally even death. It also reveals that in recent years, club drugs have been used increasingly to commit sexual assaults. In combination with alcohol, these drugs are even more dangerous. It is extremely difficult to determine the toxicity or medical consequences of these drugs because of uncertainty over the sources, chemicals, and possible contaminants used to manufacture them. These drugs can be addictive.

Some of the signs you might see are confusion, depression, chills or sweating, slurred speech, problems with short-term memory, loss of coordination, dizziness or fainting, and drowsiness due to sleep problems.

Stimulants

Nicotine is highly addictive. Approximately 3.8 million young people ages 12 to 17 smoke tobacco in the United States (Substance Abuse and Mental Health Services Administration, 2003). Research suggests that teens are generally resistant to antismoking messages. While nicotine is popular among youth, educators are focusing little attention on this drug.

Diet pills and over-the-counter medications are also popular stimulants among our youth. For more information, see the Companion Website.

Examples of strong stimulants are powder cocaine, crack cocaine, amphetamines, and methamphetamines. Some of the behaviors you might see are intense agitation, unreasonable suspiciousness, bizarre behavior, hostility and aggression, extreme talkativeness, and flushed skin. Appetite loss, stomachache, headache, and insomnia are common side effects.

Steroids

Steroids affect a person's heart, appearance, and mood. They also pose a risk of infection from needles. Steroids are illegal to possess without a prescription from a physician. Steroids can be addictive. Steroids stay in the body anywhere from a couple of weeks to more than 18 months. See Table 11-1 for more information.

If a student is under the influence of drugs or alcohol or in any identifiable stage of withdrawal, remove the student from class. Do not attempt a power struggle with a student who appears to be under the influence of a drug. Certain drugs elicit combative behavior that can often be avoided if you do not respond impulsively. Do not confront the student with an accusation of drug use in front of peers. This may lead to opposition, resistance, or combativeness.

After you have removed the student from class, explain why you are concerned and ask if you can help. School authorities and parents should be notified, as should medical agencies if intoxication or withdrawal is severe.

Do not hesitate to seek emergency medical treatment for a student who appears to be experiencing a physical or emotional crisis. Sources of emergency care services, such as poison control, crisis intervention, and the police department, are often listed in the human services section of the telephone directory.

Prevention and identification are important activities for educators. Once you've established drug use, make individual referrals to proper agencies, especially if it is the basis for disruptive behavior or poor academic performance. Table 11-1 summarizes the lure and risks of the major drugs. To learn more about drug and alcohol abuse, visit the Companion Website.

EATING DISORDERS

According to the National Institutes of Health, "Eating is controlled by many factors, including appetite, food, availability, family, peer, and cultural practices, and attempts at voluntary control" (National Institutes of Health, 2003, p. 1). **Eating disorders** are not due to a failure of willpower. This medically treatable illness involves maladaptive patterns of eating that assume lives of their own. People who struggle with this disease can experience an assortment of health complications that may lead to death.

Professionals who work with adolescents need to be familiar with the major eating disorders: anorexia nervosa and bulimia nervosa. People with any eating disorder experience a preoccupation with weight, size, and body image. Often, they also feel guilt and shame. Eating disorders typically coexist with other psychiatric disorders, such as depression, anxiety, and substance abuse. Denial plays a part, as people suffering with this illness do not recognize or admit they are ill. They think they can change or control their eating patterns on their own.

The *DSM-IV-TR* (American Psychiatric Association, 2000) lists the criteria for anorexia nervosa as follows:

- Refusal to maintain body weight at or above a minimally normal weight for age and height
- Intense fear of gaining weight or becoming fat, even though underweight
- Infrequent or absent menstrual period
- Unwillingness to believe that low body weight is a serious problem (p. 263)

Bulimia, which often follows anorexia nervosa, is defined by the *DSM-IV-TR* (American Psychiatric Association, 2000) as recurrent episodes of binge eating. A binge is defined as follows:

- Quickly eating an amount of food that is considerably larger than most people would eat during a similar period of time
- Lack of control during the binge (e.g., inability to stop eating or to control type or quantity of food)
- Recurrent inappropriate behavior, such as self-induced vomiting; misuse of laxatives, diuretics, or enemas to prevent weight gain; fasting; or excessive exercise
- Frequency of at least two binges a week for 3 consecutive months
- Undue influence of body shape and weight on self-esteem and self-confidence

You will probably not succeed by encouraging or admonishing the student to eat better. Rather, your role is to inform parents and mental health professionals of your concerns. Above all, do not ignore the problem; the mortality rate for eating disorders can be as high as 25% (American Psychiatric Association, 2000). School nurses often notice students who are compulsive overeaters. Generally, nurses will work with the family and the students. They will attempt to involve outside agencies that treat this disorder as an illness rather than as a lack of willpower.

ANXIETY DISORDERS

Children and adolescents can experience several types of **anxiety disorders,** including separation anxiety, generalized anxiety, social anxiety, obsessive-compulsive anxiety, and posttraumatic stress anxiety (American Psychiatric Association, 2000).

The primary feature of **separation anxiety disorder** is developmentally inappropriate anxiety sufficient to cause the child or adolescent to experience distress or impairment when faced with separation from home or major attachment figures in their lives (American Psychiatric Association, 2000). Children and adolescents with anxiety disorders may refuse to go to school because of difficulty making friends, then complain that their peers mistreat them. They may complain repeatedly of physical symptoms, such as headaches or stomachaches, when they anticipate separation from major attachment figures. Children and adolescents may exhibit persistent refusal or reluctance to transition into a classroom because of fear of separation from a major attachment figure, such as their favorite homeroom teacher.

Children and adolescents with **generalized anxiety disorder** experience multiple excessive, persistent worries and fears. They worry about life occurrences beyond their control, such as who their math teacher will be next year, as well as matters of personal performance, such as a poor grade they made weeks ago. Children and adolescents with anxiety disorders may be conforming and perfectionist. They are unsure of themselves and tend to repeat tasks because they are dissatisfied with their imperfect performance. This leads them to require excessive reassurance about their performance from teachers, friends, and family members.

Children and adolescents with **social anxiety disorder** will avoid unfamiliar places and people even if doing so attracts undesirable scrutiny (American Psychiatric Association, 2000). Besides experiencing a fear of public speaking—a common social phobia—students with this disorder may fear using public bathrooms, eating in the cafeteria, or going to a party. They also may feel lonely, develop low self-esteem, and begin to see themselves as different from the other children in the classroom.

Obsessive-compulsive disorder in children and adolescents is characterized by the presence of an obsession (persistent, disturbing, intrusive thoughts or impulses that are illogical or irresistible) or a compulsion (obsessive rituals or actions that the person feels urgently compelled to engage in) (American Psychiatric Association, 2000). In the school environment, you might observe these students engaging in repeated hand washing because of an obsession with dirt and germs. Or you might notice that a student is preoccupied with counting the lines of a story instead of focusing on the content or constantly arranging things in a certain symmetrical order. Such perfectionism from children or adolescents may interfere with the progression and completion of homework, classroom learning, and extracurricular activities.

Posttraumatic stress disorder (PTSD) may be present in children and adolescents who have experienced a traumatic event or pattern of abuse. These could include kidnapping, a serious car or airplane accident, a violent attack such as rape or torture, or physical or sexual abuse (American Psychiatric Association, 2000). Children and adolescents who experience PTSD may lose interest in their favorite things. They may avoid going to places or seeing things that remind them of the traumatic event. Anniversaries of traumatic events are often very difficult. In addition, some children and adolescents with PTSD may relive their trauma repeatedly via nightmares, flashbacks, or intrusive images of the traumatic event.

When a child's anxiety interferes with normal school and social functioning, consider a referral to a mental health professional. Treatment for anxiety disorders can be multifaceted, including various psychotherapeutic techniques, cognitive behavioral therapy, individual psychotherapy, behavioral relaxation, desensitization techniques, and psychopharmacological interventions as well as psychoeducation for supporting teachers, families, and friends.

For classroom interventions, review the school survival skills described in Chapter 8. They may be helpful in alleviating children's anxieties about school demands and deadlines. Time management can be especially helpful for an overanxious child. Ask the child's therapist for suggestions and be sure to report back any progress or problems.

SPECIFIC PHOBIAS

A **specific phobia** is an intense and persistent fear of a particular object or situation that may involve irrational aversion to certain things or situations, such as heights, animals, escalators, injections, storms, enclosed places, tunnels, flying, insects, death, water, or seeing blood (American Psychiatric Association, 2000).

Psychotherapeutic treatment of phobias usually involves establishing a relationship with a therapist, identifying the feared object or situation, and offering ways for the youngster to become desensitized to the feared object or situation. The final goal is to help the child face the feared object or situation. If one of your students experiences **school refusal,** sometimes called school phobia, your role in addressing it could be extensive.

Children and adolescents may avoid attending school because of anxiety or fear. Anxiety-based school refusal is a clinical problem in which children and adolescents are motivated by specific fears to avoid going to school. This is different from truancy. Truant students are not fearful of the school situation, whereas a school refuser may show signs of fear and anxiety, such as problems with sleep, withdrawal from social interactions with other children, and a general inability to cope with demands at home and at school.

On the first day that a school refuser returns to the classroom, it is important to provide the child and the parents the opportunity to talk during the day. This way, parents and teachers can gauge the child's comfort level and suggest strategies for handling any new anxieties that might arise. Contact during the day also reduces the student's ability to manipulate parents and to avoid school. If the parents are able to manage unaided on successive mornings, they will assume full responsibility for keeping their child in school. But support from clinic or school must be available if the student falters or if either child or parents demonstrate a loss of resolve. After a week, interview the child at school to sort out any existing or potential anxieties.

SUMMARY

- Do not hesitate to discuss a worrisome child with a colleague. You do not need to be absolutely certain about your concerns to make an inquiry.
- Be sure to document your concerns so that future professionals will have a good understanding of the child's history.
- Today, schools have an opportunity to work in tandem with mental health agencies.
- There is an unserved population of undiagnosed children and adolescents with psychiatric illness that does not seek treatment even though treatment would improve their quality of life.
- Students are experimenting with drugs at an earlier age than 10 years ago.
- Students who suffer with a mental health disorder or a substance abuse problem are less successful in school, are more susceptible to negative health consequences, and have fewer skills at socializing.

The following case study describes an adolescent's problems with binge eating and alcohol abuse. As you read about Helen's struggle with eating and drinking problems, identify observable behaviors.

Come into My Classroom: A Case Study

Helen, 16, found solace in comfort foods high in fat, sugar, flour, and salt. She remembers reaching for Coca-Cola and cookies as a small child and, as an early teen, discovering junk food and alcohol. Both of her parents are obese. When she was 10, she knew she was fat but refused to diet despite the school nurse's recommendation.

Helen recalled the euphoria she felt after drinking her first beer, describing a sense of calm reminiscent of the feeling she got after binging on high-calorie food. She loved numbing herself, then drifting off to sleep.

At school, things seemed normal enough. She tried eating like everybody else but had trouble resisting pizza and cheeseburgers. She arrived home to an empty house every day. After walking through the door, she would head straight to the refrigerator, then to the pantry. She rarely brought her book bag inside because she was too tired to bother. She began with milk and cereal, then moved on to cookies, cake, ice cream, leftovers, or anything available. Three hours later, she ate a large meal with her family.

On Thursdays and Fridays, Helen's ritual changed because her parents worked later and there was no family dinner. On those nights, she went to her parents' liquor cabinet, had a few drinks, climbed upstairs to her bedroom, and passed out.

As the amounts of food and alcohol increased, Helen's social life decreased. She began isolating herself from her friends. She felt more relaxed with food and alcohol than with people, even her friends. Once a counselor suggested she might be depressed. She did not understand what that meant. She did not care about much and wished people would leave her alone.

Case Study Reflection Questions

1. Based on what you've learned about talking to a student, how might you help Helen?
2. How do you help a resistant student?
3. To whom would you refer this student?
4. What would be your key concerns?

DISCUSSION/APPLICATION IDEAS

1. How would you talk with a student who appears to be depressed? Why is it so important for teachers to recognize depression?
2. What are the warning signs for suicide? Have you known students who exhibited them?
3. What are the psychotherapeutic treatments for phobias?
4. What behavioral indicators might alert you to a student's use of alcohol, marijuana, cocaine, stimulants, narcotics, hallucinogens, or inhalants?
5. What are the warning signs for anorexia nervosa and bulimia nervosa?
6. What are the steps to take when an intoxicated student comes to your class?

REFERENCES

American Psychiatric Association. (2000). *Diagnostic and statistical manual of mental disorders* (4th ed.-TR). Washington, DC: Author.

Anderson, R. N., & Smith, B. L. (2003). Deaths: Leading causes for 2001. *National Vital Statistics Report, 52*(9), 1–86.

Brent, D. A., Baugher, M., Kolko, D. J., & Bridge, J. (2000). Compliance with recommendations to remove firearms in families participating in a clinical trial for adolescent depression. *Journal of American Academy of Child and Adolescent Psychiatry, 39,* 1220–1226.

Fertman, C., Tarasevich, S., & Hepler, N. (2003). *Retrospective analysis of the Pennsylvania student assistance program outcome data: Implications for practice and research.* Retrieved on December 17, 2004, from http://www.nasap.org/sap_booklet_3.pdf.

Forness, S. R., Walker, H. M., & Kavale, K. A. (2003). Psychiatric disorders and treatments: A primer for teachers. *Teaching Exceptional Children, 36*(2), 42–49.

Garland, A. F., Hough, R. L., McCabe, K. M., Yeh, M., Wood, P. A., & Aarons, G. A. (2001). Prevalence of psychiatric disorders in youths across five sectors of care. *Journal of the American Academy of Child and Adolescent Psychiatry, 40,* 409–418.

Gould, M., Greenberg, T., & Velting, D. (2003). Youth suicide risk and preventive interventions: A review of the past 10 years. *Journal of the American Academy of Child and Adolescent Psychiatry, 42*(4), 387–405.

Lambert, D.L. (2004) *Abused drugs: Appeal and risks.* Unpublished manuscript.

National Household Survey on Drug Abuse. (2001). *Infofax.* Rockville, MD: Author.

National Household Survey on Drug Abuse. (2002). *Binge drinking among underage persons.* Rockville, MD: Author.

National Institute on Drug Abuse. (2004) *NIDA info facts: High school and youth trends.* Retrieved December 17, 2004, from http://www.nida.nih.gov/Infofax/HSYouthtrends.html

National Institutes of Health. (2003). *Eating disorders: Facts about eating disorders and the search for solutions.* Washington, DC: Author.

Substance Abuse and Mental Health Services Administration. (2003). *Overview of findings from the 2002 National Survey on Drug Use and Health* (Office of Applied Studies, NHSDA Series H-21, DHHS Publication No. SMA 03-3774). Rockville, MD: Author.

U.S. Surgeon General. (2001). *U.S. Public Health Service Report to the Surgeon General's conference on children's mental health: A national action agenda.* Retrieved from http://www.surgeongeneral.gov.

CHAPTER 12 EXTENDING INTERVENTION EFFECTS

OUTLINE

Introduction
Principles of Maintenance and Generalization
Transition Planning
Effective Collaboration

OBJECTIVES

After completing this chapter, you should be able to

- Describe the relationship between the restrictiveness of treatment settings and the extent to which intervention effects generalize to other environments.
- Identify and describe obstacles to the maintenance and generalization of treatment effects.
- Describe strategies for achieving the maintenance and generalization of specific behaviors.
- Describe procedures for assessing the expectations and tolerances of less restrictive settings for desired and maladaptive behaviors.
- Indicate factors to consider when planning for the transition of students to other environments.
- Suggest strategies for accomplishing the successful transition of students to these other settings.
- Explain the role of the special education teacher in working with families and other professionals.

KEY TERMS (refer to the Glossary on the Companion Website for definitions)

cognitive behavior modification
community-based training
criterion of ultimate functioning
generalization plan
levels system
primary treatment settings
response generalization
response maintenance
schedule of reinforcement
self-mediated strategies
stimulus generalization
thinning reinforcement
transenvironmental programming
transfer of training
transition plan
trapping effect
treatment integrity
vicarious reinforcement

The major focus of this text has been on accomplishing changes in students' problem behaviors in settings where the primary intervention agent directly implements or supervises intervention procedures. In many cases, these **primary treatment settings** are individual classrooms that afford a high degree of stimulus control over pupils' behavior. As you have seen, there is a varied and powerful technology for accomplishing desired behavioral changes in settings in which intensive treatment can be applied. However, unless strategies to facilitate the maintenance and generalization of behavior changes are used, the effects of even carefully designed and implemented classroom interventions often do not generalize to other settings, nor do they tend to persist in primary treatment settings once intervention procedures are withdrawn. The failure of intervention effects to maintain and generalize is a serious problem, especially for students whose behavior poses significant challenges to school personnel. Therefore, in this final chapter, we present a number of strategies that are considered best practice with respect to facilitating the maintenance and generalization of desired behavior changes.

Many of the strategies we describe are dependent on other service providers and caregivers, so the guidelines and suggestions presented in the preceding chapter are relevant here as well. Because transition planning is an important process that incorporates a variety of maintenance and generalization strategies, we begin by illustrating a transition plan for a special education student.

COME INTO MY CLASSROOM: A CASE STUDY

A TRANSITION PLAN FOR EILEEN

Kristine Jolivette
Georgia State University

Eileen, now 16 years old, has received special education services since the third grade as a student with emotional and behavioral disorders (EBD). In her school records, Eileen was described as "having experienced significant difficulties during her transition from middle school to high school. As a result, she was suspended for a day due to hitting and pushing a peer in the hallway and was in in-school suspension for a total of 6 days her first month in high school for making verbal threats toward her math and English teachers and overt noncompliance in other academic subjects." During this transition period, Eileen's grades were lower than expected but steadily improved over the course of the year. Given her difficulty during this transition, Eileen's parents have begun to voice concern over her impending transition from school to a work environment.

From the age of 14, Eileen has had a transition plan embedded in her individualized education plan (IEP). The purpose and goals of that transition plan centered on Eileen and her family beginning discussions regarding what Eileen will do after she completes high school, where she will live, and whether she wants to further her education. The goals on this transition plan were purposely written in vague yet measurable terms so as to provide Eileen and her family a starting point in their discussions of Eileen's future. Now that Eileen is 16 years old and 2 years from her expected graduation date, teachers, support staff, Eileen, and her family are meeting once again for her yearly IEP review and to more precisely outline responsibilities for the transition component.

Eileen has been present at her IEP meetings since the seventh grade, as her parents and teachers felt that allowing her to have an active voice in her schooling may positively affect her rates of noncompliance and aggression. In the past several years, Eileen has been charged with detailing her strengths, preparing academic and social goals, and providing input on her future goals. This year, Eileen and the guidance counselor she meets with twice weekly have been working on Eileen's presentation of her transition goals and areas in which Eileen has concerns. In addition, Eileen's teachers and vocational counselor have assessed her strengths and weaknesses in the areas of academic, social, and vocational skills and have begun to assess community options in the domains of employment, housing, recreation, medical services, higher education, and postschool support systems (i.e., social services, rehabilitation services). At home, Eileen and her family have begun talking about what each sees the other doing after her graduation. Following are brief summaries of the actions/decisions and information from Eileen, her teachers, and family.

Eileen

Eileen has told both her family and guidance counselors that she is apprehensive about her life after graduation. She is unclear as to her specific career goals, whether she wants to attend the local community college, and where she would like to live. Eileen accurately portrays her job skills, as she is currently working at various employment sites in her hometown in the afternoons with support from a job coach. She has done well at the sites where she is permitted to work independently on repetitive tasks. In these situations, she has received positive evaluations, most notably for her accuracy and attention to detail. In addition, at these sites she has displayed positive and proactive social skills during "down times." However, she has had difficulties, mostly social in nature, when the job requires her to work as part of a team or when she needs to rely on another individual to complete a task. When Eileen has experienced situations like these, she has verbally threatened her coworkers, thrown supplies or products on the floor, and left the site without permission. She states that when she has questions and cannot find someone to help her, she gets mad and will then find a coworker to "be mean to." She also acknowledges that she does not seem to get along with coworkers if she has to work directly with them on a common goal. Eileen is unsure about her work preferences with regard to responsibilities, supervision, and so on.

Eileen has stated that she wants to remain in her community; however, she would like to live as independently as possible in her own apartment, mobile home, or house with or without roommates. In addition, she has expressed concern regarding what she will do for "fun" after graduation and wants to explore recreational opportunities. Eileen also has acknowledged her difficulty in maintaining long-term friendships and is willing to continue to work on her social skills in the community to improve employment and social options.

Eileen's Teachers

Based on assessments recently conducted with Eileen, her teachers conclude that Eileen will be able to make a successful transition into the community postschool as well as reach goals she sets for herself. Since her involvement in her IEP Team meetings has steadily increased the past couple of years, her teachers report that Eileen is learning to be an effective self-advocate. Moreover, in doing so, she has been more compliant with her IEP goals and more strident in her desire to improve her social skills. Eileen's most recent data suggest the following: (a) that she has the motivation and commitment to support herself in postschool employment; (b) that she has significantly improved on the skills of turn taking, problem solving, asking for help, and clearly stating needs;

Page 1 of 2

Transition Plan

Student: Eileen Jacobs **D.O.B.:** 12/20/89 **Grade:** 10th

Goal Statement: The purpose of this transition plan is to better prepare Eileen for her transition from school to work in terms of the following domains: academics, employment, housing, and recreation. The specific goals are categorized by domain and the person(s) primarily responsible for action. These goals will be assessed at each grading period (3 per year) and each participant has agreed to meet at such times for follow-up.

Persons Invited	In Attendance	Agree with Plan
Special education teacher	yes	yes
Vocational counselor	yes	yes
Guidance counselor	yes	yes
Business manager	yes	yes
Eileen	yes	yes
Eileen's mother	yes	yes
Eileen's father	yes	yes
Job coach	no	N/A
Rehabilitation counselor representative	yes	yes

ACADEMICS

Eileen

1. Eileen will self-enroll in the courses outlined in her program of studies (see IEP course list).
2. Given a three-ring binder and dividers and after visiting various community agencies as part of community-based instruction, Eileen will organize agency materials by domain employment, housing, recreation.
3. Eileen will continue to work with the guidance counselor on social skills and anger management 2 hours 2x/week.
4. Eileen will continue to participate in the assistive employment program at school.

School

1. Given a weekly budget and a shopping list, Eileen (via classroom simulation) will purchase the groceries within the budget.
2. Given the family weekly budget, money, and a shopping list, Eileen (with the special education teacher) will purchase the groceries within the budget.

Family

1. Eileen's family will continue to provide Eileen with a math and reading tutor 3x/week.

EMPLOYMENT

Eileen

1. Given Eileen's interests and past employment experiences, she will write a goal statement for postschool employment.
2. Given a list of Eileen's past and current employment history, she will identify preferred employment characteristics for each placement.
3. Given the list of preferred employment characteristics created by Eileen, she will write a job description for her postschool employment.

FIGURE 12–1 Eileen's Transition Plan

4. Given the list of employee attributes, Eileen and the vocational counselor will circle the attributes in which she has demonstrated competency.
5. Given the list of employee attributes, Eileen and the guidance counselor will work on areas to improve.

School

1. In partnership with local businesses and community outreach, the special education teacher and vocational counselor will list supported employment options for Eileen and her family.
2. The guidance counselor will make three joint appointments during the school year with Eileen and a rehabilitation counselor to discuss short- and long-term goals and support systems available to Eileen in the community.
3. In partnership with local businesses, the special education teacher, vocational counselor, and business managers will create a list of employee attributes prospective employers seek.
4. Given local community agencies, the special education teacher and vocational counselor will list community contacts (agency, contact name, address, phone) for various supported and nonsupported employment options for Eileen and her family.

Family

1. Eileen's family will continue to encourage and reinforce Eileen's independent securement of babysitting jobs.

HOUSING

Eileen

1. Given Eileen's housing options, she will write a goal statement for postschool living arrangements.

School

1. Given local community agencies, the special education teacher and vocational counselor will list community contacts (agency, contact name, address, phone) for various housing options for Eileen and her family.

Family

1. Given the local newspaper rental section, Eileen's family will cut out housing options (mobile homes, apartments, assistive living, rental homes) for Eileen's three-ring binder.
2. Given the housing options notebook section, Eileen's family, with Eileen, will visit two options per month.

RECREATION

Eileen

1. Given the local recreational newsletter and paper, Eileen will sign up for one recreational class provided by the community per semester.

School

1. Given local community agencies, the special education teacher and vocational counselor will list community contacts (agency, contact name, address, phone) for various housing recreation options for Eileen and her family.

Family

1. Eileen's family will provide Eileen with transportation to and from evening and weekend recreational classes.

FIGURE 12–1 (Continued)

and (c) that she has many prerequisite skills needed for independent to semi-independent living, securing full-time employment, and pursuing further educational opportunities. These data also suggest that Eileen needs improvement in the following: (a) anger management and problem solving in work settings, (b) interview skills and how to accurately complete job applications, and (c) support in exploring community options matched with her long-term goals.

Eileen's Family

Eileen's family states that they are having difficulty viewing Eileen as an independent adult able to successfully and independently live in the community and who also is happy. As a result, the family admits that they have spent little time formally preparing Eileen for life after high school. When asked to describe Eileen's responsibilities at home, her family stated that (a) she independently cleans her room, (b) she can be left alone, (c) she helps her mother grocery shop once a week and can stay within the budget, (d) she pays for her own phone line with babysitting money, (e) she takes turns with her sibling with the dinner dishes and vacuuming, and (f) she has to tell her parents where she is and who she is with. The family also stated their concerns regarding Eileen's lack of friends, future living options, and inability to independently seek out and follow through with recreational activities. In addition, her family expressed concern over their lack of knowledge of what their community has to offer Eileen.

Based on this information, the school, family, and Eileen wrote a yearlong transition plan. It was decided that the specific goals to be achieved would be broken into three areas (school, family, Eileen) so as to empower Eileen and clarify family responsibilities with the understanding that they all share responsibility for goal achievement. Eileen's transition plan is shown in Figure 12–1.

INTRODUCTION

You can see from the summary of Eileen's experience in special education that she has made a great deal of progress; however, she still has a long way to go to meet the goals that she, her family, and her teachers have established. What do you think of Eileen's plans for her life after high school? Are they realistic? How does the **transition plan** that she and her transition team developed fit her strengths, needs, and aspirations? As you read this chapter, think about how the strategies we describe might be used to accomplish the goals listed in Eileen's transition plan.

Extending the effects of both academic and behavioral interventions beyond a single classroom is a critical task. For students with academic and behavioral challenges, including EBD, this task is rendered more complex by the difficulties of including them in general education programs (Guetzloe, 1999). Nevertheless, there are practical reasons for attempting to generalize behavioral changes across settings and over time. These are described on the Companion Website.

If you are working with students who are 16 and older, the Individuals with Disabilities Education Act (IDEA) requires that a transition plan be in place to address their needs in adult living and working environments. To accomplish these goals, you must involve a variety of other persons (e.g., other teachers, school administrators, bus drivers, family members, human service agency representatives, employers) in planning and implementing transition procedures.

Note the persons who were involved in developing Eileen's transition plan. If you are involved in transition planning for students, do teams include representatives of all relevant life domains?

This chapter describes strategies for extending the effects of interventions to other settings in which improved behavior also is desired. We present these in three sections. The first presents some important principles of maintenance and generalization and describes procedures that have been validated through research. The second section addresses strategies to facilitate the transition of pupils to other environments. The last section describes strategies for working with parents and professionals outside primary treatment settings and therefore is a logical extension of the preceding chapter. Obviously, the procedures we describe in the following sections overlap considerably. Throughout the discussion, we raise issues that affect attempts to work across educational and other settings. No doubt you have encountered some of these yourself.

PRINCIPLES OF MAINTENANCE AND GENERALIZATION

The question of whether desired behavior changes extend across settings is one of generality. As Baer, Wolf, and Risley (1968) explained, "A behavior change may be said to have generality if it proves durable over time, if it appears in a wide variety of possible environments, or if it spreads to a wide variety of related behaviors" (p. 96). Generality therefore may be defined in terms of three effects. **Response maintenance** is the continuation or durability of behavior in treatment settings after the intervention has been withdrawn. Thus, if a student continues to exhibit the social skills she acquired through instruction in the classroom and continues to improve after social skills training procedures are discontinued, response maintenance has occurred. **Stimulus generalization** refers to the transfer of behaviors that have been trained in one setting or in the presence of specific discriminative stimuli to settings or stimuli in the presence of which they have not been taught. An analogous term, **transfer of training,** more aptly describes the transfer of behavior changes accomplished in one situation to new settings or in the presence of new discriminative stimuli (e.g., cues, persons, physical objects). For example, a student may use a social skill taught in the classroom with her peers in the cafeteria. **Response generalization** involves changes in untreated behaviors that are related to those behaviors targeted for intervention. For example, if a pupil is taught to suppress her physical attacks on other students and her rate of verbal aggression also decreases (even though this behavior was not treated directly), response generalization has occurred. Such generalization across behaviors is more likely in responses that serve the same function (i.e., produce the same outcomes) as the target behavior.

Important considerations regarding the maintenance and generalization of intervention effects are presented in Box 12-1. Think about the behavior changes you are attempting to facilitate in your students and consider whether you can answer the questions affirmatively.

You can promote maintenance and generalization on two fronts: one focuses on working with the student to ensure that desired behavior will occur in other settings, and the other focuses on preparing other settings to support the pupil's behavior. If you are unable to influence what goes on in other settings, for example, you still can use strategies in your own classroom that focus on working with the student directly. However, it is clear that maintenance and generalization programming is most effective when employed on both fronts, especially with students with more severe disabilities (Rutherford & Nelson; 1988). Consider these issues when reviewing the maintenance and generalization strategies we describe here.

Stokes and Baer (1977) identified nine strategies in the research literature that address generalization and maintenance. A decade later, Stokes and Osnes (1986) refined these into 11 tactics grouped into three categories that emphasize the general principles underlying the classification. These are listed in Table 12-1, and each is described and illustrated in the following sections. On the Companion Website, you will find a link to a PowerPoint® presentation on these strategies.

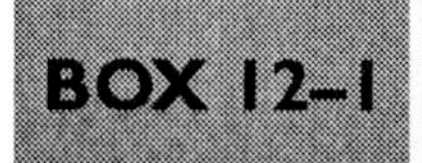

Considerations for Maintenance and Generalization of Behavior Change

1. Will desired behavior changes persist when students leave structured, highly controlled training settings?
2. Will students exhibit newly learned behaviors in nontraining settings, in the presence of other teachers or peers, and over time?
3. Will learning new skills facilitate the acquisition of similar behaviors that were not targeted for training in the original setting (Rutherford & Nelson, 1988)?

TABLE 12–1 Principles and Strategies for the Maintenance and Generalization of Behavior

1. Take advantage of natural communities of reinforcement
   a. Teach relevant behaviors
   b. Modify environments supporting maladaptive behaviors
   c. Recruit natural communities of reinforcement
2. Train diversely
   a. Use sufficient stimulus exemplars
   b. Use sufficient response exemplars
   c. Train loosely
   d. Use indiscriminable contingencies
   e. Reinforce unprompted generalization
3. Incorporate functional mediators
   a. Use common physical stimuli
   b. Use common social stimuli
   c. Use self-mediated stimuli

Source: *Stokes, T. F. & Osnes, P. G. (1986). Programming the generalization of children's social behavior. In P. S. Strain, M. J. Guralnick, & H. M. Walker (Eds.).* Children's social behavior: Development, assessment, and modification *(pp. 407–443). Orlando, FL.: Academic Press.*

The Early Childhood Behavior Project posts "Tip Sheets" on its Website. A link to tips for generalization and maintenance of behavior changes also is on the Companion Website.

Take Advantage of Natural Communities of Reinforcement

The strategies incorporated in this principle emphasize using reinforcement normally available in natural settings. For example, appropriate social behaviors usually are followed by pleasant social responses from other persons, which is reinforcing to most individuals. Thus, the first strategy, *teach relevant behaviors,* involves teaching skills to students that are likely to set up interactions that support their continued use of these behaviors in other settings. Examples of socially relevant behaviors include greetings and other positive social initiations as well as effective language, communication, and interpersonal skills. Behaviors that are useful in generalization settings for gaining attention, inviting interactions, or generating praise effectively "trap" reinforcement; thus, the term **trapping effect** is used to describe the tactic of increasing behaviors that effectively capture naturally contingent reinforcement.

To optimize this strategy, you should assess generalization settings to identify skills and behaviors that are required or are likely to result in reinforcement. A skill that is taught in one setting (e.g., greeting every pupil in the class with a handshake) may not be necessary or even desirable in other settings. Also ensure that the student is proficient in relevant skills by teaching her to a level of fluency necessary in the generalization setting. If the student does not use the skill as fluently as other students in the generalization setting, she is less likely to be reinforced when she does use it. One way to increase the probability of reinforcement in generalization settings is to prompt it. In an early study, teachers had to prompt preschool children to interact with a withdrawn child in order to increase her social initiations enough to occasion their responses naturally (Baer & Wolf, 1970). It also is important to go beyond teaching skills in only the primary treatment setting and not simply hope that the target behavior occurs in other environments. In fact, it is much more efficient and logical to teach social skills in the settings where they are needed initially (Scott & Nelson, 1998). Finally, do not assume that the naturally occurring consequences in a setting will be reinforcing to the student. Remember that reinforcers are determined by individual preferences.

As you know, peers sometimes directly reinforce undesired student behaviors, and adults and peers in generalization settings may not adequately reinforce desired behaviors. In such cases, it may be necessary to *modify environments supporting maladaptive behavior.* This tactic entails controlling the consequences that peers provide for undesired behavior. Given the number of students and settings that may be involved, managing peer reactions can be extremely difficult. If peers are supporting the student's undesired behavior, consider using peer-mediated procedures, such as dependent group contingencies and peer feedback, to shift reinforcement contingencies so that desired replacement behaviors are supported instead. For example, when Juanita uses appropriate behavior to seek teacher attention, she and the students around her earn a reinforcer (e.g., point). Under such contingencies, desired behavior becomes the discriminative stimulus for peer group reinforcement. However, you also may need to prevent reinforcement of undesired behavior by teaching peers, other staff, or parents to ignore maladaptive behavior and to attend systematically to replacement behaviors. Obviously, this strategy requires intervention in generalization settings, and conducting a functional behavioral assessment will improve correspondence between the function of target and replacement behaviors.

Another strategy that can be used is to teach the target pupil to *recruit natural communities of reinforcement.* This consists of teaching the student not only to use behaviors desired in generalization settings but also to draw positive adult or peer attention to these behaviors. This strategy has been effective in recruiting adult attention (e.g., Graubard, Rosenberg, & Miller, 1971; Hrydowy, Stokes, & Martin, 1984), but its success with peers has not been as well documented. However, Gaylord-Ross, Haring, Breen, and Pitts-Conway (1984) taught adolescent boys with autism to operate socially desirable objects (e.g., a video game and a tape player) and then to use them in social interactions with typical peers. The researchers observed generalized maintenance of those students' social interactions with typical pupils. To increase the likelihood that this strategy will be effective, it may be necessary to specifically teach the student how to recruit reinforcement.

> Revisit the goals written in Eileen's transition plan. Select some strategies described in the previous section and tell how you would use them to facilitate the success of her transition plan.

Train Diversely

The objective of this principle is to arrange teaching conditions and response and reinforcement criteria to cover a range of possible circumstances that occur in generalization settings. The strategies included here may be applied in the primary treatment setting, but they are much more effective when instruction occurs in generalization settings as well. The first strategy, *use sufficient stimulus exemplars,* tells you to arrange for more than one or a small set of discriminative stimuli to control the target behavior. Thus, you should provide instruction in more than one setting or under more than one set of training circumstances. One way to apply this strategy involves using typical peers as discriminative stimuli for targeted social behaviors. For example, teach the student to initiate social interactions on the playground. Naturally, this tactic will be much more effective if peers have been taught to respond to the student when she exhibits appropriate behavior.

You also should augment peer-mediated interventions with direct instruction of the skills the student is to use in generalization settings (Shores, 1987). A written **generalization plan** is a useful tool for making sure that instruction has incorporated the necessary and appropriate stimulus examples. Figure 12–2 presents a sample format. Decide where and with whom generalization is desired and tailor your strategy according to the characteristics of these persons, stimuli, and settings.

The response analogue of the previously mentioned strategy is to *use sufficient response exemplars,* which involves including more than one example of the target behavior(s) in teaching. Using multiple-response examples is particularly important when attempting to generalize a complex

Student ______________________ Target Behavior ______________________

Primary Treatment Setting ______________________

Intervention Plan (Include objective, procedures, data decision rules, review dates, etc.)

Outcome (Narrative description, dates plan reviewed/revised, data summaries or graphs, etc.)

Generalization Plan

Objective

Terminal Behavior

Conditions (Settings, persons, reinforcers, schedule, etc.)

Criteria

Strategy (Procedures used, resources needed, etc.)

Evaluation Plan (Data to be collected, when it will be collected, who will collect it, who will summarize/evaluate data, data decision rule, etc.)

Outcome (Narrative description, dates plan reviewed/revised, data summaries or graphs, etc.)

FIGURE 12–2 Sample Generalization Plan Format

behavior such as holding a conversation. In applying this strategy, the pupil is taught a range of correct responses that are appropriate for the situation and is reinforced for using them. Teaching several acceptable response variations also is useful for situations in which students may be required to exhibit different types of behavior in different stimulus settings. For example, some greeting behaviors may be appropriate for a male coming up on a group of adolescent boys (e.g., "How's it going?" or "What's up?"), while other expressions are preferred for use in greeting members of the opposite sex (e.g., "Hi!" or "Hello, Sandy."). Getting a drink of water requires different response topographies when at a drinking fountain or a restaurant.

Train loosely is closely related to the previous two strategies. To use this strategy, you should relax your control over the circumstances in which desired behavior is expected to occur and over the behavior itself. More tightly controlled initial teaching conditions will require greater attention to ultimately loosening stimulus control. Consequently, you should try to create the least tightly controlled yet effective initial teaching environment. If you have your students work in study carrels, deliver their daily assignments in folders, time their seat work assignments, and have very specific behavioral requirements for earning reinforcement, you will need to loosen this stimulus control to facilitate their success in less structured environments.

The objective of the strategy *use indiscriminable contingencies* is to loosen control over the consequences of behavior. The most common application is to use an intermittent **schedule of reinforcement** to lessen the predictability of reinforcement while increasing the durability of target behaviors. That is, instead of following each correct response with a specific reinforcer, make reinforcement less predictable and more sporadic. To make reinforcement less predictable, delay its delivery for some time after the target behavior has occurred. Another term used to describe this process is **thinning reinforcement.** One note of caution, however: you should be certain that desired behaviors are well established and that they receive systematic and plentiful reinforcement before making the discriminative stimuli for reinforcement less easy to identify. You will find a tutorial on schedules of reinforcement and their effects on behavior on the Companion Website.

Another application of this strategy is to use **vicarious reinforcement.** For example, if one student is praised for appropriate behavior, other pupils who observe this model are more likely to imitate the desired behavior (Kazdin, 1977; Strain, Shores, & Kerr, 1976). This has been referred to as a *ripple,* or *spillover, effect.* When you publicly praise a student who is showing good behavior, you are using this tactic. The last strategy in this category, *reinforce unprompted generalization,* involves monitoring in generalization settings and reinforcing spontaneous generalization of desired target behaviors when they occur or reinforcing the omission of maladaptive behaviors. Obviously, this strategy requires that persons in generalization settings be aware of target behaviors, monitor their occurrence, and apply appropriate reinforcement.

Incorporate Functional Mediators

The strategies included in this group attempt to take advantage of potential discriminative stimuli that are common to training and generalization settings. Again, assessment and training in generalization settings are critical to the success of these strategies. *Use common physical stimuli* means to ensure that physical discriminative stimuli are present in all settings in which target behavior is desired. Common work or play materials may be used to facilitate generalization. Marholin and Steinman (1977) found that by reinforcing the academic response rate and accuracy of special education students when the teacher was present, the academic materials became discriminative stimuli that occasioned working even when the teacher was not present. However, when the teacher merely reinforced on-task behavior, work productivity dropped when the teacher was out of the room, apparently because the adult was the discriminative stimulus for academic responses in this condition.

Peers are logical common stimuli in the next strategy, *use common social stimuli.* Significant peers and adults present in generalization settings may participate in teaching sessions in the primary treatment setting. For example, Gunter, Fox, Brady, Shores, and Cavanaugh (1988) brought typical peers (who were present in generalization settings) into the primary treatment setting, where they served as discriminative stimuli for the appropriate social initiations of students with disabilities. This tactic is an option when trainers cannot work in generalization settings but assessment is necessary to ensure that interactions in these settings are consistent with the generalization plan.

A readily available source of common stimuli is the student herself. Thus, the final strategy, *use self-mediated stimuli,* involves having the student carry or deliver stimuli that are discriminative of appropriate responses. Instructions, reminders written on a card, or a string on a finger are tangible discriminative stimuli, whereas teaching the student to self-administer a verbal instruction or cue is less obvious. Teaching students **self-mediated strategies,** such as self-recording, self-evaluation, and self-reinforcement, is another example of using self-mediated stimuli. This set of strategies is potentially one of the most useful and least intrusive for promoting transfer of training, but it also is hard to evaluate the extent to which students use self-mediated procedures. Consequently, it is difficult to say that these procedures are responsible for some of the gains attributed to them. It also is important to realize that prior training in using self-mediated strategies is critical to ensuring their effectiveness in generalization environments (Polsgrove & Smith, 2004). Nevertheless, a number of studies have involved teaching students to self-monitor their performance. For example, Clees (1995) taught students with learning and behavioral disorders to self-record their daily schedules and observed significant and durable increases in the number of teacher-expected behaviors exhibited, even after withdrawing the self-recording intervention. Levendoski and Cartledge (2000) improved the on-task behavior and academic productivity of four elementary students with EBD by teaching them to use a simple self-monitoring strategy.

Cognitive behavior modification involves teaching students cognitive strategies to help them solve problems. These strategies incorporate an analysis of the tasks to be performed (or the social problems to be solved) and teaching the strategy through modeling, self-instruction, and self-evaluation (Polsgrove & Smith, 2004). For example, if a student needs to learn how to control her temper, the teacher might teach her—through modeling, role-playing, and individual or group discussions—a set of steps to rehearse when she finds herself losing control (e.g., count to 10, leave the situation, repeat to herself that the other person is not trying to "get" her).

A variety of curricula exist for teaching students cognitive problem-solving strategies. Specific steps include recognizing that a problem exists, identifying a goal for dealing with the problem, generating alternative solutions and evaluating their likelihood of success, designing and carrying out a problem-solving plan, and evaluating the outcome (Polsgrove & Smith, 2004). Even young children have been able to learn and apply a problem-solving strategy (e.g., Buie Hune & Nelson, 2002). However, less formal approaches also are effective. For example, teachers provide a powerful model for students when they "think out loud" about how they approach problem-solving (Polsgrove & Smith, 2004).

The strategies that you design to extend treatment effects to other settings, persons, or specific discriminative stimuli over time will depend on your objectives for the student and situation. It is likely that a combination of strategies will be more appropriate to specific circumstances than a single procedure. Use the format presented in Figure 12–2 to develop a generalization plan. You also can use a checklist like the one on the Companion Website to identify resource persons to assist in generalization programming. Once you have gained fluency in writing intervention and generalization plans, you may find it more convenient to incorporate the latter into your intervention plan from the beginning.

In discussing maintenance and generalization strategies, we have emphasized the importance of assessment and intervention in the environments where skills are expected or needed. Interventions that fail to address the idiosyncrasies of generalization settings are not likely to produce effects that persist in these environments. Thus, severe limitations are imposed on intervention agents who are unable to gain access to these settings because their direct teaching responsibilities prohibit it, because other teachers will not tolerate other adults in their classrooms, or because staff members will not cooperate with intervention procedures. The organization of most public schools can be a significant obstacle to effective maintenance and generalization of treatment effects. Although you are not likely to have the authority to change such factors as teacher's class loads, you can identify resources in the school to facilitate generalization objectives. Your own enthusiasm and dedication to helping your students will assist in recruiting reinforcement and support for your efforts. We have known educators who, by modeling hard work and determination, evoked similar efforts from their colleagues. As more school districts adopt teaming strategies that support both students and teachers, better mobilization of the many resources available in schools (and communities) will follow.

TRANSITION PLANNING

In this section, we describe strategies directed toward moving students to less restrictive educational settings, to other programs or facilities where services are delivered, or to postsecondary school environments. The maintenance and generalization procedures just presented also apply to this goal. Our rationale for presenting transition strategies separately is that the transition of pupils to less restrictive and postschool environments is a common educational goal, and it involves transferring students and their entire repertoires of behavior to new settings. Thus, it is a broader task than that of programming for the maintenance and generalization of specific target behaviors. Furthermore, the movement of students among instructional settings is an activity peculiar to schools. Each classroom teacher has individual expectations for the behaviors required in her setting. Transition planning must take these expectations into account, and strategies for accomplishing the movement of pupils into less restrictive settings must involve a broad range of activities.

Procedures have been developed for the specific purpose of facilitating this movement, especially in the case of students with disabilities. We describe strategies to facilitate transitions to less restrictive educational settings and other educational or treatment settings and to adult environments separately, although many procedures, including those discussed in the previous section, are appropriate for any of these goals. We also consider follow-up assessment procedures because these are important for evaluating both pupils' status after leaving treatment settings and the effectiveness of the programs they received. State departments of education have developed descriptions of transition plan requirements for students with disabilities as well as implementation guidelines.

The key element in all transition activities is a transition plan. In effect, the eligibility assessment and determination process conducted prior to students' entry into special education programs involves transition planning from general to special education. All systematic transitions must include strategies for moving both the student and appropriate data from one location to another. Transition plans most often are associated with movement of students with disabilities from secondary school programs to postsecondary settings, but the components of all transition plans are the same: a statement of the goals and objectives to be achieved by the transition and the procedures for their implementation, including the responsibilities of the sending and receiving program, the information to be transferred, and follow-up procedures.

Transitions to Less Restrictive Educational Settings

While the movement toward including students with disabilities in general education settings has had dramatic effects on the classroom placement of many pupils with special education needs, recall that students who exhibit emotional and behavioral challenges are the least likely to be successfully included of any group. Furthermore, they are the most likely of any group of students with disabilities to be educated in settings outside the educational mainstream (Bradley, Henderson, & Monfore, 2004). Contrary to popular belief, research does not support claims that inclusion settings are beneficial for all students with disabilities while more restrictive settings are never beneficial (Klinger, Vaughn, Hughes, Schumm, & Elbaum, 1998; MacMillan, Gresham, & Forness, 1996).

Nevertheless, returning students with EBD to general education classroom settings is a laudable but complex goal. If you are the practitioner who is contemplating such a transition for a student, you must not only evaluate and develop appropriate pupil behaviors but also coordinate a number of environmental variables: schedules, curricula, materials, school staff, and other students, just to name a few. A technology for achieving this change on behalf of students with disabilities is developing; however, as Guetzloe (1999) has observed, the attitudes, strategies, and resources needed for achieving the successful full inclusion of students with significant behavioral challenges are not in place in the vast majority of school districts in the United States. Yet federal law is clear, and Box 12–2 presents what IDEA has to say about inclusion.

A recommended process for accomplishing the reintegration[1] of students with EBD into regular classrooms is **transenvironmental programming** (Anderson-Inman, Walker, & Purcell, 1984), a comprehensive set of strategies that include four components: assessing the behavioral expectations of specific generalization settings, teaching skills related to these expectations to students in the special education environment, selecting and using techniques for promoting the transfer of skills across settings, and monitoring and evaluating student performance in generalization settings. Only the second component can be accomplished entirely in the primary treatment setting, and even so, it requires assessment data from the generalization setting. Following is a detailed description of each step.

Assessing Mainstream Classrooms. The task of locating an appropriate general education class into which to reintegrate a student is greatly facilitated in schools with a climate that supports full inclusion. It is true that the mechanics and dynamics of such a climate are not in place on a large scale. Until they are, students who are hard to teach and to manage will not be welcome or successful in

BOX 12–2 IDEA's Requirement with Regard to Inclusion

To the maximum extent appropriate, children with disabilities, including children in public or private institutions or other care facilities, are (to be) educated with children who are not disabled, and special classes, separate schooling, or other removal of children with disabilities from the regular educational environment occurs only when the nature or severity of the disability of the child is such that education in regular classes with the use of supplementary aids and services cannot be achieved satisfactorily. (§ 612[a], (5)(A)) general education classes regardless of lip service given to having "full inclusion" school programs.

Fortunately, research is beginning to identify the factors that characterize such a climate. For example, Rock, Rosenberg, and Carran (1994) identified variables that influence the reintegration rate of students with EBD. They found three sets of variables that predicted higher rates of reintegration. To review these sets of variables and a discussion of their role in successful inclusion, go to the Companion Website.

As we explained in Chapter 1, a lively and sometimes contentious debate has developed regarding the participation of students with EBD in full inclusion programs. We believe that full inclusion is a desirable goal for these students but is not an appropriate strategy for all. Rather, as Edgar and Siegel (1995) observed, the needs of many pupils with EBD (and their families) require a wide range of services that exceed those typically provided by the schools. Furthermore, without extended services, school programs are not likely to be successful. Edgar and Siegel (1995) also advised that teachers should argue "for programs that achieve desired outcomes regardless of the degree of inclusion, concede that no one program will ever meet the needs of all students, and advocate for the proactive testing of many program types rather than continued debates on what should be" (p. 252).

Preparing the Student. In describing strategies for developing students' competence with regard to the expectations and freedoms of the general education classroom, we begin with the assumption that you have improved the student's academic and social functioning to the point where she is able to profit from a less restrictive environment. If this assumption is met, the issue is one of generalization and maintenance of behavior change, which of necessity involves arrangements with other persons.

To help the student prepare for inclusion in a mainstream class, develop a hierarchy of student competencies and classroom structure that increasingly approximates the pupil behaviors and teacher expectations found in general education classrooms (Maag & Katsiyannis, 1998). One strategy to organize these variables is to establish a **levels system,** which we described in Chapter 2. Ideally, a levels system is coordinated with a continuum of placements in the school building. The likelihood that students will retain and generalize critical behaviors outside restrictive settings is enhanced by having a complete continuum of services available in the building (MacMillan et al., 1996; Rock et al., 1994). That is, rather than going directly from a self-contained, highly individualized program into a group-oriented general education classroom, students enter a class that more closely approximates the setting, demands, and expectation of the regular classroom (e.g., a resource room) and are phased into mainstream classrooms from there.

Entry and exit competencies for each level of program in this continuum can be specified. For example, Taylor and Soloway (1973) devised a service delivery system consisting of four levels of student competence. *Preacademic competencies* include such skills as paying attention, starting an assignment immediately, working continuously without interruption, following task directions, doing what one is told, taking part verbally in discussions, getting along with others, and demonstrating adequacy in perceptual-motor and language skills. *Academic competencies* include proficiency in all core subjects as well as being accurate, neat, efficient, and well organized. *Setting competencies* involve learning to profit from instruction provided in settings found in mainstream classrooms (independent work, large- and small-group work), and *reward competencies* range from responding to tangible reinforcers at the most basic level to being reinforced by social recognition and the acquisition of new knowledge and skills. Pupils move up through the levels as they demonstrate more advanced competencies. The environments corresponding to each level consist of a self-contained setting, a resource room (with increasingly greater time spent in general education classrooms), and the mainstream classroom. You will find a table summarizing Taylor and Soloway's (1973) levels system on the Companion Website. Similar levels systems have been developed for secondary programs (e.g., Braaten, 1979; Vetter-Zemitsch et al., 1984) and for children and adolescents with severe behavior disorders in residential programs (e.g., Bauer & Shea, 1988; Hewett & Taylor, 1980; LaNunziata, Hunt, & Cooper, 1984).

It is doubtful that you will have the prerogative of developing a complete delivery system. However, most levels systems are designed to operate in the context of an individual classroom (e.g., Cruz & Cullinan, 2001). Therefore, you can arrange your own expectations for student behavior in terms of a hierarchy of competencies. If progress through the levels is associated with increasing independence and powerful (and natural) reinforcers, student motivation to advance will pose few problems. However, your system will work only if it is based on skills your pupils actually *need* for success in the less restrictive environments within your school or institution. Therefore, you should begin by determining the minimum requirements of each environment. For example, what skills do pupils need to be successful in mainstream classes in your building? Which behaviors are more likely to successfully trap reinforcement in the less restrictive environment? In general, we believe these consist of appropriate social behavior, compliance with teacher requests and directions, and basic language proficiency. You can facilitate student progress within a given level by teaching the skills needed at the next-higher level. You will find an example of one teacher's levels system on the Companion Website.

These basic skills, as well as the school survival skills described in Chapter 8, suggest some target behaviors for students you are considering moving to less restrictive settings. However, each classroom teacher's specific skill requirements vary, just as competence in and motivation to perform these skills vary from student to student; therefore, assess each environment separately. For these reasons, steps 1 and 2 of transenvironmental programming are ongoing and interactive.

In selecting target behaviors for intervention with the goal of the full inclusion of pupils with EBD in mind, assign appropriate social skills a high priority. The social skill deficits of students with disabilities, including EBD, are well documented. Lack of effective social skills appears to be a factor that discriminates between children with disabilities and their peers who are not disabled (Gresham, Elliott, & Black, 1987). Use rating scales such as those discussed in Chapter 4 to evaluate pupils' social skills relative to normative standards and to select target behaviors for training prior to mainstreaming placement.

Of course, students also should be prepared to meet the academic expectations of less restrictive environments if they are to have successful experiences in these settings. The delineation of academic instructional strategies is beyond the scope of this book; consult Darch and Kame'enui (2004) or Mercer and Mercer (2001) for information on best practices in this area. Your approach should be the same as for preparing students to meet the social demands of less restrictive settings: identify the academic expectations, assess the student with regard to these expectations, teach the pupil in the more restrictive setting up to the criterion levels expected in the less restrictive environment, provide generalization training in the new setting, and follow up to determine whether the student is meeting expectations and to provide ongoing support and technical assistance to the general education teacher.

Implementing Transition Strategies. In the process of assessing the less restrictive classroom environment and establishing a match between the student's characteristics and the reintegration setting, you will develop relationships with the other building staff. Your relationship with the potential receiving teacher will be strengthened if you plan the student's academic program with her. In view of the likely possibility that the pupil may need special support and assistance that isn't readily available in the setting, be prepared to help the teacher adapt instruction by providing special materials, arranging for peer tutoring, or training the teacher in errorless or mastery learning procedures. If your school has formed Behavior Support Teams, staff may be available to assist teachers in adapting instruction and management practices.

Use these teacher support services to facilitate the transition of your pupils to less restrictive settings. The more that dealing with students with behavior problems is seen as a responsibility shared by all professional educators and not just by those who are certified as "special," the more quickly professionals will learn the necessary skills and accept responsibility for guaranteeing these students their educational rights.

The settings in which social skills instruction takes place are important to consider. As we have emphasized before, the most effective maintenance and generalization strategies involve training in generalization settings. For example, the use of multiple peer exemplars is a critical social skill generalization strategy, and research clearly supports involving typical peers who are specifically trained to prompt and support appropriate social interactions (Gresham, 1998; Hollinger, 1987; McEvoy & Odom, 1987; Simpson, 1987). In turn, more durable patterns of interactions occur when students with disabilities are taught to make social initiations toward trained peers (Gaylord-Ross & Haring, 1987; Gresham, 1998).

These strategies require that reciprocal social interactions between students occur in generalization settings. This requirement is difficult for many school districts to implement because other responsibilities restrict the staff members with expertise in social skills training (e.g., special education teachers) from working in settings with students who are not disabled. The most economical solution to this dilemma is to make social skills training the responsibility of general education staff, but given the current pressures on regular classroom teachers, this is not likely to happen. The development of collaborative teaching models, in which general and special education teachers work together in full inclusion classrooms, is a promising compromise (Walsh & Jones, 2004). Whether you seek employment as a general or special education teacher, we strongly recommend that you investigate the amount of time and opportunity you will have to work with other educators as well as the school's strategies for promoting collaborative relationships.

Wong, Kauffman, and Lloyd (1991) developed procedures, based on the effective teaching literature, for establishing a match between the characteristics of teachers in general education classrooms and students who are being considered for inclusion. Their strategy involves observing and interviewing teachers to determine the degree of match between their expectations and students' classroom behavior, as well as the degree of technical assistance they would require to support the student. A brief explanation of Wong et al.'s system is provided on the Companion Website.

Monitoring and Follow-Up Assessment. The purposes of follow-up assessments are to monitor and evaluate the student's current status with regard to IEP or intervention objectives, to evaluate how well the program prepared the student for integration, or to evaluate the accuracy with which staff members implement transition procedures. Follow-up data thus serve three functions: to certify that objectives have been reached, to provide feedback for use in revising programs for future students, and to determine whether strategies are being properly implemented.

If the student has been certified previously as having a disability, follow-up data regarding IEP goals and objectives may be used as a basis for deciding that special education classification is no longer needed. In Chapter 1, we recommended that IEP Teams specify criteria for decertification of pupils once conditions that caused them to be certified have been resolved. The IEP should contain goals and objectives related to successful integration or reintegration into the educational mainstream; therefore, follow-up assessment in mainstream settings is needed for making decertification decisions. Follow-up evaluation of the maintenance and generalization of intervention effects is more specific and precise because the focus of assessment is on targeted behaviors. These assessments may or may not occur in settings outside the educational program.

The specific follow-up assessment procedures used depend on the student's current educational placement. If the pupil is in your classroom, follow-up may involve conducting measurement probes of targeted behaviors after an educational program or intervention strategy has been terminated. If the student has been moved to another setting, the same behaviors should be monitored, but the measurement strategy used will be influenced by the setting and the person using it. For example, if you must rely on a regular classroom teacher to do the assessment, you probably will select a less technically demanding procedure than you would if you were monitoring the behavior yourself. In such circumstances, you may elect to have the teacher complete a behavior rating scale or evaluate the student against criteria for behaviors in her classroom (e.g., is the target pupil's frequency of disruptive behavior higher than, about the same as, or lower than that of the average student?). Frequency counts of discrete behaviors are preferable, and these data are even better when rates of similar behaviors collected on nontarget peers are available for comparison (see Chapter 5). However, such procedures require trained observers.

Although data obtained from these procedures cannot be compared to the graphs and charts used to analyze the student and her program while in your classroom, they can serve to socially validate that behavioral changes have taken place. Because the perceptions of other persons regarding the student's behavior in her natural environment is the ultimate test of success in adjusting, these data should not be treated lightly. However, using measures that are more comparable to the data you collected during intervention phases can be important if target behaviors once again are problematic or you need to assess their occurrence in the new environment. If you are unable to collect these data or if your presence in the environment influences the pupil's behavior, follow the guidelines presented in Chapter 5 for training other observers.

Finally, the length and schedule of follow-up monitoring should be geared to the student, the behaviors, and the settings in which assessments are conducted. If you follow the suggestions in Chapter 5, follow-up data collection should not be unduly time consuming. You may want to monitor some behaviors closely (e.g., verbal threats having a history of leading to physical aggression); others may require less regular scrutiny because they are less important to the pupil's success in the new setting. Some data are easy to collect (e.g., number of assignments completed), whereas other data require more time and effort (e.g., use of appropriate social skills). In general, use data that are readily available and that the classroom teacher, employer, or caregiver keeps and uses anyway.

Data pertaining to the student's adjustment to the expectations of the mainstream classroom environment thus can be as specific or general as necessary. The important point is to establish a feedback loop in which you and your colleagues collect and respond to information about the student's performance. Figure 12-3 illustrates a simple daily evaluation form. The format may be adapted to suit the student's age, grade, or subject, or the student may evaluate herself and have the mainstream teacher sign it. Depending on circumstances, the student can bring the cards to you, or the classroom teacher may keep them for periodic review with you. You also may ask the classroom teacher to rate the frequency of behaviors she previously identified as critical or unacceptable with a scatter plot. Regardless of the procedure chosen, be sure that you and the teacher meet regularly to review these data and design collaborative strategies to intervene when needed. As students demonstrate increasingly consistent adjustment, decrease the frequency of monitoring. Another strategy is to have the student rate or tally her own behavior (see Chapter 5).

If the student has been transferred out of your building or even farther away, follow-up will be

Student's Name ____________ Date ____________ Class ____________

Yes	No		Comments
_____	_____	Followed classroom rules	
_____	_____	Demonstrated appropriate social behavior	
_____	_____	Completed work on time	
_____	_____	Tried his/her best	

Teacher's Signature ______________________________

FIGURE 12–3 Sample Daily Teacher Report Card

sporadic, at best. Few agencies are interested in the status of clients once their direct service responsibilities have ended. Still, you may make telephone, e-mail, or conventional mail contacts to assess former pupils' current status. No matter where former students are located, schedule follow-up contacts on your calendar so you will not forget. Initially, follow-up intervals should be short (e.g., 1 to 3 weeks). Thin the schedule as time passes (e.g., 1-, 6-, and 18-month intervals). At some point, you will be able to decide to discontinue evaluation. As with other phases of assessment, your data will suggest when you reach this point.

Another reason for conducting follow-up assessments is to evaluate the implementation of maintenance and generalization training procedures. These evaluations address the question of **treatment integrity** (Lane, Bocian, MacMillan, & Gresham, 2004), or the extent to which intervention procedures have been followed. Recommended formats for such assessments include behavioral checklists or rating scales that list intervention components. Items are checked or rated by an observer familiar with the intervention according to whether they are implemented properly. Figure 12–4 illustrates a treatment integrity checklist for a DRO (differential reinforcement of other behavior) intervention. Intervention steps that are not being properly implemented indicate a need for feedback or retraining of the responsible persons. Assessment of treatment integrity is important, especially for identifying implementation failures when staff members report that a procedure "is not working." Having a plan for sustaining accurate implementation of the intervention procedures also is important, especially when treatment integrity data indicate that procedures are not being implemented as planned. Noell et al. (2000) demonstrated that general education teachers improved their implementation of a peer tutoring reading comprehension program when they received brief daily performance feedback from consultants.

Obviously, effective transition to less restrictive educational environments involves much more than physically placing students who appear ready to make the necessary adjustments. To improve the educational performance of students with EBD, it is necessary to work closely with general education staff, acknowledging and responding to their expectations and needs for support. Few individual special education teachers have the time or authority to serve in this capacity. This is another reason for having Behavior Support Teams in schools.

Transitions to Other Settings

As a group, children and youth with significant behavior challenges are involved in numerous transitions. Although they are the last group of students

Observer ______________________ Observation Dates ______________________

	Observations		
	1	2	3
1. Length of DRO interval is set (interval length _____ secs/mins).	_____	_____	_____
2. Teacher accurately observes occurrence/nonoccurrence of target behavior during interval.	_____	_____	_____
3. Behavior *does not* occur during interval.	_____	_____	_____
3.1 Teacher delivers reinforcer immediately upon end of interval.	_____	_____	_____
3.2 Teacher resets interval timer.	_____	_____	_____
4. Behavior *does* occur during interval.	_____	_____	_____
4.1 Teacher does not respond to behavior.	_____	_____	_____
4.2 Teacher resets interval timer.	_____	_____	_____

FIGURE 12–4 DRO Treatment Integrity Checklist

with disabilities to be identified and placed in special education programs (U.S. Department of Education, 2000), they often have histories of multiple placements in the regular educational system prior to their referral to special education (Walker, Shinn, O'Neill, & Ramsey, 1987). The transitions they make include changes in school districts, classrooms, and programs (e.g., Title 1, remedial classes, alternative education programs). Presumably, these alternate placements are attempts to meet students' needs, but it is likely that the motivation is to reduce disruptions to the settings from which the students were removed.

Students who have been identified as having EBD also are extremely mobile. Although in the previous section we discussed transitions to less restrictive educational settings, their transitions typically involve movement to more restrictive educational settings (Rock et al., 1994; Stephens & Lakin, 1995). Moreover, in their study of students in separate facilities for children and youth with disabilities, Stephens and Lakin (1995) found that facilities primarily serving students with EBD reported considerably greater turnover and shorter average lengths of stay than did facilities serving children with varying disabilities. In addition, compared with day programs for students with varying disabilities, nearly twice as many students leaving day programs for students with EBD either had no next placement or the placement was unknown to the staff. Approximately 20% of those leaving day or residential programs for students with EBD were transferred to another, separate facility.

Homeless youth are another highly mobile population. Transition planning for homeless youth with EBD in particular requires intense levels of support (Wilder, 2003). Thus, teachers of children and youth with EBD, whether in public school or separate day or residential programs, should expect the management of transitions to be a significant component of their job.

Transitions to and from More Restrictive Settings. As we have just indicated, a typical movement of public school students with EBD is toward more restrictive environments. These settings include segregated special classes, special day programs in the public schools, day treatment programs, residential school programs, residential psychiatric facilities, and juvenile correctional programs.

Unfortunately, such transitions often appear to be made for the convenience of the school and community rather than to meet the needs of the student. You can learn more about transition and other issues affecting youth with disabilities who are involved with the juvenile justice system on the Website of the National Center for Education, Disabilities, and Juvenile Justice.

Frequently, movement to more restrictive settings entails transitions between separate agencies (e.g., public schools and juvenile correctional or residential treatment programs). Edgar, Webb, and Maddox (1987) identified three components to the transition process: (a) a sending agency, which has the student who is being transferred elsewhere; (b) a receiving agency, which gets the student; and (c) the handoff, which is a process and a set of procedures for moving the student and her records from one agency to another. According to Edgar et al. (1987), six issues are involved between agencies when making transitions (see Box 12-3).

If these issues are not addressed when making transitions from one agency to another, students experience a lack of continuity in their educational programming, which may express itself in terms of repeating a curriculum they have completed already or being exposed to a curriculum that is inappropriate for their skills and needs. As a classroom teacher, you should be involved in transition activities at either the sending or the receiving level to help ensure continuity of instructional and behavioral interventions. Your participation in site-based management teams will help you ensure that your agency's policies include important collaborative interagency linkages.

Also bear in mind that the vast majority of incarcerated youth return to their home communities and that IDEA applies equally to students with disabilities who are incarcerated. Appropriate transition planning for these youth is especially important to their successful engagement in work and school in their communities (Bullis, Yovanoff,

BOX 12-3 Transition Issues Between Agencies

1. **Awareness.** Sending and receiving agencies need to learn about each other's programs and services. Unfortunately, most agencies operate without such information.
2. **Eligibility criteria.** The sending agency should have a working knowledge of the eligibility criteria of the agencies whose services may help their students or clients. Obviously, a lack of information about other agencies suggests that knowledge of eligibility criteria also is lacking.
3. **Exchange of information.** The receiving agency needs information before the client arrives. The transfer of student records is a universal problem. Often, records do not arrive in time to be used in placement or planning, and in many cases, the student has left the agency before her school records are obtained.
4. **Program planning before transition.** This should involve both sending and receiving agencies so that students are prepared for the programs they are about to enter and so their new programs will capitalize on the gains made in the old ones.
5. **Feedback after transition.** Feedback to the sending agency is essential for program evaluation and modification. Without it, agencies are left to repeat the mistakes of the past, which often is the case.
6. **Written procedures.** Formal written procedures ensure that important handoff activities take place. If only one staff person knows the procedures, there will be nothing in place should that person leave unless procedures are formalized in writing (Edgar et al., 1987).

& Havel, 2004). If you are working with incarcerated youth or in a community-based aftercare program, become a member of interagency wraparound planning teams for your students. Intensive aftercare services for youth returning to their communities that include wraparound service coordination and an emphasis on school and work have had promising results (Altschuler & Armstrong, 2001).

Transitions to Postschool Environments. IDEA requires that schools serve children and youth with disabilities through age 21 and that, beginning not later than the first IEP to be in effect when the student is 16, the IEP must include appropriate postsecondary goals related to training, education, employment, and (where appropriate) independent living skills, as well as the transition services needed to assist the student in reaching these goals (§614[d] (1) (A) (i) (VIII)).

Unfortunately, follow-up studies of the postschool status of youth with disabilities indicate that the special education enterprise has not been overwhelmingly successful in terms of preparing these young persons for successful postschool adjustment, particularly students with EBD (Malmgren, Edgar, & Neel, 1998; McLaughlin, Leone, Warren, & Schofield, 1994; Sitlington & Neubert, 2004).

For nearly three decades, the **criterion of ultimate functioning** (Brown, Nietupski, & Hamre-Nietupski, 1976) has influenced curriculum planning for pupils with moderate to severe disabilities. This top-down approach to curriculum design begins with the assessment of the skill demands of the least restrictive adult environments in which the student is likely to function, and the curriculum is developed around pupils' strengths and needs based on these expectations. However, determining which adult environments are least restrictive for students exhibiting widely varying levels of cognitive, academic, and social functioning is complex in itself and must be accomplished before the expectations of these settings can be assessed. Therefore, specific postschool objectives for students with less severe disabilities, based on assumptions about the limits of their future capabilities, are more difficult to develop while they are still in school. We are not suggesting that objectives relevant to postschool living cannot be established for these youth; appropriate social behaviors are useful in all adult settings and are needed by persons at all levels of cognitive functioning. Students who interview for jobs or admission to postsecondary schools, who go out on dates, or who visit their local hair salon need to employ these skills every day.

Unfortunately, the lack of such skills is a common denominator among individuals who display chronic emotional and behavioral problems (Nelson, Leone, & Rutherford, 2004; Shinn, Ramsey, Walker, Stieber, & O'Neill, 1987; Walker et al., 1987). Walker and Stieber (1998) found that teacher ratings of social skills in grade 5 were significant predictors of police contacts and arrest status through grade 11. Thus, early maladaptive social behavior patterns appear to be predictive of lifelong patterns of social failure (Conroy & Brown, 2004). Early identification and remediation of social skills deficits in children who are at risk should be a major educational priority.

Review again the transition plan developed for Eileen. Which of her transition goals involve the need for appropriate social skills?

Planning for transitions to adulthood may not prevent the failure of all (or even many) students with behavior problems, but neither should it be assumed that the existence of problem behaviors condemns pupils to lives of crime or institutionalization. Transition programs for adolescents are useful for bridging the gap between school and productive adult experiences. If a transition plan is to be meaningfully linked to the student's postschool life, it should be initiated well before graduation.

Research has identified several promising transition practices, including (a) interagency collaboration; (b) the presence of a strong transition coordinator; (c) comprehensive educational programming that includes vocational preparation, social skills, and self-awareness training as well as effective academic instruction; (d) identification of school and community services to meet individual needs; (e) parental involvement; and (f) supported employment (Maag & Katsiyannis, 1998; Sample, 1998; Sitlington & Neubert, 2004). If you are involved in transition planning for students, we recommend that you become familiar with these practices and advocate for their use.

Transition plans must be developed with persons who have a stake in the pupil's postschool adjustment (e.g., parents, the student), and they should involve agencies and service providers who can address the student's likely postschool needs. Transition plans also should take into account the wide range of options the student may consider as an adult. Therefore, a team of persons who know and care about the student should develop transition plans, and community-based service providers should be involved well before the student leaves school. Including the student's parents or primary caregivers throughout the process provides greater assurance that the transition plan will address life domains that are relevant, and this strategy also increases the likelihood of their ongoing involvement and cooperation.

Maag and Katsiyannis (1998) argue that school personnel are best suited to assume the role of transition coordinator because of their greater familiarity with the student and because IDEA requires that transition strategies be initiated well before students leave school. Unfortunately, the high dropout rate of students with EBD poses a significant barrier to the implementation of school-based transition activities (Maag & Katsiyannis, 1998; Sitlington & Neubert, 2004). Therefore, a critical element of effective transition is keeping the student in school. Linking students' academic experience with vocational education through secondary vocational-technical education programming is a logical approach to preventing high school students with special needs from dropping out (Harvey, 2001). Rylance (1997) found that students with EBD who received counseling and vocational education had significantly higher graduation rates than those who did not receive these services.

It would be naive to assume that school-based interventions alone are sufficient to enable adolescents with emotional and behavior problems to successfully enter adult living and working environments. Ideally, they also should have the benefit of **community-based training** during their public school years. Community-based instruction has played an important role in the curriculum of pupils with moderate and severe disabilities, and many good models are available (e.g., see Goetz, Guess, & Stremel-Campbell, 1987; Taylor, Bilken, & Knoll, 1987). Much less attention has been paid to teaching social skills to students with so-called mild disabilities in the community settings where these skills are critical to their successful adjustment. Given that many adolescents with EBD fail to make adequate adjustments to adult life (Frank & Sitlington, 1997; Malmgren et al., 1998; McLaughlin et al., 1994), appropriate changes in the secondary school curriculum for these students clearly are needed.

It is important to recognize that EBD is extremely durable and has deleterious long-term effects. Therefore, one aspect of postschool transition is maintaining service coordination with agencies and the family to ensure that students continue to receive adequate support. Sample (1998) observed that, relative to students with other disabilities, fewer adult services are available to students with EBD after they leave school, and these individuals are more likely to refuse to attend eligibility meetings with potential adult service providers. As Walker and Bullis (1996) indicate, the goal for working with older adolescents and young adults with EBD probably should be accommodation, that is, to reduce the negative impact of their disability on successful adjustment. Alarm regarding the costs of a community-based support system to achieve the necessary level of accommodation should be balanced by the realization that these are no greater (and probably much less) than the staggering costs of long-term institutionalization. At this level, the transition plan might better be conceptualized as a wraparound plan because it emphasizes providing ongoing support to the individual across multiple life domains. Moreover, youths involved in a community-based system of care are far less likely to be a financial burden to their families or society. Illinois has a particularly active system of care. You can learn more about it on the Illinois State Board of Education Emotional and Behavioral Disabilities/Positive Behavioral Interventions and Supports Network.

Clark, Unger, and Stewart (1993) describe four domains that should be considered in transition planning for students with EBD (see Table 12-2). Alternatives such as college, military service, and independent living should be considered in addition to employment. Support services likely to be needed (e.g., mental health counseling, daily living support, vocational training) should be indicated, and representatives from agencies that provide services (e.g., community mental health, developmental disabilities council, vocational rehabilitation) should participate in drafting the transition plan. Implementation of the plan should begin during the pupil's secondary school experience and should continue until the structure and support provided by the plan are no longer needed. Bearing in mind that individuals with EBD appear to be

TABLE 12-2 Transition Domains

A. Employment
   1. Competitive employment
   2. Supported employment (individual and enclave)
   3. Transitional employment opportunities
   4. Work experience opportunities

B. Education opportunities
   1. Workplace educational programs
   2. High school completion or GED certificate
   3. Vocational or technical certification
   4. Associate's degree
   5. Bachelor's degree or beyond

C. Independent living
   1. Independent residence
   2. Residence with natural, adoptive, or foster family
   3. Semi-independent living (e.g., nonlive-in case manager assists)
   4. Supported living (e.g., supervised apartment)
   5. Group home or boarding home

D. Community life: Skill development and activities related to domains A, B, and C
   1. Leisure time activities and fun
   2. Social interaction and problem-solving skills (e.g., self-advocacy)
   3. Relationship development (e.g., friendships, intimate relationships)
   4. Peer support groups
   5. Emotional/behavioral management (e.g., anger control, relapse prevention, self-medication management)
   6. Safety skills (e.g., prevent victimization, avoid dangerous situations)
   7. Daily living skills (e.g., eating nutritious food, leasing an apartment)
   8. Health care and fitness (e.g., stress management, physical activity)
   9. Substance abuse prevention and maintenance
   10. Sex education and birth control (e.g., prevention of sexually transmitted diseases and unwanted pregnancies)
   11. Community resources (knowledge and utilization)
   12. Transportation skills
   13. Cultural/spiritual/religious resources

Source: *Clark, H. B., Unger, K. V., & Stewart, E. S. (1993). Transition of youth and young adults with emotional/behavioral disorders into employment, education and independent living.* Community Alternatives: International Journal of Family Care, 5*(2), 19–46. Copyright Human Services Associates, Inc. Reproduced with permission.*

extremely resistant to intervention (Sample, 1998), ensure that the plan is relevant, supportive, and responsive to the youth's evolving needs.

EFFECTIVE COLLABORATION

As we have emphasized throughout this chapter, the successful maintenance and generalization of behavioral improvements requires the involvement of persons in other settings. Especially if you are working with students who present serious psychiatric disorders, you can expect to be part of interagency wraparound planning teams. (You can learn more about wraparound planning on the Illinois State Board of Education's Website mentioned earlier.) Even if you serve students with behavior problems in a single classroom setting, your work will lead you into other environments both within and outside the school. In this section, we suggest strategies to increase your effectiveness with other professionals and laypersons in these settings.

Working with School Personnel

In a typical school building, residential facility, or institution, there are a number of people who can be resources for students with emotional and behavioral problems. The extent of their involvement may range from praising a student's achievement to taking pupils on after-school trips, from simply rating performance as acceptable or unacceptable to taking frequency data, and from following a plan worked out by you to collaborating in the development of a complete intervention strategy. Different persons may prove useful for different functions, and the checklist provided on the Companion Website should help you develop a profile of various personnel resources in your school or facility.

Before you approach anyone to assist you with a pupil or program, get your objective clearly in mind. Do you want to assess the generalization of change in a target behavior? Do you want to evaluate a trial regular classroom placement? Do you want to establish other persons as social reinforcers? Do you want to increase the availability of reinforcement outside your classroom? Do you need assistance with potential emergency situations? Each objective indicates different tactics. When you enlist the cooperation of other people, explain clearly what you would like them to do as well as when and how they are to communicate to you regarding their work with the pupil or pupils. It is especially important to agree on the student outcomes to be achieved and how these will be monitored. As Gable, Mostert, and Tonelson (2004) observed, evaluations of collaboration typically focus on the process and ignore outcomes.

Once again, a written plan is the best approach, especially if the program is complex. Conflicts may arise between involved parties, such as teachers and school administrators; each party may want to impose its agenda on your program (e.g., the teacher wants the student to suit up for gym, the principal wants her to arrive at school on time). A written plan clarifies agreements reached in team meetings. Remember too that the *student* is your client (the person who is to benefit from the program). This focus is somewhat different from the one you use when you are serving as a consultant, where your client is the person who comes to you with the problem. Many a good teacher has been rendered ineffective by trying to serve too many clients with conflicting demands. A written plan should specify objectives and roles at the outset, thereby preventing such episodes.

A student's Behavior Support Team can be expanded to include other school personnel and family members who know and care about the student. This team can develop a school-based wraparound plan to address the student's typical day and provide behavioral support where it is needed as well as systematic reinforcement in settings in which the student typically behaves appropriately. Like interagency wraparound plans, a school-based wraparound plan is driven by the needs of the student rather than the services traditionally available in the school. It also typically addresses services and supports that extend to life domains beyond the school. Thus, the resources, structure, and supports for each targeted student must be flexible and creative. For example, if managing unstructured times and settings (e.g., hallways, cafeteria, bus waiting areas) is a difficult task for the student, a wraparound plan might consist of enlisting the aid of a member of the school staff to escort her to her locker and then the classroom. Several peer "buddies" or mentors may be recruited to accompany her on the bus, in the halls and cafeteria, and to the restroom. Or teachers may stand outside their classroom doors during class breaks to monitor her behavior during transitions. As she makes progress, this structure may be loosened so that the pupil maintains a self-monitoring checklist that is reviewed several times daily with her wraparound coordinator.

In working with school staff, remember that adults need support and reinforcement too; therefore, find out what teachers need, set up communication channels, and be sure to show your appreciation for their assistance. You can increase the likelihood of a plan being followed by meeting staff needs (e.g., arrange to help supervise difficult transition times) or providing materials (e.g., a checklist for classroom teachers to complete, a roll of smiley-face stickers for the cafeteria cashier or bus driver to put on the shirts of well-behaved students, a wrist counter for the librarian to use in counting disruptions).

Students (and teachers) often regard the school principal as the major disciplinarian for a building. In view of this, having the principal deliver reinforcement can be a potent tactic. Building administrators can give recognition and praise or provide opportunities to engage in preferred activities contingent on appropriate school behaviors. Also consider enlisting the services of school counselors, psychologists, social workers, and other staff (e.g., office personnel, custodians, cafeteria workers, bus drivers, school safety officers). Involving staff who know the student or her family or who have similar cultural backgrounds or experiences not only widens the support base for the student but also expands your network of support in the school.

Other staff may be helpful in additional ways. For example, many reinforcing activities occur around the school office: pupils can deliver attendance slips or notes, answer the telephone, run the copy machine, file, or perform other office tasks as reinforcement for desired behaviors. The main reason such opportunities are not taken is that teachers seldom think of them. Few persons will refuse to facilitate such experiences if you ask them (and remember to follow up with reinforcement for doing so).

Involving yourself has the further advantage of increasing your visibility to and interaction with school staff, which lessens the stigma attached both to teachers and to students who spend much of the day in segregated special classrooms. Volunteering to sponsor all-school activities such as clubs and social events will improve your standing with pupils outside your classroom. In addition, do not shirk cafeteria or bus duty, and don't do all your work in the classroom, where you are isolated from your colleagues. Instead, spend some of your time working in the teachers' lounge. In our experience, the more successful special education teachers are actively involved in the total school environment. When you are working with pupils with EBD, visibility and involvement are especially important because of the fear and misconceptions regarding persons with such disabilities.

In developing intervention plans that encompass a student's school day, it is important to recognize that schools are rich in intervention resources. In addition to the school staff mentioned previously, other students may be used as models, tutors, reinforcing agents, and monitors for intervention plans. For students who need this level of structure, it is essential that environmental assessments be performed to identify those settings and times of the day when behavior support is needed. It also is important to schedule regular meetings with the team to ensure that the plan is being implemented properly and the student is making progress.

Working with Families

Those who provide daily care of children with EBD, as well as those who live with them, need as much (if not more) support than do professional service providers. They also have unique perspectives on the strengths and issues these children present. At the same time, the blame that has been assigned to parents of students with EBD, as well as the disruptions created by living with children who exhibit such great challenges, has caused them to refrain from vigorously advocating for their children. The development of community system-of-care approaches for children and families with the most intensive level of needs and the emergence of strong family organizations (e.g., the PACER Center, PEAK Parent Center, Federation of Families for Children's Mental Health) are changing this picture for the better. Go to their Websites for information and resources. Family members now are acknowledged as essential to effective wraparound teams. Two specific ways in which education professionals can improve outcomes for students and assist families include (a) helping them address a child's behavior in their home or neighborhood and (b) helping families support academic and behavioral improvements made at school. Each goal calls for a slightly different approach.

Family Implementation of Positive Behavior Support. If you and the parents agree on the need for positive behavior support at home, you are putting yourself in a consultative relationship. Because caregivers have learned to expect teachers to deal directly with their children and, consequently, may be less prone to let you help them, this relationship can be a difficult one. In addition, parents of children with behavior problems (especially children who have been certified as having EBD) may be defensive about admitting their problems because, in the past, it was fairly common to attribute children's behavior disorders to faulty parenting. Fortunately, as mentioned previously, families are becoming empowered to work actively on behalf of their children and are being included as equal partners with professionals in planning and implementing services. Comprehensive systems of care have a distinctly family-centered focus in which families are regarded as a source of support and strength, not of dysfunction and pathology (Duchnowski, Berg, & Kutash, 1995). Such national organizations as the Federation of Families for Children's Mental Health and the National Alliance for the Mentally Ill—Children and Adolescent Network have provided strong political advocacy where none has existed before. Visit the Websites of these organizations as well as that of the PACER Center for more information and resources.

Nevertheless, some professionals still hold the view that parents are the cause of their children's emotional and behavioral disorders, and because parents' interactions with school personnel tend to be negative, they may avoid working with school staff. One way around this problem is to treat the task of helping parents more effectively address the needs of their child as an educational issue rather than as a problem requiring psychotherapy or analysis. Parents are essential partners for students who need the structure of wraparound service plans. Such plans should be based on needs identified by the family as well as on educators' expectations. By including parents on the behavior support or wraparound planning team for their child, professionals not only gain important information about the child and her needs but also enlist an important ally in their efforts to help the student. When families are full participants in developing a team-based plan, their resistance tends to disappear. The wraparound emphasis on strength-based planning and the focus on strengthening desired replacement behaviors that is inherent in positive behavior support also help break down barriers. Another suggestion is to maintain a focus on the child. Presenting ideas and techniques to help the parents address their child's behavior problems at home is likely to meet with less resistance than giving them the impression that their parenting skills need a major overhaul.

When parents do recognize a problem or agree to help, the team has several options. One is to set up a specific home-based positive behavior support program, following the steps delineated in Chapter 4. There is evidence that parents can successfully implement such procedures with professional guidance. For example, Strain and Danko (1995) taught caregivers to implement a social skills training program and to encourage positive interactions between three 3- to 4-year-old children with autism and their siblings. The caregivers were quite successful in applying the interventions and reported that they were simple to learn, easy to apply, and enjoyable.

If you have several interested parents, a parent education group may be a useful strategy. Several formats have been used. The format we prefer combines instruction in behavioral principles and procedures with specific problem-solving consultation. Parents show more interest in learning principles when they can immediately apply them to their children's behaviors. However, a short-term parent course may be insufficient without long-term follow-up consultation for other problem behaviors. In addition, aggressive children who display problems outside the home may require more extensive community-based intervention. If you need to go this far, consider developing a comprehensive wraparound plan or involving other agencies.

Parental Support of Classroom Goals. If caregivers are to support classroom goals, they should have input in identifying target behaviors and interventions. It also requires a school–home communication system, for parents can hardly be expected to support the objectives of a behavior change program if they do not understand them or have little access to information regarding their child's progress. Traditional reporting systems (e.g., grade cards) are unsuitable for this type of communication because they are infrequent and tend to communicate only summary information. Parental response to an unsatisfactory report card may be inappropriate, or caregivers may fail to respond at all to good reports. Therefore, we suggest a frequent (daily or weekly) reporting system that conveys meaningful information to parents and to which they may respond in a systematic manner. This implies that you have worked out a plan with the family beforehand. Tell them what to expect (e.g., a daily or weekly report containing points their child has earned for academic work and for social behavior each day), when to expect it (e.g., every day after school), and how to respond to each report (e.g., praise when the point total is above 35 and for each subject or area for which 4 or more points are awarded). Davern (2004) provides guidelines for using school-to-home notebooks to communicate with families about their children.

Where more solid home support is needed, work with parents to set up explicit home contingencies based on their child's school performance. For example, they may provide extra privileges for good reports (specify the criteria for a "good" report) or lose privileges for a poor report. If required, you may even work out a menu of backup home consequences similar to a classroom menu of backup reinforcers. This provides for differential reinforcement and long-term savings for special privileges or treats (e.g., a movie, a fishing trip). It is preferable to work out the details of more elaborate systems with a simple contract among the pupil, parents, and you. All parties should sign and receive copies of the contract.

Figure 12–5 shows a variety of daily report cards (these also could be weekly). Panels A and B present forms useful for preschool and primary-age students. Panel C is a simple checklist for middle-grade students, and Panel D shows a form for reporting daily points. Panel E is a checklist for upper-level or secondary pupils and may be used with students in general education classrooms. One problem with daily report cards is that students may lose them. If you advise parents to respond to a missing report as though it were poor or below criterion, this problem seldom persists. If you are concerned that parents fail to read the report, include in the contract an agreement that they are to sign reports and return them the next

Date ________

Classroom Work

☐ Good ☺

☐ Bad ☹

____

Teacher's Signature

A

Date ________

Classroom Behavior

☐ Good ☺

☐ Bad ☹

____

Teacher's Signature

B

Date ________

Social Behavior

☐ Acceptable

☐ Unacceptable

Academic Work

☐ Completed on time

☐ Not completed

☐ Accuracy acceptable

☐ Accuracy unacceptable

____

Teacher's Signature

C

Date ________

Reading ________

Math ________

Spelling ________

Science ________

P.E. ________

Lunchroom ________

Playground ________

Social Behavior ________

Bonus Points ________

Fines ________

Total Points ________ Total Possible ________

____

Teacher's Signature

D

Subject ________________________ Date ________

________ Is doing acceptable work and is keeping up with assignments

________ Is not doing acceptable work

________ Is behind on assignments

________ Exhibits acceptable social behavior

________ Exhibits unacceptable social behavior

Comments:

____

Teacher's Signature

E

FIGURE 12–5 Daily Report Cards

day. Graphs and charts such as those presented in Chapter 6 also may be sent home on a daily or weekly basis.

Home-school communication systems that use backup home contingencies offer several advantages. First, they provide contingent consequences at home for performance in school. This can be a great help for students who do not respond well to school consequences (e.g., pupils who "do not care" if they miss recess or backup reinforcers available at school). Second, they keep caregivers informed of their child's progress and get them involved in what is going on at school. Third, by emphasizing reinforcing consequences for good performance, they break down the common expectation among parents of children with behavioral problems that all school reports will be bad reports. Furthermore, by teaching parents to reinforce their children, you may help break the criticism-punishment cycle that is prevalent in families with children who exhibit behavioral problems.

Strategies for working with parents can be as varied as the students and caregivers themselves. Each situation calls for different measures, but behavior in the home obeys the same principles as that in school.

Working with Community Professionals and Agencies

Your work with children and youth exhibiting behavior problems will lead you into the domain of other professionals and agencies. Federal, state, and local efforts have been launched to reform systems of children's services toward greater coordination and integration. As pointed out in Chapter 1, a system of care for children and youth with EBD and their families emphasizes more community services, less reliance on restrictive child placements, prevention of hospitalization and out-of-home placements, interagency collaboration, flexible and individualized services, and cost containment and efficiency (Stroul, Goldman, Lourie, Katz-Leavy, & Zeigler-Dendy, 1992).

The lack of interagency collaboration has been a major obstacle to achieving continuity of programming between public schools and other human service agencies. Remember that discontinuity in services contributes to the failure of treatment effects achieved in one setting to be generalized and maintained in other settings where these effects are expected and needed. As a professional attempting to extend the effects of interventions applied in education settings or attempting to plan interventions across settings, you may work with a number of agencies, such as the juvenile court, child welfare agencies, mental health centers, organizations serving children and youth with developmental disabilities, vocational rehabilitation agencies, medical clinics, and service organizations such as Big Brothers or Big Sisters, in addition to working with parents and family groups. The professionals in these agencies (or in private practice) include social workers, psychologists, psychiatrists, physicians, dentists, and lawyers. Whether or not a system of care exists in your community, it is likely that your work will bring you into contact with professionals and agencies outside the school. Therefore, we offer a few practical guidelines for effective interaction and collaboration.

First, you should be aware of political realities. One of the foremost of these is that outside the school, special education is not viewed as the salvation of children with learning and behavior problems. Do not expect other professionals to greet your suggestions and views with automatic respect and admiration. Your credibility with these people will come from your record with their clients. If you succeed in accomplishing goals with students and parents that are in accord with the agency's goals or if you have solved problems addressed by the agency or professional, you are more likely to be viewed as effective. However, it is foolhardy to set up programs that oppose those established by another agency if you want to enjoy credibility with that agency. For example, if you develop a behavioral program with parents to address their child's noncompliance while a psychiatrist has prescribed medicine to treat the same problem, you are not likely to establish a good working relationship with that professional. A better tactic would involve demonstrating the effectiveness of your programs with other behaviors or students and to offer suggestions as requested. Alternately, a strategy developed collaboratively by a wraparound planning team that includes the psychiatrist could provide greater consistency throughout the child's day.

Second, learn to channel credit away from yourself and toward the other professional whenever appropriate. However, do not suggest that the other professionals possess qualities or powers they do not have and do not give credit where credit is not due. A good strategy is to follow the principle of contingent reinforcement of practices with which you concur. For example, if you approve of a psychologist's plan for dealing with school phobia, say, "I like this plan," not "You're a terrific psychologist" or "You have so much insight into this client." At times, you need to overlook that it was you who suggested a particular plan in the first place.

Third, you should recognize that other professionals may not speak your language. You must be tolerant of the jargon of other professions while minimizing the use of your own. This is particularly important in the case of behavior analysis terminology. By selecting nontechnical but meaningful words (e.g., "reward" instead of "positive reinforcement"), you can avoid both semantic confusion and value clashes.

Fourth, you should realize that most human service agencies often do not communicate well with one another. That is, juvenile court personnel may seldom contact the school, and there may not be an automatic communication link between the school and the local mental health clinic. Communication among agencies requires someone to initiate and maintain it. Although interagency linkages are improving rapidly, frequently effective communication results from a dynamic individual rather than from agency policy. Thus, if you desire communication with other agencies, be prepared to take the initiative and follow through. In addition, remember that communication will continue only as long as it is reinforced and functional. Therefore, you need to acknowledge your appreciation of others' attempts to communicate and to make use of the communicated information. Further, be sure to communicate information that is useful to the treatment program being followed by the other agency. Irrelevant comments about a child's social history or the criminal record of her brother serve only to cloud issues and professional judgment.

Finally, whether you approach another agency or professional or they approach you, clarify the purposes of the involvement and your mutual responsibilities. Interagency memoranda of agreement formally commit agencies to working together, but these do not ensure effective collaboration among frontline staff and parents. A major advantage of a written integrated (or wraparound) service plan for a particular child and family is its clear delineation of roles and responsibilities. If an agreement is plainly spelled out and understood by all (you are to count the frequency of Romey's appropriate bids for social attention during school hours, her parents are to record it at home, and both parties are to call in their data to the mental health service coordinator every Friday), there is a greater likelihood that interactions will be efficient, productive, and mutually reinforcing.

As you work with other professionals and human service agencies, you will learn which are most useful for specific purposes. You may find it helpful to maintain a checklist, using a format similar to that presented on the Companion Website, to keep track of your contacts and the outcomes of your involvement. When working outside the school, keep in mind the limitations of your role. If you overextend yourself or intrude too far into another's territory, you may experience unpleasant consequences. At the least, you are apt to find that your efforts do not produce the effects you desire. The range of persons and professional or volunteer agencies in the local community that can assist your students is virtually endless. Each community has its own array of resources. These may be enlisted in the same manner as parents or in-school resources, and the guidelines we presented for working in those settings apply here as well. Particularly when working with professional agencies, make your requests consistent with the functions and philosophy of those within the agency (do not ask a psychoanalytically inclined social case worker to follow a sophisticated behavioral procedure) unless you are able to provide sufficient training and consultation to ensure reliable performance.

Again, we must emphasize that the complex issues faced by many students with EBD, their families, and the educators who serve them are such that schools are not, *nor should they be,* able to deal with them alone. As public schools become more active participants in developing integrated, comprehensive services for children and youth with EBD, new models of service delivery are emerging in the schools. These include intensive wraparound planning, collaborative day treatment programs, and family-linked services (see Illback & Nelson, 1996). These models compel educators to learn new skills and to assume increasingly more collaborative roles with parents and other professionals.

SUMMARY

- Extending the effects of interventions that have been successfully applied in primary treatment settings is a complex task requiring intensive programming within these settings as well as assessment and intervention in those settings where these behavior changes also are needed and desired.
- Research has demonstrated that generalization of desired intervention outcomes can occur when it is systematically planned and implemented.
- Achieving for the successful transition of students to other education and noneducation settings involves preparing both the student and the receiving education program or agency.
- Postsecondary transition planning is required by law, and must address daily living, vocational, and social domains to facilitate students' adaptation to adult living.
- To improve outcomes for students with EBD, educators must work effectively with persons outside primary treatment settings.

DISCUSSION/APPLICATION IDEAS

1. Meet with a small group of peers and make a list of specific practices to facilitate the maintenance and generalization of student behavior based on the principles and strategies described in this chapter. Collectively evaluate this list and rate each practice in terms of (a) whether it would be likely to work and (b) how feasible it would be to implement.
2. Assume that you are a member of Eileen's IEP Team that is responsible for implementing her transition plan. Eileen's work-study supervisor has reported that she has been displaying angry outbursts toward coworkers. Suggest some strategies you could use to help Eileen monitor and reduce these outbursts.
3. Interview a general education teacher into whose classroom students with EBD have been placed. Ask about his or her experiences with inclusion, including what information was provided beforehand about the student, how much input he or she had on the process of placing the student, and what, if any, support he or she received once the student was placed.
4. Talk with a parent of a student who is exhibiting behavioral difficulties at school. How does he or she characterize interactions with the school concerning this child? What are the parent's goals for this child, and how does the school contribute to these? What could the school do to improve the relationship?

NOTES

1. Because these students are the last group of students with disabilities to be identified—in terms of age and grade level—and placed in special education programs (U.S. Department of Education, 2000), their entry into the educational mainstream is more accurately characterized as reintegration than integration.

REFERENCES

Altschuler, D. M., & Armstrong, T. L. (2001). Intensive aftercare for the high-risk juvenile parolee: Issues and approaches in reintegration and community supervision. In T. L. Armstrong (Ed.), *Intensive interventions with high-risk youths: Promising approaches in juvenile probation and parole* (pp. 45-84). Monsey, NY: Criminal Justice Press.

Anderson-Inman, L., Walker, H. M., & Purcell, J. (1984). Promoting the transfer of skills across settings: Transenvironmental programming for handicapped students in the mainstream. In W. R. Heward, T. E. Heron, D. S. Hill, & J. Trap-Porter (Eds.), *Focus on behavior analysis in education* (pp. 17-39). Upper Saddle River, NJ: Merrill/Prentice Hall.

Baer, D. M., & Wolf, M. M. (1970). The entry into natural communities of reinforcement. In R. Ulrich, T. Stachnik, & J. Mabry (Eds.), *Control of human behavior: Vol. II. From cure to prevention* (pp. 319-324). Glenview, IL: Scott, Foresman.

Baer, D. M., Wolf, M. M., & Risley, T. R. (1968). Some current dimensions of applied behavior analysis. *Journal of Applied Behavior Analysis, 1,* 91-97.

Bauer, A. M., & Shea, T. M. (1988). Structuring classrooms through level systems. *Focus on Exceptional Children, 21*(3), 1-12.

Braaten, S. (1979). The Madison School program: Programming for secondary level emotionally disturbed youth. *Behavioral Disorders, 4,* 153-162.

Bradley, R., Henderson, K., & Monfore, D. A. (2004). A national perspective on children with emotional disorders. *Behavioral Disorders, 29,* 211-223.

Brown, L., Nietupski, J., & Hamre-Nietupski, S. (1976). The criterion of ultimate functioning and public school services for severely handicapped students. In A. Thomas (Ed.), *Hey, don't forget about me: New directions for serving the severely handicapped* (pp. 2-15). Reston, VA: Council for Exceptional Children.

Buie Hune, J., & Nelson, C. M. (2002). Effects of teaching a problem-solving strategy on preschool children with problem behavior. *Behavioral Disorders, 27,* 185-207.

Bullis, M., Yovanoff, P., & Havel, E. (2004). The importance of getting started right: Further examination of the facility-to-community transition of formerly incarcerated youth. *Journal of Special Education, 38,* 80-94.

Clark, H. B., Unger, K. V., & Stewart, E. S. (1993). Transition of youth and young adults with emotional/behavioral disorders into employment, education, and independent living. *Community Alternatives: International Journal of Family Care, 5*(2), 19-46.

Clees, T. J. (1995). Self-recording of students' daily schedules of teachers' expectancies: Perspectives on reactivity, stimulus control, and generalization. *Exceptionality, 5,* 113-129.

Conroy, M. A., & Brown, W. H. (2004). Early identification, prevention, and early intervention with young children at risk for emotional or behavioral disorders: Issues, trends, and a call for action. *Behavioral Disorders, 29,* 224-236.

Cruz, L., & Cullinan, D. (2001). Awarding points, using levels to help children improve behavior. *Teaching Exceptional Children, 33*(3), 16-23.

Darch, C. B., & Kame'enui, E. J. (2004). *Instructional classroom management: A proactive approach to behavior management* (2nd ed.). Upper Saddle River, NJ: Merrill/Prentice Hall.

Davern, L. (2004). School-to-home notebooks: What parents have to say. *Teaching Exceptional Children, 36*(5), 22-27.

Duchnowski, A., Berg, K., & Kutash, K. (1995). Parent participation in and perception of placement decisions. In J. M. Kauffman, J. W. Lloyd, D. P. Hallahan, & T. A. Astuto (Eds.), *Issues in educational placement: Students with emotional and behavioral disorders* (pp. 183-195). Hillsdale, NJ: Lawrence Erlbaum Associates.

Edgar, E., & Siegel, S. (1995). Postsecondary scenarios for troubled and troubling youth. In J. M. Kauffman & D. P. Hallahan (Eds.), *The illusion of full inclusion: A comprehensive critique of a current special education bandwagon* (pp. 251-283). Austin, TX: PRO-ED.

Edgar, E. B., Webb, S. L., & Maddox, M. (1987). Issues in transition: Transfer of youth from correctional facilities to public schools. In C. M. Nelson, R. B. Rutherford, Jr., & B. I. Wolford (Eds.), *Special education in the criminal justice system* (pp. 251-272). Upper Saddle River, NJ: Merrill/Prentice Hall.

Frank, A. R., & Sitlington, P. L. (1997). Young adults with behavior disorders—before and after IDEA. *Behavioral Disorders, 23,* 40-56.

Gable, R. A., Mostert, M. R., & Tonelson, S. W. (2004). Assessing professional collaboration in schools: Knowing what works. *Preventing School Failure, 48*(3), 4-8.

Gaylord-Ross, R., & Haring, T. (1987). Social interaction research for adolescents with severe handicaps. *Behavioral Disorders, 12,* 264-275.

Gaylord-Ross, R. J., Haring, T. G., Breen, C., & Pitts-Conway, V. (1984). The training and generalization of social interaction skills with autistic youth. *Journal of Applied Behavior Analysis, 17,* 229-247.

Goetz, L., Guess, D., & Stremel-Campbell, K. (Eds.). (1987). *Innovative program design for individuals with dual sensory impairments.* Boston: Paul H. Brookes.

Graubard, P. S., Rosenberg, H., & Miller, M. B. (1971). Student applications of behavior modification to teachers and environments or ecological approaches to social deviancy. In E. A. Ramp & B. L. Hopkins (Eds.), *A new direction for education: Behavior analysis: 1971* (pp. 80-101). Lawrence: University of Kansas Support and Development Center for Follow Through.

Gresham, F. M. (1998). Social skills training: Should we raze, remodel, or rebuild? *Behavioral Disorders, 24,* 19-25.

Gresham, F. M., Elliott, S. N., & Black, F. L. (1987). Teacher-rated social skills of mainstreamed mildly handicapped and nonhandicapped children. *School Psychology Review, 16,* 78-88.

Guetzloe, E. (1999). Inclusion: The broken promise. *Preventing School Failure, 43,* 92-98.

Gunter, P. L., Fox, J. J., Brady, M. P., Shores, R. E., & Cavanaugh, K. (1988). Nonhandicapped peers as multiple exemplars: A generalization tactic for promoting autistic students' social skills. *Behavioral Disorders, 13,* 116-126.

Harvey, M. W. (2001). Vocational-technical education: A logical approach to dropout prevention for secondary special education. *Preventing School Failure, 45,* 108-113.

Hewett, F. M., & Taylor, F. D. (1980). *The emotionally disturbed child in the classroom: The orchestration of success* (2nd ed.). Boston: Allyn & Bacon.

Hollinger, J. D. (1987). Social skills for behaviorally disordered children as preparation for mainstreaming: Theory, practice, and new directions. *Remedial and Special Education, 8*(4), 17-27.

Hrydowy, E. R., Stokes, T. F., & Martin, G. L. (1984). Training elementary students to prompt teacher praise. *Education and Treatment of Children, 7,* 99-108.

Illback, R. J., & Nelson, C. M. (Eds.). (1996). *Emerging school-based approaches for children and youth with emotional and behavioral disorders: Research or practice and service integration.* New York: Haworth Press.

Kazdin, A. E. (1977). Vicarious reinforcement and direction of behavior change in the classroom. *Behavior Therapy, 8,* 57-63.

Klinger, J. K., Vaughn, S., Hughes, M. T., Schumm, J. S., & Elbaum, B. (1998). Outcomes for students with and without learning disabilities in inclusive classrooms. *Learning Disabilities Research and Practice, 13,* 153-161.

Lane, K. L., Bocian, K. M., MacMillan, D. L., & Gresham, F. M. (2004). Treatment integrity: An essential—but often forgotten—component of school-based interventions. *Preventing School Failure, 48*(3), 36-43.

LaNunziata, L. J., Hunt, K. P., & Cooper, J. O. (1984). Suggestions for phasing out token economy systems in primary and intermediate grades. *Techniques: A Journal for Remedial Education and Counseling, 1,* 151-156.

Levendoski, L. S., & Cartledge, G. (2000). Self-monitoring for elementary school students with serious emotional disturbances: Classroom applications for increased academic responding. *Behavioral Disorders, 25,* 211-224.

Maag, J. W., & Katsiyannis, A. (1998). Challenges facing successful transition for youths with EBD. *Behavioral Disorders, 23,* 209-221.

MacMillan, D. L., Gresham, F. M., & Forness, S. R. (1996). Full inclusion: An empirical perspective. *Behavioral Disorders, 21,* 145-159.

Malmgren, K., Edgar, E., & Neel, R. S. (1998). Postschool status of youths with behavioral disorders. *Behavioral Disorders, 23,* 257-263.

Marholin, D., & Steinman, W. (1977). Stimulus control in the classroom as a function of the behavior reinforced. *Journal of Applied Behavior Analysis, 10,* 465-478.

McEvoy, M. A., & Odom, S. L. (1987). Social interaction training for preschool children with behavioral disorders. *Behavioral Disorders, 12,* 242-251.

McLaughlin, M. J., Leone, P. E., Warren, S. H., & Schofield, P. F. (1994). *Doing things differently: Issues and options for creating comprehensive school-linked services for children and youth with emotional or behavioral disorders.* College Park: University of Maryland and Westat, Inc.

Mercer, C. D., & Mercer, A. R. (2001). *Teaching students with learning problems* (6th ed.). Upper Saddle River, NJ: Merrill/Prentice Hall.

Nelson, C. M., Leone, P. E., & Rutherford, R. B. (2004). Youth delinquency: Prevention and intervention. In R. B. Rutherford, M. M. Quinn, & S. R. Mathur (Eds.), *Handbook of research in emotional and behavioral disorders* (pp. 282-301). New York: Guilford.

Noell, G. H., Witt, J. C., LaFleur, L. H., Mortenson, B. P., Ranier, D. D., & LeVelle, J. (2000). Increasing intervention implementation in general education following consultation: A comparison of two follow-up strategies. *Journal of Applied Behavior Analysis, 33,* 271-284.

Polsgrove, L., & Smith, S. W. (2004). Informed practice in teaching self-control to children with emotional and behavioral disorders. In R. B. Rutherford, M. M. Quinn, & S. R. Mathur (Eds.), *Handbook of research in emotional and behavioral disorders* (pp. 399-425). New York: Guilford.

Rock, E. E., Rosenberg, M. S., & Carran, D. T. (1994). Variables affecting the reintegration rate of students with serious emotional disturbance. *Exceptional Children, 61,* 254-268.

Rutherford, R. B., Jr., & Nelson, C. M. (1988). Generalization and maintenance of treatment effects. In J. C. Witt, S. N. Elliott, & F. M. Gresham (Eds.), *Handbook of behavior therapy in education* (pp. 277-324). New York: Plenum.

Rylance, B. J. (1997). Predictors of high school graduation or dropping out for youths with severe emotional disturbance. *Behavioral Disorders, 23,* 5-17.

Sample, P. L. (1998). Post-school outcomes for students with significant emotional disturbance following best-practice transition services. *Behavioral Disorders, 23,* 231-242.

Scott, T. M., & Nelson, C. M. (1998). Confusion and failure in facilitating generalized social responding in the school setting: Sometimes 2 + 2 = 5. *Behavioral Disorders, 23,* 264-275.

Shinn, M. R., Ramsey, E., Walker, H. M., Stieber, S., & O'Neill, R. E. (1987). Antisocial behavior in school settings: Initial differences in an at risk and normal population. *Journal of Special Education, 21,* 69-84.

Shores, R. E. (1987). Overview of research on social interaction: A historical and personal perspective. *Behavioral Disorders, 12,* 233-241.

Simpson, R. L. (1987). Social interaction of behaviorally disordered children and youth: Where are we and where do we need to go? *Behavioral Disorders, 12,* 292-298.

Sitlington, P. L., & Neubert, D. A. (2004). Preparing youths with emotional or behavioral disorders for transition to adult life: Can it be done within the standards-based reform movement? *Behavioral Disorders, 29,* 279-288.

Stephens, S. A., & Lakin, K. C. (1995). Where students with emotional or behavioral disorders go to school. In J. M. Kauffman, J. W. Lloyd, D. P. Hallahan, & T. A. Astuto (Eds.), *Issues in educational placement: Students with emotional and behavioral disorders* (pp. 47-74). Hillsdale, NJ: Lawrence Erlbaum Associates.

Stokes, T. F., & Baer, D. M. (1977). An implicit technology of generalization. *Journal of Applied Behavior Analysis, 10,* 349-367.

Stokes, T. F., & Osnes, P. G. (1986). Programming the generalization of children's social behavior. In P. S. Strain, M. J. Guralnick, & H. M. Walker (Eds.), *Children's social behavior: Development, assessment, and modification* (pp. 407-443). Orlando, FL: Academic Press.

Strain, P. S., & Danko, C. D. (1995). Caregivers' encouragement of positive interaction between preschoolers with autism and their siblings. *Journal of Emotional and Behavioral Disorders, 3,* 2-12.

Strain, P. S., Shores, R. E., & Kerr, M. M. (1976). An experimental analysis of "spillover" effects on the social interaction of behaviorally handicapped preschool children. *Journal of Applied Behavior Analysis, 9,* 31-40.

Stroul, B., Goldman, S., Lourie, I., Katz-Leavy, J., & Zeigler-Dendy, C. (1992). *Profiles of local systems of care for children and adolescents with severe emotional disturbances.* Washington, DC: Georgetown University Child Development Center, CASSP Technical Assistance Center.

Taylor, F. D., & Soloway, M. M. (1973). The Madison School plan: A functional model for merging the regular and special classrooms. In E. Deno (Ed.), *Instructional alternatives for exceptional children* (pp. 145-155). Reston, VA: Council for Exceptional Children.

Taylor, S. J., Bilken, D., & Knoll, J. (Eds.). (1987). *Community integration for people with severe disabilities.* New York: Teachers College Press.

U.S. Department of Education. (2000). *21st annual report to Congress on the implementation of the Individuals with Disability Education Act.* Washington, DC: U.S. Department of Education, Office of Special Education and Rehabilitative Services.

Vetter-Zemitsch, A., Bernstein, R., Johnson, J., Larson, C., Simon, D., Smith, D., et al. (1984). The on campus program: A systematic/behavioral approach to behavior disorders in high school. *Focus on Exceptional Children, 16*(6), 1-8.

Walker, H. M., & Bullis, M. (1996). A comprehensive services model for troubled youth. In C. M. Nelson, B. Wolford, & R. B. Rutherford (Eds.), *Developing comprehensive systems that work for troubled youth* (pp. 122-148). Richmond, KY: National Coalition for Juvenile Justice Services.

Walker, H. M., Shinn, M. R., O'Neill, R. E., & Ramsey, E. (1987). A longitudinal assessment of the development of antisocial behavior in boys: Rationale, methodology, and first year results. *Remedial and Special Education, 8*(4), 7-16, 27.

Walker, H. M., & Stieber, S. (1998). Teacher ratings of social skills as longitudinal predictors of long-term arrest status in a sample of at-risk males. *Behavioral Disorders, 23,* 222-230.

Walsh, J. M., & Jones, B. (2004). New models of cooperative teaching. *Teaching Exceptional Children, 36*(5), 14-20.

Wilder, L. K. (2003). Transitioning homeless youth with emotional and behavioral disorders. *Beyond Behavior, 13*(1), 17-19.

Wong, K. L. H., Kauffman, J. M., & Lloyd, J. W. (1991). Choices for integration: Selecting teachers for mainstreaming students with emotional or behavioral disorders. *Intervention in School and Clinic, 27,* 108-115.

EPILOGUE: TAKING CARE OF YOURSELF

You have studied this textbook because of your interest in helping students with emotional and behavioral disorders. Now we'd like to offer a few final words on how you can help *yourself* avoid burnout. Burnout is not an individual problem but rather the result of a dislocation between who you are and what is expected of you at work. Left unchecked, burnout is "a malady that spreads gradually and continuously over time, putting people into a downward spiral" (Maslach & Leiter, 1997, p. 17). Studies have shown that six factors cause burnout:

1. Work overload
2. Lack of control
3. Insufficient reward—this refers to both psychological rewards as well as tangible compensation
4. Unfairness
5. Breakdown of community
6. Value conflict

As you read the following statement, see if you can identify these six factors.

> The most effective behavior managers are teachers who acknowledge that reinforcement and punishment occur naturally and, consequently, analyze and modify environmental, curricular, and instructional variables to promote appropriate behavior. These teachers worked hard to positively reinforce appropriate students' behavior and ignore misbehavior when it does not interfere with other students' learning, classroom routines, or is otherwise reinforcing. They also sparingly use reprimands and only in an even-handed, matter-of-fact tone. Students view these teachers as people whose attention is valued, whom they want to be around, whom they enjoy . . . rather than as a watchdog to be feared because of the punishment they may dole out.
>
> Perhaps there are not more teachers who engage in these activities because they are not reinforced for doing so. Teachers are paid whether or not students display such appropriate behaviors. Their workloads are not based on how effective[ly] they manage behavior or on how much their students learn. More conceivably, teachers who use positive reinforcement techniques effectively may be punished: Administrators may see them as the likely candidates to deal with students with the most challenging behaviors. These teachers, in turn, may receive the preponderance of these students and that represents a daunting task, even for special educators trained in behavior management with small case loads and paraeducator assistance. The unintended result may be to punish good behavior management skills. (Maag, 2001, p. 185)

The good news is that you can prevent burnout through work habits that counteract the six risk factors. Here are a few examples; check the Companion Website for additional Web resources and examples. *Effective time management,* for example, can ease your workload. Speak up when you are getting more than your fair share of assignments: saying "no" and *setting limits* can help you cope with unfairness and the feeling that situations are out of your control. Keep in mind, however, that the stress of a *well-managed* challenge is actually helpful in preventing burnout. Don't assume that merely avoiding big assignments or challenging students will be a panacea. When you *adopt proven strategies* instead of fads, you increase your effectiveness and the psychological reward of a job well done. *Build a sense of community* through informal activities (e.g., humorous exchanges, celebrations, informal gatherings, joint study of lessons or readings, and tackling workplace problems as a team). Studies have shown that employees working together can guard against the feelings of isolation and cynicism that characterize burnout (Maslach & Leiter, 1997).

As colleagues for nearly 30 years, we hope that you, too, will have lasting professional relationships. May *your* peers safeguard you through the rough times and join you in celebrating your many future accomplishments.

REFERENCES

Maag, J. (2001). Rewarded by punishment: Reflections on the disuse of positive reinforcement in schools. *Exceptional Children, 67,* 173–186.

Maslach, C., & Leiter, M. (1997). *The truth about burnout: How organizations cause personal stress and what to do about it.* San Francisco: Jossey-Bass.

INDEX

AAMD; *See* American Association of Mental Deficiency (AAMD)
Aarons, G.A., 319
(A-B-C); *See* Antecedent-behavior-consequence (A-B-C) assessment
A-B-A-B designs, 185–186
Abolishing operations (AO), 295
Academic assessment, and EBD certification, 23, 24, 25
Academic competencies, 349
Academic intervention, 263
Academic precorrection, 55
Accommodation plan, 13
Achenback, T. M., 18
Acquisition deficit, 238
Acquisto, J., 294
Activity reinforcement, 77
ADA; PL 101-336, 13
Adaptive Behavior Scale, School Edition, 25
Adelins, J. D., 299
ADHD; *See* Attention-deficit hyperactive disorder (ADHD)
Aggressive behavior
  academic intervention, 263
  anger management training, 266, 272–273
  conflict resolution strategies, 272
  contingency management strategies, 266, 269
  crisis intervention, 270–272
  documenting and understanding, 261–262
  peer confrontation, 272
  peer-mediated strategies, 272–273
  self-mediated strategies, 273–274
  social competence training, 266
  student characteristics, 264
  teacher-mediated strategies, 262–272
  time-out, 270
  token reinforcement, 269–270
  verbal deescalation, 263, 265–266
  psychological skills area, 243–245
Ahearn, W. H., 289, 291
AIMS; *See Assessment for Integration into Mainstream Settings* (AIMS)
Alberto, P.A., 58, 69, 72, 74, 75, 178, 179, 185, 186, 188, 189
Albin, R.W., 110, 119
Alcohol, 325, 327
Alder, N., 56
Algozzine, B., 223
Algozzine, R., 17, 22
Alternating treatments design, 188–189
Altschuler, D. M., 356
American Association of Mental Deficiency (AAMD), 25
American Psychiatric Association, 20, 22, 321, 322, 323, 329, 330, 331
Americans with Disabilities Act of 1990, 13
Amundson, D., 41
Analog measure, 238
Anderson, J.A., 52
Anderson, K., 90
Anderson, R. N., 323
Anderson-Inman, L., 349
Anger management training, 266
Anger thermometer, 267–269
Antecedent-behavior-consequence (A-B-C) assessment, 98, 114–116, 261
  example record, 115
  types of, 59–60
Antecedent stimuli, 69
  setting events, 60
Antecedents, Behaviors, and Consequences for Discrimination Training, 275
Antisocial behavior, introduction to, 260–261; *See also* Aggressive behavior; Teacher-mediated strategies
Anxiety, principles of remediation, 229
Anxiety disorders, 330–331
AO; *See* Abolishing operations (AO)
Applied behavior analysis, 69–73
  principle I, 69–71
  principle II, 71–72
  principle III, 71–72
  principle IV, 72–73
  principle V, 73
  principle VI, 73
Argulewicz, E. N., 88
Arllen, N. L., 272, 273
Armstrong, T. L., 356
Asmus, J. M., 197
Assessment
  descriptive, 118
  direct behavior, 107
  emotional or behavior disorder certification, 19–27
  indirect, 119
  indirect behavioral, 107
Assessment-based intervention planning, 110–128; *See also* Behavioral assessment
  functional methods, 117
  step 1 assess student behavior, 111–116
  step 2 hypothesis, 116–118
  step 3 validity of hypothesis, 118–120
  step 4 design intervention, 120–124
  step 5 data collection, 124
  step 6 intervention objectives, 125–128
Assessment for identification, behavioral disorder identification, 18–19

Assessment for Integration into Mainstream Settings (AIMS), 108
Assignments
and behavior, 54-55
principles of remediation, 229
Astuto, T.A., 58
Attention, principles of remediation, 229
Attention and praise, effective use of, 56-58
Attention-deficit hyperactive disorder (ADHD), 6-7
Attkisson, C.A., 11
Ault, M.J., 126
Austin, G.A., 223
Autographing, 164-167
Automatic reinforcement, 299-300
Aversive procedures, legal and ethical guidelines, 85
Aversive stimulus, 71

Baer, D. M., 69, 139, 341, 342
Bailey, D. B., 73, 79
Bailey, J. S., 82, 296
Balla, D.A., 25
Bambara, L., 89
Bandura, A., 73, 76
Bantz, J., 58
Bar graph, 168
Barnett, D.W., 16
Barrett, H. C., 154
Barrett, S. B., 50
Barton, L. E., 74, 86
Barton-Arwood, S., 52
Baseline, 170-171
Baseline data, 178
guidelines for, 178
Bates, P., 227
Baugher, M., 324
Bauman, K. E., 301
Baumeister, A.A., 289, 305
Beard, K., 90
Becker, W. C., 18, 57, 71
Behavior
consistently and immediately, 73
controlled by stimuli, 69-71
escape or avoid, 118
gain access, 118
identifying problem, 103-110
modeling, 73, 76
and punishment, 72-73
and reinforcement, 71
systematic procedures for influencing, 73-84
withholding the consequences, 71-72
Behavior change; *See* Maintenance and generalization; Transition plan
Behavior contract, 76-77
Behavior disorders; *See also* Emotional or behavioral disorder (EBD)
identifying students, 16-28
or problem behaviors, 14-16
Behavior enhancement
activity reinforcement, 77
contingency contract, 76-77
current trends, 88-90
edible reinforcement, 78-79
introduction to, 73-74
modeling, 76
procedures for, 73-79
social reinforcement, 75-76
tactile and sensory reinforcement, 79
tangible reinforcement, 78
token reinforcement, 77-78
Behavior incident data, 45-47
Behavior intervention plan (BIP), 9; *See also* Assessment-based intervention planning; Behavioral assessment
criteria for effective, 10
example of, 99-100
positive behavior support, 7, 9-11
Behavior management, 42-44; *See also* Problem behavior
Behavior observation record, 105
Behavior problems
data about, 45-47
own the problem, 42-43
prevention and early intervention, 43-44
school, 41-44
Behavior rating scales, 107
Behavior reduction
current trends, 88-90
differential reinforcement, 80-81
extinction, 81
introduction, 79-80
legal and ethical guidelines, 85-88
other procedures, 84
overcorrection, 83
physical aversives, 83-84
procedures for, 79-84
response cost, 82
time-out, 82-83
verbal aversives, 81-82
Behavior report, data from, 45-47
Behavior specialist, 27
Behavior support team, and behavior intervention planning, 10, 19
Behavioral assessment, 102-103
antecedent-behavior-consequence (A-B-C) assessment, 98, 114-116
data collection, 124
direct observation, 114-116
functional methods, 117
guidelines for, 103
hypothesis proposal, 116-118
and intervention planning, 110-116
interviews, 112-114
long- and short-term objectives, 125-128
operational definition, 111
scatter plot, 112-113
school records, 113-114
target behaviors, 111-112
task analysis, 126
Behavioral context, 102
Behavioral interventions
introduction to, 69
principles of, 69-73
Behavioral interviews, 112-114
Behavioral objectives, 111-112, 125-128
Behavior-specific praise, 76
Behavior-specific praise statement (BSPS), 76
Belanoff, P., 154

Berg, K., 361
Berkson, G., 291
Best, A. M., 26
Beyond Behavior, 134
Bicanich, P., 205
Bijou, S., 139
Bilken, D., 357
Binge drinking, 327
BIP; *See* Behavior intervention plan (BIP)
Bipolar disorder, 323
Black, F. L., 350
Blair, K., 55
Blakeley-Smith, A. B., 305
Block-Pedego, A., 18, 25, 113
Bocian, K. M., 353
Bodfish, J. B., 289, 291, 292, 293
Bolig, A. A., 228
Borthwick, S., 291
Bos, C., 55
Bower, B., 154
Boyd, K., 212
Braaten, S., 86, 87, 350
Bradley, R., 26, 349
Brady, M. P., 346
Breen, C., 343
Brent, D. A., 324
Brewer, D. M., 154
Bridge, J., 324
Brigham, F. J., 13
Brodigan, D., 60
Brooks, K., 41
Browder, D., 223
Brown, C. H., 42
Brown, G., 223, 224
Brown, K. A., 295
Brown, L., 356
Brown, P., 57
Brown, W. H., 356
Brulle, A. R., 74, 86
Bry, B. H., 90
BSPS; *See* Behavior-specific praise statement (BSPS)
Buie, J. D., 83
Buie Hune, J., 346
Bulimia, 329-330
Bullis, M., 355, 357
Burton, C., 223
Butt, K., 234
Cade, T., 227
Callahan, K., 134, 175, 196
Cameron, S., 303
Carden-Smith, L. K., 207
Carlyon, W. D., 228
Carr, E. G., 57, 74, 89, 294
Carr, S., 234
Carr, V. G., 59
Carran, D. T., 348, 349, 354
Carta, J., 233
Cartledge, G., 89, 234, 239, 240, 263, 272, 346
Case study
  anger management skills lessons, 276-284
  behavior plan, 306-311
  eating disorder, 332
  psychiatric problems, 318
  self-stimulatory behavior (SSB), 289
  transition plan, 336-339
Cash, M. E., 212
Casto, G. W., 232
Cavanaugh, K., 346
CEC; *See* Council for Exceptional Children
Certification
  archival student data, 25
    and behavioral disorder identification, 19-27
    and IDEA, 19
  medical, 26
  mental health assessment, 20, 22-23, 24
  school-based assessment, 23-27
  social and linguistic functioning, 24, 25
Changing criterion design, 186-188
Chapman, D., 45
Chart, 162; *See also* Graphing and charting
Checklists, 107
Childs, K. E., 112
Choutka, C. M., 52, 55
Chung, B. I., 289, 291
Cicchetti, D. V., 25
Cipani, E., 52
Clark, H. B., 358
Clark, K. M., 289, 291
Clarke, S., 112
Classroom
  antecedents and consequences, 59-60
  attention and praise, 56-58
  effective behavior management, 52-53
  group management systems, 58-61
  instruction and student behavior, 52-58
  levels systems, 60-61
  negative behavior management strategies, 59
  positive behavior support, 50-61
  precorrection, 55
  promoting success, 51-52
  prompts and cues, 55-56
    and school-wide rules, 51
    and school-wide systems design, 50-51
  tangible reinforcers, 52
Classroom behavior management; *See* Classroom
Classroom measurement; *See also* Monitoring and evaluation; Student progress
  overview of, 137-142
  student progress monitoring, 137-142
Classroom procedures, 227
Clees, T. J., 346
Club drugs, 328
CMO; *See* Conditioned motivation operation (CMO)
Cognitive behavior modification, 346
Colavecchia, B., 81
Cole, L., 25
Collaboration and communication, 359-366
  community professionals and agencies, 364-366
  families, 360-366
  family and classroom goals, 362-364
  school personnel, 359-360
Collaborative effort, and positive behavior support, 9
Colletti, L., 90
Colvin, G., 10, 19, 55, 270, 273
Comarata, A., 223

Combs, C., 223
Common physical stimuli, 345-346
Common social stimuli, 346
Communication; *See* Collaboration and communication
Communicative function, 6
Community-based training, 357
Community professionals and agencies, collaboration and communication, 364
Competing explanations, 184
Condition lines, 170-171
Conditioned motivation operation (CMO), 295
Conditioned reinforcer, 57
Conditions, 170-171
Conduct disorder; *See* Antisocial behavior
Cone, J. D., 166, 167
Connell, J. E., 213
Conoley, J. C., 264
Conroy, M.A., 110, 112, 197, 356
Consequences, and behavior, 70-71
Consequent stimuli, 69
Consulting teacher, 27
Contingency, 73, 76-77, 208-210, 228, 231, 266, 269
Contingency contract, 76-77, 202, 208-210
Contingent observation, 83
Continuous behavior, 143
Contract
  behavior, 76-77
  contingency, 76-77, 202, 208-210
  home-based, 202
Cook, S. B., 232
Cooke, N. L., 139
Cooley, C., 52
Cooper, J. O., 145, 350
Cooperative learning, 233
Copeland, S. R., 71, 75, 76
Coprophagia, 292
Corporal punishment, 85
Correct responding, calculating of, 135
Council for Behavioral Disorders, 85
Council for Children with Behavioral Disorders (CCBD), 20, 85
Council for Exceptional Children, 12, 13, 83
Courson, F. H., 139
Court, D., 239
Coutinho, M. J., 26
Cowdery, G. E., 304
Cowen, E. L., 223
Cox, P., 212
Coyle, E. M., 210
Crawford, T. W., 289, 292
Crenshaw, T., 43
Crimmins, D. B., 112, 294
Criscitiello, E., 232
Crisis intervention, 270-272
Crisis management, 123-124
Criterion of ultimate functioning, 356
Crone, D.A., 118
Cruz, L., 350
Cullinan, D., 18, 350
Cumblad, C., 10
Cummings, A., 305
Cumulative graph, 168-169

Daly, E. J., III, 16, 119
Danko, C. D., 362
Darch, C. B., 52, 53, 54, 74, 80, 170, 350
Data analysis, 175
  analyzing level, 179
  data trends, 179, 181, 182, 183-184
  formative evaluation, 175, 177, 178
  functional relationships, 178
  summative data, 176
Data collection
  behavior incident, 45-47
  behavior report, 45-47
    and behavioral assessment, 124
    and classroom measurement, 137-142
  data analysis, 175
  decision making, 175-184
  office discipline referral (ODR), 45-47
  summary of, 46-47
Data collection form, 45-47
Data decision rules, 137
  steps for implementing, 182
Data trend analysis, 179, 181, 182, 183-184
Data-based decision making, 162, 175-184; *See also* Data analysis; Data collection
Data-based evaluation, and positive behavior support, 9
Daunic, A. P., 272
Davern, L., 228, 362
Davis, C.A., 200
Dawson-Rodriques, K., 227
Dealing with Anger, 266
Decreasing trend, 181
Dedrick, C., 79, 84
Dejud, C., 55
Del'Homme, M., 18
Delia, M. D., 299
Delquadri, J., 233
Denny, R. K., 57, 74, 75, 79, 136, 140, 175, 270
Deno, S. L., 105, 140, 162, 169, 170, 173, 181
DePaepe, P., 57
Dependent group contingency, 209
Depression, 321-323
Derby, M., 295
Descriptive function, 178
Devany, J., 300
Diagnostic and Statistical Manual of Mental Disorders, 4th Edition (DSM-IV), 20, 321
  diagnostic classifications, 22
Dickson, M., 154
Dietz, D. E., 80
Differential reinforcement, 57, 80-81
Differential reinforcement of alternate behavior (DRA), 81
Differential reinforcement of incompatible behavior (DRI), 81
  guidelines for, 304
Differential reinforcement of low rates of behavior (DRL), 80, 201
Differential reinforcement of other behavior (DRO), 80, 200
  guidelines for, 304
  SSB & SIB, 298, 304
DiGangi, S.A., 234
Direct assessment of behavior, 107

Disciplinary policies
controlled procedures, 86
legal and ethical guidelines, 85-88
permitted procedures, 86
prohibited procedures, 86
Discipline regulations, 12-13
Discrete behavior, 143
Discrete learning trials, 147
Discriminative stimulus, 54
Disruptive behaviors, reasons for, 194-195
Distributed trials, 147
Dodd, J. M., 211
Dodge, K., 234
Donnellan, A. M., 6
Dorsey, M. F., 294, 301, 303
Downing, J. A., 202
Doyle, P. M., 126
DRA; *See* Differential reinforcement of alternate behavior (DRA)
DRI; *See* Differential reinforcement of incompatible behavior (DRI)
DRL; *See* Differential reinforcement of low rates of behavior (DRL)
DRO; *See* Differential reinforcement of other behavior (DRO)
Drug and alcohol abuse, 324-329
appeal and risks, 325-326
DSM-IV; *See Diagnostic and Statistical Manual of Mental Disorders, 4th Edition (DSM-IV)*
Dube, W. V., 289, 291
Duchnowski, A. J., 52, 361
Duhon, G. J., 213
Dunlap, G., 43, 55, 112, 299
Durand, V. M., 112, 294
Duration, and progress monitoring, 142
Duration recording, 147
Dysthymia, 321
symptoms of, 322-323

Eating disorders, 329-330
EBD; *See* Emotional or behavioral disorder (EBD)
Eber, L., 10, 14
Ecological ceiling, 181
ED; *See* Emotional disorders (ED)
Eddy, J. M., 285
Edgar, E., 349, 355, 356, 357
Edible reinforcers, 58, 78-79
Education of the Handicapped Act of 1975, 11
Educational placement, emotional or behavioral disorder (EBD), 29-31
Educational progress, and EBD certification, 23, 25
Effective behavioral support, 7
Egar, E. B., 354, 355
Egel, A. L., 299
Elbaum, B., 348
Eldridge, N. 204
Elective mutism, 238
Eligibility determination checklist, 21
Elliott, D., 41
Elliott, R., 57
Elliott, S. N., 350
Ellis, C., 89
Emotional disorders (ED), IDEA defined, 14-15
Emotional or behavioral disorder (EBD)
assessment for identification, 18-19
assessment process, 16
behavior support, 27-28
certification, 19-27
educational placement, 28-31
IDEA defined, 14-15
identifying students with, 16-28
and instruction, 52
introduction to, 5-6
pupil identification assessment process, 24
systematic screening, 17-18
Enhancement procedures, 73-74
Environment, SIB & SSB, 300, 301-303
Environmentally mediated interventions, 195-197
rules, 195-197
teacher movement patterns, 197
EO; *See* Establishing operations (EO)
Epstein, M. H., 10, 18, 25, 42, 227
Equal interval graph, 168-169
Equal ratio graph, 168-169
Esbensen, A. J., 292
Escape and avoidance behaviors, 71, 118
Establishing operations (EO), 295
Ethics; *See* Legal and ethical guidelines
Evans, C., 18
Evans, M. B., 57
Exclusionary time-out, 83
Experimental control, 184
External validity, 184
Externalizing behavior patterns, 18
Extinction, 57, 71-72, 81, 298
SSB & SIB, 298, 304-305
Eyman, R., 291

Fabre, T. R., 18, 20, 27
Fabry, B. D., 166, 167
Fair pair rule, 72-73
Falk, G. D., 112
Falk, K. B., 52
Families
classroom support, 362-364
collaboration and communication, 360-366
positive behavior support, 361-362
Farber, J. M., 301
Farra, H., 224
Farrell, D.T., 60
Farrington, D. P., 261
Favell, J. E., 292, 298, 303
FBA; *See* Functional behavioral assessment (FBA)
Federal Register, 15
Feedback, 57
Feil, E. G., 13, 18, 43
Fertman, C., 319
Fetrow, R.A., 272
Fisher, D., 223
Fisher, W. W., 294, 299
Fluency deficit, 238
Fogt, J., 89
Foley, R. M., 227
Formative evaluation, 137
Forness, S. R., 15, 22, 26, 43, 319, 348, 349
Fowler, M., 231
Fowler, S.A., 207
Fox, J. J., 80, 107, 110, 112, 346

Fox, S. L., 103, 121, 181
Foxx, R. M., 82
Frank, A. R., 89, 263, 357
Franklin, M. E., 239
Frequency, and progress
monitoring, 142-143
Frequency polygon, 168-169
Frequency recording, 147
Frey, K. S., 90, 240
Friedman, R.A., 10
Friman, P. C., 228, 305, 307
Fuchs, D., 137, 138, 139, 233
Fuchs, L.A., 233
Fuchs, L. S., 137, 138, 139, 143, 169
Full inclusion, 30
Functional analysis, 119, 294
brief, 119
extended, 119
Functional behavioral assessments
(FBAs), 6, 294; *See also*
Assessment-based intervention
planning; Behavioral
assessment
Functional mediators, 345-347
Functional relationship, 119-120
and data collection, 178

Gable, R.A., 80, 110, 119, 120, 128,
272, 273, 359
Gain access behavior, 118
Galand, B., 7
Gardenier, N. C., 289, 291
Garland, A. F., 319
Gast, D. L., 83, 137, 157, 164, 169,
179, 181, 184, 186, 189
Gast, K. B., 175
Gatti, S. L., 213
Gaylord-Ross, R. J., 343, 351
Generalization plan, writing of, 344
Generalized anxiety disorder, 330
Gerber, B. L., 136, 175
Giek, K., 208
Gilbertson, D., 13, 52, 53, 55, 74
Gipson, B., 266
Givon, S., 239
Goetz, L., 357
Goff, G.A., 305
Goh, H. L., 299
Golden, R. N., 289, 292
Goldman, S., 364
Goldstein, A. P., 242, 245, 264
Golly, A., 90
Gonzalez, J. E., 25, 42
Gonzalez, M., 18
Good, R. H., 55
Good behavior game, 210-211
Gordon, B. D., 82
Gorham, G., 90
Gould, M., 324
Grant, S. H., 75
Graph, 162; *See also* Graphing and
charting
Graphing and charting
autographing formats, 164-167
decision graph, 183
defined, 167-168
for program monitoring and
evaluation, 172-175
guidelines for construction,
170-171
student performance, 164-175
types of, 168-169
Graubard, P. S., 343
Green, G., 299
Greenberg, M., 42
Greenberg, T., 324
Greenwood, C. R., 108, 233
Gresham, F. M., 16, 20, 25, 29, 42, 43,
51, 55, 56, 71, 75, 77, 85, 110,
234, 238, 240, 348, 349, 350,
351, 353
Gresham, R., 201
Group contingencies, 208-210,
228, 231
Group goal setting and feedback,
206-207
Group management systems, and
classroom management, 58-61
Guess, D., 357
Guetzloe, E., 340, 348
Gunter, P. L., 28, 43, 56, 57, 74, 75,
79, 89, 136, 137, 138, 140, 175,
197, 198, 227, 233, 270, 346
Guzzo, B.A., 90, 240

Hagopian, L. P., 294
Hall, R. V., 153, 186
Hall, T. E., 228
Hallahan, D. P., 29, 58
Hallucinogens, 327
Hamburg, B., 41
Hamm, C., 223
Hammond, R. W., 266
Hamre-Nietupski, S., 356
Handler, M. W., 90
Handwriting, principles of
remediation, 230-331
Hanley, G. P., 299, 305
Hansen, D. J., 223, 240, 241
Happy Valley Elementary school,
problems at, 38-41
Haring, N. G., 108, 179, 181, 182
Haring, T. G., 343, 351
Harper, G. F., 125
Harris, F. R., 57
Harrison, J., 57
Harrison Middle School (2001), 226
Hartman, R., 270
Hartmann, D. P., 186
Harvath, B., 45
Harvey, M. W., 357
Haugen, L., 90
Hausafus, C. O., 156
Havel, E., 356
Hayes, S. C., 307
Heffner, T., 154
Henderson, K., 26, 348
Hendrickson, J. M., 272, 273
Henry, D., 75
Hepler, N., 319
Heroin, 327
Heward, W. L., 139
Hickman, C., 291, 298, 299
Hieneman, 43
High-probability behavior, 77
High-probability request
sequences, 200
Hirschstein, M. K., 90, 240
Hoffman, C. C., 119, 128
Hofweber, C., 45
Hollinger, J. D., 351
Home-based contract, 202
Homework strategies, 227-228
Honig v. Doe, 85
Hooper, S. R., 25
Hopkins, B. L., 57
Hopkins, R., 223

Hops, H., 108
Horner, R. H., 6, 7, 8, 10, 19, 43, 45, 110, 118, 119, 195, 238
Hosp, J. L., 26, 140
Hosp, M. K., 140
Host environments, 7
Hough, R. L., 319
Howell, K. W., 103, 119, 121, 128, 181
Hoyson, M., 206
Hoyt, R., 301
Hrydowy, E. R., 343
Hudson, S., 52, 57, 90
Hughes, C., 272
Hughes, H. H., 210
Hughes, M. T., 348
Hummel, J. H., 43, 74, 89, 134
Hundert, J., 82
Hune, J. B., 89-90, 234
Hunt, K. P., 350
Hunter, J., 9, 10
Hypersomnia, 321
Hypothesis
  and behavioral assessment, 116-118
  validity of, 118-120

Ialongo, N., 210
IDEA; *See* Individuals with Disabilities Education Act (IDEA)
IEP; *See* Individualized education plan (IEP)
IEP Team; *See* Individualized Education Program Team (IEP Team)
Illback, R. J., 10, 366
Inclusion, 30
Independent group contingency, 209
Indirect behavioral assessment, 107
Indiscriminable contingencies, 345
Individualized education plan (IEP), 6, 12
  performance chart, 166
Individualized Education Program Team (IEP Team), 12, 17
  behavior support, 27
  eligibility decisions, 28
Individuals with Disabilities Education Act (IDEA), 6, 11-13, 109
  emotional disorders, 14-15
Individuals with Disabilities Education Improvement Act of 2004, 6-7
Inhalents, 327-328
In-school suspension, 84, 270
Institute of Education Sciences, 90
Instruction
  and stimulus control, 53-54
  and student behavior, 52-58
Instructional objectives, acceptable and unacceptable, 125
Intellectual assessment, and EBD certification, 23, 24
Intensity, and progress monitoring, 142
Intensive intervention plan, 7-8, 10-11
  positive behavior support implementation, 44-45
Interdependent group contingency, 209
Interim alternative educational setting, 11
Internal validity, 184
Internalizing behavior patterns, 18
Interobserver agreement, 144
Interruption and redirection, 304
Interval recording, 149, 150, 151
Intervention conditions, 170-171
Intervention planning
  assessment process, 102-103
  assessment-based, 110-128
  behavior plan for Rodney, 98-102
  and behavior problems, 43-44
  designing of, 120-124
  identifying problem behavior, 103-110
  introduction, 101-102
Intervention strategies; *See also* Intervention planning
Interviewing, and psychological problems, 319-321
Instructional agents, peers as, 242
Intrusiveness, 73
Irvin, D. S., 305
Irvin, L. K., 86
Itkonen, T., 295
Iwata, B. A., 82, 294, 298, 299, 301, 303, 304, 305

Jack, S. L., 28, 57, 74, 75, 79, 80, 118, 197, 198, 270
Jacobson, J. W., 291
Jantzen, N. R., 208
Jarzynka, J., 212
Jenson, W. R., 303
Johns, B. H., 59
Johnson, A., 52
Johnson, C. T., 272
Johnson, H., 83
Johnson, J., 90, 349
Johnson, K., 289
Johnson, N., 52, 57, 90
Johnston, M. K., 57
Jolivette, K., 8, 9, 52, 55, 90
Jones, D. B., 201
Jones, E. J., 16
Jones, M. L., 303
Joseph, G. E., 57, 206, 240
Journal of Applied Behavior Analysis, 294

Kam, C. M., 42
Kame'enui, E. J., 52, 53, 54, 74, 170, 350
Kamphaus, R. W., 154
Kamps, D. M., 89
Kartub, D. T., 195
Karvonen, M., 223
Kasanen, K., 234
Katsiyannis, A., 12, 13, 349, 356, 357
Katz-Leavy, J., 364
Kauffman, J. M., 13, 14, 18, 22, 28, 29, 42, 43, 58, 138, 351
Kavale, K. A., 15, 22, 43, 319
Kazdin, A. E., 69, 73, 74, 76, 77, 82, 83, 88, 345
Keenan, S., 10, 14
Keeney, K. M., 305
Kellam, S., 210
Keller, F. S., 295
Keller, H. R., 263
Kellner, M. H., 90
Kelly, C. S., 57
Kennedy, C. H., 289, 292, 295, 298
Kern, L., 52, 55, 71, 89, 112

Kerr, M. M., 77, 207, 223, 224, 345
Kesler, J., 303
Kissel, R. C., 301
Klinger, J. K., 348
Knies, W. C., 60
Knoll, J., 357
Knoster, T., 45
Koegel, R. L., 299
Kohen, A., 57
Kolko, D. J., 324
Kroeger, S., 223
Kubany, E. S., 151, 152
Kuhn, T. S., 234
Kusche, C., 42
Kutash, K., 52, 361

Lacourse, M., 227
Ladwig, C. N., 197
LaFleur, L. H., 353
Lambert, D. L., 223, 326
Lambert, M. C., 239
Lambert, N., 25
Landrum, T. J., 14, 89
Lane, K. L., 42, 52, 353
Langer, S. N., 112, 149
LaNunziata, L. J., 350
Larkin, K. C., 354
Larson, C., 349
Larson, S., 7, 175
Latency, and progress monitoring, 142
Lavay, B., 234
LaVigna, G. W., 6
Law; *See* Legal and ethical guidelines
LEA; *See* Local educational agency (LEA)
Leadership, and positive behavior support, 9
Least restrictive environment, 30
  transition to, 348–353
LeBlanc, L. A., 294, 299
Lee, J. W., 239, 240
Lee, Y., 55
Leedy, A., 227
Legal and ethical guidelines, 85–88
Leiter, M., 371, 372
Lenkner, D. A., 223
Lentz, F. E., Jr., 16
Leone, P. E., 41, 356, 357
Level change, 179
Level stability, 179
Level trend, 181
LeVelle, J., 353
Levels system, 349
  and classroom management, 60
  considerations for, 61
Levendoski, L. J., 90, 112, 119, 346
Levendoski, L. S., 234
Lewis, M. H., 289, 292
Lewis, T. J., 43, 52, 57
Lewis-Palmer, T., 7, 43, 45, 175
Liaupsin, C. J., 8, 9, 41, 43, 128
Lichter, L. S., 41
Lichter, S. R., 41
LIFT; *See Linking the Interests of Families and Teachers* (LIFT)
Lindauer, S. E., 299
Lindberg, J., 299
Line of progress, 180
Linking the Interests of Families and Teachers (LIFT), 272
Llewellyn, G., 45
Lloyd, J. W., 28, 58, 351
Lo, Y., 89
Local educational agency (LEA), 12
Locus, and progress monitoring, 142
Loe, S. A., 89, 239, 263
Loeber, R., 261
Lohrmann-O'Rourke, S., 43, 83, 86
Long, E. S., 305
Long- and short-term objectives, and behavioral assessment, 125–128
Long-term suspension, 85
Lourie, I., 364
Lovaas, O. I., 291, 292, 298, 299
Low-probability behavior, 77
LSD, 327
Luce, S., 299
Luiselli, J. K., 83
Lund, K., 139

Maag, J. W., 12, 57, 200, 234, 349, 356, 357, 371
MacDonald, R. F., 112, 149
MacKenzie-Keating, S. E., 81
MacMillan, D. L., 348, 349, 353
Maddox, M., 356
Madsen, C. H., Jr., 57, 71
Mager, R. F., 124
Magnitude, and progress monitoring, 142
Maheady, L., 125
Maintenance and generalization
  effective collaboration, 359–366
  incorporate functional mediators, 345–347
  natural communities of reinforcement, 342–343
  principles and strategies, 341–347
  strategies for, 342
  train diversely, 343–345
Major depression, 321
Malaby, J., 82
Mallette, B., 125
Malmgren, K., 41, 356, 357
Maloney, M., 86
Malott, M. E., 69
Malott, R. W., 69
Mamlin, N., 29
Manifestation determination, 12
Mannella, M. C., 204
March, E. R., 205
Marchand-Martella, N., 8, 52
Marcus, B., 294
Marholin, D., 345
Marijuana, 327
Martella, R., 7
Martella, R. M., 8
Martens, B. K., 88
Martin, G. L., 343
Martin, J. E., 212
Martin, S., 154
Marzano, R. J., 233
MAS; *See* Motivation assessment scale (MAS)
Maslach, C., 371, 372
Massed trials, 147
Mastropieri, M. A., 232
Mathur, S. R., 233
Mayer, M. J., 41
Mazaleski, J. L., 298
McCabe, K. M., 319
McConaughy, S. M., 18
McConnell, S. R., 25, 223, 234, 242
McCullough, J., 58

McCurdy, B. L., 204
McDowell, J. J., 294
McEvoy, M.A., 234, 351
McFetridge, M., 212
McGimsey, J. F., 298, 303
McGinnis, J. C., 228
McInerney, D., 114
McIntyre, T., 15, 26, 106
McKain, Brian W., 267
McLaughlin, M. J., 82, 356, 357
McQuiston, S., 291
Meador, S.A., 265
Meadows, N. B., 29, 80
Measurement probes, 140
Medical assessment
and EBD certification, 24, 26
and problem behaviors, 104
Meisel, S. M., 41
Mellard, D., 85
Melloy, K. J., 69, 72, 74, 75, 77, 82, 83, 84
Mental health assessment
and *DSM-IV*, 20-22
and EBD certification, 20, 22-23
projective techniques, 23
Menzies, H. M., 52
Mercer, A. R., 52, 350
Mercer, C. D., 52, 350
Meyer, K.A., 240, 241
Michael, J. L., 295
Milburn, J. F., 239
Miller, A., 90
Miller, K.A., 89
Miller, L. J., 212
Miller, M. B., 343
Miltenberger, M. G., 304
Miltenberger, R. G., 305
Mirkin, P., 105
Misidentification, and IDEA 2004, 13
Mithaug, D. E., 212
MO; *See* Motivative operations (MO)
Mock, D. R., 13
Modeling, 73, 76
Modify environments supporting maladaptive behavior, 343
Momentary DRO, 81
Momentary time sampling, 149
Monfore, D.A., 26, 348
Monitoring and evaluation; *See also* Progress monitoring; Recording strategies
format and procedures, 142-146
frequently asked questions, 139-141
graphing and charting, 172-175
recording strategies, 146-157
school-wide data, 40
student behavior, 137-142
student progress, 142-157
teacher objection to, 138-139
Mood disorder, 321; *See also* Depression
Morehead, M. K., 103, 121, 181
Morgan, P. L., 140, 273, 275
Mortenson, B. P., 353
Mostert, M. R., 359
Motivation assessment scale (MAS), 112, 294
Motivative operations (MO), 295-296
Movement patterns, 197
Movement suppression procedures, 305
Mulick, J., 301
Multiple baseline design, 186
Multiple probe design, 186

Nagle, D.W., 240, 241
Nakasato, J., 45
Narcotics, 328
National Center for Education Statistics, 41
National Center for Students with Intensive Social, Emotional, and Behavioral Needs (Project Reach), 79
National Council for Accreditation of Teacher Education (NCATE, 2000), 136, 139
National Household Survey on Drug Abuse (2001), 325, 327
National Institute on Drug Abuse (NIDA, 2004), 328
National Institutes of Health (2003), 329
National Technical Assistance Center for Positive Behavioral Interventions and Support, 11
Natural communities of reinforcement, 342-343
Nau, P.A., 81, 301
NCATE; *See* National Council for Accreditation of Teacher Education (NCATE, 2000)
NCLB; *See* No Child Left Behind Act (NCLB)
Neel, R. S., 2, 356, 357
Negative behavior management strategies, 59
Negative reinforcement, 71
Nelson, C. M., 10, 13, 41, 43, 45, 57, 74, 75, 80, 83, 89-90, 111, 112, 118, 122, 124, 128, 164, 234, 245, 342, 343, 346, 356, 366
Nelson, G. H., 211
Nelson, J. R., 7, 8, 52, 110, 119
Nelson, M., 270
Neubert, D.A., 356, 357
Newsom, C. D., 291, 298, 299
NIDA; *See* National Institute on Drug Abuse (NIDA, 2004)
Nietupski, J., 356
Nishioka, V. M., 13
No Child Left Behind Act (NCLB), 13-14
Noell, G. H., 119, 213, 353
Noncompliance, principles of remediation, 230
Noncontingent reinforcement (NCR), SSB & SIB, 298, 304
Nordness, P. D., 25, 42
Northup, J., 119

O'Brien, F., 291, 292
Obsessive-compulsive disorder, 330
Ochoa, T., 29
Odom, S. L., 351
Odom, S. R., 234, 242
ODR; *See* Office discipline referral (ODR)
Office discipline referral (ODR), 39
behavior incident data, 45-47
O'Leary, K. D., 57, 79
O'Neill, R. E., 110, 119, 354, 356
Operational definition, 111
Opportunities to respond, increasing of, 56

Organization of thought, principles of remediation, 230
Osnes, P. G., 341
Oster-Granite, M., 292, 301
Oswald, D. P., 26
Overcorrection, 83
Over-identification, and IDEA 2004, 13
Overlapping data points, 179
Oxycodin, 328

Pace, G. M., 294, 301, 303, 304
Parker, D. E., 289, 292
Parker, F. C., 201
Parker, G., 29
Partin, M., 60
Patching, B., 55
Patton, J. R., 17, 22, 227
Payne, L. D., 90
Pearson, C. A., 88
Peck, S. M., 295
Pederson-Seelye, V. A., 196
Peer confrontation, 208, 272-273
Peer management, 208
Peer manager strategy, 208, 242
Peer monitoring, 207-208
Peer trainer steps, 274
Peer tutoring, 232-233
Peer-mediated intervention, 206-211
  goal setting and feedback, 206-207
  good behavior game, 210-211
  group contingencies, 208-210
  peer management, 208
  peer monitoring, 207-208
Peer-mediated strategies
  aggressive behavior, 272-273
  cooperative learning, 233
  peer tutoring, 232-233
Peer-monitoring procedures, 207
Penno, D. A., 89, 263
Permanent products, 141
Perpetual reinforcement, 298
Performance deficit, 238
Performance graph, 169
Peterson, B. P., 303
Peterson, L. Y., 212
Peterson, R. L., 7, 85, 86
Pfiffner, L. J., 79
Phase change lines, 171
Physical arrangements, 48-49
Physical aversives, 83-84
Physical interaction, with students, 200
Piazza, C. C., 299, 305
Pica, 292
Pickering, D. J., 233
Pigott, R. L., 223
Pinpoint, 266, 269
Pitts-Conway, V., 343
PLACHECK, 149, 153
Plager, E., 71
PL94-142, 11; *See* Individuals with Disabilities Education Act (IDEA)
Planned ignoring, 82
Poduska, J., 210
Poling, A., 305
Pollock, J. E., 233
Polloway, E. A., 227
Polsgrove, L., 10, 29, 75, 82, 83, 102, 346
Popkin, J., 208, 209
Portfolios, 141
Positive behavior support, 6-11, 123, 124, 128
  behavior incident data, 45-47
  classroom, 50-61
  families, 361-362
  identifying students, 16-17
  implementation of, 8-9, 44-61
  intervention planning, 9-11
  model of school-based, 8
  primary prevention plans, 7
  school-wide implementation, 44-50
  school-wide systems design, 47-50
  secondary prevention plans, 7
  seven key features, 50
  tertiary prevention, 7-8, 10-11
Positive practice overcorrection, 83
Positive reinforcement, 56-57, 71
Posttraumatic stress disorder, 330
Potter, M. L., 26
Powell, S. B., 289, 292
Powell, S. R., 233
Pragmatic language skills, 25
Praise-and-ignore approach, 200
Preacademic competencies, 349
Precorrection, and classroom management, 55
Predictive function, 178
Premack, D., 77
Prereferral intervention, 15
  assessment for identification, 19
Presley, J. A., 272, 274
Prevention strategies, and behavior problems, 43-44
Primary prevention strategies, 7
Problem behavior pathway, 120
Problem Behavior Questionnaire, 112
Problem behaviors
  or behavior disorders, 14-16
  data about, 45-47
  identifying of, 103-110
  medical explanations, 104
  own the behavior, 42-43
  prevention and early intervention, 43-44
  and school, 41-44
  screening, 106-110
  social validation of, 104-106
  universal interventions, 42
Problems, school, 41-44
Progress graph, 169
Progress monitoring; *See also* Monitoring and evaluation; Recording strategies
  accuracy of recording, 156-157
  behaviors and setting limitations, 144-145
  duration, 142
  format and procedures, 142-152
  frequency or rate, 142
  guidelines and frequency, 145
  intensity, 142
  latency, 142
  locus, 142
  magnitude, 142
  novice observer suggestions, 145
  observe and record immediately, 143-144
  observe and record over time, 143
  recording strategies, 146-157
  select direct and sensitive format, 143
  specific behavior, 144

Projective techniques, 23
Promoting Alternative Thinking Strategies (PATHWAYS), 241-242
Prompts and cues, classroom management, 55-56
Psychiatric problems
anxiety disorders, 330-331
bipolar disorder, 323
depression, 321-323
drug and alcohol abuse, 324-329
eating disorders, 329-330
identifying of, 319-320
interviewing of student, 319-321
introduction to, 318-319
mental health prevention services, 319
specific phobias, 331
suicide, 323-324
Psychotropic medication, 43
Public posting, 201-202
Purcell, J., 348
Putnam, R. F., 90
Pyles, D.A. M., 296

Quinn, K., 10
Quinn, M. M., 119, 128, 233

Rademacher, J.A., 196
Ragland, E. U. (1979), 207
Ramasamy, R., 185
Ramsey, E., 29, 42, 43, 55, 56, 270, 273, 354, 356
Rand, M. S., 298, 304
Ranier, D. D., 353
Rankin, R., 223
Rapp, J.T., 305
Rate, and progress monitoring, 142
Rate data summary sheet, 165
Rate per minute, 147
Räty, H., 234
RC; *See* Response cost (RC)
RE menu; *See* Reinforcing event menu
Readiness drill, aggressive events, 271
Recording strategies
accuracy of, 156-157
counting permanent products, 146
discrete learning trials, 147
duration recording, 147
frequency or tally methods, 147
interval recording, 148-149, 150, 151
multiple behaviors, 153-154
and progress monitoring, 146-150
student portfolios, 153-154
technology use for, 156
time sampling, 149
Recruit natural communities of reinforcement, 343
Reductive procedures, 73-74
Reed, E. S., 239
Reed, T. M., 57
Referral-driven identification procedures, 18
Regan, R. R., 26
Reichle, J. E., 200
Reid, J. B., 272
Reid, R., 25, 42, 110
Reinforce unprompted generalization, 345
Reinforcer sampling, 78
Reinforcing event menu (RE menu), 77
Reisberg, L., 60
Remediation, principles of, 229-230
Ramierez-Platt, C. M., 90
Ramsey, E., 71, 75, 77, 85
Reith, H. J., 82, 83
Replacement behavior, 72-73, 120-123
functional, 121
increasing of, 121-123
long-term objective, 122
short-term objective, 122
successive approximations, 122
Report Card, 363
Repp, A. C., 74, 80, 86, 305
Reprimands, 199
Reschly, D. J., 25, 26, 51, 134
Research designs, single-subject, 184-189
Research-validated practices, 7
Response cost (RC), 82, 270
Response efficiency, 120
Response equivalency, 120
Response generalization, 341
Response latency recording, 148
Response maintenance, 341
Response to intervention, 16-17
Response-reinforcer procedure, 299
Restitutional overcorrection, 83
Restraint devices, 305
Restrictive educational settings, transition to, 354-356
Restrictiveness, 74
Reversal designs, 185
Reverse-role tutoring, 232
Reward competencies, 349
Reynolds, C. J., 210
Reynolds, C. R., 156
Rhode, G., 270
Richards, R., 185
Richards, S., 185
Richman, D. M., 295
Richter, M., 52, 57, 90
Rinaldi, C., 25
Rincover, A., 81, 299, 300
Ringdahl, J. E., 294
Riordan, M. M., 296
Ripple effect, 345
Risley, T. R., 69, 341
Ritualistic; *See* Self-stimulatory behavior (SSB)
Roane, H. S., 294
Roberts, M., 119
Roberts, R. E., 11
Robertson, E., 42
Robinson, S, 57, 74, 89
Rock, E. E., 349, 354
Rodgers, T. A., 294
Rodgers-Adkinson, D. L., 25
Rojahn, J., 292, 301
Rolheiser, C., 154
Rolider, A., 305
Rollings, P., 305
Roscoe, E. M., 304
Rosenberg, H., 343
Rosenberg, M. S., 349, 354
Rosenblatt, A., 11
Rotheram, M. J., 269
Rourke, D.A., 294
Routines, 48
Rovner, L., 303
Ruef, M., 43

Rules, 48, 195-197
guidelines for, 195, 196
list of, 196
Rutherford, R. B., Jr., 80, 83, 119, 128, 233, 234, 245, 341, 356
Rylance, B. J., 357
Ryser, G., 18

Sabatine, K., 45
Sacca, M. K., 125
Safran, S. P., 227
Sage, S.A., 270
Sailor, W., 43
Salend, J. S., 208
Salend, S. J., 82, 210
Salvia, J., 19, 23
Sameoto, D., 81
Sample, P. L., 356
Sanders, D., 10
SAP; *See* Student Assistance Program (SAP)
Sasso, G. M., 110, 295
SBS Inventory of Teacher Social Behavior Standards and Expectations, 107-108
Scatter plot, 112, 113
Schaeffer, A. L., 223, 224
Schedule of reinforcement, 345
Schell, R. M., 298
Scheuermann, B., 60
Schiraldi, V., 41
Schnaps, L,, 139
Schoenfeld, W. N., 295
Schofield, P. F., 356, 357
School Archival Record Search, 25, 113-114
School personnel, working with, 359-360
School problems, 41, 42
School refusal, 331
School survival skills
assessing of, 222-225
direct teaching of, 228
improving, 222
introduction to, 222
School-based assessment
and EBD certification, 23-27
educational progress, 23, 25
intellectual assessment, 23
School-wide data
collection system, 40
monitoring and evaluation, 40
School-wide implementation, positive behavior support, 44-50
School-wide rules
adapting of, 47-48
big ideas, 47-48
for classroom, 50
strategies for, 39-40
School-wide system design
for classroom, 50-61
and positive behavior support, 47-50
Schroeder, S. R., 292, 301
Schumm, J. S., 348
Schutte, R. C., 57
Schwartz, I., 206
Scott, C. M., 29
Scott, T. M., 7, 8, 9, 10, 41, 43, 45, 50, 52, 74, 75, 83, 90, 111, 112, 118, 122, 124, 128, 341, 343
Screening, 106-110
and behavioral disorder identification, 16-17
responsiveness to intervention, 16-17
self-report, 108
student ranking form, 109
teacher expectations, 107-108
teacher rankings, 108
Scruggs, T. E., 232
Seclusionary time-out, 83
Secondary intervention plans, 7
Section 504, 13
Self-determination, promoting of, 223
Self-esteem, principles of remediation, 230-231
Self-evaluation, 212-213
Self-graphing, 213
Self-injurious behavior (SIB), 81, 292-294
assessment and intervention, 292-293, 300-306
differential reinforcement of other behavior (DRO), 303
environmental changes, 301-303
functional relations, 294
interruption and redirection, 304
motivational conditions for, 294
movement suppression procedure, 305-306
noncontingent reinforcement (NCR), 304
restraint devices, 305
weakening of, 304-305
Self-injury and Self-Restraint (SIB-C), 292, 293
Self-Injury Trauma (SIT) scale, 301
Self-instruction, 213
Self-management strategies, 211-213; *See also* Self-mediated interventions
self-evaluation, 212-213
self-graphing, 213
self-instruction, 213
self-monitoring, 211-212
self-recording, 211
Self-mediated stimuli, 346
Self-mediated strategies, 234, 242, 245, 247, 346
aggressive behavior, 273-274
Self-monitoring, 211-212
Self-mutilating; *See* Self-injurious behavior (SIB)
Self-recording, 211
Self-report, 108
Self-stimulatory behavior (SSB), 71-72, 289, 291-292
assessment and intervention, 292-293, 296-300
automatic reinforcement, 299-300
differential reinforcement of other behavior (DRO), 298
enriching the environment, 298
environment safety considerations, 300
functional relations, 294
noncontingent reinforcement (NCR), 298
perceptual reinforcement, 298
response-reinforcer procedure, 299
sensory extinction procedure, 300
sensory preferences, 299
sensory reinforcement, 299
social reinforcement, 298
stimulus variation, 299

Sellers, J. A., 197
Semilogarithmic, 168
Sensory extinction, 81
Sensory extinction procedure, 300
Sensory preferences, 299
Sensory reinforcement, 299
Sentelle, J., 239
Separation anxiety disorder, 330
Serna, L., 17, 22
Setting competencies, 349
Setting events, antecedent stimuli, 60
Severson, H. H., 13, 18, 25, 43, 108, 113
Seybert, L., 85
Shaping, 70
Shapiro, S. T., 82
She, H-C, 223
Shearer-Lingo, A., 52
Sherman, M., 272
Shinn, M. R., 354, 356
Shippen, P., 80
Shores, R. E., 28, 57, 74, 75, 77, 79, 80, 118, 197, 198, 270, 344, 346
SIB; *See* Self-injurious behavior (SIB)
SIB-C; *See* Self-injury and self-restraint (SIB-C)
Sickmund, M., 41
Sidman, M., 309
Siegel, S., 349
Simon, D., 349
Simpson, R. L., 351
Sinclair, E., 18
Singer, G. S., 86
Singh, N. N., 305
Single-subject research design, 162, 184–189
  alternating treatments design, 188–189
  changing criterion design, 186–188
  requirements of, 185
  withdrawal and reversal design, 185–186
Sitlington, P. L., 356, 357
Skiba, R. J., 34, 85, 90
Skinner, C. H., 208, 209
Slifer, K. J., 301
Slogett, B. B., 151, 152, 153
Smith, B. L., 323
Smith, C. R., 13
Smith, D. J., 45, 119, 211, 273, 275, 349
Smith, J., 154
Smith, R. G., 294, 298, 301, 303
Smith, S. W., 60, 75, 272, 346
Snyder, H. N., 41
Social and linguistic functioning, and EBD certification, 24, 25
Social anxiety disorder, 330
Social behavior, standards for, 103–104
Social competence, 25
  strategies to improve, 234
  training, 266
Social maladjustment, 15
Social reinforcement, 57, 75–76
Social skills, 108, 234, 236–238
  instruction, 239–242
  teacher-mediated strategies, 239–242
Social skills instruction, 239–242
  assessment, 239
  competing behaviors, 239–240
  cultural sensitivity, 239
  generalization and maintenance, 240–242
  modeling, 240
  performance feedback, 240
  role playing, 240
  setting, 239
Social validation, 104–106
Social withdrawal, 238–239
Socially skilled, assessment of, 234, 236–238
Sociometric procedures, 108
Sokol, N. G., 52, 55
Soloway, M. M., 349
Southard, K. L., 200
Sparrow, S. S., 25
Specific phobias, 331
Spillover effect, 345
Split-middle line of progress, 179
Spooner, E., 139
Sprague, J. R., 6, 7, 90, 110, 119
Spriggs, M., 90
SSB; *See* Self-stimulatory behavior (SSB)
Stagg, V., 223
Stainback, S., 79, 84
Stainback, W., 79, 84
Static measures, 173
Staub, R. W., 201
Steege, M. W., 119
Steinman, W., 345
Stephens, S. A., 354
Stereotypy; *See* Self-stimulatory behavior (SSB)
Stereotypy Checklist (STY-C), 290–291
Steroids, 328
Stevahn, L., 154
Stevens, K. B., 80
Stewart, E. S., 357
Stichter, J. P., 110
Stieber, S., 356
Stimulants, 328
Stimulus, 54
Stimulus generalization, 341
Stimulus variation, 299
Stimulus-response relationship, 55
Stokes, T. F., 139, 341, 343
Storey, K., 110, 119
Strain, P., 236, 237, 242
Strain, P. S., 57, 77, 206, 212, 223, 240, 345, 362
Strauss, M. A., 79
Stremel-Campbell, K., 357
Stroul, B. A., 10, 364
Student Assistance Program (SAP), 319
Student behavior
  introduction to, 5–6
  legislation affecting, 11–14
Student discipline, 41–42
Student portfolios, 153–154, 156
Student progress; *See also* Monitoring and evaluation; Progress monitoring; Recording strategies
  measuring of, 142–157
  objections to monitoring, 138–139
  recording strategies, 146–150
  teacher monitoring of, 137–142
Sturmey, P., 294
Subject evaluation form, 226
Subsequent event, 71

Substance Abuse and Mental Health Services Administration (2003), 328
Successive approximations, 122
Sudargas, R.A., 57
Sufficient response exemplars, 344-345
Sufficient stimulus exemplars, 343
Sugai, G. M., 6, 7, 8, 10, 19, 43, 45, 53, 54, 55, 73, 79, 112, 119, 123, 175, 176, 177, 238
Suicide, 323-324
Sullivan, M.T., 294
Summative evaluation, 137
Survival skills
  peer-mediated strategies, 232-233
  self-determination, 223, 225
  self-mediated strategies, 234
  social, 234, 236-238
  teacher-mediated strategies, 225-231
Survival skills scale, 224
Susan, J. L., 197
Suspension
  in-school, 84
  long-term, 85
Sutherland, K. S., 56, 71, 75, 76, 140, 198, 199, 233
Sweeney, D. P., 43
Swicegood, P., 153, 154, 155
Symons, F. J., 75
Syndrome, 20
Systematic school-wide screening, 18
Systematic screening, 17-18
Systems of care, 10

Tactile and sensory reinforcement, 79
Talbott, E., 71, 75
Tangible reinforcers, 52, 78
Tankersley, M., 14, 89
Tapasak, R. C., 263
Tapp, J.T., 156
Tarasevich, S., 319
Target behaviors, 103
  reducing, 123-124
Targeted intervention, 7, 9-10
  positive behavior support implementation, 44-45
Task analysis, 126
Tasks
  and behavior, 54-55
  principles of remediation, 230
Tawney, J. W., 137, 157, 169, 174, 179, 181, 184, 186, 189
Taylor, F. D., 350
Taylor, J. C., 57, 74, 89
Taylor, R., 185
Taylor, S. J., 357
Teach relevant behaviors, 342
Teacher expectations, checklist and rating scales, 107-108
Teacher movement patterns, 197
Teacher rankings, 108
Teacher-mediated interventions, 198-206
  contingency contracting, 202
  differential reinforcement of low rates of behavior (DRL), 80, 201
  differential reinforcement of other behaviors (DRO), 80, 200
  high-probability request sequences, 200
  monitoring verbal and nonverbal behavior, 198-199
  physical interaction with students, 199-200
  praise-and-ignore approach, 200
  public posting, 201-202
  reprimands, 199
  token economy programs, 202-206, 213-218
Teacher-mediated strategies, 225-231, 239-242, 262-272; *See also* Teacher-mediated interventions
  academic intervention, 263
  anger management training, 266
  contingency management, 228, 231, 266, 269
  contingency management strategies, 266, 269
  crisis intervention, 270
  general guidelines, 225, 227
  homework strategies, 227-228
  instructional modifications, 228
  managing routines, 227
  school survival skills, 228
  social competence training, 266
  social skills instruction, 239-242
  time-out, 82-83, 270
  verbal deescalation, 263, 265-266
    effective behaviors, 54
    monitoring student progress, 137-142
    movement patterns, 197
Teitelbaum, P., 295
Tertiary prevention plans, 7-8, 9-10
Test, D. W., 139, 223
Tharinger, D., 25
Think First, 241
Thinning reinforcement, 345
Thomas, D. R., 57, 71
Thompson, R. H., 299
Thompson, T. J., 292, 301, 305
Thwarting, 295
Time sampling, 149
Time-out, 82-83, 270
Tindal, G.A., 53, 54, 176, 177
Todd, A. W., 10, 19, 43, 45, 90
Todis, B., 18, 25, 113
Token economy, 77-78, 202-206, 213-218, 269-270
Token reinforcement, 77-78, 202-206, 213-218, 269-270
Tokens, 58, 77-78, 202, 204-206, 213-218, 269-270
Tonelson, S. W., 359
Tools for Getting Along, 272
Torrie, M., 156
Touchette, P. E., 112, 149
Tournaki, N., 232
Train diversely, 343-345
Train loosely, 345
Transenvironmental programming, 348
  classroom assessment, 348-349
  monitoring and follow-up assessment, 351-353
  student preparation, 349-350
  transition strategies implementation, 350-351
Transfer of training, 341

Transition plan, 347-359
adulthood, 356-357
domains, 358
effective collaboration, 359-366
introduction to, 340-341, 347
less restrictive educational setting, 348-353
postschool environments, 356-359
restrictive educational settings, 354-356
transenvironmental programming, 348-354
Trapping effect, 342
Treatment integrity, 353
Trend lines, 179, 180
Trials-to-criterion data sheet, 148
Trice, A. D., 201
Trojan, E.A., 69
Trout, A., 25, 42
Trout, D. D., 164
Troutman, A. C., 58, 69, 72, 74, 75, 178, 179, 185, 186, 188, 189
Turnbull, A. P., 43
Turnbull, H. R., III, 43
Turner, W. D., 305
Twyman, J. S., 83

Umbreit, J., 55
UMO; *See* Unconditioned motivative operation (UMO)
Unconditioned motivative operation (UMO), 295
Unger, K.V., 358
Universal intervention, 7
positive behavior support implementation, 44-45
and problem behaviors, 42
U.S. Surgeon General, 318, 319, 323
U.S Public Health Service, 4
U.S. Department of Education, 11, 13, 16, 85, 348, 354

Valcante, G., 197
Van Acker, R., 71, 75
VanDerHyden, A. M., 13, 52, 53, 55, 74
Van Dycke, J. L., 212
Van Houten, R., 81, 201, 305
Variable-interval recording form, 152
Vaughon, S., 348
Velting, D., 324
Venn, M. L., 43, 74, 89, 134
Verbal aversives, 81-82
Verbal confrontation, avoidance of, 263, 265-266
Verbal deescalation, 263, 265-266
Vetter-Zemitsch, A., 350
Vicarious reinforcement, 345
Vicodin, 328
Vineland Adaptive Behavior Scale, 25
Vision, and positive behavior support, 8-9
Vocational Rehabilitation Act of 1973, Section 504, 13
Vollmer, T. R., 294, 298, 299, 301, 303

Wacker, D. P., 89, 263, 295
Walker Problem Behavior Identification Checklist, 107
Walker, H. M., 6, 7, 13, 18, 20, 25, 27, 29, 42, 43, 55, 56, 71, 75, 77, 85, 90, 107, 108, 198, 223, 270, 273, 319, 348, 354, 356, 357
Walton, T.W., 138
Warren, S. H., 356, 357
Watkins, D. E., 233
Watkins, P. C., 210
Webb, S. L., 355
Webber, J., 60
Wehby, J. H., 52, 55, 71, 75, 76, 115, 118, 156, 198, 198, 199
Wentzel, K. R., 233
Werthamer, L., 210
West, R. P., 273, 275
White, O. R., 137, 169, 179, 182
Whole interval DRO, 81
Wickham, D., 43
Wilcox, B., 43
Wilder, L. K., 354
Wiley, L. P., 89
Williams, D. E., 305
Williams, G., 60
Williams, J.A., 299
Williams, K., 38
Williams, L., 305
Williams, T., 7, 85
Williamson, D.A., 210
Williamson, S. H., 210
Wilson, K. G., 307
Windmiller, M., 25
Withdrawal and reversal design, 185-186
Withdrawal design, 186
Withholding attention, 57
Witt, J. C., 13, 52, 53, 55, 74, 119, 354
Witt, W. C., 88
Wolery, M. 73, 79, 126
Wolf, M. M., 7, 8, 69, 104, 341, 343
Wolfe, P. S., 228
Wolford, B. I., 245
Wong, H. K., 195, 227
Wong, K. L. H., 351
Wong, R.T., 195, 227
Wood, F. H., 86, 87
Wood, P.A., 319
Wood, W. M., 223
Worchester, J., 55
Worsdell, A. S., 299, 305
Wraparound plan, 8, 11

Yazdian, L., 233
Yeh, M., 319
Yell, M. L., 85, 86
Yoder, P. J., 198
Young, K. R., 273, 275
Young, R. K., 211
Yovanoff, P., 355
Ysseldyke, J. E., 19, 23, 26
Yung, B. R., 266

Zarcone, J. R., 294, 298, 301, 303
Zeigler-Dendy, C., 364
Zeller, R., 13
Zhou, L., 305
Ziedenberg, J., 41
Zigmond, N., 29, 30, 223, 224
Zimmerman, E. H., 57
Zimmerman, J., 57
Zirkel, P.A., 83, 86
Zirpoli, T. J., 69, 72, 74, 75, 77, 82, 83, 84
Zwald, L., 201